*The Principles
of Auto Body Repairing
and Repainting*

Fourth Edition

THE PRINCIPLES OF AUTO BODY REPAIRING AND REPAINTING

A.G. DEROCHE and N.N. HILDEBRAND

Instructor in Auto Body Repairing and Repainting
Red River Community College
Winnipeg, Manitoba, Canada

PRENTICE-HALL, INC., Englewood Cliffs, New Jersey 07632

Library of Congress Cataloging-in-Publication Data

Deroche, A. G.
   The principles of auto body repairing and repainting.

   Includes index.
     1. Automobiles—Bodies—Maintenance and repair.
2. Automobiles—Painting. I. Hildebrand, N. N.
II. Title.
TL255.D47 1986   629.2′6′0288   86-20527
ISBN 0-13-708173-1

Editorial/production supervision and
  interior design: Tom Aloisi
Cover design: 20/20 Services, Inc.
Manufacturing buyer: Rhett Conklin

*The authors would like
to dedicate this book
to the memory of their parents.*

Printed in the United States of America

10 9 8 7 6 5 4 3 2 1

ISBN: 0-13-708173-1   025

Prentice-Hall International (UK) Limited, *London*
Prentice-Hall of Australia Pty. Limited, *Sydney*
Prentice-Hall Canada Inc., *Toronto*
Prentice-Hall Hispanoamericana, S.A., *Mexico*
Prentice-Hall of India Private Limited, *New Delhi*
Prentice-Hall of Japan, Inc., *Tokyo*
Prentice-Hall of Southeast Asia Pte. Ltd., *Singapore*
Editora Prentice-Hall do Brasil, Ltda., *Rio de Janeiro*

Contents

Acknowledgments

The authors wish to acknowledge the help and encouragement of the many companies and individuals that helped to make this book possible. Special credit is due to the following companies:

Applied Power (Canada), Rexdale, Ontario, Canada
Bear Manufacturing Co., Rock Island, Illinois, U.S.A.
Black & Decker Manufacturing, Brockville, Ontario, Canada
Canadian Industries Ltd., Montreal, Quebec, Canada
Canadian Liquid Air, Winnipeg, Manitoba, Canada
Chart Industries, Ltd.
Chrysler of Canada, Windsor, Ontario, Canada
DeVilbiss Company, Barrie, Ontario, Canada
Dupont of Canada, Ltd.
Ford Motor Company, Dearborn, Michigan, U.S.A.
General Motors of Canada, Oshawa, Ontario, Canada
Minnesota Mining and Manufacturing Co., London, Ontario, Canada
Petersen Manufacturing Co. Inc., DeWitt, Nebraska, U.S.A.
H. K. Porter Inc., Somerville, Mass., U.S.A.
Sherwin-Williams Canada, Inc.
Snap-On Tools of Canada, Winnipeg, Manitoba, Canada
Spae-Nauer Products Ltd.,
Union Carbide Corporation of Canada

Preface

As a result of the constant, continual changes being made in the design and construction of the modern automobiles by the car manufacturers, in an attempt to cope with the problems of ecology (air pollution) and in conserving the unrenewable natural resources throughout the world, we, the authors and publisher, in order to keep abreast with the above-mentioned changes, have found it necessary to revise our auto body textbook for the third time.

In making the necessary revisions, we have conferred with the major manufacturers of automobiles and trucks, with the manufacturers of the latest auto body servicing equipment and paint products used in refinishing and also with the bodyshop owners and mechanics in the auto body trade.

With an ever-growing number of women entering the labor force and working side by side with men, in occupations and trades previously held and done by men, we, the authors and publisher, would like to here and now disclaim any prejudice against either of the sexes, be it male or female, and that whereever masculine connotations are used in our textbook, they also equally apply to the feminine sex.

The textbook has been revised and presents all theoretical knowledge and outlines and describes the different practical repair operations for the auto body student or apprentice in clear and simple terms, and makes it possible for him to learn the basic repair operations quickly and enables him to become a fully qualified and proficient tradesman. It can also be used as a reference manual by the journeyman. The following paragraphs briefly outline and summarize the changes we have made in our revised fourth edition.

Chapter 1 has been revised and updated to include the trends in design and construction of automobiles today. It describes and illustrates the older types of "mild steel" body and frame and unitized construction, and how they differ from the latest type of unitized, "high strength" steel (HSS) as well as the "Space Frame" construction still in the initial stages of production. Many of the body parts, such as decorative moldings, trim panels, body assemblies and component parts and the more common fastening devices, including information on how to differentiate metric from the customary "inch" bolts, nuts and screws, are dealt with in detail.

In Chapter 2 the oxyacetylene welding, brazing and cutting section has been retained, but the arc welding section, having become outdated with the introduction and extensive use of high strength (HSS) steel in automobile construction, has been deleted and replaced with the metal inert gas (MIG) welding process, as recommended by all automobile manufacturers.

Chapter 3 deals with the use of the many different hand-tools used in metal-working in the auto body trade and describes and illustrates how each hand-tool is used most efficiently in the repairing of different types of sheet-metal damage.

Chapter 4 describes and clearly illustrates some of the latest up-to-date hydraulic equipment used in conjunction with auto body hand-tools. It not only covers all of the basic set-ups such as "pulling," "pushing," "spreading" and "clamping" corrective forces, but has been revised to include the latest types of portable and stationary body and frame straighteners available and used in the auto body trade at the present time. The care and maintenance of all equipment and how to use it safely is fully covered in this chapter.

Chapter 5 deals with the properties of metal, the effects that the "forces of expansion and contraction" have on metal when it is heated such as in welding and then allowed to cool and how these forces can be controlled and used advantageously by an auto body repairman. The different method used in controlling heat-distortion when welding a simple break or tear in a panel, a patch, or the installation of a partial repair panel on an automobile are clearly described and illustrated in Unit 1.

Unit 2 deals with the advantageous use of heat in the shrinking of excessively stretched areas on autobody panels. A step by step procedure of how to shrink a small stretched area or dent, a gouge, the edges of panels, fender flanges, flat, low high-crown and reverse-crowned panels, with and without a backing-up tool or dolly, and the shrinking of "false-stretched" areas on hoods and deck-lids is described in detail.

Chapter 6 is devoted to how abrasives are manufactured, the various types of abrasives used in metal-working and in refinishing of automobiles and the most efficient methods of sanding the different body panels on an automobile, the types and grit of abrasives used in sanding and all safety aspects are discussed in detail.

Chapters 7 and 8 outline the recommended procedures and operations to be followed in the solder and plastic-filling of inacessible areas or dents that cannot be repaired in the usual manner (hammer-out), because of either the light gauge of sheet-metal used in a particular panel or the sheet-metal having become too thin, weak or rusted-out.

Chapter 9 deals with all aspects of fiberglass repair. It describes and illustrates the step-by-step procedures used in the repairing of both minor and major damage of fiberglass bodies on automobiles and trucks. Unit 2 has been added to Chapter 9, in which plastic, its uses and methods of repairing thermo-plastic and thermo-setting type of plastic parts and panels, by means of welding or with the use of structural adhesive is fully covered.

Additional new information has been added to Chapter 10. It supplies the reader with information on how to diagnose and repair both standard and unitized older bodies and frames (prior to 1980) and the newer unitized, high strength steel (HSS) bodies; frame and wheel misalignments and methods used to correct them; wheel-balancing and its importance, are all discussed in detail.

In Chapter 11 adjustments of different adjustable body panels are explained, the adjustment of hoods, doors and trunk lids has been expanded by the use of drawings, new pictures and illustrations.

In Chapters 12 and 13 obsolete material was removed and other material was updated as well as new illustrations were used where necessary.

Chapter 14 has been updated with new illustrations. The use of urethane adhesive for windshields and some side windows, as well as some new types of weatherstripping are described and illustrated. A new section on the removing and replacing of adhesive-backed moldings and wood-grain transfers has been included.

Chapter 15 has been revised completely. All of the individually described auto body repair operations of the preceding chapters are presented in the proper sequence in which each must be carried out in the repairing of major front-end, side, turret-top and rear-end collision damage. Many of the illustrations have been improved or updated, and new ones added to clearly show actual on-the-job applications of some of the latest hand tools, hydraulic jacking equipment, portable and stationary body and frame-straighteners. Variations in the alignment, welding and metal-working procedure necessary in repairing the new unitized, high strength steel (HSS) automobiles, as recommended by the manufacturer, have been inserted throughout the entire chapter.

Chapters 16 through 19 supply information on automobile refinishing. New material has been included and expanded, such as down-draft spray booths and air make-up units and pressurized respirators, acrylic enamel, polyurethane enamel, their uses and methods of application; acrylic enamel and acrylic lacquer base and clear coats are all fully dealt with. The sand blasting method is also introduced for the removal of surface rust on panels. Vinyl Guard as well as trunk splatter paint has also been introduced as well as its application. The refinishing of vinyl and plastic parts is also included as well as the methods to recognize what type of material that the parts are made from. The use of spray equipment and its application for certain types of work is well illustrated and explained. A troubleshooting section on guns and paint defects is also included.

The care and maintenance of the exterior and interior of an automobile, including the elimination of dust and water leaks, rattles and cleaning of upholstery, are described in Chapter 20. Shop management, estimating, and shop safety are covered in Chapter 21. Estimating has been expanded somewhat.

The appendices have been rearranged and revised and clearly describe the uses of the more common hand-tools used in auto body repairing. They also contain a SI conversion chart and a comprehensive glossary. The appendices, if used in conjunction with Chapter 3 by the student in his studies, will be of great help in acquainting him with the terms used in the auto body trade and enable him or her to become more proficient in the use of hand tools.

Winnipeg, Manitoba   A. G. DEROCHE
Canada   N. N. HILDEBRAND

*The Principles
of Auto Body Repairing
and Repainting*

1

Body Construction

The repair of automobiles and trucks has become one of the fastest-growing and most important industries in the modern world. Since almost every family in America owns and operates at least one automobile (if not two or more) today, the amount of money that is spent annually to repair them is enormous. This sum includes not only expenditures by the owners themselves but also large sums spent by the automobile manufacturers for repairs, labor, parts, new machinery, and tools.

Repairing and refinishing of automobile bodies should, of course, only be carried out by people trained in this particular type of work. Such craftsmen need a thorough understanding of the operation of the various tools and equipment as well as of the many different types of automobile bodies (sections, assemblies, and component parts) in order to work efficiently and properly.

To meet this need for fully qualified craftsmen in the automobile industry, a certain percentage of the labor force must be trained to build, maintain, and repair the vast number of motor vehicles on our highways. This is where the auto body repairman and the refinisher enter the picture, and the part that these craftsmen play is of great importance to the nation's economy.

When motor vehicles become tied up, and these tie-ups may be due either to general wear and tear or to accidents (collision damage), they must be repaired and put back on the road as quickly as possible. Most of the damaged parts on motor vehicles involved in accidents are generally repaired with a substantial saving realized, unless the cost of repairing, and in some cases the loss suffered by the owner of the vehicle, exceeds the actual value of the vehicle. A good craftsman, whether he is an auto body repairman or an automobile refinisher, is meticulous in the way he carries out the repair operations necessary in restoring a damaged vehicle to its original condition or sometimes even in modifying it.

A good craftsman need not worry about being unemployed, for there is a great shortage of qualified people in the auto body repairing and refinishing trade. The amount of repair work available is tremendous, and statistics show that out of every dollar spent on service and repair work, 45 cents is spent in the auto body shop.

A good craftsman will earn a very good wage, enabling him and his family to enjoy a rather high standard of living. It is possible for him to become a shop owner, a shop foreman, or even an insurance adjuster, depending on his desires and ambition.

A good craftsman must be proficient in his work. In order to reach and maintain a high degree of proficiency, he must study hard, work diligently, and constantly keep up with all the changes in construction and repairing that manufacturers incorporate into new models every year. Such information may be obtained from the manufacturers themselves or by attending the yearly *factory field-training courses* that are held throughout the country. In the final analysis, a craftsman is only as good as the amount of pride that he has in his work. Any repair job worth doing, whether large or small, should be of as high a standard as possible and at a fair price. There is no better advertisement for any auto body and refinishing shop and the people it employs than the quality of work that they turn out.

UNIT 1-1: DETAILS OF BODY CONSTRUCTION

The first automobiles, or self-propelled (steam-powered) *horseless carriages* as they were then called, were actually built from much the same materials and hardware that were being used in the construction of the horse-drawn carriages, wagons, or buggies of the nineteenth century. In the beginning, this type of motorized vehicle was usually equipped with only one seat, which could hold only the driver and one passenger. It offered little in the way of comfort and safety because it was completely open, with no top, windshield, fenders, pneumatic balloon tires, or paved roads on which it could travel.

As time went on, however, and with the invention of the internal-combustion engine, the automobiles became larger and more stylish. They were equipped with windshields, canvas tops, side doors, fenders, and rubber-tired wheels. People also began thinking of improving the roads on which these automobiles could travel. The bodies were gradually closed in completely, but since the modern sheet-metal forming techniques had not yet been invented, the bodies were built almost entirely of wood.

With the invention of more modern methods of metal forming and manu-facturing of automobile body parts (see Chapter 3), a *skin* of sheet metal was used to cover the automobile's wooden framework.

Later, in the 1930s, as the demand for and the use of the automobile in-creased, still better methods of body construction were developed and the all-steel body came into being. Most automobile bodies manufactured up until the early 1980s were built mainly of mild steel, some were built partially of alu-minum, and others had bodies made of fiberglass. (Fiberglass body repair pro-cedures are described in Chapter 9.)

In the early 1980s, as a result of the worldwide energy crises and the spiraling cost of fuel, automobile manufacturers have attempted, and are contin-uing their efforts, to eke out the maximum distance from a gallon of fuel, not only by downsizing but also by cutting the gauge thickness of the structural members and body panels, thereby decreasing the overall weight of their models.

To accomplish this without jeopardizing the strength and safety of their automobiles, design engineers have turned more and more to the use of light-weight plastics, aluminum, and high-strength steel (HSS), also known as high-strength low-alloy steel (HSLA).

Steel is produced from iron, carbon, and certain additional alloy materials, such as chromium, manganese, nickel, and others, each mixed according to a specific formula, giving it certain properties. One of these properties is yield strength, the resistance that a particular type of steel possesses to permanent stretching.

Steel possessing a yield strength of up to 35,000 psi (241,000 kPa) is called mild steel and up until 1980 was used extensively in manufacturing automobiles of standard or conventional as well as unitized body construction (described later in this chapter).

Steel with a yield strength of 40,000 to 150,000 psi (276,000 kPa to 1034 MPa) is called high-strength steel and is used on all late-model automobiles of unitized body construction.

Steel, when examined under a microscope, is found to be composed of small particles or grains, arranged in a general pattern or structure (Fig. 1-1). When precise amounts of certain alloys are added to basic steel at the furnace in the steel mill, this grain structure is altered, imparting special qualities to the steel, qualities such as greater yield strength, hardness, flexibility, or resistance to corrosion. Mild steel is composed of large grains that are widely spaced; high-strength steel has far smaller grains that are more densely packed together (Fig. 1-2). It is the interlocking of the grains and the forces of attraction of the grains to each other that gives high-strength steel its superb strength.

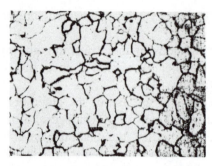

1977 Pontiac frame rail (mild steel) grain structure before heating. Note the large grains and loose arrangement. (400X magnification)

FIGURE 1-1 (Courtesy of Blackhawk, Division of Applied Power, Canada, Ltd.)

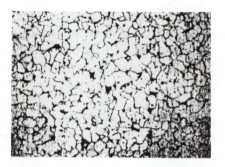

Ford Escort front inner rail (HSS) grain structure before heating. Note the smaller grains and tighter arrangement than in the mild steel (400X)

FIGURE 1-2 (Courtesy of Blackhawk, Division of Applied Power, Canada, Ltd.)

There are three main reasons why automobile manufacturers are using high-strength steel wherever possible:

1. It enables them to reduce the weight of the vehicle by cutting down the gauge or thickness of its structural members and sheet-metal panels, without sacrificing strength.

2. Most auto body parts can be made of high-strength steel without changing existing dies or tooling.

3. Manufacturers have found high-strength steel to be the cheaper method of reducing the weight of the automobile than aluminum or plastics.

Following is a brief description of some of the different high-strength steels produced and for what body parts each type is used:

• Rephosphorized steel, which has a yield strength of 40,000 psi (276,000 kPa), is used in rear rails, rear seat backs, seat cushions, A pillars, and various suspension parts.

• Nitrogenized steel, which also has a yield strength of 40,000 psi (276,000 kPa), is used in front side rails, tie-down reinforcements, and various brackets.

- High-strength low-alloy steel, which has a yield strength of 50,000 psi (345,000 kPa), is used for window regulator arms and suspension brackets.

- High-strength low-alloy steel, which has a yield strength of 80,000 psi (552,000 kPa), is used for rear suspension cross-members and track bars.

- Ultrahigh-strength steel, which has a yield strength of 85,000 psi (586,000 kPa), is specially processed (cold rolled, full hard) and used for rear door guard beams. When processed, with a yield strength of 120,000 psi (827 MPa), it is employed in front and rear bumper reinforcements, and when processed with a yield strength of 140,000 psi (965 MPa), it is used for front door guard beams.

- Martensitic steel, which has a yield strength of 150,000 psi (1034 MPa), is the strongest, hardest, and most brittle steel produced and is used for front door guard beams.

All auto manufacturers recommend that all welding on late-model automobiles of high-strength-steel construction be done using only the MIG (metal inert gas) welding process, and that the use of the oxyacetylene torch be restricted and limited to heating only in the repair of automobiles, and that it be used very carefully and sparingly and only when absolutely necessary (discussed in Chapter 15). Manufacturers recommend that no heat whatsoever be used on parts made of martensitic or ultrahigh-strength steel. Some high-strength-steel parts should not be heated beyond 1200°F (643.3°C) for more than 3 minutes; others, made of high-strength steel and high-strength low-alloy steel, if heated beyond 700°F (371.1°C), begin to lose strength, and if heated to 1000°F (537.7°C), revert to the strength level of plain, low-carbon steel (Fig. 1-3).

If this loss of strength can lead to future failure of a structural member or part, insurance claim adjusters, auto body repair shops, and body repairmen all have an interest in seeing to it that proper repair methods are used.

Structural failure on a repaired automobile will occur, if at all, after the car is back on the road. The failure will be in the metal adjoining the weld, leading to a critical loss of strength which causes the part to crack and tear under stress or load.

In the standard or conventional body construction (Fig. 1-4), the body and the frame are two entirely separate units and are held together at various points by means of body bolts that are usually tightened with torque wrenches to the manufacturer's specifications. Rubber insulators and various thicknesses of shim stock separate the body and frame at these points; they prevent squeaks from

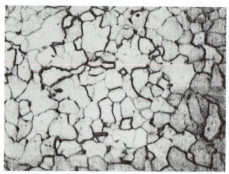

1977 Pontiac frame rail (mild steel) grain structure before heating. Note the large grains and loose arrangement. (400X magnification)

Pontiac rail after heating to 1700°F for 2 minutes and air cooling. Note that the structure is almost unchanged from the unheated sample. (400X)

Ford Escort front inner rail (HSS) grain structure before heating. Note the smaller grains and tighter arrangement than in the mild steel. (400X)

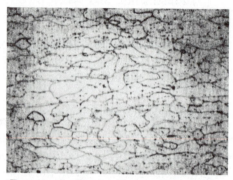

Escort rail after heating to 1050°F for 2 minutes and air cooling. Note that the grains have grown larger and the arrangement has gotten looser. (400X)

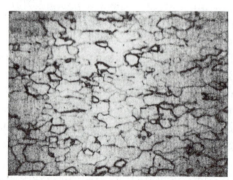

Escort rail after heating to 1200°F for 2 minutes and air cooling. Note that the grains have remained about the same size, but don't appear to fit together as well. (400X)

Escort rail after heating to 1700°F for 2 minutes and air cooling. Note that both grain size and structure have deteriorated almost to the level of mild steel. (400X)

FIGURE 1-3 Effect of heat on the granular structure of mild and high-strength steel. (Courtesy of Blackhawk, Division of Applied Power, Canada, Ltd.)

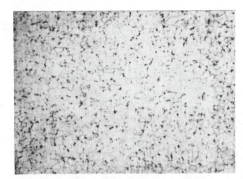

General Motors X-car front rail (HSS) grain structure before heating. Note the still smaller grains and even tighter arrangement (400X)

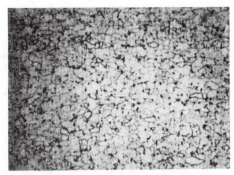

X-car rail after heating to 1050°F for 2 minutes and air cooling. Note that there is almost no change in grain size or structure at this temperature. (400X)

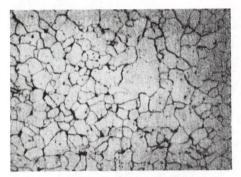

X-car rail after heating to 1200°F for 2 minutes and air cooling. Note that the grains have started to gobble each other up, and that the arrangement has gotten slightly looser. (400X)

X-car rail after heating to 1700°F for 2 minutes and air cooling. Note that some parts have deteriorated more than others despite the even heating, and some areas are approaching the appearance of mild steel. (400X)

FIGURE 1-3   (cont.)

developing, and road noises from being transmitted through the frame to the body. If necessary, by either removing or adding shims at these points, easy and accurate alignment of the body and frame is obtained. Frames used in this type of construction can be of the perimeter or ladder type; these are described and illustrated in Chapter 10.

In the unitized body construction, and that includes the newer unitized (HSS)-constructed automobiles, both the frame and the body are made from a large number of sheet-metal panels of varying sizes and shapes (Fig. 1-5). These are assembled and welded into a single unit. This type of construction gives an overall rigidity to the integral body construction. The strength that these bodies possess is drawn from each of the many individual panels, which, after they

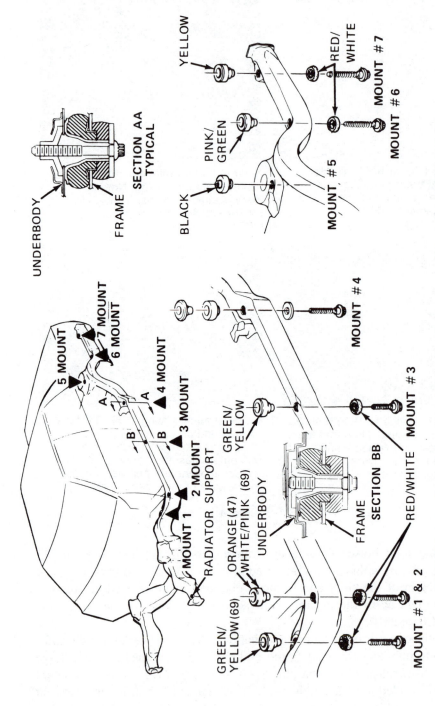

FIGURE 1-4 Typical frame and body mounts: two-door coupe (47) and four-door sedan (69). (Courtesy of General Motors of Canada, Ltd.)

have been welded together, make up the body shell. The necessary attachments required to hold the power train and the suspension system are built into the reinforced floor pans, side rails, and cross-members; these are called the *under-body* section. It is this section that provides the greatest amount of strength to the body. This type of construction eliminates the independent body and frame and is dealt with in detail in Chapter 10.

One of the latest types of unitized body construction, employing "space-frame" technology, gives great structural strength to the automobile and also keeps its overall weight to a minimum (Fig. 1-6). The all-steel framework, composed of six modular units (Fig. 1-7), each made up of many smaller parts of different types of high-strength steel, is automatically welded together. The welded space frame is clamped in a "mill and drill fixture" that drills holes in their exact location on all mounting pads, to which the exterior Enduroflex panels (Fig. 1-8) are then attached.

Some manufacturers also employ what is known as a modified form of unitized body construction (Fig. 1-9), consisting of half frame and half unitized body construction. The frame consists of short, stubby side rails that usually extend from behind the front doors to the front of the vehicle and are joined by lateral cross-members. This frame provides support for the front wheel suspension, engine, transmission, steering mechanism, and front-end sheet metal. The rear section of the vehicle has the frame built into the underbody section and forms an integral part of the body.

When an automobile is brought into the auto body shop for repairs, the auto body repairman should know the correct name of all the many parts, assemblies, and sections of an automobile body. Not only will this knowledge enable him to repair, align, and replace damaged parts in accordance with the shop estimate, but it will enable him to order parts intelligently, thereby eliminating the needless delivery of wrong repair parts and greatly assisting him in preparing estimates when the opportunity arises. Figure 1-10 shows typical sheet-metal body parts, panels, and assemblies.

An automobile body is generally divided into four sections: the front, the upper or top, the rear, and the underbody. These sections are further divided into small units, called *assemblies*, which in turn are divided into even smaller units, called *parts*.

The front section is composed of a number of assemblies, such as the grille, the hood, the right and left fender, and the cowl assembly.

The cowl assembly, one of the largest of all assemblies, is composed of the shroud upper panel, shroud vent panel, windshield glass support, instrument panel, front body hinge pillar to rocker panel, and the dash panel.

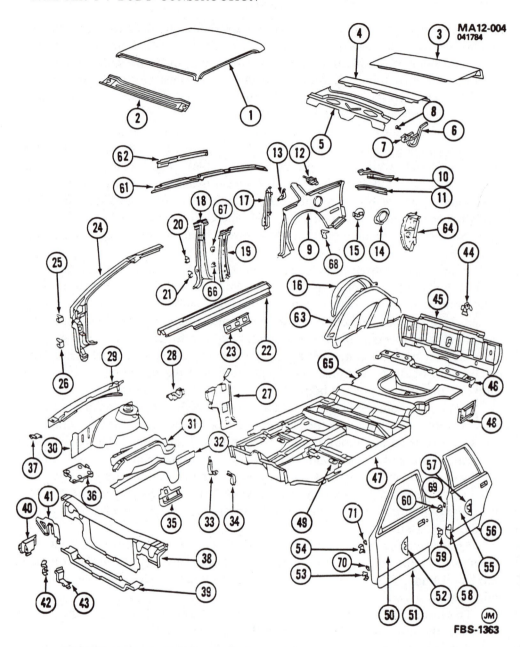

FIGURE 1-5 1982–1985 A19 body sheet metal. (Courtesy of General Motors of Canada, Ltd.)

1. **PANEL:** Roof (Exc AD3)
   PANEL: Roof (1982 W/AD3)(1985 W/ AD3)
   PANEL: Roof-W/FULL VINYL (CB5) (1984-85)
2. **FRAME:** W/S Inr Upr
3. **LID:** Compt
4. **PANEL:** Compt Frt
5. **PANEL:** R/Seat To Bk Wdo
6. **STRAP:** Hge C/Lid & Supt
7. **BOX:** Hge C/Lid-RH
   BOX: Hge C/Lid-LH
8. **PIN:** Compt Lid Hgw
9. **PANEL:** Qtr Otr-RH
   PANEL: Qtr Otr-LH
10. **EXTENSION:** Q/Otr To R/Pnl-RH
    EXTENSION: Q/Otr To R/Pnl-LH
11. **RETAINER:** Tr On R/Pnl-RH (1982)
    RETAINER: Tr On R/Pnl-LH (1982)
12. **EXTENSION:** Q/Otr Pnl At B/W-RH
    EXTENSION: Q/Otr Pnl At B/W-LH
13. **FILLER:** Q/Wdo Lwr Cor-RH
    FILLER: Q/Wdo Lwr Cor-LH
14. **FILLER:** Q/Otr Pnl At Tank
15. **DOOR:** Fuel Tank Fil
16. **PANEL:** W/H Otr-RH
    PANEL: W/H Otr-LH
17. **PANEL:** Lk Plr Inr Upr-RH
    PANEL: Lk Plr Inr Upr-LH
18. **PANEL:** C/Plr Otr-RH
    PANEL: C/Plr Otr-LH
19. **PANEL:** C/Plr Inr-RH
    PANEL: C/Plr Inr-LH
20. **STRAP:** Hge Upr Bdy Si-RH
    STRAP: Hge Upr Bdy Si-LH
21. **STRAP:** Hge Lwr Bdy Si-RH
    STRAP: Hge Lwr Bdy Si-LH
22. **PANEL:** Rkr Otr-RH
    PANEL: Rkr Otr-LH
23. **REINFORCEMENT:** Rkr Otr Pnl
24. **PANEL:** Hge Plr-RH
    PANEL: Hge Plr-LH
25. **STRAP:** Hge Upr Bdy Si-RH
    STRAP: Hge Upr Bdy Si-LH
26. **STRAP:** Hge Lwr Bdy Si-RH
    STRAP: Hge Lwr Bdy Si-LH

27. **REINFORCEMENT:** Hge Plr Inr Pnl-RH
    REINFORCEMENT: Hge Plr Inr Pnl-LH
28. **HINGE:** Hood-RH
    HINGE: Hood-LH
29. **RAIL:** M/Compt Si Upr-RH
    RAIL: M/Compt Si Upr-LH
30. **PANEL:** M/C Si & W/H-RH
    PANEL: M/C Si & W/H-LH
31. **RAIL:** M/Compt Si Otr-RH
    RAIL: M/Compt Si Otr-LH
32. **RAIL:** M/Compt Si Inr-RH
    RAIL: M/Compt Si Inr-LH
33. **EXTENSION:** M/C Si Otr F/Rail-RH
    EXTENSION: M/C Si Otr F/Rail-LH
34. **EXTENSION:** M/C Si Inr Rail-RH
    EXTENSION: M/C Si Inr Rail-LH
35. **RAIL:** Mtr Comps Si Otr-RH
    RAIL: Mtr Comps Si Otr-LH
36. **TRAY:** Battery (1982-83 W/4.3T Exc H.D. Bat)
    TRAY: Battery (1982-83 W/4.3T & H.D. Bat)
    TRAY: Battery (1984-85 W/4.3T Exc H.D. Bat)
    TRAY: Battery (1984-85 W/4.3T & H.D. Bat)
37. **EXTENSION:** Mtr Compt Frt To Upr Rail-RH
    EXTENSION: Mtr Compt Frt To Upr Rail-LH
38. **PANEL:** Mtr Compt Frt
39. **BAR:** R/End Lwr Tie
40. **EXTENSION:** Mtr Compt Si Rail Frt-RH
    EXTENSION: Mtr Compt Si Rail Frt-LH
41. **EXTENSION:** Mtr Compt Frt Pnl To Rail-RH
    EXTENSION: Mtr Compt Frt Pnl To Rail-LH
42. **SUPPORT:** Bar F/End Lwr
43. **REINFORCEMENT:** F/End Lwr Tie Bar-RH
    REINFORCEMENT: F/End Lwr Tie Bar-LH
44. **STRIKER:** Lid C/Lid
45. **PANEL:** R/End
46. **SUPPORT:** R/End Fin Pnl (OLDS Only)

47. **PAN:**   Compartment
48. **FILLER:**   Pan Compt To Qtr Pnl-RH
    FILLER: Pan Compt To Qtr Pnl-LH
49. **COVER:**   Floor Pan Gage & Drn Hole
    COVER: Compt Pan Gage & Drn Hole
       (1982-83)
    COVER: Compt Pan Gage & Drn Hole
       (1984-85)
50. **DOOR:**   Frt-RH
    DOOR: Frt-LH
51. **PANEL:**   F/D Otr-RH
    PANEL: F/D Otr-LH
52. **BAR:**   F/D Otr-RH
    BAR: F/D Otr-LH
53. **STRAP:**   Hge F/D Lwr Door Si-RH
    STRAP: Hge F/D Lwr Door Si-LH
54. **STRAP:**   Hge F/D Upr Door Si-RH
    STRAP: Hge F/D Upr Door Si-LH
55. **DOOR:**   Rr-RH
    DOOR: Rr-LH
56. **PANEL:**   R/D Otr-RH
    PANEL: R/D Otr-LH
57. **BAR:**   R/D Otr-RH
    BAR: R/D Otr-LH
58. **PLATE:**   Anc R/D Lwr Hge Dr Si
59. **STRAP:**   Hge R/D Lwr Do Si-RH

STRAP: Hge R/D Lwr Do Si-LH
60. **STRAP:**   Hge R/F Upr Do Si
61. **RAIL:**   Si Rf Inr-RH
    RAIL: Si Rf Inr-LH
62. **RAIL:**   Si Rf Otr-RH
    RAIL: Si Rf Otr-LH
63. **PANEL:**   W/H Inr-RH
    PANEL: W/H Inr-LH
64. **EXTENSION:**   Q/Otr to R/End Pnl Lwr-RH
    EXTENSION: Q/Otr to R/End Pnl Lwr-LH
65. **PAN:**   Compartment
66. **PLATE:**   R/D Lwr Hge Body Si Anc-RH
       (1983-85)
    PLATE: R/D Lwr Hge Body Si Anc-LH
       (1983-85)
67. **PLATE:**   R/D Upr Hge Body Si Anc-RH
       (1983-85)
    PLATE: R/D Upr Hge Body Si Anc-LH
       (1983-85)
68. **SUPPORT:**   Filler Neck Stone Shield
       (1983-85)
69. **PLATE:**   R/D Upr Hge Dr Si Anc
70. **PLATE:**   F/D Lwr Hge Dr Si Anc
71. **PLATE:**   F/D Upr Hge Dr Si Anc

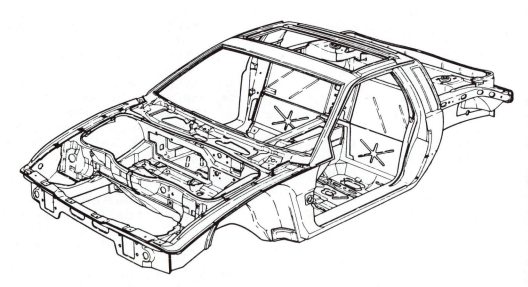

FIGURE 1-6   Space frame. (Courtesy of General Motors of Canada, Ltd.)

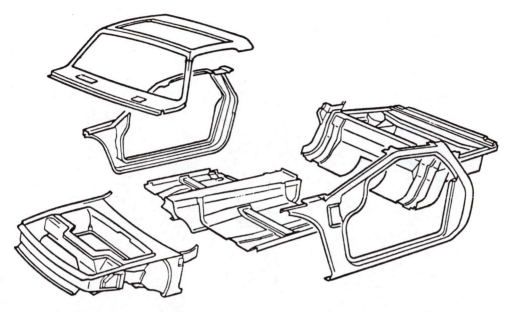

FIGURE 1-7 Space-frame modules. (Courtesy of General Motors of Canada, Ltd.)

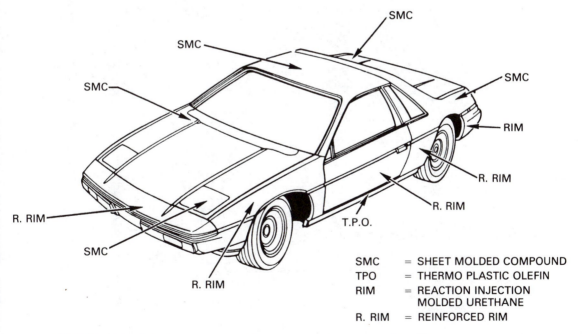

SMC	=	SHEET MOLDED COMPOUND
TPO	=	THERMO PLASTIC OLEFIN
RIM	=	REACTION INJECTION MOLDED URETHANE
R. RIM	=	REINFORCED RIM

FIGURE 1-8 All-plastic Enduroflex exterior body panels. (Courtesy of General Motors of Canada, Ltd.)

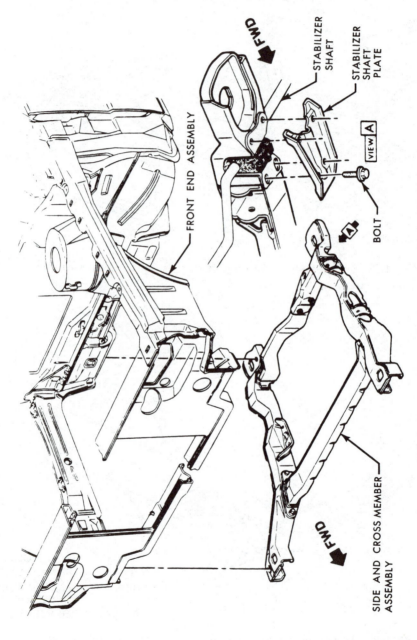

STABILIZER SHAFT

STABILIZER SHAFT PLATE

VIEW A

BOLT

FRONT END ASSEMBLY

FWD

FWD

SIDE AND CROSS MEMBER ASSEMBLY

FIGURE 1-9 Side and cross-member assembly.

The roof panel is usually the largest of all body panels and is supported by the upper inner windshield frame, the front body hinge pillars, the longitudinal roof bows on its sides, and the inner back window panel at the rear. The center of the roof panel is reinforced by the roof bow.

The quarter-panel assemblies are located in the rear section of the automobile and are composed of the lower inner rear quarter panel, wheelhouse panel, and outer rear quarter side panel.

The automobile body is divided into three distinctly separate compartments and these are serviced by the following assemblies. Doors provide easy access to the body compartment, hoods to the engine compartment, and the deck lids to the luggage compartment. They are all similar in design and construction in that each is made with an outer panel whose flanged edges are not only folded over but are also spot-welded to a box-type frame or inner construction, thus giving them a great deal of strength. All are mounted on hinges and equipped with locks for easy opening and closing.

Rocker panels are rust-proofed assemblies of box-type construction and are composed of the outer door-opening rocker panel, the rear outer rocker panel reinforcement, and the front outer-rocker panel reinforcement. They are located directly below the doors and are not only spot-welded to the sides of the floor pans, thereby greatly reinforcing the underbody section, but also to the cowl assembly in front and the rear quarter-panel assembly at the rear.

The front and rear bumpers (Figs. 1-11 and 1-12) not only provide a certain amount of protection to the automobile but also enhance its appearance. The bumpers are held in position by means of brackets, shock absorbers or isolators that are bolted to each end of the frame side rails, commonly called *frame horns*.

Slotted holes, either in the brackets or in the frame horns, off-center washers, and cam-equipped bolts are employed in the installation and adjustment of automobile bumpers. (For further information, see Chapter 11.)

On automobiles of standard or conventional body construction, most of the front-end sheet-metal parts (Fig. 1-13) are bolted together, but in automobiles of unitized body construction most of the parts (except those that have to be removed for periodic servicing) are spot-welded together. These methods vary somewhat from model to model and from year to year, however, and are predetermined by the design and styling of a particular automobile and the assembly system employed by the manufacturer.

The grilles are usually held in place by screws, bolts, or even rivets and are die-cast or made out of plastic, aluminum, or stamped sheet metal, which is then chrome-plated. Figure 1-14 shows a typical grille assembly and the method used in securing it to the sheet metal.

Front-end sheet metal refers to all the panels from the cowl assembly forward, such as the right and left fender panels and their inner skirts, sometimes

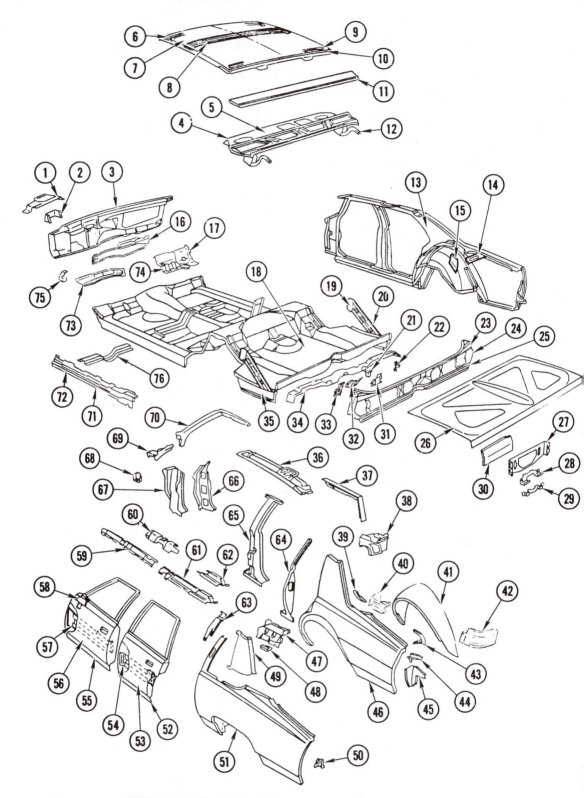

FIGURE 1-10 Body shell components and sheet metal. (Courtesy of General Motors of Canada, Ltd.)

"B69" BODY SHEET METAL

1. **PLATE ASM:** Fender on Dash Mounting.
2. **SUPPORT ASM:** Fender Skirt (exc. Olds & Cadillac).
3. **PANEL ASM:** Dash.
4. **REINFORCEMENT:** Rear Seat to Back Window.
5. **PANEL:** Rear Seat to Back Window.
6. **FRAME:** Windshield Inner Upper.
7. **PANEL:** Roof Outer.
8. **BOW:** Roof No. 1
9. **PANEL:** Back Window Inner Upper ("C" Styles).
10. **PANEL:** Back Window Upper ("B" Styles).
11. **PANEL:** Compartment Front.
12. **BOX ASM:** Rear Compartment Lid Hinge.

   STRAP & LINK ASM: Rear Compartment Lid Hinge.

   ROD: Compartment Lid Hinge Torque.

   PIN: Rear Compartment Lid Hinge.

13. **PANEL:** Quarter Inner Upper.
14. **BRACE:** Compartment Gutter to Wheelhouse (Chev.).
15. **BRACE:** Compartment Lid Hinge to Wheelhouse.
16. **REINFORCEMENT:** Dash Panel (Cadillac).
17. **FILLER:** Floor Pan to Rocker Inner Front.
18. **PAN ASM:** Compartment.
19. **BRACE:** Wheelhouse to Compt. Pan Diagonal Front (Cadillac).
20. **BRACE:** Wheelhouse to Compt. Pan Diagonal (Cadillac).
21. **PLATE:** Compartment Lid Mechanical Closing (Cadillac).
22. **STRIKER:** Compartment Lid Lock.
23. **PANEL:** Rear End Upper (Buick).
24. **PANEL:** Rear End.
25. **PANEL:** Rear End Lower (Buick "C").
26. **PANEL ASM:** Compartment Lid.
27. **POCKET ASM:** License Plate. Mounting (Chev. & Pontiac).
28. **SUPPORT:** License Plate (Pontiac).
29. **SUPPORT:** Tail Lamp & Rear End Panel Mounting (Pontiac).
30. **PANEL:** Rear End Finish (Pontiac).
31. **SUPPORT ASM:** Rear Bumper Skid (Olds).
32. **REINFORCEMENT:** Rear End Panel Center (Buick).
33. **REINFORCEMENT:** Rear End Panel At License Plate (Chev. & Pontiac)
34. **BAR ASM:** Compartment Pan Rear Cross.
35. **FILLER:** Quarter Panel to Compartment Pan.
36. **RAIL:** Side Roof Inner.
37. **RAIL ASM:** Side Roof Outer.
38. **EXTENSION:** Rear Seat to Back Window ("C" Styles).
39. **FILLER:** Quarter Panel at Back Window Lower ("C" Styles).
40. **REINFORCEMENT:** Quarter Outer Panel.
41. **PANEL:** Wheelhouse Outer.
42. **SHIELD:** Tailpipe & Frame-On Wheelhouse.
43. **FILLER:** Quarter Outer to Rear End Panel Upper (Pontiac).
44. **SUPPORT:** Rear End Finish Panel to Rear End (Pontiac).
45. **EXTENSION:** Compartment to Quarter Panel Filler ("B" Styles).
46. **PANEL:** Quarter Outer.
47. **GUTTER:** Quarter Window Run ("D" Styles).
48. **FILLER:** Quarter Panel to Back Window Reinforcement ("D" Styles).
49. **PANEL:** Quarter Outer Rear ("D" Styles).
50. **SUPPORT:** Rear End Finish Panel (Cadillac).
51. **PANEL:** Quarter Outer Front ("D" Styles).
52. **DOOR ASM:** Rear.
53. **PANEL:** Rear Door Outer.
54. **BAR ASM:** Rear Door Outer.
55. **DOOR ASM:** Front.
56. **PANEL:** Front Door Outer.
57. **BAR ASM:** Front Door Outer.
58. **REINFORCEMENT:** Front Door Outer Panel-At Mirror.
59. **RAIL ASM:** Front Side Roof Outer ("D" Styles).

60. **RAIL ASM:** Front Side Roof Inner "D" Styles).
61. **RAIL ASM:** Rear Side Roof Outer ("D" Styles).
62. **RAIL:** Rear Side Roof Inner ("D" Styles)
63. **PANEL ASM:** Body Lock Pillar Inner Upper ("D" Styles).
64. **PANEL ASM:** Body Lock Pillar Outer
65. **PILLAR ASM:** Center.
66. **REINFORCEMENT ASM:** Front Body Hinge Pillar.
67. **PANEL:** Front Body Hinge Pillar Lower
68. **PLATE:** Front Fender on Pillar Mounting.

69. **BRACE:** Windshield Lower Frame Reinforcement.
70. **RAIL ASM:** Windshield Side Frame & Reinforcement-Front.
71. **PANEL:** Rocker Outer ("B, C" Styles)
72. **PANEL:** Rocker Outer-Front ("D" Styles).
73. **REINFORCEMENT:** Dash Panel (Cadillac).
74. **BRACE ASM:** Dash to Chassis Frame.
75. **SUPPORT ASM:** Dash Panel Reinforcement to Chassis (Cadillac).
76. **REINFORCEMENT:** Front Seat Cross Bar Underbody (Exc. Buick).

called wheelhouses (Fig. 1-15); the hood panel; stone deflector panel; and so on.

These panels, when assembled, cover the front sections of the frame and front wheel suspension system, keeping water, dirt, and dust raised by the wheels from splashing and covering the outer panels and windows of the body and making driving more comfortable and less hazardous. They also form a suitable compartment in which the engine can operate. The front-end sheet metal is held in position by such parts as the radiator support, the tie bar assembly, and the valance panel (Fig. 1-16).

The top mounting bracket or flange, located near the rear end of many front fender panels, is bolted to the upper section of the lower shroud side panel (cowl assembly) (Fig. 1-17) and to the rocker panel at the bottom.

The front of the fender panel is attached to the radiator support, which in turn is attached to the front of the frame horn. Shims are used to vary the height of the front of the fender between the frame and the radiator support (Fig. 1-18).

The hood panel not only serves as a finish panel to fill in the large space between the two front fenders but it also prevents water from falling on the engine. It pivots on large hinges that are usually attached to either the cowl or front fender or both. It is held down at the front by a locking mechanism composed of a lock bolt and a lock plate (Fig. 1-19) or a remote control hood latch (Fig. 1-20). Stationary as well as adjustable rubber bumpers are used to keep it cushioned and aligned in its opening and at the correct height (level) with the front fenders and the upper shroud (cowl) assembly panel. In order to perform the necessary adjustments and to obtain proper alignment of the body and the front-end sheet metal, the reader should study Chapter 11 thoroughly.

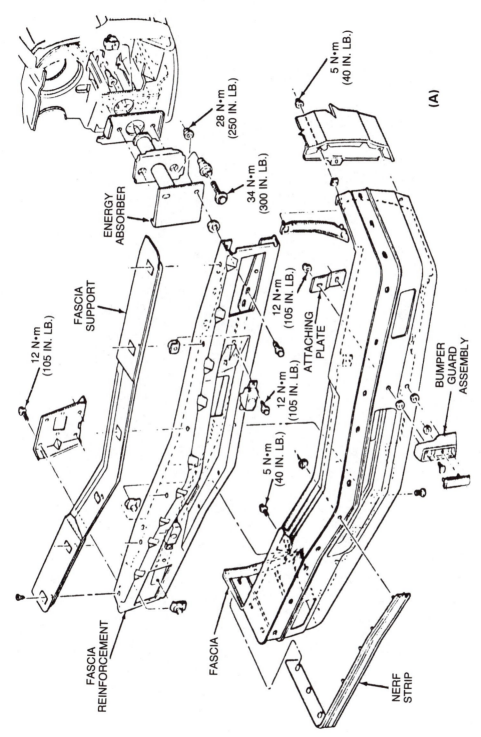

FIGURE 1-11 Front (A) and rear (B) bumpers and supports. (Courtesy of Chrysler Canada Ltd.)

28 N·m
(250 IN. LB.)

34 N·m
(300 IN. LB.)

5 N·m
(40 IN. LB.)

(A)

ENERGY
ABSORBER

12 N·m
(105 IN. LB.)

12 N·m
(105 IN. LB.)

ATTACHING
PLATE

FASCIA
SUPPORT

12 N·m
(105 IN. LB.)

12 N·m
(105 IN. LB.)

BUMPER
GUARD
ASSEMBLY

5 N·m
(40 IN. LB.)

FASCIA
REINFORCEMENT

FASCIA

NERF
STRIP

19

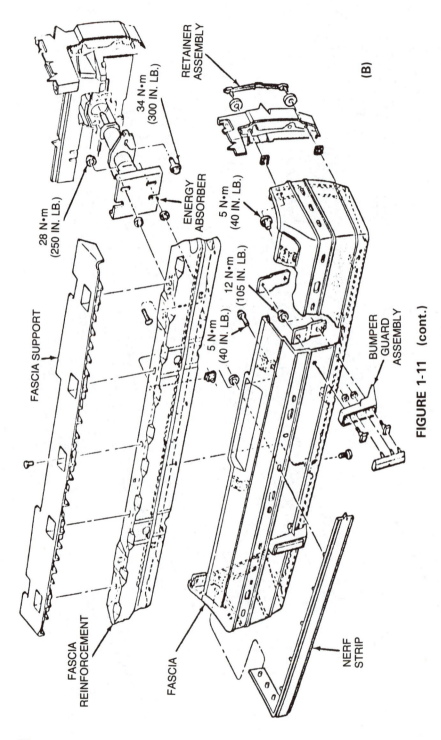

FASCIA SUPPORT

RETAINER ASSEMBLY

34 N•m (300 IN. LB.)

28 N•m (250 IN. LB.)

ENERGY ABSORBER

5 N•m (40 IN. LB.)

12 N•m (105 IN. LB.)

5 N•m (40 IN. LB.)

BUMPER GUARD ASSEMBLY

FASCIA REINFORCEMENT

FASCIA

NERF STRIP

(B)

FIGURE 1-11   (cont.)

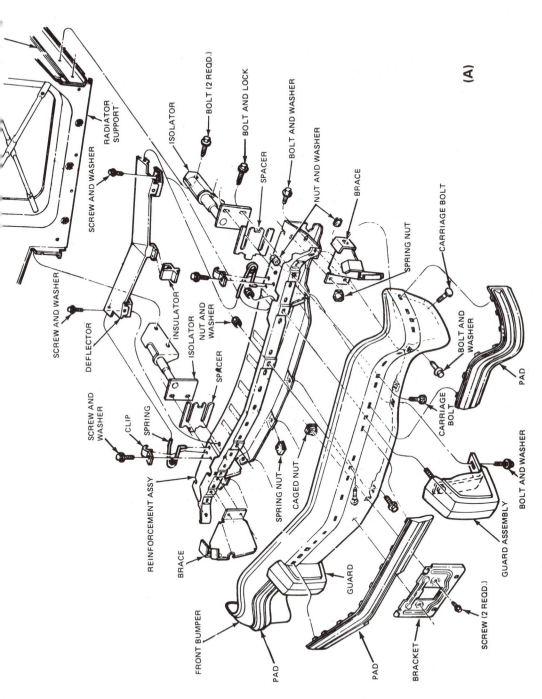

FIGURE 1-12 Front (A) and rear (B) bumper assemblies. (Courtesy (A) of Ford Motor Company of Canada, Ltd.) (Courtesy (B) of General Motors of Canada, Ltd.).

21

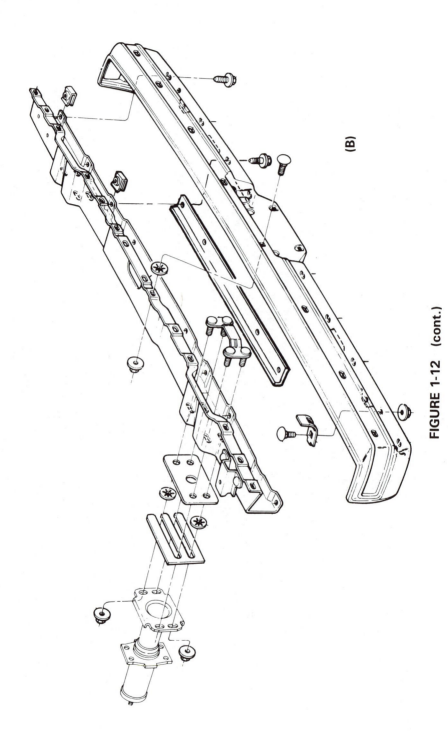

(B)

FIGURE 1-12 (cont.)

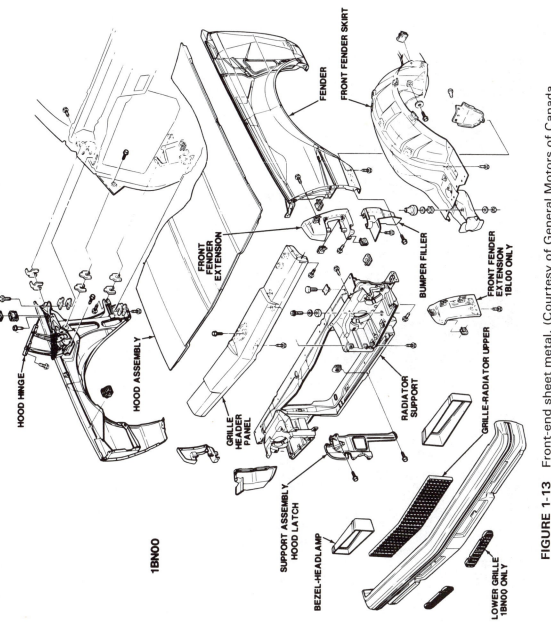

FIGURE 1-13 Front-end sheet metal. (Courtesy of General Motors of Canada, Ltd.)

HOOD HINGE

HOOD ASSEMBLY

1BN00

FRONT FENDER EXTENSION

GRILLE HEADER PANEL

SUPPORT ASSEMBLY HOOD LATCH

BEZEL-HEADLAMP

RADIATOR SUPPORT

GRILLE-RADIATOR UPPER

FRONT FENDER EXTENSION 1BL00 ONLY

BUMPER FILLER

FRONT FENDER SKIRT

FENDER

LOWER GRILLE 1BN00 ONLY

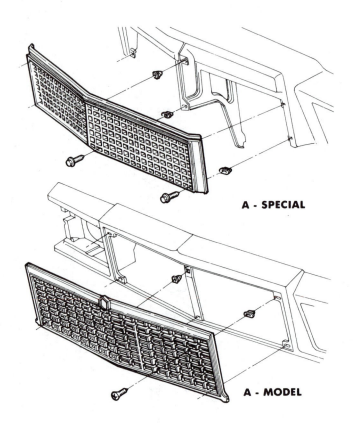

A - SPECIAL

A - MODEL

FIGURE 1-14 Grille assembly. (Courtesy of General Motors of Canada, Ltd.)

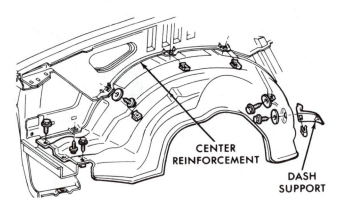

CENTER REINFORCEMENT

DASH SUPPORT

FIGURE 1-15 Fender and skirt assembly. (Courtesy of General Motors of Canada, Ltd.)

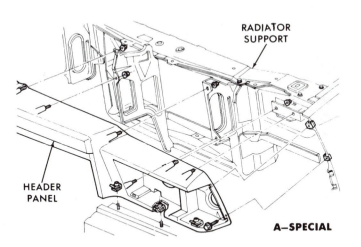

RADIATOR
SUPPORT

HEADER
PANEL

A—SPECIAL

FIGURE 1-16 Header panel to radiator supportment. (Courtesy of General Motors of Canada, Ltd.)

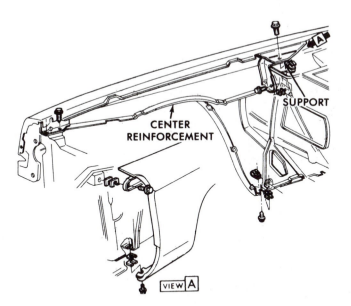

SUPPORT

CENTER
REINFORCEMENT

VIEW A

FIGURE 1-17 Attachment of front fender to cowl and rocker panel. (Courtesy of General Motors of Canada, Ltd.)

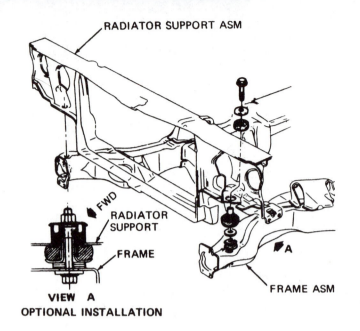

RADIATOR SUPPORT ASM

FWD

RADIATOR
SUPPORT

FRAME

VIEW A
OPTIONAL INSTALLATION

A

FRAME ASM

FIGURE 1-18 Attachment and shimming of radiator support to frame. (Courtesy of General Motors of Canada, Ltd.)

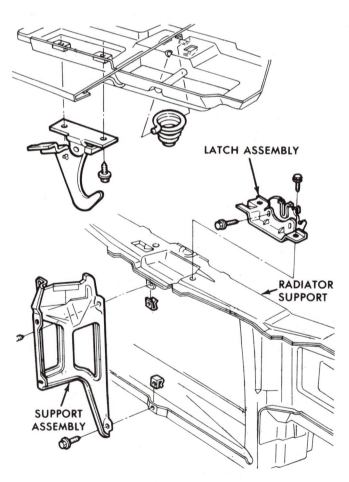

LATCH ASSEMBLY

RADIATOR
SUPPORT

SUPPORT
ASSEMBLY

FIGURE 1-19 Hood latch and support. (Courtesy of General Motors of Canada, Ltd.)

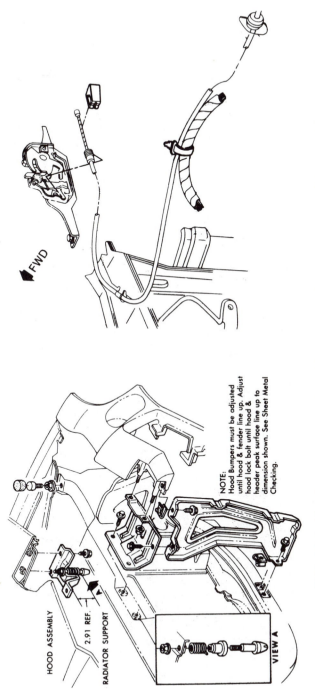

FIGURE 1-20 Remote control hood latch assembly. (Courtesy of General Motors of Canada, Ltd.)

FWD

NOTE:
Hood Bumpers must be adjusted until hood & fender line up. Adjust hood lock bolt until hood & header peak surface line up to dimension shown. See Sheet Metal Checking.

HOOD ASSEMBLY

2.91 REF.

RADIATOR SUPPORT

VIEW A

UNIT 1-2: FASTENING DEVICES, MOLDINGS, AND CLIPS

Many different methods are used in attaching exterior and interior parts, such as moldings, letters, emblems, and nameplates to an automobile; it is impossible to show every single type of clip used in the industry today. In the following illustrations, a few of the more common types are shown and their uses briefly described. First, however, it is important for the student to know the names of the different body moldings and their exact location on an automobile body (Fig. 1-21). Moldings that are fastened and held in place by means of screws [Fig. 1-22(A)] are usually die-cast (white metal) and are equipped with threaded holes

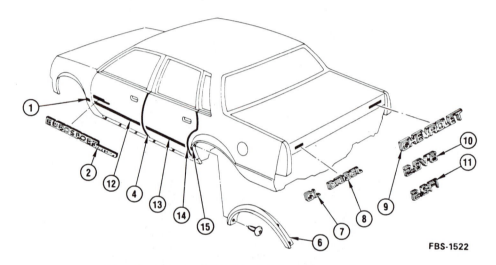

FBS-1522

1984-85 "A19-27" SIDE MOLDINGS BELOW BELT
  1. MOLDING, F/Fdr-RH (Exc B88)
  2. PLATE, Na F/D Otr Pnl "EUROSPORT"
  3. MOLDING KIT, F/D Ctr-RH)Exc B88)
  4. MOLDING, F/D Edge Guard-RH
  5. MOLDING KIT, Rr Q/Frt Of Whl Opg-RH (Exc B88)
  6. MOLDING KIT, Rr Whl Opg-RH (W/B96)(1984)
  7. PLATE, Na Rr Compt Lid "CL" (Bla/Red)
  8. PLATE, Na Rr Compt Lid "DIESEL"
  9. PLATE, Na Rr Compt Lid "CHEVROLET"
10. PLATE, Na Rr Compt Lid "2.8V-6" (Bla/Red)
11. PLATE, Na Rr Compt Lid "2.5-FI" (Bla/Red)
12. MOLDING KIT, F/D/ Ctr-RH (Bla/Gray)
13. MOLDING KIT, R/D-RH (Bla/Gray)
14. MOLDING, R/D Edge Guard-RH
15. MOLDING KIT, Rr Qtr Frt of Whl Opg-RH (Bla/Gray)

FIGURE 1-21 1984–1985 A19-27 side moldings below belt. (Courtesy of General Motors of Canada, Ltd.)

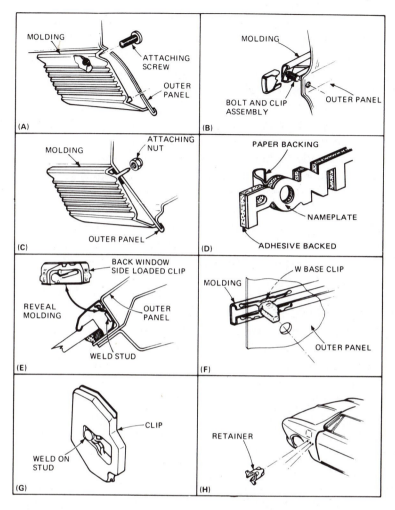

FIGURE 1-22   Exterior molding attachments. (Courtesy of General Motors of Canada, Ltd.)

to take screws. Others are equipped with unthreaded holes that take *self-tapping* screws.

The bolt and clip assembly method of attaching moldings has been used for many years and is one of the strongest ways of fastening moldings [Fig. 1-22(B)]. The clips must first be installed and positioned in the molding before the bolts are pushed through the holes in the outer panel; the nuts are started and then tightened, gradually drawing up the molding. Easy access to the inner side of the outer panel and sufficient working room must be available in order for this method to be used.

Moldings that are equipped with the integral stud and attaching nut [Fig. 1-22(C)] may be made of die-cast metal or steel and are generally used in panels that have ample room in the back for drawing them up. The accommodating holes in the outer panel must be drilled very accurately, however, or great difficulties in installation will result.

A *retainer*, similar to the one shown in Fig. 1-22(H) is often used in place of the self-threading nut. This type of retainer allows the molding to be installed on a totally enclosed outer panel.

Back window side-loaded clips are positioned around the windshield and back window openings and are held in place by weld studs [Fig. 1-22(E)]. The reveal moldings are inserted between the side-loaded clips and the outer panel and pushed down into place; this causes them to lock firmly.

Weld-on stud-type clips [Fig. 1-22(G)] are made of nylon and slide into position on studs spot-welded onto the outer panels on automobiles. The moldings are then correctly positioned and *snapped* over the clips, as previously described (see bathtub clips).

The clips must first be installed on the outer panel. Then the molding is positioned correctly and hooked over the upper lip of the clip. With a sliding downward thump on the molding with the palm of the hand, the molding is *snapped* over the bottom lip of the bathtub clip. It is always advisable, however, to use at least one or two (one at either end of the molding) bolt and clip assemblies with these clips to keep the molding from sliding out of place should it get bumped on either end.

These clips have become very popular with automobile manufacturers because they are not affected by corrosion. Moreover, nylon, because it is a softer material than steel, does not puncture the underlying coats of paint as some of the metal clips do.

Bayonet-type stud fasteners are used for fastening emblems, nameplates, and even letters. The pointed studs are positioned in holes, equipped with retainers [Fig. 1-23(I)], and then gently and evenly bumped or hammered in until the emblem, nameplate, or letter is snugly against the outer panel.

Various types of snap-in clips are used in fastening moldings. Some are stamped out of sheet metal [like the W-base clip shown in Fig. 1-22(F)], while others are made of nylon [see Fig. 1-24(A)]. They are easily installed and positioned in the molding before the molding is snapped into its position on the outer panel. They should also be used with one or two threaded stud-type fasteners to keep them from shifting easily.

The ends of many moldings, which are stamped out of stainless steel and aluminum, are held down tightly to the panels they are mounted on by means of a threaded stud-type molding fastener [Fig. 1-24(B)], which is equipped to take an attaching screw. The remaining in-between portions of the molding are fas-

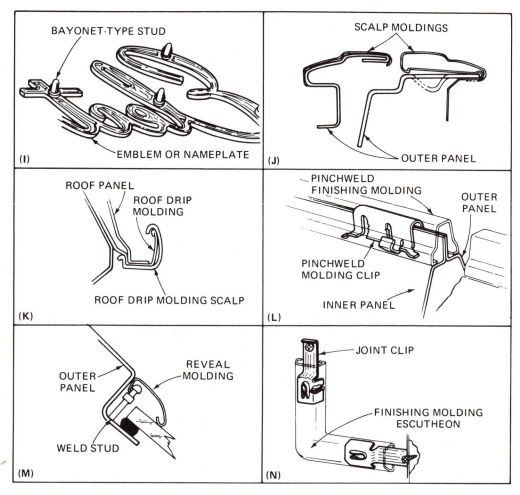

FIGURE 1-23 Exterior molding attachments. (Courtesy of General Motors of Canada, Ltd.)

tened by means of a bolt clip assembly [Fig. 1-22(B)], sometimes by W-base clips [Fig. 1-22(F)], or even by a variety of different-shaped wire-formed types of spring clip (Fig. 1-25). These clips are sometimes also called snap-in clips and must first be installed in the molding, correctly positioned and spaced, before they can be pressed or snapped into the accommodating holes in the outer panel.

Two-sided adhesive tape on moldings and nameplates [Fig. 1-22(D)] are very popular today and are easy to remove when damaged by cutting the adhesive with a sharp object, such as a putty knife (Fig. 1-26).

Bayonet-type studs are also frequently tightened by means of speed nuts (Fig. 1-27) or self-threading steel nuts (Fig. 1-28). Scalp moldings are made to

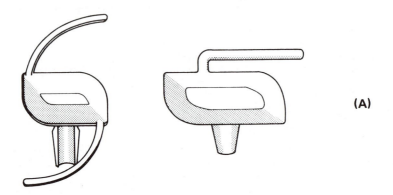

(A)

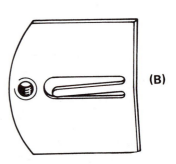

(B)

FIGURE 1-24   (A) Nylon snap-in clips; (B) threaded stud-type molding fastener. (Courtesy of Spae-Naur Products, Ltd.)

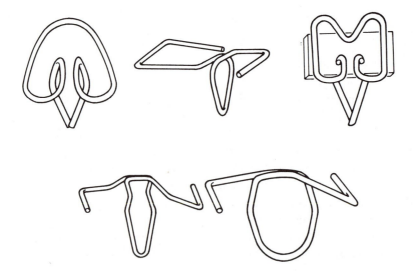

FIGURE 1-25

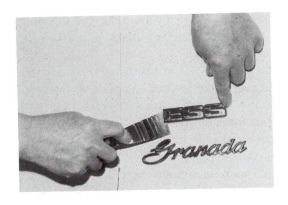

FIGURE 1-26 Removal of adhesive taped nameplate.

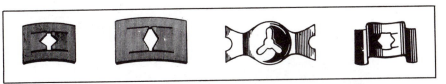

FIGURE 1-27 Speed nuts. (Courtesy of Spae-Naur Products, Ltd.)

fit tightly over various sections or parts on an automobile body and are self-retaining [Fig. 1-23(K)]. They are slipped over roof drip moldings and door window frames, greatly adding to the appearance of many automobiles.

A *weld stud*, such as that shown in Fig. 1-23(M), is used to hold stationary glass reveal moldings in place. The moldings are properly positioned between the round head of the weld stud and the outer panel and then gently thumped into place.

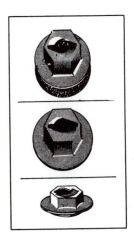

FIGURE 1-28 Self-threading steel nuts. (Courtesy of Spae-Naur Products, Ltd.)

Joint clips, like those shown in Fig. 1-23(N), are used to hold finishing molding escutcheons in their proper positions, and they make it possible for corner joints to be made neatly and accurately.

Nylon plug-type molding fasteners (Fig. 1-29) are becoming very popular. They are similar to nylon snap-in clips except that they are equipped with tapered plugs that must be tapped in completely to expand and seat them tightly. If fasteners are undamaged and accessible from the back, they can easily be removed by tapping the tapered plugs back out with a drift punch and reinstalled when necessary.

Nylon plugs and rivets are used on many late-model cars. Nylon rivets are used to connect the lower channels to door and quarter window glasses (Fig. 1-30).

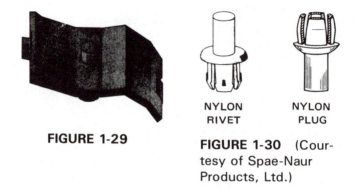

NYLON
RIVET

NYLON
PLUG

FIGURE 1-29

FIGURE 1-30 (Courtesy of Spae-Naur Products, Ltd.)

Trim panels are held in place using a variety of fasteners (Fig. 1-31). These are generally mounted on or near the outer edges of the trim panels in stamped-out slots or holes or by means of nails (older models) spot-welded to metal-retaining strips that are crimped around the outer edges of the cardboard inner panels. A number of the newer automobiles have plastic door trim panels and use a new type of nylon fastener [Fig. 1-32(A)].

When removing trim panels, damage to both the panel and fasteners can be minimized by using the proper trim removal tool [Fig. 1-32(B)]. A gentle lifting pressure should be applied in the immediate area or directly under each fastener until the trim panel is freed.

All electrical wiring, brake lines, and gasoline lines are supported and held in place by various types of rubber grommets, tube fasteners, and wiring fasteners

FIGURE 1-31 Trim panel fasteners. (Courtesy of Spae-Naur Products, Ltd.)

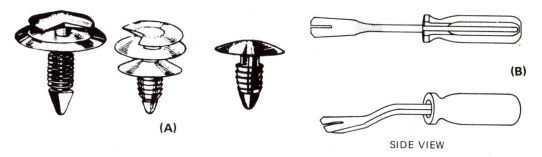

FIGURE 1-32 (A) Nylon trim fasteners; (b) trim removal tool. [(A) Courtesy of Spae-Naur Products, Ltd.)

(Fig. 1-33). *Rubber* grommets are used to protect wiring and tubing from abrasion wherever they have been routed through holes in body panels or frame members. Tube and wiring fasteners are used to keep brake and gasoline lines from vibrating and breaking.

RUBBER GROMMETS

BRAKE AND GASOLINE LINE FASTENERS

WIRING FASTENERS

FIGURE 1-33 Grommets, tube fasteners, and wire fasteners. (Courtesy of Spae-Naur Products, Ltd.)

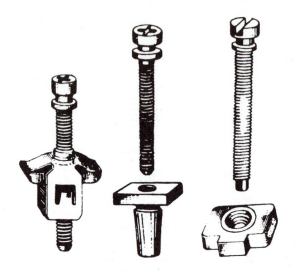

FIGURE 1-34 Self-lock-ing-type fasteners.

Headlight sealed-beam units are held in place and adjusted by means of screws equipped with nylon nuts (Fig. 1-34) that lock securely into accommodating rectangular holes in the headlight body or radiator support panel. On older-model cars the threaded nylon blocks (Fig. 1-35) are fastened by means of small rivets or bolts.

Hose clamps are used to tighten radiator and heater hoses and flexible gasoline lines; they are available in many sizes. There are three types used on

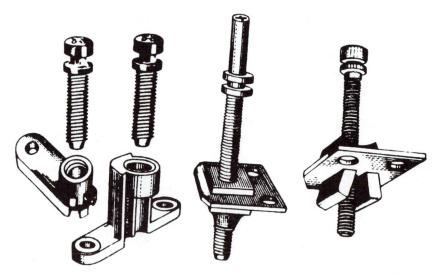

FIGURE 1-35 Rivet or bolt-on-type fasteners. (Courtesy of Spae-Naur Products, Ltd.)

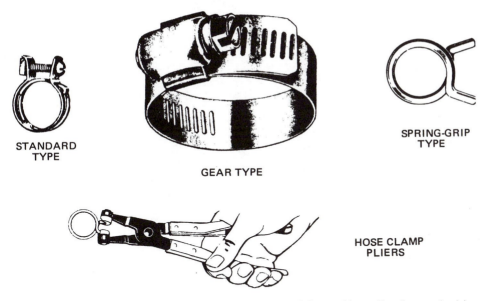

STANDARD
TYPE

GEAR TYPE

SPRING-GRIP
TYPE

HOSE CLAMP
PLIERS

FIGURE 1-36 Hose clamps. (Courtesy of Spae-Naur Products, Ltd.)

automobiles, namely the standard, the gear, and the spring-grip type (Fig. 1-36). A regular flat-blade screwdriver is used to install the first two types, while hose clamp pliers are used with the spring-grip type.

Pop rivets are precision-made, high-strength hollow rivets that are made of aluminum, Monel steel, or stainless steel and assembled on solid mandrels. They are available in various sizes and in two types: open end and closed end. They are especially useful for blind-fastening parts on automobiles where there is no access to the reverse side of the work. On many late models, pop rivets are used instead of bolts in fastening window regulators, inside remote controls, and power door lock actuators in position on the inner panels of doors. They are installed and set from the same side by means of a setting tool (Fig. 1-37). The retracting jaws of the tool pull the round head of the mandrel into the rivet, mushrooming its end until the mandrel breaks under tension.

Cushion clips or hog rings, as they are frequently called, are used to fasten seat padding, seat fabrics, and seat covers to the seat frame and its spring work. They are clinched (closed) firmly in place by means of cushion clip pliers (Fig. 1-38).

On some late-model automobiles, both metric and the customary (inch-type) bolts, nuts, and screws are used on the same car. In an attempt to reduce the number of sizes and yet retain the best strength characteristics of fasteners used, manufacturers adopted a portion of the standard metric fastener sizes, which are nearly the same in diameter as customary inch fasteners, but their thread pitch

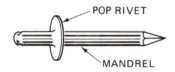

POP RIVET

MANDREL

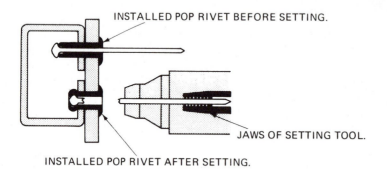

INSTALLED POP RIVET BEFORE SETTING.

JAWS OF SETTING TOOL.

INSTALLED POP RIVET AFTER SETTING.

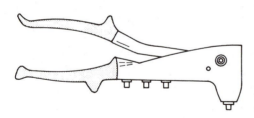

POP RIVET SETTING TOOL.

FIGURE 1-37

is in between the customary coarse and fine pitches, making identification very difficult. When servicing the automobile, care should therefore be taken to guard against cross-threading and improper retention (tightening), due to interchanging of metric with customary (inch) bolts and nuts.

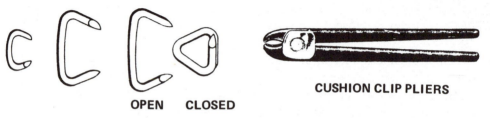

OPEN   CLOSED

CUSHION CLIP PLIERS

FIGURE 1-38 (Courtesy of Spae-Naur Products, Ltd.)

METRIC BOLT AND NUT IDENTIFICATION

Common metric fastener strength property classes are 9.8 and 10.9 with the class identification embossed on the head of each bolt. Customary (inch) strength classes range from grade 2 to 8 with line identification embossed on each bolt head. Markings correspond to two lines less than the actual grade (i.e. grade 7 bolt will exhibit 5 embossed lines on the bolt head). Some metric nuts will be marked with single digit strength identification numbers on the nut face. The following figure illustrates the different strength markings.

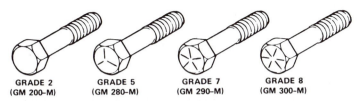

GRADE 2
(GM 200-M)

GRADE 5
(GM 280-M)

GRADE 7
(GM 290-M)

GRADE 8
(GM 300-M)

Customary (inch) bolts – Identification marks correspond to bolt strength – Increasing numbers represent increasing strength.

Metric Bolts – Identification class numbers correspond to bolt strength – Increasing numbers represent increasing strength.

MANUFACTURERS
IDENTIFICATION

NUT STRENGTH
IDENTIFICATION

CROSS RECESS
SCREW HEAD

IDENTIFICATION MARKS (4)

1943

FIGURE 1-39 Metric bolt and nut identification chart. (Courtesy of General Motors of Canada, Ltd.)

Any bolts, nuts, and screws removed from the car should be saved and reused, whenever possible, and if not reusable, should be replaced with one matching the original and bearing the same identifying mark or number, as illustrated in the identification chart (Fig. 1-39). Common metric fastener strength property classes are 9.8 and 10.9 with the class identification embossed on the head of each bolt. Customary (inch) strength classes range from grade 2 to 8 with line identification embossed on each bolt head. Markings correspond to two lines less than the actual grade (that is, grade 7 bolt will exhibit five embossed lines on the bolt head). Some metric nuts will be marked with single-digit strength identification numbers on the nut face.

QUESTIONS

1-1 How can an auto body repairman or refinisher become a good craftsman and maintain a high degree of proficiency in his chosen trade?

1-2 What is the best advertisement for an auto body repair and refinishing shop and the people it employs?

1-3 What material was mainly used in manufacturing automobiles until the 1980s?

1-4 What brought about the change in design and materials used in the manufacture of automobiles?

1-5 What difference is there in the granular structure of mild and high-strength steel?

1-6 State the three main reasons why manufacturers are using high-strength steel.

1-7 List six different types of high-strength steel used in unitized automobiles today.

1-8 What two types of high-strength steel should never be heated?

1-9 What happens to high-strength steel when heated beyond 700°F (371.1°C)?

1-10 Why should it be of great importance to the repairman and all concerned that proper methods be used in the repairing of automobiles of high-strength-steel construction?

1-11 What different types of body construction are used today?

1-12 How are squeaks kept from developing and road noises from being transmitted through the frame to the body in automobiles of standard or conventional construction?

1-13 In what way is accurate alignment of the body and frame obtained?

1-14 What accounts for the overall rigidity in unitized body construction?

1-15 In unitized construction, what section of the body possesses the greatest amount of strength?

1-16 How is the latest type of unitized automobile employing space-frame technology built?

1-17 How does the modified form of unitized body construction differ from the unitized body construction?

1-18 Why is it important for an auto body repairman to know the names of all the body sections, assemblies, parts, and fastening devices?

1-19 What is the front section of the body called, and what are its principal parts?

1-20 What is the largest body panel on an automobile? How is it supported and reinforced?

1-21 In what section of the body are the quarter-panel assemblies located, and what are their component parts?

1-22 Doors, hoods, and deck lids provide easy access to various compartments. Give the names of these compartments.

1-23 Describe how doors, hoods, and deck lids are similar in design and construction.

1-24 How are the front and rear bumpers held in position on an automobile?

1-25 The installation and adjustment of bumpers are made in three different ways. Name them.

1-26 What different materials are grilles made of, and how are grilles held in place?

1-27 When speaking of front-end sheet metal, what different panels or parts are included?

1-28 What useful functions do the preceding panels perform?

1-29 By what parts is the front-end sheet metal held down and reinforced?

1-30 To what panels is the rear end of many front fender panels bolted?

1-31 Describe how the front of the fender panel is attached and held in place.

1-32 How is the hood panel mounted and held in its proper position on most automobiles?

1-33 In what way are die-cast moldings attached to the body?

1-34 Why is it that the bolt and clip assembly method of attaching moldings cannot be used on all outer panels?

1-35 What is used to attach moldings and nameplates to panels when no clips or nuts are used?

1-36 Why have weld-on stud-type clips become popular with automobile manufacturers?

1-37 What type of fastener is used in attaching emblems, nameplates, and letters?

1-38 Describe briefly the different ways in which stamped stainless steel and aluminum moldings are attached to an outer panel.

1-39 How are finishing molding escutcheons attached, and where are they used?

1-40 Once nylon plug-type molding fasteners have been installed, how can they be removed and reinstalled?

1-41 What type of fastener is used in connecting lower channels to door and quarter-window glasses?

1-42 When removing a trim panel, how can damage to the panel and its fasteners be minimized?

1-43 How are electrical wiring, brake lines, and gasoline lines supported and held in place?

1-44 What kind of fasteners are used in the mounting and adjustment of automobile headlight sealed-beam units?

1-45 List three types of hose clamps used on automobiles, and describe how each is tightened.

1-46 What fastening device and special tool are employed in the fastening of parts on body panels that are inaccessible from the reverse side?

1-47 How are the seat padding, seat fabrics, and seat covers fastened to the seat frame and its spring work?

1-48 What difference is there between metric and customary (inch) bolts, nuts, and screws?

1-49 How can cross-threading and improper retention be avoided?

2

Welding

---

1. Never convert an acetylene regulator to oxygen use, or vice versa.

2. Never use cylinder gas without a regulator.

3. Always stand to the side of an oxygen regulator when the valve is opened.

4. Always open the oxygen valve slowly until the pressure reaches the maximum; then finish opening the valve.

5. Always check to see that the pressure-adjusting screw is released before opening the cylinder valve.

6. Never use a hose that is dirty or that has talc inside; blow it out with oxygen. Dirt or talc could clog the torch.

7. Never use more than hand pressure to open cylinder valves. If the valve is too tight, the cylinder should be replaced.

8. Heating a cylinder with a flame could cause it to explode.

9. Never try to fill a small cylinder from a large one.

10. Observe all fire-prevention practices. Have water and a fire extinguisher handy for use if necessary.

11. Always wear welding goggles when welding or cutting.

12. Never try to repair regulators or torches unless you know how to do so. A poor job could cause a serious explosion.

13. Always protect the hose from fire, slag, or sharp edges. It is made of rubber and burns or can be cut easily.

14. Always take good care of your welding equipment. It is a good servant if used properly.

15. When a welding torch is not being used, it should be shut off because it could set a fire or seriously burn a fellow worker if he should come in contact with it. One of the most dangerous things to weld is a gas tank that has not been steamed properly, for there is a good chance that it will explode on contact with the flame. One of the best methods to repair a gas tank is to use a soldering iron and do a solder repair instead; it is much safer.

UNIT 2-1: OXYACETYLENE WELDING

Body repairs can rarely be carried out without the use of welding equipment, such as the common oxyacetylene torch. Oxyacetylene equipment, which is used quite extensively in any body shop, has various uses—welding, cutting, and heating to normalize metal, to shrink metal, to forge or shape metal, and to solder. Other types of welding, like arc and spot welding, are also used, but they have specific applications.

Before turning to oxyacetylene welding, however, let us discuss some of the equipment and gases used in the welding process. The gases used for oxyacetylene welding are usually acetylene and oxygen. When mixed together in the proper proportions, and with the proper equipment, these two gases produce a flame that is hot enough to melt most commercial metals.

Oxygen

Oxygen is obtained from the air via a liquefaction process. The air that we breathe contains different gases that can be separated. The air is compressed and cooled until it turns liquid. The gases evaporate at different temperatures and thus can be separated by special rectifying apparatus. As each gas reaches its boiling point, it is separated from the others. Oxygen has a boiling point of $-182.9°C$. When the liquid gas reaches this temperature, the oxygen starts to boil and becomes a gas. It is then collected and stored in cylinders built for this purpose.

The Oxygen Cylinder

The oxygen cylinder is made seamless by drawing it from a solid piece of high-grade steel, which is heat-treated so as to resist abuse and also to have great strength; the wall thickness is about 5/16 in. (8 mm). The cylinder is equipped with a double-seated valve, which is designed to operate at high pressure without any leaks. The valve seat seals the oxygen in the cylinder when it is closed. When it is open, the valve seals and prevents any leaks from occurring at the valve stem. The valve should always be opened fully when in use and closed completely when not in use. When the cylinder is not in use, the safety cap should always be in place to protect the valve from damage during shipping or handling. The valve also has a safety disk that will rupture, thus releasing the oxygen if the pressure should become excessive—for example, from a fire. This safety disk would prevent an explosion by releasing the pressure in the oxygen cylinder.

The cylinders are generally filled to a pressure of 2200 psi (15,180 kPa) at 70°F (21.1°C). If the temperature goes down, the pressure will go down. If the temperature goes up, the pressure will go up. Usually, three different sizes of cylinders are used: the large size, which holds approximately 244 cu ft (7076 liters) (Fig. 2-1); the medium size, which holds approximately 122 cu ft (3538 liters); and the small size, which holds approximately 80 cu ft (2320 liters).

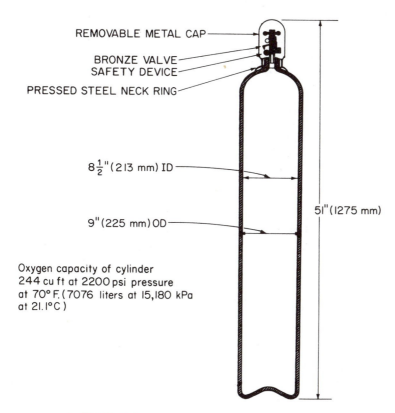

REMOVABLE METAL CAP

BRONZE VALVE
SAFETY DEVICE
PRESSED STEEL NECK RING

$8\frac{1}{2}$" (213 mm) ID

9" (225 mm) OD

51" (1275 mm)

Oxygen capacity of cylinder
244 cu ft at 2200 psi pressure
at 70°F. (7076 liters at 15,180 kPa
at 21.1°C)

FIGURE 2-1 Oxygen cylinder construction.

Acetylene

Acetylene is made when calcium carbide cakes are immersed in water in a generator. A chemical reaction occurs, giving off acetylene. Calcium carbide is produced by smelting coke and lime in an electric furnace; the smelting produces a gray stonelike material.

The acetylene is then collected and stored in cylinders. Free acetylene cannot be used at pressures that exceed 15 psi (103.5 kPa) because it becomes unstable and could explode. Acetylene can also explode under the right conditions if it is released in a room and mixes into the air; a spark could set it off. A mixture of between 2.6 and 80 percent of acetylene in the air could possibly explode.

The Acetylene Cylinder

The acetylene cylinder is quite different from the oxygen cylinder. It is made from steel but is usually welded at the seams. The walls are thinner, it is shorter in length, and the diameter is larger than that of the oxygen cylinder. Two different types of cylinders are used; one is shown in Fig. 2-2. The second type is similar except that the top of the cylinder is recessed and does not require a safety cap to protect the valve, for the high side or extension at the top of the cylinder protects the valve from damage.

Since free acetylene becomes very unstable when compressed above 15 psi (103.5 kPa), the method used to compress acetylene to a higher pressure is as follows: The cylinder is filled with a porous material, such as asbestos, charcoal, or balsa wood. This material is saturated thoroughly with liquid acetone. Acetone will absorb and dissolve great quantities of acetylene, much like a blotter absorbs water. When acetylene is stored in this manner, it is very stable and will not change its composition.

The valve used is a single-seated valve and should not be opened more than a turn and a half. If it should leak around the stem, the gasket can usually be tightened to stop the leak. If this step does not stop the leak, the cylinder should be left in an open-air area and shipped to the supplier as soon as possible. The cylinder is protected from explosion by safety fuse plugs that melt at about 220°F (104°C), thus releasing the pressure.

Regulators

Regulators are instruments designed to reduce high cylinder pressure to a low pressure, which is required for welding or cutting operations. The regulators are attached to the cylinder valves by threaded fittings.

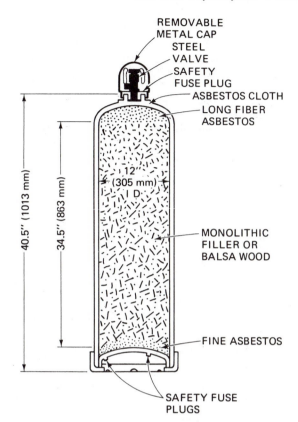

REMOVABLE
METAL CAP
STEEL
VALVE
SAFETY
FUSE PLUG
ASBESTOS CLOTH
LONG FIBER
ASBESTOS

12"
(305 mm)
D.

MONOLITHIC
FILLER OR
BALSA WOOD

FINE ASBESTOS

SAFETY FUSE
PLUGS

40.5" (1013 mm)

34.5" (863 mm)

ACETYLENE CAPACITY
APPROX. 275. cu ft
AT 250 psi PRESSURE
AND 70° F. (7975 LITERS
AT 2325 kPa AND 21.1°C.)

FIGURE 2-2 Acetylene cylinder construction.

Oxygen regulators are designed to withstand a pressure of around 3000 psi (20,700 kPa). The cylinders are usually filled to a pressure of around 2200 psi (15,180 kPa). The fittings on this regulator are always right-hand thread. Acetylene regulators are very similar to oxygen regulators, but they are not designed to withstand high pressure because it is not required. The cylinder pressure gauge only registers to 350 psi (2415 kPa) and the working pressure gauge is only graduated to 15 psi (103.5 kPa). Acetylene regulator fittings and accessories have left-hand thread with a groove cut in the nut; this eliminates the danger of interchanging any of the fittings. Each regulator is equipped with a screw that is used to adjust the pressure required. The regulators are designed to give an accurate and nonfluctuating pressure to the blowpipe or torch.

Two types of regulators are manufactured, the two-stage and the single-stage regulator. The two-stage regulator uses two stages to reduce cylinder pressure to a working pressure at the torch. The single-stage regulator reduces the high pressure to a working pressure in one stage. The two-stage regulator has two diaphragms and the single stage has one diaphragm. These diaphragms are commonly made of rubber or even stainless steel.

Since the cylinder pressure will not remain constant while being used, the regulator must be able to take whatever pressure is in the cylinder, whether 2000 or 200 psi (13,800 or 1380 kPa), and must be able to deliver the required pressure, which could be 10 psi (69 kPa) at the torch. Therefore, when the welding outfit is to be used, the adjusting screw is turned clockwise to adjust the pressure. This step applies pressure to a spring that is seated on the diaphragm; the diaphragm moves back and pushes the valve seat away from the high-pressure nozzle. The gas from the cylinder enters and pressures the chamber, gradually overcoming the pressure applied on the diaphragm by the spring. This operation, in turn, closes the valve seat. As the gas is used up, another cycle takes over and the whole operation is repeated.

The operation of a double-stage regulator is a little more complicated. The double-stage regulator has a high-pressure chamber and a low-pressure chamber. The high-pressure chamber tension spring is preset, thus allowing gas to flow in when the cylinder valve is opened. It only closes when sufficient pressure over-comes the spring tension on the diaphragm. As the adjusting screw is turned clockwise, the low-pressure chamber valve opens, allowing gas to enter and bleed the high-pressure chamber. When sufficient pressure has entered, it pushes against the diaphragm and closes the valve. When the gas is used, the cycle repeats itself. All regulators are equipped with a safety relief valve which will release excessive pressure which could build up in the regulator chamber due to a leaking valve.

Certain precautions should be followed when operating regulators. Before opening the supply cylinder, check the adjusting screw to see if it is released; then open the cylinder valve. To adjust the working pressure, the valves on the torch body should be opened slightly as the adjusting screw is turned to adjust the pressure on the regulator that is required for the job. When a regulator is not being used overnight or is idle for a long period, the pressure should always be relieved on the delivery pressure valve seat.

Most regulators are equipped with two gauges (Fig. 2-3); one gauge shows the pressure left in the cylinder and the other shows the pressure used at the torch. These gauges use a Bourdon tube; as the gas enters the tube, it tends to straighten it out. The tube is connected to a mechanism with a moving needle that moves on a calibrated dial. The reading on the dial is given in pounds per square inch (psi) or kilopascals (kPa) per square centimeter.

These gauges are fragile and care must be taken to have the adjusting screw released before opening the cylinder valve. If the screw is not released, the

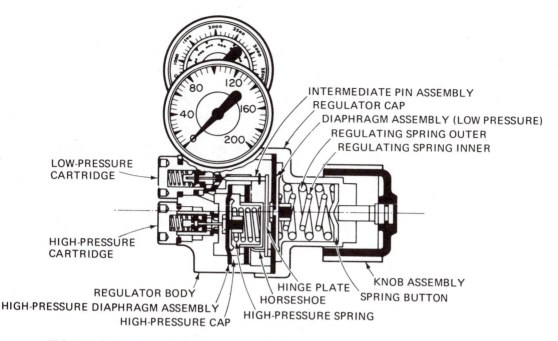

FIGURE 2-3 Cross section of double-stage regulator. (Courtesy of Canadian Liquid Air.)

sudden rush of gas could rupture the tube or diaphragm. The screw must always be turned to the left in order to relieve the pressure on the diaphragm.

Hoses

Only an approved type of welding hose should be used. These hoses are usually joined by a web. Oxygen hoses are green in color and acetylene hoses are red. These colors are generally the same on the regulators. Hoses should be fitted with the proper fittings and ferrules. The oxygen fittings have right-hand thread; acetylene fittings have a left-hand thread and, in general, a groove cut in the nut. Hoses should be checked periodically for leaks and they should never be repaired with anything other than approved fittings or splicers. Be sure that all dust and talc are blown out before using.

Torches

The torch consists of a torch body that is equipped with acetylene and oxygen shutoff valves. These valves are either incorporated in the torch body or are a separate section of the body. The torch found in most shops is a medium-pressure

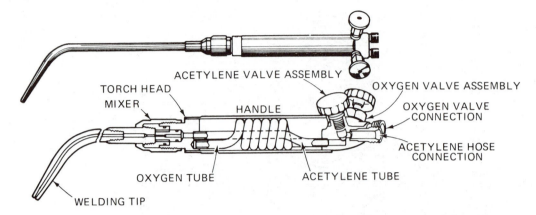

FIGURE 2-4 Torch body. (Courtesy of Union Carbide of Canada, Ltd.)

type that uses from 1 to 15 psi (6.9 to 103.5 kPa) of acetylene pressure (Fig. 2-4). The oxygen and acetylene are fed at different pressures to the mixer nozzle, depending on the various specifications incorporated by manufacturers. All torch bodies are sold with an assortment of tips of different sizes so that a wide variety of jobs can be handled.

Equipment Required

A welding and cutting outfit consists of the following parts:

1. Oxygen cylinder
2. Acetylene cylinder
3. A suitable truck to hold cylinders
4. Welding torch and cutting attachment
5. Acetylene and oxygen regulators
6. Hoses
7. Friction lighter
8. Welding goggles

The first steps required to set up an oxyacetylene outfit are that the cylinders be placed in a specially built truck and then that the safety caps be removed. Next, the valves on the cylinders must be opened slightly, one at a time, to

(A)   (B)

FIGURE 2-5 Cracking the cylinder valves. (Courtesy of Union Carbide of Canada, Ltd.)

remove dust accumulation in the valves (be sure that no one is in the way of the blast of the escaping gas). Then shut the valve. The term used for this operation is usually called *cracking* the valve (Fig. 2-5).

The regulators are then connected to the cylinders. Be sure that they are perfectly clean—free of grease, oil, and dirt (Fig. 2-6). Before the cylinder valve is opened, the pressure-adjusting screw should be checked to see that it is released, so that no pressure is exerted on the diaphragm. The valve should then be opened slowly and as far as required. When the valve is opened slowly, the pressure builds up gradually in the regulator and in this way the diaphragm will not be damaged.

The hoses are then connected to the regulators (Fig. 2-7); they should be blown out, each independently, to remove all traces of dust and talc that might be present. Before blowing the hoses out, check to see that no open fires, oil, or grease are present. The hoses are blown out by turning each regulator-adjusting screw in and then out. The loose end of the hoses is then attached to the torch body and the welding tip is inserted into the torch (Fig. 2-8). All connections should be checked to ensure that they are tight. They must not be overtightened, however—only tight enough so that no leaks will be present.

(A)

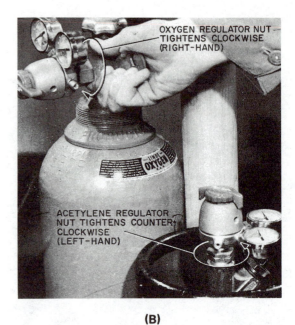

OXYGEN REGULATOR NUT—
TIGHTENS CLOCKWISE
(RIGHT-HAND)

ACETYLENE REGULATOR
NUT TIGHTENS COUNTER-
CLOCKWISE
(LEFT-HAND)

(B)

(C)

FIGURE 2-6 Attaching regulators to cylinders.

FIGURE 2-7 Attaching supply hoses to regulators. (Courtesy of Union Carbide of Canada, Ltd.)

FIGURE 2-8 (A) Attaching supply hoses to blowpipe; (B) attaching welding or cutting tip. (Courtesy of Union Carbide of Canada, Ltd.)

(A) **(B)**

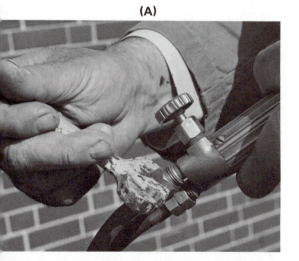 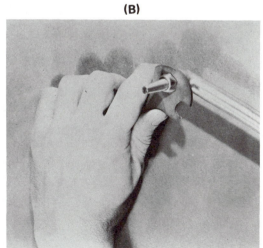

The acetylene valve on the torch body is opened slightly and the adjusting screw on the regulator is turned clockwise until the proper working pressure is obtained (see Table 2-1). Then the valve is closed (Fig. 2-9). This step is repeated for the oxygen valve; then all connections should be checked with an oil-free soap and water solution. If any leaks are present, investigate the reason and correct it.

Welding goggles must always be worn to protect the eyes from the heat of the torch's flame. If no goggles are worn, the eyeballs become very dry and the operator runs the risk of getting pieces of slag embedded in his eyes.

The oxygen valve is opened slightly and then the acetylene valve. A flint striker is used to light the torch. Never use a match or a lighter, for the result may be burned fingers (Fig. 2-10).

TABLE 2-1 Welding chart.

Metal Thickness (Steel)	Welding Tip Size No. *	Oxygen Pressure [psi (kPa)]	Acetylene Pressure [psi (kPa)]
Less than 1/32 in. (0.8 mm)	2		
1/32 in. (1 mm) (22 gauge)			
1/16 in. (2 mm) (16 gauge)	6		
3/32 in. (2 mm) (13 gauge)			
1/8 in. (3 mm) (11 gauge)	6 or 15	5 (34.5)	5 (34.5)
1/16 in. (5 mm)	15		
1/4 in. (6 mm)	15		
1/4 in. (6 mm)	20		
3/8 in. (10 mm)	20	6 (41.4)	6 (41.4)
3/8 in. (10 mm)	30	9 (62.1)	9 (62.1)

Welding tip cleaning drill sizes.

Tip Size No.	Drill Size
2	75
6	60
15	53
20	50
30	44

*Gas flows: The size number of each tip represents the approximate consumption of each gas. That is, a No. 15 tip will consume about 15 cu ft (375 liters) of oxygen and 15 cu ft (375 liters) of acetylene per hour.

Source: Courtesy of Union Carbide of Canada, Ltd.

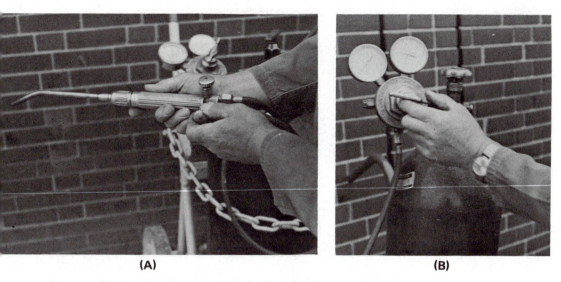

(A)   **(B)**

FIGURE 2-9   (A) Adjustment of blowpipe valves; (B) adjustment
of regulators. (Courtesy of Union Carbide of Canada, Ltd.)

The acetylene valve is opened enough so that the flame is bright, with no black carbon soot visible. If it is not opened enough, black soot will result; if opened too much, the flame will leave the end of the tip. There will be a gap between the tip and the flame and the torch may go out.

Tips and Sizes to Use

Manufacturers make a wide range of tips available to the welder. The tips recommended for the Prest-O-Lite 420 Welding and Cutting Outfit supplied by Union Carbide of Canada, Ltd. (or any distributor of welding equipment) are shown in Table 2-1. Welding tips should always be cleaned carefully with a proper tip cleaner or twist drill. They must never be reamed or filed.

The Flame and Its Uses

The acetylene valve is opened until the flame is ready to leave the tip; then the oxygen valve is opened farther until the desired flame is adjusted. Three types of flames are used: the neutral flame, the oxidizing flame, and the carbonizing flame.

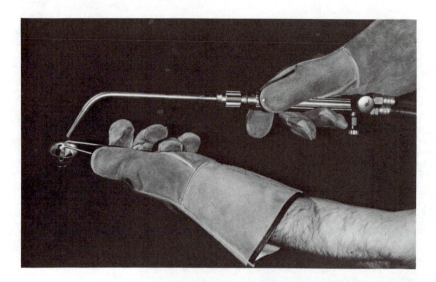

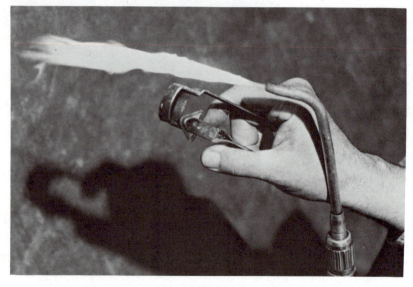

FIGURE 2-10 Lighting the torch.

Neutral Flame

Used for most steel welding, the neutral flame burns approximately one part of oxygen to one part of acetylene through the blowpipe, but it also burns a part and a half of oxygen from the air. Adjust the torch until the inner cone is as blunt as possible and the feathery edges have disappeared. Figure 2-11 shows a neutral flame; the temperature is approximately 5900°F (3260°C).

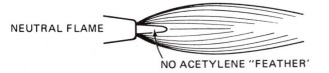

NEUTRAL FLAME

NO ACETYLENE "FEATHER'

FIGURE 2-11 Neutral flame. (Courtesy of Union Carbide of Canada, Ltd.)

Excess Oxygen or Oxidizing Flame

A slightly oxidizing flame is used for brazing. It is obtained by opening the oxygen slightly more than for the neutral flame. The inner cone gets shorter and pointed and it becomes purplish (Fig. 2-12). The temperature is approximately 6300°F (3482°C).

OXIDIZING (EXCESS OXYGEN) FLAME

INNER CONE BECOMES SHORTER
FLAME BECOMES NOISIER

FIGURE 2-12 Oxidizing (excess oxygen) flame. (Courtesy of Union Carbide of Canada, Ltd.)

Excess Acetylene Flame or Carbonizing Flame

An excess acetylene flame is used mostly for heating parts or for soldering. It burns more acetylene than oxygen through the torch; therefore, its inner cone has a feather. The inner cone is also whitish. The envelope around it would have much the same appearance as the neutral flame (Fig. 2-13). The temperature is approximately 5700°F (3154°C).

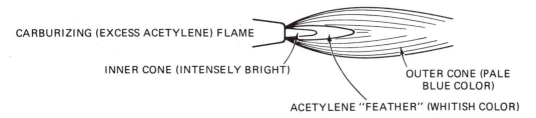

CARBURIZING (EXCESS ACETYLENE) FLAME

INNER CONE (INTENSELY BRIGHT)

OUTER CONE (PALE BLUE COLOR)

ACETYLENE "FEATHER" (WHITISH COLOR)

FIGURE 2-13 Carbonizing (excess acetylene) flame. (Courtesy of Union Carbide of Canada, Ltd.)

Flashback

A flashback, a malfunctioning of the torch, occurs when the flame goes inside the torch. When this happens, close the oxygen valve immediately. When the flame goes inside the torch, it will start to hiss or squeal. Closing the oxygen valve stops the flame. Next, close the acetylene valve. The regulators should then be closed and the torch allowed to cool. When a flashback occurs, it is usually because the torch is used improperly or insufficient gas pressure is being used on the orifice of the tip.

Backfire

If the torch is operated improperly, it may cause the flame to go out with a loud snap or pop, which is called a *backfire*. The torch valves should be shut off and connections and valves checked for leaks. If everything is in satisfactory condition, the torch may be relit.

A backfire is generally caused by the following factors: the tip touching the work, overheated or dirty tip, lower than recommended gas pressure, loose torch head or tip, or a poor seal between the torch body and mixing chamber.

General Rules

1. Always clean tips with tip cleaners or proper twist drills.

2. Always use strikers to light torches.

3. Always use proper wrenches on connections.

4. Never use oxygen as a substitute for compressed air or as a source of pressure.

5. Before starting to weld or cut, make certain that there is no material nearby or openings leading to material that flame, sparks, hot slag, or metal might ignite.

6. Be sure to keep a clear space between cylinders and the work.

7. Always repair hoses with splicers; never use wire, tape, or copper tubing.

8. Always use a water–soap solution to test for leaks; check hose and connections regularly for leaks.

9. Cylinders should always be used and stored in an upright position.

10. Cylinders should always be handled with great care; they should not be dropped or knocked about. Never use cylinders except for the specific purposes they were meant to be used for. Your life may depend on it.

11. Never move cylinders without having safety caps on. The valve could be knocked off if one should fall down.

12. If clogged with ice, the valve should be thawed out with lukewarm water only. If boiling water is used, the safety plug could melt and release the gas.

13. Never use oil on welding equipment. Oil and oxygen under pressure could cause a violent explosion. When changing cylinders, make sure that hands are clean at all times.

UNIT 2-2: FUSION WELDING SHEET METAL

The first thing a student in auto body repairs has to master is the welding of sheet metal. Learning how to weld it is difficult because the metal is thin and the heat travels quite fast. Therefore, special precautions have to be taken to control the forces of expansion and contraction. High-crowned areas are always easier to weld than flat or low-crowned areas. Thorough penetration must be obtained. The buildup on the bead must be kept to a minimum, so the bead is sunk to the bottom to obtain the proper penetration in the weld (Fig. 2-14).

The proper sized tip should be inserted into the torch body. The regulators should be adjusted to the right pressure for the particular type of torch used. A welding bench with bricks on top should be used as a place to lay some body sheet metal or 20-gauge sheet metal, cut into reasonably sized pieces by a shear.

The torch is then lit with a striker and the flame adjusted to a neutral flame. The torch is held in the hand that is normally used, whether right or left. If held in the right hand, the torch should be positioned on the right side of the piece of metal and the work should progress toward the left. The end of the tip should be held at approximately a 45° angle to the metal and directly in line with the

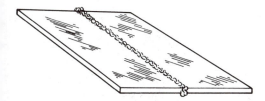

FIGURE 2-14

FIGURE 2-15 Position of blowpipe. (Courtesy of Union Carbide of Canada, Ltd.)

direction of travel (Fig. 2-15). The cone is held 1/16 in. (2 mm) from the metal until the metal turns from red to white and a puddle forms. The torch should not be moved until the puddle has become between 3/16 to 1/4 in. (5 to 6 mm) wide; then it is slowly advanced in a slightly oval circle of 5/16 in. (8 mm) in diameter. Each circle should overlap the other as the torch is advanced by about a 1/16 in. (2 mm) (Fig. 2-16). The puddle must be watched—not the torch—because the speed at which the puddle melts will determine the speed of travel. The puddle is then moved ahead on the sheet metal. If moved at the right speed, it will leave a bead with a slight trough having even and smooth ripples on the top and thorough penetration at the bottom of the bead. Penetration is the complete melting of the sheet metal where the bead was run (Fig. 2-17). If the movement of the torch is too fast, it will leave only a slight trace of a bead on the metal.

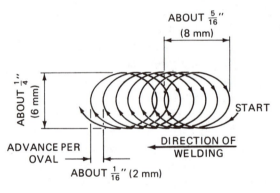

FIGURE 2-16 Blowpipe motion for practice puddle. (Courtesy of Union Carbide of Canada, Ltd.)

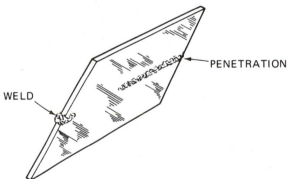

FIGURE 2-17 Underside of bead.

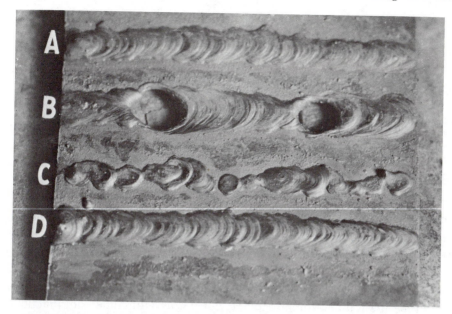

FIGURE 2-18 (A) and (D) are examples of good puddles. Excess heat caused holes in (B). Puddle (C) shows insufficient heating. (Courtesy of Union Carbide of Canada, Ltd.)

If it is moved too slowly, however, the puddle will get too large and the metal will melt completely, forming a hole in the sheet. Beads should be run at different speeds and examined carefully to determine the proper speed the bead should be run (Fig. 2-18). When the running of the bead has been mastered in the flat position, they should then be run in the vertical, horizontal, and overhead positions, because a body man must be able to weld in all positions.

The next step is to incorporate a welding rod to add filler metal to the weld. The movement of the torch remains the same, but the rod is held in the other hand (that is, the torch in one hand and the rod in the other). The rod should be held at a 45° angle to the sheet metal and in a direct straight line to which the bead is to be run. The rod is inserted into the envelope of the flame. This step preheats the end of the rod, and as soon as the puddle is formed, the rod is lowered into the center of it (Fig. 2-19). The movement of the torch and rod must be timed together so that the rod is lowered when the torch is moved ahead, not vice versa. The amount of filler rod must also be controlled so that the results are a bead with good penetration and only a slight buildup (Fig. 2-20). This control makes it easier for the body man because if there is a buildup, it has to be ground or filed off.

The same exercises as before should be done; the torch should be adjusted

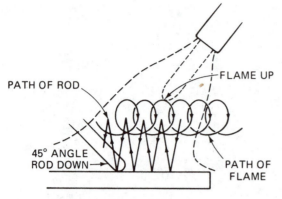

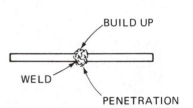

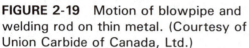

FIGURE 2-19   Motion of blowpipe and welding rod on thin metal. (Courtesy of Union Carbide of Canada, Ltd.)

FIGURE 2-20   Slight buildup.

and a 1/16 in. (2 mm) mild steel rod used as filler metal. It will be difficult at first to time the rod and torch together, but timing will come with practice. The torch, as it moves forward, will melt off a piece of the rod, which is deposited in the base metal. The rod should just be pulled out of the puddle so that the end of the rod remains near a molten state. The movement of the torch and the rod must be timed together so that the rod enters into the puddle as the torch moves to the advancing edge of the puddle. Examples of good and bad welds are shown in Fig. 2-21.

The puddle must be kept at the correct width, for if it becomes too large, a hole will be made; if it is too small, the weld will have poor penetration. These welds should also be made in the four positions mentioned; a slight decrease in the torch angle to the metal might be necessary for the horizontal and vertical positions.

The Butt Weld

The most common type of welding is the butt weld, which is frequently used to join two pieces of metal together. The torch is lit and a neutral flame used. Two pieces of metal are aligned closely edge to edge, but a gap of one thickness of the metal is allowed to counteract expansion and contraction. The edges at one end of the slit are heated. When the corners start to melt, the rod is added to bridge the gap; the same is done at the other end (Fig. 2-22). The tack welds should be kept fairly close together, a step that will help to control the distortion of the weld. The weld can then be started at the right-hand side of the metal.

FIGURE 2-21   (A) and (D) are examples of good welds. Weld (B) shows overheating. Weld (C) shows insufficient heating. (Courtesy of Union Carbide of Canada, Ltd.)

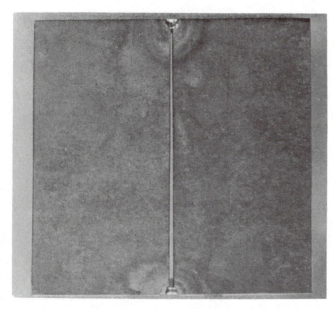

FIGURE 2-22   Tack-welding metal. (Courtesy of Union Carbide of Canada, Ltd.)

Care must be taken to dip the rod in the center of the puddle; otherwise, the rod will stick to the sides. If the metal threatens to melt through, the torch should be raised for an instant to allow the metal to cool slightly; then the welding can be resumed. When doing the horizontal butt weld, more heat should be applied to the bottom sheet than the top. To do so, hold the torch tip slightly downward.

Filler rod should never be added until a molten puddle has been formed. Also, the leading edge of the puddle must be watched to ensure that it is melted so that thorough fusion will result. It is also necessary to reach around in front of the rod with the flame and melt the edges to obtain fusion and penetration. The rod must always be deposited evenly, by melting it into the puddle and not by applying the flame to the rod.

When a few samples have been completed, they should be checked for even ripple, buildup, and penetration. Figure 2-23 shows a completed butt weld from the top view. This type of weld should also be practiced in all four positions.

FIGURE 2-23 Butt weld. (Courtesy of Union Carbide of Canada, Ltd.)

Lap Weld or Fillet Weld

The lap weld is used in the joining of panels or in putting patches over rusted-out areas. One piece of sheet metal is laid on top of another, overlapping it about 1 in. (25 mm) (Fig. 2-24). The torch is then lit and adjusted to a neutral flame. Next, the sheets are tacked to prevent the top sheet from lifting away from the bottom sheet. If it is not tacked properly, the edge of the top sheet will rise and melt away faster than it can be welded.

The torch is held in much the same manner as before, but the bottom sheet is heated more by holding the cone of the flame a 1/4 in. (6 mm) away from the top plate. When the puddle forms, move the cone closer to the edge of the top plate. Also, when the puddle forms, the welding rod is applied. The rod should be kept close to the top plate and slightly between it and the flame. The cone should be directed more toward the bottom than the top plate. More rod is going to be required to fill and form a strong even bead than for other types of welds.

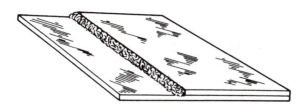

FIGURE 2-24 Lap weld.

Tee Weld

The tee weld is similar to the lap weld except that one piece of sheet metal stands on edge on top of the other (Fig. 2-25). The sheets must also be tacked properly. It is easier to weld, for the heat is distributed evenly on both sheets. The flame has a tendency to pop as the tip is confined and overheats slightly, usually because cool air is not able to reach and cool it. When welding sheet metal, always remember to use a method that counteracts distortion as much as possible.

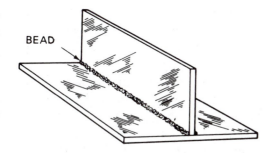

FIGURE 2-25 Tee weld.

Generally, sheet metal does not require preheating; the weld should be started and completed as soon as possible. The angle of the torch may also be decreased so as to spread the heat to a wider area and, also, so as not to force the puddle through. Another method that is very effective is to stagger the tacking and then weld from one area to the other. This procedure helps to control distortion, for only a small area is heated and welded at one time. Directing more of the flame on the rod by moving the cone slightly ahead will also help to control the heat.

UNIT 2-3: WELDING PLATE METAL

Now that techniques for welding sheet metal have been learned, they must be applied to plate metal. Plate metal is any piece of metal that is over 1/8 in. (3 mm) thick. Instead of moving the torch in a series of overlapping circles, a side-

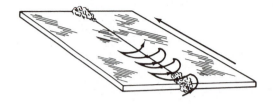

FIGURE 2-26 Suggested blowpipe motion. (Courtesy of Union Carbide of Canada, Ltd.)

to-side weaving technique must be used (Fig. 2-26). This process allows the movement of the puddle to receive proper penetration and a good bead.

The torch is held in the same way as for sheet-metal welding. A neutral flame is used. The only differences are that a tip with a bigger orifice is used and a mild steel rod of a larger diameter. Also, the acetylene and oxygen pressure is increased. Consult a chart from a welding equipment manufacturer or distributor for proper tip and gas pressures. The first exercise should be the running of the puddle without a rod. When this step is accomplished satisfactorily, a rod is then used until a proper bead with penetration is obtained. Be sure that the inner cone is 1/8 in. (3 mm) from the surface; keep the puddle a reasonable width. If the puddle becomes too wide and the metal sparks, too much heat is being used. Keep in mind that the puddle must be kept as small and uniform as possible and that the rod must be kept in the center of the puddle as the puddle is moved ahead with a weaving motion.

Butt-welding plate metal is similar to the process used for welding sheet metal except that the metal is thicker. When a weld is finished, the welded section should be put in a vise down to the bead and the vise tightened. The welded section should be bent to a 90° angle, with the top of the bead being on the inside of the angle. If the root of the weld does not break, the weld is good. When welding metal that is thicker than 1/8 in. (3 mm), the edges must be beveled in order to obtain thorough penetration (Fig. 2-27). Various methods can be used to bevel the metal, such as grinding, filing, or using the oxyacetylene cutting torch. Using the torch will require practice before this technique can be mastered. An angle of approximately 90° should be formed by the two edges when joined (Fig. 2-28). The edges are tack-welded as usual, and the welding is done in two passes. The root of the weld is done first; this should be approximately half the thickness of the metal. Then a second layer is laid on top of the root weld to complete the operation (Fig. 2-29). If the weld is more than 12 in. (0.30 m) long, a small section of the root weld is done first; then the section of the finish weld is done. The welding should progress by overlapping the root welds and finishing welds much like a bricklayer lays bricks. The advantage of this method is that the heat left in the root is used to good advantage as each section of the finish weld is done.

It must be remembered that when the bead is run, the tack welds must be

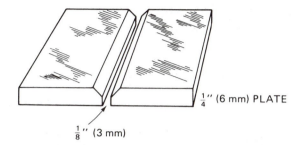

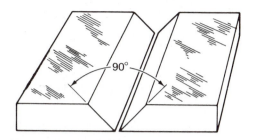

FIGURE 2-27 Single-vee butt weld with square nose.

FIGURE 2-28 Single-vee butt weld with a feather edge. (Courtesy of Union Carbide of Canada, Ltd.)

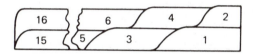

FIGURE 2-29 Welding in layer sequence. (Courtesy of Union Carbide of Canada, Ltd.).

thoroughly melted and incorporated in the bead. The filler rod should never be added until a molten puddle has been formed and then should only be added to the puddle in a smooth, regular pattern.

Backhand Welding

Most welding is done via the forehand method, but sometimes it is practical to do it the opposite way. That is, the torch is moved from left to right instead of right to left. This method is normally used to weld near chrome moldings, glass, rubber, and so on. The heat does not travel over the area to be welded but over the welded area (Fig. 2-30). When used for plate or sheet metal, backhand

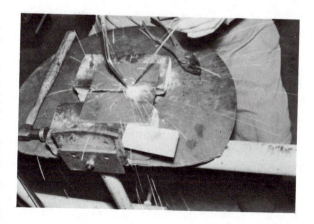

FIGURE 2-30 Backhand welding.

welding usually provides better penetration and puddle control as well as less distortion, for the heat zone does not travel as far ahead of the weld as in forehand welding.

UNIT 2-4:   BRAZE WELDING

Braze welding, or brazing as it is commonly called, can be defined as a group of welding processes where adhesion or bonding is produced by heating the base metal to an appropriate temperature above 800°F (426°C) and then adding a nonferrous filler metal that has a melting temperature lower than the base metal. The molten filler metal (rod) is distributed and flows out over the heated base metal by what is called capillary attraction, which is the power that a heated metal has to draw and spread the molten filler metal between the closely fitting surfaces of the joint.

The difference between braze welding and fusion welding is that the metal is heated only to a cherry red in braze welding. A bronze welding rod melts at approximately 1600°F (871°C) and when deposited in a molten stage, gives a strong bond between similar or different types of metal. This process could be compared to soldering except that bronze requires more heat to melt and is much stronger. Braze welding can be performed on many types of metals, such as galvanized iron, cast iron, and carbon steels, as long as their melting point is higher than the bronze.

The types of joints used in braze welding are the same as those used for fusion welding. The technique or method used is also the same as for fusion welding, but with the important exception that the base metal is not melted but only raised to the tinning temperature. (*Tinning* means to prepare the metal by flowing a light bead of brass on it. This will help the succeeding beads to adhere properly to the base metal.)

In the braze-welding process, bronze will flow on a properly prepared surface of metal and have a molecular union, thus providing a good bond without melting the base metal; in turn, this gives a joint comparable to that obtained from fusion welding.

Since the metal is only heated to a cherry red, much less distortion occurs and the bronze filler rod, which is approximately 60 percent copper and 40 percent zinc, is melted onto the metal joint, thus providing a good bond.

A flux is used in braze welding to clean the surface of impurities and oxides. It also provides a coating to protect the molten rod and hot metal from the air until the weld has cooled down. The rods can be bought both bare or flux-coated. The end of the bare rod that is to be used is heated and then dipped into a can of flux. A sufficient amount of flux is going to adhere to the rod. When this part of the flux-coated rod has been used up, the process is repeated.

Clean metal should be used for practice. The torch should be ignited and the flame adjusted to slightly oxidizing—just so the inner cone becomes sharp. For this flame, simply increase the oxygen slightly or decrease the acetylene slightly. Flux-coated bronze rods should be used because the right amount of flux is deposited automatically on the metal in the right proportions.

The slightly oxidizing flame forms a thin oxide shield over the molten bronze; this prevents the zinc in the rod from burning or fuming. The oxidizing flame is also a little hotter, thereby bringing the metal to the proper temperature faster, which helps to control expansion.

The procedure for brazing is similar to fusion welding, but with a difference—the metal should be tinned by running a light bead first (Fig. 2-31). The reason is to provide a good base for the bead. The rod is brought into the envelope as soon as the metal becomes cherry red. Then it can be either inserted in and out of the envelope or dragged along the metal, depending on the amount of metal to be deposited. After the tinning is completed, a bead of bronze is deposited to build up the area sufficiently. If one bead is not enough, another can be run over it (Fig. 2-32).

The puddle should be moved slowly and steadily, and enough bronze rod should be deposited to obtain a good strong bond. Proper torch motion will ensure the right amount of heat on the piece to be welded, so that the bronze is deposited with an even flow and good adherence (Fig. 2-33). If the metal is underheated, the bronze will not stick properly; but if it is overheated, it will burn. If a problem with overheating occurs, the tip should be changed for a smaller one. If this does not cure it completely, the torch angle is reduced and the flame can be raised up and down and concentrated more on the rod. The same projects used for fusion welding should be used with bronze, for a body man must be able to weld in all positions. It is very necessary to do a good job at all times. When welding in a horizontal position, hold the tip at an upward angle to the weld area. The force of the gas will help to keep the bronze from sagging down.

Because braze welding has no penetration like fusion welding, its use is somewhat limited in the auto body industry. Lap joints and spot plug welds are the types that are done, chiefly because braze welding needs a slight buildup for strength. Braze welding should never be used on supporting panels, members, or any areas that are subject to severe vibration or strain. A butt weld in bronze has very little strength after filing or grinding is done on the area. Also, it is impossible to fusion-weld over braze welding. A piece of metal that has bronze welding cannot be shrunk in the area of the weld.

FIGURE 2-31   Tinning. (Courtesy of Union Carbide of Canada, Ltd.)

FIGURE 2-32　A good bead. (Courtesy of Union Carbide of Canada, Ltd.)

(A)

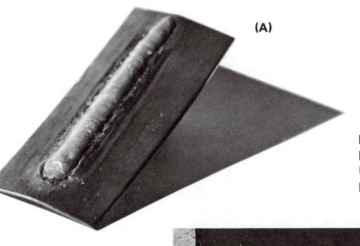

FIGURE 2-33　Finished braze weld. (Courtesy of Union Carbide of Canada, Ltd.)

(B)

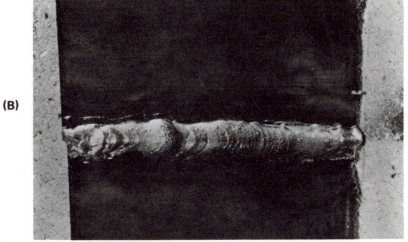

Braze welding is used to repair rusted-out panels, by lap-welding a patch of metal on top of it with bronze. The braze welding provides a fast repair without too much distortion because of the low amount of heat required to do the welding.

Many of the lower panels used in the manufacture of automobiles are zinc-coated. This zinc coating is used to prevent the rusting of the panels. The panels can be fusion-welded or braze-welded in the ordinary way except that care must be taken not to inhale the fumes, which can cause illness. Any type of welding of zinc should be done in a well-ventilated area. Milk is a good antidote for any illness that may occur. It should be taken before, during, and after the welding job.

Spot welds are often used in the replacement of panels. The holes are drilled through the top piece and then the torch is applied to heat the bottom piece through the holes to a cherry red. The brazing rod is next applied and the hole is filled. This procedure provides a quick method, in the shop, of duplicating factory welds usually done by spot welders.

Welding Aluminum

Methods that differ from those employed in steel welding are used to weld aluminum. Aluminum does not give any warning by changing color as it becomes hot enough to weld. When this metal gets too hot, it will collapse, for aluminum is weak when it is hot. It conducts and absorbs a terrific amount of heat before the area can be brought to the necessary welding temperature.

Aluminum oxide will coat the aluminum as a result of oxidation from the air. This oxide must be removed by wire brushing and the use of flux, which will float to the top after the weld is finished. Because it is corrosive, the flux must be washed off the part once the welding is finished.

An excess acetylene flame is used with an aluminum rod and the flux to weld aluminum. The blowpipe tip should be held at an angle of 30° and the tip of the inner cone should be approximately 1/2 in. (3 mm) from the surface of the metal. The operator must watch the metal, for a slight depression will form on the surface when it becomes hot enough for welding.

The first step in the welding operation is to clean the metal in order to remove the oxides. Next, apply the flux to the prepared joint. Using an excess acetylene flame, heat the joint to the proper temperature. Watch for a slight depression to form in the sheet. Then apply the rod to the flame on the puddle and run the puddle the length of the weld, inserting enough rod metal to fill the joint properly. The same tip used for fusion welding should be used and the panel should be preheated. Make sure that the welding is done in a well-ventilated area. Figures 2-34 to 2-36 show the different types of joints used to weld aluminum.

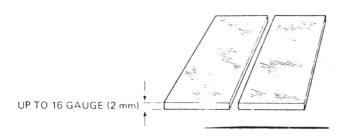

UP TO 16 GAUGE (2 mm)

FIGURE 2-34 The simple butt-type joint is suitable for welding aluminum up to 16 gauge (2 mm). Just cut the edges straight and square. (Courtesy of Union Carbide of Canada, Ltd.)

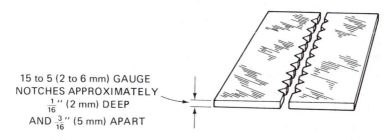

15 to 5 (2 to 6 mm) GAUGE
NOTCHES APPROXIMATELY
$\frac{1}{16}$″ (2 mm) DEEP
AND $\frac{3}{16}$″ (5 mm) APART

FIGURE 2-35 Notch the edges of butt-type joints in aluminum from 15 to 5 gauge (2 to 6 mm) thick. (Courtesy of Union Carbide of Canada, Ltd.)

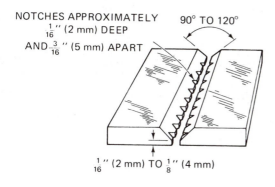

NOTCHES APPROXIMATELY
$\frac{1}{16}$″ (2 mm) DEEP
AND $\frac{3}{16}$″ (5 mm) APART

90° TO 120°

$\frac{1}{16}$″ (2 mm) TO $\frac{1}{8}$″ (4 mm)

FIGURE 2-36 Use the single-vee joint with notched straight nose for aluminum plate up to 7/16 in. (2 mm) thick. (Courtesy of Union Carbide of Canada, Ltd.)

Welding White Metal

In the automotive industry, white metal is used in castings—in grille parts, door handles, and so on. White metal welding will not prove difficult if aluminum welding has been mastered.

If the part is chrome-plated, the plating must be removed because it has a higher melting point than white metal. Remove only enough to facilitate the welding operations. On thin parts, a jig made of clay is useful in holding the shape of the part. White metal does not change color before it reaches its mushy stage.

An excess acetylene flame is used to heat and weld the metal. When the metal becomes mushy, a white metal rod is melted into the mushy puddle. To make the puddle mix properly, it is sometimes necessary to use a steel welding rod to help the mushy puddle flow.

UNIT 2-5: CUTTING WITH OXYACETYLENE

The cutting attachment is used extensively in any body shop to cut bolts, rivets, panel assemblies, and mangled sheet metal that must be removed if repairs are to be made.

The cutting of ferrous metals is actually the result of a chemical reaction of an oxygen stream, which, when thrust on metal that is heated to its kindling temperature, will oxidize the metal. In other words, we say the oxygen stream has cut or severed the piece of metal. Flame cutting is widely used because of its fast, versatile, and rather inexpensive properties. Replace the welding head with a cutting attachment and then consult Table 2-2 for the pressure that should be used.

Figure 2-37 shows the preheat holes and the hole from which pure oxygen is injected into the hot metal. The flame is controlled by the torch valves; but when the cutting attachment is being used, the oxygen valve on the torch body is opened completely. The oxygen for the preheat flames is controlled by the valve on the cutting attachment. The torch acetylene valve is opened slightly and a striker is used to light it. The acetylene is increased until the flame burns brightly. Then the oxygen valve on the attachment is opened to give a neutral

TABLE 2-2 Cutting chart.

Metal Thickness [in. (mm)]	Cutting Tip Size No.	Cleaning Preheat	Drill Sizes Cutting	Cutting Oxygen Pressure [psi (kPa)]	Acetylene Pressure [psi (kPa)]
1/8 (3)	2	77	76	15-20 (104-138)	
1/4 (6) 3/8 (10)	3	75	68	20-35 (138-242)	3-5 (21-35)
1/2 (13)	4	73	60	30-40 (207-276)	
1 (25)	4	73	60	40-50 (276-345)	
2 (50)	4	73	60	60 (414)	

Source: Courtesy of Union Carbide of Canada, Ltd.

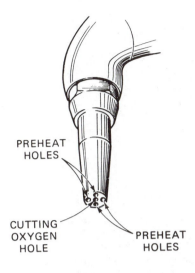

PREHEAT
HOLES

CUTTING
OXYGEN
HOLE

PREHEAT
HOLES

FIGURE 2-37 Close-up
of a cutting tip.
(Courtesy of Union
Carbide of Canada, Ltd.)

flame on the preheat flames. It will be noticed that when the lever on the cutting
attachment is depressed, the full flow of oxygen comes out of the center orifice.

A piece of plate metal is cleaned and marked with soapstone or chalk.
Welding goggles must be worn for cutting as well as for welding. The torch is
held with two hands, as in Fig. 2-38, and the edge of the plate is preheated. The

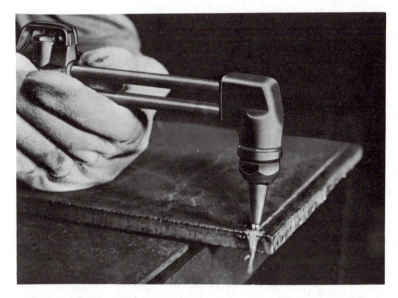

FIGURE 2-38 Preheating the top and edge of the plate.
(Courtesy of Union Carbide of Canada, Ltd.)

FIGURE 2-39   As soon as the plate is preheated, turn on the cutting oxygen. (Courtesy of Union Carbide of Canada, Ltd.)

torch tip is held at a 90° angle to the metal and the pale blue cone of the preheat flame is kept about 1/16 in. (1.6 mm) away for the best results. The tip is kept perpendicular to the plate until the spot under the preheat flame begins to melt. The tip is tilted so that the preheat flame will point toward the edge of the plate, and then the cutting oxygen valve is depressed (Fig. 2-39). When the cutting starts, the tip is slowly straightened. When the cut has penetrated through the plate, the tip is tilted in the direction to which the cutting is taking place. The tip should be tilted to a 60° to 70° angle to the metal, which helps to make the cut easier. When the cut is started, the torch is moved ahead. The speed of the movement is important, for if the movement is too slow, the cut will fuse; if the movement is too fast, the cut will be lost. If the cut is lost, the oxygen valve is released and the metal is heated to its kindling point before the process is started again.

Cutting Heads of Bolts or Nuts and Rivets

When it is necessary to cut the bolts or nuts and rivets that hold the different parts of the automobile together, it is very important that the cutting be done with caution. For example, if the bolts or nuts holding the bumper brackets to the frame in the back of the car are to be cut off, the gas tank should be examined carefully to see if there are any leaks, for gasoline and its fumes are extremely flammable. A fire extinguisher of the proper type should be close at hand if there is no leakage of gasoline. If there is any leakage, the tank should be removed or the cutting of the bolt or nut should be done with a pneumatic tool or a nut splitter.

The cutting torch is then lit in the normal fashion. Lying down on a creeper and keeping your body as far away as possible from the slag that will fall, the

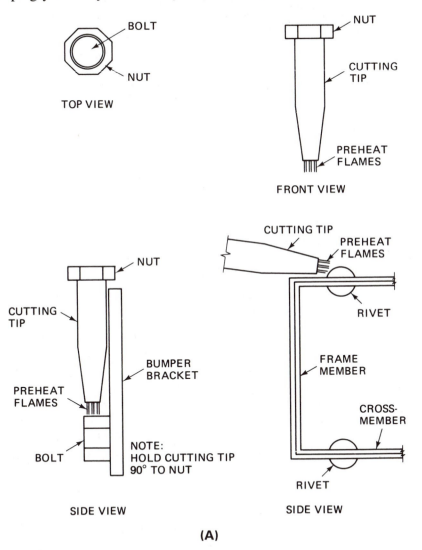

FIGURE 2-40   (A) Cutting bolt heads, nuts, and rivets; (B) cutting sheet metal.

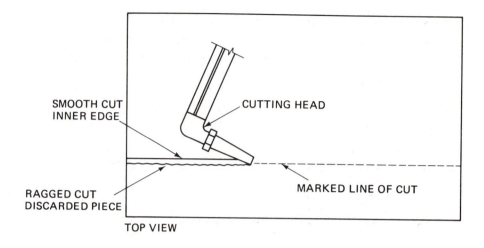

SMOOTH CUT
INNER EDGE

CUTTING HEAD

RAGGED CUT
DISCARDED PIECE

MARKED LINE OF CUT

TOP VIEW

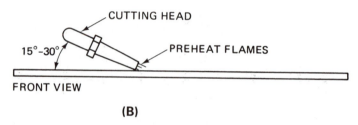

CUTTING HEAD

15°-30°

PREHEAT FLAMES

FRONT VIEW

(B)

FIGURE 2-40   (cont.)

bolt head or nut is preheated at the edge. When it becomes red in color, the oxygen lever is pressed to allow the oxygen to flow and oxidize the metal. It should be remembered that when cutting bolts, nuts, or rivets the cutting tip is held as close as possible to the bracket or frame member, thus forming as close as possible to a 90° angle (Fig. 2-40). This is done so that only the bolt head, nut, or rivet head will be cut off and the surrounding metal will not be damaged. To finish cutting the head, it might be necessary to tip the torch slightly less than 90°, but great care must be taken so as not to damage the other parts which the bolt or rivets hold together. The preheat flames are held approximately 1/8 in. or 3 mm away from the bolt, nut, or rivet until it is cherry red. When the oxygen lever is pressed down, the oxygen cuts off the bolt, nut, or rivet. The torch must travel at the proper speed or the cut will be lost and the metal will have to be reheated.

Cutting Sheet Metal

When sheet metal has to be cut, lower pressure and a different torch angle to the sheet metal must be used. The preheat flames are adjusted to a neutral flame, and the torch tip is held at a 90° angle to the sheet metal to get the cut started. As soon as the metal is hot enough, the oxygen lever is pressed down and the cut is started. As this happens the torch is tipped at a 15° to 30° angle, depending on the area that has to be cut. The oxygen pressure coming from the oxygen orifice blows the slag away. The torch should also be pointed toward the metal to be discarded because this will give a clean line on the piece that is to be kept. The forward movement of the torch is much faster because it is easier and faster to cut sheet metal [see Fig. 2-40(B) for details].

UNIT 2-6:   METAL INERT GAS WELDING

Metal inert gas (MIG) welding, also called gas metal arc welding (GMAW), uses a continuous, consumable, bare wire that is automatically fed through the torch unto the work, at a constant preset speed. As the wire makes contact with the work, it short-circuits; an arc is established and a small portion of the end of the wire melts, drops down on the work (forming a puddle), and the arc goes out. However, while the arc is out, the molten metal (puddle) begins cooling and flattening out; the wire continues to be fed, contacting the work and short-circuiting out again. This procedure of heating and cooling is repeated time after time, an average of up to 90 times per second, and each time a small amount of molten metal is transferred to the work (Fig. 2-41). The molten metal or puddle is protected from atmospheric contamination by a shielding gas, such as carbon dioxide (CO_2), or a mixture of 75 percent argon and 25 percent carbon dioxide. The latter, although more costly, has been found most suitable for welding mild and high-strength steel, because argon produces a much more stable arc than CO_2, resulting in a neater bead, with less spatter and burn-through, especially when welding very thin sheet metal.

Most MIG welders, as shown in Fig. 2-42(A), come set up from the factory for 0.023 or 0.030 in. (0.6 and 0.8 mm) wire, available in 8 to 12 in. (203 to 305 mm) spools, at most welding supply outlets. They require a constant voltage power source to operate with optimum efficiency, and should be used, employing a direct-current reverse polarity (DCRP) circuit [Fig. 2-42(b)], in order to get the maximum penetration possible, with a minimum of heat transfer to the base metal or work.

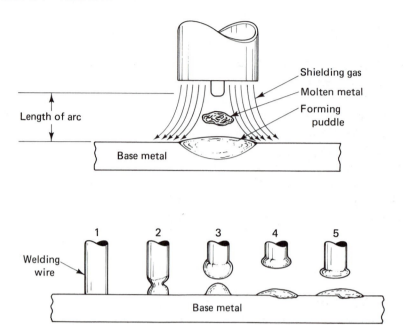

FIGURE 2-41 Transfer of welding wire to work.

However, it is possible, and sometimes desirable, to reverse the direction of electron flow, by changing from a direct-current reverse polarity (DCRP) circuit to a direct-current straight-polarity (DCSP) circuit. Each circuit has its advantages.

When a DCRP circuit is used, one-third of the heat generated in the arc is released at the base metal and two-thirds is released on the wire-electrode metal and the surrounding shielding gas, causing them to be superheated. As a result, the molten metal in the arc travels at a far higher rate of speed across the arc to the base metal. Deep penetration, with little or no warping of the base metal, results.

When a DCSP circuit is used, just the opposite occurs. One-third of the heat generated in the arc is released on the wire electrode and two-thirds is released on the base metal. A weld with less penetration, greater heat buildup in the weld zone, and more warping of the base metal results.

Advantages of MIG Welding

MIG welding has the following advantages compared to other methods of welding:

(A)

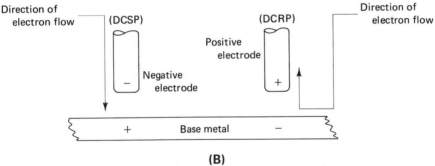

FIGURE 2-42 (A) Typical MIG welder; (B) direct-current straight polarity and direct-current reverse polarity circuits. [(A) Courtesy of Blackhawk, Division of Applied Power, Canada Ltd.]

Direction of electron flow   (DCSP)

(DCRP)   Direction of electron flow

Positive electrode

Negative electrode

Base metal

(B)

1. It makes faster high-speed welding possible.

2. Because welding can be done at a higher speed, distortion and warping are greatly reduced.

3. It provides a narrower, more concentrated, and controlled heat, making it ideal for mild-steel, high-strength steel (HSS), and aluminum welding.

4. It is much easier to learn, making possible faster operator training.

5. Less waste of welding wire (filler rod) is realized.

6. No slag or flux has to be removed from welds, resulting in considerable saving in labor costs.

7. Perfect penetration in fusion and spot welding of sheet metal.

8. Less dismantling is required for the prevention of fire.

Using the MIG Welder

Setting Up the Welding Gun

The welder must first select the proper liner for the gun. The type of liner used in the gun is determined by the wire being used. A Teflon liner is used for aluminum wire and a steel liner for all other types of wire (Fig. 2-43).

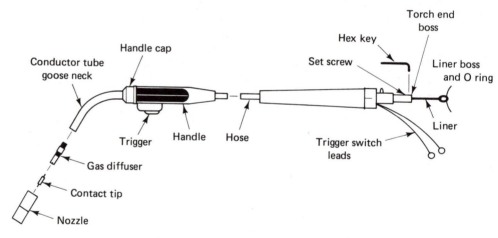

FIGURE 2-43 Liner change installation. (Courtesy of Blackhawk, Division of Applied Power, Canada Ltd.)

Selecting the Contact Tip

The size of contact tip required in the gun is determined by the size of wire used. A contact tip that is too small will hinder wire feed, and a contact tip that is too large will not provide sufficient electrical contact for the weld wire (Fig. 2-44). For easy identification, each contact tip is stamped with its proper size. To install the tip, just screw it clockwise into the end of gun and tighten.

Wire size (in.)	Contact tip size [(in.) mm]
0.023	0.023 (0.6)
0.030	0.030 (0.8)
0.035	0.035 (1.0)

FIGURE 2-44 Contact tip size chart. (Courtesy of Blackhawk, Division of Applied Power, Canada Ltd.)

Selecting the Gas Nozzle

Two gas nozzles are provided with each machine: a standard welding nozzle and a spot welding nozzle (Fig. 2-45). The standard nozzle is used for applications other than spot welding.

NOTE: Gas nozzles should be kept clean. Use a small piece of wood to remove spatter buildup. Antispatter spray on the gas nozzle and contact tip before operation will make the removal of spatter easy. Nozzles thread on and off and should only be hand-tightened.

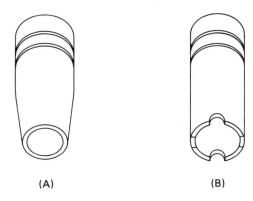

(A)   (B)

FIGURE 2-45 Gas nozzles: (A) standard; (B) spot weld.

Selecting the Welding Wire

The type and size of welding wire required is determined by the type and thickness of the metal to be welded (Fig. 2-46). Many welding machines come set up from the factory for 0.023 in. (0.6 mm) wire, and with only minor modifications will also accept 0.030 and 0.035 in. (0.8 and 0.9 mm) wire.

Only premium wire meeting AWS Spec. A5.18, electrode classification E70-S6, should be used for all automotive steel welding, including high-strength steel (HSS) and high-strength low-alloy steel (HSLA). The electrode classification number E70-S6 conveys the following information:

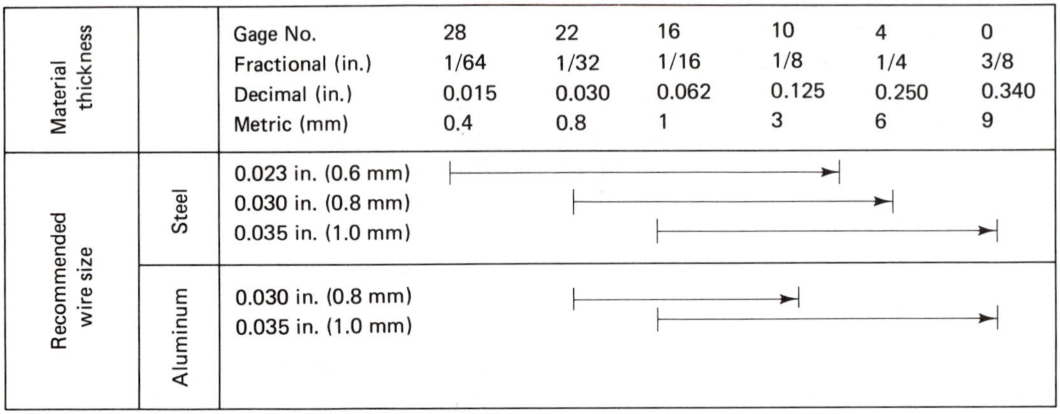

Material thickness	Gage No.	28	22	16	10	4	0
	Fractional (in.)	1/64	1/32	1/16	1/8	1/4	3/8
	Decimal (in.)	0.015	0.030	0.062	0.125	0.250	0.340
	Metric (mm)	0.4	0.8	1	3	6	9

Recommended wire size		
Steel	0.023 in. (0.6 mm)	⊢—————————————→
	0.030 in. (0.8 mm)	⊢———————————→
	0.035 in. (1.0 mm)	⊢———————————→
Aluminum	0.030 in. (0.8 mm)	⊢————————→
	0.035 in. (1.0 mm)	⊢——————————→

FIGURE 2-46 Wire size selection chart. (Courtesy of Blackhawk, Division of Applied Power, Canada Ltd.)

- E identifies the wire to be used as an electrode.

- 70 stands for 70,000 psi (483,000 kPa) tensile strength.

- S denotes a solid, bare steel welding wire.

- 6 specifies the chemical composition of the welding wire in accordance with American Welding Society specifications.

Two common filler wires are recommended for aluminum welding: type 5356 and type 4043. Either type should be compatible with automotive applications of aluminum, but filler wire 0.035 in. (1 mm) in diameter is recommended for heavy applications.

Installing the Welding Wire

1. The power switch should be flipped to *off* before the door on the left side of the cabinet is opened.

2. The wire tension lever is then flipped out, and the spool hub flange nut is removed (Fig. 2-47).

3. Unpack the wire very carefully. If narrow spools are used, put wire on first; then install the spool spacer. Make sure that the wire unwinds from the top in a clockwise direction and that the guide pin on the wire spindle lines up with the hole in the back side of the wire spool. To verify that the guide pin is in position, rock the wire spool back and forth on the spindle.

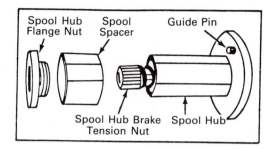

Spool Hub Flange Nut   Spool Spacer   Guide Pin

Spool Hub Brake Tension Nut   Spool Hub

FIGURE 2-47 Wire spool installation. (Courtesy of Blackhawk, Division of Applied Power, Canada Ltd.)

4. Reinstall the spool hub flange nut to hold the spool on the hub (Fig. 2-47).

5. Adjust the spool hub brake tension by turning the nut clockwise to increase, or counterclockwise to decrease, braking (Fig. 2-47).

6. Carefully loosen the wire from the spool so that it does not unravel, keeping a firm grip on the wire throughout the cutting and threading operation. Straighten the wire and cut the end off straight.

7. Check the drive wheel groove for proper size. The small groove is used for wire 0.023 in. (0.6 mm) in diameter and the large groove for wire 0.030 and 0.035 in. (0.8 and 0.9 mm) in diameter.

8. Thread the wire through the brass guide tube of the drive assembly, past the drive and idler rollers into the torch end, making sure that the wire is properly started in the liner of the torch assembly.

NOTE: Check that the correct gun liner and contact tip are being used for the wire size selected.

9. Close the wire drive pressure wheel assembly by moving the tension lever.

10. Remove the gas nozzle and contact tip from the end of the welding gun, to prevent an obstruction to the welding wire end, to be fed through the torch assembly (Fig. 2-48).

11. Push the power switch into the *on* position. Set the wire feed control to number 4, and pointing the gun away from the welding machine and yourself, press the gun control trigger until the welding wire emerges from the torch.

12. Check the wire spool brake tension, by holding the spool with your hand. While turning the spool, you should feel a slight amount of resistance, just enough tension to prevent unraveling of the wire when

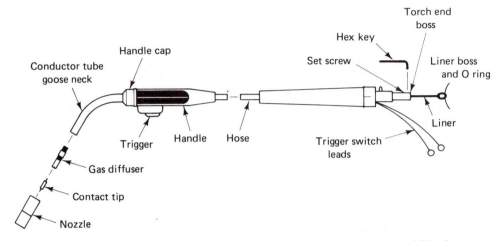

FIGURE 2-48 MIG welding torch assembly. (Courtesy of Blackhawk, Division of Applied Power, Canada Ltd.)

drive is stopped. Spool brake tension should be checked frequently, not only when changing wire, but also as the spool is used.

13. Install the proper contact tip (the size is marked on its side) and the desired gas nozzle. Antispatter should now be applied to help keep the spatter from sticking.

14. Cut off the extra wire protruding so that the end of the welding wire extends about 1/4 in. (6 mm) from the tip of the gun (Fig. 2-49).

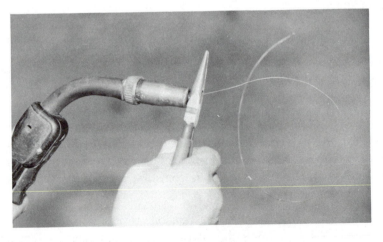

FIGURE 2-49 Cutting off the welding wire.

Selecting the Shielding Gas

The type of gas to be used is determined by the type of metal to be welded. Be sure to use a welding-grade gas. Local welding suppliers can advise you as to the shielding gas for auto body welding (Fig. 2-50).

NOTE: Pure carbon dioxide (CO_2) shielding gas is not recommended for auto body welding. Shielding gas does not produce heat.

Material	Gas	Flow rate with gun control trigger depressed
All steels	75% Argon 25% CO_2 Stargon 100% CO_2	12–20 cfh* 12–20 cfh* 16–24 cfh*
Aluminum	100% Argon	16–24 cfh*

FIGURE 2-50 Shielding gases and flow rates. (Courtesy of Blackhawk, Division of Applied Power, Canada Ltd.)

Connecting the Gas Regulator to the Shielding Gas Cylinder

Basically the same procedure is followed in connecting a gas regulator to a shielding gas cylinder as in oxyacetylene welding (described and illustrated in Unit 2.1).

Connecting the Ground Clamp

All paint, rust, scale, oil, and other nonconductive or flammable material must be removed from the welding area and the area where the ground connection is to be made. Clamp the ground cable as close to the weld area as possible.

A good, clean ground clamp connection is very important in all arc welding. A poor connection not only wastes power but results in poor welder performance.

Steps to Be Followed before Welding Is Attempted

1. Place power switch in the *on* position.

2. Open the shielding gas cylinder very slowly but fully.

3. Adjust the heat and wire speed control.

4. Move the weld selector switch to the manual weld position.

5. Adjust the regulator flow rate.

6. Clamp the ground cable to the work.

7. Extend the welding wire about 1/4 in. (6 mm) beyond the contact tip.

8. Follow all necessary safety precautions. Place the torch in position; wear gloves and proper clothing; lower the helmet or use a shield; press the trigger and proceed to weld.

Welding Positions

As in oxyacetylene welding, MIG welding can be done in all four positions: flat, horizontal, vertical, and overhead. Welding in the flat position is usually the easiest, fastest, and allows for better penetration; overhead welding is the most difficult, requiring many hours of practice to perfect. Wherever possible, position the work so that welding can be done in the flat position, especially if the operator has little or no MIG welding experience.

Clamp workpieces firmly in position to prevent them from shifting or moving around while tack welding and running of a bead is carried out.

Holding the Gun

The gun should be held with the nozzle at an angle of 45 to 60° to the work (Fig. 2-51) and as the wire is not energized until the gun control trigger is pressed, the wire can be positioned on target before the helmet or face shield is brought over or up to the face. The gun should be held so that the contact tip is about 1/4 in. (6 mm) from the work. To enable the operator to maintain this distance, the wire must be extended to be about 1/4 in. (6 mm) beyond the gas nozzle before striking the arc. Holding the gun too close or too far from the work will result in poor welds, increased spatter, and will cause the torch to operate with an erratic sound (Fig. 2-52).

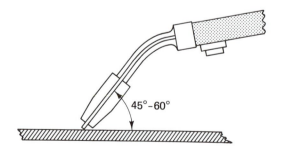

45°–60°

FIGURE 2-51 Holding gun to work.

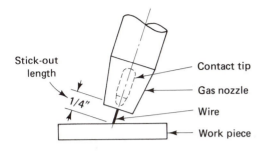

FIGURE 2-52 Initiating the arc. (Courtesy of Blackhawk, Division of Applied Power, Canada Ltd.)

Travel Methods and Travel Speed

Two different methods of travel, in the running of beads, are employed in MIG welding: the pulling method and the pushing method. The gun is held at an angle of about 60° to the work (Fig. 2-53), and moved with little or no weaving motion, except in the welding of poorly fitted edge joints, where some weaving is desirable. Wherever possible, the pulling method is used for welding light-gauge metal; the pushing method is used for heavy metal and all-aluminum welding because of the greater shielding gas protection required in combating contamination.

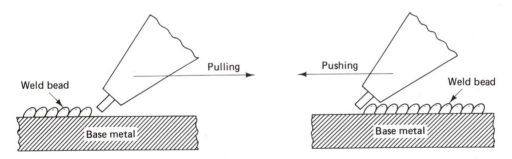

FIGURE 2-53 Methods of travel.

The speed of travel is regulated by the type of weld bead required. While learning, travel at a speed that allows you to maintain a bead of uniform width. Never allow the bead width to be less than the thickness of the metal or to become too wide. Too wide a bead, especially when welding high-strength steel, may cause overheating of the metal and result in the destruction of the base metal properties.

A good bead requires a steady gun movement along the weld seam. Moving the gun too rapidly or straying off the seam will result in improper metal-to-metal fusion and an uneven, poor-looking, and generally weaker weld bead.

Continuous Welding

In continuous welding, as in other MIG welding, the heat selector switch, having nine positions, must be accurately set for the job on hand. Generally, the thicker the metal to be welded, the higher the heat setting (Fig. 2-54).

The wire speed control is used for fine tuning the welding operation. An increase in heat will require an increase in wire speed. The chart (Fig. 2-55) will help with the basic settings of the machine, but fine tuning of the operation, using similar metal, will be required until the correct "sizzling" sound is obtained. It is similar to the sound of tearing a linen sheet or the frying of eggs. If the wire speed setting is too low, the torch will develop a "hiss" and the wire will burn, forming a ball; if too high, the wire will push the torch away from the work, accompanied by a loud, crackling arc.

Continuous welding is used mostly for welding thicker metal. For thinner metals, such as sheet metal, stitch or spot welding is recommended. It should, however, be used in welding aluminum, because a continuous weld is more likely to have fewer contamination imperfections than a stitch-welded weld.

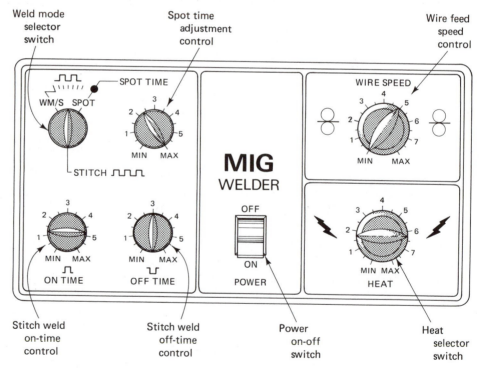

FIGURE 2-54 Control panel. (Courtesy of Blackhawk, Division of Applied Power, Canada Ltd.)

Material thickness		Gage No.	28	22	16	10	4	0
		Fractional (in.)	1/64	1/32	1/16	1/8	1/4	3/8
		Decimal (in.)	0.015	0.030	0.062	0.125	0.250	0.340
		Metric (mm)	0.4	0.8	1	3	6	9
Settings*	0.023 in. Wire	Heat wire	2-3 2-4	3-4 2-5	5-7 3-5	7-8 4-6	Not recommended; use 0.030 in. wire	
	0.030 in. Wire	Heat wire	Not recommended; use 0.023 in. wire	3-5 1-3	5-6 4-5	6-7 3-5	8 3-6	8 3-6
Aluminum 0.030		Heat wire	Not recommended	3-4 4-5	4-5 5-7	5-6 7-Max	Not recommended	

*Your settings may vary depending on the input voltage, material used and operator preference.

FIGURE 2-55 Base setting chart for wire speed control. (Courtesy of Blackhawk, Division of Applied Power, Canada Ltd.)

Preparing the Metal for MIG Welding

Clean the area to be welded. Using either a power wire brush or a disk grinder, remove any nonconductive or flammable materials, such as rust, undercoating, primer, paint, putty, plastic filler, solder, galvanized or zinc coatings, oil, grease, or dirt.

WARNING: Exposure to the welding arc is extremely dangerous and harmful to the eyes and skin and prolonged exposure can cause blindness and severe burns. Never start arc welding unless you are adequately protected by wearing flameproof welding gloves, a heavy long-sleeved shirt, cuffless trousers, high-top shoes, and a welding helmet or shield. Never bring a butane lighter with you into the weld area.

Using a perfectly clean piece of sheet metal or body panel, firmly clamped in a flat position, practice running beads about 3 in. (76 mm) in length. Holding the gun at the correct angle and on target, using the pulling method of travel, strike the arc and move along at a uniform speed. On reaching the end of the bead, release the gun control trigger, which cuts off the welding current and stops the wire feed, but keep the gun over the weld bead until the shielding gas stops flowing. This protects the puddle from contamination. Practice welding by repeating the operation, frequently examining specimens for defects, until you are able to make reasonably good weld beads, before attempting longer beads.

Filling Holes in Body Panels

Small holes in body panels can easily be filled by reducing the heat setting one or two steps lower than for continuous welding. Make a short tack weld on the outer edge of the hole and allow it to cool until the orange color disappears. Proceed, making short tack welds, alternating from side to side, until the hole is filled (Fig. 2-56).

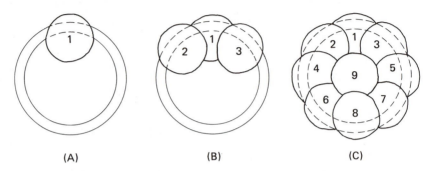

(A)   (B)   (C)

FIGURE 2-56 Steps used in filling holes. (Courtesy of Blackhawk, Division of Applied Power, Canada Ltd.)

Seam-Welding Tears and Gaps

In seam-welding tears and gaps, the heat setting is also reduced one or two steps lower than for continuous welding. Bridge the gap at intervals about 1/2 in. (12 mm) apart, by making short tack welds on each side of the gap, and let each cool before proceeding with the next weld (Fig. 2-57). Fill in the remaining gaps using the hole-filling technique. If required, the appearance of the filled tear or gap can be improved (smoothed out), by stitch welding over the area, using the normal heat setting.

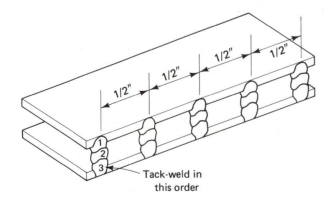

Tack-weld in this order

FIGURE 2-57 Seam welding tears and gaps. (Courtesy of Blackhawk, Division of Applied Power, Canda Ltd.)

Spot and Plug Welding

Spot/plug welding is used extensively on unitized body cars, because welds can be made at the identical factory locations and through two different thicknesses of metal. It is recommended, whenever possible, that the lighter metal be welded to the heavier metal, that both pieces make good contact with each other, and that the overlapping surfaces be clean.

A spot weld is a small, round, localized weld that penetrates through one piece of metal into the other (Fig. 2-58).

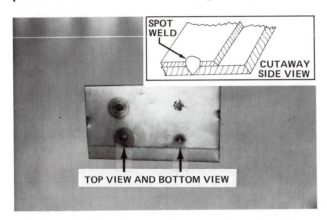

FIGURE 2-58 Sheet-metal spot welds.

A plug weld is similar to a spot weld, except that holes are first punched into the top piece of metal, with a hole-punching tool, before the two pieces of metal are spot-welded together (Fig. 2-59). It produces the strongest spot weld possible, requiring a minimum amount of heat.

Spot and plug welding can be done either manually or automatically, with or without the spot weld gas nozzle. Spot welding should be done manually when only a few welds have to be made or when the metals to be welded vary in thickness. Automatic welding should be used when making many welds on metals of equal thickness.

Automatic Spot and Plug Welding Procedure

1. Remove the standard nozzle, attach a spot weld nozzle to the gun, and apply antispatter spray to the gun nozzle and contact tip.

2. Adjust the heat and wire speed control base settings, as shown in Fig. 2-55. Settings should be based on combined metal thicknesses.

3. Fine tuning of control settings is done by making welds manually on pieces of similar scrap metal.

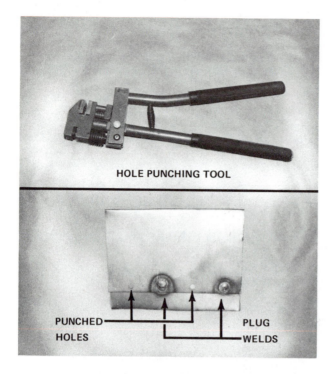

FIGURE 2-59 Hole-punching tool and plug welds.

4. Move the weld selector switch to the spot weld position (Fig. 2-54), adjust the spot time adjustment control, and fine-tune the setting using similar scrap metal. An ideal spot weld is small in diameter, with penetration clearly visible on the back side of the metal.

5. Extend and then cut the wire so that it is flush or within the end of the spot weld nozzle (Fig. 2-60).

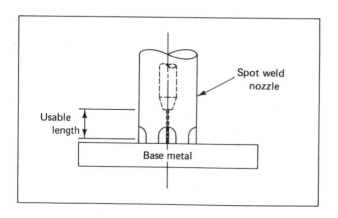

FIGURE 2-60 Wire cut flush with end of spot weld nozzle. (Courtesy of Blackhawk, Division of Applied Power, Canada, Ltd.)

6. Hold the nozzle perpendicular to the work, allowing the nozzle to rest on the work. If spot welding using a punched hole, aim the wire at the center of the hole before dropping the helmet over the face and pressing the gun control trigger. The welding machine will stop automatically when the spot weld has been completed. Then move to the next area and continue spot welding.

Another type of spot welder used in auto body repairing is the resistance spot welder (Fig. 2-61), which will make two spot welds at the same time. This machine has two cables, each having its own electrode holder; different types of electrodes are supplied to perform welds in different locations. The two electrodes are held one in each hand and pressed against the area to be spot-welded (Fig. 2-62). One electrode has a pushbutton that is pressed whenever spot welds are to be performed. There is a variable timer on the machine to provide and to select the desired heat to complete the spot welds. Figure 2-63 shows a drawing of the typical spot weld done by this machine.

FIGURE 2-61 Resistance spot welder.

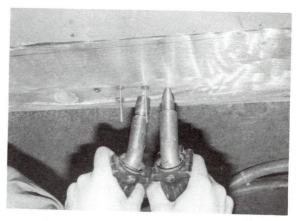

FIGURE 2-62 Electrodes positioned on panel for spot welding.

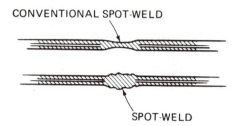

CONVENTIONAL SPOT-WELD

SPOT-WELD   **FIGURE 2-63**

Stitch Welding

Stitch welding is used in welding thin or rusty metal, where warpage and burn-through is a problem. Basically, it consists of a series of overlapping spot welds, each being allowed time to cool before the next weld is made (Fig. 2-64). Stitch welding is comparable in quality and penetration to a continuous weld, with less heating of the metal. It can be done either manually or automatically. Stitch welding should be done manually when only a few welds are to be made or when welds must be made on metals varying in thickness.

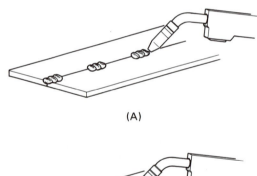

(A)

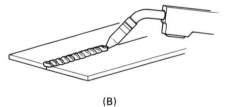

(B)

FIGURE 2-64 Manual stitch (A) and skip (B) welding. (Courtesy of Blackhawk, Division of Applied Power, Canada Ltd.)

Automatic stitch welding should be used when many welds are to be made on metal of the same thickness. The operating techniques followed are very similar to those used in automatic spot welding, except that the weld selector switch is moved to the stitch weld position. Start spot welding with a time base setting of 2 on both stitch *on* time and stitch *off* time controls. Then test the weld. The orange color of the weld should disappear completely before the next cycle begins. Fine tuning of the operation is done on similar metal, by adjusting the weld *on* time control to get the desired puddle size, and the weld *off* time control for the proper cooling-off time.

Skip Welding

Skip welding is employed to further reduce distortion problems. It requires the running of very short beads, about 1/2 in. (12 mm) in length; stopping; and restarting another short bead about 1/4 in. (6 mm) farther up the seam (Fig. 2-64). It is used primarily where spot welding is not enough and distortion is a major problem.

Controlling Overheating and Burn-Through

Overheating will cause large, thin auto body panels to warp, and if the heat is concentrated on a very small area, as it is in welding, it will often cause burn-through.

To minimize burn-through, stop the running of the bead occasionally, as in stitch welding, and before starting again, allow the weld to cool until it loses its orange color. If burn-through continues, adjust to a lower heat setting.

Burn-through and warping can also be controlled by properly tack-welding the metal (Fig. 2-65), followed by alternate welding, using the same procedural steps as in oxyacetylene welding (described and illustrated in Chapter 5).

The Heat-Shrinking Attachment

This attachment is used in shrinking stretched areas on thin-gauge body panels and is done without the use of shielding gas or weld wire. The gas nozzle must be removed from the gun and a carbon rod attached by means of a special attachment (Fig. 2-66). The heat control is set between 1 and 4, depending on the thickness of the panel, and the weld selector switch is moved to the manual weld position.

The tip of the carbon rod is then placed on the outer edge of the stretched area, the face is covered with the helmet or shield, and the trigger is pressed. Moving in a circular pattern, work your way round and round, in a slow but steady manner, to the center of the stretched area and stop when the area starts changing color. Then quench the area with a cold, water-soaked rag. Do only a small area at a time. However, there is a limit to the amount of shrinking possible with this attachment.

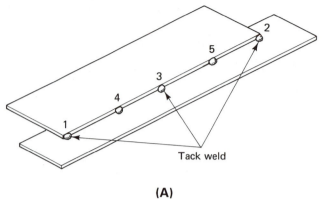

(A)

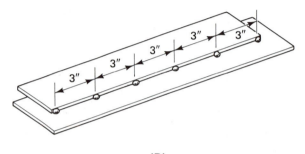

(B)

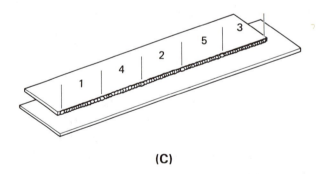

(C)

FIGURE 2-65 (A) Procedure of tack welding; (B) tack welds should be 3 in. or less apart; (C) alternate welding: stitch, skip, or spot in the order indicated. (Courtesy of Blackhawk, Division of Applied Power, Canada Ltd.)

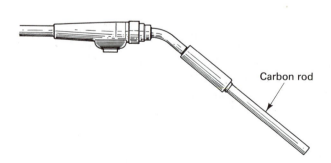

Carbon rod

FIGURE 2-66 Heat-shrinking attachment. (Courtesy of Blackhawk, Division of Applied Power, Canada Ltd.)

Maintenance of the MIG Welder

Regular maintenance and adjustments are needed to keep the MIG welder in top operating condition and to provide years of trouble-free service. The gun and torch assembly is the most important part of a MIG welder and must be properly cared for and maintained by observing the following general rules:

1. Never make sharp bends with the gun hose and frequently check it for signs of abrasion and other defects or damage.

2. Keep the gun nozzle and contact tip free of spatter using a wooden stick to remove spatter deposits. Use antispatter spray, as recommended, after each operating period.

3. Always replace the contact tip when the hole is abraded too large or when there is excessive dirt buildup, generally after one-third of the spool of wire has been used.

4. The gas nozzle should be replaced with a new one when the insulator begins to get brittle or when it does not provide even shielding.

5. Check the wire conduit or liner occasionally for free wire movement. To clean it, remove and soak the liner in solvent and blow it dry with compressed air.

6. Clean the inside of the cabinet regularly with a vacuum cleaner and a soft-haired brush.

7. Check the wire spool brake tension and adjust, if necessary, at least every time one-third of a spool of wire has been used.

Aluminum Welding

The setup for aluminum welding is similar to that for steel welding, with the following exceptions:

1. Suitable aluminum wire must be used; type 5356 and type 4043 are recommended (see the wire selection chart, Fig. 2-46).

2. A Teflon liner should be used in the torch assembly, which allows the aluminum wire to slide easily through the torch assembly and will not have any steel particles on it to contaminate the aluminum weld.

3. Only pure argon shielding gas should be used, at 16 to 24 cu ft/hr (38 to 56 liters/hr).

NOTE: When welding aluminum, surface preparation is extremely important. The weld area should be cleaned with a suitable solvent, such as lacquer thinner or enamel reducer, and brushed vigorously, just before welding, with a clean stainless steel brush to remove any surface oxidation.

Contamination from dirt, grease, oil, water, and other foreign material is the biggest enemy of aluminum welding. For this reason it is best to use a new, unopened spool of aluminum wire, and because it cannot be kept from contamination very long, the smallest spool possible should be purchased from the supplier.

Aluminum Welding Technique

The basic operating techniques are the same as those for steel welding, with the following differences:

1. The stick-out length of the aluminum wire is increased to 5/16 in. (8 mm).
2. The travel speed will be much faster for aluminum welding.
3. The base setting of the wire feed speed will be higher per heat setting than for steel (see the base setting chart, Fig. 2-55).
4. While welding aluminum, it is recommended that the work area be free of drafts.

After the aluminum welding project is completed, the MIG welder is shut off following the same procedure as that used in steel MIG welding.

Different Types of Joints Used

Several types of joints are used to weld sheet metal on auto bodies. The most common are the butt joint, the recessed lap joint, the lap joint, and the flange joint (see Figs. 2-67 and 2-68).

Recessed Lap Joint

The recessed edge is usually shaped with a special flanging tool. It is an attachment that fits a pneumatic tool. Where the patch is desired, a hole is cut with a special chisel that fits in the same tool. In corners, a dolly and hammer are used to finish the flange. The patch is cut to size and is held there by using

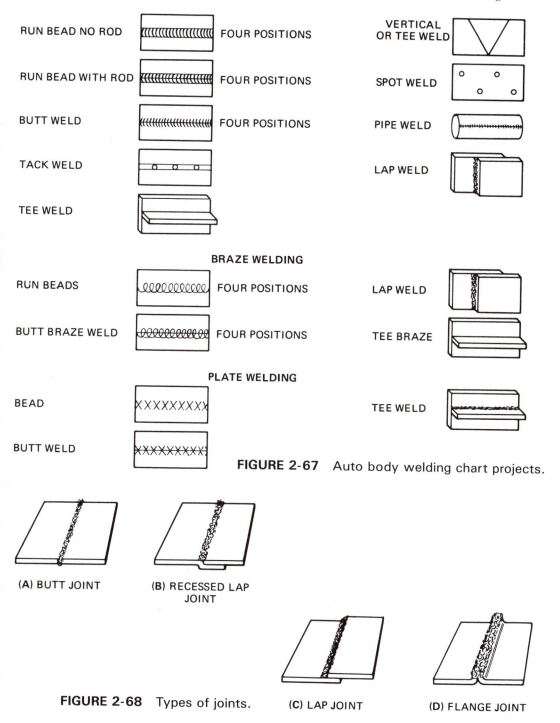

RUN BEAD NO ROD — FOUR POSITIONS

RUN BEAD WITH ROD — FOUR POSITIONS

BUTT WELD — FOUR POSITIONS

TACK WELD

TEE WELD

VERTICAL OR TEE WELD

SPOT WELD

PIPE WELD

LAP WELD

BRAZE WELDING

RUN BEADS — FOUR POSITIONS

BUTT BRAZE WELD — FOUR POSITIONS

LAP WELD

TEE BRAZE

PLATE WELDING

BEAD

BUTT WELD

TEE WELD

FIGURE 2-67   Auto body welding chart projects.

(A) BUTT JOINT

(B) RECESSED LAP JOINT

(C) LAP JOINT

(D) FLANGE JOINT

FIGURE 2-68   Types of joints.

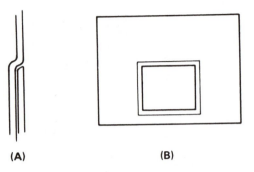

(A)

(B)

FIGURE 2-69 Plate added on top of member: (A) side view; (B) front view.

self-tapping metal screws or pop rivets. Then it is secured by gas welding, arc welding, or spot welding. The spot weld would be the best, for almost no distortion is caused. The edges of the patch can then be filled with solder. This type of joint, once properly finished, would not permit moisture to seep through easily (Fig. 2-69).

Fish Plate

Another type of joint, which is generally used only when doing frame repairs, is the addition of plate on top of the member (Fig. 2-70). Plate is added to reinforce a frame rail that has cracked. Since the frame is the main reinforcing part of a car body, the part on which the alignment of the wheels and body depend, it is important that the rail be put back in correct alignment before it is welded. The reinforcement is added so that the frame will not flex as much, for it could crack again.

Another way to cut metal on automobile bodies is with the pneumatic tool and a cutting chisel (Fig. 2-71). This tool is versatile; by changing the accessories, it can be used to help break spot welds (Fig. 2-72).

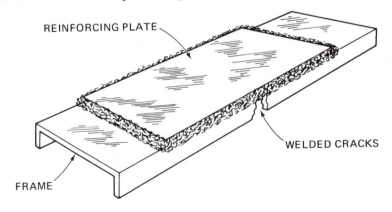

REINFORCING PLATE

WELDED CRACKS

FRAME

FIGURE 2-70

FIGURE 2-71 Using a metal cutter.

FIGURE 2-72 Breaking spot welds.

Another useful attachment is the flanger. A flanged patch is easier to install than a butt joint because less metal protrudes above the surface (Fig. 2-73) and therefore minimizes to a great degree the amount of filler required to taper the edges and to keep a straight surface in relation to the panel.

Some of the more common welding rods and fluxes used in fusion and braze welding of different types of metals are shown in Figure 2-74.

FIGURE 2-73 Flanging tool.

FIGURE 2-74 Gas welding rod and flux data.

Type of Welding	Material to Be Welded	Rod to Use	Flux to Use
Fusion welding	Steel and steel alloys	OXWELD No. 1 H.T. (High-Test) Steel Rod	None
	Thin plate or sheet steel (less than 1/4 in. (6 mm) thick)	OXWELD No. 7 Drawn iron rod	None
	Cast iron	OXWELD No. 9 Cast-iron rod	FERRO
	Stainless steel	OXWELD No. 28 (Pat.) Columbium bearing 18-8 Stainless steel rod	CROMALOY*
	Aliminum and aluminum alloys	OXWELD No. 14 Drawn aluminum rod	OXWELD*† Aluminum
	Brass and bronze	OXWELD No. 25M Bronze rod or	BRAZO
		OXWELD No. 25M Flux-coated bronze rod (Pat.)	None
Braze welding	Steel-, iron-, copper-, and nickel-base alloys	OXWELD No. 25M Bronze rod or	BRAZO
		OXWELD No. 25M Flux-coated bronze rod (Pat.)	None

*These fluxes must be mixed with water to form a paste. The paste is then painted on the rod and base metal.

†Aluminum flux, when heated, give off fumes irritating to eyes, nose, and throat. Use in well-ventilated places with the draft away from the operator. Avoid contact with eyes or skin.

Source: Courtesy of Union Carbide of Canada, Ltd.

QUESTIONS

2-1 What gases are generally used for welding with a torch?

2-2 How is oxygen obtained from the air?

2-3 What material is used to make an oxygen cylinder? How?

2-4 How many seats does the oxygen valve have?

2-5 An oxygen cylinder is filled to what pressure and temperature?

2-6 What is the highest pressure at which free acetylene can be used?

2-7 What is inside an acetylene cylinder?

2-8 What is the purpose of using a pressure regulator?

2-9 What types of threads are used on an oxygen regulator: left-hand or right-hand?

2-10 What is the color of the acetylene hose?

2-11 What types of torches are normally used in body shops?

2-12 What equipment is required to set up an oxyacetylene welding outfit?

2-13 What is *cracking the valve*?

2-14 How should the torch be ignited?

2-15 Why should a flint striker be used to ignite a torch?

2-16 What type of flame is used to weld mild steel?

2-17 What type of flame is used for brazing?

2-18 What is a flashback?

2-19 At what angle should the torch be held in relation to the metal?

2-20 How far away from the metal should the inner cone be?

2-21 Where should the rod be dipped?

2-22 What type of torch motion is used to weld plate metal?

2-23 What is done to plate metal before welding so that the weld will penetrate properly?

2-24 Why should the metal be tinned before a heavy bead of bronze is melted on the metal?

2-25 What are the uses of the preheat flames on the tip of a cutting torch?

2-26 Why is so much heat required when welding aluminum?

2-27 For what operations is the cutting attachment used in an auto body shop?

2-28 What actually occurs when a piece of metal is cut with an oxyacetylene cutting attachment?

2-29 When the lever on the cutting attachment is pressed, from which orifice does the pure oxygen flow?

2-30 What type of flame is used to preheat the metal, and how is it controlled and adjusted?

2-31 When cutting metal, why is the speed at which the torch is moved so important?

2-32 What safety precautions should be taken before any cutting is attempted?

2-33 When cutting sheet metal, at what angle should the torch be held once the cut has been started?

2-34 How is the torch held so that the piece of sheet metal to be kept has a clean line or edge?

2-35 Briefly explain how a MIG welder works.

2-36 What shielding gas is most suitable for welding mild and high-strength steel?

2-37 For what size of welding wire are most MIG welders set up at the factory?

2-38 What type of electrical circuit should be used to get maximum penetration?

2-39 Why is deeper penetration of the base metal achieved when a direct-current reverse-polarity circuit is used in MIG welding?

2-40 State the advantages of MIG welding over other methods of welding.

2-41 What different types of liners are used in MIG welders?

2-42 What determines the size of contact tip to be used, and how is tip size identified?

2-43 What gas nozzles are provided with every welding machine?

2-44 How are gas nozzles cleaned and maintained?

2-45 What information does the electrode classification number convey?

2-46 How is the spool hub brake tension adjusted?

2-47 Why should the gun liner and contact tip be checked for size before attempting to install the welding wire?

2-48 Once the spool of wire has been installed, how is the wire spool brake tension checked?

2-49 How is a good ground connection made, and why is it necessary?

2-50 In what position, whenever possible, should MIG welding be done to make it easier?

2-51 How is the gun held in striking the arc?

2-52 What two methods of travel are used in MIG welding, and for what welding is each method most suitable?

2-53 What regulates the speed of travel in MIG welding?

2-54 How is the wire speed control used in fine tuning the welding operation?

2-55 What sound should the MIG welder make when in operation and fine tuned?

2-56 What different types of welding are used in welding thicker and thinner metals?

2-57 What safety precautions must be taken before any MIG welding is attempted?

2-58 How are holes in body panels filled?

2-59 What is the difference between a spot weld and a plug weld?

2-60 When should spot and plug welding be done manually and when automatically?

2-61 What type of spot welder makes two spot welds at the same time?

2-62 What is stitch welding, and where is it used?

2-63 Where is skip welding employed?

2-64 What attachment makes shrinking of stretched areas with a MIG welder possible, and how is it carried out?

2-65 What general rules must be observed in maintaining a MIG welder?

2-66 What surface preparation is required in welding aluminum?

2-67 Name the tool used in shaping or recessing the edge in recessed lap joints.

2-68 How is a frame rail reinforced?

2-69 What tool and attachments are used in cutting sheet metal and in breaking spot welds?

3

Repairing Damaged Panels and Metalworking Methods

Years ago automobile bodies were relatively plain, simple, and much smaller in design and construction compared to the auto bodies of today. Their inner construction or framework was made almost entirely of hardwood, generally birch or maple, to which the outer heavy-gauge sheet-metal panels (having little or no contour) were fastened by means of body nails. The fenders and frames were also of *heavy* metal construction and were not welded together to form an integral part or assembly as they are at the present time; instead they were joined by means of bolts and rivets. This method of automobile manufacturing was rather slow. Better and faster ways of making parts had to be found if the new (at that time) concept of assembly-line production was to be fully utilized.

The wood-and-steel type of body construction was soon replaced by the all-steel body. This step was brought about when a new, more efficient method of producing auto body parts was discovered, one still in use today.

Parts of varying sizes and shapes are *stamped* out of flat sheets of light-gauge steel by presses, each using its own particular set of dies. The set of dies is made in the shape of the part it *stamps*. The lower die is stationary. The upper die moves down over it, and the flat sheet of steel, which is placed in the press, is squeezed between the dies and comes out of the press in the form of the finished part. Presses are used in forming, piercing, bending, and punching. Very often a die is designed to perform several operations at one time.

Presses enable the car manufacturer to make light (yet strong), low-cost parts, such as fenders, hoods, turret tops, doors, grilles, and trunk lids. These parts, although formed out of light-gauge steel sheets, acquire their exceptional strength and rigidity from a number of different contours into which they are formed.

One of the most common methods of strengthening a flat-sheet-metal panel or surface is to curve it or give it *crown* when it is press-formed (Fig. 3-1). Through experimentation it was found that a far greater amount of force was required to change the shape of a *crowned* sheet-metal surface than it took to bend a flat sheet-metal surface. Experimentation also revealed that the amount of resistance offered by a crowned surface in changing its shape is directly proportional to the amount of crown it possesses. The resistance to bending, or *strength* as it is commonly called, is attributed to a number of changes that occur when sheet metal is bent or crowned in a press (Fig. 3-2).

Notice that before a piece of sheet metal is curved in a press, its top, center, and bottom surface measurements are all the same and its grain or molecular structure is the same throughout the entire sheet. When the sheet metal is bent beyond its *elastic limit*, however, its shape is permanently changed or set. Its outer surface stretches and lengthens; its inner surface shrinks and shortens, while its through-center length remains the same. The pressure exerted on it by the

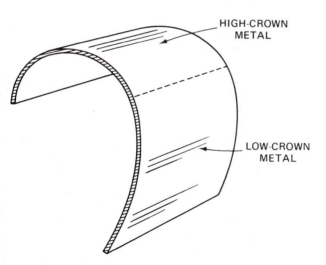

HIGH-CROWN
METAL

LOW-CROWN
METAL

FIGURE 3-1

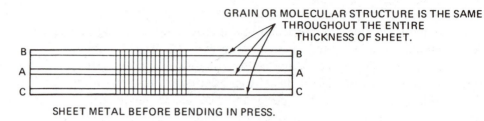

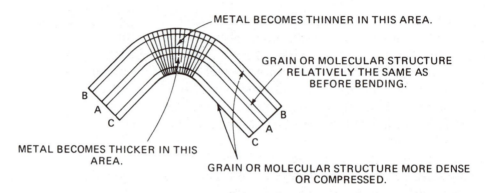

FIGURE 3-2

press also brings about changes in the grain and molecular structure of both the outer and inner surfaces of the sheet metal, causing them to become denser. This procedure is generally called *work hardening* (see Fig. 3-2).

Various other methods of shaping metals are employed in strengthening automobile panels and parts. Right-angle bends are used in making the strong framework or inner construction that supports and reinforces the outer body panels (Fig. 3-3). *Outer* body panels, which are unsupported over large areas, are given strength and stiffness by *right-angle* bending their outer edges, called *flanging*, or by curving them either concave or convex (Fig. 3-4). Large inner-construction panels that do not require smooth, flat surfaces are usually strengthened by means of angular depressions of various sizes and shapes, or ribs (Fig. 3-5).

A narrow piece of flat sheet metal has very little strength and bends quite easily, but when it is bent up at right angles on both sides, into a U shape (Fig. 3-6), it becomes very strong. It is for this reason that many frames, supporting braces and brackets, inner construction, and glass channels on an automobile are made of U channels. When two U channels are fitted and welded together (Fig. 3-7), a strong type of *box construction* is obtained. It is used in building automobile frames, roof rails, rocker panels, and so on.

FIGURE 3-3

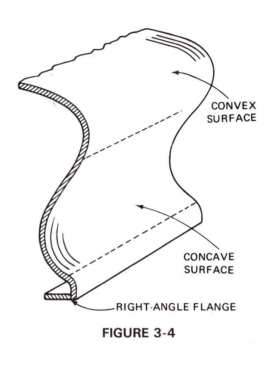

CONVEX
SURFACE

CONCAVE
SURFACE

RIGHT-ANGLE FLANGE

FIGURE 3-4

FIGURE 3-5

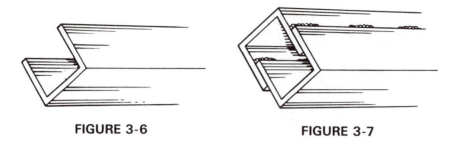

| FIGURE 3-6 | FIGURE 3-7 |

Types of Collision Damage

It is essential that a repairman clearly understands the underlying principles involved when automobile sheet metal becomes damaged or bent if he is to analyze properly the damage that has taken place and to decide on the correct and most efficient way of repairing the particular job on hand.

Either or both of two types of sheet-metal damage generally occur when an automobile is involved in a collision, namely direct or indirect damage (Fig. 3-8). Direct damage can be defined as the damage that occurs to the area that is in direct contact with the damaging force or impact. Indirect damage can be defined as the damage that occurs as a result of the direct damage. When a sheet-metal panel is bent in by a force or impact, it does not merely bend in the area

FIGURE 3-8

of direct impact; the damaging force is transmitted throughout the surrounding areas of the panel until it is used up, leaving a series of V channels, valleys, or buckles whose outermost edges form distinctive ridges. The ridges thus formed are hard rigid areas created by the bending of the sheet metal beyond its elastic limit and thereby give a permanent set to each individual valley or buckle.

Types of Buckles Formed

Four different buckles are formed when auto body sheet metal is bent in beyond its elastic limit and becomes permanently deformed. The type of buckle formed depends on the shape and contour of the sheet metal. The four different buckles formed are the simple hinge, the collapsed hinge, the simple rolled, and the collapsed rolled.

A simple hinge buckle is formed when flat sheet metal is forced to bend either inward or outward by a damaging force or impact (similar to the bending of a hinge on a door). The change in the grain or molecular structure of the metal or work-hardening that occurs will vary greatly, depending on the sharpness of the bend (Fig. 3-9).

Straightening a simple hinge buckle is done most efficiently by applying a stretching pull (as in opening up a door hinge) and then rearranging the molecular structure of the buckled metal by means of on- and off-the-dolly hammering, as shown in Fig. 3-10, rather than by pushing or bumping it out, which generally only creates additional damage to the already damaged metal and also to the surrounding elastic metal.

A collapsed hinge buckle is formed when a simple hinge buckle created by a damaging force or impact extends and crosses over a stamped-in reinforcing flange, bead, or ridge on a flat or reverse-curved (concave) surface of an auto body panel, causing the surface to bend, buckle, and collapse and causing a shortening up in the overall length of the panel to take place (Fig. 3-9).

FIGURE 3-9

FIGURE 3-10

Collapsed hinge buckles are formed not only when flanges, beads, and ridges, generally considered as being of partial box construction, suffer damage, but also on box-constructed members and assemblies such as the siderails on automobile frames, rocker panels, roof rails, and a variety of body pillars.

The damage to the metal in the area of a collapsed hinge buckle, which is work-hardened initially in the stamping process, is far more extensive and severe than a simple hinge buckle (Fig. 3-9). Therefore, a far greater and stronger stretching pull must be applied in order to straighten it and if the panel or assembly is to be restored to its original overall length. Simultaneously, as the stretching pull is applied, (Fig. 3-10), it requires a great deal of metal shaping (roughing out and accurately aligning of the collapsed flange, bead, or ridge) by the repairman, and it must be completed before the simple hinge buckle can be straightened and the applied stretching pull is released.

Two types of rolled buckles are formed whenever a hinge buckle, created by a damaging force or impact, extends and crosses over the crowned surface of an auto body panel (Fig. 3-11). For example, take an ordinary round tin can and apply pressure on its side with your thumbs. As the crowned surface of the can is bent in, the metal in the area of the buckle formed collapses and shrinks severely (Fig. 3-12). As you increase the pressure on the can with your thumbs, the outer ridges formed at either end of the buckle continue to spread and roll out farther and farther across the crown of the can and into the adjacent metal, pulling the ends of the can closer together, and the can collapses. It is for this reason that the resulting buckle is called a collapsed rolled buckle. You will also

FIGURE 3-11

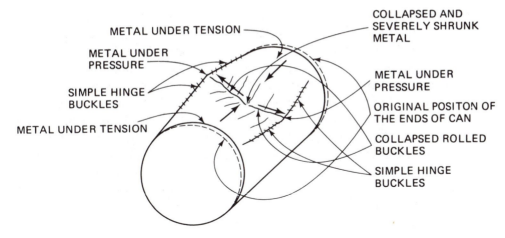

FIGURE 3-12

observe that at either end of the collapsed rolled buckle (in the area of indirect damage) two additional smaller buckles have formed. These are commonly called simple rolled buckles.

Rolled buckles, either simple or collapsed, are generally roughed out and straightened most efficiently by applying a stretching pull, as shown in Fig. 3-13. You will find that as the stretching pull is applied on either side of the collapsed rolled buckle, the metal in the area of the collapsed rolled buckle begins to rise and straighten out, and the buckle becomes shallower and shallower.

FIGURE 3-13

Simultaneously, the simple rolled buckles also begin to roll back out, leaving a series of ridges that are straightened out next, either by spring-hammering them or by on- and off-the-dolly hammering. You will observe that the collapsed rolled buckle will continue to rise and its overall size and depth diminish until all of the tension exerted by the first stretching pull has been exhausted. All of the damaged crowned metal cannot be brought out in one step or stage by applying one single stretching pull. The damaged metal (buckles) must be brought up very gradually, as slowly and as smoothly as possible, if a great deal of unnecessary work is to be avoided. Therefore, the straightening procedure described above will generally have to be repeated a second, third, fourth, or as many times as may be required until all of the damaged crowned metal has been brought out smoothly to its original shape and contour (Fig. 3-35).

When straightening collision damaged parts and assemblies in which both the outer panel and its supporting framework or inner construction have been damaged, the damage to the framework is generally corrected first whenever possible or simultaneously as the damage to the outer panel is brought out. By following the repair procedure above, sufficient room is provided for the outer panel to move back up and out unrestricted to its original size and shape, making the repair operation much easier. Next, the crowned surface of the outer panel (simple and collapsed rolled buckles) is roughed out and straightened by applying a stretching pull (Fig. 3-14). Any existing beads and ridges in the crown of the panel are also simultaneously brought out and straightened at this time. The more flat, lower portion of the outer panel (collapsed hinge buckle) is roughed out and

FIGURE 3-14

FIGURE 3-15

straightened next. Caulking irons, driving spoons, and on- and off-the-dolly hammering, whichever is most practical, is used in this operation. The simple hinge buckles above and below the ridge in the panel (Fig. 3-15), which have already been partially brought out as the collapsed hinge buckle is removed, are straightened last. The entire door panel is then metal-finished, starting with the crowned upper portion of the panel, followed next by metal-finishing all flanges, beads, ridges, and the outer edges on the door panel. Any and all still remaining roughed out and straightened areas on the flat, low, and reverse-crowned lower portions of the panel are metal-finished last.

As a rule, in repairing collision damage, the outer edges of the damaged panel and its supporting, reinforcing framework, which may be of single, double- or triple-layer construction, are generally roughed out first, followed by any beads, ridges, or contour lines in the panel. All double-crowned areas are then brought out, followed by single-crowned areas. Reinforcing flanges, U's, or reverse-crowned metal at the outer edges of the front and rear fenders and quarter-panels are roughed out next. All remaining flatter areas on the panel are done last.

Another important factor to be considered by the repairman is the direction of the damaging force or impact because in nearly all cases sheet-metal damage is corrected in exactly the opposite sequence to which it occurred. As a rule, the indirect damage is corrected first and the direct damage last.

Before the predetermined repair procedure can be carried out, however, both inner and outer surfaces of the particular sheet-metal panel must be thoroughly cleaned of all deadeners, undercoatings, and other foreign materials that might interfere with the application of corrective forces. Most of the deadeners and undercoatings used today can be removed quite easily with a scraper or putty knife, after they have been softened by heating the outside of the panel with a large-tipped torch and a mild reducing flame (Fig. 3-16) or with a pneumatic cutting tool adjusted to a very low setting and equipped with a wide, fairly dull chisel attachment. The outer surface of the panel must be cleaned of sand, gravel, and other gritty materials by washing with clear water. Asphalt, oil, and road tar deposits can easily be removed by dissolving and wiping them off with a solvent-soaked rag. These steps will enable the repairman not only to carry out corrective procedures more efficiently but also to make his hand tool straightening operations more effective. It will also save hand tools from unnecessary wear and tear.

All parts that interfere with the straightening operation must also be removed. For example, a front fender that has been badly damaged around the headlight will probably require the removal of the headlight assembly, fender side molding, front side medallion, and other parts located in the front section of the fender.

Once the damaged sheet-metal panel or part has been properly prepared, the straightening operation, which is carried out in a number of different stages or steps, follows. The first step in the straightening operation is to unlock the metal in the damaged area. The purpose of unlocking the metal is to unfold the

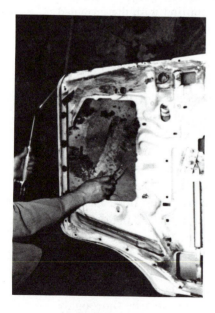

FIGURE 3-16

FIGURE 3-17

V channels, valleys, and buckles as gently as possible, without further stretching, creasing, or upsetting them, as they are brought up, one after another, to roughly their original position and contour. They have not been bent beyond their elastic limit but are held or *locked* in their distorted shapes by ridges of nonelastic or permanently deformed metal located at their outer-most edges (Fig. 3-17). The metal is unlocked by a gradual reshaping of these ridges at the same time as the V channels, valleys, and buckles are slowly raised up in line, level with the surrounding sheet metal. This step is accomplished by applying a corrective force to the damaged area, starting at the outer edges of the indirect damage and working toward the center of the direct damage until all damaged sheet metal has been unlocked (Fig. 3-18).

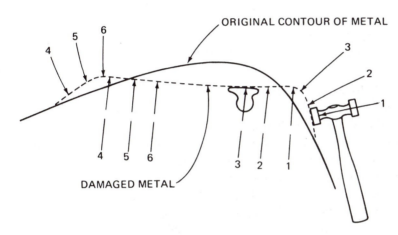

FIGURE 3-18

The type of corrective force used in the *unlocking* or roughing-out operation, as it is also called, is determined by the amount of damage that has occurred. When the damage to a particular panel is only slight, and the panel is not reinforced by some kind of framework or inner construction, the metal is generally unlocked by merely *bumping* out the V channels, valleys, or buckles with a suitable dolly (Fig. 3-18).

Metalworking Procedures

Hammers of sufficient size and weight (such as roughing-out, ball, and cross-peen hammers and sledgehammers) are frequently used either alone or in conjunction with an appropriate sized piece of hardwood in raising *elastic* metal areas. The *nonelastic* outer ridges are then reshaped by first spring-hammering them wherever possible or by the *on-* and *off*-dolly hammering technique shown

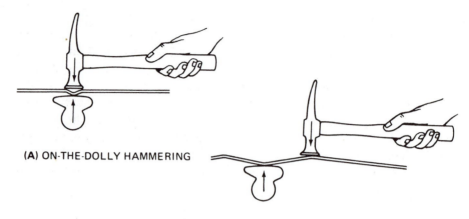

(A) ON-THE-DOLLY HAMMERING

(B) OFF-THE-DOLLY HAMMERING

FIGURE 3-19

in Fig. 3-19. However, where a damaged panel's elastic metal areas are subjected to extra-heavy stresses and strains, caused by excessive stretching of the sheet metal, additional indirect damage or distortion of its supporting and surrounding framework or inner construction, or a combination of both, the unlocking or roughing-out operation becomes too difficult for hand tools. Therefore, a corrective force consisting of either a push or pull is exerted on the outer panel by means of hydraulic equipment (Fig. 3-20). As a result, not only are the damaged areas in the outer panel raised up but, at the same time, the framework or inner construction is repositioned and straightened. All nonelastic ridges found on either the outer panel or inner construction must be spring-hammered and re-shaped by means of on- and off-dolly hammering, called *dinging*, before the applied hydraulic corrective force is released. A good rule for the repairman to remember is to use a pulling force wherever possible when unlocking or roughing-out damaged auto body panels. It has been found to be the best and most efficient method of unlocking damaged automobile panels.

Sometimes, in order to straighten a large, unsupported panel properly so that it keeps its shape after it has been straightened, not only must the corrective hydraulic force or pressure be used in the unlocking operation, but it must be maintained until all straightening and metal-finishing operations have been completed and the panel is ready for refinishing (Fig. 3-21). Not until then should the corrective pressure be released.

After the metal has been unlocked and straightened to roughly its original shape and contour, it is straightened and leveled still more, shrinking its stretched areas wherever necessary until all surface irregularities that can be detected by

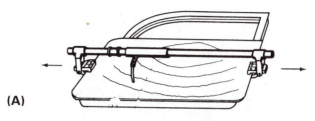

(A)

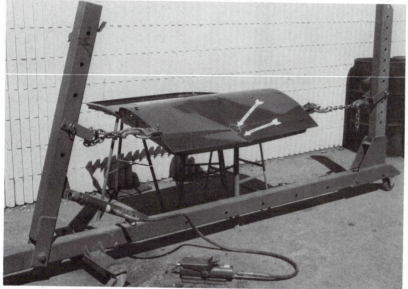

(B)

FIGURE 3-20   (A) Applying hydraulic corrective force on a door; (B) applying hydraulic corrective force with a pulldozer.

FIGURE 3-21

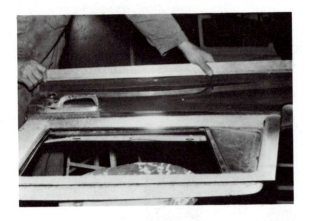

FIGURE 3-22

sight, feeling with the hand, or the use of a straightedge when repairing straight-surface panels are eliminated (Fig. 3-22).

How to Hold and Use a Balanced Dinging Hammer

In using a balanced dinging hammer (and this also applies to any other type of body hammer) for straightening operations, the hammer is grasped about one-quarter of the distance from the end of the handle and held loosely in the hand (Fig. 3-23). All blows are made by swinging the hammer with a wrist action, in a circular motion, rather than with a follow-through, as used when driving a nail (Fig. 3-24). This gives the repairman greater control of the hammer. The face of the hammer should land squarely on the sheet metal, with a sort of sliding blow—not too hard, for a few hard blows tend to stretch the metal more than many lighter blows. Because most body hammers are equipped with slightly curved faces, the actual area of contact between the face of the hammer and the

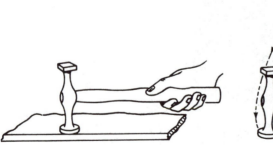

FIGURE 3-23

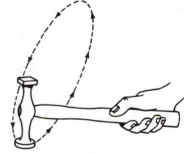

FIGURE 3-24

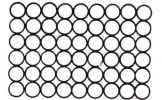

FIGURE 3-25

metal is approximately 3/8 to 1/2 in. (10 to 13 mm) in diameter. Therefore, in all dinging operations, the hammer blows should be spaced approximately 3/8 in. (10 mm) apart and in rows one beside the other (Fig. 3-25), until all the damaged metal has been hammered and leveled out. An experienced repairman will make approximately 100 to 120 light hammer blows per minute when dinging metal.

How Various Types of Dollies Are Used in Shaping and Straightening Sheet Metals

In all dinging and straightening operations, the dolly is placed on the inside of the damaged panel and held against its surface by means of pressure exerted on it by the forearm (Fig. 3-26). By varying this pressure, surface irregularities on the panel can be raised or lowered at will by the repairman as he proceeds in dinging out the damaged panel. The dolly acts as an anvil on which the metal is straightened when its surface is subjected to well-placed hammer blows. In selecting the proper dolly for a particular job, always remember to choose one with the same or slightly smaller radius than the curve of the sheet metal being repaired (Fig. 3-27).

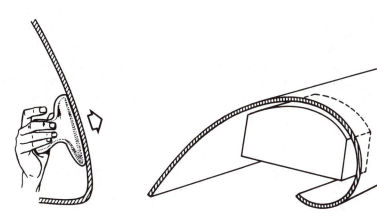

FIGURE 3-26   **FIGURE 3-27**

How to Straighten Flat Sheet-Metal Surfaces, Using a General-Purpose Dolly

When using the general-purpose dolly in straightening flat surface metals, great care must be taken not to stretch the metal, because of the slight contour of the dolly. The dolly should be offset, that is, not held directly underneath the ridge or high area of the metal (Fig. 3-28). A moderate amount of upward pressure is then exerted on the dolly by the repairman while, at the same time, the ridge or high area is hammered down. The hammer blows used in the dinging operation should, however, be kept to a minimum if unnecessary stretching of the metal is to be avoided.

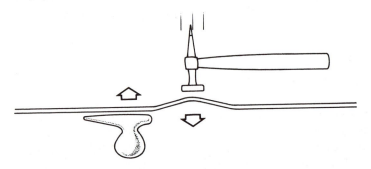

FIGURE 3-28

What actually happens when metal becomes stretched is as follows: When a piece of flat sheet metal is exposed to excessive on-the-dolly hammering, the metal in that particular area becomes thinner and larger in area with each succeeding hammer blow. Because it is held firmly in place by the surrounding unhammered metal and not allowed to spread out sideways in any direction, the extra metal has no alternative but to move either upward or downward from its straight and level position (Fig. 3-29). Low areas or troughlike depressions in flat sheet-metal panels are straightened by applying an upward pressure on the dolly, placed directly underneath the center of the depression (Fig. 3-30), while the two ridges or high areas are alternately hammered down, until the metal in

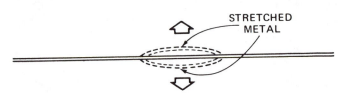

STRETCHED
METAL

FIGURE 3-29

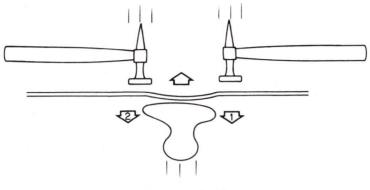

FIGURE 3-30

the low area is raised and brought in line with the surrounding sheet metal. Very small dents, shallow pop-out valleys, and light creases can be straightened in this manner without damaging the paint.

Method Used in Turning a Flange

The general-purpose dolly is placed in the damaged flange, or what is left of it, and a downward as well as outward pressure is applied on the dolly (Fig. 3-31). The flange is then formed or reshaped by on-the-dolly hammering started at the outer edge of the fender flange and gradually working toward its inner

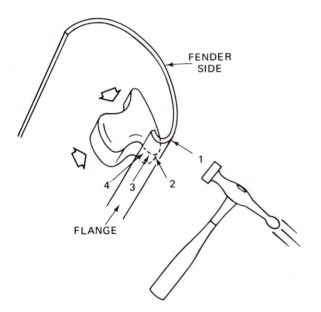

FIGURE 3-31

edge, as indicated by the arrows, until it is perfectly round and smooth. It is of the utmost importance that this flange be perfectly reshaped and any breaks in it welded and properly reinforced if the side of the panel is to retain its original strength and shape.

Method Used in Shaping Crowned Metals

If the crown of a panel has been damaged, the metal must first be unlocked or roughed-out. The roughed-out areas are then leveled and smoothed out by on- and off-dolly hammering (Fig. 3-32). Make sure that you hold the dolly tightly against the metal as you move it back and forth across the crown, occasionally bumping up existing low areas with the face of the dolly; at the same time hammering is continued.

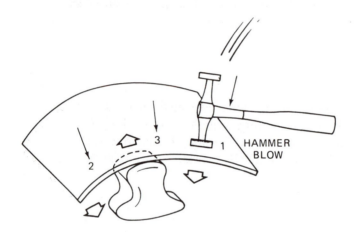

FIGURE 3-32

Method of Using Pointed Corner of General-Purpose Dolly

Low areas are often raised by using the sharp-pointed corner of the dolly (Fig. 3-33). This method is especially useful when a section of a weld that is too low has to be raised. The point of the dolly is held directly underneath the welded low area and is then struck a blow with the hammer from on top. This step raises the low metal, which is supported by the point of the dolly, and causes the surrounding high and unsupported welded areas to be driven down. The method can also be used in roughing-out and metal-finishing operations.

Method of Forming a Bead

In order to form a bead more easily on a panel, its size and shape should be clearly marked out on the panel, as illustrated in Fig. 3-34 by the dashed

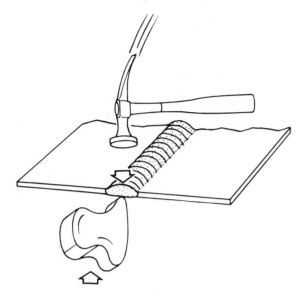

FIGURE 3-33

outline. The dolly is held tightly underneath the center line of the marked-off metal, and it is hammered until slightly stretched. The outer edges and ends of the bead are then formed by alternate off-the-dolly hammering, using the square face of either a bumping or balanced dinging hammer, until the metal becomes stretched enough and the bead is fully formed. Care must be taken to keep the metal from caving in while the bead is being formed, by applying enough upward pressure on the dolly, and also to avoid nicking the metal with the square-faced end of the hammer.

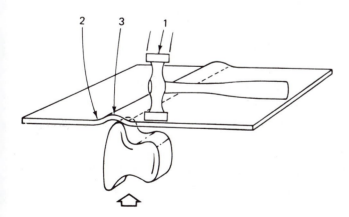

FIGURE 3-34

Using the Low-Crown Dolly in Shaping Metals

The low-crown dolly is used in unlocking or roughing-out damaged sheet metal by striking the elastic metal with one or a number of blows with the dolly, starting at its outer edges and working toward its center until all metal has been raised to approximately its original shape (Fig. 3-35). After dolly blows 1 and 2 have raised the metal to the contour, outlined by the dotted line, the outer ridges are eliminated by either spring-hammering or off-the-dolly hammering. This action relieves and releases many of the stresses and strains in that particular area of the metal, making it much easier to unlock and raise the remainder of the elastic metal.

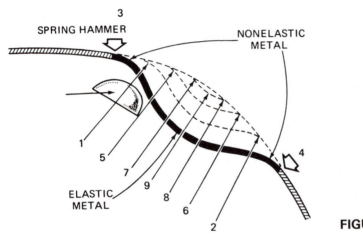

FIGURE 3-35

The roughed-out metal is then thoroughly straightened by on- and off-dolly hammering. Any areas found to be high or *stretched* are brought to the level of the surrounding sheet metal by means of *shrinking* (see Chapter 5).

Forming Beads with a Beading Dolly

In repairing a damaged bead, using a beading dolly, the end with a shape most closely resembling the inner surface of the bead should be selected and held tightly against the metal (Fig. 3-36). The square-faced end of the balanced dinging hammer is then used in hammering the adjoining surfaces of the panel as indicated by 1 and 2. This step causes the metal to stretch and shape itself around the face of the dolly. Any deformations and dents will spring out, and with additional on-the-dolly hammering, as indicated by 3, 4, and 5, the bead is reinforced (permanently shaped), aligned, and gradually straightened.

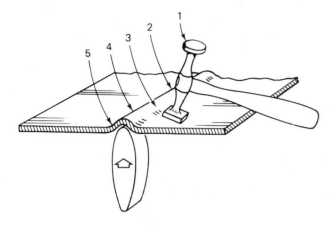

FIGURE 3-36

Different Ways of Using the Heel Dolly

Both the flat side and the flat end of the dolly are used in straightening flat surface metals, while the low-crown side is used in repairing low-crown metals. Straightening of the V (crease) is accomplished by means of hammering either on or off the dolly (Fig. 3-37).

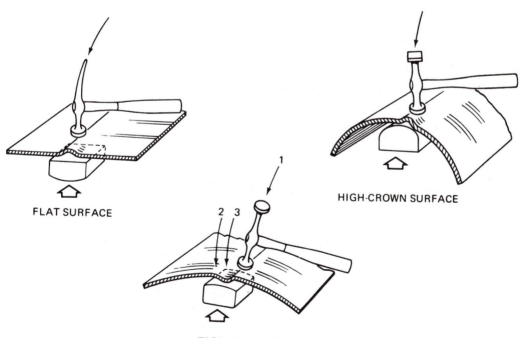

FLAT SURFACE

HIGH-CROWN SURFACE

FIGURE 3-37

The high-crown end of the dolly is used in shaping and straightening high-crown metals on fenders, doors, and especially headlight openings, as shown in Fig. 3-37. The dolly is held tightly against the inside of the metal while the metal is hammered into its proper shape and contour from on top.

Method of Using the Toe Dolly

The toe dolly is used in straightening flat or near-flat metal surfaces. The flat side of the dolly is used in shrinking operations, as described in Chapter 5. The toe dolly is used in straightening panels that are reinforced by inner construction, where there is very little working room between the outer panel and the inner construction.

The dolly is held in the palm of the hand and pressed tightly against the outer panel. All ridges and high spots in the panel are then carefully hammered down and low areas raised by using the on- and off-dolly hammering technique. This step minimizes stretching of the metal and a great deal of unnecessary work for the repairman (Fig. 3-38).

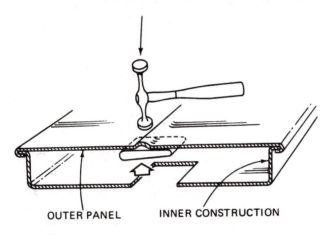

OUTER PANEL   INNER CONSTRUCTION   **FIGURE 3-38**

Method of Forming a Bead or Molding Using the Toe Dolly

The toe dolly is placed in the damaged bead and pressed firmly against its inner surface, while hammering of the metal on each side of the bead is carried out as indicated by 1 and 2 in Fig. 3-39. This step helps to shape the metal around the face of the dolly. The hammering is continued over the entire surface of the bead until it attains its proper shape indicated by 3, 4, and 5 in Fig. 3-39. This preceding method is also used in repairing many of the *rolled* flanges on unsupported body panels.

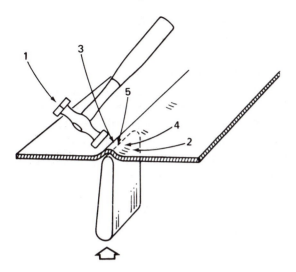

FIGURE 3-39

Raising a Low Spot with a Wedge Dolly

Hold the dolly against the metal, as shown in Fig. 3-40. Hammer *off* the dolly, as indicated by 1 and 2. Doing so will lower the ridges at the outer edges of the low spot and, at the same time, raise the metal, supported from underneath by the wedge dolly. The low spot, if it still remains lower than the surrounding sheet metal, is then struck one, two, or a series of blows with the dolly, until it is raised to its proper level. The dolly is turned on its side and its low-crown face is used in on- and off-dolly hammering of the metal until straightening is completed.

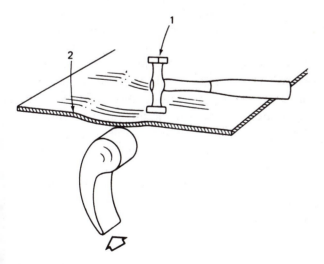

FIGURE 3-40

Straightening Crown Metal on Turret Top with Wedge Dolly

The tapered edge of the wedge dolly is used in raising and shaping the crown metal on a turret top, just above the roof rail (Fig. 3-41). The wide tapered end, when used in this manner, spreads the force of the blows over the wide area of the sheet metal and enables the repairman to raise up the crown metal very smoothly and with surprising ease. The low-crown face of the dolly is then held tightly against the roughed-out metal, and straightening is completed by means of on- and off-dolly hammering.

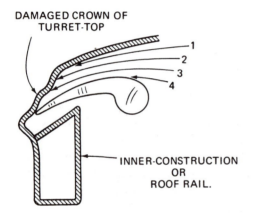

DAMAGED CROWN OF TURRET-TOP

1
2
3
4

INNER-CONSTRUCTION
OR
ROOF RAIL.

FIGURE 3-41

Roughing-Out and Straightening Double-Crowned Metal

In repairing damaged double-crowned metal (Fig. 3-42) the roughing-out operation is carried out by means of a gradual, step-by-step procedure of unrolling (bumping out) the badly collapsed and severely shrunk collapsed rolled buckles, starting with the largest buckle A, bringing it up and out until its overall surface area is considerably smaller than the second largest collapsed rolled buckle B. Next, buckle B is partially bumped out until it is considerably smaller in size than partially bumped out buckle A. Bumping out of the buckles is continued, working round and round from the largest buckle to the next largest, as indicated by the numbers (Fig. 3-42), until only the center of the damaged area (direct damage number 10) is left, which is bumped out last. The roughed-out, double-crowned metal is then straightened by on- and off-the-dolly hammering and shrinking of all excessively high (stretched) metal.

It is then metal-finished by eliminating all surface irregularities or low spots

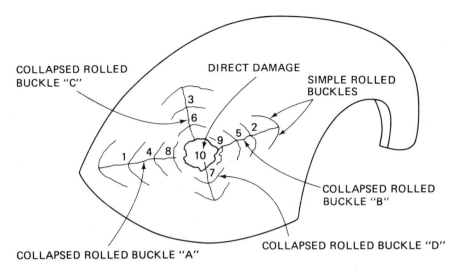

FIGURE 3-42 Roughing-out double-crowned metal.

by bringing them up (picking) with a suitable pick hammer, depending on the height of the double-crown. An adjustable file and holder, properly adjusted to conform to the convex surface of the double-crown (see Appendix A) or the straight standard-cut file and holder, which is pushed with a curving, sweeping stroke across or over the crowned metal, is used in outlining and locating minor surface irregularities or low spots until all have been eliminated.

Roughing-Out a Door Panel with Double-End Lower Back and Quarter-Panel Spoon

A door panel that has been damaged without any damage occurring to its inner construction can be roughed-out and straightened by supporting the door at its outer edges with two pieces of wood (Fig. 3-43). This method prevents the door panel from resting on the floor and gives the panel room to move or spring out as pressure is exerted on it by the double-end lower back and quarter-panel spoon. This spoon is used in raising elastic metal areas on damaged quarter panels, back panels, and many other panels that are reinforced by inner construction.

After the panel has been roughed-out, the flat faces of the spoon are used in completing the straightening of the panel by on- or off-the-spoon hammering. Where practical and convenient, however, different types of dollies can also be used in conjunction with the spoon in completing the straightening operation.

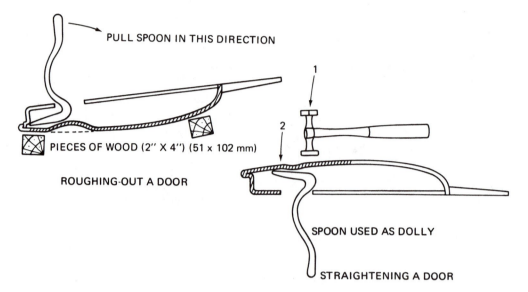

PULL SPOON IN THIS DIRECTION

PIECES OF WOOD (2″ X 4″) (51 x 102 mm)

ROUGHING-OUT A DOOR

SPOON USED AS DOLLY

STRAIGHTENING A DOOR

FIGURE 3-43

Roughing-Out Crowned Metals and Sides of Turret Top

The double-end door and side apron spoon has a longer and wider face and is used in the same manner as the wedge dolly. It is used for roughing-out and straightening metals that are sealed off by inner construction (Fig. 3-44).

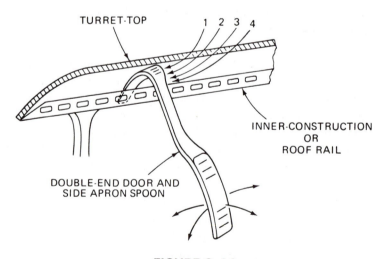

TURRET-TOP

1 2 3 4

INNER-CONSTRUCTION
OR
ROOF RAIL

DOUBLE-END DOOR AND
SIDE APRON SPOON

FIGURE 3-44

How the Double-End Heavy-Duty Driving and Fender-Beading Tool Is Used

This tool is used in straightening hood and fender flanges by placing its most suitable end in the flange of the fender or hood and striking down the reinforced square seat, especially designed for this purpose. It is similarly used in shaping headlight openings (Fig. 3-45). Either one of its ends can also be used as a dolly in straightening high-crown metals (Fig. 3-46).

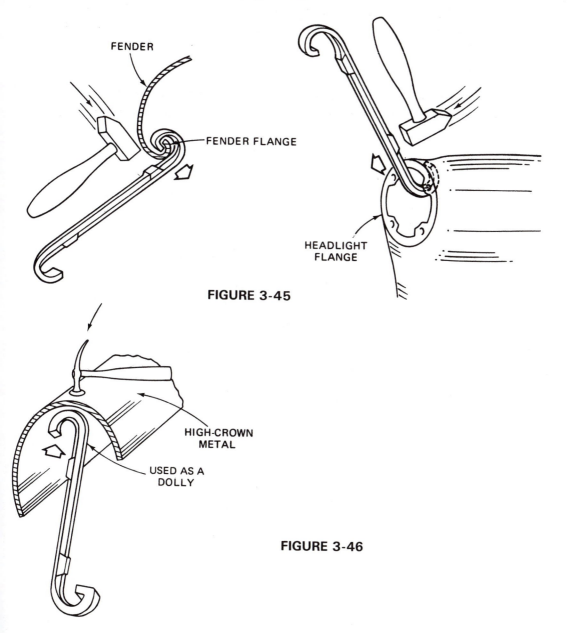

FIGURE 3-45

FIGURE 3-46

Double-End Heavy-Duty Driving Spoon and Its Uses

This spoon is used in separating outer panels from inner construction when these have been damaged and squashed together. It is inserted by driving it in between the two panels, prying either sideways or up and down on the opposite end of the spoon until the panels are roughed-out and then used as a dolly in straightening both the outer panel and the inner construction (Fig. 3-47). It is an excellent tool for breaking spot welds and opening panel flanges on doors and quarter panels, after the spot welds have been weakened by drilling them, using a 1/8 or 1/4 in. (3 or 6 mm) high-speed drill bit, depending on the size of the spot weld (Fig. 3-48).

Quite often this spoon is also used in releasing (normalizing) the stresses and strains set up in sills, door pillars, roof rails, and header bars, when door and window openings become damaged and distorted. They are then repositioned and corrected by using hydraulic jacking equipment (Fig. 3-49).

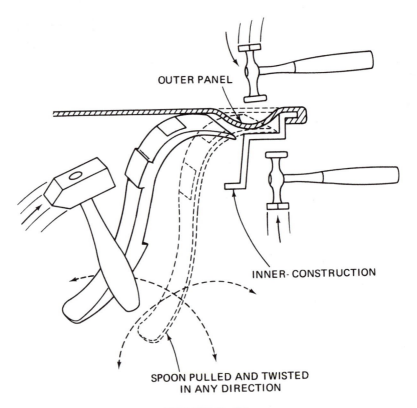

OUTER PANEL

INNER-CONSTRUCTION

SPOON PULLED AND TWISTED
IN ANY DIRECTION

FIGURE 3-47

FIGURE 3-48

FIGURE 3-49

Most of the curves and beads in the openings have to be reworked and normalized if the corrected opening is to retain its proper shape and size permanently. This operation must be done while the hydraulic jacking pressure is being applied. It is accomplished by gently heating the distorted areas with a carburizing flame until the metal turns bluish in color and letting it cool, by hammering the distorted areas cold, or by heating the metal and then hammering down any ridges or buckles that may have formed.

How Caulking Irons Are Used

Caulking irons with chisel-shaped ends of varying degrees of sharpness and width (see Fig. 3-50) are used in conjunction with ball or cross-peen hammers in the reshaping of flanges, beads, straight-line ridges, and bends on body panels and frames, as illustrated by the arrows in Fig. 3-51. Because of the restricted location or complicated shape, this cannot be carried out as fast or efficiently with conventional driving spoons, hammer and dolly, or the chisel-bit pick hammer.

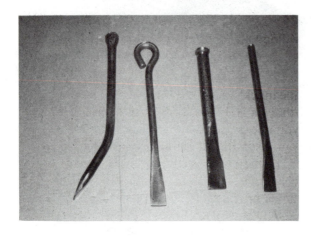

FIGURE 3-50

Spring-Hammering a Ridge or Simple Hinge Buckle

The best method of straightening the long and fairly high ridges, generally located at the outer edges of bent-in and buckled body panels (commonly referred to as *indirect damage*), and also many of the simple hinge buckles a repairman encounters is by spring-hammering them while the stresses and strains in the panel are being removed, either by the step-by-step gradual bumping-out method (Fig. 3-35) or by applying a stretching pull (Fig. 3-10). Spring-hammering of the ridge is started (using the appropriate surfacing spoon and a ball-peen hammer of sufficient weight) at the outer ends and alternately working from side to side in toward the center or highest portion of the ridge (Fig. 3-52).

The procedure above eliminates the danger of the ridge collapsing, which as it is hammered down would form two or more smaller ridges and spread the

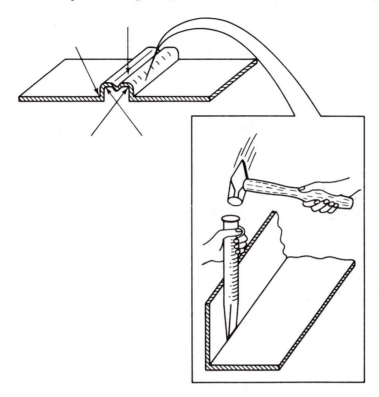

FIGURE 3-51

damage out over a larger area, which in turn would create more work for the repairman.

After the damaged metal has been roughed-out and straightened as accurately as possible by eye and by feeling its surface, it is ready for the metal-

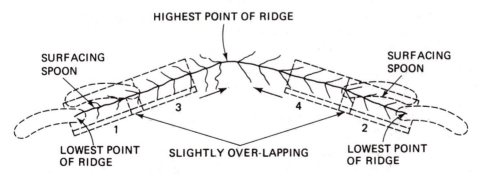

FIGURE 3-52 Spring-hammering a ridge or simple hinge buckle.

finishing operation. This operation involves the removal of any hidden surface irregularities by the repairman as he removes the paint from the metal surface by filing the area with a body file. All low spots are eliminated by *picking* the metal, using the picking hammers, pick bars, or short picks, until a perfectly smooth and level surface is obtained.

Method of Using Pick Hammer in Raising Low Spots in Metal Finishing

Small low areas are raised by using the side of the round face of the pick hammer first. Then, once the metal has been checked for levelness with the body file, any remaining tiny low spots are raised by striking each one individually with a blow or a series of tiny blows with the pick end of the hammer (Fig. 3-53).

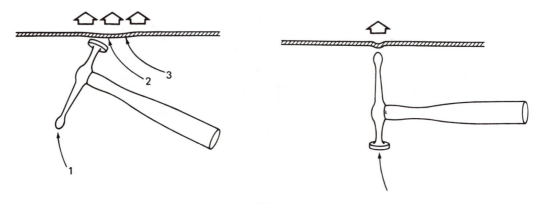

FIGURE 3-53

Care must be taken not to strike the low spots too hard; otherwise, they will become rough (pimply) and stretched and additional dinging and shrinking of the metal may be necessary. There is also the ever-present danger of cutting holes in the metal when using the body file if the low spots have not been picked up smoothly or softly. This operation requires a great deal of skill, accuracy, and a good eye if it is to be carried out efficiently and is only acquired with a considerable amount of patience and practice.

Method of Using Picks and Punches

Picks and punches are used in raising low areas that are inaccessible because of inner construction and therefore cannot be raised in the regular manner with the pick hammer. Instead, the low spots are raised by exerting an upward prying

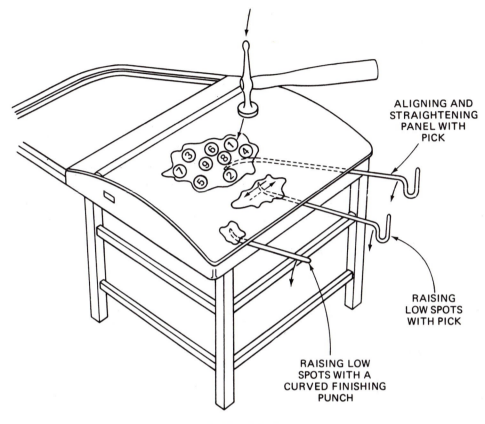

FIGURE 3-54

pressure directly underneath the low spots (Fig. 3-54). Quite often the piercing punch is used to pierce holes in the inner construction; directly underneath the weather stripping, the pick or punch is inserted, and the low spots are raised by applying pressure on its protruding end.

Picks, because they are longer in length than punches and therefore have a longer reach, are used in raising low spots in inner sections of panels; while punches, because of their short reach, are used in the outer areas or edges of body panels.

There are three ways of accurately positioning a pick or finishing punch on a particular low spot you want to raise or eliminate. It can be done by looking for a slight rise, movement, or pimpling in the metal; by laying the pick across the outer side of the panel at the insertion hole and using the pick to measure the distance between a particular low spot and the outer edge of the panel; or by moving the pick or finishing punch around, after having pushed it through the insertion hole, and applying an upward pressure, simultaneously hammering down on the outer surface of the panel until the lightly applied hammer blows are felt landing directly on the point of the pick or finishing punch and on the exact and desired area of the low spot.

Method of Filing a Fender

The crown of the fender is filed by pushing the file forward over its surface, using long strokes and a moderate amount of pressure on the file, as indicated by the arrows in Fig. 3-55. The file is drawn back over the crown, using the same length of stroke but with little or no pressure on the file, as indicated by the arrow directly below the file at A. The file is also pushed forward at a 35° angle over the crown's surface as shown at B. It is then drawn back, as indicated by the arrow, until the crown has been completely filed. This process will not only keep the metal level lengthwise but will also give a smooth curving surface to the metal as the crown of the fender is metal-finished.

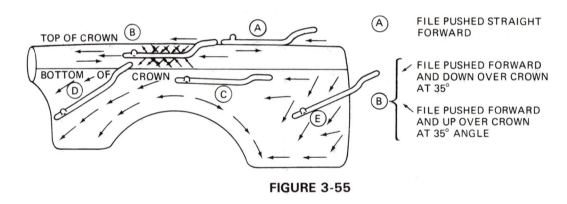

FIGURE 3-55

The center section of the side of the fender is filed by pushing the file across its surface at as near to a 35° angle as possible (shown at C); however, this step will depend entirely on the type of flange the fender has. The front and rear sections of the fender's side are filed by holding the file at a 35° angle also, as shown at D and E, respectively. The fender flange is filed with the most suitable file available, holding it straight and pushing it forward with a sort of curving motion, as indicated by the arrows.

After all low spots have been removed and the fender has been restored to its original shape, the fender is disk-sanded to its final finish (described in Unit 6-2).

Method of Filing a Door

A similar procedure is used in filing the crown on a door. The crown area on a door is filed by using long strokes (Fig. 3-56). The filing is continued until the entire surface of the crown has been filed. Both left and right sides of the door panel are then filed downward, at approximately a 35° angle, away from the crown and toward the center of the door panel, as shown in B and C, respectively. This process makes filing much easier, draws the metal from the crown portion of the door, and locates high and low spots much faster and more accurately. The lower portion of the panel is also filed straight across its entire length, making doubly sure that all irregularities have been corrected. All outer edges of the door panel are also checked by filing them, as indicated by the arrows. After the damaged door has been restored to its original shape, it is disk-sanded to its final finish (see Unit 6-2).

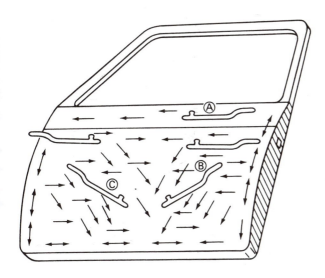

FIGURE 3-56

Method of Filing a Turret Top

The high-crowned outer areas of the turret top are filed using the same method as when filing the crown on a fender or a door and as illustrated by arrows 1, 2, 3, and 4 in Fig. 3-57. The straighter and slightly curved center section of the turret top is filed using long strokes and pushing the file at a 35° angle away from the crown, toward the center of the turret top, as indicated by arrows 5, 6, 7, and 8. The center section is then cross-filed (arrows 9, 10, 11,

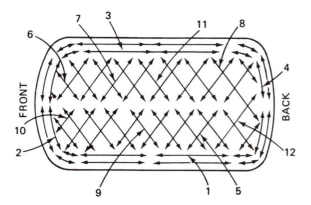

FIGURE 3-57

and 12) until all surface irregularities and low spots have been detected and eliminated.

Forging Welds

Sizable tears and breaks in automobile fenders and body panels, whose inner surfaces are not obstructed by framework or inner construction, that can be reached quite easily with a dolly are often repaired by butt-welding them in the usual way and then smoothing the welds (beads) by means of forging. Forging is a repair operation used in restoring welded butt joints to as near as possible the same thickness and molecular structure as that possessed by the surrounding sheet metal. If properly carried out, the forging operation not only increases the strength of the welded area but also eliminates the use of plastic fillers or body solder in metal finishing.

After the tear or break has been welded, the tip on the welding torch is changed to one at least one size (preferably two sizes) larger than that used in welding that particular gauge of sheet metal. The torch is lit and adjusted to a slightly carburizing flame, which is used in heating up approximately 1 to 1½ in. (25 to 38 mm) of the bead to a bright red color. The torch is quickly laid aside (without shutting it off) and the red-hot bead immediately smoothed out by means of on-the-dolly hammering, using a suitable dolly and a heavy-duty bumping hammer (Fig. 3-58). The amount of pressure exerted on the dolly by the forearm from the inside must be just right and must match the hammer blows if the red-hot bead is to remain level (which it must) with the surrounding sheet metal in the forging operation. It has been found that a greater number of light-to-medium-hard hammer blows will do a better job in forging welds than fewer harder blows. Next, another 1 to 1½ in. (25 to 38 mm) of the bead is heated to a bright red color. Be sure that it overlaps the already forged first area before it is forged.

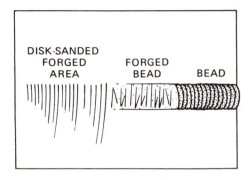

DISK-SANDED
FORGED   FORGED
AREA   BEAD   BEAD

FIGURE 3-58

This procedure is repeated over and over until the entire weld (bead) has been forged. It is then allowed to cool slowly before it is metal-finished, using the disk sander, body file, dolly, and pick hammer.

In repairing rust or collision damaged automobiles, many of the smaller partial replacement repair panels are not always readily available for the different makes and models of automobiles manufactured, or using the partial repair panels that are available is not economically feasible. Therefore, the repairman must become fully skilled in making up (shaping) the smaller partial repair panels from ordinary straight, flat sheet metal if he wishes to become a fully qualified tradesman.

How to Bend a Short and Long Right-Angle Flange

A short right-angle flange can easily be bent by placing a short piece of sheet metal, with the exact width of the flange clearly marked or scribed, between two pieces of angle iron supported in a vise or between an I-beam and an angle iron (Fig. 3-59), allowing enough metal (the width of the marked-off flange) to extend beyond the outer edges of the clamped together angle iron. A body ham-

FIGURE 3-59

FIGURE 3-60

mer with a large and round flat face or a mallet is used to bend the extending sheet metal over to an angle of 90°.

In bending a long flange, a long piece of sheet metal is clamped between two pieces of angle iron or I-beam and angle iron, of the same or longer length, and the scribed, extending sheet metal (Fig. 3-60) is gradually bent over with a heavy roughing-out hammer (either ball or cross-peen) and a piece of hardwood approximately 1 ft (305 mm) long.

Making a Series of Right-Angle Bends in Sheet Metal

After the first right-angle flange on the outer edge of a piece of sheet metal has been made, as already described, the location of the second, third, or fourth bends are laid out and clearly marked off on the sheet metal. The sheet metal is then clamped down again and the same procedure (repeated again and again) is used to bend the second, the third, the fourth, and each succeeding right-angle bend. On panels where the bends are closely spaced, a piece of plate steel 1/8 or 3/16 in. (3 or 6 mm) thick is used instead of a piece of hardwood to make the right-angle bends (Fig. 3-61).

How to Crown and Reverse Crown Sheet Metal

A piece of flat sheet metal can be bent or curved to the desired crown or reverse crown, depending on which side is facing up or out, by placing it between a length of pipe or tubing, approximately 3 to 4 in. (76 to 102 mm) in diameter, and angle iron (Fig. 3-62) and applying hand pressure to the extending portion of sheet metal. The sheet metal is then unclamped, shifted slightly, and re-

FIGURE 3-61

FIGURE 3-62

clamped. Pressure is again applied to the extending sheet metal. This procedure is repeated again and again until the sheet metal has taken on the right amount of curve or crown.

On repair jobs in which very sharply crowned and reverse crowned metal is required and in which very little sheet metal extends beyond the clamping edge, making bending by hand pressure impossible, bending or curving of the sheet metal is accomplished by placing a piece of hardwood lengthwise over the short extending edge of the metal and hammering it down with either a ball or cross-peen hammer until the desired curve or crown is obtained (Fig. 3-63).

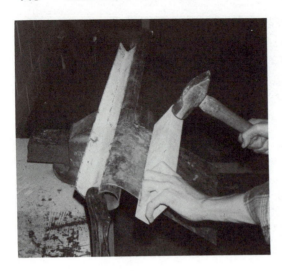

FIGURE 3-63

Flanging a Single-Crowned Panel

Before attempting to flange a single-crowned panel, the width of the desired flange must be clearly marked off. A dolly with a curved face closely conforming to the curvature of the crowned panel is accurately positioned and firmly held in place to support the metal as the body hammer is used in the gradual, step-by-step bending of the metal in forming and shaping the right-angle flange (Fig. 3-64). A series of wrinkles or buckles in the flange metal will be noticed, as the partial turning (bending) of the flange, by shifting the dolly from one position to the next and indicated by the numbers, is carried out. The wrinkles and buckles in the roughly shaped flange, which have become progressively larger throughout the flanging operation, are eliminated by means of oblong shrink spots, as de-

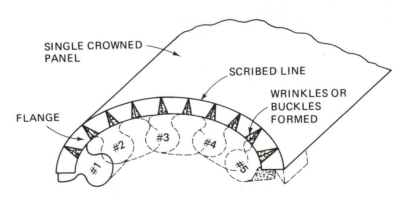

FIGURE 3-64

scribed in the shrinking of a flange (see Chapter 5). The flange is then accurately straightened to its final shape and finish by on- and off-the-dolly hammering.

Flanging a Reverse-Crowned Panel

Although the flanging of a reverse-crowned panel is far more difficult and slower, it can be done. The procedure is basically the same as that used in flanging a single-crown panel, except that as the flange is being bent or turned, the flange metal has to stretch extensively (Fig. 3-65). Heat, supplied by a welding torch equipped with a welding tip at least two sizes larger than that used in welding the flange metal, is evenly applied directly on the flange in order to make it stretch much easier. After the flange has been completely bent and roughly shaped, it is straightened in the usual manner.

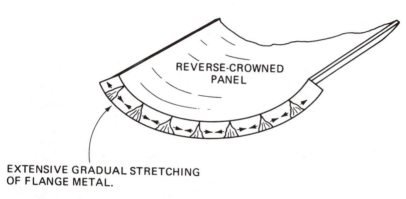

EXTENSIVE GRADUAL STRETCHING
OF FLANGE METAL.

FIGURE 3-65

Another method of flanging the repairman frequently uses is to cut an entirely separate flange out of another piece of sheet metal and edge-weld it to the reverse-crowned panel (Fig. 3-66).

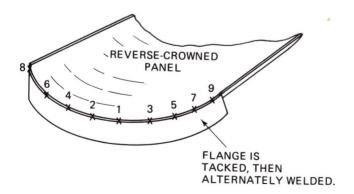

FLANGE IS
TACKED, THEN
ALTERNATELY WELDED.

FIGURE 3-66 Sequential order of tack-welding a reverse-crowned panel.

Procedure Followed in Making and Installing Patches or Partial Repair Panels

Before a patch or partial repair panel can be made for the particular job on hand, a template (paper pattern) has to be made. Masking paper, masking tape, and chalk or marking pencil are used to make the template. The overall size of the metal to be repaired, including the exact location and width of all beads, ridges, and flanges (Fig. 3-67), is traced onto the template. The template is transferred onto clean sheet metal and the patch is cut out by using either a panel cutter, snips, or power shear, whichever is available or most suitable. All body lines, beads, rolled curves, such as crowns and reverse crowns, are formed or bent as described above. The flanges on the outer edges of the patch or partial repair panel are usually bent on the automobile if the outer panel and inner construction are sound and in good shape. If they are unsound, badly damaged, or rusted, they are preformed off the car.

FIGURE 3-67

The disk grinder and the electric or pneumatic drill with a grinding attachment are used to clean (to remove) all paint, putty, plastic filler, and rust from the outer edges of the area the patch will overlap on the car body or panel and also the inner and outer edges of the patch or partial repair panel. The patch is then placed and positioned on the automobile panel. The patch should be made to fit so that a minimum of forcing is required as it is firmly clamped in place. The electric spot welder or welding torch and brazing rod together with a patch holder are now used in tack-welding the patch (see Chapter 5).

The outer flanges of the patch, if not preformed already, are bent with the aid of heat supplied by the welding torch before the patch is solidly and completely braze-welded in place. The repairman should not forget to lightly hammer the already-run and cooling bead in order to relieve the forces of contraction and to minimize warping of the patch and the surrounding metal.

The patch or panel and all adjacent areas are straightened and metal-finished by removing all surface irregularities by either picking or filling them with either body solder (a rather expensive and not too frequently used filler) or plastic filler, whichever is more practical.

Repairing Aluminum Body Panels

Most of the repairing of aluminum body panels on late-model automobiles is done by the *roughly aligning and filling* method.

Roughing-Out and Straightening Aluminum Panels

Polyester filler is used for attaching *pull or tension plates* to the damaged panel in applying the corrective stretching pull. Heating of buckles, if done very carefully and cautiously while the stretching pull is applied, has the same effect on aluminum as it has on steel. Aluminum possesses elastic qualities similar to those of steel, but aluminum's ductility is much lower. Spring-hammering, roughing-out, and straightening with body spoons and picking can be done reasonably well, but they must be done very carefully if additional damage is to be avoided.

Stretched or high areas on panels can be *heat shrunk* to a degree, but since the shrinking operation is not as effective on aluminum as it is on steel, it must be done very carefully, making certain that the heat applied is kept below the 1200°F (549°C) level. As on steel, quenching of shrink spots should be done very gradually, to avoid excessive distortion.

Metal-Finishing Aluminum Panels

Aluminum, being much softer than steel, responds very rapidly to on-the-dolly hammering, but there is always the danger of overstretching the metal. Picking of aluminum has been found to be much safer, but aluminum does not respond as well as steel does to off-the-dolly hammering. Hammer blows on high metal areas may result in local indentations unless the blows are applied very cautiously. If the indentations are not too sharp and too deep, hailstone damage can be removed easily by applying heat (Fig. 3-68).

In outlining high and low spots with the body file, it is recommended that the edges (sharp corners on the milled teeth) of the body file be rounded to avoid scratching and gouging the metal.

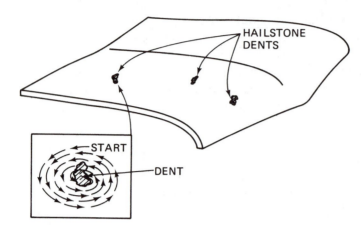

FIGURE 3-68. Circular movement of torch used in removal of hailstone damage.

In disk-sanding an aluminum panel, nothing coarser than a No. 80 (1/0) grit disk with a foam backing pad should be used, to minimize heat buildup. A high-rpm electrical polisher with a speed of approximately 2000 to 2500 rpm does a good job. If a pneumatic disk sander is used, its speed can be controlled with the trigger. A random-orbit sander, with a 6 in. foam pad and a No. 100 (2/0) grit disk, works well in final finishing.

In the fast removal (stripping) of paint from an aluminum panel a No. 36 (2) grit open-coat disk can be used, but the removal of metal should be avoided. Intermittent quenching of the metal while disk-sanding an area is recommended to reduce heat buildup and prevent possible distortion. Torch-heated areas should be quenched very carefully to avoid tension draws created by the *forces of contraction*.

Plastic filler used in eliminating minor surface irregularities adheres as well to aluminum as it does to steel if the surface is free of wax, oil, grease, and so on. In the initial shaping of the plastic-filled area, a cheese-grater file can be used if the surrounding base metal is not gouged. The final shaping of the plastic-filled area is done with the same type and grit of sandpaper as on steel.

Brazing and Soldering Aluminum Panels

In brazing aluminum the joint is created by surface bonding. Fusing of the base metal should not be attempted. The base metal and filler rod must be at approximately the same temperature if the filler rod is to bond. If they are not, the filler rod will roll off the surface of the base metal. Because pure aluminum melts at 1218°F (659°C), the filler rod used in the brazing operation must melt below this temperature.

Water-soaked rags, placed approximately 1 in. (25 mm) on each side of the joint, are used as *heat sinks* to allow more time for the brazing operation and minimize heat distortion. The raw edges of a tear in an aluminum panel are hard to tack-weld unless they can be clamped. Heat causes the raw edges of the butt-joint to misalign.

For best results, the base metal should be clean, free of all oil and grease, and abraded to remove oxidation. A low-volume, slightly carburizing flame is used in brazing aluminum. The base metal has reached the correct brazing temperature when a slight ashen cast appears on the base metal. The most suitable aluminum brazing rod, available in either *bead-forming* or *thin-flowing* type, is used in braze-welding the joint. The weld is then allowed to cool slowly. Remember, rapid quenching causes distortion and tension draws similar to those in steel. After the braze-welded joint has cooled, it and all adjacent metal should be water-rinsed to neutralize and remove the highly corrosive brazing flux from the base metal.

Aluminum solders, melting within the range of 320 to 700°F (160 to 371°C) are also available. Some may be applied without the use of flux, but the surface to be soldered should be cleaned with solvent and abraded before soldering is attempted. The flame produced by a soldering tip at approximately 4800°F (2650°C) is more than adequate.

Bar solder is not available for filling irregularities on aluminum panels. Plastic filler is the most practical substitute.

QUESTIONS

3-1 How are auto body parts manufactured?

3-2 What are the changes that occur when sheet metal is stamped out in presses?

3-3 In what different ways is sheet metal given resistance to bending or strength?

3-4 Define clearly *direct* and *indirect* damage.

3-5 What four different types of buckles are formed when sheet metal is bent in beyond its elastic limit?

3-6 In what specific areas on a damaged body panel are each of the buckles formed or located, and how is each roughed-out and straightened most efficiently?

3-7 Describe the step-by-step procedure used to straighten collision damaged parts and assemblies whose outer panels and supporting framework or inner construction have both been damaged.

3-8 In what order are the two types of sheet-metal damage corrected?

3-9 How are damaged sheet-metal panels prepared for the straightening operations?

3-10 What is the first step in the straightening operation, and how is it carried out?

3-11 How are high ridges on the outer edges of large V channels or valleys reshaped?

3-12 How are the extra-heavy stresses and strains on elastic metal areas released?

3-13 What kind of force should be used in *unlocking* or *roughing-out* damaged auto body panels?

3-14 How is a large unsupported panel straightened so that it keeps its shape?

3-15 By what means are surface irregularities in the straightening operation detected?

3-16 Describe how a body hammer is held and how it is used.

3-17 What is *dinging*?

3-18 How is the proper dolly for a particular job selected?

3-19 How can stretching of flat surface metals be minimized when the general-purpose dolly is being used?

3-20 Explain what actually takes place when sheet metal becomes stretched.

3-21 How are the dolly and hammer used in straightening low areas or troughlike depressions and light creases in flat sheet-metal panels?

3-22 How are fender flanges turned and reshaped, and why is it so important to weld and straighten them properly?

3-23 How is the general-purpose dolly used in straightening crown metals?

3-24 Describe how the pointed corner of the general-purpose dolly is used.

3-25 What kind of hammer is used in forming a bead?

3-26 Illustrate by means of a drawing how a large V channel or valley is unlocked or roughed-out, using a low-crown dolly.

3-27 How are deformations and dents in a bead eliminated?

3-28 The heel dolly is used in straightening what kind of metal surfaces?

3-29 In what straightening operations is the toe dolly used?

3-30 Illustrate with a drawing and describe how the wedge dolly is used in straightening the crown metal on a turret top.

3-31 How is double-crowned metal roughed-out and straightened?

3-32 In what operations can the double-end lower back and quarter-panel spoon be used, and how is it used?

3-33 Show and describe how the double-end door and side apron spoon is used in roughing-out and straightening crown metal in a turret top.

3-34   What kind of hammer is used with a double-end heavy-duty driving spoon, and what are its uses?

3-35   How are door and window openings *normalized*?

3-36   How and in what operations on damaged body panels and frames are caulking irons used?

3-37   How is the straightening of a long and fairly high ridge or simple hinge buckle by spring-hammering carried out?

3-38   What repair operation follows the straightening operation?

3-39   Is the pick end of the pick hammer used in raising the smaller low areas in damaged sheet metals? If not, how is it used?

3-40   Describe how picks and punches are used in metal finishing.

3-41   In metal finishing, what are the three ways of determining the exact location of a pick or finishing punch?

3-42   Describe and illustrate with a sketch the proper method used in filing a fender.

3-43   Describe and illustrate with a sketch how you would file a door.

3-44   Describe and illustrate with a sketch how you would file a turret top.

3-45   What is *forging a weld* in auto body repairing?

3-46   Describe in detail how a weld is forged and what type of body hammer is used in the operation.

3-47   How is a forged weld metal-finished?

3-48   How would you proceed to bend a right-angle flange?

3-49   How does the bending or curving procedure used in crowning a short piece of sheet metal vary from the procedure used in crowning a long piece?

3-50   In flanging a single-crowned panel, what changes must occur in the flange metal?

3-51   Briefly describe the methods used in flanging a reverse-crowned panel.

3-52   Describe the step-by-step procedure used in making and installing a patch or partial repair panel.

3-53   What method is used to repair aluminum panels on late-model automobiles?

3-54   How are pull plates attached to an aluminum body panel?

3-55   Can aluminum panels be heat shrunk? If so, how is the operation performed?

3-56   How does aluminum react to on- and off-the-dolly hammering?

3-57   What method is used to repair hailstone damage if the indentations are not too sharp and too deep?

3-58 How can scratching and gouging of the aluminum panel be avoided when outlining high and low spots with a body file?

3-59 What type of sander should be used in disk sanding and in final finishing of repaired areas?

3-60 How is the aluminum panel stripped of its paint with a disk sander?

3-61 What precautions should be taken if a cheese-grater file is used in the initial shaping of the plastic filler?

3-62 At what temperature must the filler rod melt in order to braze aluminum?

3-63 How can heat distortion be minimized in the braze-welding operation?

3-64 What two types of aluminum brazing rod are used in brazing aluminum?

3-65 Why should the braze-welded joint and all adjacent metal be water-rinsed after they are cooled?

3-66 If a joint on an aluminum panel is to be soldered, how is the surface prepared for the soldering operation, and what type of flame is used?

4

Hydraulic Equipment

In the correction of both minor and major auto body damage, hydraulic equipment, as well as hand tools, is used in the restoration of damaged sections, assemblies, and parts to their original positions and shape. All outer body panels are supported, held in place, and strengthened by some type of framework or inner construction, which is generally formed from heavier-gauge sheet metal. The framework also becomes distorted, bent, or pushed out of position when the vehicle is involved in a collision. To repair this particular type of damage properly and efficiently, both the outer panel and the framework or inner construction must be roughed-out and aligned at the same time. This process can only be done by the application of an even and uniform corrective force, which can be increased or decreased at will, as required in different repair operations. This force is produced for the repairman by an hydraulic jacking unit (Fig. 4-1), consisting of a hydraulic jack with all its parts and attachments.

Hydraulic jacking units are manufactured in a variety of sizes. Light-duty jacking units generally have capacities of 1½ to 2 tons (1361 to 1814 kg) *pulling* and up to 4 tons (3629 kg) *pushing*. They are lightweight and ideally suited for the lighter repair operations, such as repairing doors, cowls, fenders, grilles, hoods, and quarter panels. They are especially handy in making adjustments required in the replacement of new parts.

Standard jacking units are of heavier, more rugged construction and have from 5 to 10 tons (4536 to 9072 kg) of pushing capacity, which makes them suitable for practically all jobs in auto body repairing. They can be used for

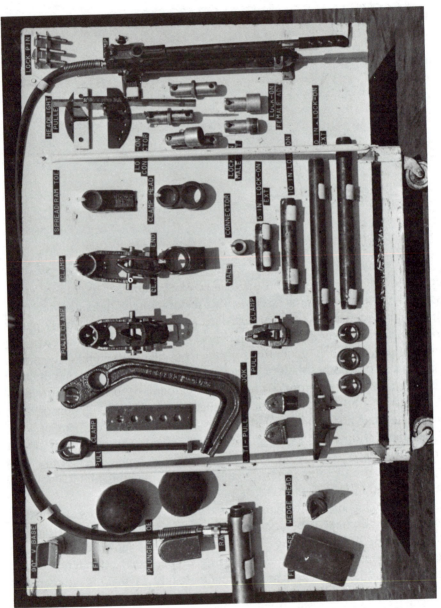

FIGURE 4-1

158

pushing, pulling, clamping, and spreading the stronger reinforced sheet-metal sections and assemblies on auto bodies and minor repairs on frames.

Heavy-duty hydraulic jacking units are of extra-heavy construction, having from 12 to 50 tons (10,886 to 45,360 kg) of pushing power. They are used on the most difficult body and frame reconditioning jobs, on both cars and trucks, where extremely large amounts of hydraulic power are required. These units are also capable of pushing, pulling, spreading, clamping, lifting, and pressing, depending on how they are set up. Every hydraulic jacking unit is equipped with a hydraulic jack. The jack consists of the pump (1), the hose (2), the quick detachable coupler (3), and the ram (4), as shown in Fig. 4-2. The pump is equipped with a hydraulic oil reservoir and a handle [Fig. 4-3(A)], which when operated by hand, activates a piston, which, in turn, pumps the oil from the reservoir into the hose.

FIGURE 4-2 (Courtesy of Blackhawk, Division of Applied Power, Canada, Ltd.)

FIGURE 4-3 (Courtesy of Blackhawk, Division of Applied Power, Canada, Ltd.)

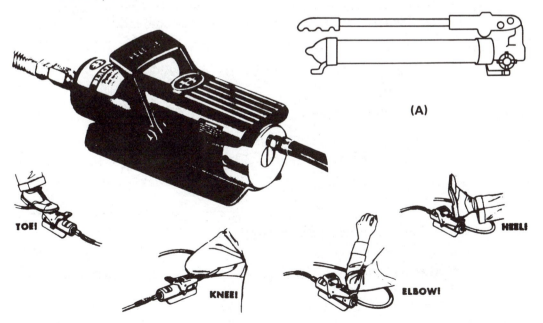

(A)

An air hydraulic pump can also be used to activate the ram [Fig. 4-3(B)]. This pump enables the repairman to use hydraulic jacking equipment easily, more accurately, and faster than with the hand pump, because both hands are free and enable him to reposition setups more readily, observe the work more closely, and hammer out wrinkles and folds in metal as stresses and strains are released.

The hose, which is made of special oil-resistant rubber embedded with steel-wire reinforcement, is approximately 6 ft (1.83 m) in length and quite flexible. It transfers the hydraulic oil from the pump to the ram and lets the repairman work where he can best observe the results as jacking progresses (Fig. 4-4).

The quick detachable coupler permits the removal of the coupler tube without the loss of hydraulic fluid from the ram (Fig. 4-5) and makes it possible to use the same pump with a variety of rams and spreaders (Fig. 4-6) by simply selecting the best-suited ram or spreader for the particular job on hand and

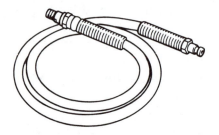

FIGURE 4-4 (Courtesy of Blackhawk, Division of Applied Power, Canada, Ltd.)

FIGURE 4-5 (Courtesy of Blackhawk, Division of Applied Power, Canada, Ltd.)

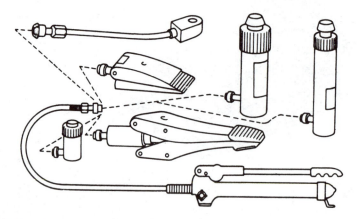

FIGURE 4-6 (Courtesy of Blackhawk, Division of Applied Power, Canada, Ltd.)

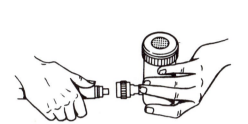

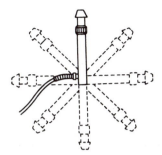

FIGURE 4-7 (Courtesy of Blackhawk, Division of Applied Power, Canada, Ltd.)

FIGURE 4-8 (Courtesy of Blackhawk, Division of Applied Power, Canada, Ltd.)

connecting the ram to the hose by tightening the female connector with a twirl of the finger (Fig. 4-7). Furthermore, the coupler allows the ram to swivel freely, enabling the repairman to use it in any position (Fig. 4-8) and to apply pressure in any direction and at any angle.

The ram (Fig. 4-9), which is made out of a single piece of high-grade steel, is generally cylindrical in shape. Its base is equipped with inside threads into which attachments can be turned. The opposite end of the ram (body) is also threaded for attachments, as is the *plunger*. The plunger is fitted into an accurately bored-out cylinder that receives the hydraulic oil from the pump. The pressure in the cylinder is built up as the amount of hydraulic oil pumped into it increases; as a result, the plunger is moved out of the cylinder a short distance with each stroke of the pump handle.

To harness the power developed by the hydraulic jack, a variety of threaded attachments must be used. These attachments can be threaded to the ram plunger or into the ram base (Fig. 4-10). An alternative and faster method of connecting attachments to the hydraulic jack is by the use of lock-on connectors, male and female lock-on adaptors (Fig. 4-11). When *direct pulling* setups are made using the method above, however, locking pins must be slipped through the drilled holes that are especially provided for this purpose.

FIGURE 4-9 (Courtesy of Blackhawk, Division of Applied Power, Canada, Ltd.)

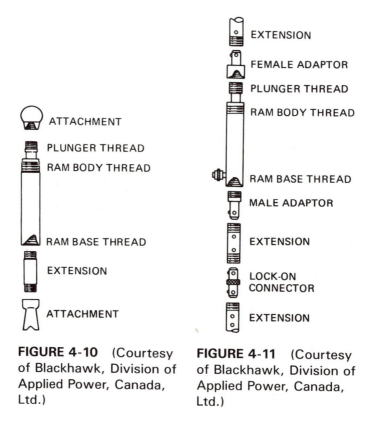

FIGURE 4-10 (Courtesy of Blackhawk, Division of Applied Power, Canada, Ltd.)

FIGURE 4-11 (Courtesy of Blackhawk, Division of Applied Power, Canada, Ltd.)

UNIT 4-1: BASIC PUSHING SETUPS

When the hydraulic jack is coupled with a number of different attachments, it becomes an extremely versatile tool that helps the repairman to do hundreds of jobs and operations quite easily—jobs that, without hydraulic equipment, he would not be able to handle at all. When the hydraulic jack is to be used in repair operations that require *pushing* power, the attachments shown in Fig. 4-12 are used in making basic pushing setups.

Light-duty pushing combinations are made by using either 3/4 in. (19 mm) threaded or 3/4 in. (19 mm) lock-on extension tubing, which is available in different lengths, generally 23, 15, 10, 5, and 3 in. (584, 381, 254, 127, and 76 mm) long. Lengths can be connected by threaded couplers or lock-on connectors. The ends of each *pushing* combination are fitted with special attachments. These attachments not only protect the threads on the extension tubing and the ram plunger from being damaged when pressure is applied but also tend to distribute or spread this pressure over a larger area of the work, thereby minimizing if not completely preventing any additional damage from occurring.

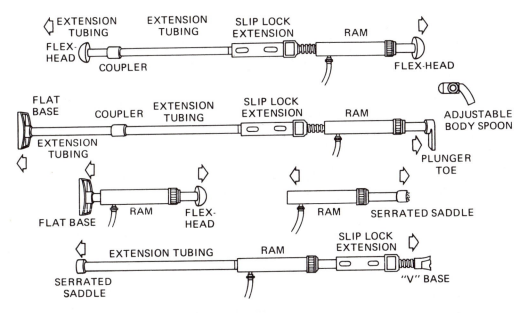

FIGURE 4-12 Light-duty pushing combination (Courtesy of Blackhawk, Division of Applied Power, Canada, Ltd.)

Flex heads, or rubber bases as they are sometimes called, conform to any contour and are most often used as a terminal point for pushing against concave surfaces. Flex heads fit any curve on door and window openings, inside window frames, and other crowned body sections. They provide positive contact, yet do not mar painted surfaces when under hydraulic pressure. They are made in different sizes: 2¾ in. (70 mm) used with the light-duty [4 ton (3629 kg)] jack and the 3¼ and 5 in. (83 and 127 mm) flex head used with the standard [10 ton (9072 kg)] pushing combinations shown in Fig. 4-13.

Their dome design enables setups to be positioned in compact places and at different angles. Although flex heads are most frequently used in pushing and spreading operations in the repairing of turret tops, quarter panels, door pillars, wheel housings, and back panels, they are also occasionally used in clamping operations. Slip-lock extensions enable the repairman to change setup lengths faster, without any disassembly. They are a great timesaver because they adjust the length of hookup as much as 5¼ in. (133 mm), providing the exact length needed to fit a particular job. The extension works equally well in all types of setups—pushing, pulling, spreading, or clamping.

Flat bases are available with plain steel or rubber facing. They are attached to the ram base by means of a male connector or onto extension tubing, providing a good wide base from which pressure can be exerted. The rubber-faced flat base gives a completely nonskid footing for pushing operations where hydraulic power

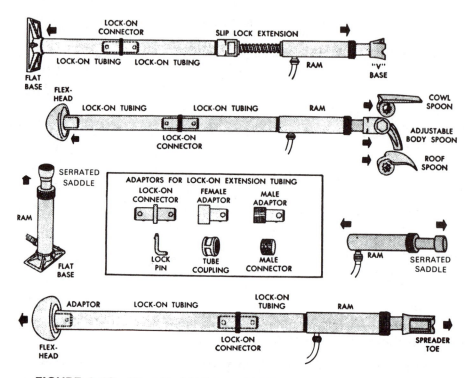

FIGURE 4-13 Standard (10 ton, 9072 kg) pushing combination. (Courtesy of Blackhawk, Division of Applied Power, Canada, Ltd.)

is exerted at odd angles, such as is used in the roughing-out of turret tops and quarter panels. It also prevents the marring or scratching of painted surfaces. The flat base can be used with the hydraulic *wedgie* by means of the swivel connector for spreading damaged doors, cowls, quarter panels, and so on.

The serrated saddle is used to protect the threads on the extension tubing and the ram plunger, and its serrated face serves as a base that does not slip or slide easily when pressure is applied. Bases, wedge heads, and spreader toes are designed to anchor combinations against frame members, braces, and the heads of body bolts.

Adjustable body spoons are used in pushing out all types of different-shaped body panels. The fork and hexagon pin serve three body spoons, each shaped to handle different contours. Each spoon can be adjusted on the fork to 14 practical working positions. With three spoons, this makes a total of 42 separate positions in which the repairman can apply hydraulic power. Each spoon is made of drop-forged steel so that it may also be used as a dolly in roughing-out and aligning body panels.

Pushing combinations of 20 tons (18,144 kg) use the same attachments as

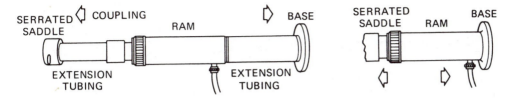

FIGURE 4-14   Heavy-duty (20 ton, 18,144 kg) pushing combinations. (Courtesy of Blackhawk, Division of Applied Power, Canada, Ltd.)

standard pushing combinations of 10 tons (9072 kg), except that the wall of the extension tubing is extra heavy (Fig. 4-14). These pushing setups are primarily used in extra-heavy work, such as shifting entire assemblies and sections on badly damaged cars and trucks and in the repairing of frames, where extra amounts of pushing power are required.

UNIT 4-2:   PULLING SETUPS

Many body panels and parts are more easily roughed-out and brought into alignment with adjacent parts by the application of a pulling force. It will be noticed that by changing the attachments of each end of the pushing combinations and by using offset pull toes, yokes, adaptors, pull ram connectors, and a number of different clamps (Fig. 4-15), many different pulling combinations can be set up.

Fender clamps, when used with the adaptors (Fig. 4-15) or with a chain, can be employed for many pulling operations. Clamp jaws are serrated, which gives them positive gripping action and enables them to hold the lighter-gauge metals without slipping or sliding. They are easily attached in any holding position by simply tightening two bolts. They are designed to fit over deep flanges and raised edges, such as beads found on the outer edges of panels, without causing any damage to the metal.

Offset (notched) pull toes make pulling setups completely adjustable and exert a pull across either high- or low-crown body sections, without any danger of the jack crushing undamaged metal (Fig. 4-16).

Pull clamps hold their grip under hydraulic pressure and withstand hammer vibrations because of their sharp, forged, cross-milled jaws, which are equipped with twin bolt adjustability for a sure grip. Because of the shallowness of their jaws, however, they can only be employed on straight or nearly straightedged sheet-metal panels. They can be used with a pull plate in series (two at each end of the combination), as shown in the preceding figures.

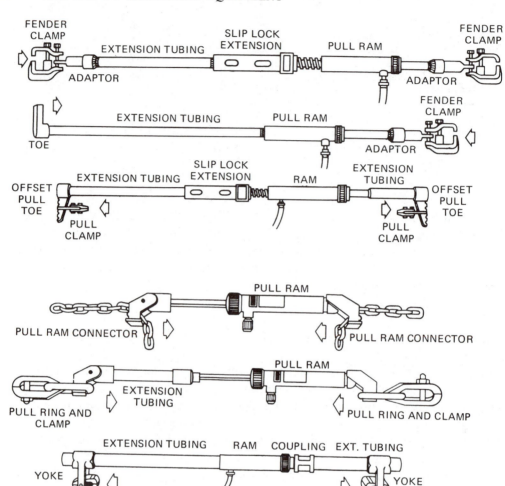

FIGURE 4-15 Light-duty pulling combinations. (Courtesy of Blackhawk, Division of Applied Power, Canada, Ltd.)

FIGURE 4-16

Standard (10 Ton, 9072 kg) Pulling Combinations

Standard (10 ton, 9072 kg) pulling combinations are set up in the same way as the light-duty combinations except that all the equipment used is more rugged and consequently, more hydraulic pulling power is developed (Fig. 4-17).

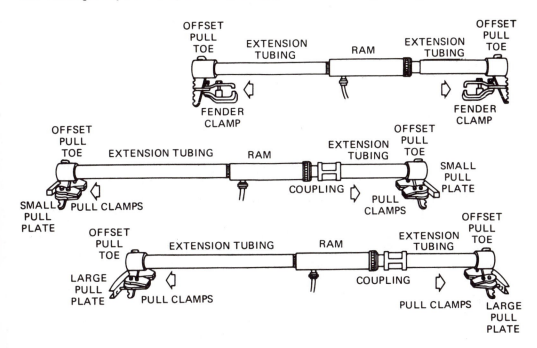

FIGURE 4-17 (Courtesy of Blackhawk, Division of Applied Power, Canada, Ltd.)

Occasionally, the repairman is confronted with a particular job in which it is impossible to use pull clamps because the pulling force has to be exerted on the center portion of a panel, where there are no panel edges on which pulling clamps can be mounted. To apply a pulling force on such an area, that is, relieving the tension and bringing the metal back to its original position without stretching or distorting it, *solder plates*, sometimes called *tension plates*, work well when used with the standard (10 ton, 9072 kg) pushing combination (Fig. 4-18). The solder plates are positioned on the panel and their exact location marked off. All paint is removed well beyond the marked-off areas by using the disk grinder. The cleaned areas and the faces of the pull plates are then properly tinned. Bar solder is deposited and flowed out over the areas to approximately 1/8 in. (3 mm) deep. The solder plates are held near the soldered areas and

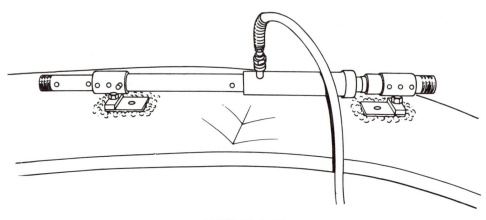

FIGURE 4-18

heated up at the same time. The solder and the plates must be at the right temperature, not too cold to form a strong bond. The softness of the solder can easily be tested with the corner of the plate. Once the right temperature is reached, the torch is quickly laid aside and the hot plate is pressed down into the solder. The plate and solder are then quickly quenched by laying a wet rag or sponge on the hot plate. Once the solder plates and the panel are completely cold, the pulling pressure can be applied. The solder plates must, however, be mounted as close to the damage as possible and be aligned accurately, so that a minimum of twisting will occur in the pulling operation. The solder plates can easily be removed from the panel by a moderate application of heat on the plates; however, the plates must be retinned after each pulling operation.

The 10 ton (9072 kg) pulling combinations that employ one or two chains (Fig. 4-19) are chiefly used on very tough pulling operations, where body and frame sections and parts have to be drawn back into their proper positions. The combinations are quite heavy in weight; because the hydraulic jack and attachments must be held up in its pulling position while the chains are hooked up and adjusted, two men are generally required to make these setups. The chains must also be padded when wrapped around sharp corners to prevent their links from bending frame members when pressure is applied.

Heavy pulling is made possible by using chains and pull plates. These attachments provide a fast, efficient method of pulling when repairing frames or reinforced sheet-metal sections and parts. Chains of varying lengths allow infinitely adjustable setups for heavy-duty pulling with full hydraulic power. The pull plate used in Fig. 4-19 is turned onto the ram threads after the thread-protecting collar has been removed. This collar should be replaced, however, once the pulling operation has been completed and the setup disassembled. Its

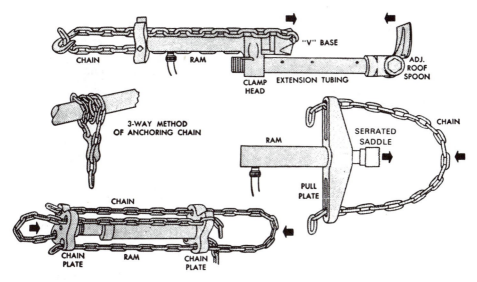

FIGURE 4-19 (Courtesy of Blackhawk, Division of Applied Power, Canada, Ltd.)

design allows chain adjustments to be made quickly and easily. A serrated saddle is used on the ram plunger to protect its threads and provide a suitable base that will neither slip nor slide when under hydraulic pressure.

When the two chain-pulling setups are used, the chain plates are threaded onto the ram plunger and onto the bottom of the ram body by means of a male connector. The large round holes in the chain plates act as guides through which the chains slide. The other two *slotted* holes provide an easy way of adjusting chain length by simply inserting the chain links adjacent to the slots after the chains have been completely stretched out.

UNIT 4-3: SPREADING SETUPS

When the hydraulic jack is inserted and positioned in between two body sections, panels, or parts and hydraulic pressure is then applied, the foregoing parts will be moved farther apart, causing them to spread. Spreading pressure can often be applied in very restricted areas when *spreading toes* and flat bases are attached to the 4 ton (3629 kg) ram (Fig. 4-20).

The *wedgie ram* can be used alone in spreading operations (Fig. 4-21) or it can be used with various attachments, such as flex heads, V and flat bases, or serrated saddles, and the swivel connector to rough-out the lighter outer body

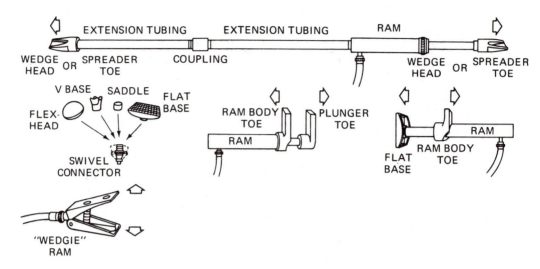

FIGURE 4-20 (Courtesy of Blackhawk, Division of Applied Power, Canada, Ltd.)

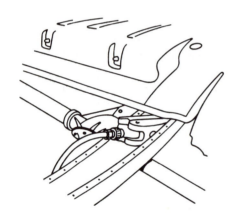

FIGURE 4-21 (Courtesy of Blackhawk, Division of Applied Power, Canada, Ltd.)

panels that are largely closed off by braces, reinforcement, or inner construction of one kind or another, as found on fenders, doors, cowls, sills, and quarter panels.

All the spreading combinations in Fig. 4-22 are set up in the same manner as the light-duty combinations previously described except that the jacks and attachments employed are larger and stronger. The spreader ram is ideal for roughing-out deep creases in the wide flaring fenders and body panels on late-model cars. It has an approximate spreading range of 10 to 11 in. (254 to 279 mm) and reaches into deep, narrow openings. Consequently, the preceding combinations are primarily used in repair operations where greater amounts of spreading power are required.

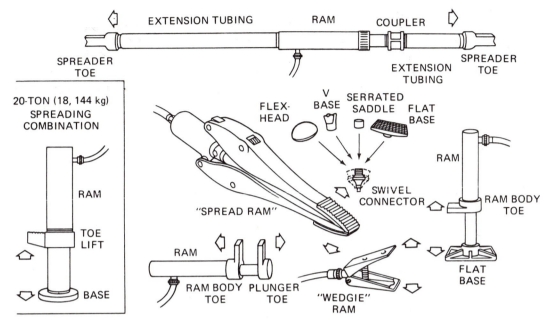

FIGURE 4-22 Standard (10 ton, 9072 kg) and heavy-duty (20 ton, 18,144 kg) spreading combinations. (Courtesy of Blackhawk, Division of Applied Power, Canada, Ltd.)

UNIT 4-4: CLAMPING SETUPS

Often sections, assemblies, and parts that are being repaired must be clamped together and the ordinary C clamps cannot be used. However, when a clamp head (which is turned onto the ram body threads), one or several extension tubes, and a plunger toe are coupled together with a hydraulic jack (Figs. 4-23 and 4-24), an effective clamping combination is established. In addition to the preceding clamping combinations, C clamps, of heavy and strong construction (Fig. 4-24) are frequently used with a variety of adaptors or pusher pins in the removal of shackle pins on leaf-type truck springs. These clamps can also be used in frame straightening and many other clamping jobs.

Hydraulic presses are used as another means of clamping work. They speed up and make short work of all types of removal and installation jobs. They are particularly handy in the reshaping and aligning of damaged bumper face bars, when they have to be repaired and sent out for rechroming. The hydraulic press in Fig. 4-25 is powered by an ordinary 10 ton (9072 kg) hydraulic jack that is positioned in between the two upper solid steel bars, which are held up in place by thick steel rods. These rods, in turn, are anchored in a heavy press bed, which

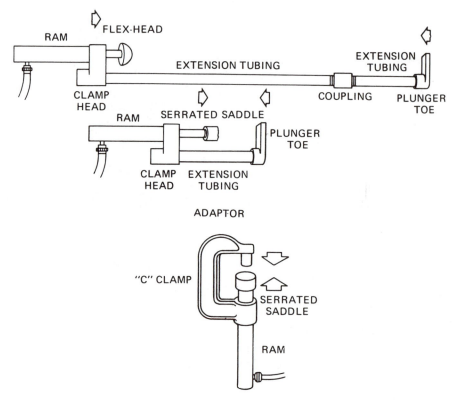

FIGURE 4-23 Light-duty (4 ton, 3629 kg) clamping combination. (Courtesy of Blackhawk, Division of Applied Power, Canada, Ltd.)

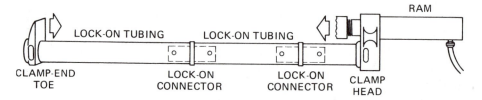

FIGURE 4-24 Standard (10 ton, 9072 kg) clamping combinations. (Courtesy of Blackhawk, Division of Applied Power, Canada, Ltd.)

also consists of steel bars. The work is placed in the press and the hydraulic jack (plunger) is fitted with attachments most suitable for the job on hand. Presses are frequently used as vises in body shops. The bumper face bars, after being roughed-out and aligned, are then held down securely in the press while the metal-finishing operation is completed.

FIGURE 4-25

UNIT 4-5: CARE OF HYDRAULIC EQUIPMENT

It is extremely important that hydraulic equipment be used and taken care of properly. It is hoped that the following suggestions will not only make hydraulic equipment last longer but will also enable it to give better and more trouble-free service.

Rams should not be overloaded. Choose the right capacity ram for the job on hand. Cracked cylinders, blown seals, and bent plungers can result from overloading (Fig. 4-26). Rams should also not be overextended, for it is possible (because of the terrific hydraulic power developed by the pump) to push the plunger right out of the ram (Fig. 4-27).

FIGURE 4-26 (Courtesy of Blackhawk, Division of Applied Power, Canada, Ltd.)

FIGURE 4-27 (Courtesy of Blackhawk, Division of Applied Power, Canada, Ltd.)

The spring retaining screw at the bottom of the ram, which holds the spring that pulls back the plunger, should not be tampered with. Any turning on this screw is liable to unhook the spring; as a result, the plunger will not automatically pull back into the ram once the pressure has been released (Fig. 4-28).

All threads on hydraulic equipment should be protected at all times and kept in excellent condition (Fig. 4-29). The proper attachments should be used and should be turned on completely.

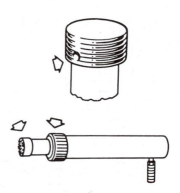

FIGURE 4-28 (Courtesy of Blackhawk, Division of Applied Power, Canada, Ltd.)

FIGURE 4-29 (Courtesy of Blackhawk, Division of Applied Power, Canada, Ltd.)

Oil lines should be kept clean at all times and dust caps should be installed on coupler halves when rams, spreaders, or wedgies are not connected to the pump (Fig. 4-30). This will prevent dirt and other foreign matter from entering the hydraulic system.

When using attachments like the notched pull toe, the edge clamp, the adjustable body spoon, or the toe lift, where the load is off-center, hydraulic equipment should be used very carefully. Stop frequently to adjust the load to a less off-center position and then continue with the corrective procedure (Fig. 4-31). Doing so will reduce the strain on the plunger, extension tubing, and attachments being used. Care should be taken not to drop heavy, sharp objects

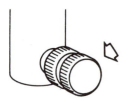

FIGURE 4-30 (Courtesy of Blackhawk, Division of Applied Power, Canada, Ltd.)

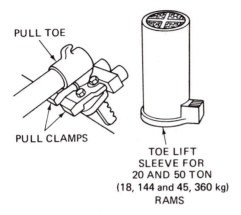

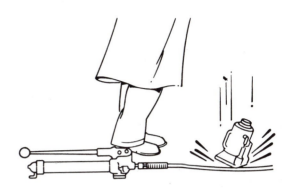

FIGURE 4-31 (Courtesy of Black-hawk, Division of Applied Power, Canada, Ltd.)

FIGURE 4-32 (Courtesy of Black-hawk, Division of Applied Power, Canada, Ltd.)

on the hydraulic hose (Fig. 4-32). Doing so will kink the hose, often causing a break in it. The ram and pump should not be lifted and carried by the hose.

When using the hydraulic jack, allow enough clearance for the hose (Fig. 4-33) and the quick detachable coupler (Fig. 4-34), so that no pressure will be exerted on them by the work. Avoid heating up of hydraulic equipment when using the oxyacetylene torch (Fig. 4-35), for this will weaken and often cause damage to the hose, flex heads, and seals in the rams, spreaders, and wedgies.

When refilling the hydraulic jack with hydraulic oil, first collapse the ram if it is connected to the pump. The pump is then placed in a vise (Fig. 4-36).

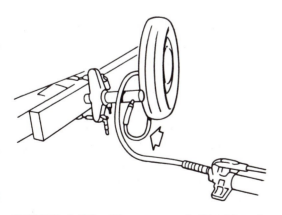

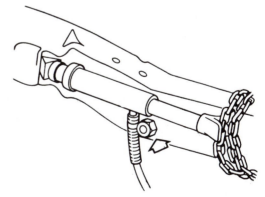

FIGURE 4-33 (Courtesy of Blackhawk, Division of Applied Power, Canada, Ltd.)

FIGURE 4-34 (Courtesy of Blackhawk, Division of Applied Power, Canada, Ltd.)

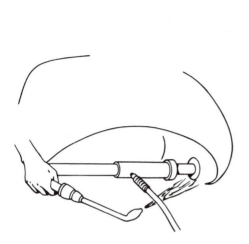

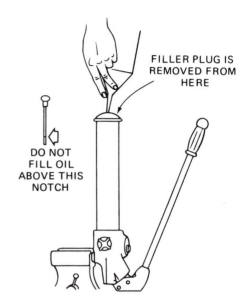

FILLER PLUG IS
REMOVED FROM
HERE

DO NOT
FILL OIL
ABOVE THIS
NOTCH

FIGURE 4-35 (Courtesy of Blackhawk, Division of Applied Power,
Canada, Ltd.)

FIGURE 4-36 (Courtesy of Blackhawk, Division of Applied Power,
Canada, Ltd.)

Next, the filler plug is removed from the end of the pump and hydraulic oil is
added until the proper level is reached. This level is determined by frequent
checking of oil level with the dipstick attached to the filler plug. Do not overfill
the pump or it will not have sufficient air space to function properly.

See Fig. 4-37 for hydraulic combinations for basic setups.

UNIT 4-6: BODY AND FRAME STRAIGHTENERS

As a result of the gradual change that has occurred in the design and construction
of automobiles and trucks over the past 30 years, new methods of body and
frame straightening have been developed; these make the repair of collision-
damaged vehicles much easier and less time consuming.

Repairmen found that the hydraulic jacking equipment that had worked
reasonably well on the older automobiles was no longer satisfactory as the number
of *unitized constructed* vehicles increased. Fewer pushing points were available;
many body parts were inaccessible and could no longer be removed, repaired,
and then replaced as had been the practice; consequently, the frame and body
sheet metal had to be straightened at the same time.

The demand for better and more efficient methods of repairing automobiles

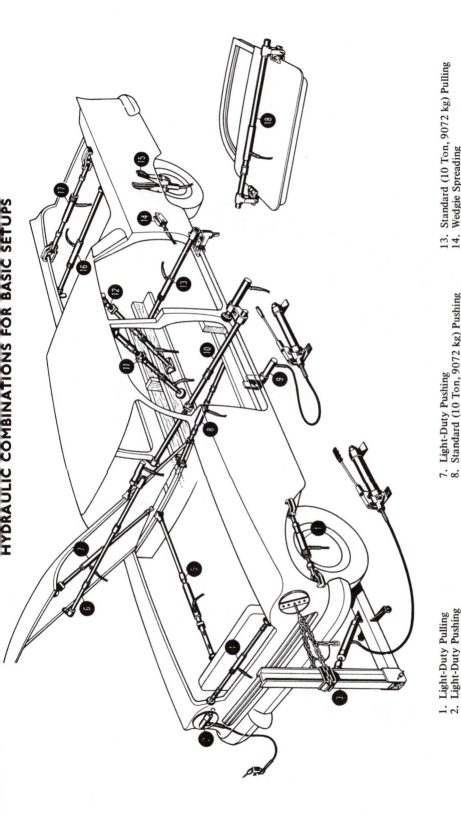

1. Light-Duty Pulling
2. Light-Duty Pushing
3. Dozer Pulling
4. Light-Duty Spreading
5. Standard (10 Ton, 9072 kg) Pushing
6. Light-Duty Clamping

7. Light-Duty Pushing
8. Standard (10 Ton, 9072 kg) Pushing
9. Standard (10 Ton, 9072 kg) Spreading
10. Standard (10 Ton, 9072 kg) Clamping
11. Standard (10 Ton, 9072 kg) Pushing
12. Standard (10 Ton, 9072 kg) Pushing

13. Standard (10 Ton, 9072 kg) Pulling
14. Wedgie Spreading
15. Spread Ram Spreading
16. Light-Duty Pushing
17. Light-Duty Pulling
18. Standard (10 Ton, 9072 kg) Pulling

FIGURE 4-37 (Courtesy of Blackhawk, Division of Applied Power, Canada, Ltd.)

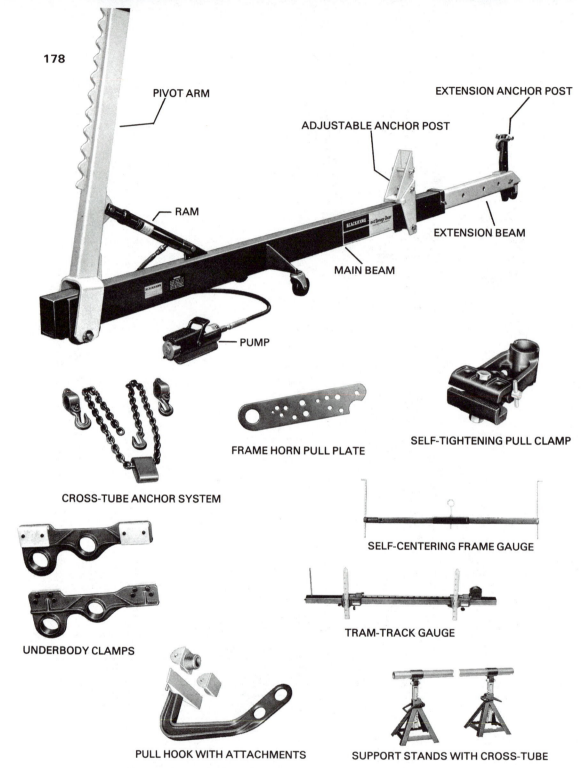

PIVOT ARM

EXTENSION ANCHOR POST

ADJUSTABLE ANCHOR POST

RAM

EXTENSION BEAM

MAIN BEAM

PUMP

FRAME HORN PULL PLATE

SELF-TIGHTENING PULL CLAMP

CROSS-TUBE ANCHOR SYSTEM

SELF-CENTERING FRAME GAUGE

TRAM-TRACK GAUGE

UNDERBODY CLAMPS

PULL HOOK WITH ATTACHMENTS

SUPPORT STANDS WITH CROSS-TUBE

FIGURE 4-38 Blackhawk dozer, portable body, and frame straightener. (Courtesy of Blackhawk, Division of Applied Power, Canada, Ltd.)

brought about the introduction of the portable body and frame straightener or *pulldozer*, as it is commonly called (Fig. 4-38). It is used in the roughing-out and alignment of both the frame and body sheet metal at the same time and makes it possible to apply a *corrective pull* in almost any desired direction. It not only minimizes but entirely eliminates the removal of damaged parts on some automobiles.

The straightener consists of a *main beam* that is equipped with wheels or casters so that it can be moved about easily from one job to another in the shop. A *pivot arm*, located at one end of this beam, is activated by means of a 10 ton (9072 kg) hydraulic ram having either a 6 or 10 in. (152 or 254 mm) stroke. The other end of the main beam is equipped with an *adjustable anchor post* (Fig. 4-39) that can be positioned and firmly locked on any portion of the beam, depending on the length required. The extension beam is also fitted with an anchor post that adjusts to three separate heights, enabling easy anchoring of the straightener to almost any area on an automobile.

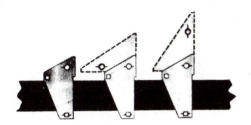

FIGURE 4-39 Adjustable anchor post. (Courtesy of Blackhawk, Division of Applied Power, Canada, Ltd.)

Because of the height of the main beam (especially on the longer, larger models), *support stands* and *cross tubes* are used to raise the automobile off the floor. When they are used with *underbody clamps*, as shown in Fig. 4-40, they provide a large base to which the straightener can be anchored.

The *pivot arm*, or *tower* as it is sometimes called, is connected to the damaged area that must be repositioned and pulled back into its original position and shape (Fig. 4-41). Frame-horn pull plates, self-tightening pull clamps, pull or tension plates, and the body pull hook with a variety of attachments are used with chains to make the required *pulling* setups.

The *frame-horn pull plate* is equipped with numerous holes by which it can be bolted to bumper bracket mounting holes in the side rails or to any other parts or areas on an automobile; it has an extra-large end hole or eye through which a chain is passed and wrapped around the pivot arm when making a pulling setup (Fig. 4-42).

Self-tightening pull clamps are also used in applying corrective pulls on parts equipped with flanges (Fig. 4-43).

The *pull hook* and its attachments are used to hook up the straightener to

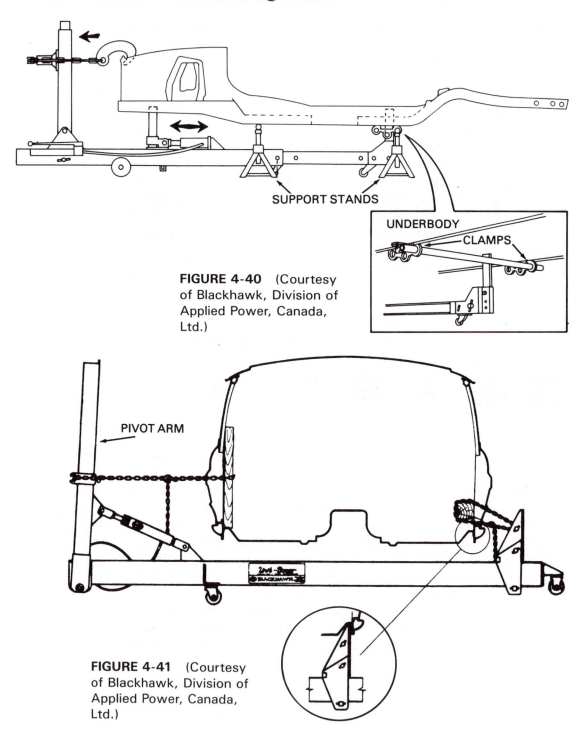

SUPPORT STANDS

UNDERBODY
CLAMPS

FIGURE 4-40   (Courtesy of Blackhawk, Division of Applied Power, Canada, Ltd.)

PIVOT ARM

FIGURE 4-41   (Courtesy of Blackhawk, Division of Applied Power, Canada, Ltd.)

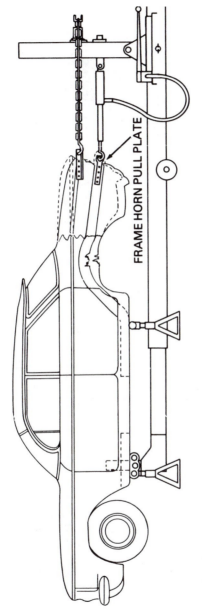

FRAME HORN PULL PLATE

FIGURE 4-42 (Courtesy of Blackhawk, Division of Applied Power, Canada, Ltd.)

181

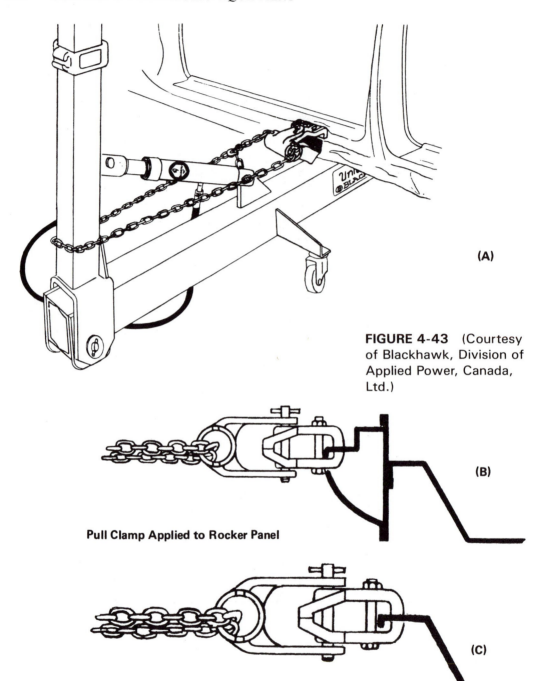

(A)

FIGURE 4-43 (Courtesy of Blackhawk, Division of Applied Power, Canada, Ltd.)

(B)

Pull Clamp Applied to Rocker Panel

(C)

out-of-the-way pull points. It prevents damage to the body and frame from wraparound chain hookups and frequently eliminates the cutting of access holes in body floor panels. Its wide mouth makes it possible to pull car trunk wells and other deep-contoured sections, such as cowl posts, body panels, and fenders (Fig. 4-44). Hook attachments consist of one large and one small plate, which help to spread the pressure of the applied pull over a large area, and an adaptor, which accommodates standard 10 ton (9072 kg) hydraulic attachments such as flex heads, flat bases, the serrated saddle, and wedge heads.

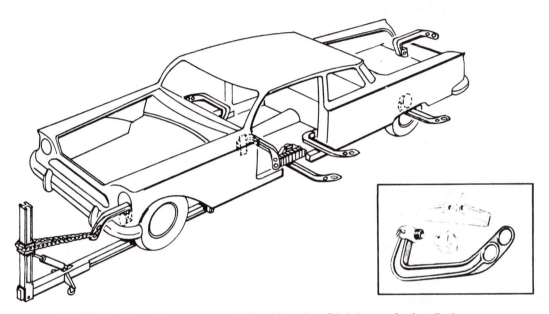

FIGURE 4-44 (Courtesy of Blackhawk, Division of Applied Power, Canada, Ltd.)

Unitized body anchor clamps can be fastened to grip firmly practically anywhere along body pinch-weld flanges on automobiles; when used with a cross tube and support stands as shown in Fig. 4-40, they provide a solid anchor for the body and frame straightener.

Self-centering frame gauges are shown in Fig. 4-45; three or more are generally required to diagnose and correct frame damage accurately on an automobile.

The *tram-track* gauge (illustrated in Fig. 4-38) is composed of three sections and assembles in 32, 70, and 134 in. (0.80, 1.8, and 3.35 m) lengths. It is equipped with three 1/16 in. (2 mm) graduated pointers, which when used with a clip-on pointer bracket holding a measuring tape, makes it possible for underbody, frame, and tracking measurements to be easily made.

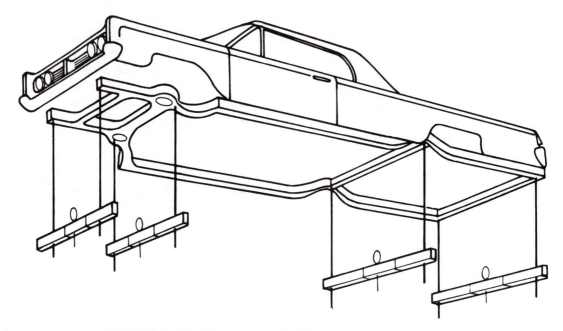

FIGURE 4-45 (Courtesy of Blackhawk, Division of Applied Power, Canada, Ltd.)

The *cross-tube anchor system* [Fig. 4-46(A)] consists of a 9 ft (2.79 m) one-hook chain that is fitted with an adjustable anchor-pin adaptor and two cross-tube hooks to make anchoring of the straightener possible without altering the length of the extended main beam.

One of the latest and strongest methods of anchoring portable body and frame straighteners on unitized automobiles, especially later models of high-strength steel construction, is the quadri-clamp anchoring rack [Fig. 4-46(B)]. The rack is equipped with four underbody clamp assemblies that mount to the rocker panel pinch-weld flanges on either side of the center section of the automobile. It is used as an anchor in applying single or multiple corrective pulls in repairing front-end, rear-end, side collision, and turret-top damage, and will prevent unwanted damage to the underbody of the automobile while pulling.

One of the largest and most up-to-date stationary types of body and frame straighteners (Fig. 4-47) consists of a heavy base unit embedded in the cement floor of the shop; this allows easier anchoring and corrective pulling than the previously described portable straightener.

The damaged vehicle can be driven or rolled onto the flat, floor-level base unit by means of a floor jack; then it can be positioned near its center (which

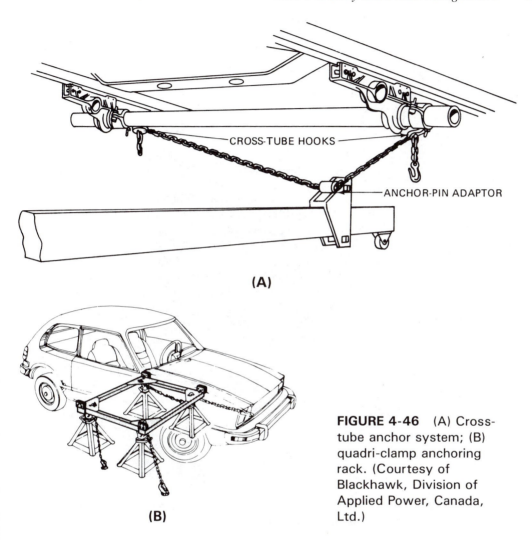

CROSS-TUBE HOOKS

ANCHOR-PIN ADAPTOR

(A)

(B)

FIGURE 4-46 (A) Cross-tube anchor system; (B) quadri-clamp anchoring rack. (Courtesy of Blackhawk, Division of Applied Power, Canada, Ltd.)

provides a maximum number of *anchoring* and *pulling* points) or (if preferred) anywhere on the base unit, depending on the particular job on hand.

The pulling arrangement for this straightener is determined by a simple triangle, as illustrated in Fig. 4-48(A). The base unit, ram, and chain are hooked up in the form of a triangle. When the ram is extended and because the top of the ram is securely locked in position by means of attachments called the *chain head* and *cross pin*, the one side of the triangle is made longer than it was. Consequently, it and anything attached to it is forced to swing or move up and over to the right. Where a more *straight-out* pull is required, the ram is placed

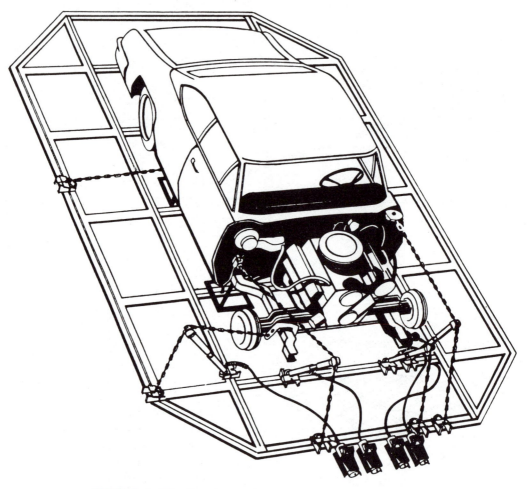

FIGURE 4-47   Korek stationary body and frame straightener. (Courtesy of Applied Power, Inc.)

at an angle to the right from the true vertical [Fig. 4-48(B)]. This type of straightener is capable of exerting *corrective pulls* in every direction from any point around an automobile as well as from underneath it.

Pulls are applied by means of a chain anchored to the base unit, which is moved by a 10 ton (9072 kg) hydraulic ram. It is possible to locate (position and exert a pull) both with a chain and ram at any point around and underneath an automobile by means of a ram foot and chain anchor. The *ram foot* and *chain anchor* are one and the same attachment and it fits into the slots of the base unit [Fig.4-48(B)]. When the ram is placed in the socket of this attachment, it is

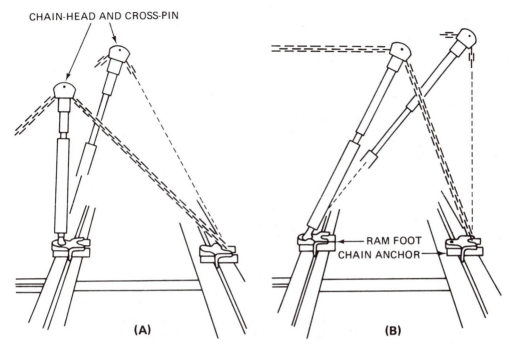

CHAIN-HEAD AND CROSS-PIN

RAM FOOT
CHAIN ANCHOR

(A)   (B)

FIGURE 4-48   (Courtesy of Applied Power, Inc.)

called and becomes the ram foot and allows the ram to be positioned at any desired angle. When it is used for holding a chain, however, it becomes a *chain anchor*.

In making a corrective pulling setup, the chain is attached to the damaged section of an automobile and stretched out in the desired direction. The ram foot and chain anchor are placed directly below the chain and locked in the base unit with steel wedges (Fig. 4-49). The ram is positioned in the ram foot and properly angled to exert a force in the desired direction. The chain is pulled tight and locked in the chain head with a cross pin. The remaining length of chain is then stretched out and hooked into the chain anchor [Fig. 4-48(B)]. It is very important that the attachment point on the automobile, the ram foot, and the chain anchor, form a straight line in the direction of the pull required.

Upward, downward, and outward pulling setups are easily made by simply altering the angle of the ram and by adjusting the length of the extension tubing used with the ram. In order to make an upward pulling setup, a longer length of tubing will be required than in a downward pulling setup in which the ram is placed at an angle low to the floor.

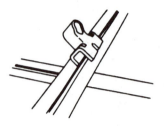

Insert ram foot/anchor into
base keeping socket on top.

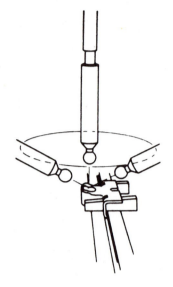

Place the ram into the ram foot
at any angle you may need.

FIGURE 4-49 Installing a ram foot or chain anchor. (Courtesy of Applied Power, Inc.)

Following are some of the most frequently used pulling setups:

By positioning the ram at an approximate angle of 45° to the floor and at the same height as the attachment point, as in Fig. 4-50(A), a straight-out pulling setup is made.

A down and outward pulling setup is made by positioning the ram lower than the attachment point and nearer to the floor [Fig. 4-50(B)].

A downward pulling setup on the front portion of an automobile frame is made by tying down the frame with chains to the base unit [Fig. 4-50(C)] and applying a lifting upward pressure at the cowl.

For a horizontal pulling setup on the cowl of an automobile, enough extension tubing is added to the ram, which when placed at an angle as shown in Fig. 4-50(D) will bring the *chain head* to approximately the same height as the cowl attachment point.

A downward and slightly forward pulling setup is quite often required. This consists of a firmly anchored *bridged* chain to which a force is applied [Fig. 4-50(E)].

When a ram with sufficient extension tubing is placed in a vertical position as illustrated in Fig. 4-50(F), an upward and slightly outward pulling force can be exerted.

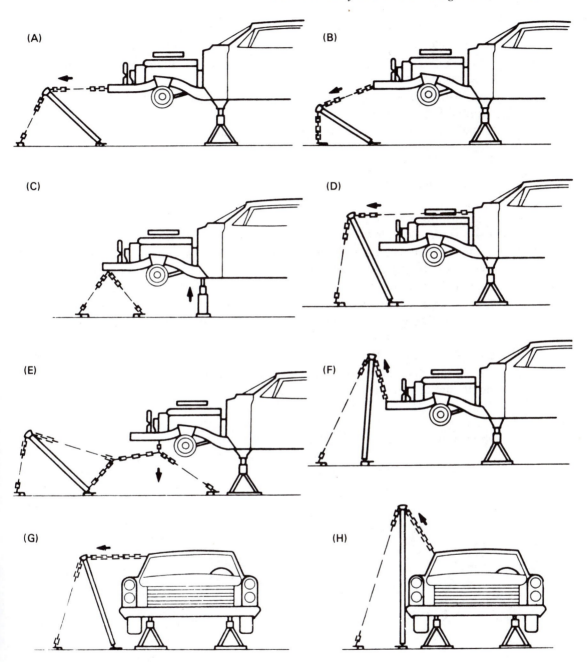

FIGURE 4-50   Korek pulling setups. (Courtesy of Applied Power, Inc.)

The ram, when used with sufficient extension tubing, positioned, and locked at an angle to a chain attached to the roof line of an automobile as shown in Fig. 4-50(G), makes an effective horizontal pulling setup used in the repairing of turret tops.

Wherever an upward and also an outward pulling setup on a turret top is required [Fig. 4-50(H)], a longer chain and sufficient extension tubing is added to make the ram strut considerably higher than the attachment point on the roof area.

Pushing Setups

Pushing setups are made as easily as *pulling* setups. For pushing upward, downward, and sideways, a tripod setup is used. It employs a *push attachment* through which a chain is passed and hooked onto two chain anchors to form two legs of the tripod [Fig. 4-51(A)]. A ram fitted with extension tubing forms the third leg. One end of another length of extension tubing fitted with a *lock-on adaptor* and a serrated saddle, flat base, or other suitable attachment makes contact with the vehicle while the other end is fitted into the push attachment.

When the ram is extended, the top of the tripod moves away from the ram and pushes against the automobile. The direction of push is controlled by positioning the chain anchors on the base unit by adjusting the ram extension tubing length and also the chain length.

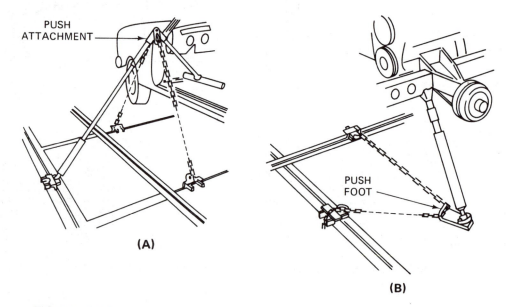

(A)

(B)

FIGURE 4-51 Korek pushing setups. (Courtesy of Applied Power, Inc.)

An upward push can also be exerted from anywhere on the floor by attaching a slack chain to two chain anchors locked in the base unit, so that it forms a sling on the floor [Fig. 4-51(B)]. A *push foot*, which provides a solid anchor for the *ram ball*, is hooked to the sling; by adjusting the length of the chain or position of the chain anchors, the direction of the push can be controlled.

Before it is possible to apply a corrective pull or push on an automobile, however, it must be properly anchored. The car is placed on car/truck stands that not only provide sufficient clearance but also working convenience [Fig. 4-52(A)]. The stands are constructed to accommodate a cross tube and underbody clamps. *Cross-tube anchor clamps* are then placed over the cross tube and tightened securely. Chains are attached to the cross-tube anchor clamps, stretched out, and hooked to the chain anchor attachment in the base unit. Any slack in the chains can easily be removed by simply sliding the chain anchors along the slotted base unit before the tapered steel wedges are driven in place.

For maximum stability and the prevention of additional damage during corrective pulling or pushing operations, a sufficient number of anchoring points should always be employed. Some of the most commonly used anchor locations are illustrated by means of arrows in Fig. 4-52(B).

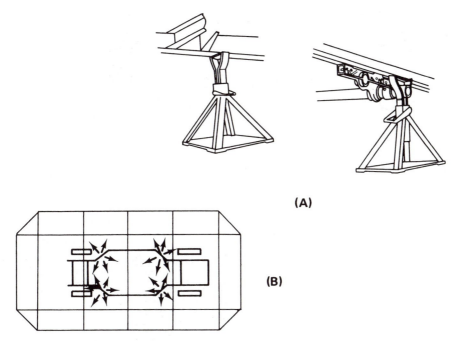

(A)

(B)

These are the most commonly used tie-down locations.
Full 360° anchoring is easy and unrestricted.

FIGURE 4-52 (Courtesy of Applied Power, Inc.)

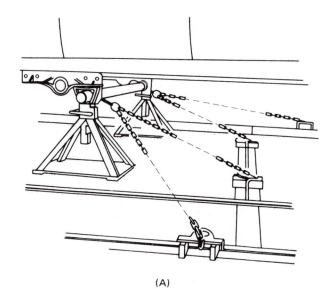

(A)

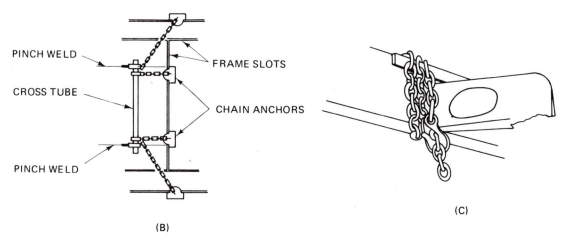

PINCH WELD

CROSS TUBE

PINCH WELD

FRAME SLOTS

CHAIN ANCHORS

(B)

(C)

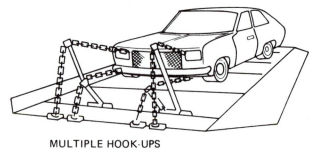

MULTIPLE HOOK-UPS

FIGURE 4-53 (Courtesy of Applied Power, Inc.)

A double-anchor arrangement [Fig. 4-53(A)] makes it possible to pull both side rails on a damaged frame and sheet metal simultaneously [Fig. 4-53(D)] without any forward or sideward movement of the automobile.

When chains are used to make heavy pulls on box frame members, the frame should be padded with angle iron with the chain wrapped around the member two or three times, as shown in Fig. 4-53(C). This spreads the pressure exerted by the pull over a larger surface area and prevents the chain from digging into and kinking the frame member.

How to Use Chains Properly

Before attempting to use chains the repairman should make sure they have been freed of all twists, knots, and kinks. Pads should be used whenever chains are placed over hard, sharp corners, such as box or U-shaped frame members. Chains with locked or stretched links or without free-moving links should not be used. Never should a hammer be used to straighten a kinked link or to force a link into position. Chains that have become excessively pitted, corroded, or worn should be taken out of service.

Care and Storage of Chains

Chains should be cleaned (preferably washed) of all grit and grime and allowed to dry by suspending them on an A-frame or rack before they are stored in a clean, dry place. When chains are put in prolonged storage, they should be oiled thoroughly in order to protect them from corrosion. Chains should be regularly inspected for twists or bends, nicks or gouges, stretch, excessive wear at bearing points, and for damaged or distorted master links, coupling links, and chain attachments, especially the spreading in the throat openings of hooks. Chains having any of these defects should not be used but should be replaced with new chains.

Important Safety Precautions

To prevent serious personal injury, it is wise not to stand in line with a chain being subjected to a load or under a load or tension. A chain should never be crossed, kinked, knotted, or shortened with a pin. Chains should not be left lying on the ground where heavy loads can pass over them. When a chain is being passed over sharp corners, protective padding should be used.

A loop should not be formed by inserting the point of a hook into a link. Welding and cutting torches should not be used near a chain because heating a chain greatly reduces its strength.

Another very popular and versatile body and frame straightener or *power pull* (Fig. 4-54), becomes a portable straightener when used by itself or a stationary straightening machine when used with *anchor pots*.

The straightener is similar in construction to other types available, except that it has a stationary *vertical beam* or *tower* instead of a *pivot arm*. The horizontal frame (main beam) is equipped with stabilizer jacks and casters for easy maneuverability and on-the-job positioning (Fig. 4-55). It is also equipped with a rigid front wheel and a keyhole at the end of the telescopic main beam, making instant low anchoring with a chain possible (Fig. 4-55). A 12 in. (305 mm) and an 18 in. (457 mm) compression (anchoring) bar is provided for higher anchoring of the straightener (Nos. 17 and 30 in Fig. 4-55).

The *tower* is fitted with a winch-operated *power box* that can be adjusted to the exact height required (Fig. 4-56). The power box is equipped with a standard 10 ton (9072 kg) hydraulic ram which can be operated by means of a hand pump or a *remote control* air hydraulic pump and an 8 ft (2.34 m) chain which freely passes over two pulleys (Fig. 4-57). It develops the *pulling power* and is the heart of the straightener. When the lower chain is locked by means of a *flat grab hook* at the L position and the ram is extended, then a pull will be exerted by the upper section M of the chain. If the upper section of the chain is locked at the M position and the retracted ram is once more extended, however, a pull will be exerted by the lower section L of chain.

The power unit can be operated to supply 5 tons (4536 kg) of power at a fast speed, such as required for sheet-metal pulling; 10 tons (9072 kg) of power at a standard speed, such as used on sheet-metal and frame corrective pulling; and 20 tons (18,144 kg) of power at a low speed, such as used in extra-heavy pulling. It will pull up or down (Fig. 4-58).

The power box can also be set up to supply a continuous pull without releasing tension on the already partially pulled out area or section of an automobile (Fig. 4-59). After the ram has been fully extended, the lower flat grab hook (N) is used to lock the chain at P. The ram is then retracted, the slack in the chain is taken up, and the upper flat grab hook (O) is repositioned. By slightly extending the ram, a sufficient amount of pressure is reapplied to loosen the lower flat grab hook (N), which is then removed, and pulling is continued.

The straightener, when set up with a combination compression beam as shown in Fig. 4-60, will supply a lifting, straight upward pull when used by itself. When it is used in conjunction with chain R, however, a lifting and forward pulling force can simultaneously be exerted.

The setup mentioned above is made by raising the power box to the blue paint mark (T) on the vertical beam (Fig. 4-61) and locked by inserting pin A. The ram (J) is retracted; the *compression beam* is lifted into position; and the *pivot pin* is inserted at Q. The beam is allowed to rest on top of the *slide box*

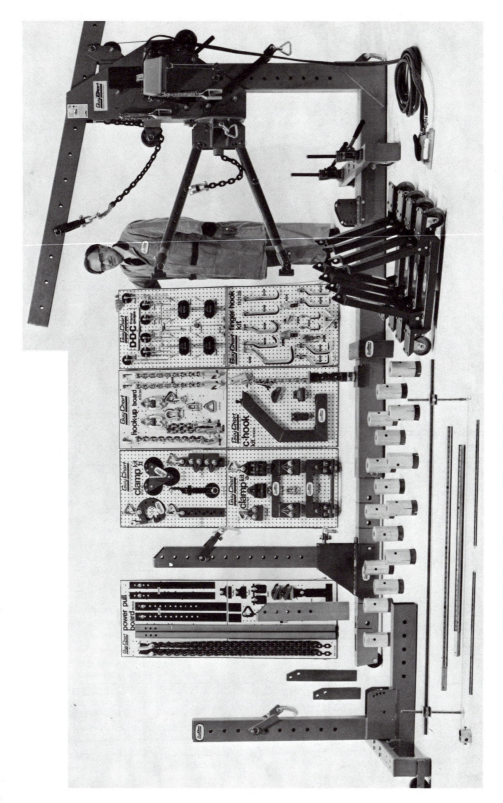

FIGURE 4-54 Power pull body and frame straightener. (Courtesy of Guy-Chart Sales, Ltd.)

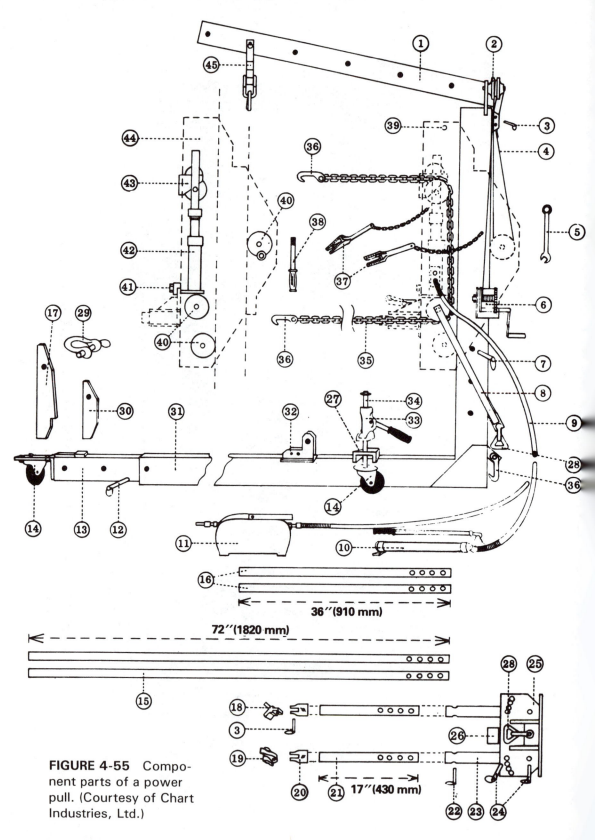

FIGURE 4-55 Component parts of a power pull. (Courtesy of Chart Industries, Ltd.)

36″(910 mm)

72″(1820 mm)

17″(430 mm)

1. Combination Compression Beam, 6 ft
2. Upper Winch Pulley with sleeve, nut, and washer
3. Practi Pin, ½ in. × 2½ in.
4. Winch Cable
5. Wrench, 15/16 in. combination
6. Winch complete with handle less cable
7. Practi Pin, 5/8 in. × 6 in.
8. Anchor Bracket complete
9. Hose, 6 ft with half coupling
10. Hand pump with handle, hose, and half coupling
11. Air pump with hose and half coupling
12. Practi Pin, ¾ in. × 5¾ in.
13. Inside Telescopic Beam
14. Swivel Caster
15. Center Pull Arm, 72 in.
16. Center Pull Arm, 36 in.
17. Compression Bar, 19½ in.
18. V Tip
19. Universal Flat Tip
20. Wrist Action Housing complete with lock screws
21. Center Pull Arm, 17 in.
22. Practi Pin, ½ in. × 3¼ in.
23. Center Pull Arm Housing, 12 in.
24. Practi Pin, ½ in. × 4 in.
25. Swivel Box Housing Assembly only
26. Center Retainer Coupling for above
27. Stabilizer Axle
28. Practi Shackle with Nut, Bolt, and Triangle
29. Practi Shackle, ¾ in. with Practi Pin
30. Compression Bar, 12 in.
31. Power-Pull Frame domestic welded
32. Bracing Plate
33. Stabilizer Jack Assembly complete with washer and handle
34. Stabilizer Shaft with ¼ in. body washer and cap screw less caster
35. Alloy Chain, 8 ft less hook
36. Practi Hook
37. Flat Grab Hook Assembly with chain
38. Handle for Power Pull
39. Power Box Retainer Bolt Assembly with bushing
40. Pulley less sleeve
    Bolt Assembly with sleeve
41. Center Pull Lock Plate with bolt and washer
42. Ram, 10 Ton
43. Slide Box Housing
44. Power Box Housing only
45. Clevis Assembly for Combination Beam

FIGURE 4-55 (cont.)

FIGURE 4-56 (Courtesy of Chart Industries, Ltd.)

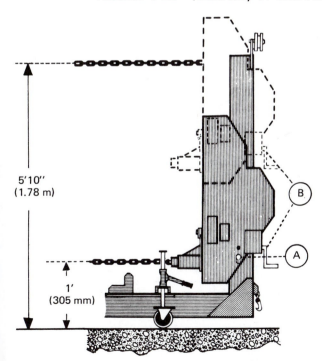

13'10" (4.2 m)
WITH EXTENSION

5'10"
(1.78 m)

5'10"
(1.78 m)

1'
(305 mm)

1'
(305 mm)

(A) IMPORTANT: Always support power box with pin before use.

(B) Winch adjusts power box to exact height desired.

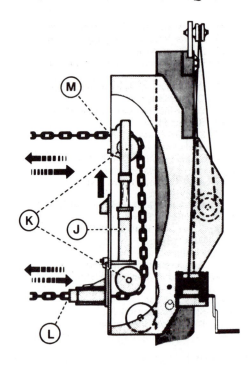

FIGURE 4-57 (Courtesy of Chart Industries, Ltd.)

FIGURE 4-58 (Courtesy of Chart Industries, Ltd.)

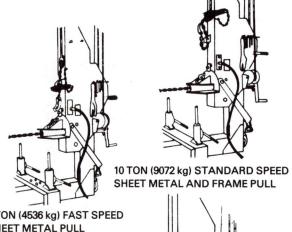

5 TON (4536 kg) FAST SPEED
SHEET METAL PULL

10 TON (9072 kg) STANDARD SPEED
SHEET METAL AND FRAME PULL

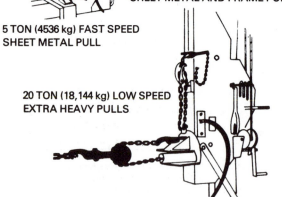

20 TON (18,144 kg) LOW SPEED
EXTRA HEAVY PULLS

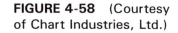

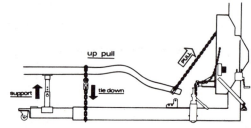

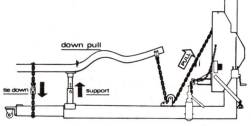

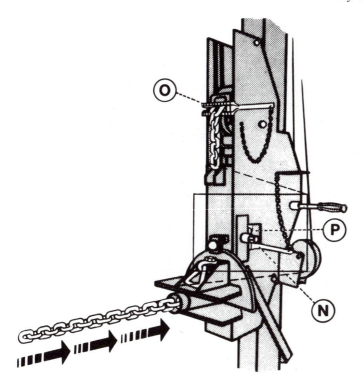

FIGURE 4-59 (Courtesy of Chart Industries, Ltd.)

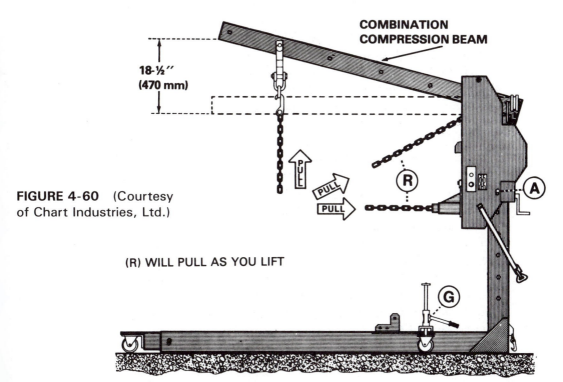

COMBINATION COMPRESSION BEAM

18-½"
(470 mm)

PULL

PULL

PULL

(R) WILL PULL AS YOU LIFT

FIGURE 4-60 (Courtesy of Chart Industries, Ltd.)

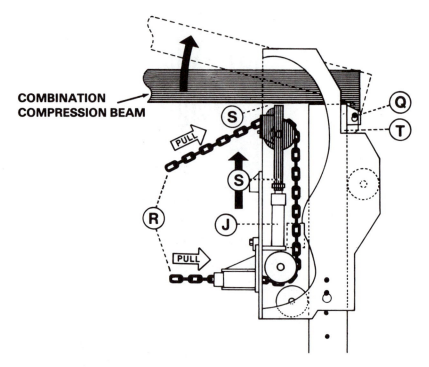

FIGURE 4-61   (Courtesy Chart Industries Ltd.)

(S). As the ram is extended, the compression beam is pushed up, lifting anything connected to it (Fig. 4-62).

Before any lifting or pulling is attempted, however, the stabilizer jacks on the power pull *must* be lowered, allowing the unit to rest on the floor and *never under any circumstances should the machine be repositioned when under load*.

Extremely powerful *center-pull* hookups can also be made with the power pull (Fig. 4-63). Center pulls are made by means of the swivel-box housing, attached to the front of the power box, which rotates a full 360° and accommodates 17 in. (0.43 m), 36 in. (0.91 m), and 72 in. (1.82 m) adjustable pull arms that can be spread out from 0 to 60°.

The ends of the *pull arms* making contact with the work areas on an automobile are fitted with a *wrist-action housing and lock screw* to which a *universal flat tip* or V tip can be connected (Fig. 4-63). The pull arms stabilize and restrict the *corrective pulling forces* to the areas being worked on.

Center pulls are very useful in repairing twisted cross-members and bumpers, straightening side panels, pushing from the heads of body bolts, bending of door pillars, and pushing body parts back into position when used as a bracing support (Fig. 4-64).

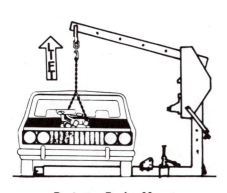

Replacing Engine Mounts

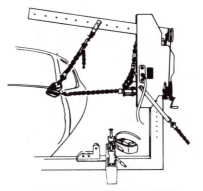

Vertical and Horizontal Pull

FIGURE 4-62   (Courtesy of Chart Industries, Ltd.)

FIGURE 4-63   (Courtesy of Chart Industries, Ltd.)

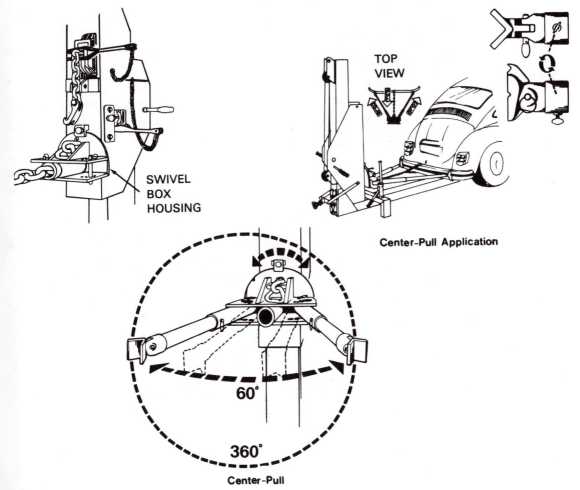

SWIVEL
BOX
HOUSING

TOP
VIEW

Center-Pull Application

60°

360°

Center-Pull

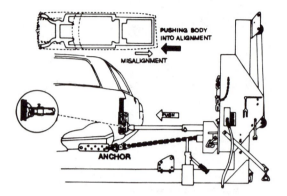

Pushing

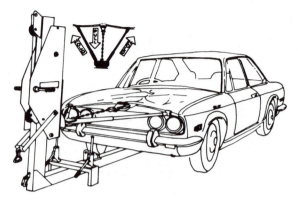

Using Center-Pull on hood

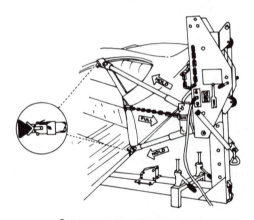

Center – Pull – Pillar application

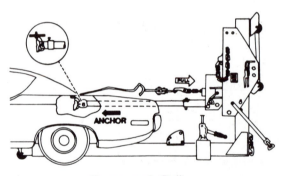

Brace and Pull

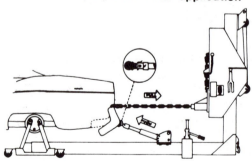

Twisting a bumper

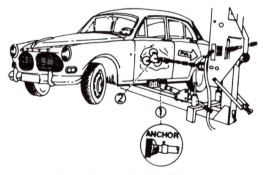

Removing a dent with tri-cups

FIGURE 4-64   Center-pull applications. (Courtesy of Chart Industries, Ltd.)

Anchoring and Hooking Up the Power Pull

Anchoring of the power pull, when it is used as a portable straightener, is greatly simplified when it is done with one of the clamping kits provided.

Clamp kit A consists of one single Scott clamp, one single Scott clamp and special triangle, one Scott clamp with shackle and pin and special triangle, and two double Scott clamps with bars [Fig. 4-65(A)].

Clamp kit B consists of a practi clamp, tri-cup assemby, draw bar, heavy-duty pulley, and rack clamp [Fig. 4-65(B)].

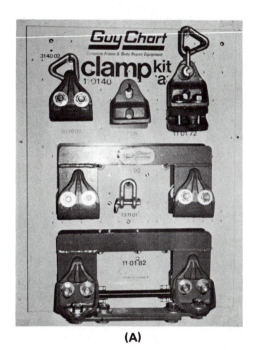

(A)

(B)

FIGURE 4-65 (Courtesy of Chart Industries, Ltd.)

Scott clamps are used singly or in pairs (double arrangements) to anchor the power-pull (Fig. 4-66). They are positioned easily, tightened by means of an impact wrench and adjustable; hookup lengths can readily be altered when used with practi hooks, because every link in the chain means another adjustment. The teeth in Scott clamps are milled in opposite directions to prevent shearing of the metal and yet to provide a maximum amount of grip during clamping and pulling operations.

The *practi clamp* [Fig. 4-67(D)] is designed for high-crowned and flanged

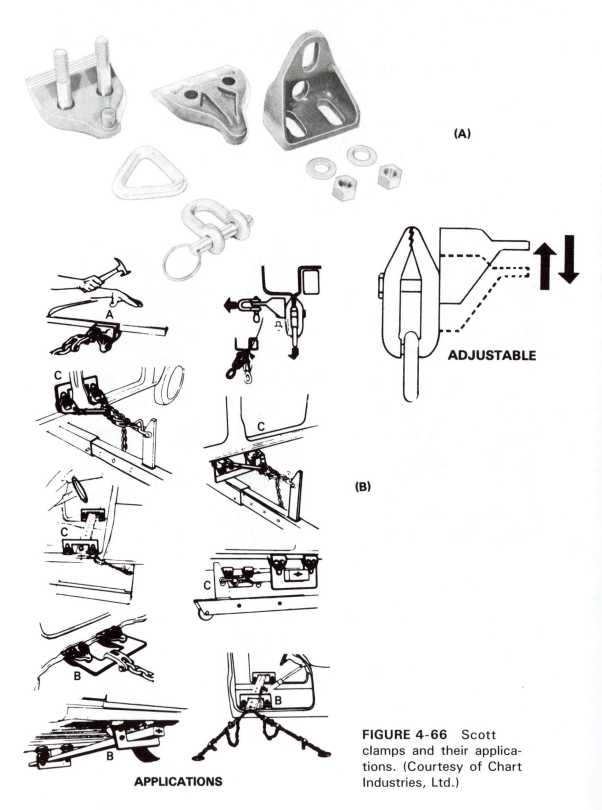

(A)

ADJUSTABLE

(B)

APPLICATIONS

FIGURE 4-66 Scott clamps and their applications. (Courtesy of Chart Industries, Ltd.)

204

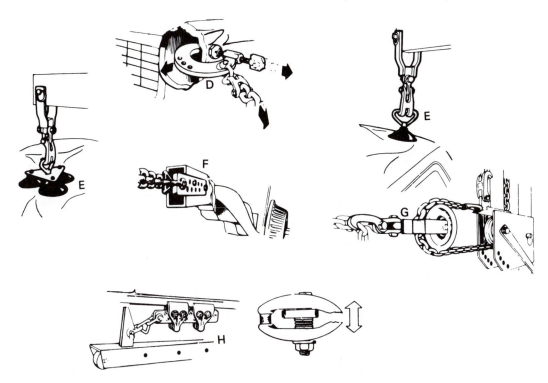

FIGURE 4-67 Anchoring and hookup attachments. (Courtesy Chart Industries, Ltd.)

sheet-metal applications. The deep-throated body of the clamp allows it to go over an obstruction and pull in any direction.

The *tri-cup assembly* [Fig. 4-67(E)] is capable of exerting 600 lb (272 kg) of pull on uneven contoured areas, such as door or roof panels whose outer surfaces are in reasonably good (smooth) condition. The tri-cup assembly can be used as an assembly composed of three, two, or one suction cups, depending on the size and shape of the damaged area.

The *draw bar*, or pull plate as it is often called, is constructed of plate steel with 10 differently spaced holes to facilitate bolting [Fig. 4-67(F)]. The Scott clamp also fits into the holes of the draw bar for parallel anchoring [Fig. 4-66(B)].

The *heavy-duty pulley assembly* is used to increase the power of the power pull from 10 ton (9072 kg) to 20 ton (18,144 kg); when it is used with the power post [Fig. 4-67(G)], from 5 ton (4536 kg) to 10 ton (9072 kg). For downward pulling, the pulley is positioned by itself on the main beam of the power pull. For vertical lifting and for underbody application, the pulley frame is positioned by itself on the combination beam.

The *rack clamp* is an assembly that anchors directly to a pinch-weld flange [Fig. 4-67(H)]. Springs keep the jaws of the clamp open to make installation easy. The shackle, pin, and triangle may be used on either end of the rack clamp, so that the bolts always face out, making mounting of the clamp much easier.

Two different hookup kits are available for the power pull, namely the finger-hook kit and the hookup kit (Fig. 4-68).

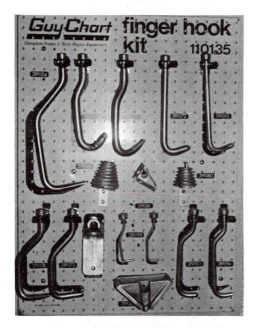 

FIGURE 4-68 Hookup attachment kits. (Courtesy of Guy-Chart Sales, Ltd.)

The *finger-hook kit* consists of two basic types of hooks. One is the bullet nose, with a cone-shaped tip that can be hammered into an existing undersized hole if a hole of exactly the same size is not available or a hole can easily be drilled or punched if an insertion hole cannot be found. The other is the chisel tip, which is excellent for working on flat surfaces, pinch-weld flanges, etc.

Finger hooks are easily attached to the power pull by means of practi-hooks (Fig. 4-69) and when they are inserted into such accessories as the spiral screw (B), wedge tip (C), hook extension (D), utility tip, and extension wedge (E), their applications are greatly increased.

The *hookup kit* is composed of such attachments as the bumper-hook assembly, lock-clamp assembly (G), two chain shorteners (H), one 3/4 in. (18 mm) shackle with pin, one 1/2 in. (12 mm) shackle and pin with a special

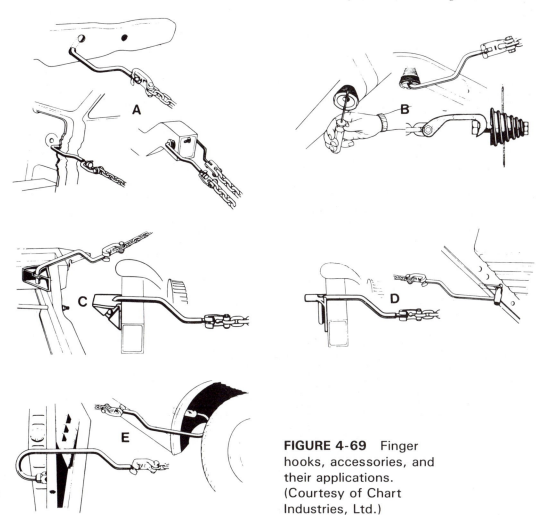

FIGURE 4-69 Finger hooks, accessories, and their applications. (Courtesy of Chart Industries, Ltd.)

triangle, one 1/2 in. (12 mm) practi-shackle and pin, and two plug-hook assemblies (F) (Fig. 4-70).

The attachments above are used virtually every day by an auto body repairman and enable him to make pulling, anchoring, twisting, and tying down hookups (Figs. 4-69 and 4-70) easily and in the shortest time possible.

NOTE: To avoid any possibility of injury, it is recommended that during the application of a pull a rubber mat or blanket be used to cover up a pulling hookup in which finger hooks or any other hook accessories are employed.

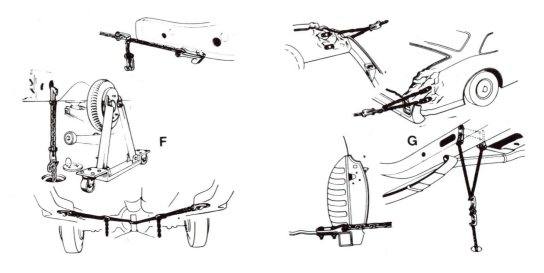

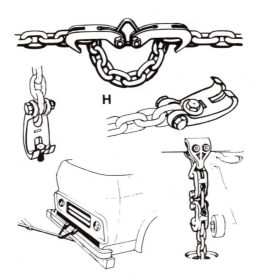

FIGURE 4-70 Hookup chain, clamps and their application. (Courtesy of Chart Industries, Ltd.)

The *C-hook kit* consists of a large hook that can be fitted with either a universal flat or V tip (Fig. 4-71) or with standard hydraulic push jack fittings. It is used in a straight line around an obstruction pulling of sheet-metal panels and frames. It comes with a stress-equalizer attachment that firmly fastens to

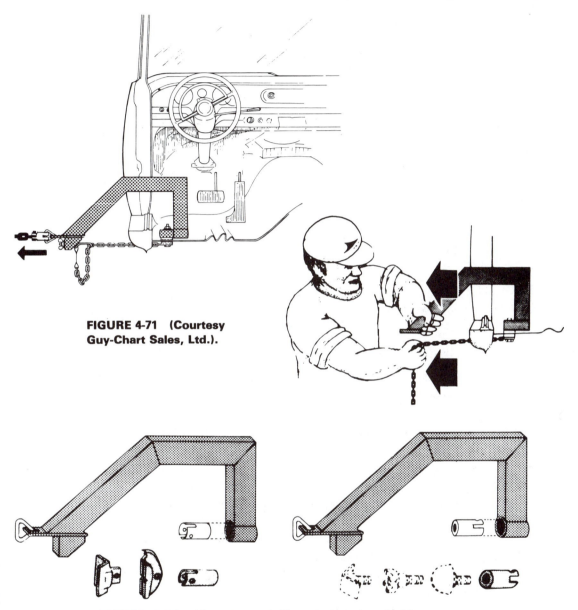

**FIGURE 4-71   (Courtesy
Guy-Chart Sales, Ltd.).**

FIGURE 4-71   (Courtesy of Chart Industries, Ltd.)

both sides of sheet metal and makes heavy pulling possible without stressing the hook body.

A *bracing tower assembly*, which can be securely locked to the telescopic beam (Fig. 4-72), makes the restriction of the corrective forces to the higher-up

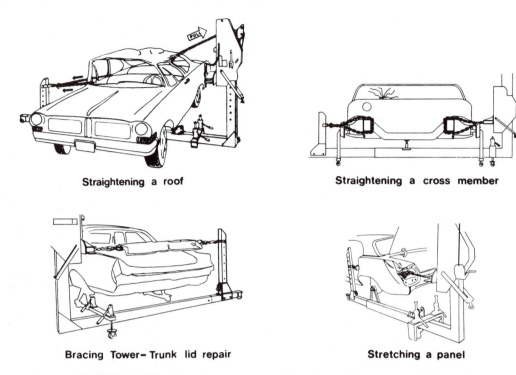

Straightening a roof

Straightening a cross member

Bracing Tower— Trunk lid repair

Stretching a panel

FIGURE 4-72 Bracing tower applications. (Courtesy of Chart Industries, Ltd.)

panels on an automobile that are being worked on possible and leaves the working area clear of obstructions.

The anchor post, another accessory, can be used to exert a push or a pull. In pushing, it is anchored to an anchor pot by means of a practi hook [Fig. 4-73(A)] and one end of a standard pushing setup is positioned against the anchor post and the other end against the automobile. In pulling, any type of pulling device such as a simple turnbuckle, a come-along, or a standard pulling setup employing an hydraulic pull ram can be used [Fig. 4-73(B)].

The anchor post, when equipped with a power conversion kit, becomes a *power post* (Fig. 4-74). Although it is short in length and light in weight and can only be used with anchor pots as a stationary straightener, it will handle all sheet metal as well as many frame jobs.

Mobile axle stands fit all stud-mounted wheels (Fig. 4-75) and provide more safe working space under an automobile for use when estimating or repairing underbody damage. The stands, equipped with rugged swivel casters, are made to support the heaviest vehicle and it will line up automatically by itself during pulling operations. The automobile can be pushed by hand to any desired position

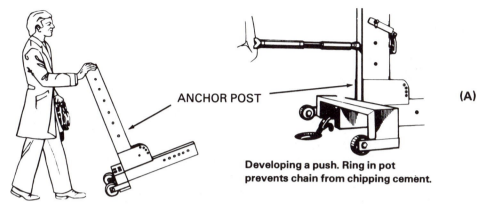

ANCHOR POST

(A)

Developing a push. Ring in pot prevents chain from chipping cement.

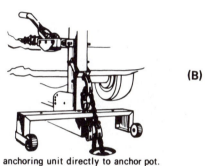

(B)

FIGURE 4-73 (A) Pushing with hydraulic ram; (B) pulling with come-along. (Courtesy of Chart Industries, Ltd.)

anchoring unit directly to anchor pot.

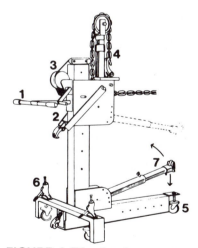

1 Steering Handle
2 Anchor Bracket
3 Winch (raising & lowering of Power Head)
4 Ten Ton (9072 kg) Ram
5 Caster (retracts under load)
6 Spring-Loaded Stabilizer Jack
7 Center-Pull Assy. (Adjustable and Interchangeable)

FIGURE 4-74 Anchor post (equipped with power conversion kit) and its application. (Courtesy of Chart Industries, Ltd.)

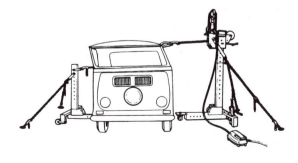

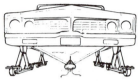

Mobile Axle Stands

FIGURE 4-75 (Courtesy of Guy-Chart Sales, Ltd.)

for faster anchoring and tie-downs. Since the weight of the automobile is kept on the suspension, as specification book measurements require, frame gauge readings will be accurate.

A complete set of datum, diamond, and center frame gauges and a tram and track gauge are provided (Fig. 4-76) to diagnose and correct any misalignment condition on a car or truck accurately to the exact specifications.

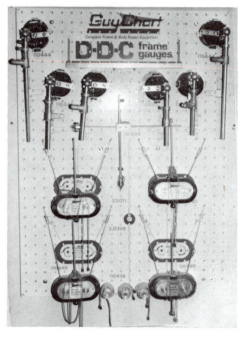

(A)

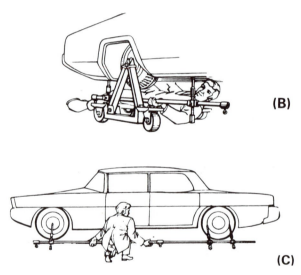

(B)

(C)

FIGURE 4-76 (A) Frame gauges; (B) using a tram gauge; (C) using a traction gauge. (Courtesy of Chart Industries, Ltd.)

Advanced Body and Frame Straightening Equipment

With all the changes taking place in the automobile industry, it is inevitable that a lot of updating of equipment will have to be done in order to repair the newer unitized high-strength steel (HSS) constructed automobiles competitively and properly. The equipment manufacturers have introduced a lot of new equipment on the market. The dedicated bench body and frame straightener with fixtures manufactured to fit the numerous types of automobiles built (Fig. 4-77) was introduced from Europe. The dedicated bench body and frame straightener is equipped with fixtures made to fit jig holes and reference points on the underbody of an automobile, which are adjusted according to blueprints supplied by the manufacturer and employed in restoring the damaged automobile to factory specifications.

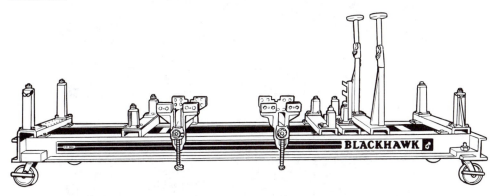

FIGURE 4-77 Dedicated bench with fixtures. (Courtesy of Blackhawk, Division of Applied Power, Canada, Ltd.)

All of the new body and frame straighteners have one feature in common. They are all designed and constructed using the pinch-weld flanges on the rocker or sill panels on the automobile to tie it down and hold the vehicle on the straightener.

The rocker or sill panels are the backbone of an automobile and when exerting or applying corrective pulls, care must be taken that the multiclamp sets are properly positioned (on perfectly clean and straight areas of the rocker or sill panel flanges) and tightened securely, to prevent tearing or damaging the rocker or sill panels (Fig. 4-78). A variety of other hold-down, anchoring, and clamping systems are illustrated in Figs. 4-79 and 4-80.

One manufacturer of body and frame straighteners also has available universal measuring devices, as shown in Fig. 4-81.

The universal measuring gauges, once set up under the automobile in their proper positions and height according to specifications, will eliminate the need for repeated tape measuring during the straightening process and will monitor all control points simultaneously. They will also provide continuous information on the movement and position of body members and sheet metal as the corrective pulls are applied in the desired areas of correction. They will monitor all control points desired, even the location or position of strut towers and spindles.

FIGURE 4-78 Underbody clamping system.

FIGURE 4-79 P4 Anchoring clamps. (Courtesy of Chart Industries, Ltd.)

The Tri-Scan Universal Laser Gauge Measuring system (Fig. 4-82), one of the latest, more sophisticated systems, will verify an automobile's underbody in three dimensions simultaneously, such as height, width, and length. It also has side body dimension monitoring capabilities, enabling the repairman to check the alignment of strategic areas on the body, such as door hinges, cowls, bumpers, and so on.

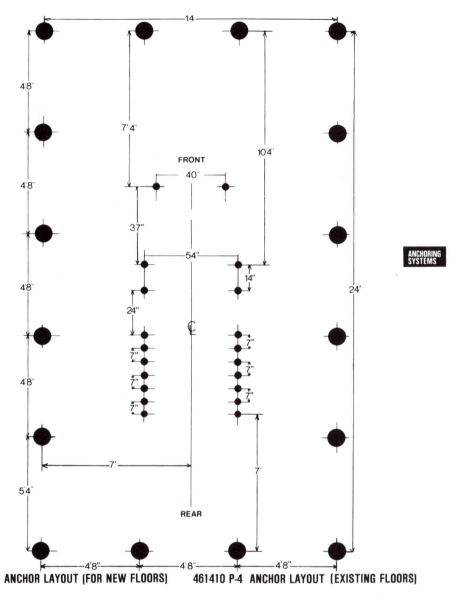

ANCHORING SYSTEMS

ANCHOR LAYOUT (FOR NEW FLOORS)   461410 P-4   ANCHOR LAYOUT (EXISTING FLOORS)

FIGURE 4-80   Floor anchoring system. (Courtesy of Chart Industries, Ltd.)

There are so many different types of body and frame straighteners on the market today that it is impossible to describe and illustrate them all. When contemplating what type of body and frame straightener to purchase, it is advisable to get all the information possible from the manufacturers' representatives

FIGURE 4-81 Exacto 3D measuring gauge and Porta Bench. (Courtesy of Chart Industries, Ltd.)

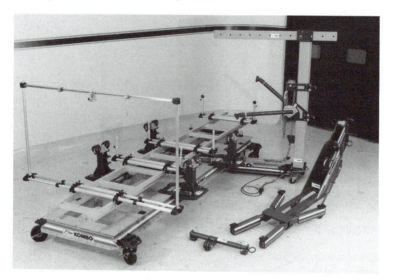

FIGURE 4-82 Porta bench system with tri-scan laser gauge. (Courtesy of Chart Industries, Ltd.)

about every type of straightener on the market and then to select the straightener with the features that makes it most suitable for the type of work that a particular body shop will handle.

QUESTIONS

4-1 What supplies an even and uniform corrective force to both the inner construction and outer body panels for the repairman?

4-2 Make a list of the various sizes in which this equipment is made and its uses.

4-3 What six operations can be performed with this equipment?

4-4 List the four principal parts of a hydraulic jack and describe their functions.

4-5 What two methods are employed in harnessing the power produced by the hydraulic jack?

4-6 What size of extension tubing is used with the light-duty (4 ton, 3629 kg), hydraulic jacking units?

4-7 What attachments are most often used as terminal points for pushing against concave metal surfaces?

4-8 What attachment is used in altering setup lengths quickly?

4-9 How are flat bases attached to the ram?

4-10 What attachment is used to provide a nonskid footing in odd-angle pushing operations?

4-11 How can the flat base be used in spreading damaged doors, cowls, and quarter panels?

4-12 How is the serrated saddle used?

4-13 What attachments are generally used in anchoring pushing combinations?

4-14 What attachment is used by the repairman to push out all types of different-shaped body panels from many different positions?

4-15 What is the difference in the attachments used in the standard (10 ton, 9072 kg) and heavy-duty (20 ton, 18,144 kg) pushing combinations?

4-16 For what type of work are heavy-duty pushing setups primarily used?

4-17 In what way are pushing combinations changed to pulling combinations?

4-18 What attachments are used in exerting a pull across high- or low-crown body sections, without any danger of crushing undamaged metal areas?

4-19 How do fender clamps differ from pull clamps?

4-20 How do standard (10 ton, 9072 kg) pulling combinations differ from the light-duty (4 ton, 3629 kg) pulling combinations?

4-21 How is a pulling force exerted on the center portion of a panel when pull clamps cannot be clamped to its outer edges?

4-22 What type of pulling setup is used on very tough jobs, where body and frame sections must be drawn into their proper positions?

4-23 How can chain links be protected from bending and breaking when the chain is wrapped around sharp-cornered frame members?

4-24 How are ram threads protected when the pull plate is not being used?

4-25 Describe how you would make a two-chain pulling setup.

4-26 In what ways can spreading pressure generally be applied in restricted areas?

4-27 What type of (10 ton, 9072 kg) ram is ideal for roughing-out deep creases in wide-flaring fenders and body panels?

4-28 Can a spreading combination also be used for lifting?

4-29 Describe how a clamping combination is set up.

4-30 Is it necessary to use locking pins with lock-on connectors when they are used in clamping combinations?

4-31 In what way can damaged bumper face bars be reshaped and aligned?

4-32 Are hydraulic presses also used as vises in body shops? If so, explain how.

4-33 Give two reasons why hydraulic equipment should be used and looked after properly.

4-34 What protective measures should be taken to ensure trouble-free service from rams?

4-35 How are oil lines protected against dirt?

4-36 How should hydraulic jacking equipment be used when notched pull toes are being used and the load is off-center?

4-37 In what ways can the hydraulic hose be protected from unnecessary abuse?

4-38 Describe how a hydraulic jack should be refilled with hydraulic oil.

4-39 What important single factor brought about the introduction of portable body and frame straighteners?

4-40 Briefly explain the construction of a pull dozer and how it functions.

4-41 What accessories are used to raise and support an automobile off the floor?

4-42 How is a pull dozer anchored?

4-43 What attachments are employed in making pulling setups?

4-44 What attachment is used in hooking up the pull dozer to out of the way pull points?

4-45 What attachment is designed to grip body pinch-weld flanges firmly?

4-46 What does the cross-tube anchor system consist of, and how does it make anchoring of the straightener easier?

4-47 What equipment provides the strongest method of anchoring portable body and frame straighteners and prevents unwanted damage from occurring to the underbody on unitized and, especially, high-strength-steel automobiles?

4-48 What type of body and frame straightener makes anchoring and corrective pulling even easier than with the pull dozer?

4-49 How is a Korek pulling setup made, and what parts go into its makeup?

4-50 Briefly describe in your own words how you would make (a) a straight-out pulling setup; (b) a down and outward pulling setup; (c) a downward and slightly forward pulling setup; (d) a horizontal pulling setup used in the repairing of turret tops.

4-51 What attachments are used in making a pushing setup?

4-52 How is the direction of push controlled?

4-53 What attachment provides a solid anchor for the ram ball in an upward pushing setup?

4-54 When anchoring, how can slack in the chains attached to underbody anchor clamps be removed?

4-55 On a particular job, where both side rails on a damaged frame and also the sheet metal have to be pulled simultaneously, how is the automobile kept from moving forward and sideways?

4-56 How does the power-pull straightener differ in construction from other types of straighteners available?

4-57 How is the power-box height adjustment made?

4-58 Describe how pulling power is developed in the power box.

4-59 At what power and speed can the power unit be operated?

4-60 How is the power box set up to supply a continuous pull?

4-61 What part on the power-pull straightener, when mounted and used by itself, will supply a lifting, straight-upward pull?

4-62 Where is the swivel-box housing located, and what parts can it accommodate?

4-63 What attachments greatly simplify the anchoring and hooking up of the power pull when it is used as a portable straightener?

4-64 What attachment is used in altering the length of chains?

4-65 What attachment is designed for pulling high-crowned and flanged sheet metal?

4-66 To increase the pulling power of the power pull from 10 tons (9072 kg) to 20 tons (18,144 kg), what attachment is employed?

4-67 What built-in feature do Scott clamps possess that makes their installation so easy?

4-68 What are the two basic types of finger hooks, and for what is each type used?

4-69 How are finger hooks attached to the power pull?

4-70 What safety precautions must be taken when finger hooks and their accessories are employed in pulling operations?

4-71 What does the C-hook kit consist of, and for what is it used?

4-72 To what part of the power pull does the bracing-tower assembly attach, and for what pulling operations is it used?

4-73 How is an anchor post stabilized or anchored?

4-74 How can an anchor post be used as a power post, and can it be used as a portable straightener?

4-75 What accessories are used with the power pull to diagnose and correct misalignments on cars and trucks accurately?

5

Expansion, Contraction, and Shrinking of Metal

UNIT 5-1: EXPANSION AND CONTRACTION

To clearly understand why a piece of metal expands when it is heated, as in fusion and braze welding, and contracts when it is allowed to cool, often causing it to distort and lose its shape, a repairman must know something about the properties of the particular metal he is working with, the changes that each undergoes, and the peculiarities that each possesses.

Scientists have established that all substances, whether liquids or solids, are made up of tiny particles called *molecules* which are in a state of constant motion or vibration (bombardment with each other) and are kept from separating or breaking apart by a force of attraction. This force of attraction determines the *tensile strength* of a substance.

Tensile strength can therefore be defined as the amount of smoothly applied, direct pull, or tension a material (be it metal, plastic, rubber, etc.) will stand before the material breaks. It is the measurement of this strength a particular metal possesses that enables design engineers to calculate the overall dimensions of a particular part so that it will safely carry or bear a specified load or weight.

Furthermore, it was discovered that when heat is evenly applied over the entire surface of a sheet of metal, not only do the molecular motion and vibrations in the sheet increase but the bombardment of the molecules against each other also becomes more violent as the metal becomes hotter, causing them to spread (bounce) farther apart. As a result, an overall minute increase in the length, width, and thickness is observed. In other words, if the sheet of metal is heated up uniformly to an even temperature over its entire surface and allowed to expand unrestricted, its entire surface will expand evenly and in all directions or dimensions. It was also found that if the sheet of metal is then allowed to cool off and contract unrestricted, it will return to its original size and shape.

A repairman, when either heating or welding, must know how to control the forces of expansion and contraction; otherwise, his work will be spoiled. In certain cases, however, the body man can use these forces to his own advantage. For example, the forces of expansions are frequently put to good use in the removal of a tight-seated (seized) nut on a badly rusted bolt. By a quick application of *controlled* heat using a large welding tip adjusted to a slightly oxidizing flame, the nut is heated to a cherry red color, causing it to expand slightly and make its removal relatively easy.

Another good example is shrinking sheet metal (which is fully dealt with in the latter part of this chapter). When a spot is heated, the metal in that particular area expands. When the metal is hammered down against the flat face of a dolly, its surface area is reduced slightly. Then by rapid cooling with a water-soaked rag or sponge, the metal contracts still further and its area is reduced even more.

If a metal bar is positioned so that it is free to expand and contract evenly in all dimensions, one finds that when the bar is heated evenly and allowed to cool uniformly, it will return to its original size. But if the bar is held along one axis, such as when placed in a vise and heated uniformly, it will expand along the other axis but will not be able to expand in length. Then when it cools it will contract evenly along all axes. This process causes the bar to become shorter but thicker. When the bar has completely cooled it will fall out of the vise (Fig. 5-1). One factor that must be kept in mind is that as the metal is heated, the forces of expansion are exerted; as the metal cools, the forces of contraction take effect in all directions. However, as the metal is heated, it loses its strength and becomes more ductile. A ductile material is one that can be worked or bent without its breaking. For example, a piece of metal will bend easier when it is hot than when it is cold and it will retain its new shape better.

In sheet-metal welding, as with any welding, the area that is being welded will expand. Consequently, special precautions must be taken; otherwise, the distortion would spoil the job that is being welded. If a sheet of metal is heated along the edge, it will expand along the edge. Since the entire sheet does not expand at the same rate, however, heating will cause the metal to warp on the heated edge (Fig. 5-2). Because the metal on the edge was restricted from expanding in all directions when it was heated, the metal will warp. When it cools, it will be found to be slightly wavy and not as wide as before.

The phenomenon that occurs when metal is restricted from expanding in all directions, yet allowed to contract in all directions when it cools, is called *up-*

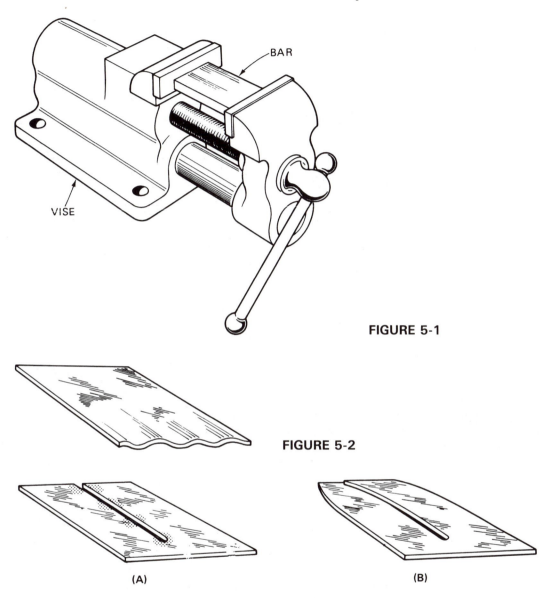

BAR

VISE

FIGURE 5-1

FIGURE 5-2

(A)　　　　　　　　　　　　　　　(B)

FIGURE 5-3 (Courtesy Union Carbide of Canada, Ltd.).

setting (Fig. 5-3). Figure 5-4 shows a piece of sheet metal that is cut nearly in two. After the shaded areas are heated red hot, the metal is allowed to cool. This process is repeated several times along the slit; the ends will soon overlap each other. This change in shape is due to upsetting the molecular structure of the metal and is called the *hinge effect*.

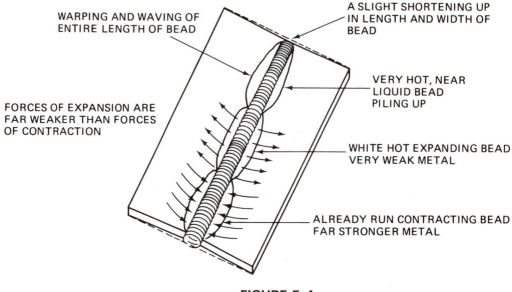

WARPING AND WAVING OF ENTIRE LENGTH OF BEAD

A SLIGHT SHORTENING UP IN LENGTH AND WIDTH OF BEAD

FORCES OF EXPANSION ARE FAR WEAKER THAN FORCES OF CONTRACTION

VERY HOT, NEAR LIQUID BEAD PILING UP

WHITE HOT EXPANDING BEAD VERY WEAK METAL

ALREADY RUN CONTRACTING BEAD FAR STRONGER METAL

FIGURE 5-4

When a piece of sheet metal is heated in one spot, it expands. But since it is restricted in one direction by the rest of the sheet, the metal will expand in its free areas and thus pile up. As it cools, however, the metal will contract evenly and remain thicker in the spot where it was heated. The result is that when the sheet metal has completely cooled, the edge that was heated has become shorter.

Let us now take two pieces of sheet metal, place them edge to edge, and attempt to fusion-weld them together. We find that as we progress in running a bead, the metal in the area of the already run bead is beginning to solidify and contract, while the white hot metal in the puddle area, being in its liquid or molten state, is expanding and is far weaker. Consequently, as the metal in the completed portion of the bead continues to cool, the forces of contraction cause the metal in the very hot and near liquid portion of the bead to pile up (get thicker). They also cause the two sheets to be drawn closer and closer together until they overlap and cause an overall shortening in length of the bead to occur. This, in turn, causes the metal in the weld area to warp and wave (Fig. 5-4).

Special techniques are needed to overcome the forces of expansion and contraction when welding or heating metal. Although heat distortion, caused as a result of these forces, cannot be eliminated completely, it can be greatly minimized and controlled.

Different Methods Employed in Controlling Heat Distortion

When fusion butt welding, distortion can be controlled by allowing a gap between the two sheets being joined and then tack-welding first, before attempting to run the bead (Fig. 5-5). After tack-welding make sure the edges of the sheet metal to be joined are accurately and properly aligned before attempting to weld. Generally, any slight distortion in the area of the tack welds can easily be corrected by on- and off-the-dolly hammering (Fig. 5-6).

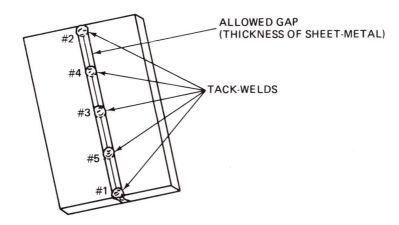

FIGURE 5-5 Tack welds illustrated in sequential order.

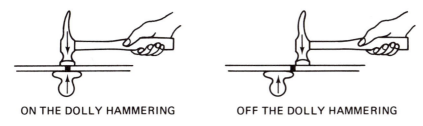

ON THE DOLLY HAMMERING   OFF THE DOLLY HAMMERING

FIGURE 5-6 Aligning sheet metal after tack welding.

Distortion while tack-welding can be eliminated by clamping edges down with welding clamps, C clamps and jigs, or with pop rivets or metal screws (Fig. 5-7). When making long panel joints, distortion can be controlled by first tack-welding and then welding in alternate areas or by staggering the fusion or braze welding process (Fig. 5-8).

In braze welding operations such as lap joints and spot brazing, it is of utmost importance that an absolute minimum amount of heat be used in perform-

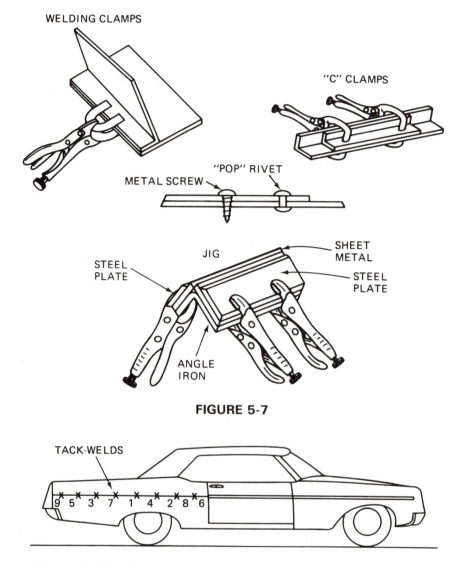

FIGURE 5-7

FIGURE 5-8 Alternating or staggering fusion or braze welding.

ing the welding operation. The area must not be preheated. The welding flame must be kept directly on the work, the torch must be as close to the work as possible, and the welding must be done as quickly as possible (Fig. 5-9).

Distortion resulting from the pull exerted on the surrounding sheet metal by the forces of contraction can be eliminated and also prevented from occurring by lightly hammering (on-the-dolly technique is most effective) the weld metal (bead) as it is cooling (Fig. 5-10).

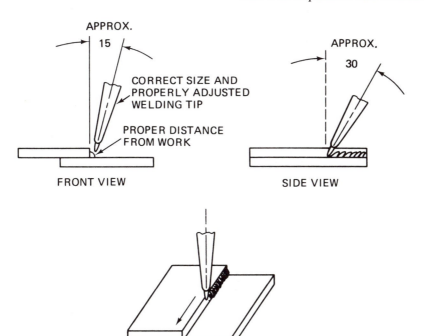

WELD QUICKLY

FIGURE 5-9

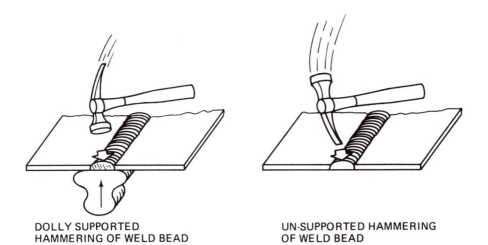

DOLLY SUPPORTED
HAMMERING OF WELD BEAD

UN-SUPPORTED HAMMERING
OF WELD BEAD

FIGURE 5-10

When welding large flat or low-crowned sheet metal, heat can be kept from radiating into the surrounding metal and distortion can be controlled by placing water-soaked rags, cotton waste, or powdered asbestos (often called a *heat-sink*) in the immediate area of the weld (Fig. 5-11). Any minor warping and waving, however, will have to be corrected by on- and off-the-dolly hammering and metalworking.

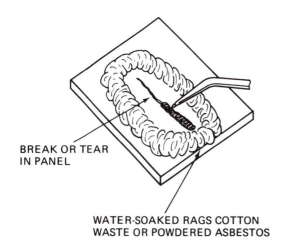

BREAK OR TEAR
IN PANEL

WATER-SOAKED RAGS COTTON
WASTE OR POWDERED ASBESTOS   **FIGURE 5-11**

Frequently, when welding in unobstructed easy-to-reach areas, the forces of contraction can easily be controlled and metal distortion can be eliminated by forging the weld as the bead is cooling (see the section ''Forging Welds,'' Chapter 3).

How to Weld a Simple Break or Tear in a Fender or Body Panel

Before attempting to weld a break or tear in a fender or body panel, the raw edges must be properly aligned so that the outer edge and corner of the wheel opening flange and any other character lines, such as beads and ridges, match exactly. Welding clamps are then securely locked into position as shown in Fig. 5-12. Tack welding, or *tacking* as it is often called, should then be started, working from the inner end of the break toward the outer edge of the flange, and spaced approximately 1 in. (25 mm) apart. When excess metal is encountered, it should be allowed to overlap and eliminated just before or during tack welding. Welding is completed by first running a very neat bead (of approximately the same thickness as the panel metal) in from the edge of the panel to the corner of the flange, then by alternately welding, an inch at a time, working

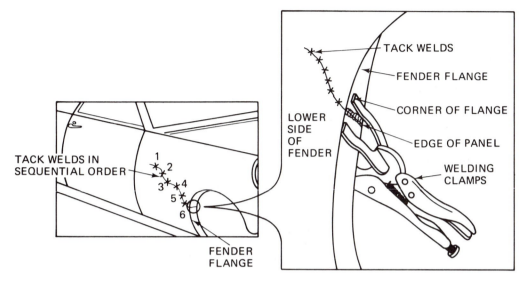

FIGURE 5-12   Welding a simple break or tear.

from the inner end of the tear out toward the flange. *Remember:* All metal in the weld area must be kept in perfect alignmemt throughout the entire welding operation by on- and off-the-dolly hammering.

Welding Procedure for Patching a Rusted-Out Area

Wherever possible, the removal of all paint from the sheet-metal patch (if discarded body panel metal is being used) and at least 4 in. (100 mm) beyond the outer edges of the rusted-out area is recommended. This step not only makes the welding of the patch much easier, because less heat will be required in tack welding and running the bead, but it also enables the repairman to determine more accurately the condition of the surrounding metal and detect any other deteriorations, for example, pinholes.

A piece of sheet metal of sufficient size is cut to completely cover and overlap the entire rusted-out area and any unsound areas in the surrounding metal. All its corners are rounded-off, as shown in Fig. 5-13, so that the heat required in welding these areas (corners) will be less concentrated and spread out over a larger area, resulting in a minimum of heat distortion.

Tack-welding is then started in the center of one side, working alternately from side to side toward the rounded corners. Tack welds are spaced approximately 1 in. (25 mm) apart. The metal is allowed to expand more freely out toward the corners, and the forces of expansion and contraction are kept in more equal balance; consequently, less distortion occurs. Welding of the entire outer

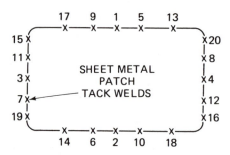

FIGURE 5-13 Tack-welding sequence in patch installation.

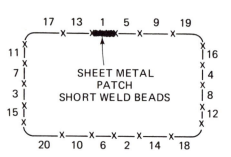

FIGURE 5-14 Alternate welding sequence in patch installation.

edge of the patch is then completed by alternately welding, approximately 1 in. (25 mm) at a time, as indicated by the numbers in Fig. 5-14.

Welding Procedure in the Installation of a Partial Repair Panel

After the repair panel has been cut to its required size, it must be fitted into its proper position on the automobile so that all its outer edges accurately match those of adjacent panels and so that the correct size and shapes of the body openings each is a part of or helps form is maintained. Metal screws, pop rivets, welding clamps, and C clamps (depending on the panel being installed and its location) are used to hold the panel in position.

Panel flanges A and B and metal extending approximately 1/2 to 3/4 in. (13 to 19 mm) inward from each corner (fitted beforehand to form perfectly level butt joints) are first tacked and then fusion welded together (Fig. 5-15). Tack-welding of the overlapping inner edge (lap joint) is done next by using a slightly oxidizing flame and a 1/8 in. (3 mm) brazing rod or an electric arc spot welder, starting approximately an inch in from the ends of the fusion welds (beads) and alternately working horizontally across and vertically up toward the rounded-off corner. The rounding of a corner on a partial repair panel, especially when it is in the more central portion of a large, flat or very low-crowned panel, prevents welding heat from building up excessively in a small area, thus resulting in less distortion. Tack welds are spaced approximately 1 in. (25 mm) apart and the metal is allowed sufficient time to cool before welding of the joint is completed by alternately lap brazing (running short beads) between the tack welds. The door pillar flange, the wheel opening flange, and the floor lower extension panel flange are then spot brazed into position every 2 to 2½ in. (50 to 63 mm).

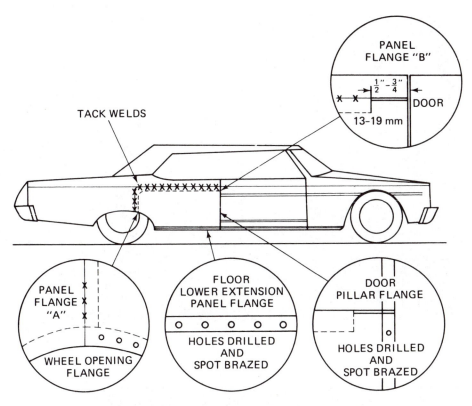

FIGURE 5-15   Installation of a partial repair panel.

UNIT 5-2:   SHRINKING

The forces of expansion and contraction, when properly applied, can be used advantageously by the repairman in the shrinking of metal, as stated in Unit 5-1. In auto body repairing, shrinking is an operation where stretched areas on damaged auto body parts and panels are disposed of and brought back, as nearly as possible, to their original shape and size. This process is accomplished by the application of *controlled* heat to the stretched area. Although tricky at times, once the operation has been mastered by the repairman, he will not only save a lot of time and hard work but also be able to handle many jobs that would otherwise be impossible.

When a body panel is damaged, a certain amount of stretching of the metal takes place and this stretching generally occurs in the area of direct impact (Fig. 5-16). It is in this area that the shrinking operation must be carried out. If

FIGURE 5-16

FIGURE 5-17

skillfully performed, it will minimize both the bumping and metal-finishing operations. If done improperly, however, it will make the repair even more difficult.

Therefore, it is important that the damaged panel be roughed-out properly. This step not only prevents any additional damage (stretching and distortion) to the already stretched area but also enables the repairman to determine the exact location, size, and shape of the area that he will have to shrink. He does so by *hand feeling* (running the palm of the hand over the roughed-out metal), by *eye* or (in the case of a large, straight, flat surface, like a door panel) by using a straightedge (Fig. 5-17).

Shrinking a Dent

In shrinking a dent, the center or highest point of the stretched area must be determined. The welding torch should then be lit and adjusted to a neutral flame, using the same size tip as required in welding that particular gauge of metal. A spot, right on the highest point of the stretched area, should then be heated to a cherry red color. The size of this spot should never be larger than a dime (18 mm). The torch should be held far enough from the metal to avoid overheating and burning a hole in it.

It will be noticed that as the spot is being heated, the metal expands and rises (bulges up) above the surrounding area. This bulge is then given several quick, sharp, squarely placed blows with a dinging hammer; this causes it to collapse or *upset* (Fig. 5-18).

A backing-up tool, either a dolly or a body spoon, is then held, with slight upward pressure directly underneath the bulge or heated spot. The dinging hammer is next used on the top side to level and smooth out the ridge and wrinkles in and around the heated spot or upset area (Fig. 5-19). The hammer blows are placed directly on the ridge, with a slapping or sliding motion toward the center of the heated spot, until it and all the wrinkles are smoothed out (Fig. 5-20).

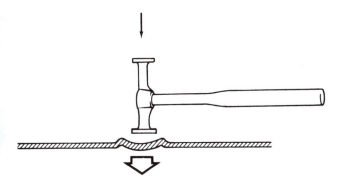

FIGURE 5-18

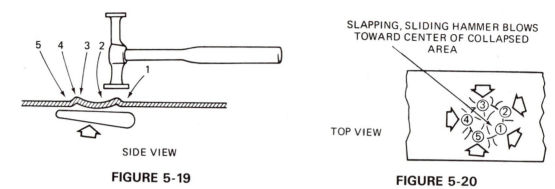

SIDE VIEW

FIGURE 5-19

SLAPPING, SLIDING HAMMER BLOWS
TOWARD CENTER OF COLLAPSED
AREA

TOP VIEW

FIGURE 5-20

Because the metal in the heated area is softer and also weaker, the excess metal tends to shift into the heated spot, causing it to become thicker. The hammer blows should, however, be kept to a minimum because excessive hammering in this leveling operation will tend to thin out and restretch the metal.

In choosing the proper dolly or body spoon for a particular shrinking (leveling) operation, it must be remembered that a *flat* dolly or body spoon is used in shrinking low-crowned metal, while a low-crowned dolly or body spoon is most suitable for shrinking high-crowned metal (Fig. 5-21).

The preceding steps should be carried out as quickly as possible, preferably before the heated metal loses all its reddish color and turns black. Once the heated spot has turned black, it should be quenched with a water-soaked sponge

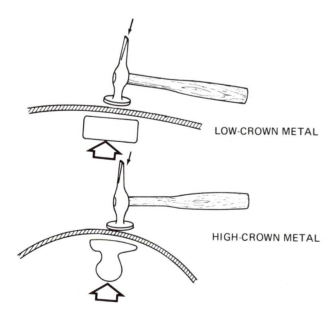

LOW-CROWN METAL

HIGH-CROWN METAL

FIGURE 5-21

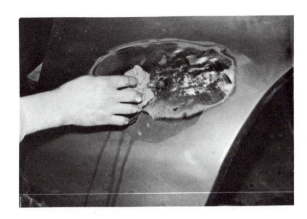

FIGURE 5-22

or rag (Fig. 5-22). Quenching causes the heated spot to cool off more rapidly; thus it contracts still more and a greater shrinking of the metal takes place. This quenching also draws out the heat expansion from the metal, enabling the repairman to determine to what extent the stretched area has shrunk and also if more shrinking is required.

NOTE: Never quench the heated spots before the metal has turned black or the metal will crystallize and harden, making it very difficult to metal-finish and, if severe enough, to *crack* and fail completely.

If the metal surrounding the already shrunken spot is still high, the shrinking operation must be repeated on the remaining high spots, until all have been brought down to the required level. This operation (Fig. 5-23) is referred to as *shrinking in sequence* and is generally used on large flat panels that have been stretched. In sequence shrinking, the heat spots should be kept as small as possible and widely spaced, so that enough sound metal is left between the heat

FIGURE 5-23

points. The heat used in shrinking causes the sheet metal to *deaden* somewhat; therefore, whenever possible, the heated spots should be separated by an ample amount of sound metal. It is *always* better to use a number of small shrinks rather than one large shrink because the metal will remain more stable (level) and tight during the shrinking process and heat buildup and distortion will be kept to a minimum.

Several repair jobs require a great number of heated spots in order to bring them into proper shape and contour—for example, repairs to the large, unsupported quarter panels and hoods found on modern automobiles. These areas are extremely difficult to shrink successfully; even when the shrinking in sequence is done most carefully, the heat buildup in the panels is extremely high. This buildup is transferred through the entire panel, often causing it to distort and warp the undamaged panel sections while the repairman is preoccupied with shrinking the stretched area.

This hazard can be minimized, if not entirely eliminated, by providing a *heat sink* (Fig. 5-24), which draws surplus heat out of the panel and prevents it from spreading into the undamaged sections. Wet asbestos furnace cement is ideal for this purpose. When packed against the side of the panel adjacent to the damaged area, it acts like a dam, preventing the heat from spreading to the undamaged sections. Instead the excess heat is drawn into the wet asbestos and dries it out very quickly, so it must be kept wet throughout the shrinking operation, particularly when the heat buildup is very great.

Wet asbestos is also adaptable to a number of other body shop repair functions where heat insulation is required. It is ideal for confining heat when small spot repairs are needed on outer panels and inner construction, such as filling of trim clip and nameplate holes, antenna openings, and the rewelding of inner construction that had to be removed before repairs to outer panels could be made. It prevents the paint from burning and the metal from warping. The wet asbestos

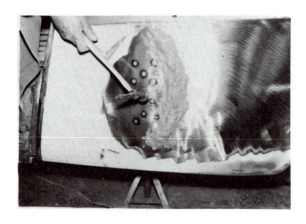

FIGURE 5-24

FIGURE 5-25

is formed into the shape of a pancake and applied directly over the work area. The center portion is then moved back, exposing the area on which the repair must be made (Fig. 5-25). It is important that the metal be kept in alignment throughout the shrinking operation. If any portion of the already shrunken metal collapses, while the remaining stretched metal is being shrunk, it must be brought into alignment by reworking (bumping) it, using the dinging hammer and dolly.

When shrinking the edges of panels, fender flanges, or bumper face bars, oblong shrinks must be used. Otherwise, the shrinking operations are the same except that the proper or correct shape and contour of the metal must be maintained during the entire shrinking operation (Fig. 5-26). Before attempting to shrink a badly gouged or creased panel, it should be brought up above the overall surface level of the panel. This step can be done by using the same tools employed in roughing-out operations. If the metal is extensively stretched and very stiff, the crease can often be roughed-out and brought up more easily if it is heated to a cherry red color. Heating to this color softens the metal and makes

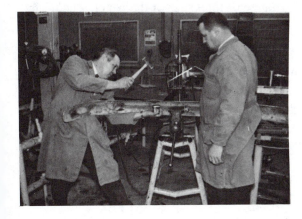

FIGURE 5-26

FIGURE 5-27

the task much easier. The shrinking operation should then be started by placing a shrink at each end of the crease, which often prevents the stretched (excess) metal from moving into the undamaged section of the panel (Fig. 5-27). The remainder of the creased metal is then brought into alignment by means of sequence shrinking. Great care should be exercised in subsequent dinging and grinding, for the thickness of the metal will vary throughout the shrunk areas and it is often possible by heavy filing and grinding to penetrate right through it.

If the metal has become very thin, metal thickness can be restored by building up the area with body solder, but a great deal of care is still required.

In aligning and metal-finishing flat, low-, and high-crowned panels, small stretched areas (no more than 1/16 in. (1½ mm) higher than the surrounding metal) are encountered. Generally, these areas can be shrunk successfully without using a back-up tool. In this method of shrinking, the metal (heat spots) is not brought to a cherry red but only to a blue color and kept very small, approximately 1/8 in. (3 mm) to 1/4 in. (6 mm) in diameter, depending on the amount of stretched metal present and on the gauge or thickness of the panel. The heated spot is immediately hammered down with a dinging hammer as shown in Figs. 5-18 and 5-20 and then quenched.

NOTE: Because the metal is only heated to a blue color, only a very small amount of collapsing and upsetting occurs when the heat spot is hammered down; the metal remains relatively straight and level throughout the entire operation. For the operation to be most effective (and this applies to all other operations), it must be carried out with the greatest of speed.

If any portion of the already shrunken metal collapses (generally a sign of overshrinking) while the remaining stretched metal is being shrunk, it must be brought into alignment by reworking (bumping and restretching) with the dinging hammer and dolly.

Oblong shrinks are used to shrink the edges of panels, fender flanges, and bumper face bars of single-layer construction. Oblong shrinks are also used in shrinking stretched outer edges on doors, deck lids (often called *hems*), and "double" flanges on hoods, front fenders, and most body openings on an automobile. They are constructed of two and three layers of metal and frequently are of varying thicknesses. Therefore, a large welding tip that supplies a greater amount of heat will be required.

If the metal is gouged so badly that it is near its breaking point, it is often more expedient to make a cut down the center (deepest portion) of the gouge with a pneumatic tool and cutting chisel, bring up and align the two edges, trim off any excess metal, so that they butt up neatly, and then reweld the break. If the badly gouged metal is in an area that does not structurally weaken the panel, it can be repaired more speedily by welding a patch of sufficient size over the gouged area. Because of the forces of expansion and contraction, the metal in the area of the weld beads frequently has a tendency to rise slightly and remain higher than the surrounding metal after it cools. These high areas can be shrunk (brought down) by indenting the weld beads, as shown in Fig. 5-28.

SHIFT DOLLY FROM SIDE TO SIDE OF BEAD AS YOU FIND NECESSARY.

FIGURE 5-28 Indenting weld bead.

Shrinking stretched metal on a reverse-crowned panel can be very difficult, tricky, and trying at times, even when it is done with great care and caution. If the panel is extensively damaged, replacement is recommended. If the panel is repairable, the stretched metal or crease must be brought up above the general contour of the panel without disturbing any of the surrounding metal (by applying heat directly on the crease if necessary) before it is shrunk. One or a number of very small "pin shrinks" rather than large heat spots are used in the shrinking operation.

NOTE: To repair reverse-crowned body panels successfully, the overall surface area of the stretched metal must be reduced precisely the right amount so that it can take its proper shape and position on the panel. For it to do so, it must be brought back (shrunk) to its original size, as shown in Fig. 5-29. It can be neither undershrunk nor overshrunk; therefore, it requires a high degree of skill and accuracy on the part of a repairman.

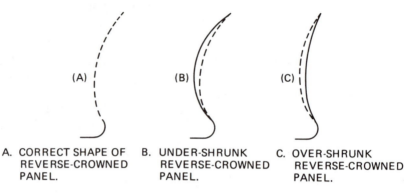

(A)	(B)	(C)
A. CORRECT SHAPE OF REVERSE-CROWNED PANEL.	B. UNDER-SHRUNK REVERSE-CROWNED PANEL.	C. OVER-SHRUNK REVERSE-CROWNED PANEL.

FIGURE 5-29

If the stretched area on a reverse-crowned panel is easily accessible from the back, the shrinking operation is often performed in reverse. Instead of the dolly's being held on the inside of the panel, it is held on the outside. Hammering of the heat spot is done from the inside, as shown in Fig. 5-30.

If the inner construction and outer panel on a hood, deck lid, or door have been damaged simultaneously and so extensively that the crown of the outer

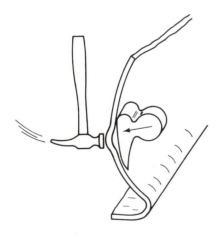

FIGURE 5-30 Shrinking in reverse manner.

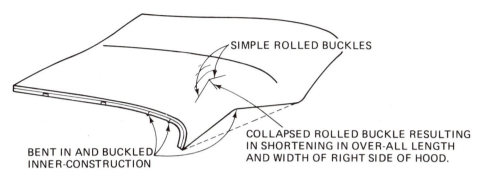

SIMPLE ROLLED BUCKLES

BENT IN AND BUCKLED INNER-CONSTRUCTION

COLLAPSED ROLLED BUCKLE RESULTING IN SHORTENING IN OVER-ALL LENGTH AND WIDTH OF RIGHT SIDE OF HOOD.

FIGURE 5-31

panel has been pushed in causing the resulting indirect damage (outer edges of the simple rolled buckles formed) to travel and extend into the large, more flat area of the panel, the metal in this area rises and bulges up, as shown in Fig. 5-31. The bulge formed makes the metal appear to be badly stretched in this area, but in reality it is not. The rolled buckles, as they form across the crown of the panel, cause the extra metal that is required in the forming of a crowned panel to shift into the weaker, flatter area of the panel and a general shortening up in the overall length of the crown to occur. The inner construction is also bent in and buckled at the same time, confining (holding) the outer panel into a smaller area and restricting it from spreading out or springing back.

Generally, this type of damage is difficult to repair because it is almost impossible to straighten all bends and buckles perfectly in both the inner construction and outer panel and to relieve all stresses and strains built up in the metal in the roughing-out and straightening operations. Consequently, the bulging, high area in the panel, commonly called a *false stretch*, can by very carefully and simultaneously roughing-out and accurately aligning the inner construction and crown of the outer panel (as described in the section "Types of Buckles," Chapter 3) be brought down to near its original height and contour. In most cases, however, it cannot be completely eliminated.

The repairman has no alternative but to shrink the still remaining high metal. The shrinking operation is started in the more or less undisturbed, straight, and flatter area of the panel by using a series of tiny *pin shrinks* to *fence off* the false stretch (see Fig. 5-32).

NOTE: The fencing-off procedure keeps the excess metal in the false stretch area from shifting into the flat and weaker, more central metal of the panel as the excess metal is brought down (shrunk) and blended in to conform with the general height and contour of the crown.

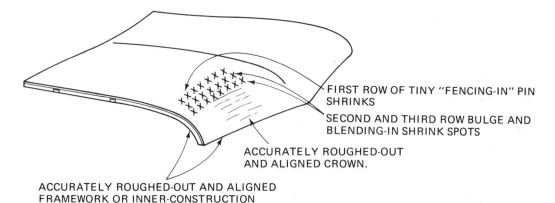

FIRST ROW OF TINY "FENCING-IN" PIN SHRINKS

SECOND AND THIRD ROW BULGE AND BLENDING-IN SHRINK SPOTS

ACCURATELY ROUGHED-OUT AND ALIGNED CROWN.

ACCURATELY ROUGHED-OUT AND ALIGNED FRAMEWORK OR INNER-CONSTRUCTION

FIGURE 5-32

Shrinking the false stretch is done next. A series of pin shrinks, placed in rows that are generally spaced approximately 3/4 to 1 in. (19 to 26 mm) apart, are used. The repairman works from the "fence" out toward the direct damage or crown. It is very important that each shrink spot be thoroughly quenched and cooled before proceeding with the next shrinking if overshrinking of the panel is to be avoided.

The undersides of hot-shrunk panels are particularly prone to rapid rusting and, wherever possible, should be given a coat of primer, undercoating, or a similar preservative. Otherwise, these areas will corrode much faster than the surrounding panel sections and may even rust out completely within a short time if the metal is very thin.

QUESTIONS

5-1 What determines the tensile strength of a material?

5-2 What causes a sheet of metal to expand when heat is applied evenly over its entire surface?

5-3 If a sheet of metal is heated uniformly to an even temperature and is allowed to expand unrestricted, will it expand evenly in all directions or dimensions?

5-4 Will a sheet of metal return to its original size and shape if it is allowed to cool and contraction is restricted?

5-5 Give two examples of how a body man uses the forces of expansion and contraction to his advantage.

5-6 What happens when a steel bar, heated uniformly, is restricted from expanding evenly in all directions but is allowed to cool and contract unrestricted?

5-7 Define *ductility*.

5-8 What happens to a sheet of metal when it is heated only along its outer edge?

5-9 What is *upsetting*?

5-10 What happens when two pieces of sheet metal are placed edge to edge and fusion welding is attempted?

5-11 List the different methods used to control heat distortion.

5-12 Describe in detail how you would fusion-weld a simple break or tear in a fender.

5-13 Describe how you would weld a patch over a rusted-out area.

5-14 What is the welding procedure in the installation of a partial repair panel?

5-15 What does the shrinking operation accomplish in auto body repairing?

5-16 What kind of heat is used in shrinking?

5-17 Describe and illustrate how a small dent is shrunk.

5-18 Why should red-hot shrink spots not be quenched before they have turned black in color?

5-19 What method of shrinking is generally employed when shrinking large, flat panels?

5-20 What are the advantages of using a number of small shrinks instead of one large shrink, and why should the shrink spots be separated or spaced whenever possible?

5-21 How can heat buildup be kept from being transferred through the entire panel?

5-22 How are the edges of panels, fender flanges, and bumper face bars shrunk?

5-23 How can the spreading of the stretched metal be prevented when shrinking a badly creased panel?

5-24 What method is used to restore the thickness of a metal panel when it has become very thin?

5-25 How can the small stretched areas that are frequently encountered in aligning and metal finishing be shrunk successfully without using a back-up tool?

5-26 How is a badly gouged metal area that is near its breaking point shrunk and brought back into alignment?

5-27 How is a slightly high weld bead brought down into alignment with the surrounding metal?

5-28 In shrinking a reverse-crowned stretched panel, why should small pin shrinks be used instead of large shrink spots?

5-29 How is shrinking in a reverse manner carried out?

5-30 What is a false stretch? How is the shrinking operation used to eliminate it performed?

5-31 Are hot-shrunk panels highly susceptible to rusting? If so, how can rusting on the inner side be prevented?

6

Abrasive and Power Tools

UNIT 6-1: ABRASIVES

An abrasive is any hard, sharp material that will wear away a softer, less-resistant surface when the two are rubbed together. The term *abrasive* is generally applied to sharpening stones, grinding wheels, and, when used on flexible backings, *coated abrasives.*

Five different minerals are used in the manufacturing of abrasives today. Three minerals—flint, garnet, and emery—are classified as *natural mineral abrasives* because they are used in their natural state. The remaining two—aluminum oxide and silicone carbide—are classified as *synthetic mineral abrasives* because they are man-made.

Flint or flint quartz is found in large quantities all over the world, but not all flint can be used as abrasives. The best type for this purpose varies in color from a dull gray to a faint pink. The lumps, when crushed, break up into sharp crystals that are graded as to size and fastened to paper by means of an adhesive, giving us what is commonly called *flint sandpaper.* This paper does not, however, hold its sharpness for very long.

In addition to being an abrasive, garnet (in its larger, purer forms) is used as a semiprecious stone in making jewelry. The smaller, more imperfect stones are crushed. The crystals formed are also graded and fastened to paper by means

245

of an adhesive. Garnet possesses toughness and a hardness that is second only to diamond. When it breaks down, each break produces new sharp edges. It is this breaking down that gives garnet sandpaper its superior cutting action and longer life.

Emery, because of its great hardness, is used in the form of powder, grain, or larger masses for grinding and polishing. It is black in color and composed of iron oxide and corundum (aluminum oxide). When emery is crushed, its grain shape is more rounded than either flint or garnet. For this reason emery sandpaper is more frequently used as a polishing paper than for cutting.

Silicon carbide is a synthetic mineral made by processing a mixture of sand and carbon in an electric arc furnace. Its crystals are very hard and sharp (needle-like); when first manufactured they were used for polishing gems. As manufacturing costs dropped, however, its use as an abrasive in the manufacture of sandpaper increased.

Aluminum oxide, another synthetic mineral, is produced from a form of clay called *bauxite*; it is mixed with coke and iron filings and heated to a high temperature in an electric arc furnace. The resulting material, reddish-brown in color, is then crushed. The crystals formed are coarse and chunky, do not break very readily, and therefore can withstand greater working strains. Aluminum oxide is especially suited for cutting and grinding operations on steel and other hard surfaces and is considered the toughest and longest lasting of all abrasives.

It should be mentioned that, of the preceding abrasives, flint and emery are more suitable for household use, while garnet, silicone carbide, and aluminum oxide are used extensively in industry. In repairing and refinishing auto bodies, silicone carbide and aluminum oxide abrasives are most commonly used.

Coated abrasives are flexible backings that are made of either rope or kraft paper cloth or a combination of paper and cloth. Rope paper backings are made from old rope and are the strongest paper backings available. Kraft paper backings are made from wood pulp and are used where a weaker paper backing can be employed.

Two grades of cloth backings (light and heavy) are used where extra strength and flexibility are required. Combination backings (cloth and paper) are made for jobs that require a stronger flexibility than cloth backings give. A vulcanized fiber backing is also made; it is used in the manufacturing of special disks for high-speed grinding operations on rough work.

The abrasives placed on backings are crushed and then put through steel rollers. The grit is screened and graded for size. Grit sizes are designated by symbols or mesh number, or both. Abrasives used in auto body repairing all employ the mesh number in describing the grit size. The finer grits, called *flours*, are graded by the sedimentation of the air flotation process. The abrasive particles or grains are then cleaned chemically or by heating, thereby removing any surface contaminations that result in poor bonding with the adhesive.

Huge rolls of different-type backings are then passed through the machine that makes the sandpaper; it prints the brand names on the back, coats the top surface with the adhesive, and applies the abrasive either by gravity or electrostatically. Two types of adhesive are used for fastening the abrasive grains to backings: hide glue to make abrasives used only in *dry* sanding and grinding work, and synthetic resins for abrasives that can be used in either *dry* or *wet* sanding and grinding operations. The amount of grain is very accurately controlled, making it possible to manufacture either thinly spaced open-coat or very densely spaced closed-coat abrasive materials. The material is then transferred to a drying room on drying racks. After drying it is wound into very large rolls from which a variety of abrasive items, such as sandpaper and sanding disks and belts, are then cut.

UNIT 6-2: POWER-SANDING TOOLS

Three different types of power sanders are generally used in auto body repair shops today—the disk, the oscillating, and the belt sander. All are driven by either electricity or compressed air and are used in performing the many grinding, sanding, buffing, and polishing operations required before a damaged vehicle is restored to its original shape and appearance.

Disk sanders are manufactured in either 7 in. (178 mm) standard or the 7 and 9 in. (178 and 229 mm) heavy-duty models. They are light in weight and have extra-powerful motors that run at high no-load speeds ranging from 4200 to 5000 rpm. The heavy-duty models eliminate the possibility of overheating when they are subjected to extra-heavy sanding for a prolonged period of time and will maintain a constant speed even when under heavy pressure.

Disk sanders are available with round, flexible, molded rubber backing pads in 5, 7, and 9 in. (127, 178, 229 mm) diameters. When the sanding disk used on the backing pad becomes worn-out and dull at its outer edge, it can be cut down to a somewhat smaller-sized disk with a fresh cutting edge by using a special tool called a disk trimmer (Fig. 6-1).

Method of Attaching Backing Pad and Sanding Disk

The rubber-molded backing pad has a metal hub that threads onto the sander spindle, marked B in Fig. 6-2. The spindle is kept from turning while the backing pad is turned onto it by depressing the spindle locking button marked A. The

DISK TRIMMER

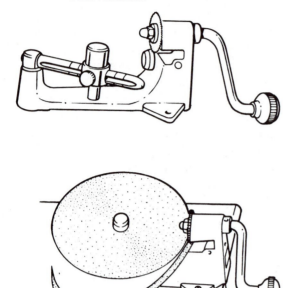

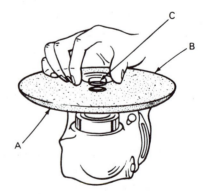

FIGURE 6-1 (Courtesy of Black & Decker Co., Ltd.)

pad should be turned down all the way on the spindle and firmly tightened by hand—not by running the motor. The sanding disk, which is marked B in Fig. 6-3, is then laid on the rubber backing pad marked A, and the clamp nut marked C is placed on the spindle with the flange up. The clamp nut, after having been started one or two turns, is then turned into the metal hub until tight by holding

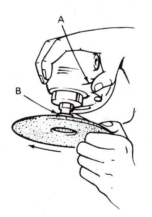

FIGURE 6-2 (Courtesy of Black & Decker Co., Ltd.)

FIGURE 6-3 (Courtesy of Black & Decker Co., Ltd.)

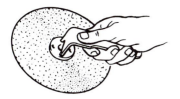

FIGURE 6-4 (Courtesy of Black & Decker Co., Ltd.)

the backing pad with one hand and the sanding disk with the other. The disk is turned clockwise until the clamp nut is completely turned down. The clamp nut is kept from turning in the center hole of the sanding disk because of the gripping action of the abrasive on the clamp nut. A wrench, which can also be used for tightening and removing the sanding disk (Fig. 6-4), is available as an accessory.

Using the Disk Sander

Electric disk sanders are equipped with *off-on* switches of the plunger, toggle, or compression type, depending on the manufacturer. The disk sander is lifted from the floor and held by grasping the control handle firmly with one hand and the side handle with the other. The side handle can easily be changed for either left- or right-hand use, whichever is most natural or comfortable for the repairman. The disk sander is turned *on*; the disk is kept off the work and sufficient room for it to revolve freely is allowed. It is then held against the work and moved across its surface via long, sweeping, back-and-forth strokes, with just enough pressure to keep it from chattering and bouncing. The application of heavy pressure on the disk sander will not increase its cutting action; rather, it will slow it down and greatly reduce the life of the abrasive. To operate the disk sander at maximum efficiency, it must be held against the work at an angle of

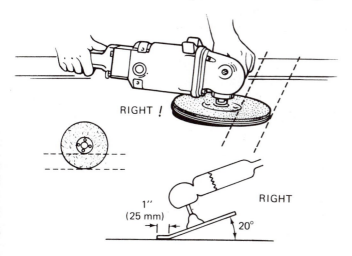

RIGHT !

RIGHT

1"
(25 mm)

20°

FIGURE 6-5 (Courtesy of Black & Decker Co., Ltd.)

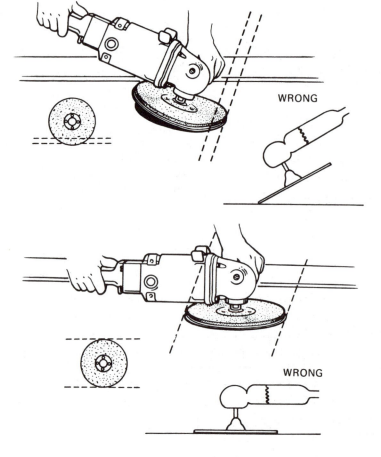

FIGURE 6-6 (Courtesy of Black & Decker Co., Ltd.)

FIGURE 6-7 (Courtesy of Black & Decker Co., Ltd.)

approximately 20°, so that the maximum amount of abrasive makes contact with the work and yet does not affect the smooth cutting action of the disk sander (Fig. 6-5).

Where sanding operations are performed using only the outer edge of the abrasive disk (Fig. 6-6), a rough-cut, burred, and often deeply gouged surface is obtained. On the other hand, if the disk sander is held directly flat against the work (Fig. 6-7), the sanding action is very rough and bumpy and the disk sander is hard to control.

Selection of Sanding Disks

Two types of sanding disks are employed in metal finishing and feather edging: namely, open-coat and closed-coat abrasive disks (Fig. 6-8). Open-coat abrasive disks are designed for removing heavy coats of paint, glazing putty,

(A)   **(B)**

FIGURE 6-8 (A) Closed-coat disk; (B) Open-coat disk.

and plastic filler from metal surfaces and for work on wood and other coarse fibrous materials having a tendency toward *loading up* the sanding disk. They are manufactured in various grits ranging from No. 16 (4), very coarse; No. 24 (3) coarse; No. 36, No. 50, and No. 60, (2, 1, and 1/2), fine; and No. 80 to No. 120 (1/0 to 3/0), very fine, abrasive disks, which are used primarily in feather edging (Fig. 6-9). Closed-coat abrasive disks are designed for metal finishing. No. 16 (4), very coarse; and No. 24 (3½), coarse, grit disks are used for grinding and rough cutting in metal repair work. Grinding not only removes paint and rust (Fig. 6-10) but also outlines the damaged area for the repairman. After the disk sander has been carefully passed over the entire lower portion of the panel (Fig. 6-11), all surface irregularities are clearly visible. Bare metal areas indicate high spots, while areas where the paint has not been removed indicate low spots.

The low spots are raised by further dinging and bumping of the area, frequently passing the disk over it, to check for high and low spots (Fig. 6-12) until a large percentage of the paint has been removed and the size of the low spots has been minimized. The panel is then more accurately rechecked by cross-filing it, and any remaining low spots are raised with the pick hammer. When this step

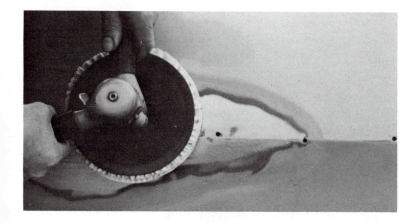

FIGURE 6-9

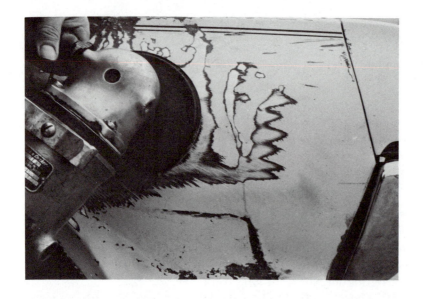

FIGURE 6-10

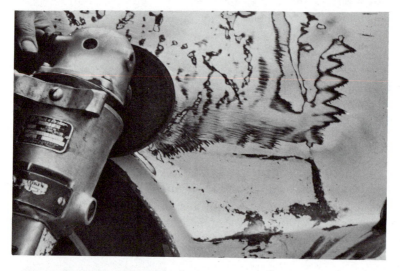

FIGURE 6-11

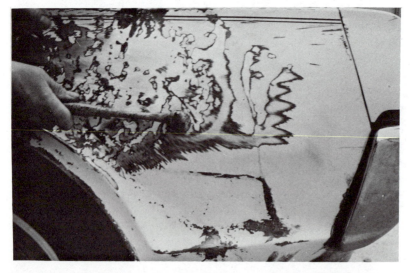

FIGURE 6-12

has been completed, the repaired metal is disk-sanded again, first with No. 36 (2), fine, grit abrasive disk, which is followed by a No. 50, No. 60 (1, 1/2), or even a No. 80 (1/0), very fine, grit disk (Fig. 6-13(A)). Finishing the metal in this manner removes the disk scratch pattern left from previous disk sanding and polishes it, keeping the costs of refinishing materials and preparatory work down to a minimum.

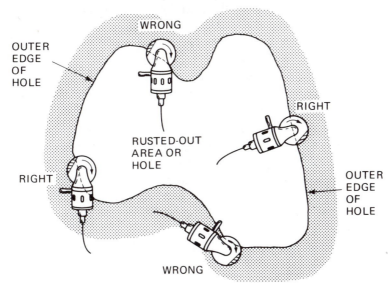

FIGURE 6-13 Disk sanding around a rusted-out area or hole.

In order to obtain the best quality finishes, it is recommended that disk grinding, sanding, and polishing be done in steps. If, on a particular job, a No. 24 (3) grit open-coat sanding disk was first used to remove the paint, it should be followed by cross-cutting the area with a No. 36 (2) closed-coat sanding disk and finished by sanding the area (polishing) with a No. 50, No. 60, or No. 80 (1, 1/2, or 1/0) closed-coat disk. The removal of metal in disk-sanding operations should be kept to a minimum so that the original strength and thickness of the sheet metal are maintained as much as possible.

Any-size grit closed-coat disk may be used for cross-cutting, sanding, and polishing; however, it depends entirely on the job and the type of refinishing materials used in its repair.

Safety Precautions for Disk Sanding

When using the disk sander, or when in the immediate area where one is being used, the repairman should protect the eyes by wearing either grinding goggles or plastic eye shields.

Always notify others near you before starting disk-sanding operations.

Loose-fitting clothes and long neckties should not be worn when using a disk sander.

The portable disk sander should always be started off the job and should be stopped on the job.

Before connecting the disk sander to the power supply, make sure that it is grounded properly and that it is in its correct position (sanding disk facing up), with the operating switch in the *off* position.

Before operating the disk sander, make sure that the disk is installed properly, and when changing from one disk to another, make sure that the lead is *pulled out* from the power supply. This will prevent accidental starting of the sander while disks are being changed.

When the sander is not in use in metal finishing it should be laid on the floor, thereby preventing accidental dropping and breaking.

When using the disk sander near drip moldings, sharp panel edges, loose clips and bolts, lap-joint constructions, and badly rusted-out panels, great care must be exercised to prevent the sanding disk from being caught and torn, which often causes serious injury to the operator. This can be prevented by disk sanding potentially dangerous areas, by switching the disk sander on and off and allowing the built-up momentum to do the sanding, or by operating the disk sander in such a way that the sanding disk does not rotate or turn into the edge of the metal but away from it instead [Fig. 6-13(B)].

Method of Sanding Crown Surface on a Fender

On any crown area, disk sanding should always be done with long, sweeping, back-and-forth strokes along the crown, as shown by the dotted lines in Fig. 6-14. Disk sanding is started at the top of the crown. The disk sander is moved from left to right in making the first forward stroke, with just a slight amount of pressure being exerted on the sanding disk.

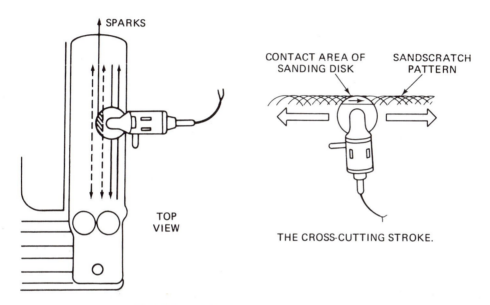

FIGURE 6-14 Cross-cutting stroke.

At the end of the forward stroke, the return stroke is started immediately without any hesitation or stopping by passing the disk sander over the already sanded surface but in the opposite (right to left) direction and without applying any pressure whatsoever on the sanding disk.

If disk sanding is done in this manner, generally called a *cross-cutting* stroke (because of the intricate crisscross sand scratch pattern it creates), the return stroke will remove any burrs left by the cutting action of the abrasive disk in the preceding forward stroke and will result in a smoothly sanded surface.

It will be noticed that the area of contact between the abrasive disk and the crown is much smaller than when disk-sanding flat surface metals. Therefore, the second and all subsequent forward and return strokes must be spaced more closely together and must be more numerous before a crown area has been completely covered and smoothly sanded.

Method of Disk Sanding Side of Fender

After the crown area of the fender has been sanded, the entire fender, including the headlight opening, can also be disk-sanded. Disk sanding is started at the top or lower edge of the crown area, as shown by the dashed line in Fig. 6-15. With the application of a small amount of pressure, the sander is moved down the side of the fender up to about 1 in. (25 mm) of the bottom edge. It is then moved up again over the same area, but without applying any pressure on the sanding disk. This procedure, generally called a *buffing* stroke (used in the fast removal of paint and the sanding down or leveling of flat and low-crowned surfaces), is continued until the whole side of the fender has been completely

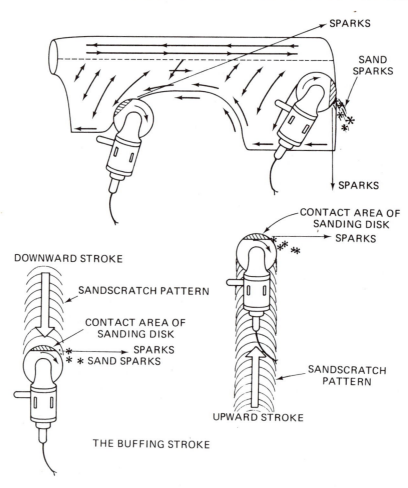

FIGURE 6-15   Buffing stroke.

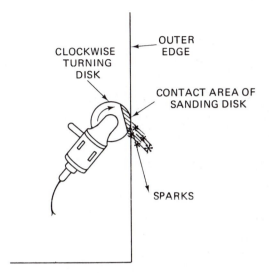

FIGURE 6-16

sanded. All outer edges at the rear, bottom, as well as the wheel-opening fender flange, are sanded by holding the disk sander in such a position that the abrasive disk turns in a direction away from the particular edge being sanded and the sparks given off shoot away from the fender instead of onto it (Fig. 6-16). This method will prevent the sanding disk from turning into and catching the edge of the fender, shattering, and causing personal injury to the repairman as well as others near him.

The flange on the front of headlight openings and surrounding surfaces must be sanded very cautiously. These surfaces are generally sanded by utilizing the built-up momentum of the disk sander after it has been turned *on* and then immediately turned *off*.

Hard-to-reach concave surfaces around headlights, fender flanges, and trim moldings are frequently sanded by changing the flat backing pad and sanding disk for a cone mandrel and abrasive cone (Fig. 6-17).

Method of Disk Sanding a Door

An automobile door is sanded in much the same way as a fender. The crown area of the door is sanded first, starting at the top near the glass opening and gradually working down using cross-cutting strokes until the crown has been completely sanded (Fig. 6-18). The flatter, lower portion of the door panel is sanded next, to within approximately 1½ in. (38 mm) of its outer edges, using long up-and-down vertical buffing strokes and the same procedure described for sanding the side of a fender. Notice how flat the disk sander is held, with just a

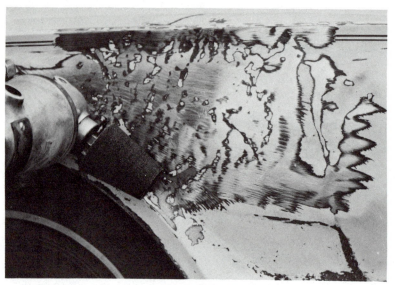

FIGURE 6-17

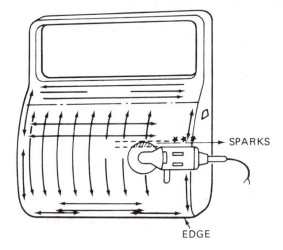

SPARKS

EDGE   **FIGURE 6-18**

slight curving motion as it is moved first down and then up, as the sanding is carried out. The outer edges of the door, like the fender, are sanded so that sparks run away from the door, which will prevent the disk from cutting into the outer edge of the panel.

Method of Disk Sanding a Turret Top

After the turret top has been properly roughed-out, aligned, and straightened, its outer high-crowned areas, which as a rule are generally metal-finished

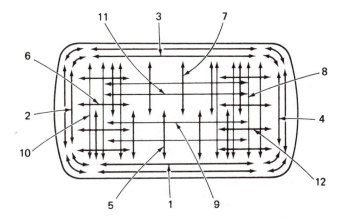

FIGURE 6-19

first, are disk-sanded in the same manner as the crown on a fender or a door employing long back-and-forth cross-cutting strokes, as indicated by arrows 1, 2, 3, and 4 in Fig. 6-19. The straighter or low-crowned center section is disk-sanded using buffing strokes as indicated by arrows 5, 6, 7, and 8. When the turret top has been completely metal-finished, its center section is also often disk-sanded by passing the sander back and forth over the metal, cross-cutting as shown by arrows 9, 10, 11, and 12. This step will give the repaired turret top an even finer final finish and will cut down the costs in both labor and materials.

Frequently, the disk sander is also used with long, sweeping, back-and-forth horizontal cross-cutting strokes (Fig. 6-18) over a portion or over all of the roof panel. This particular method of disk sanding is not only used in highlighting the damaged area for the repairman but is also used with the finer closed-coat abrasive disk, such as No. 36, No. 50, No. 60 (2, 1, 1/2), and sometimes, No. 80 (1/0) grit, employed in buffing and polishing coarsely sanded surfaces to give an extra-fine finish before they are repainted.

Orbital Sanders

Orbital sanders are used extensively in such auto body refinishing operations as feather edging, sanding, and polishing. They are manufactured in various sizes and models—light, standard, and heavy-duty—which operate on either electricity (Fig. 6-20) or compressed air. Those operating on compressed air can be used in wet as well as dry sanding operations, while electrically operated oscillating sanders can only be used in dry sanding operations. They oscillate at anywhere from 3400 to 4500 orbits per minute, are generally equipped with pads that hold one-third of a 9 × 11 in. (227 × 279 mm) abrasive sheet of paper, and make it possible for a repairman to perform feather edging, sanding, and polishing operations many times faster than he can manually.

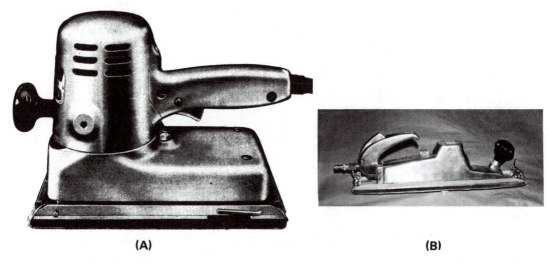

(A)   (B)

FIGURE 6-20   (Courtesy of Black & Decker Co., Ltd.)

The straight-line sander shown in Fig. 6-20(B) is primarily used by an auto body repairman in sanding down the larger repaired areas on auto bodies that are inaccessible and very difficult to metal-finish without the use of small amounts of plastic filler or body solder.

The sander is operated by compressed air and works with a back-and-forth straight-line stroke. It is equipped with a long, wide backing pad that is designed and fitted with clamps to hold 2¾ by 17½ in. (70 by 445 mm) strips of sandpaper.

NOTE: For better operation and longer life, pneumatic tools should be lubricated regularly with the right lubricant and operated at air pressures no higher than recommended by the manufacturer.

Polishers

Polishers are very similar in construction to the disk sanders. They are also powered by either electricity or compressed air and, like disk sanders, are manufactured in a variety of sizes and models. Polishers, when used with the proper type of backing pad and the right kind of sandpaper (generally No. 80 (1/0) grit dry sanding abrasive disk sandpaper) are one of the fastest methods of feather edging developed to date (Fig. 6-21).

By changing to another type of backing pad, fitted with an extra-heavy wool buffing bonnet, the polisher can be used in buffing, cleaning, and polishing operations (Fig. 6-22).

FIGURE 6-21

FIGURE 6-22

Belt Sanders

Belt sanders are primarily used on large, flat, easy accessible areas. They are driven by electricity and are used in removing paint, glazing putty, sanding solder, and plastic-filled areas and in feather edging (Fig. 6-23). Because they are equipped with a vacuum system, they almost eliminate all sanding dust, which is especially heavy when fiberglass sanding operations are carried out via other methods.

FIGURE 6-23 (Courtesy of Black & Decker Co., Ltd.)

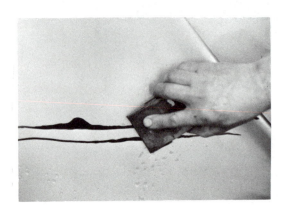

FIGURE 6-24

Feather edging is also frequently done by either dry or wet hand-sanding, using a rubber sanding block (Fig. 6-24). No. 80, No. 100, No. 120, and No. 150 (1/0, 2/0, 3/0, and 4/0) grit dry sanding paper is used in dry feather edging while No. 120, No. 150, and No. 180 (3/0, 4/0, and 5/0) grit sandpaper, which can be used with or without water, is used in wet feather-edging operations.

Primer surfacers are generally wet-sanded by hand, using No. 320 (9/0) grit sandpaper, if the work is to be refinished in enamel.

If, however, the work is to be refinished in either nitrocellulose or acrylic lacquer, the primer surfacer is wet-sanded using No. 400 (10/0) grit sandpaper.

Glazing putty is generally wet-sanded with No. 120, No. 150, No. 180 (3/0, 4/0, or 5/0) sandpaper, using a rubber sanding block. It is sometimes also sanded dry, using No. 100, No. 120, or No. 140 (2/0, 3/0, or 4/0) with the orbital sander, but this can only be done if the glazing putty has been allowed to dry thoroughly.

When preparing an automobile for painting, the old finish has to be thoroughly cleaned first by washing it down with water and then with a silicone wax

FIGURE 6-25   Sandpaper used in vehicle refinishing.

Type	Grit No.	Uses
Wet and dry sanding	120 (3/0)	Feather edging and sanding glazing putty
	150 (4/0)	
	180 (5/0)	
	220 (6/0)	Rough sanding of paint on trucks and other
	280 (8/0)	commercial vehicles
	320 (9/0)	Sanding primer surfacer and old finishes on cars to be refinished in enamel
	400 (10/0)	Feather edging, sanding primer surfacer, and old finishes to be refinished in nitrocellulose or acrylic lacquer
Dry sanding	40 (1½)	Sanding plastics and for rough work on wood, other fibrous materials, etc.
	60 (1/2)	
	80 (1/0)	
	100 (2/0)	Sanding glazing putty or plastics, wood, and other fibrous materials after having cut them down with No. 40, No. 60, or No. 80 (1½, 1/2, or 1/0) grit sandpaper
	120 (3/0)	
	150 (4/0)	

and polish-removing solution. Then it must be thoroughly sanded in order to roughen the old paint's surface, so that the new paint will properly adhere to it when applied with the spray gun. If the automobile is to be refinished in enamel, the old paint is wet-sanded by hand, using No. 320 (9/0) sandpaper. If it is to be refinished in nitrocellulose or acrylic lacquer, the old paint is wet-sanded by hand, using No. 400 (10/0) sandpaper.

The different types and grits of sandpaper and for what sanding operations each is used in automobile refinishing are shown in Figure 6-25.

QUESTIONS

6-1   What is an abrasive?

6-2   Name three natural mineral abrasives.

6-3   What abrasives are classified as synthetic or man-made?

6-4   Briefly describe how silicone carbide and aluminum oxide are made.

6-5   Which of the five abrasives are extensively used in industry and which are suitable for household use?

6-6   What abrasives are most commonly used in the repairing and refinishing of automobiles?

6-7   Which of the synthetic abrasives is the toughest and longest lasting: aluminum oxide or silicon carbide?

6-8   From what materials are the flexible backings on coated abrasives made?

6-9   How are grit sizes designated?

6-10   Describe briefly how coated abrasives are made.

6-11   What three types of power sanders are generally used in auto body repair shops?

6-12   What operations can be performed with power sanders?

6-13   In what sizes and models are disk sanders manufactured?

6-14   What type of backing pads are used on disk sanders?

6-15   How is a sanding disk given a fresh cutting edge?

6-16   In what way is the sanding disk attached to the backing pad?

6-17   How is the clamp nut kept from turning in the center hole of the sanding disk?

6-18   What available accessory can be used in tightening and removing the sanding disk?

6-19   How should the disk sander be lifted and held?

6-20   Electric disk sanders are equipped with what type of *off-on* switch?

6-21   How should the disk sander be passed over the work's surface?

6-22   At what approximate angle to the work's surface should the disk sander be held?

6-23   When only the outer edge of the disk sander is used in power sanding a metal surface, what results are obtained?

6-24   What kind of sanding action is obtained when the disk sander is held flat against the work?

6-25   Open-coat sanding disks are designed for what specific purpose?

6-26   Closed-coat sanding disks are designed for what specific purpose?

6-27   What type and grit of abrasive disks are used in removing paint and rust and outlining high and low spots for the repairman?

6-28   What type and grit of abrasive disks are used in sanding repaired or metal-finished areas?

6-29   What is accomplished by final disk-sanding the work in steps?

6-30 Why should the removal of metal in disk-sanding operations be kept to a minimum?

6-31 In what way should the eyes of the operator and those in the immediate area be protected?

6-32 What type of clothing should be worn when power sanding?

6-33 How should the disk sander be started, and how should it be stopped when it is no longer required?

6-34 What necessary precautions should be taken before the disk sander is connected to the power supply?

6-35 Why should the lead be pulled out of the power supply when the sanding disk is being changed?

6-36 How can accidental dropping and breaking of the disk sander be prevented when it is not being used?

6-37 What areas on an automobile need special care when being power sanded?

6-38 Describe and illustrate with a sketch the proper method used in disk-sanding a fender.

6-39 Describe and illustrate with a sketch the proper method used in disk-sanding a door.

6-40 Describe and illustrate with a sketch how to disk-sand a turret top properly.

6-41 Orbital sanders are used extensively in what kind of repair operations?

6-42 Can orbital sanders, driven by electricity, also be used in wet-sanding operations?

6-43 What type of orbital sander can be used in both wet- and dry-sanding operations?

6-44 What size of sandpaper is used on an orbital sander?

6-45 How can feather-edging, sanding, and polishing operations be performed faster: by hand or with an orbital sander?

6-46 Are polishers used in feather-edging operations? If so, what changes must be made, and what type of abrasive is used?

6-47 Can feather edging be done faster or slower by means of the polisher rather than an orbital sander?

6-48 What type of pad is used on the polisher in buffing, cleaning, and polishing operations?

6-49 On what surfaces are belt sanders primarily used?

6-50 Why are vacuum-equipped belt sanders so popular in sanding fiberglass?

6-51 How is wet or dry feather edging done by hand?

6-52 What type and grit of sandpaper are used (a) in wet feather edging? (b) in dry feather edging?

6-53 What type of sandpaper is used in sanding primer surfacers?

6-54 How is glazing putty generally sanded, and what type of sandpaper is used?

6-55 What type of sandpaper is used in preparing the old painted surface of an automobile for refinishing (a) in enamel? (b) in nitrocellulose or acrylic lacquer?

7

Filling Dents with Body Solder

When dented, quite a number of inaccessible areas on an automobile body cannot be repaired in the usual way. These are generally located in the upper sections of doors (framework around window and door openings), door pillars, cowl and rocker panel areas, and on other outer body panels that are reinforced and held in position by some kind of framework or inner construction, including all panel-joint welds. When these areas become dented, they can be repaired by one of two methods, either by filling them with body solder or by cold filling.

Composition of Body Solder

Body solder is an alloy of lead and tin. Its properties may vary, but the most common mixture consists of 30 percent tin and 70 percent lead, or 30/70 solder, as it is usually called.

The property of body solder that makes it an ideal and practical metal for filling dents is its ability to change from a solid to a liquid state when heat is applied. Tin has a melting point of 450°F (232°C) and lead, 620°F (327°C).

It has been found that any mixture of tin and lead has a melting temperature considerably lower than the melting point of lead. Also, any mixture containing from 16 to 63 percent tin becomes soft or plastic at approximately 361°F (182.7°C) and does not change to a liquid state until a much higher temperature is reached. 30/70 tin and lead solder has a soft, plastic range of 361 to 496°F (182.7 to 257.7°C), at which temperature it changes to a liquid. It is this property that enables the repairman to work and shape it by means of a soldering paddle.

Solder-Filling Equipment

Body soldering requires the application of controlled heat, which is supplied by using the following equipment: The oxyacetylene welding torch with a medium-sized welding tip is adjusted to a carburizing flame. This flame is ideal for solder filling because the heat given off is low in intensity and spreads out gently over a large area. The welding torch, with a slip-on soldering tip, can also be used. The slip-on soldering tip slips over the regular welding tip and uses only one gas—acetylene—with oxygen is supplied from the atmosphere. The welding torch with a slip-on soldering tip produces a low-temperature, light blue flame, which also spreads heat over a wide area. The required acetylene operating pressure is 4 to 5 lb (27.6 to 34.5 kPa), and because no oxygen cylinder is required, a saving of oxygen gas is realized. The size of the flame is varied by adjusting the acetylene valve on the torch body.

A third method of soldering is by using a specially designed soldering torch. This torch is light in weight and is used solely for soldering. It also operates on acetylene gas and has only one shutoff valve, which adjusts and varies the size and intensity of the flame. The oxygen is supplied from the atmosphere, through holes located near the base of the tip. This torch is connected to an ordinary acetylene regulator by means of the standard acetylene hose and operates at 4 to 5 lb (27.6 to 34.5 kPa) pressure.

The soldering iron is sometimes used in solder-filling small areas, such as antenna, sign, and nameplate holes in turret tops, cowls, and other sections on auto bodies. These areas can be filled by countersinking the hole edges and sweating a thoroughly tinned, sheet-metal plug over the countersunk hole. If additional solder buildup is required, it can be applied by careful manipulation of the same soldering iron. This soldering procedure eliminates the danger of fire and the removal of head linings, insulation, sealers, and many other combustible materials.

Before attempting to solder-fill a dented surface, it should be roughed out and aligned to as near its original shape as possible. This step will retain the original strength of the panel, framework, or inner construction and allow all interacting parts to function and operate properly, as well as cut solder consumption down to a minimum.

The roughed-out surface must then be thoroughly cleaned. All traces of paint, scale, rust, grease, and other foreign materials must be removed. Paint, rust, and scale can be removed by running the power grinder with a suitable sanding disk or a cup-shaped wire brush over the area. Paint can also be removed quite easily by burning it with a torch and, while still hot, brushing it away with a steel wire brush. The area to be solder-filled should be cleaned from 1 to 2 in.

FIGURE 7-1

(25 to 51 mm) beyond the rim of the dent, ensuring a large enough surface on which the body solder can be applied (Fig. 7-1).

By using a 5 in. (127 mm) backing pad and a special eight-sided, star-shaped disk, cut from either a 7 or 9 in. (178 or 229 mm) sanding disk (Fig. 7-2), it is possible to remove paint, rust, and other foreign materials from low spots on roughed-out metal surfaces that must be thoroughly cleaned for solder or plastic filling. This disk is ideal for sanding concave surfaces without any danger of excessively cutting or gouging the metal.

The thoroughly cleaned surface must then be tinned. *Tinning* involves coating the surface with a thin layer of solder, which provides a suitable base over which additional body solder buildups can be made. It requires the use of special

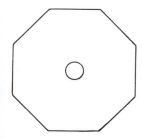

FIGURE 7-2

FIGURE 7-3

materials, called *soldering fluxes*, which when liberally applied over the cleaned and preheated metal (Fig. 7-3) not only clean the surface chemically by removing and preventing oxides from forming on the metal but also increase solder flow out and bond strength between it and the metal. Different types of acid and nonacid fluxes are available today. One type of nonacid flux frequently employed in tinning is prepared by dissolving soldering salts in water. The strength of the salt solution may be varied to meet job requirements by increasing or decreasing the amount of water added to a fixed amount of soldering salts. For best results, however, it is always advisable to follow the directions supplied by the manufacturer.

Muriatic acid is acid-type tinning flux that is often used. Straight muriatic acid is excellent for cleaning and descaling sunken panel-joint welds, as well as many other metal surfaces. After the scale has been removed, cut muriatic acid is then applied to the surface by means of an acid brush or swab made from a piece of rag and welding rod. To cut muriatic acid, drop zinc bar into it, until all chemical action (boiling) ceases (Fig. 7-4).

NOTE: The fumes given off in cutting muriatic acid are very harmful, inflammable, and corrosive. Inhalation of fumes should be avoided and kept away from tools and equipment. Water must never be added to muriatic acid, for it can cause a violent chemical reaction. It is clearly marked *poisonous* and should be treated as such.

FIGURE 7-4

Another product very popular with auto body repairmen is a nonacid type of tinning flux that consists of a powdery mixture of solder and flux. It is applied by means of dipping a steel wool pad into the flux. The flux-coated pad is then rubbed back and forth over the preheated metal (Fig. 7-5), which, when heated sufficiently, will melt the solder and flux and cause them to flow out and coat the entire surface with a thin, bright layer of solder. This flux is excellent for tinning panel-joint welds and other very thin and badly corroded areas that cannot be metal-finished in the usual manner. Furthermore, it enables the repairman to clean and tin the metal in one operation.

Acid-core solder is also quite frequently used in tinning operations. The hollow core of the solder is acid-filled and not only cleans and tins the metal in one operation but requires less heat than all other tinning fluxes, because the tin content of acid-core solder is higher (50 percent tin and 50 percent lead). When soldering fluxes (such as soldering salts and cut muriatic acid, containing no solder whatsoever) are used in tinning metal, the solder must be added to the already preheated and flux-coated surface, by reheating it to the melting point of solder. A bar of body solder is then rubbed over the hot metal (Fig. 7-6), depositing just enough melted solder over the surface so that it can be spread over the entire area by wiping it with a clean cloth. Care should be taken not to overheat and burn the surface of the metal. Solder wiping should be done very carefully, just hard enough to remove all excess flux and other impurities from

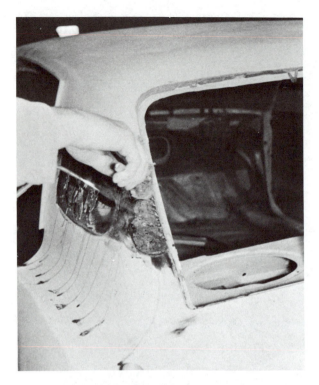

FIGURE 7-5

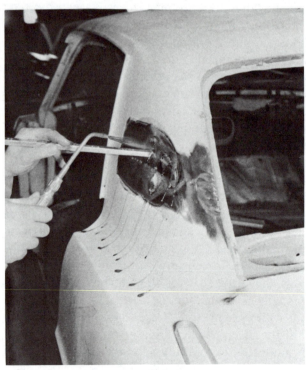

FIGURE 7-6

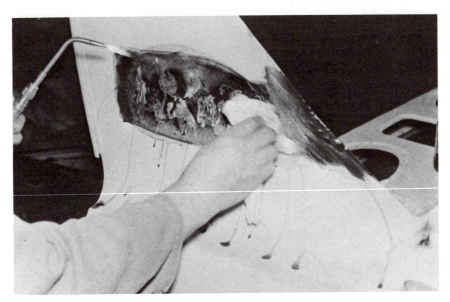

FIGURE 7-7

the metal (Fig. 7-7). This step will leave the tinned surface silvery white in color and the tin coating exactly the right thickness. The tinned area is then built up by applying additional amounts of body solder. The solder is applied by alternately heating approximately 1 in. (25 mm) of the end of a bar of solder and the tinned surface. The bar of solder is heated until it becomes soft, and the soft end of the bar is pressed against the hot tinned metal. The softened solder is deposited in this way on the hot surface of the metal (Fig. 7-8). This procedure is repeated until enough solder is deposited on the tinned surface as needed to fill and smooth out completely all depressions to a level slightly higher than the surrounding metal.

The solder deposits are spread and smoothed out over the entire tinned area by means of a soldering paddle (Fig. 7-9) after the solder deposits have been softened by reheating. Reheating is done by running a carburizing flame back and forth over the deposits until they become soft and a slight sagging of the solder occurs. This sagging is an indication that the solder has reached its proper temperature or plastic state and can now be shaped and worked with the soldering paddle (Fig. 7-10). Two kinds of paddles are used in soldering. The flat-face paddle is used in soldering all surfaces except concave surfaces; the curved-face paddle is used for concave surfaces (Fig. 7-11). Paddles are generally made of fine-grained hardwood, such as maple, and must be kept clean and well lubricated. Beeswax, light oil, and mutton tallow are commonly used as lubricants.

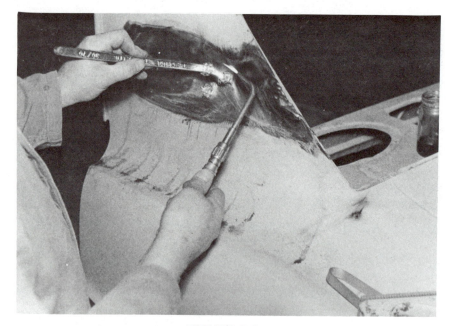

FIGURE 7-8

FIGURE 7-9 (Courtesy of J & J Auto Repair, Ridgefield Park, N.J.)

FIGURE 7-10 Flat-face paddle.

FIGURE 7-11 Curved-face paddle.

These lubricants prevent the hot solder from sticking to the paddle and result in a smooth, flawless fill, free of pinholes and other imperfections. The soldered area must be allowed enough time to cool completely before it can be metal-finished. The cooling-off time can be shortened considerably by quenching the area, thereby enabling the repairman to continue with the metal finishing sooner.

Quenching, when properly carried out, will help to prevent panel distortion. Panel distortions, such as warping, waving, and bulging (especially common when soldering a large low-crowned surface that requires solder filling in more than one area), are caused by heat buildup throughout the panel and the rapid expansion of the metal in the immediate area of the solder fill. These distortions can be controlled by properly preheating the metal, solder-filling each area separately and then quenching it, before proceeding to solder-fill the remaining areas of the panel (Fig. 7-12).

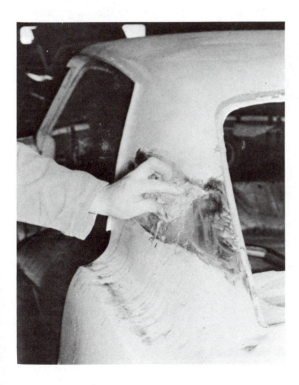

FIGURE 7-12

FIGURE 7-13 (Courtesy of Snap-On Tools of Canada, Ltd.)

All solder-filled areas are then metal-finished by removing any excess body solder from the area and bringing it down to the same level as the surrounding metal by means of the body file (Fig. 7-13). Great care must be taken, however, not to undercut or gouge the soldered surface because the body file tends to bite far deeper into the soldered area than into the surrounding steel. It is for this reason that many repairman prefer finishing a soldered area with a slightly dull or used file.

Filing should be done from all angles, starting at the outer edges of the soldered area and gradually working toward its center (Fig. 7-14), until it is brought into alignment with the surrounding sheet metal. The body file must be kept clean at all times. Long, smooth strokes should be used whenever possible, with just enough pressure on the forward stroke to prevent the file from sliding

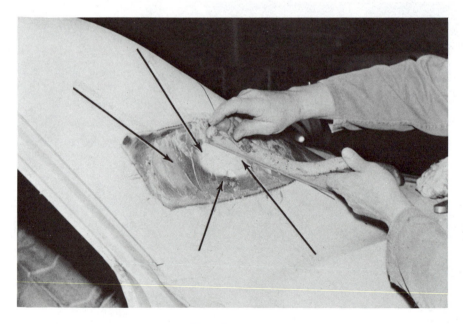

FIGURE 7-14

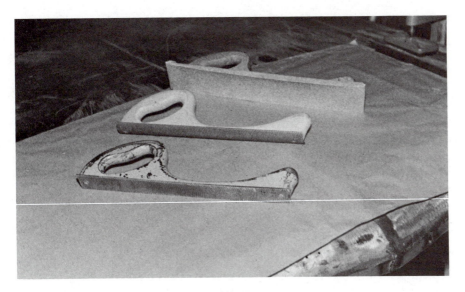

FIGURE 7-15

over the soldered area without cutting. The file should be lifted slightly on the return stroke to prevent scratching or marking the smooth surface.

Final finishing of the soldered area is done by sanding it, using No. 80 or No. 100 (1/0 or 2/0) grit strip sandpaper wrapped around an ordinary flat body file, the half-round file or the extra-wide-backed speed file (Fig. 7-15). Very small areas are sometimes finished by hand sanding, but again great care should be taken not to remove too much solder and thereby spoil the contour of the filled area.

Once the dented panel has been repaired by solder filling, it can be painted. Before any painting can be done, however, the soldered area must be treated with a metal conditioner.

QUESTIONS

7-1 In what way are damaged inaccessible areas on automobiles repaired?

7-2 What is the composition of the most common mixture of body solder?

7-3 What makes body solder an ideal and practical metal for filling dents?

7-4 List four different ways used in supplying controlled heat in body soldering.

7-5   Why should a dented surface be roughed-out and aligned before it is solder-filled?

7-6   How is a roughed-out surface cleaned?

7-7   What is *tinning*?

7-8   What different types of tinning agents are used in body soldering?

7-9   What important part do tinning fluxes play in the tinning operation?

7-10   Describe how each of the tinning fluxes are used.

7-11   How is muriatic acid processed (cut) for soldering?

7-12   What method is employed in spreading the solder over the cleaned and flux-coated bare metal?

7-13   Describe how the additional body solder is applied to the tinned surface.

7-14   What tools are used in spreading and shaping body solder?

7-15   Why should soldering paddles be kept clean and well lubricated?

7-16   What are the most common lubricants used on soldering paddles?

7-17   State the reasons for quenching solder-filled areas.

7-18   How can low-crowned surfaces be kept from warping and waving when they are being soldered?

7-19   In what manner are solder-filled areas metal-finished?

7-20   How should a solder-filled area be filled?

7-21   What type and grit of sandpaper are used in final finishing of a soldered area?

8

Plastic Filler and Its Uses

Another method used in auto body repairing for filling surface depressions and irregularities is with a material called *plastic* (cold) *filler*. This filler is available in either quart or gallon (1 liter or 4 liter) quantities and is mixed with a hardener or catalyst, supplied in separate plastic tubes or bottles, in either cream or liquid form.

The surface preparation is similar to that used in solder filling. All paint and rust must be removed from the surface to be filled by sanding or grinding it, using either a No. 16 (4) or a No. 24 (3) grit open-coat sanding disk (Fig. 8-1). If the surface is covered with oil, grease, or heavy coats of wax, these items must *first* be removed before any grinding is done. Removing these im-

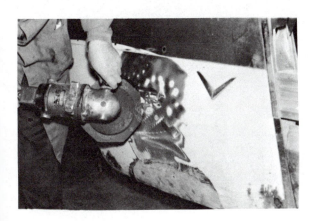

FIGURE 8-1

purities will prevent them from being spread and worked down through the paint onto the bare metal and contaminating it as the grinding operation is carried out. Surface grinding should be extended over an area at least 2 in. (51 mm) beyond the outer rim of the damage area; once this is completed the area should not be touched with anything but the plastic filler, which should then be immediately applied. For best results, manufacturers recommend that the plastic filler, the shop, and the metal repair area be an equal temperature, 70°F (21°C) minimum and 90°F (32°C) maximum. On days of high humidity, the area to be filled should be warmed with heat lamps to drive off any moisture from the metal before the plastic filler is applied.

Before removing any portion of the plastic filler from its container, it must be thoroughly stirred with a stirring paddle until all ingredients are uniformly dispersed throughout the filler. Stirring will eliminate the occurrence of *wet* spots in the fill once it has been applied and hardened.

The desired amount of plastic filler should then be taken from the container with a putty knife and placed on a clean smooth surface, on which it is again mixed thoroughly with the catalyst or hardener. A flat piece of sheet metal or glass, approximately 8 in. (227 mm) square in size, will provide a suitable surface on which the mixing can be done (Fig. 8-2). Only the correct proportion of catalyst should be used in the mixing process and different brands should not be

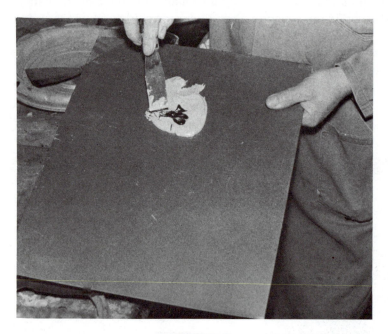

FIGURE 8-2

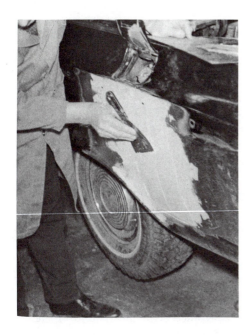

FIGURE 8-3

interchanged. Only enough plastic filler should be mixed with the catalyst as can be easily applied before it hardens.

The (mixed) plastic filler is then applied to the clean, bare metal by means of a putty knife or a squeegee (Fig. 8-3), with sufficient pressure to ensure a good bond by spreading an initial thin layer of plastic filler over the area. Upon hardening, additional layers of filler are immediately applied over the first layer, until it is just a little higher than the surrounding surface. This step will allow a little extra filling material for filing and sanding down, required in the final finishing of the area. *Caution:* Any mixed plastic filler that is left over must *not* be returned to the container, for it will harden the remaining contents.

Plastic fillers harden from the inside out and are generally ready for filing and sanding in about 20 minutes at average shop temperatures (68 to 70°F, 20 to 21.1°C) or when the filler has hardened enough to resist finger-nail scratching. When hard, the area can be filed, sanded, and feather-edged to the desired contour and finished just like any solder-filled area, except that any low spots found in the filled area must be filled with additional plastic filler instead of being raised by means of *picking* or *prying*, as done on solder-filled areas.

The application of plastic filler is not recommended on the outer edges of doors, hoods, fenders, trunk lids, and door posts, however, because these parts are vulnerable to vibration and bumping, which tend to break the bond between the filler and the sheet metal. When the bond is broken, it causes moisture to enter under the fill and corrosion to develop until the plastic filler lifts and

FIGURE 8-4

eventually drops out. The same thing occurs when rusted-out areas are ground clean and the plastic filler is applied directly over holes in rusted-out areas (Fig. 8-4). To prevent this occurrence, all edges should be solder-filled; when rusted-out areas must be repaired, a patch should be welded over the rusted-out metal and the surface depressions filled with plastic filler.

In the reconditioning of used cars, rusted-out areas are frequently repaired by using fiberglass cloth, epoxy resin, and the catalyst. Rusted-out areas require the same surface preparation as plastic filling. Grinding of the area must be done very slowly and carefully in order to prevent the grinding disk from breaking through the weak and badly corroded areas, catching on the sharp jagged edges and disintegrating. Grinding of these areas is often done by using a 1/4 in. (6 mm) electric drill with a 5 in. (127 mm) grinding disk attachment (Fig. 8-5). A number of small holes are then drilled all around the rusted-out area; these help in anchoring the fiberglass patch, which is then applied. This patch is cut large

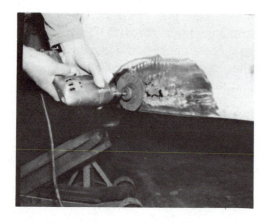

FIGURE 8-5

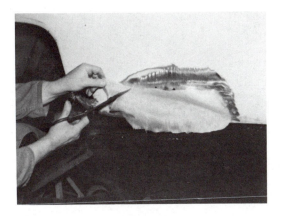

FIGURE 8-6   **FIGURE 8-7**

enough to overlap approximately 2½ to 3 in. (63 to 77 mm) beyond the rusted-out edges (Fig. 8-6). Before being placed in position over the metal, it is immersed and soaked in a glass tray that is filled with a sufficient amount of epoxy resin, to which the proportionate amount of catalyst has been added (Fig. 8-7). In dipping and applying the fiberglass cloth over the rusted-out area, rubber gloves should be worn to protect the hands from the chemical action that takes place when the resin and the catalyst are combined. The cloth should be spread out smoothly over the area (Fig. 8-8) and, in order to speed up the *curing* of the patch, additional heat can be applied by means of heat lamps. The rusted-out areas may, if necessary, be reinforced by applying one or two additional layers of fiber glass cloth (Fig. 8-9), with each layer overlapping the preceding layer or patch by about 1 in. (25 mm). Great care must be taken that all layers are completely saturated with epoxy resin and are free of air bubbles. When the fiberglass patch is completely cured (dry and hard), it can be sanded down to its final

FIGURE 8-8

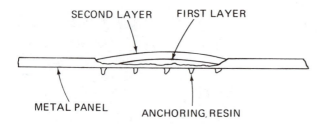

SECOND LAYER   FIRST LAYER

METAL PANEL   ANCHORING RESIN

FIGURE 8-9

FIGURE 8-10

contour and finish with the power grinder and the speed file (Fig. 8-10). Plastic-filled surfaces and fiberglass-repaired areas can be painted using the same refinishing steps and materials as those employed in the refinishing of sheet metal.

QUESTIONS

8-1 What other method of filling surface irregularities is employed in auto body repairing?

8-2 What is this material composed of?

8-3 How are the necessary surface preparations made?

8-4 Describe in detail how the plastic filler is prepared for application.

8-5 What tools are used in applying the plastic filler?

8-6 How long should the filler be allowed to harden before it is finished to its final shape and contour?

8-7 In what way should low spots in insufficiently filled surfaces be eliminated?

8-8   Why is the use of plastic filler on the outer edges of body panels not recommended?

8-9   In what other way should the outer edges be metal-finished?

8-10 How are rusted-out areas on used cars frequently repaired?

8-11 How are the weak and badly corroded areas cleaned and prepared for the patch.

8-12 What type of resin is used in bonding fiberglass cloth patches to metal surfaces?

8-13 After the patch that has been applied over the rusted-out area has hardened, how is it smoothed down?

8-14 To what size should each succeeding layer or patch be cut if more than one layer of cloth is used to reinforce the rusted-out area?

9

Fiberglass and Plastic:
Their Uses and
Repair Methods

UNIT 9-1: FIBERGLASS: ITS USES AND REPAIR METHODS

Although most of today's automobile and truck bodies are built of steel, some are also made of fiberglass.

Fiberglass, as the name implies, is a material composed of glass fibers; these fibers are impregnated and embedded in a hardened resin. When in its molten state, glass is drawn out into tiny fibers that are only a few ten-thousandths of an inch (about 0.01 mm) in diameter and anywhere from 10 to 12 in. (254 to 300 mm) in length. These fibers are very strong and quite flexible. Like other textile fibers, they can be woven into different materials, such as glass cloth, glass matting, and woven glass roving used in the manufacture and repair of reinforced fiberglass products. The glass fibers are also available in powder form (used primarily in fiberglass filler) and in very tiny short lengths called *chopped glass*.

Automobile panels and parts made from reinforced fiberglass possess extraordinary strength. They are highly resistant to fire and corrosion and are completely waterproof; when acted on by a damaging force or impact, the resulting damage is not spread out over a wide area of the panel as in the case of panels made of steel but is confined to the area of direct impact.

A procedure for repairing cracks, splintered edges, broken flanges, and sizable holes (minor damage) in fiberglass panels has been developed. Where a greater amount of damage to a particular panel has occurred, however, it is advisable to cut out the damaged panel, remove it completely, and install a replacement panel in its place. Replacement panels are available from the manufacturer. When feasible and practical, a partial replacement panel may be installed. This is done by cutting out only the damaged portion of a particular panel and replacing it with exactly the same portion cut from a replacement panel.

Fiberglass panels and parts can be repaired successfully if the following steps are taken:

1. Before attempting to repair fiberglass panels and parts, the repairman should analyze the extent and type of damage that has occurred and decide on the repair procedure most suitable for the job on hand.

2. Once the repair procedure has been determined, the damaged material should be removed.

3. The damaged area should then be properly prepared and reconstructed by filling with fiberglass and the correct mixture of resin and catalyst (hardener).

4. The catalyzed resin should be allowed to harden and cure.

5. Finally, the repaired area should be sanded down to its proper contour and final finish and painted if necessary.

A number of different materials are used in the repairing of reinforced fiberglass automobile bodies. Glass cloth, glass matting, woven glass roving, and chopped glass fibers are used as reinforcement with two types of bonding materials, called *resins*. The only difference between the resins is that the epoxy resin (recommended for maximum strength in the repair of broken fiberglass parts) bonds well with both fiberglass and metal surfaces, while polyester resin forms a more satisfactory bond with fiberglass surfaces and is less expensive.

Polyester filler is a putty-like filling material made of powdered fiberglass that is mixed with a polyester resin. It is used in filling surface irregularities on the outer side of fiberglass panels, especially repaired areas.

Powdered fiberglass is actually processed fiberglass that has been crushed into powder. It not only gives bulk and body but also strength to the filler.

A catalyst is a chemical used to start and speed up a chemical process called *hardening* (setting) of the resin used in repairing fiberglass panels and parts.

All the preceding materials are available in kit form or can also be purchased individually as required.

When fiberglass repairs are made, it is important that safety precautions be taken. Resins have occasionally been found to cause skin irritations or a rash. Therefore, it is recommended that hands be protected by either wearing rubber gloves or using a protective cream. All repair operations should be carried out in well-ventilated areas so that any toxic fumes and heat resulting from the chemical reaction between the resin and catalyst are drawn out and not allowed to remain and build up in the work area. It is this buildup that is very dangerous, for it often results in a disastrous fire. Thus any unused catalyzed resin should be disposed of as soon as possible by dropping it into a container of water. Any resin deposits on hands, tools, and clothing should be removed with lacquer thinners before the resin jells and hardens. Lacquer thinners, a highly flammable liquid, should be used with the greatest care and caution. When grinding or sanding down repaired areas, the repairman is advised to wear a respirator to avoid inhaling the fine resin dust or to use a belt sander equipped with a vacuum attachment.

Repairing Breaks and Holes in Laminated Panels

Breaks and sizable holes in laminated panels that are accessible from both sides can be repaired using the following procedure. The outer surface of the damaged panel should first be cleaned well beyond the damaged area with a good silicone wax and polish remover. All traces of paint should then be removed at least 4 in. (102 mm) beyond the damaged area, either by grinding with a No. 24 or No. 36 (3 or 2) grit disk or by hand-sanding with No. 80 (1/0) grit paper, depending on the thickness of the laminated panel.

The inner surface of the panel should also be cleaned. All foreign matter— dirt, dust, grease, and undercoating—should be removed at least 4 in. (102 mm) beyond the damaged area. The cleaned surface should then be thoroughly sanded (roughened) with No. 80 (1/0) grit paper. All cracked and fractured material along the break or hole is cut away with a hacksaw or ground out with a disk sander so that only sound material remains.

The outer surface of the panel is then beveled at an angle of approximately 30°, using a file or disk grinder (Fig. 9-1). This step provides a larger surface

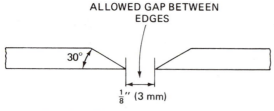

BEVELED BREAK IN FIBERGLASS PANEL   **FIGURE 9-1**

area to which the succeeding layers of fiberglass cloth or matting can readily adhere.

C clamps are then used to align panel portions, allowing approximately 1/8 in. (3 mm) between the panels to provide for proper alignment and solid bonding of the panels (Fig. 9-2). Three pieces of fiberglass cloth and two pieces of matting are cut into patches large enough to overlap the break or hole by a minimum of 2½ in. (64 mm), as shown in Fig. 9-3. The resin is then measured off into a clean, wax-free, expendable container, such as a clean juice can or glass jar, to which the proper amount of catalyst (follow the directions of the supplier) is added. The resin and catalyst are then *gently* stirred with a stick or stirring rod to remove any air trapped in the mixture as air might cause bubbling when the resin hardens.

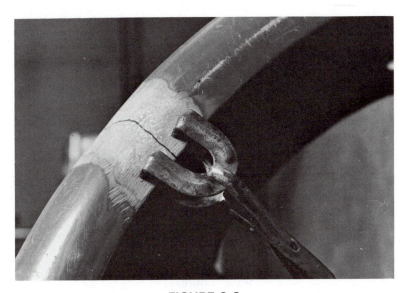

FIGURE 9-2

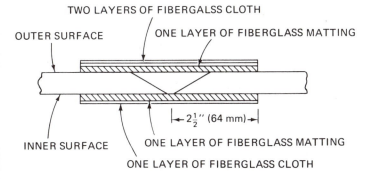

TWO LAYERS OF FIBERGALSS CLOTH

OUTER SURFACE

ONE LAYER OF FIBERGLASS MATTING

$2\frac{1}{2}''$ (64 mm)

INNER SURFACE

ONE LAYER OF FIBERGLASS MATTING

ONE LAYER OF FIBERGLASS CLOTH

FIGURE 9-3

A cellophane-covered supporting surface, made beforehand from any stiff, straight material, such as cardboard, is brought out. It is approximately 3 in. (76 mm) larger than the fiberglass cloth and matting patches, which are now placed on it. These items are saturated with the catalyzed resin by means of a paintbrush; be sure that all air bubbles are removed. The supporting surface is then picked up and tightly positioned over the roughened inner surface of the panel, which has also received a heavy coating of resin (Fig. 9-4). The patches on the outer surface of the panel are now placed in position and saturated with catalyzed resin, one after another, and allowed to harden.

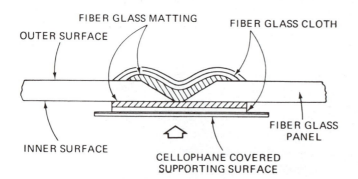

FIGURE 9-4

NOTE: To avoid hardening, only the amount of resin and catalyst needed for use should be mixed together. The hardening process can be speeded up somewhat by the application of heat—that is, infrared heating lamps. Temperatures in excess of 180°F (82.2°C) are to be avoided, however, for they tend to warp the repaired areas.

When the repaired areas have hardened (which generally takes about 30 to 40 minutes, depending on shop temperature), the supporting surface is removed from the inner side of the panel and the hardened patches are ground down with the power grinder to a slightly lower level than the surrounding contour (Fig. 9-5). The ground-down outer surface of the panel is then excessively but solidly built up with fiberglass filler, which is mixed with its catalyst in the correct proportions, as prescribed by the manufacturer (Fig. 9-6). The mixing of the filler and the catalyst, as well as the application of the catalyzed filler on the panel, is carried out by using either a squeegee or a putty knife. The filler hardens in approximately 15 minutes.

NOTE: The fiberglass filler can should be tightly closed when not in use and stored in a dry, cool place. Any unused catalyzed filler should not be returned to the can, for it will spoil the remaining contents. The repairman should wash

FIGURE 9-5   **FIGURE 9-6**

his hands after using this filler, especially before eating or smoking. Under no circumstances should it be taken internally.

When it has hardened, the fiberglass filler is sanded down to its final contour with a speed file, using No. 80 (1/0) grit strip paper, and block-sanded to an even smoother finish, using No. 100, No. 120, or No. 150 (2/0, 3/0, or 4/0) grit paper. The repaired fiberglass panel is now ready for refinishing in the usual manner.

Bonding strips, which actually are laminated fiberglass cutoffs, can frequently be used on the inner surfaces of damaged panels, eliminating the need of supporting surfaces and thereby speeding up the repair operations. Bonding strips are available with all replacement panels and are used extensively in complete panel installations (Fig. 9-7). When repairs to a damaged panel are made by using a bonding strip, the surface preparations are exactly the same as previously described. The only difference is that the fiberglass cloth and matting, as well as the supporting surface on the inside of the panel, are replaced by the bonding strip, which must be large enough to extend or overlap at least 3 in. (76 mm) beyond the edge of the hole. The bonding strip is roughened on its upper side and then held in its proper position on the inside of the panel while holes are drilled through the top to accommodate metal screws. After the inner-surface edges of the panel and the upper side of the bonding strip are heavily coated with catalyzed resin, the strip is brought up into position and the metal screws are tightened securely (Fig. 9-8).

The resin is then allowed to harden and cure. When completely hard, the metal screws are removed. Patches of sufficient size are cut from fiberglass cloth

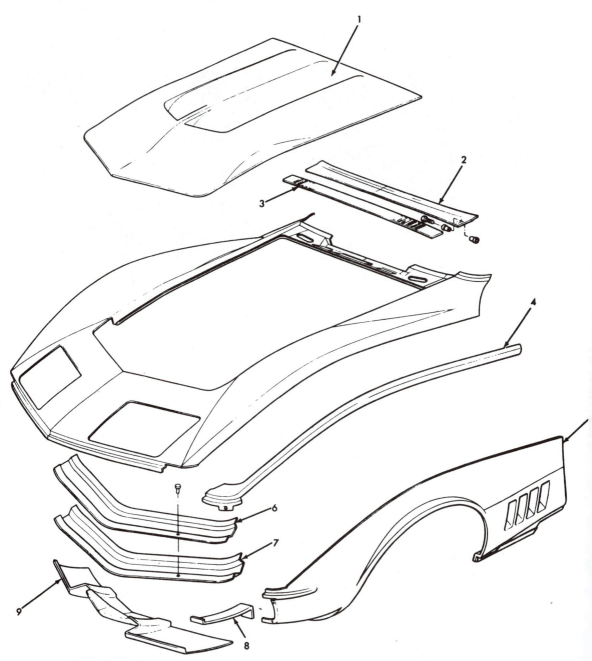

1. Panel–Hood
2. Panel–Access Door
3. Panel–Grille
4. Bonding Strip–Front Fender Upper to Lower
5. Panel–Front Fender Lower Rear
6. Reinforcement–Front Fender
7. Reinforcement–Front Fender
8. Bonding Strip–Front Fender Lower Front to Rear
9. Panel–Radiator Grille Lower

FIGURE 9-7 Front body construction. (Courtesy of General Motors of Canada, Ltd.)

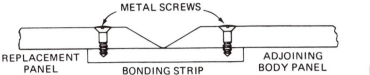

FIGURE 9-8

and matting to overlap the break by at least 2½ in. (64 mm) (Fig. 9-9). The resin mixture is prepared and the patches are individually impregnated with the resin by either using a paintbrush or dipping, as shown in Fig. 9-10.

NOTE: Any excess resin should be squeezed from the fiberglass patches, because the strength of the patch is directly proportional to its glass content. The

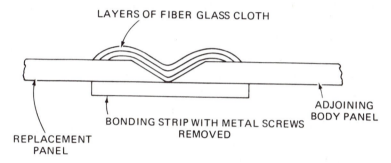

FIGURE 9-9

FIGURE 9-10

impregnated patches are then positioned over the break or hole (Fig. 9-9), covered with a sheet of cellophane wrap, pressed, and held down firmly until the resin gels.

After the patches have hardened, any excess or loose fiberglass materials protruding above the overall level of the panel are trimmed down with the disk sander to a slightly lower level than the surrounding contour of the panel. The depression is filled and excessively built up with fiberglass filler, using either a putty knife or a squeegee. It is allowed enough time to harden and is then filed and sanded down to its proper contour and finish before it is prepared for painting.

How to Repair Minor Scratches and Cracks in the Glaze Coat, Small Dents, and Pits in Fiberglass Panels

When the fiberglass panel has not been pierced or fractured, but merely requires a plastic buildup (Fig. 9-11), the following procedure is used in its repair.

The paint should first be removed from the area surrounding the damage down to the plastic with a lacquer-removing solvent. The area should then be scuffed with No. 80 (1/0) grit sandpaper to provide a good bonding surface. The scuffed area should be cleaned with Prep-Sol and the cleaning finished by wiping the area with a tack rag—to remove any lint left from cleaning.

The fiberglass body filler should now be applied with a squeegee or putty knife to fill surface imperfections. After the body filler has hardened, it should

FIGURE 9-11 Typical scratched panel.

be smoothed down, first by filing with the body file and then by sanding with either a speed file or a sanding block, using No. 100, No. 120, No. 150 (2/0, to 3/0, 4/0) or even finer grit sandpaper in preparation for painting.

Partial Panel Replacement

When fiberglass panels are damaged to such an extent that they cannot be repaired by the preceding methods, they are sometimes repaired by the installation of a partial section, cut to the required size from another replacement panel. This step will often make the repair operation much easier, eliminate the removal of many parts, and save a considerable amount of time.

A certain amount of skill on the part of the repairman in making the necessary body bonds, some of which are shown in Fig. 9-12, is involved, however. In short, a combination of the aforementioned repair procedures, as well as many of the procedural steps described below, is required.

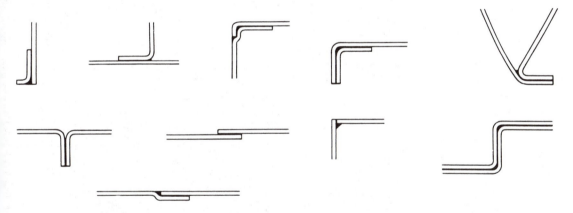

FIGURE 9-12 (Courtesy of General Motors of Canada, Ltd.)

Complete Panel Replacements

Another method of repairing a panel damaged beyond repair is by the complete removal of the damaged panel, or what is left of it, and replacing it with a completely new panel, which is supplied with all the necessary installation materials (kit), including the bonding strips (Fig. 9-13).

The first step in replacing the damaged panel is to remove it by cutting it off from the rest of the body with a hacksaw and removing all paint and dirt from the underside of the old panels for a distance of approximately 3 to 4 in. (76 to 102 mm) inward from the attaching line. The paint should be removed

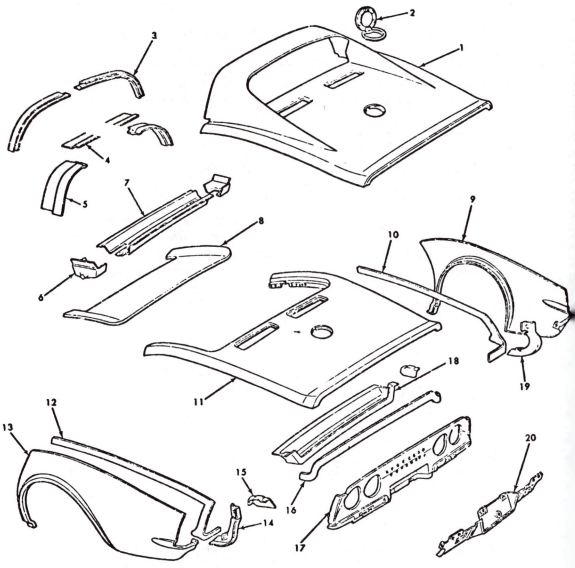

1. Panel–Body Rear Upper
2. Bezel–Fuel Tank Filler Door
3. Reinforcement Roof–Right Hand
4. Panel–Rear Roof Inner Center, Left Hand
5. Panel–Rear Roof Inner Rear, Left Hand
6. Extension–Body Rear Upper Panel
7. Support–Body Rear Upper Panel
8. Lid–Folding Top Compartment
9. Panel–Rear Quarter, Right Hand
10. Bonding Strip–Body Rear Upper Panel to Quarter Panel, Right Hand
11. Panel–Body Rear Upper
12. Bonding Strip–Body Rear Upper Panel
13. Panel–Rear Quarter, Left Hand
14. Bonding Strip–Body Lower Panel to Quarter Panel, Left Hand
15. Support–Body Rear Upper Panel
16. Bonding Strip–Body Rear Upper
17. Body Rear Lower Panel
18. Support–Body Rear Upper Panel
19. Shield–Rear Quarter Splash
20. Panel–Rear Filler

FIGURE 9-13 Rear body construction. (Courtesy of General Motors of Canada, Ltd.)

from the outer surface of the old panels for a distance of at least 3 in. (76 mm) inward from their attaching lines, using a lacquer solvent.

The cleaned underside of the old panels and the replacement panel should be scuff-sanded with No. 80 (1/0) grit sandpaper at least 2½ in. (64 mm) inward from their attaching lines and wiped clean with a tack rag. Their outer edges should then be beveled across the entire thickness of the panel, to an angle of approximately 30° (Fig. 9-14), making sure that the replacement panel and the old panels come closer together at their attaching edges.

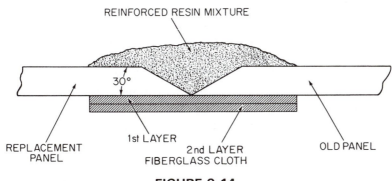

FIGURE 9-14

Two pieces of woven fiberglass cloth backing strips, each 5 in. (127 mm) wide and of sufficient length are cut to cover the underside of the attaching edges. The resin mixture is then prepared as previously described, and the replacement panel is positioned and aligned with the other body panels by means of C clamps. When C clamps cannot be used, 3/16 in. (5 mm) bolts can be used with large flat washers to hold the inner and outer surfaces of the panels in alignment. Wherever practical, steel straps and bonding strips can also be used with metal screws. The prepared cloth backing strips are now impregnated with the resin mixture by brushing or dipping, whichever is more convenient. Any excess resin on cloth backing strips should be removed by squeezing. The backing strips are positioned and pressed firmly against the underside of the panels and, if necessary, held up in place with heavy cellophane-covered cardboard until the resin has gelled.

The V groove is then filled and built up excessively with catalyzed reinforced resin material, made by mixing short [1/2 in. (13 mm)] cut glass fibers to the resin until the mixture becomes thick like putty. It can also be filled with impregnated strips of fiberglass cloth if desired. Any excess or loose fiberglass cloth must be cut down slightly below the general contour of the panel, however, after it has hardened, using the disk sander. The slight depression must be built up excessively with fiberglass filler and allowed to harden before it can be cut and sanded down, like the reinforced resin filler, to its proper contour and finish with No. 80 (1/0) grit sandpaper, using either a sanding block or the speed file. The replacement panel is then ready for refinishing in the usual manner.

UNIT 9-2: PLASTIC: ITS USES AND REPAIR METHODS

The use of plastic, when first introduced, was very limited—used mainly in the manufacturing of lenses on dash instruments, tail lamps, clearance lights, dome lights, window regulator handles, and various other small parts. However, over the years, its use has constantly increased, and today, as a result of automobile engineers' efforts to reduce the weight of their models, thereby enhancing fuel economy, more and more auto parts, such as dashboards, interior trim panels, filler panels, fender liners (wheelhousings), fan blades, fan shrouds, bumper covers and impact strips, grilles, and headlamp and tail lamp bodies and lenses, are being made of plastic.

There are more than 15 different kinds of plastics used in manufacturing auto parts (Fig. 9-15). These are either one of two types:

- *Thermoplastic:* can be softened with the application of heat, can be reshaped, and can be welded.

- *Thermosetting:* permanently set. Cannot be softened with the application of heat, cannot be reshaped, and cannot be welded. However, minor damage can often be repaired with a structural adhesive.

To determine if a material is thermoplastic, just hold a heated welder 1 in. (25. 4 mm) from the material for approximately 10 seconds. If the material begins softening, it is thermoplastic and can in most instances be welded.

To repair plastic, the repairman must first identify the material before him. This can be done by looking for a set of letters on the back or underside of the part, to match the letters on the manufacturer's identification chart (Fig. 9-15). If no letters can be found on the part, consult the manufacturer's plastic identification guide (Figs. 9-16 and 9-17).

The following tests will also help the repairman to identify five of the more common plastics used.

Symbol	Plastic material
ABS	ABS
ABS/PVC	ABS/Vinyl
PA	Nylon
PC	Lexan
PE	Polyethylene
PP	Polypropylene
PPO	Noryl
PUR	Thermoset polyurethane
PVC	Polyvinyl chloride (vinyl)
SAN	SAN
TPUR	Thermoplastic polyurethane
UP	Polyester (Fiberglass)
TPR	Thermoplastic rubber
EPDM	Ethylene propylene diene monomer

FIGURE 9-15

ABS and Polypropylene (PP) Test

Using a sharp knife, remove a sliver of plastic from the hidden back side of the part. Hold the sliver of plastic with tweezers or lay it on a clean noncombustible surface. Ignite the plastic and observe the burning closely. ABS plastic burns with a readily visible black smoke residue that will hang temporarily in the air. Polypropylene burns with no visible smoke, has its own distinguishing smell, will continue to burn when removed from flame, and will float in water.

Polyvinyl Chloride (PVC) Test

With a propane or similar torch, heat a copper wire until it begins to glow or turns red. Touch the heated wire to the hidden or back side of the plastic material so that some of the plastic adheres to the wire. Move the wire back into the flame. If the plastic on the wire burns, giving off a greenish-turquoise blue flame, it is polyvinyl chloride.

Polyethylene (PE) Test

This material will melt, swell, and drip when a flame is directed on it. Drippings may burn and will continue burning when flame is removed, giving off a burning wax odor. It will also float in water.

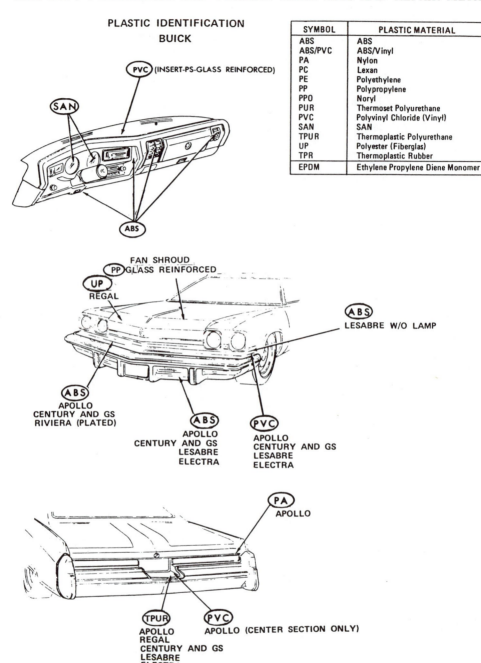

PLASTIC IDENTIFICATION
BUICK

SYMBOL	PLASTIC MATERIAL
ABS	ABS
ABS/PVC	ABS/Vinyl
PA	Nylon
PC	Lexan
PE	Polyethylene
PP	Polypropylene
PPO	Noryl
PUR	Thermoset Polyurethane
PVC	Polyvinyl Chloride (Vinyl)
SAN	SAN
TPUR	Thermoplastic Polyurethane
UP	Polyester (Fiberglas)
TPR	Thermoplastic Rubber
EPDM	Ethylene Propylene Diene Monomer

FIGURE 9-16 Plastic identification for the Buick. (Courtesy of General Motors of Canada, Ltd.)

PLASTIC IDENTIFICATION
OLDSMOBILE

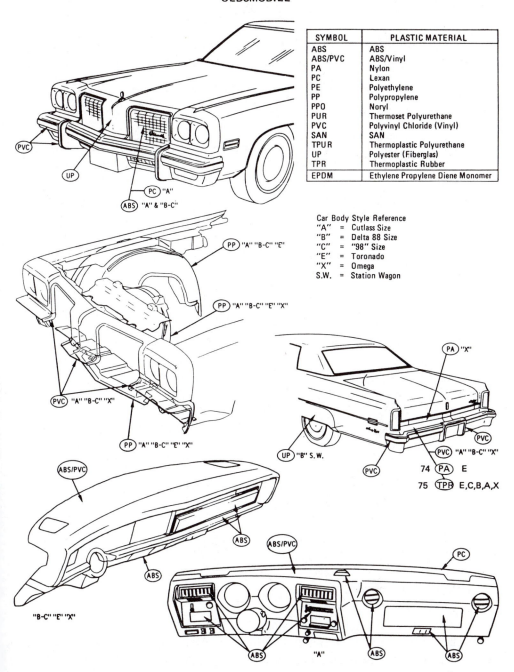

SYMBOL	PLASTIC MATERIAL
ABS	ABS
ABS/PVC	ABS/Vinyl
PA	Nylon
PC	Lexan
PE	Polyethylene
PP	Polypropylene
PPO	Noryl
PUR	Thermoset Polyurethane
PVC	Polyvinyl Chloride (Vinyl)
SAN	SAN
TPUR	Thermoplastic Polyurethane
UP	Polyester (Fiberglas)
TPR	Thermoplastic Rubber
EPDM	Ethylene Propylene Diene Monomer

Car Body Style Reference
"A" = Cutlass Size
"B" = Delta 88 Size
"C" = "98" Size
"E" = Toronado
"X" = Omega
S.W. = Station Wagon

FIGURE 9-17 Plastic identification for the Oldsmobile. (Courtesy of General Motors of Canada, Ltd.)

Thermoplastic Polyurethane (TPUR) Test

This plastic is very flexible. When set on fire, it burns with a yellow orange flame, gives off black smoke, and continues to burn with a sputter when flame is removed.

Thermoplastic Welding

The welding of plastics is done with a special torch, equipped with three tips and with a 115 volt, 300 to 500 watt element that heats low-pressure compressed air to a temperature of 400 to 700°F (260 to 371°C), hot enough to melt most thermoplastic materials (Fig. 9-18). Each manufacturer supplies its own operational instructions, and these should be carefully followed.

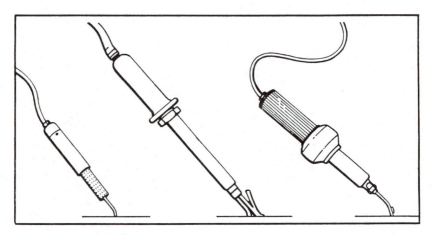

FIGURE 9-18   (Courtesy of General Motors of Canada, Ltd.)

CAUTION: The barrel of the torch, heated by the electric element, gets hot enough that skin contact could cause a burn.

Plastic Welding Rod

Plastic welding requires a welding rod made from the same material as the plastic being repaired. Welding rods are available from local plastics suppliers or can be made from clean scrap materials of the same type as that being repaired, provided that the material has not been stressed.

Preparing the Damaged Area for Welding

The break or tear should be trimmed to a V shape using a sharp knife or by sanding (Fig. 9-19). The reason for sanding the tear to a V shape is to expose a larger surface area to heat and a void to fill with softened welding rod, resulting in complete bonding or fusion. Any dust or shaving should be wiped from the joint with a dry, clean rag. Do not use solvents for cleaning, because these tend to soften the edges, causing poor welds. Figure 9-20 shows the various types of V butt welds.

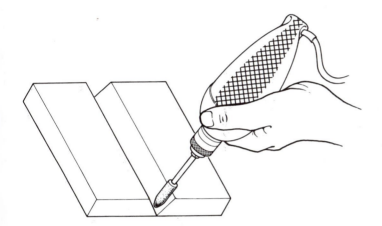

FIGURE 9-19 V shaping a tear or break using a power drill.

Starting-Up Procedure

Before starting the welding torch, make sure to use clean compressed air and that the air is flowing through the torch before the electricity is turned on.

1. Turn on the compressed air and adjust the pressure to approximately 2½ psi (17.2 kPa). The pressure setting may vary depending on the type and thickness of the plastic being welded.

2. Plug in the torch to the power supply (115 volts) and allow it to preheat for 5 to 10 minutes.

3. Check the temperature by holding a thermometer 1/4 in. (6 mm) from the hot-air end of the torch tip. The temperature should be in the range 400 to 750°F (204.4 to 399°C) for most thermoplastic welding.

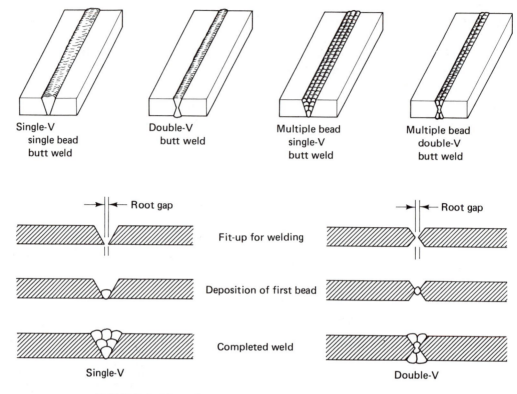

FIGURE 9-20 (Courtesy of General Motors of Canada, Ltd.)

Shutting-Off Procedure

1. Disconnect the torch from the (115 volt) power supply.

2. Allow compressed air to cool off the heating element before disconnecting the air supply.

Aligning the Tear or Break

Align the edges to be joined as necessary. If the tear is long and back-up difficult, small tack welds can be made along its entire length, to hold the two sides in place while finish welding is carried out. Tack welding is done:

1. By holding the damaged area in its correct shape and position, using clamps, fixtures, and so on.

2. Using the torch equipped with either the tack welding or round freehand welding tip, applying hot air evenly to both sides of the break or tear, until the material melts together. Adding of additional material (welding rod) should not be attempted at this time.

Starting the Weld Bead

Hold the torch 1/2 in. (12 mm) from the work and tip of the welding rod, which is held at 90° to the base material (Fig. 9-21). Play the torch between the rod and base material, evenly preheating both until shiny and tacky. Now move the rod to barely touch the base material. If preheated sufficiently, the rod will stick. Keep moving the torch between the material and rod, simultaneously pressing rod into the V weld area, with a light pressure of about 3 lb (20.7 kPa). When enough heat has been applied, a molten wave will form in the area where welding rod and base material meet, and the rod will begin to bend and move forward (Fig. 9-22).

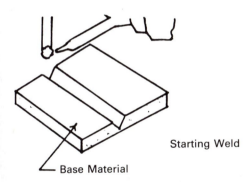

Starting Weld

Base Material

FIGURE 9-21 (Courtesy of General Motors of Canada, Ltd.)

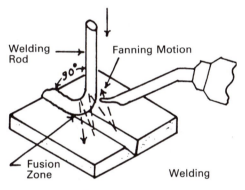

Welding Rod

Fanning Motion

90°

Fusion Zone

Welding

FIGURE 9-22 (Courtesy of General Motors of Canada, Ltd.)

NOTE: In plastic welding, a good start is essential in running a strong bead, because it is at the outer edges of the base material, where most weld failures begin. Therefore, wherever possible, the starting points on multiple-bead welds should be staggered.

Running of the bead is continued by moving the torch between the rod and the base material, with a sort of fanning motion. However, because the rod is much lighter and less bulky than the base material, it is important that more heat be directed on the base material if overheating and charring of the welding rod is to be prevented.

Feeding the Welding Rod

A constant pressure must be applied on the rod as it is being fed unto the material. A release of this pressure may cause the rod to lift away from the weld bead, and air to become trapped under the weld, resulting in a poor weld. The welder must therefore develop skill at applying a constant pressure on the rod, while repositioning his fingers. This can be done by applying pressure on the rod with the third and fourth fingers while the thumb and first fingers are repositioned higher up on the rod (Fig. 9-23). To do this, the rod must be kept cool enough. This is accomplished by careful aiming of the torch and by applying heat only to the bottom end of the rod.

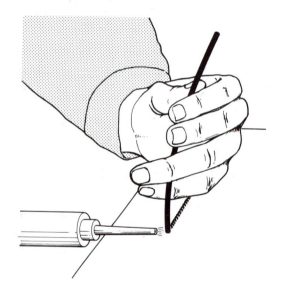

FIGURE 9-23 (Courtesy of General Motors of Canada, Ltd.)

Completing the Weld

When reaching the end of a weld, stop the fanning forward motion with the torch and direct it at the intersection of rod and base material. Remove the torch but maintain a constant downward pressure on the rod for a few more seconds. This will allow the rod to cool and prevent it from being pulled from the base material. The unused rod can then be cut from the weld.

A weld does not develop its full strength until it has completely cooled, which generally takes about 15 to 20 minutes. Cooling can be speeded by applying cold water or compressed air.

CAUTION: Any attempt to test a thermoplastic weld by bending it before it has completely cooled may result in weld separation.

Grinding Down the Weld

Excess plastic on rough welds can be removed with a sharp knife before grinding down of excessive buildup on large beads is attempted. Grinding can best be done with a 9 in. (229 mm) variable-speed polisher (5000 rpm), equipped with a No. 36 (2) grit sanding disk. Care must be exercised not to overheat the weld area, or it will become soft. Periodic cooling with water will speed up the grinding process and prevent damage to the weld.

Checking the Strength of the Weld

After the weld has been ground level and smooth, it should be examined for defects. Any pores or cracks visible before or after bend testing of the welded material will make the weld unacceptable. The weld should be just as strong as the part itself.

Finish Sanding of the Welded Area

Welded areas found acceptable are finish-sanded with either an orbital or a belt sander, or by hand-sanding with a sanding block, using No. 220 (6/0) grit sandpaper, followed with No. 320 (9/0) grit. The welded part is now ready for refinishing (described in Unit 19-8).

Semiautomatic Speed Welding

Long, straight breaks or tears can be welded much faster with the torch equipped with a speed welding tip than with a round, freehand welding tip. This tip makes it possible for the repairman to apply heat, pressure, and the feeding of the welding rod, with only one hand, once the weld has been started (Fig. 9-24).

In starting the weld, hold the torch at 90° to the base material; insert the rod into the preheating tube, and place the pointed shoe immediately on the base material at the starting point (Fig. 9-25).

Holding the torch perpendicular to the base material with one hand, push the welding rod down with the other hand until it makes contact with the base material. Applying a slight pressure on the rod and with only the weight of the torch on the shoe, slowly begin pulling the torch forward. The rod should be helped along by pushing it into the tube for the first 1 to 2 in. (25.4 or 50.8 mm) of travel. Once the weld has been started, the torch should be brought to an approximate 70° angle. The rod will then feed automatically, or hand-feeding can be continued.

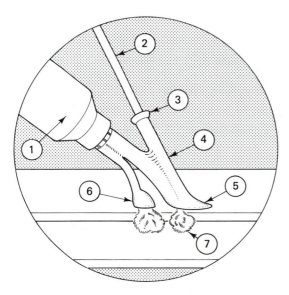

1. Electric torch
2. Welding rod
3. Speed tip
4. Rod is preheated in tube
5. Shoe provides pressure
6. Orifice preheats area to be welded
7. Heat

FIGURE 9-24 Electric torch with speed welding tip. (Courtesy of General Motors of Canada, Ltd.)

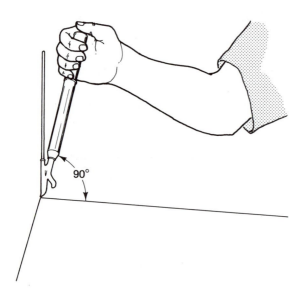

90°

FIGURE 9-25 Starting semiautomatic speed weld. (Courtesy of General Motors of Canada, Ltd.)

The quality of the weld can be visually inspected as the torch is moved along. If the welding rod has been softened too much due to overheating, it will cause the rod to stretch, break, or flatten out and the fusion lines on each side of the bead to be oversized. If no fusion lines are visible, not enough pressure is being applied on the base material or the welding speed (forward movement of the torch) is too fast.

The angle between the torch and base material determines the welding speed. Since the preheater hole in the speed tip precedes the shoe, the angle of the torch to the material determines how close the preheater hole is to the base material and how much preheating occurs. For this reason, the torch is held at a 90° angle when starting the weld (bead) and changed to approximately 45° as welding is continued (Fig. 9-26).

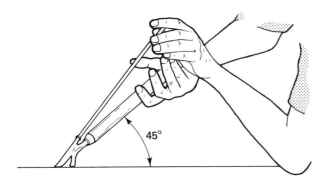

FIGURE 9-26 Continuing the semiautomatic speed weld. (Courtesy of General Motors of Canada, Ltd.)

If inspection of the bead indicates too fast a welding speed, the torch should be brought back temporarily to a 90° angle, to slow down the welding speed, and then gradually adjusted to the proper angle for the welding speed desired.

NOTE: It is very important that the torch be held so that both the preheater hole and shoe of the speed welding tip are always kept in line with the direction of the weld and that only the base material in front of the shoe is preheated. The heat pattern on the base material clearly indicates the area being preheated, and the rod should always be solidly fused in the center of that pattern.

Completing the Speed Weld

Speed welding, once started, must be continued at a relatively constant speed. When welding is to be stopped, before the rod has been used up, the torch is brought back past the 90° angle, and the rod is cut off with the shoe (Fig. 9-27). The cut-off rod must be removed immediately from the preheater tube or it will melt and char, plugging the tube and make its cleaning necessary. Welding

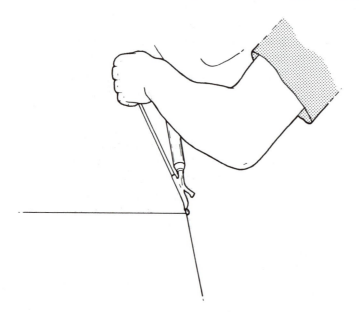

FIGURE 9-27 Finishing the semiautomatic speed weld. (Courtesy of General Motors of Canada, Ltd.)

can also be stopped by pulling the speed tip off the remaining rod, which is allowed to cool before it is cut off with a sharp knife.

The bead on a good weld will have a slightly higher crown and more uniformity than is possible in freehand welding. It will have a shiny, smooth appearance, and for best results, the speed tip must be kept perfectly clean, by occasionally cleaning it with a wire brush.

Repairing Flexible Exterior Plastic Parts

Soft plastic parts, used for exterior and cosmetic application, are made of resins that have flexible characteristics, enabling them to absorb minor impact without sustaining damage. Front and rear bumper filler panels, valance and end panels, quarter-panel extensions, front and rear bumper upper and lower covers, and bumper center moldings are typical examples. These parts, usually fabricated of

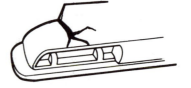

FIGURE 9-28 Types of damage. (Courtesy of Ford Motor Company of Canada, Ltd.)

thermosetting plastic, cannot be welded, but minor damage such as punctures, gouges, and tears (Fig. 9-28) can be repaired successfully with structural adhesive.

Structural Adhesive Repair Procedure

The damaged area is cleaned with a general-purpose adhesive cleaner and wax remover. Clean both sides of the part if damage extends through the entire thickness of the part. Using a No. 36 (2) grit disk, grind away all damaged material, and for best adhesion, feather-edge a large area around the damage with a No. 180 (5/0) grit desk (Fig. 9-29). Lightly singe the repair area with a gas torch for approximately 15 seconds (Fig. 9-30).

N5727-A

FIGURE 9-29 Grinding and feather-edging damaged areas. (Courtesy of Ford Motor Company of Canada, Ltd.)

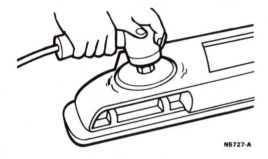

N5730-A

FIGURE 9-30 Lightly singeing repair area. Courtesy of Ford Motor Company of Canada, Ltd.)

Apply either body tape or a new or clean used adhesive-backed disk to the back side of the damage, so as to keep the patch material from falling through (Fig. 9-31). Remove all dust and any loose particles from the repair area.

Take the 3M No. 8101 Structural Adhesive Tube Kit, or equivalent, and thoroughly mix the two-component adhesive according to the manufacturer's instructions, using a putty knife or the stick enclosed in the package (Fig. 9-32). The mixing board should be made of nonporous material, such as metal, glass, or plastic, onto which equal-length beads of each component are deposited.

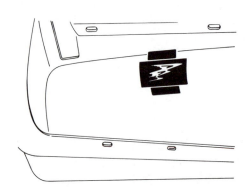

FIGURE 9-31   Tape applied for support of repair material. (Courtesy of General Motors of Canada, Ltd.)

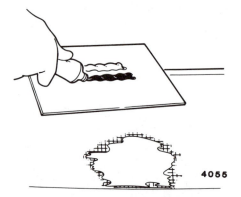

FIGURE 9-32   Measuring two-component repair material. (Courtesy of General Motors of Canada, Ltd.)

In mixing, do not lift the adhesive from the mixing board. Scrape the two components together, and with downward pressure on the putty knife or stick provided, continue spreading the components out thinly on the mixing board until a uniform color and consistency is achieved. This procedure will prevent the trapping of air (bubbles) in the adhesive.

Scrape the mixed adhesive from the mixing board and apply a thin coat over the damaged area with a soft squeegee. Mix and apply a second (heavy, filling) coat of adhesive (Fig. 9-33). Allow the filled area to cure 20 to 30 minutes at 60 to 80°F (16 to 27°C).

Sand the filling adhesive level with the surrounding area, using a flat, curve-tooth body file to establish a rough contour (Fig. 9-34), followed by disk sanding with a No. 240 (7/0) grit disk, and then wet sanding with No. 320 (9/0) grit sandpaper (Fig. 9-35). Check the area for voids and low areas, and if necessary, apply more adhesive to these areas.

Bake the repaired area for about 15 minutes at 180°F (83°C), using heat lamps (Fig. 9-36). Allow to cool before sanding down (rechecking the contour

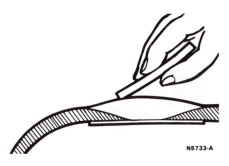

FIGURE 9-33 Applying structural adhesive material. (Courtesy of Ford Motor Company of Canada, Ltd.)

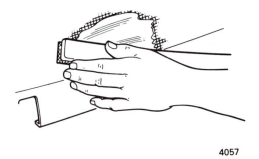

FIGURE 9-34 Establishing rough contour. (Courtesy of General Motors of Canada, Ltd.)

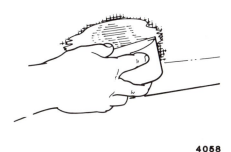

FIGURE 9-35 Block sanding for accurate contour. (Courtesy of General Motors of Canada, Ltd.)

FIGURE 9-36 Baking the repaired area. (Courtesy of Ford Motor Company of Canada, Ltd.)

and simultaneously feather-edging) the area, to its final shape and finish, using No. 320 (9/0) and No. 400 (10/0) grit wet sandpaper, respectively. The repaired part is then refinished as described in Unit 19-8.

Structural-Type Repair

The structural strength of the attaching surface (flange) of a part which is cracked or has broken away (Fig. 9-37) can successfully be repaired as follows.

Align and securely position the piece on the face side with body tape and a clamp (Fig. 9-38).

Clean the underside of the repair area with a general-purpose adhesive cleaner and wax remover before sanding each side of the break with a No. 50 (1) grit sanding disk (Fig. 9-39).

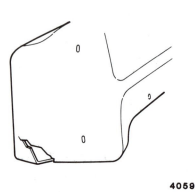

4059

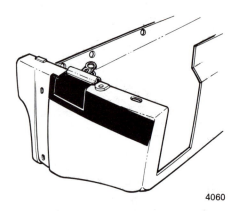

4060

FIGURE 9-37 Damaged attaching surface. (Courtesy of General Motors of Canada, Ltd.)

FIGURE 9-38 Aligning break with tape and clamp. (Courtesy of General Motors of Canada, Ltd.)

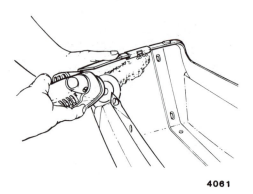

4061

FIGURE 9-39 Disk-sanding back side of damaged area. (Courtesy of General Motors of Canada, Ltd.)

Cut a piece of fiberglass cloth large enough to overlap the break 1½ in. (38 mm) (Fig. 9-40).

Mix a quantity of structural adhesive and apply a layer of the mixture, about 1/8 in. (3 mm) thick, on the back side of the part, overlapping the break at least 1½ in. (38 mm) (Fig. 9-41).

Apply the precut fiberglass cloth over the adhesive, and immediately cover the cloth with enough additional adhesive to completely fill and cover the weave (Figs. 9-42) and (9-43).

Allow the area 20 to 30 minutes curing time at 60 to 80°F (16 to 27°C) before trimming off any excess material from the edge, if necessary.

The clamp and body tape are then removed, and the face side of the part is now repaired, following the same repair procedure as that employed in repairing a puncture, gouge, or tear, and described earlier in this unit.

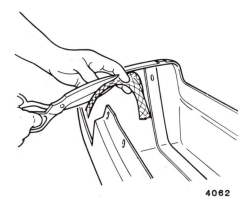

FIGURE 9-40 Cutting fiberglass cloth to size. (Courtesy of General Motors of Canada, Ltd.)

FIGURE 9-41 Applying structural adhesive material. (Courtesy of General Motors of Canada, Ltd.)

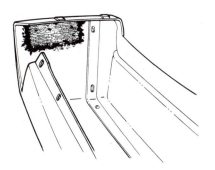

FIGURE 9-42 Applying fiberglass cloth. (Courtesy of General Motors of Canada, Ltd.)

FIGURE 9-43 Filling fiberglass cloth. (Courtesy of General Motors of Canada, Ltd.)

QUESTIONS

9-1 What is the composition of fiberglass?

9-2 Into what materials are the glass fibers woven?

9-3 What are the distinctive properties of fiberglass panels and parts?

9-4 Describe the various ways in which fiberglass panels can be repaired.

9-5 What materials are used as reinforcement with the bonding resin?

9-6   On what kind of repair jobs should epoxy and polyester resins be used?

9-7   What is polyester filler made of, and what are its uses?

9-8   What is the purpose of mixing the catalyst with the resin?

9-9   Why should fiberglass repair operations be carried out in well-ventilated areas?

9-10 In what way should unused catalyzed resin be disposed of?

9-11 What is used in removing resin deposits from hands, tools, and clothing?

9-12 What precautions should the repairman take when grinding or sanding fiberglass repair areas?

9-13 How are cracked and fractured materials along a break or hole removed?

9-14 At what angle should the outer surface of the panel be beveled?

9-15 How much gap should be allowed between the panels?

9-16 To what size should the patches of fiberglass cloth and matting be cut?

9-17 Why should the resin and its catalyst be stirred gently when they are being mixed?

9-18 In what ways are the patches held up in place on the roughened inner surface of the panels?

9-19 How can the hardening and curing process of a repaired area be speeded up?

9-20 Why should temperature above 180°F (82.2°C) be avoided?

9-21 After the patch has hardened and its outer surface sanded down, how is the repair completed?

9-22 How should fiberglass filler be stored when not in use?

9-23 Why should any unused catalyzed filler not be returned to the can?

9-24 What tools are used in sanding fiberglass filler, and what type of abrasive is used?

9-25 What is the name of another material that often speeds up fiberglass repairs?

9-26 How is a bonding strip prepared for installation on the inside of the panel?

9-27 Why should any excess resin be squeezed from the fiberglass patches?

9-28 How are the impregnated patches positioned and held over the break or hole?

9-29 After all excess and loose fiberglass materials have been removed from the hardened patch or repaired area, how and with what is the fiberglass filler applied?

9-30 Describe how minor scratches and cracks in the glaze coat, as well as small pits and dents, are repaired.

9-31 In what way can a considerable amount of time be saved when a particular panel is beyond repair?

9-32   Name the two types of plastic used in manufacturing automobile parts and how they differ.

9-33   How can a repairman identify the material to be repaired?

9-34   Describe the test used in identifying ABS and polypropylene (PP) plastic.

9-35   How can polyvinyl chloride (PVC) be identified?

9-36   How can polyethylene (PE) and thermoplastic polyurethane (TPUR) be identified when ignited?

9-37   What type of torch is used for welding plastics?

9-38   What can be used as welding rod when a particular kind of rod is not readily available?

9-39   How and why should a break or tear be trimmed to a V shape?

9-40   Briefly describe the procedure used in starting up and shutting down a welding torch.

9-41   How is the tack welding of a tear or break carried out?

9-42   At what distance from the work should the torch be held when starting the weld bead?

9-43   In plastic welding, why is a good start essential in the running of a strong bead?

9-44   How is the torch manipulated in welding once the bead has been started?

9-45   Why must more heat be directed on the base metal than on the rod?

9-46   How is a constant pressure kept on the rod as it is fed unto the material?

9-47   Once a weld has been completed, how can cooling off be speeded?

9-48   How and with what is excessive buildup on large beads ground down?

9-49   What special tip makes welding of long, straight breaks much faster?

9-50   When using the speed welding tip, how is the torch held once the bead has been started?

9-51   What appearance will a good speed-welded bead have?

9-52   What material is used in repairing minor damage on parts made of thermosetting plastic?

9-53   Describe how the surface of a damaged area is prepared for the structural adhesive.

9-54   How and on what are the two components of structural adhesive mixed?

9-55   How is the mixed structural adhesive applied?

9-56   Explain the procedure used in repairing the attaching surface or flange on a thermosetting plastic panel.

10

Frame Alignment

UNIT 10-1: FRAME ALIGNMENT AND STRAIGHTENING

Frame alignment is the procedure by which the frame of a car, truck, or bus that has been damaged in an accident or from wear is restored to the manufacturer's specifications. This procedure is usually done, without removing the body (engine, etc.) on a machine that provides for the proper positioning of the vehicle and can hold, push, or pull the frame back into alignment.

All automobiles have a frame, either the conventional frame design or the unitized body-frame construction. In the conventional type, the frame is bolted to the body and its members extend the full length of the body. The conventional frames are divided into two types: the perimeter frame and the ladder frame.

The perimeter frame is separate from the body and it forms a border that reinforces and surrounds the passenger compartment. Its front section supports the power train, front suspension assemblies, and front body mounts. The side rails extend to the back where the body and rear suspension are bolted. It is usually constructed of box or channel-type rails that are joined to torque boxes at the four corners. The primary load is transferred to the frame by the torque boxes, but the complete frame to a great extent relies on the body structure for its rigidity (Fig. 10-1).

The ladder frame is self-descriptive and was the forerunner of the various types of frames found on newer vehicles. It is similar to the perimeter frame but

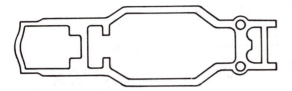

FIGURE 10-1   Perimeter frame.

its side rails do not surround the passenger compartment. Its rails are built with less offset and are constructed in a more direct line from the front to the rear wheels. This frame is constructed with several cross-members and by itself is quite rigid, forming a strong support on which the body is mounted (Fig. 10-2).

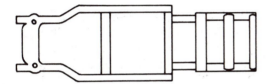

FIGURE 10-2   Ladder frame.

In unitized construction, the frame members are shorter and usually welded to the body. The underbody section is reinforced to provide the floor with enough structural strength to replace the side rail on conventional frames. There are several variations of unitized construction. In the first type (Fig. 10-3) every member is related one to the other so that all sections carry part of the load. The rocker panels, floor pans, and so on of the lower portion of the body are welded together to form a basic structure. The front of the structure where the engine and suspension are mounted is heavily reinforced and has the appearance of a separate frame except that the rails are not bolted but welded to the body structure.

In the construction of the newer type of automobiles, the vehicle has been totally redesigned (Fig. 10-4). This is due to the emphasis that has been placed on increasing the miles per gallon or liters per 100 kilometers that a particular

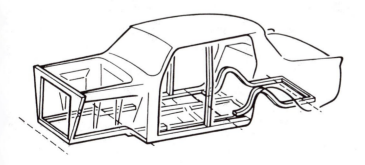

FIGURE 10-3   Unitized construction.

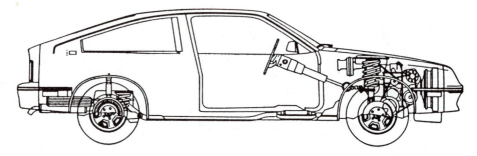

FIGURE 10-4 Unitized-body design. (Courtesy of Chart Industries, Ltd.)

vehicle will achieve. Manufacturers have downsized the automobile, and reduced its weight by using more plastics, HSS and HSLA steel, and aluminum (Fig. 10-5). Moving the total power train in the front of the vehicle and using front-wheel-drive systems have greatly reduced the weight of the automobile.

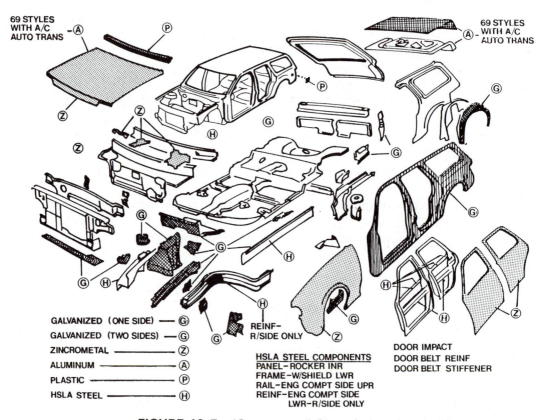

FIGURE 10-5 (Courtesy of Chart Industries, Ltd.)

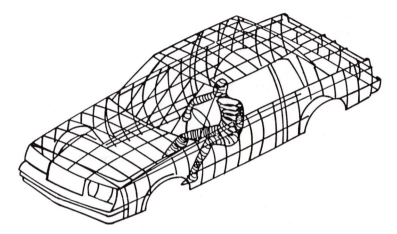

FIGURE 10-6 Passive safety design. (Courtesy of Chart Industries, Ltd.)

This new design in automobiles required total changes in engineering and styling. The new design had to be engineered to meet many safety aspects, such as the protection of passengers when involved in a collision. These vehicles are designed with what is called a passive safety design (Fig. 10-6). This means that the vehicle is designed to absorb an impact as it crushes or bends. The manufacturers design areas in the vehicle which are meant to bend and crush as the energy of the impact is absorbed. The vehicle is designed in such a way that all panels are used to reinforce the basic structure when it is involved in collision. The forces of the impact are spread out in an ever-widening area or in a cone-shaped effect (Fig. 10-7).

These lighter-gauge metals that are used throughout the structural members require finesse rather than force to correct the damage. Excessive force will only

FIGURE 10-7 Absorption of impact. (Courtesy of Chart Industries, Ltd.)

cause tearing and stretching of the members instead of correcting and straightening the damage.

The repairer must also learn the proper technique so as to be able to repair and replace the damaged section or panels in order to be competitive in the marketplace. He will also have to acquire general mechanical knowledge of wheel alignment and the mechanical disassembly of its components.

These newer vehicles have more control points, so very accurate measurement is required to bring them back to factory specifications. In the repair process great care must be used so as not to ruin or destroy the integrity of the passive safety design of these vehicles.

The fundamental approach to a basic understanding of frame construction as it relates to body-frame straightening is known as *the four controlling points*. The controlling points of any car frame are the front cross-member, the cross-member at the cowl, the cross-member at the rear door, and the rear cross-member (Figs. 10-8 and 10-9).

A frame or unitized body is divided into three sections: the front section, the center section, and the rear section (Fig. 10-10). Each is bordered by a cross-member or a controlling point. This establishes the basis for all frame-straightening procedures. Figure 10-11 is an example of unitized construction.

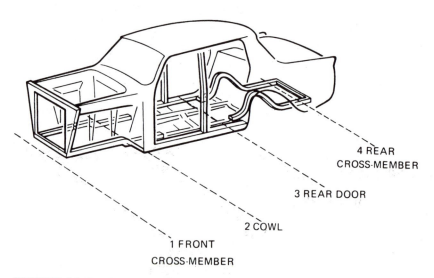

4 REAR
CROSS-MEMBER

3 REAR DOOR

2 COWL

1 FRONT
CROSS-MEMBER

FIGURE 10-8 Concept of four controlling points unitized body-frame design). (Courtesy of Bear Manufacturing Co.).

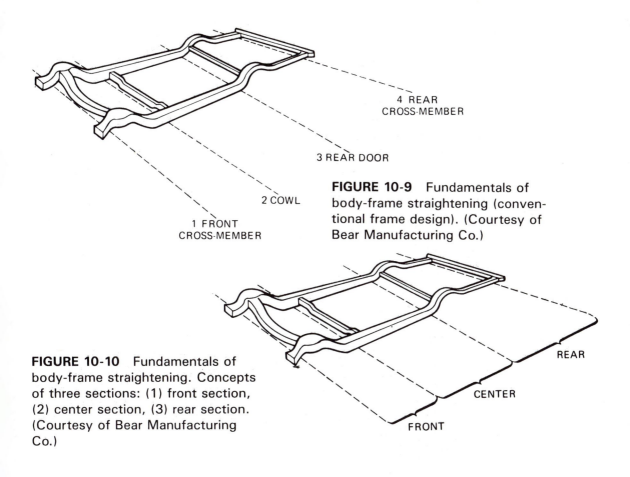

4 REAR
CROSS-MEMBER

3 REAR DOOR

2 COWL

1 FRONT
CROSS-MEMBER

FIGURE 10-9 Fundamentals of body-frame straightening (conventional frame design). (Courtesy of Bear Manufacturing Co.)

FIGURE 10-10 Fundamentals of body-frame straightening. Concepts of three sections: (1) front section, (2) center section, (3) rear section. (Courtesy of Bear Manufacturing Co.)

REAR

CENTER

FRONT

FIGURE 10-11 Lower half of unit must be stiff and strong if a frame structure A is used to support body and running gear. Unitized bottom section B can be kept light, as it depends on upper half of body to complete box section structure. Welding, instead of nuts and bolts, reduces the rattles. (Courtesy of Bear Manufacturing Co.)

WHAT . . . ?   WHY . . . ?   HOW . . . ?

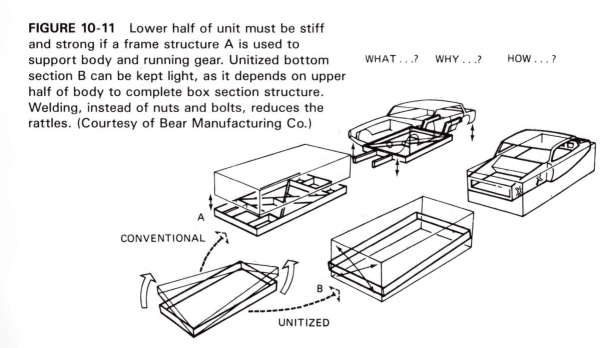

A

CONVENTIONAL

B

UNITIZED

UNIT 10-2: GAUGES

Collision damage almost always occurs at the controlling points. Upon impact, both frame side rails will move together. One possible exception is the direct impact incurred in the side of the vehicle. When there is no cross member at the controlling points, these points are then called *areas*, such as the cowl area or the rear door area. The frame-centering gauges are positioned at the controlling points. They are used to diagnose the damage that may be present in the frame.

Each frame-centering gauge is a self-centering unit that has sliding dowel pins at the tip of each leg to provide a simple means of attaching it to either the inside or the outside of box- or channel-type side rails (Fig. 10-12). On certain types of frames, it is necessary to use magnetic holders to hold the gauges, for certain holes or flanges may not be accessible. At times it is also necessary to use extensions to provide clearance and ease of sighting.

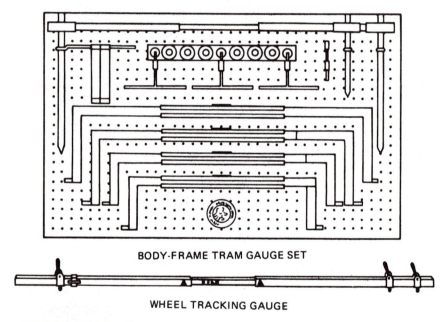

BODY-FRAME TRAM GAUGE SET

WHEEL TRACKING GAUGE

FIGURE 10-12 Step 1: Diagnosis, tools, and gauges. (Courtesy of Bear Manufacturing Co.)

When checking for sidesway, sag, mash, and twist frame damage, the gauges should be installed as in Fig. 10-13. The four locations are the front cross-member, the cowl area, the rear door area, and the rear cross-member. For easier sighting, the gauges with short legs should be attached at the cowl and rear door

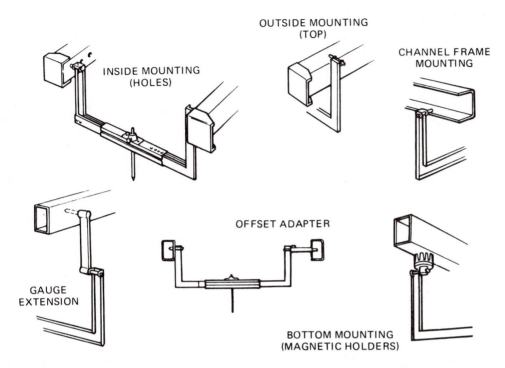

INSIDE MOUNTING
(HOLES)

OUTSIDE MOUNTING
(TOP)

CHANNEL FRAME
MOUNTING

GAUGE
EXTENSION

OFFSET ADAPTER

BOTTOM MOUNTING
(MAGNETIC HOLDERS)

FIGURE 10-13   (Courtesy of Bear Manufacturing Co.)

areas. It is important that the gauges be mounted in identical holes or areas on each side rail and that they be in contact with the side rails. This condition will allow the sighting pins to align and center themselves in the center of the gauge.

Tram Gauges

Tram gauges are used to measure car bodies and frames to help pinpoint the damage. In this case the proper measurements from blueprints must be available (Fig. 10-14). With the accurate measurements, it is easy to find where the damage in a particular area is and to repair it to specifications.

The tram gauge and measuring tape may be used to measure many types of damage if used properly. It must be remembered that all vehicles have a center-line, and this is the base for using centering gauges. The vehicle also has a lot of diagonal measurements, and this is where a tram gauge is very useful, to measure a diagonal measurement from point to point and then compare this measurement with the corresponding opposite points within a control area or length (Fig. 10-15).

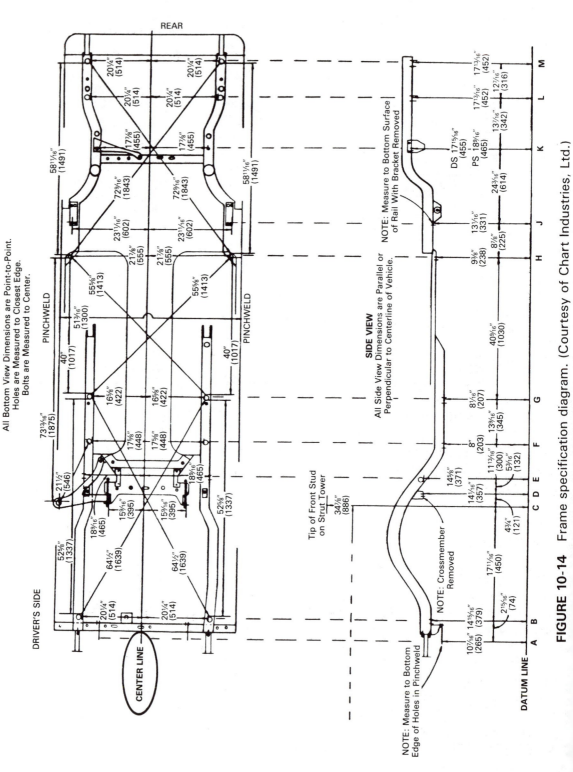

FIGURE 10-14 Frame specification diagram. (Courtesy of Chart Industries, Ltd.)

326

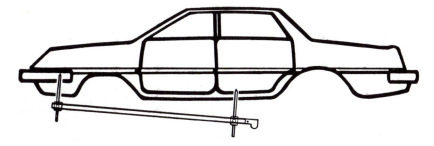

FIGURE 10-15　Point-to-point measuring. (Courtesy of Chart Industries, Ltd.)

The tram gauge may also be used for linear measurements on the datum line. To do this the tram gauge is adjusted for the proper length required and then the measurements from the datum line to the area being measured must be applied to the pointers or measuring rods on the tram gauge. (Fig. 10-16).

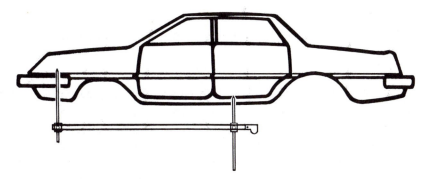

FIGURE 10-16　Linear measurement on datum line. (Courtesy of Chart Industries, Ltd.)

When doing these measurements the specifications must be checked carefully, as some of the locations or control points are symmetrical and some are asymmetrical. Check Fig. 10-34 from the strut tower to cowl; the measurements are not the same, so they are asymmetrical.

A datum line is an imaginary horizontal line that appears on frame blueprints or charts to help determine correct frame heights. Vertical measurements from specific points on the frame to the imaginary line are given on the blueprints (Fig. 10-14). When checking the datum line, the gauges should be attached to or hung from the frame at the vertical measurement locations indicated on the blueprint (Fig. 10-17).

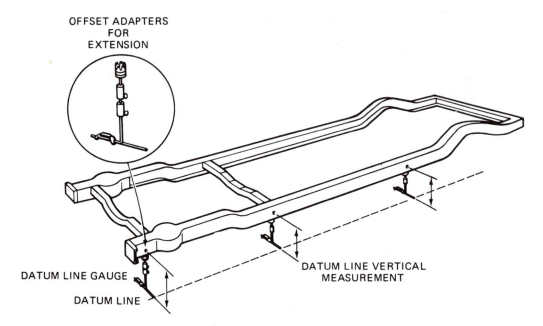

OFFSET ADAPTERS
FOR
EXTENSION

DATUM LINE GAUGE

DATUM LINE

DATUM LINE VERTICAL
MEASUREMENT

FIGURE 10-17   Datum line checking. (Courtesy of Bear Manufacturing Co.)

The cross-bars should be adjusted for the specified vertical measurement for that location. If the frame is at the correct height, the cross-bars will all be in line when they are sighted, indicating that the datum line is correct.

When the repairman is doing the different operations required to straighten a frame, he must keep in mind that the frame has to be brought back to the manufacturer's specifications (Table 10-1). If the frame is not returned to specifications, the vehicle may not drive properly or it may be impossible to fit the sheet metal on the body. Frames that have torque boxes must be returned to within 1/16 in. (1½ mm) of the specifications in the location to the rails and length from one torque box to the other.

TABLE 10-1   Factory tolerances for frame adjustment.

Passenger Cars	*Trucks*
Sidesway 1/8 in. (3 mm)	Sidesway 1/4 in. (6 mm)
Sag 1/8 in. (3 mm)	Sag 1/4 in. (6 mm)
Mash 1/16 in. (1½ mm)	Diamond 1/4 in. (6 mm)
Diamond 1/8 in. (3 mm)	Twist 1/4 in. (6 mm)
Twist 1/8 in. (3 mm)	

Tracking

After the frame has been repaired and the wheels aligned, the vehicle should then be checked to see if the wheels are tracking properly. Tracking means that the rear wheels follow the front wheels in a parallel position. To check tracking, the gauge is adjusted to the distance between the front and rear wheels on one side of the vehicle and compared with the other side (Figs. 10-18 and 10-19). The proper procedure to follow is to split the toe-in; the gauge is set to the approximate length of the wheelbase. The pointers are aligned, one at the front and two at the rear. The pointers are adjusted to make contact between the tire and rim at axle height; the setting is then compared with the other side. Hookups, hold-downs, and corrective pressures are usually applied at the controlling points, very rarely in between.

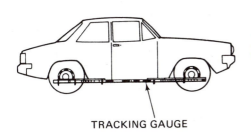

TRACKING GAUGE

TO CHECK TRACKING: ADJUST GAUGE TO THE DIS-TANCE BETWEEN THE FRONT AND THE REAR WHEELS ON ONE SIDE OF THE VEHICLE AND COMPARE WITH THE OTHER SIDE. MANUFACTURER'S SPECS. ON FRONT POINTER ONLY:

$\frac{1}{8}''$ (3 mm) TOLERANCE FOR PASSENGER CARS

$\frac{1}{4}''$ (6 mm) TOLERANCE FOR TRUCKS

NO OPEN POINTERS AT THE REAR

FIGURE 10-18   (Courtesy of Bear Manufacturing Co.)

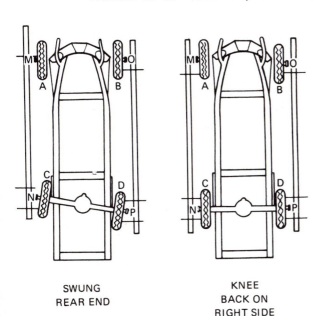

SWUNG
REAR END

KNEE
BACK ON
RIGHT SIDE

FIGURE 10-19 Tracking examples. (Courtesy of Bear Manufacturing Co.)

From a repairer's point of view, the basic difference between conventional frame and unitized construction vehicles is the difference in the correction procedure. Vehicles with unitized construction require that the body and frame be straightened and aligned together. This also applies for conventional frames, especially for rear-end and side collisions.

When repairing unitized construction vehicles, the body man must be able to measure accurately when the body or the body panels have been realigned to their proper position. This measuring is usually done via the X-checking method, which provides fast and accurate measurements (Fig. 10-20).

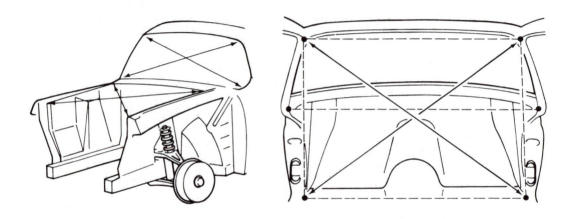

WHEELHOUSE PANEL MEASURING   TRUNK OPENING MEASURING

FIGURE 10-20   Typical body-measuring points. (Courtesy of Bear Manufacturing Co.)

Dimensions covering frames, door openings, trunk openings, and floor panels are available from manufacturers. If required, measurements can also be taken from a similar model which is not damaged.

UNIT 10-3: TYPES OF BODY-FRAME MISALIGNMENT

Five different types of frame damage can occur, depending on the type of collision—sidesway, sag, mash, diamond, and twist. Each condition is illustrated below, and each applies to both conventional frame and unitized construction vehicles.

Sidesway is when the front or rear section side rails are bent to the right or left (Fig. 10-21). Side-rail sag misalignment of the frame is caused by the buck-

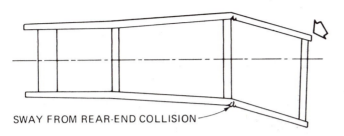

SWAY FROM REAR-END COLLISION

FIGURE 10-21 (Courtesy of Bear Manufacturing Co.).

ling of the left or right side rail, or both, upon impact (Fig. 10-22). The weight of the motor or the body usually forces the side rail to drop. The buckles in the side rail are always on the top when sag is present. When the frame receives a heavy impact, the side rail will also bend in another area or controlling point. Mash will occur behind the front cross-member or over the rear axle. In a mash, the side rail buckles underneath; the sag has the buckles on top (Fig. 10-23).

SIDE RAIL SAG FROM FRONT-END COLLISION

SIDE RAIL SAG FROM REAR-END COLLISION

FIGURE 10-22   (Courtesy of Bear Manufacturing Co.)

FRAME MASHED AND BUCKLED FROM FRONT-END COLLISION

FRAME MASHED AND BUCKLED FROM REAR-END COLLISION

FIGURE 10-23   (Courtesy of Bear Manufacturing Co.)

Diamond damage results from a heavy impact, sufficient to push the side rail back, on the corner of either side rail of the frame. As a result, the cross members are pushed out of a right angle with the side rail (Fig. 10-24).

A twisted frame usually results from a collision on a frame carrying a heavy

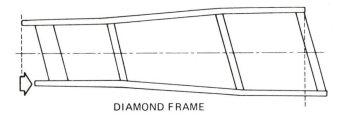

DIAMOND FRAME

FIGURE 10-24 Diamond frame. (Courtesy of Bear Manufacturing Co.)

FIGURE 10-25 Twisted frame. (Courtesy of Bear Manufacturing Co.)

load that causes it to turn over and twist the side rails out of horizontal alignment (Fig. 10-25).

When a vehicle is involved in an accident, it should always have a body-frame alignment checkup to determine the amount of damage.

When a vehicle has been struck in the front, whether it is a conventional frame or unitized, the order of damage that will result in the frame will generally be as follows: The first condition will be sidesway, then sag, mash, diamond, and twist, depending on the impact.

Regardless of the severity of the impact, a certain amount of sidesway can be expected when the frame is hit. When the vehicle is struck in a more severe collision, sag will occur. Mash will occur if sidesway exceeds 1/2 in. (13 mm) or if sag exceeds 3/8 in. (9 mm). Diamond and twist will occur in severe collisions with certain types of frames. Unitized construction is especially resistant to diamond and twist damage.

Vehicles with conventional frames when struck in the rear will probably have the following conditions: mash, sidesway, and sag. Twist could be present, but as the mash, sag, and sidesway are removed, the twist will also be corrected. Since the rear part of the frame is very elastic, it will absorb a severe impact and not diamond the center section of the frame.

Vehicles with unitized construction, when struck in the rear, will follow the same order of frame damage as when struck in the front section. These are sidesway, sag, and mash.

Sidesway

Three centering gauges are used to check the frame for sidesway. When the vehicle has been struck from the front, the gauges are attached at the front cross-member, the cowl area, and the rear door area. Since the sighting pins are self-centering, the pins are always in the center of the gauge. The best method to

SIDESWAY DIAGNOSIS (FRONT)

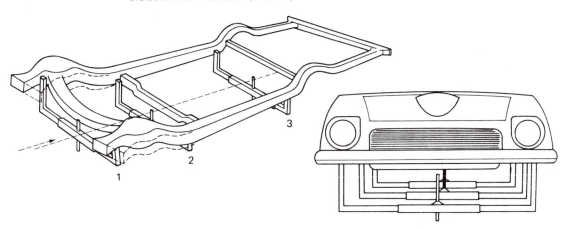

FIGURE 10-26 To check sidesway misalignment, place three frame-centering gauges at the controlling points and sight gauge pointers. The direction and amount of front sidesway are determined from the position of gauge pointer 1. (Courtesy of Bear Manufacturing Co.)

check the frame is to align the sighting pins on gauges 2 and 3. If the sighting pin on gauge 1 does not line up with the pins on the other gauges, the frame has sidesway (Fig. 10-26); if it lines up, it has no sidesway.

When the frame has been struck in the rear and sag is present at the rear door area, one gauge is attached at the cowl area, one is at the rear door area, and the gauge at the rear is installed in front of the mash condition. When checking the sag at the rear, the centering gauge is never installed at the rear cross member. A mash in the frame over the rear housing will interfere with a true sag measurement or reading. Sighting from the rear of the vehicle, the bottom bars of the first two centering gauges should be horizontally in line with each other. The sag is located on the side behind the high corner of the gauge.

Sag

Three centering gauges are used to check for a sag condition; it is a condition that can usually be noticed since the top of the front door and front fender usually overlap one another. One gauge is placed at the front cross-member, the next one at the cowl area, and the third one at the rear door area.

To find the side of the vehicle and the amount of sag present at the cowl area, the bottom bars of the first two frame-centering gauges are sighted to determine if they are horizontally in line with one another. If they are, there is

FIGURE 10-27 (Courtesy of Bear Manufacturing Co.)

no sag. If sag is present, it will be found on the side behind the high corner of the front gauge. The bars of the gauge are usually 1 in. (25 mm) wide; this helps to determine the amount of sag (Fig. 10-27).

Very often a vehicle will have both sidesway and sag. To determine the amount of sag present, the low corner of the front gauge is raised until the pointer is perpendicular; then by sighting along the centering pins the amount of sidesway will be determined when a frame also has sag.

Mash

A mash occurs directly behind the front cross-member or above the rear housing. Buckles appear on the underside of the rail; this bending will cause the rail to become shorter in length. To find the amount of mash in the front frame, it is measured from the cowl area to the front cross-member. The measurements are taken from holes or rivet heads and then compared to the other side rail. The difference in the measurement between the two rails is the amount of mash present (Fig. 10-28). A frame that has been struck in the rear is measured for mash from the rear door area to the end of the frame.

If the frame has been struck head-on and both rails are mashed, it is then necessary to refer to the manufacturer's blueprints or a similar, undamaged model for the correct specifications.

Diamond

A diamond condition in a frame always occurs in the center section between the cowl area and the rear door area. A diagonal or X-ing measurement is used through the center section of the frame. The side rail that has been pushed back will have a longer diagonal measurement than the other. The frame is always

MASH DIAGNOSIS (FRONT)

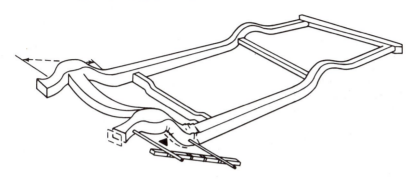

FIGURE 10-28 To check mash misalignments measure from a point at the front cross-member to a point on the side rail at the cowl area. Compare length measurement to that of opposite side rail and car blueprint specifications. (Courtesy of Bear Manufacturing Co.)

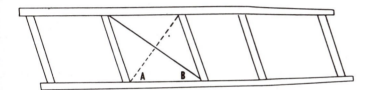

FIGURE 10-29 Diamond frame. (Courtesy of Bear Manufacturing Co.)

measured in the center; this eliminates interference from other collision damage that could make it impossible to obtain an accurate measurement (Fig. 10-29).

Twist

A twisted frame is checked by attaching two centering gauges on the center section of the frame, one at the cowl area and one at the rear door area. To check the direction and amount of twist, sight along the bottom bars of the frame-centering gauges. If the gauges are parallel, the frame is not damaged; but if they are not parallel, the frame is twisted (Fig. 10-30).

Therefore, when a vehicle is repaired, the passive safety or integrity of the design of the body shell and passenger compartment must not be compromised. The key to successful repairs will depend on an accurate diagnosis of the damage that has occurred in the collision.

In diagnosing the damage, a visual inspection is usually done first, such as

FIGURE 10-30   Twist. (Courtesy of Bear Manufacturing Co.)

checking the overall body lines, relationship of one panel to the other, the riding height of the vehicle at all four corners, and the impact angle.

The direct damage is then checked, such as buckled or wrinkled sheet metal, paint and sealer splits, and stretched and split spot welds. The indirect damage, including cracked glass, tension or pressure spots, sagged doors, uneven gaps, and poor fit on trunk lid or hood, is checked next.

On the inside, the steering column and the steering operation must be checked. The dash and lower panels, the space between the weather strip and door panels, buckled floor sections, deformed parcel shelf, and pulled spot welds must all be inspected for damage.

To determine all the damage that has occurred to the underbody, the vehicle must be checked for datum line, centerline, and all required linear references.

After completing this inspection and measurements, specific facts about the vehicle should be revealed. The inspection should show how much of the vehicle is damaged, as well as the underbody and the angle of the impact and how the forces have entered to the vehicle.

It must be realized that the damage in this type of vehicle will not be the same as in the conventional frame and body, as they respond differently to an impact to a certain degree. This is why such a careful diagnosis and inspection with a systematic approach must be carried out, so as not to miss any area of damage. Some of the most important points to remember as the diagnosis is done are the features listed in Fig. 10-31.

The information obtained by the diagnosis will determine the specific nature and type of damage, the area or location, and the extent of it in inches or millimeters. This is accomplished with complete and careful measurements of the underbody and comparing these to the factory specifications (Figs. 10-32 to 10-35).

It must be remembered that these structures are designed to transfer the damaging force of the impact into the larger adjacent panels to absorb and dis-

(I) LIGHTER GUAGE METAL THROUGHOUT STRUCTURAL MEMBERS.

(II) EXTENSIVE USE OF COATED STEELS, HIGH STRENGTH STEEL, ALLUMINUM, PLASTICS.

(III) STRUCTURAL PARTS OF BODY USED FOR ATTACHMENT OF MECHANICAL COMPONENTS.

(Iv) MORE CONTROL POINTS TO MONITOR IN DAMAGE ANALYSIS.

(v) CLOSE TOLERANCE CONSTRUCTION - LESS THE 3mm.

(vI) MORE PASSIVE SAFETY DESIGN.

(vII) FRONT WHEEL DRIVE, RACK AND PINION STEERING, MACPERSON STRUT SUSPENSION.

(vIII) IMPACT FORCES TRANSFERRED INTO LARGER ADJACENT PANELS.

(Ix) PASSENGER COMPARTMENT DESIGNED TO STAY INTACT UNDER SEVERE IMPACT.

FIGURE 10-31 Features of unitized body construction. (Courtesy of Chart Industries, Ltd.)

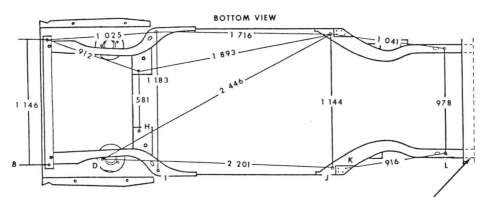

BOTTOM VIEW

1. ALL DIMENSIONS ARE METRIC (Millimeters)
2. ALL CONTROL POINTS ARE SYMMETRICAL SIDE TO SIDE
3. ALL TOLERANCES ± 3mm

X-08-11-68 STYLES SHOWN
X-37-69 STYLES ARE 71mm LONGER

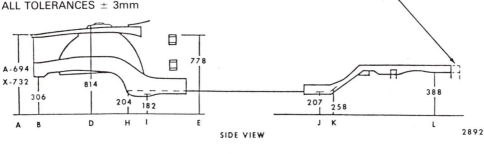

SIDE VIEW

(A)

FIGURE 10-32 (A) Horizontal and vertical dimensions. (Courtesy of General Motors of Canada, Ltd.)

BOTTOM VIEW

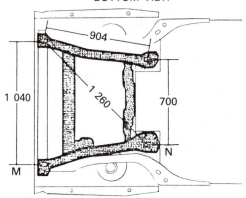

1. ALL DIMENSIONS ARE METRIC (Millimeters)
2. ALL CONTROL POINTS ARE SYMMETRICAL SIDE TO SIDE
3. ALL TOLERANCES ± 3mm

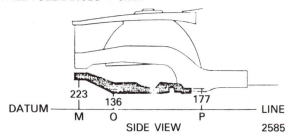

DATUM ——— LINE

SIDE VIEW   2585

(B)

(C) 1. ALL DIMENSIONS ARE METRIC (Millimeters)
2. ALL CONTROL POINTS ARE SYMMETRICAL SIDE TO SIDE
3. ALL TOLERANCES ± 3mm

TOP VIEW

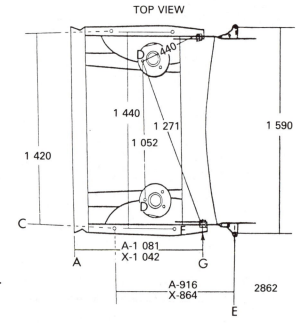

FIGURE 10-32   (cont.)
(B) Engine cradle
horizontal and vertical
dimensions; (C)
suspension strut tower
dimensions, front door
and hood hinge locations.
(Courtesy of General
Motors of Canada, Ltd.)

338

Ref.	Horizontal	Vertical	Location
A	Leading edge	Upper surface at corner	Engine compartment bar upper rail
B	Center of 16 mm (5/8 in.) gauge hole	Lower surface at gauge hole	Lower engine compartment front panel, outboard of cradle attaching hole
C	A: Center of 18 mm (11/16 in.) gauge hole X: Center of 9 mm (23/64 in.) gauge hole	None	A: Engine compartment side rail X: Engine compartment side rail in depression
D	Center of strut shock tower, front attaching hole	Upper surface at strut shock tower, front attaching hole	Strut shock tower
E	Center of front upper hinge pin hole	Upper surface at hinge pin hole	Front upper door hinge, body side
F	Center of 9 mm (23/64 in.) gauge hole	None	A: Engine compartment side rail X: Engine compartment side rail in depression
G	Top surface of hood hinge, centered with rivet	None	Hood hinge
H	Center of 16 mm (5/8 in.) gauge hole	Lower surface at gauge hole	Reinforcement No. 1 floor pan bar, inboard of cradle attachment hole
I	Center of 16 mm (5/8 in.) gauge hole	Lower surface at gauge hole	Engine compartment side rail, rearward and outboard of slot in rail
J	Front edge of 20 mm (13/16 in.) gauge hole	Lower surface at gauge hole	Compartment pan longitudinal rail, forward of control arm reinforcement
K	Center of control arm rear inboard attaching hole	Lower surface at rear inboard attaching hole	Compartment pan longitudinal rail control arm reinforcement
L	Front edge of 20 mm (13/16 in.) gauge hole	Lower surface at gauge hole	Compartment pan longitudinal rail, rearward of slot in rail
M	Center of front cradle attaching hole	Lower surface at front attaching hole	Engine cradle
N	Center of rear cradle attaching hole	None	Engine cradle
O	None	Lower surface of cradle at cross-member	Engine cradle
P	None	Upper surface of cradle at rear edge	Engine cradle

FIGURE 10-33 Horizontal and vertical locations. (Courtesy of General Motors of Canada, Ltd.)

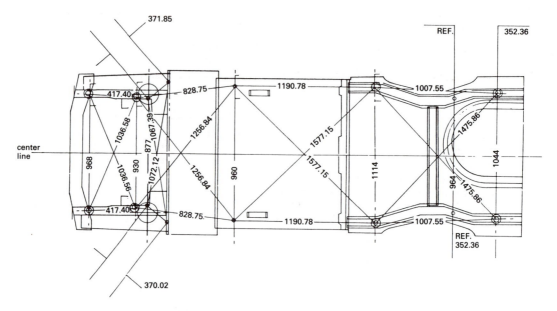

FIGURE 10-34   Underbody dimensions. (Courtesy of Ford Motor Company of Canada, Ltd.)

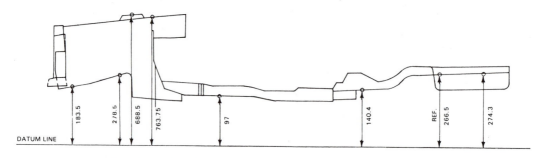

FIGURE 10-35   (Courtesy of Ford Motor Company of Canada, Ltd.)

sipate the collision forces. In cases where primary damages seem quite light, the possibility of severe extensive damage may exist. Never be fooled by the first appearance and restrict the measurements to the damaged area rather than measuring the whole vehicle, and be sure of the facts as they are gathered. This is done to determine how much of the vehicle is damaged and how much of it is free of damage. The principles of body-frame straightening have not really changed except that the repairs have to be done with greater care and precision on the new unitized HSS-constructed vehicles. Multiple hookups provide a fast and efficient method for the realignment of damaged parts. The body and frame structures must be straightened and aligned together. On unitized vehicles, whenever possible, standard or conventional body panels are not removed or replaced until the body and frame have been aligned.

Because of the design of the new automobiles, they tend to have more control points built into the vehicle, and many of them are contained within the body shell itself. A good definition of control points is reference points on each side rail, usually jig holes which allow the repairer to determine, by measurement, if the structure meets its designed specifications (Figs. 10-34 and 10-35).

All reference points must meet specifications to all other designated points by measuring within tolerance from the vehicle centerline out, from the datum line up to the member, and jig holes from each other linearly. By using this method the repairer will know that the correct alignment of the body shell is accurate when specifications are within tolerance.

Many of these control points will affect the wheel alignment and steering geometry. When the repairer does this type of correction, he must be mindful of the caster and camber, as these angles will change simultaneously when aligning the damaged sections. The repairer must be careful not to overcorrect one set of control points when trying to achieve dimensions in another area. Such situations can be controlled by constantly monitoring all the major control points, to recognize any movement, direction of movement, or nonmovement in the undamaged areas.

Because of the close tolerances of the all-welded construction, great care has to be taken that the measurements be taken with great accuracy, within 1/8 in. (3 mm) of factory specifications. Failure to achieve proper measurements may produce a vehicle that has poor panel alignment and may handle and drive poorly.

UNIT 10-4: STRAIGHTENING THE BODY AND FRAME

Depending on the type of equipment available, the shop will vary some of the hookup techniques. A manual should be obtained from the manufacturer of the equipment to obtain the proper methods to be used to correct the damage in the vehicle. The following steps will apply in most cases to the job of straightening frames for both conventional frame construction and unitized vehicles.

Conventional Frame Construction

1. The wheels, bumper, and sheet metal that will interfere with frame correction and installation of equipment attachments should be removed; body bolts should not be loosened or removed.

2. Suspension assembly or assemblies are removed.

3. A wire brush is used to clean the buckles or cracked areas.

4. All breaks in the frame are welded to avoid further tearing of the metal while it is being straightened.

5. Damaged frame horns are roughed-out in preparation for installing hookups.

Unitized Vehicles

1. Sheet metal and the bumper are removed only if absolutely required; when straightening unitized vehicles, it is required that all component parts be straightened on the vehicle as much as possible. This is to increase or gain as much support as possible when pressure is applied when straightening the body and reinforcing structures.

2. The power train and suspension assemblies on older unitized and newer unitized HSS-constructed vehicles are removed as required.

3. A wire brush is used to clean the buckled or cracked areas.

4. All breaks in the frame and body panels are welded to avoid further tearing of the metal while the frame and body are being straightened.

5. After all welding is completed, HSS welded areas are primed with a zinc primer.

Body-frame damage is always removed in the opposite direction from that of the impact. In most cases, the damage is removed by pulling instead of pushing. The use of heat is minimized; as much of the work as possible is done by cold-working. The work can be done on either a frame rack or a movable straightening system (Fig. 10-36).

With the unlimited power available the operator must be careful not to tear body panels and frame members as they are being pulled out. Thus a hammer is used to relax the buckles until a silver streak appears in the center of the buckle; then and only then is heat applied. Using a large tip and a neutral flame, the body man heats the area to cherry red as more pressure is applied to the member on conventional construction.

When a frame is being straightened, it is always necessary to overcorrect to allow for springback. Unitized construction does not require as much over-correction as the conventional type of frame. As the frame is being straightened, the body panels should also be pulled, for this saves time and helps to relieve strains on both the body and frame.

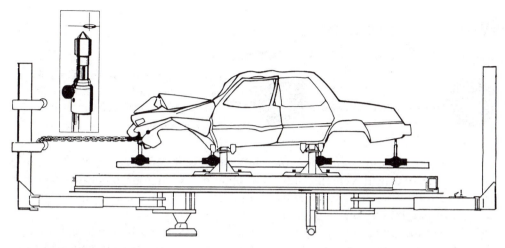

FIGURE 10-36 Accu-Rack and Exacto gauge. (Courtesy of Chart Industries, Ltd.)

The stretch and pull hookup is first attached on the side of the vehicle having the most damage. This hookup serves as the basic hookup that is used to remove all other types of frame misalignment except twist.

When a collision of any consequence occurs, damage to the structure will seldom be in a single direction (Fig. 10-37). The damage from the collision will usually affect the vehicle in several directions simultaneously and will occur in an orderly fashion. When a vehicle is hit in the front (Fig. 10-38), it will cause a shortness of length first, then height, width, side movement, and so on. Visualize the damage as it occurs because the repair will logically have to reverse the sequence. Therefore, the hookups will have to pull out the damage in the proper sequence, either along or with the other damage in the reverse order in which it happened. To avoid problems with overpulling some areas and underpulling others, this method should be followed strictly while still trying to achieve overall dimensions.

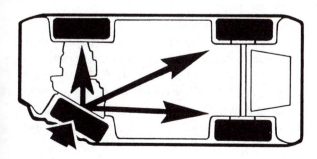

FIGURE 10-37 Direction that damage travels. (Courtesy of Chart Industries, Ltd.)

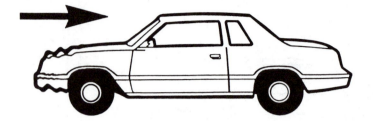

FIGURE 10-38 Crushing due to front-end collision. (Courtesy of Chart Industries, Ltd.)

The type of equipment available in the shop will vary some of the hookups, but the new unitized vehicles must be anchored with four pinch-weld clamp systems on the rocker panels. It may be necessary to have additional tie-downs to control height and side movement.

Proper alignment of the sheet metal will not occur until the internal stresses from the impact are relieved. This will allow the dimensions to remain when the corrective hookups are released. The stress relief may be done cold in some cases, and in other cases heat must be applied.

As the corrective forces are applied, movement will occur in the areas where secondary damage has occurred. As these secondary damaged areas move, work the ridges and buckles slowly while raising low metal (Fig. 10-39).

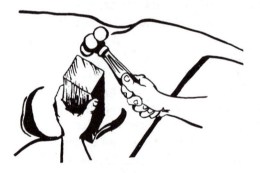

FIGURE 10-39 Relieving stresses using a block of wood and hammer. (Courtesy of Chart Industries, Ltd.)

If the metal should tear, it should be rewelded as realignment occurs. This type of construction and metal must be worked slowly to allow time for the metal to reposition itself in its proper shape or space.

Since HSS is used in most structural members, care must be used when applying heat. Heat-stress relief will work best at the critical temperature of approximately 900°F, or 371°C, or blue in color. Some manufacturers may recommend slightly higher heat but never more than 1400°F or 760°C. These ranges are acceptable for most HSS specifications depending on the domestic manufacturer, as long as the area is not heated for more than a total of 3 minutes. A heat crayon (Fig. 10-40) should be used to guide the repairer for higher-temperature exposure of panel.

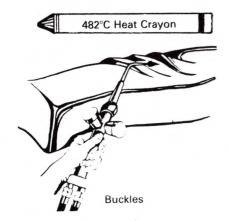

FIGURE 10-40 Heat crayon. (Courtesy of Chart Industries, Ltd.)

Heat should be applied along the edges of the damaged members, around spot welds, because this is where compression occurs (Fig. 10-41). Heat should never be applied to the side surfaces of any box-shaped members.

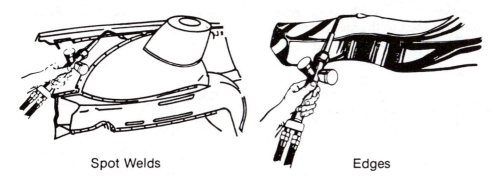

Spot Welds   Edges

FIGURE 10-41 Heat application. (Courtesy of Chart Industries, Ltd.)

The first type of frame damage that must be removed is the diamond (Fig. 10–42). During the straightening procedure, a careful diagonal measurement must be taken at the center section to ensure that the cross-members are brought back to right angles and that the diagonal measurements are equal.

Mash is the next frame condition that has to be corrected. The proper hookup is installed and the side rail is then stretched back to meet the specifications from the manufacturer's blueprint. As mash is removed it is important to check the distance from the center of the lower ball joint to the specified area on the frame. If the distance is not equal to within 1/8 in. (3 mm), one of the wheels or both wheels will not be in their proper location. This could cause the car to pull to

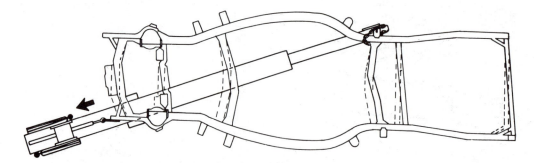

FIGURE 10-42 A diamond frame (top view) results from an impact on either corner of the car frame, sufficient to push one side rail out of square with the opposite side rail. The entire vehicle frame is affected. (Courtesy of Bear Manufacturing Co.)

the short side of the vehicle and could make a proper alignment almost impossible; this condition is often referred to as a *knee-back*. Therefore, careful measurements must be taken to assure that the proper distance from the center of the lower ball joint to the specified point on the frame is reached (Fig. 10-43).

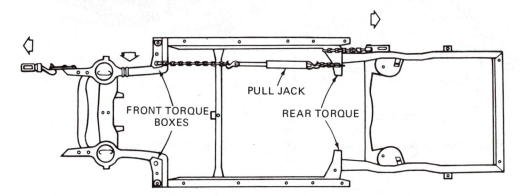

FIGURE 10-43 Torque box alignment and length measurements are most critical. With mash hookup, first restore original front-to-rear torque box dimension. Then install pull jack to prevent overpull. Continue mash correction procedures. (Courtesy of Bear Manufacturing Co.)

A mash at the rear requires the same type of hookup except that it is reversed; when removing mash on unitized vehicles, refer to sag corrections. When removing sag the rail is held as in Figs. 10-44 and 10-45, and the sagged rail is jacked up a bit past the correct height and then normalized and released to see

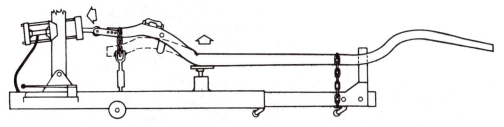

FIGURE 10-44 Sag. (Courtesy of Bear Manufacturing Co.)

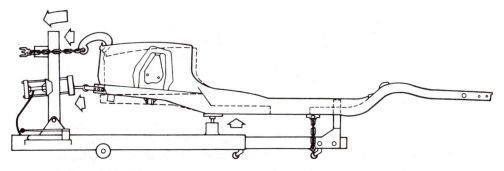

FIGURE 10-45 Front mash and sag correction hookup—unitized body. (Courtesy of Bear Manufacturing Co.)

if it is at the proper height. If the rail is not at the proper height, it must be jacked higher until proper alignment is achieved. Wood or steel plates must always be used when padding is required; otherwise, crushing of the panels can occur (Fig. 10-46).

When diamond, sag, and mash conditions have been repaired, the next condition to repair is sidesway (Fig. 10-47). The proper hookup is attached and the frame is pulled back until the sighting pins on the centering gauges remain in line. On unitized vehicles, it is necessary to correct the body or wheelhouse section at the same time (Fig. 10-48).

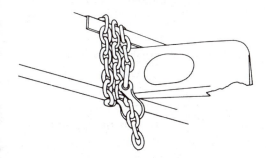

FIGURE 10-46 Padded section.

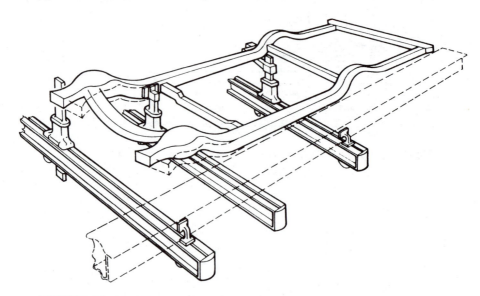

FIGURE 10-47 Sidesway (basic correction hookup). Whenever sidesway exceeds ½ in. (13 mm), use stretch and hookup pull. Sidesway has been corrected when the three pointers of the frame centering gauges are in line.

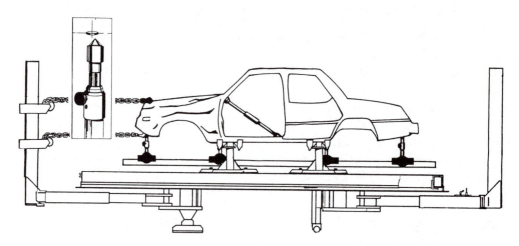

FIGURE 10-48 Sidesway correction hookup—unitized body (side view). (Courtesy of Chart Industries, Ltd.)

The last condition of frame damage to be corrected is the twist, and again the equipment available will determine the hookup. The two high points are attached to the frame machine to hold them when hydraulic pressure is applied to the two low corners. Figure 10-49 shows a typical hookup on a frame rack.

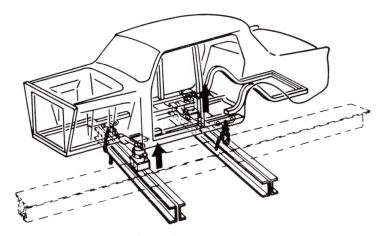

FIGURE 10-49 Unitized body frame. (Courtesy of Bear Manufacturing Co.)

The low corners will have to be raised equally high enough and the body and frame normalized as in all other conditions; if it returns after the first push, the operation must be repeated until the gauges at the cowl and rear door are parallel horizontally.

The last damage to repair is the finishing of the frame horns that were roughly aligned to facilitate the hookups necessary to start the repair of the frame. Whether the horns are repaired or replaced, they have to be returned to their proper place in relation to the frame center line and datum line. If they are not in their proper location, it will be impossible to install the front end on the car and make it to fit to the body. Figure 10-50 shows the methods used to align the horns properly by using a tape measure and the centering gauges.

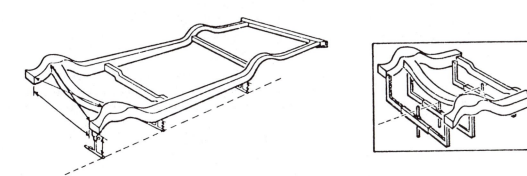

FIGURE 10-50 Frame-horn alignment is the final step in the body-frame straightening operation. To assure correct alignment, frame-centering gauges, datum-line gauges, x-ing measurements, and car factory blueprints are used.

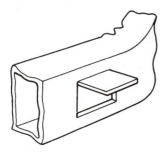

FIGURE 10-51

When the rails have been brought back to their proper location, possibly it is necessary to do metal work on some sections. Doors are sometimes cut in the rail (Fig. 10-51) to enable the straightening of the member; these are welded shut after the repair is completed. Bars forged with different curvatures and hooks are very handy to pull or push existing damage through holes on side rails so that the members or rails are returned to their proper shape for maximum strength.

UNIT 10-5:   WHEEL ALIGNMENT

When a vehicle is involved in an accident in which the frame is bent and the tires or wheels are damaged, it should receive a complete wheel alignment check. A vehicle that has poor or hard steering after an accident will certainly not please the owner. See Table 10-2 for different conditions.

When all the major controlling points on the body have been correctly aligned, the wheels must be checked for their position in relation to the body. The rear wheels should be parallel to the centerline of the vehicle. Since some of the new vehicles have solid rear axles and some have independent suspension, it is imperative that they be checked for toe. The lower ball joints must be in linear alignment to the specifications and the wheel base in proper dimensions (Fig. 10-52). Some of these checks can be done by using a tracking gauge (see Fig. 10-19).

The new unibodies employ inner fender aprons which have strut towers to which the upper part of the McPherson strut assembly is bolted. Rack and pinion steering is used on this type of suspension on most new vehicles. The strut towers have to be placed within specifications to assure that the vehicle will have the proper steering angles (Fig. 10-53). The camber adjustments are on the bottom part of the strut, which is a slotted hole (Fig. 10-53). This slot in the bracket will allow the required adjustments.

Because of the variety of wheel alignment equipment, it is impossible to describe the use of all available types. The student should receive instruction and operating manuals for the particular type of equipment that he will use.

TABLE 10-2 Wheel alignment trouble chart.

Trouble	Camber	Caster	Turning Radius	Toe-In	Steering Gear	Wheels
			Probable Causes*			
Cuppy tire wear						Bent or
Excessive tire wear	Incorrect		Incorrect	Incorrect		out of balance
Pulling to one side	Unequal	Unequal				
Wander or weave		Not enough		Incorrect	Loose or tight	
Hard steering		Too much	Incorrect		Tight	
Excessive road shock		Too much			Loose or worn	Bent
Low-speed shimmy		Too much			Loose or worn	or out of
High-speed shimmy						balance

*Other factors that cause steering trouble and excessive tire wear are faulty brakes and brake drums, bent frame, improperly adjusted front wheel bearings, improper tire inflation, faulty shock absorbers, loose spring shackles, weak springs, and out-of-round tires.

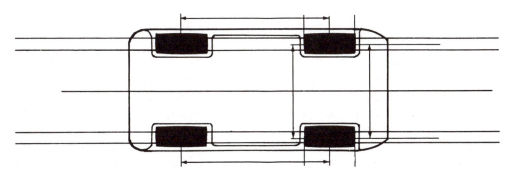

FIGURE 10-52 Wheel alignment to body. (Courtesy of Chart Industries, Ltd.)

The main purpose of wheel alignment is to make the wheels roll without scuffing, dragging, or slipping under all road-operating conditions. The result is greater safety in driving, easier steering, longer tire wear, and less strain on the parts that make up the front end of the automobile. Five simple angles are the

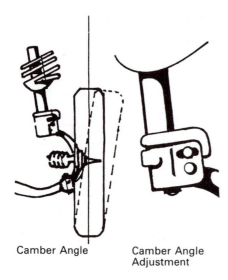

Camber Angle   Camber Angle
                      Adjustment

FIGURE 10-53 McPherson strut camber adjustment. (Courtesy of Chart Industries, Ltd.)

foundation of wheel alignment. These angles are designed by the manufacturer to locate the weight on moving parts properly and to facilitate steering.

Car manufacturers' specifications provide a range that serves as a guide for what each angle should be. Good wheel alignment service maintains the five simple angles within the range of the manufacturer's specifications.

Camber

Camber is the inward or outward tilt of the wheel at the top. It is the tire-wearing angle measured in degrees and is the amount the centerline of the wheel is tilted from true vertical.

Outward tilt of the wheel at the top from true vertical is positive camber (Fig. 10-54). Inward tilt of the wheel at the top from true vertical is negative camber. Manufacturers' specifications indicate negative and positive camber by the letters N and P. Where a letter is not indicated, it is to be regarded as positive camber.

The purpose of camber is to bring the road contact of the tire more nearly under the point of load, to provide easy steering by having the weight of the vehicle borne by the inner wheelbearing and spindle, and to prevent tire wear.

Where camber is within the range of the manufacturer's specifications, the weight of the vehicle is positioned on the spindle and wheel bearings in accordance with the design. Camber will change under weight (passengers and load) to varying degrees because of independent front-end construction. The top of the wheel is allowed to move in and out while the bottom remains stationary. When preferred specifications are given, the camber should be adjusted to the preferred setting. When preferred specifications are not shown, both wheels should be

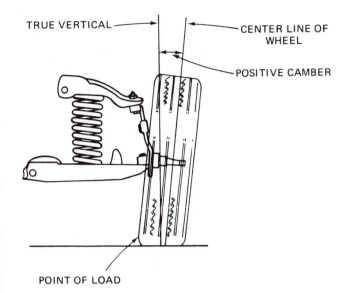

FIGURE 10-54 When the wheel is tilted outward at the top from true vertical, it is known as positive camber. (Courtesy of Bear Manufacturing Co.)

within 1/2° of each other. Generally, zero to positive camber should be maintained.

The harmful effects of incorrect camber are excessive wear to ball joints, wheel bearings, to one side of the tire tread (negative camber, inside wear; positive camber, outside wear). Excessive unequal camber will cause the vehicle to pull to one side.

Steering Axis Inclination

Steering axis inclination is the inward tilt of the king pin or spindle support arm (ball joint) at the top. Steering axis inclination is a directional control angle measured in degrees and is the amount the spindle support center line is tilted from true vertical (Fig. 10-55). This angle is not adjustable.

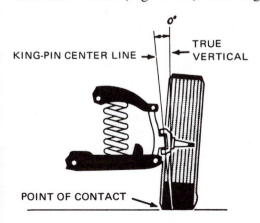

FIGURE 10-55 Steering axis inclination. (Courtesy of Bear Manufacturing Co.)

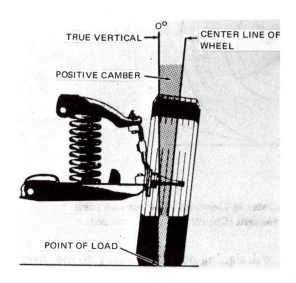

TRUE VERTICAL

0°

CENTER LINE OF WHEEL

POSITIVE CAMBER

POINT OF LOAD

FIGURE 10-56 Camber and steering axis inclination. (Courtesy of Bear Manufacturing Co.)

Figure 10-56 shows the relation of camber to steering axis inclination. This relationship does not change except when the spindle or spindle support arm (ball joint) becomes bent. The purposes of steering axis inclination are to reduce the need for excessive camber, to distribute the weight of the vehicle more nearly under the road contact point of the tire, to provide a pivot point about which the wheel will turn (thereby producing easy steering), and to aid in steering stability.

Caster

Caster is the backward or forward tilt of the king pin or spindle support arm at the top. Caster is a directional control angle measured in degrees and is the amount the centerline of the spindle support arm is tilted from true vertical. Backward tilt of the spindle support arm at the top (Fig. 10-57) is positive caster. Forward tilt of the spindle arm at the top from true vertical is negative caster. Manufacturers' specifications indicate negative and positive caster by the letters N and P. Where a letter is not indicated, it is to be regarded as positive caster.

The purposes of caster are to gain directional control of the vehicle by causing the front wheels to maintain a straight-ahead position or return to a straight-ahead position out of a turn and to offset road crown.

Tilting the spindle support arm gives front wheels the tendency to maintain straight-ahead position by projecting the centerline of the support arm ahead, and establishing a lead point ahead of the point of contact of the wheel, as shown in Fig. 10-57. Proof that the wheels tend to run straight is the fact that bicycles can be ridden without touching the handlebars.

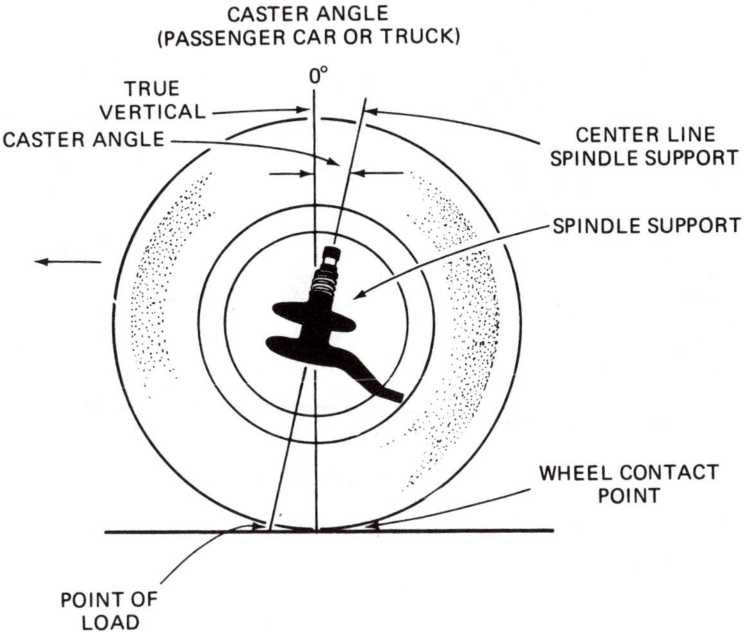

FIGURE 10-57   Principle of caster is identical in either ball joint or king-pin suspension arrangement. (Courtesy of Bear Manufacturing Co.)

Recently, car manufacturers were designing negative caster into the front wheels of their automobiles. Through wider-tread tires and the influence of another angle, steering axis inclination, directional control tendencies are maintained.

Caster is not a tire-wearing angle. Some manufacturers recommended that the right front wheel have more caster toward positive, approximately 1/2°, than the left front wheel to offset road crown. This spread in caster must stay within the range of the car manufacturers' specifications.

The harmful effects of incorrect caster are as follows: Unequal caster will cause the vehicle to pull toward the side of least caster. Too little caster causes wander and weave and instability at high speeds. Too much caster causes hard steering and excessive road shock and shimmy.

In the new unibodies, caster is a built-in feature of most strut suspension-type vehicles. Therefore, the position of the lower control arm and strut assembly in respect to the specifications becomes extremely important. Figure 10-58 shows a typical strut assembly.

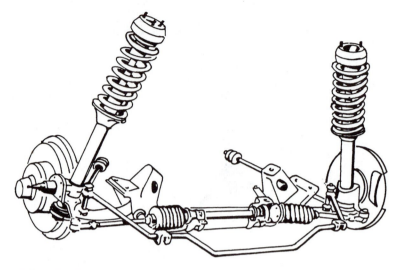

FIGURE 10-58 Strut assembly. (Courtesy of Chart Industries, Ltd.)

Turning Radius

Turning radius means toe-out on turns. The inner front wheel travels a shorter path than the outer front wheel, creating a toe-out condition when the vehicle is turned either to the right or to the left. The design of the steering arms in relation to the wheelbase of the vehicle provides this toe-out on turns.

Turning radius is a tire-wearing angle measured in degrees and is the amount by which one front wheel turns sharper than the other on a turn. The car manufacturer usually allows a difference of 1° between the inner front wheels, when measured on each turn.

Correct turning radius allows the front tires to roll free on turns. For that reason, turning radius will be correct when the other alignment angles are correct, except when a steering arm is bent. Incorrect turning angles will give excessive wear of tires on turns and squealing even at low speeds (Fig. 10-59).

Toe-In

Toe-in is the distance that the front of the front wheels (line B) are closer together than the rear of the front wheels (line A, Fig. 10-60). Toe-out is the distance that the front wheels are farther apart than the rear of the front wheels.

Toe-in is considered the most serious tire-wearing angle of the five, and it is measured in inches (millimeters). Its purpose is to compensate for widened tolerances in the steering linkage. Its characteristic tire wear appears as a feather-

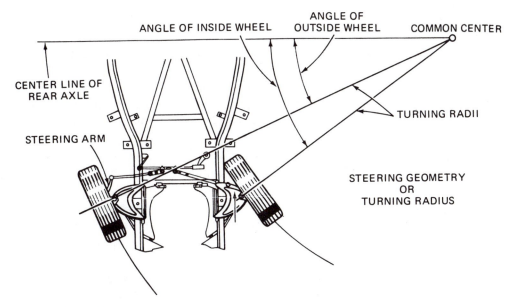

FIGURE 10-59 The wheels turn about a common center determined by the wheelbase of the vehicle. Note that with respect to the common point, the inside wheel is ahead of the outside wheel and makes a sharper angle than the outer one.

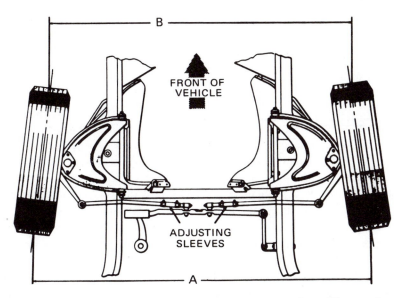

FIGURE 10-60 When the front of the wheels (line B) are closer together than the rear of the wheels (line A), they are said to have toe-in. (Courtesy of Bear Manufacturing Co.)

edged scuff across the face of both tires. It has been found, however, that a little too much toe-in will result in wearing on the outside of the right front tire only. Conversely, a little too much toe-out will result in wear appearing on the inside of the left front tire only.

Toe-in is the last of the alignment angles to be set in any wheel alignment operation. It is adjusted by turning the tie rod adjusting sleeves until the measurement taken at the front of the wheels complies with the the car manufacturer's specifications.

When the toe adjustment is completed, it would be prudent for the repairman to do one more check on the front end. This could possibly pick up a condition which is known in the trade as toe change, bump steer, or orbital steer.

This can be caused by several components, such as bent steering knuckle arms or arm, a damaged or out-of-position engine cradle, or rack and pinion steering gear clamps or brackets. This condition can cause the driver to lose control of the vehicle if it is severe enough.

The simplest way to check this condition is with a tram gauge unless the equipment available for front-end alignment is capable of measuring the toe of each front wheel separately. If a tram gauge is used, Fig. 10-61 shows how to set up the gauge and scribe the tires in the center of the tread.

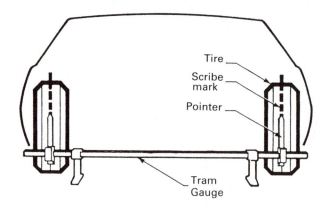

Tire

Scribe mark

Pointer

Tram Gauge

FIGURE 10-61   (Courtesy of Blackhawk, Division of Applied Power, Canada Ltd.)

What is known as a jounce/rebound test is used to check the toe deflection of each front wheel. The tram gauge is set up to the proper width with the pointers on the scribe mark. The car should be pulled down 3 in. (7.5 cm), then the toe deflection measured and registered on a chart as right wheel and left wheel.

The car should then be raised at least 3 in. (7.5 cm) above its normal riding height, and after making sure that each side of the car has been lifted equally, the amount of toe deflection measured. The reading for each wheel is added to the chart. Unless the reading for each wheel is the same as they move in and out in opposing directions, the car has a bump steer condition which must be corrected immediately by checking out what is causing the problem. Always check the manufacturer's specifications for the amount of deflection built into the steering of the vehicle.

UNIT 10-6:   WHEEL BALANCING

When an unbalanced wheel and tire assembly is jacked up, it will turn backward and forward until the heaviest part rests at the bottom. When it is revolved, the centrifugal force that acts on the heavy part will tend to lift and slam the tire down on the road with each revolution. This condition will cause wheel *hop* or bounce, which will transmit uncomfortable vibrations to the vehicle. This condition is called *static unbalance*; if uncorrected it will wear rubber from the tread of the tire in flat spots or cups (Fig. 10-62). The vibration also wears out ball joints and tie rod ends; in fact, all parts of the steering are subjected to a terrific stress and strain (Fig. 10-63).

To eliminate this condition of tire hop, weights are installed on the light side of the tire to balance the wheel; this is called *static balance* (Fig. 10-64). A wheel and tire may have static balance but still not be balanced properly if the weight of the wheel is not distributed on each side of the tire's centerline. It will have a wiggle (Fig. 10-65). A wheel and tire with this condition is dynamically unbalanced. A dynamically unbalanced wheel will not be discovered and corrected unless the wheel is revolved to simulate the conditions of being on a

EXCESS TOE-IN

DYNAMIC UNBALANCE

STATIC UNBALANCE

WORN-LOOSE PARTS

UNDER INFLATION

EXCESS CAMBER

FIGURE 10-62 Showing effects of misalignment and unbalanced wear. (Courtesy of Bear Manufacturing Co.)

FIGURE 10-63 Static unbalance results in vertical oscillations or hop of the wheel assembly. (Courtesy of Bear Manufacturing Co.)

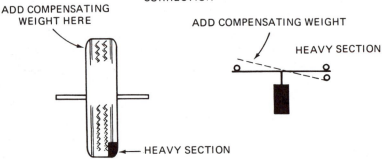

STATIC BALANCE CORRECTION

ADD COMPENSATING WEIGHT HERE

ADD COMPENSATING WEIGHT

HEAVY SECTION

HEAVY SECTION

FIGURE 10-64 A wheel that does have an unbalanced condition due to a heavy spot will tend to rotate by itself until the heavy portion of the assembly is down. Add compensating weight at top. (Courtesy of Bear Manufacturing Co.)

DYNAMIC BALANCE   BALANCING A WHEEL IN MOTION

FIGURE 10-65 A wheel that is dynamically unbalanced results in horizontal oscillations or wiggle of the wheel assembly. (Courtesy of Bear Manufacturing Co.)

vehicle. The wheel assembly is spun on a machine that will help to locate the heavy spots (Figs. 10-66 and 10-67). The necessary weights can then be installed on the opposite side of the wheel in the desired location. Locating these weights at the proper area of the wheel will make it dynamically balanced (Fig. 10-68). Wheel balancing is the proper distribution of weight around a tire and wheel assembly to counteract centrifugal forces acting on the heavy areas. The purpose of this is to maintain a true-running wheel perpendicular to its rotating axis.

DYNAMIC UNBALANCE

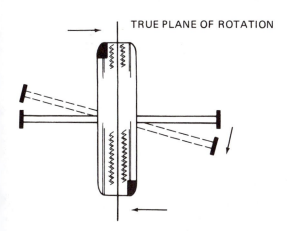

TRUE PLANE OF ROTATION

FIGURE 10-66 It is possible for a wheel to be in balance statically and be out-of-balance dynamically. Once a wheel is in motion, the static weights try to reach a point that is exactly perpendicular to the true plane of rotation due to the action of centrifugal force. (Courtesy of Bear Manufacturing Co.)

DYNAMIC UNBALANCE

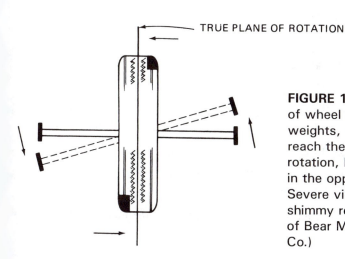

TRUE PLANE OF ROTATION

FIGURE 10-67 At 180° of wheel rotation, static weights, in attempting to reach the true plane of rotation, kick the spindle in the opposite direction. Severe vibration and shimmy result. (Courtesy of Bear Manufacturing Co.)

DYNAMIC BALANCE

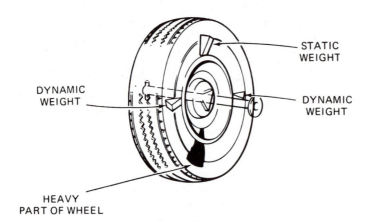

FIGURE 10-68 To eliminate this couple action, compensating weights (dynamic) are placed at 180° opposite each other. Dynamic balance is obtained while static balance remains unaffected. (Courtesy of Bear Manufacturing Co.)

QUESTIONS

10-1 What are the five frame misalignments?

10-2 In what order would the frame misalignments occur in a severe front collision?

10-3 What are the three frame misalignments that can occur in the rear of the car because of a severe collision?

10-4 Name the four controlling points in a frame.

10-5 Explain passive safety design.

10-6 Explain how collision damage is absorbed in a unitized vehicle.

10-7 Explain how a good analysis is done on a collision-damaged vehicle.

10-8 How is it determined what hookups are necessary to repair frame damage?

10-9 When checking sag with frame-centering gauges, what is used to sight from the first gauge to the second gauge: pointers, bars, or the legs of the gauge?

10-10 Where are the gauges located when checking for sag and twist?

10-11 When both side rails of the frame have been bent in a head-on collision, how is the amount of damage determined?

10-12 To check for a mash in the front sections of a frame, the measurement is taken from what section?

10-13   What is a datum line?

10-14   When the metal in a buckle starts looking silvery, what kind of heat is used: spot heat, controlled heat, or the heat of the blowtorch?

10-15   What is the maximum heat that can be used on HSS?

10-16   What can be used to relax stresses as metal sections are pulled back to specifications?

10-17   What type of flame is used when heating areas in a frame?

10-18   Name the five angles that are used for steering alignment.

10-19   What is *steering axis inclination*?

10-20   What is the purpose of caster in wheel alignment?

10-21   What is toe-in?

10-22   What is *dynamic balancing*?

10-23   What is *static balancing*?

10-24   What is the allowable tolerance for mash in a car frame?

11

Adjustments

UNIT 11-1: HOODS AND FRONT ENDS

Body panels on a car must be adjusted after a collision. Moreover, when the adjustments on certain panels are not right, this condition must also be corrected. Poorly adjusted panels can cause binding when such panels as hoods, doors, and trunk lids are opened and closed; dust and water leaks can also result from this condition.

The hood and fenders must always be aligned as a unit to fit the cowl, the door-panel edge, and the sill panel. The fenders have built-in brackets or over-sized bolt holes or elongated holes that provide for in-and-out, fore-and-aft, and up-and-down adjustments. On some vehicles shims or adjustable brackets are used to vary these adjustments, as well as the curvature of the rear part of the fender, to make it match the front edge of the door panel (Fig. 11-1). To provide the proper amount of gap between the front fender rear edge and the door panel at the bottom, it may be necessary to install or remove shims between the radiator support and the frame horns in nonunitized construction.

The hood assembly is provided with an adjustment that is built into the hinges or floating tapping plates in the hood. The hood can usually be moved up and down and fore and aft (Fig. 11-2). With these adjustments, it is usually possible to adjust the hood so that it lines up properly with the fenders. There should be a gap of approximately 5/32 in. (4 mm) between it and the fenders and enough gap at the back to clear the air-intake grille if the car has one. The

364

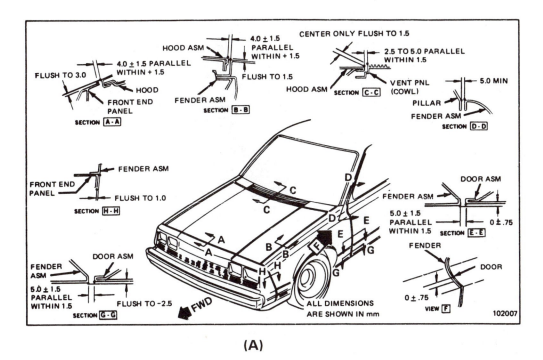

(A)

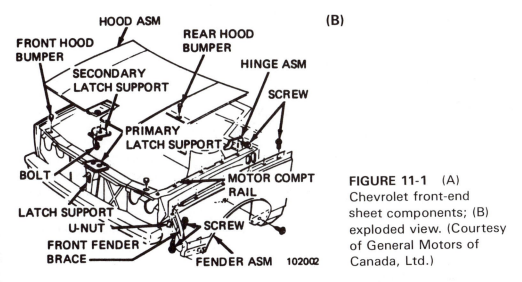

(B)

FIGURE 11-1 (A) Chevrolet front-end sheet components; (B) exploded view. (Courtesy of General Motors of Canada, Ltd.)

hood is held and adjusted by a hood latch. This latch can be adjusted to provide the proper position, so that the hood will fit tightly and line up with the fenders. The hood latch is also adjustable by means of slotted holes or threaded dowel pins (Fig. 11-3). Most cars have adjustable bumpers on the radiator support to

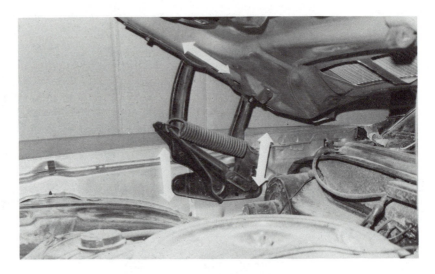

FIGURE 11-2 Hood adjustment.

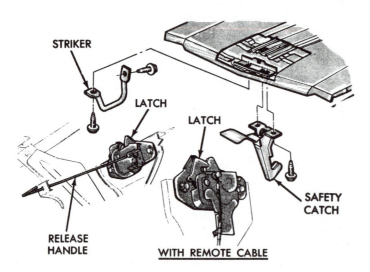

FIGURE 11-3 Hood lock and striker. (Courtesy of Chrysler Canada, Ltd.)

provide the up-and-down adjustment necessary to stop hood flutter at the front. If any of the rubber bumpers are missing on the inner edge of the fender, they should always be replaced, for these bumpers help to determine the position of the hood when it is closed.

The hood is provided with a safety catch so that if the hood should open accidentally the safety catch will prevent it from flying up to the wide open position while the car is moving. If the hood should open at high speeds and the safety catch does not hold, the hood would be damaged severely and it could possibly break the windshield. It could also cause a severe accident, which is why the body man should check to see if the safety catch holds the hood properly.

UNIT 11-2: DOORS

The doors on sedans should always be adjusted, starting at the rear door. Since the quarter panel cannot be moved, the rear door must be adjusted to fit these body lines and the opening. Once the rear door is adjusted, the front door can then be adjusted to fit the rear door; next, the front fender can be adjusted to fit the door. On hardtop models, the windows can then be adjusted to fit the weather stripping, and the two windows aligned to fit. The windows are usually adjusted starting from the front vent assembly toward the back. The vent assembly is adjusted to fit the front door pillar, and the front window is then adjusted to it. The rear door window is adjusted to the front window rear edge and the opening for the rear door assembly.

The doors are hung to the body with hinges, which can usually be moved forward and backward, up and down, and even in and out (Fig. 11-4).

It is important to remember when adjusting doors on a vehicle that the doors must be adjusted to fit the body opening. Most automobile manufacturers provide certain adjustments so that these panels can be fitted to the opening. Since most new automobiles use welded-on hinges or strap hinges, the hinges (Fig. 11-5) do not usually need adjustment except after a collision. To adjust the door to fit the body opening and the hinges after a collision, it will usually be necessary to replace the hinges or bend them back to their original shape so that the door will

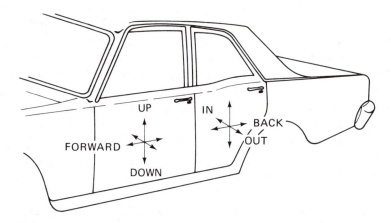

FIGURE 11-4 Door adjustments. (Courtesy of General Motors of Canada, Ltd.)

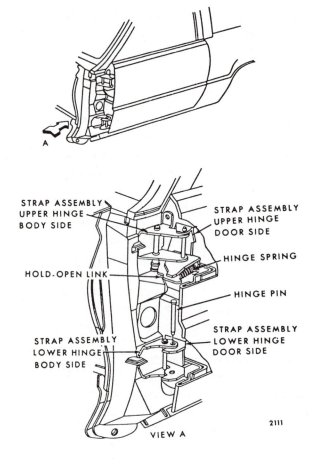

STRAP ASSEMBLY
UPPER HINGE
BODY SIDE

STRAP ASSEMBLY
UPPER HINGE
DOOR SIDE

HINGE SPRING

HOLD-OPEN LINK

HINGE PIN

STRAP ASSEMBLY
LOWER HINGE
BODY SIDE

STRAP ASSEMBLY
LOWER HINGE
DOOR SIDE

2111

VIEW A

FIGURE 11-5 Front door hinge system. (Courtesy of General Motors of Canada, Ltd.)

fit properly. To provide these adjustments in nonunitized automobiles, floating tapping or anchor plates are used in the door pillar and the door assembly.

On some makes of cars, a special wrench must be used to loosen and tighten the bolts. If the hinges are to be removed, a line should be scribed around the hinge to mark its position, which facilitates the reinstallation and positioning of the hinge. It may be necessary to loosen the fender at the rear bottom edge to enable the body man to reach the bolts.

The rear doors are hung on hinges that are bolted to the center pillar. The hinges and the door are provided with forward-and-backward, up-and-down, and in-and-out movement so that the door can be properly adjusted in the opening (Figs. 11-6 and 11-7).

Before starting to adjust the doors, the door position in relation to the opening must be checked. The gap between it and the front fender and rocker panel is checked. If it is either too low or too high, a jack with a block of wood is used

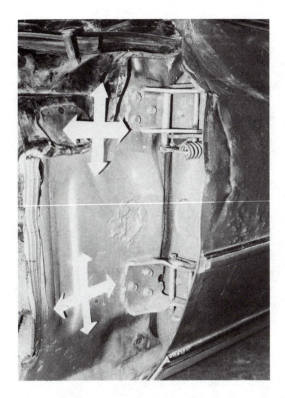 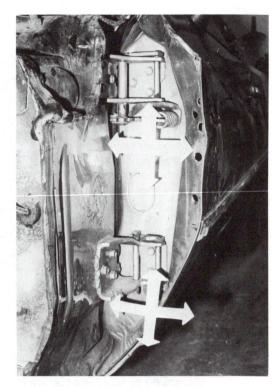

(A) **(B)**

FIGURE 11-6 (A) The arrows on the cowl side panel show how the hinges can be moved to obtain up-and-down and back-and-forth adjustments, available on automobiles that use bolt-on hinges; (B) the arrows on the front part of the door inner panel show how the door can be moved on the hinges to obtain up-and-down and in-and-out adjustments, so that the door can be adjusted to fit the body.

to lift or lower the door, as in Fig. 11-8. The block of wood is positioned under the frame to reinforce the inner door panel and prevent damaging of the outer panel. Before raising or lowering the door with the jack, the bolts are loosened on the door part of the hinge. This allows the door to be raised or lowered as required. Once the door is lifted or lowered slightly, a bolt on each hinge of the door is tightened carefully so that the in-and-out adjustments of the door will not change. The jack is lowered and the door is checked for fit to the body opening.

Back-and-forth adjustments should always be done one hinge at a time. In this way the adjustment of the door is easier to control and very often is all that

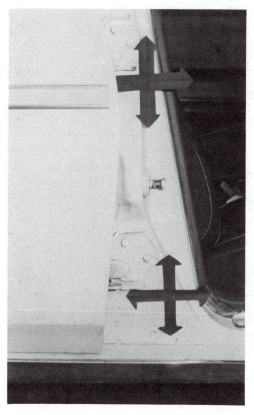

(A)   **(B)**

FIGURE 11-7   (A) The arrows on the center door post show how the hinges can be moved up and down, and back and forth, which can be used to adjust the door to fit the body opening; (B) the arrows on the front part of the door inner panel show how the door can be moved on the hinges to obtain up-and-down and in-and-out adjustment so that the door can be adjusted to fit the body.

is required. If the hinge pins are worn out, it might be necessary to change the hinges. Some hinges use bushings in the hinge around the pins. When these bushings are worn out, they can be changed. This will tighten the pin in the hinges and also readjust the door to a certain extent. Figure 11-9 shows different examples of door misadjustments and how to overcome them.

Figure 11-10(A) shows how a door can be moved ahead by first adjusting the top hinge and then the bottom hinge. The same results can be achieved by

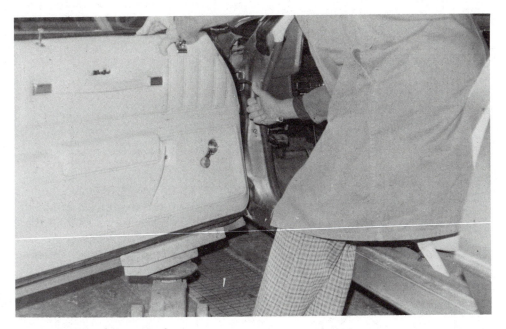

FIGURE 11-8 Raising and/or lowering the door.

FIGURE 11-9 Back-and-forth door adjustments.

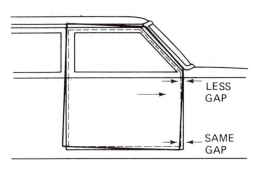

1. DOOR MOVED AHEAD AT TOP HINGE

(A)

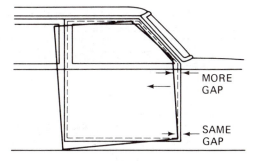

2. DOOR MOVED BACKWARDS AT THE BOTTOM HINGE.

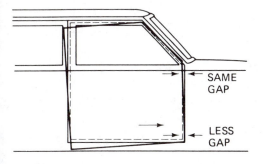

1. THE DOOR IS MOVED AHEAD AT THE BOTTOM HINGE.

(B)

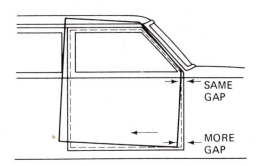

2. DOOR MOVED BACKWARDS AT THE TOP HINGE.

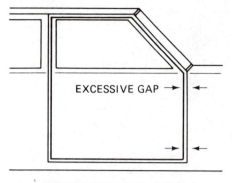

MOVING THE DOOR AHEAD

(A)

FIGURE 11-10 (A) Excessive gap; (B) moving the door ahead; (C) effect of a front collision which has sagged the frame and causes excessive gap between the front door and fender.

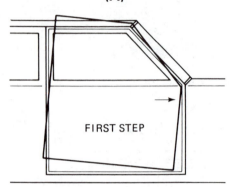

THE DOOR BEING MOVED AHEAD AT THE TOP HINGE

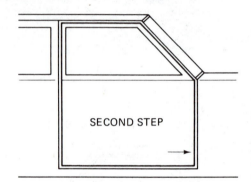

THE DOOR BEING MOVED AHEAD AT THE BOTTOM HINGE

(B)

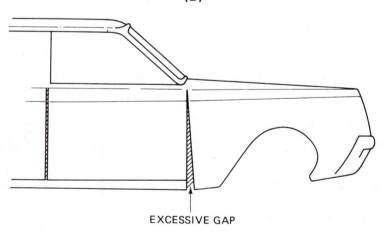

(C)

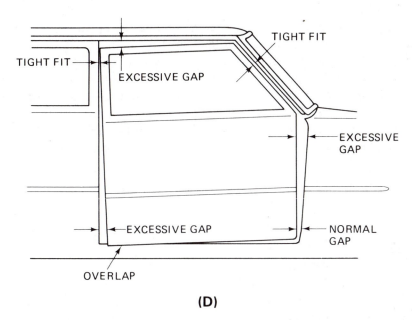

(D)

FIGURE 11-10   (cont.) (D) Effect of a front collision which has moved the front door pillar and cowl back, thereby distorting the door opening. (Courtesy of General Motors of Canada, Ltd.)

adjusting the lower hinge first and then the top hinge until the desired gap is achieved.

In-and-out adjustments are also very important because not only must the door fit the opening but it must also be reasonably aligned in and out to fit the body panels. The door must also provide a good seal between the weather stripping and the body opening. The weather stripping must be compressed sufficiently in the opening to prevent water, dust, drafts, and wind noises from occurring or entering the automobile.

Care must be taken when adjusting the in-and-out movement of the door. If the door is moved out on the top hinge, it will not only affect the top of the door but it will also move the opposite bottom corner in. If the bottom of the door is moved in on the hinge, it will move the top opposite corner out. But if the door is moved in or out equally on both hinges, it will only affect the front of the door because the amount of adjustment decreases toward the back of the door. The center door post, striker bolt, and lock will determine the position of the door at this location. The front leading edge of the door should always be slightly in on the front edge from the rear of the other panel. This will help to stop wind noises at the leading edge of the door panel. If the front edge is out past the back edge of the other panel, it will likely cause wind noises to occur.

If the vehicle has been involved in a collision and the opening is distorted, see Chapter 15 for the methods required to correct the damage.

When adjustment of doors on a car is necessary, it is sometimes advantageous to remove the striker plate. Doing so facilitates the centering of the door in the opening. The striker plate is not adjusted properly if the door rises or is forced down when the door is closed. The striker should merely provide a slight rise to the door when it is closed. The striker can be moved up and down, in and out, and back and forth. Figure 11-11 shows a General Motors striker bolt.

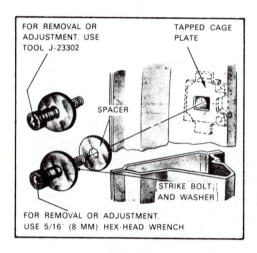

FOR REMOVAL OR ADJUSTMENT, USE TOOL J-23302

TAPPED CAGE PLATE

SPACER

STRIKE BOLT AND WASHER

FOR REMOVAL OR ADJUSTMENT, USE 5/16' (8 MM) HEX-HEAD WRENCH

FIGURE 11-11   Door lock striker installation. (Courtesy of General Motors of Canada, Ltd.)

This striker is loosened and tightened by using a 5/16 in. (8 mm) hexagon head wrench. In order to check where the striker engages into the lock, modeling clay can be used in the lock so that when it engages with the striker, an impression of the striker position will be noted (Fig. 11-12). Spacers are used to move the striker away from the post. A similar type of lock and striker is used on tailgates of station wagons.

Another type of hinge used in some models is the welded-on type that has no adjustment provisions (Fig. 11-13). A pin is provided to facilitate the removal of the door assembly for servicing of the hinges. The half of the hinge that is to be installed on the door is predrilled to permit a bolt-on installation with tapped caged plates and bolts.

When removing the door hinge pins, care must be taken to cover the spring with a rag to prevent it from flying and possibly causing damage or personal injury. The pin is then removed in each hinge and the door assembly is removed from the automobile. When the door is reinstalled, it is necessary to use a tool similar to that shown in Fig. 11-14. Again, the spring must be seated properly

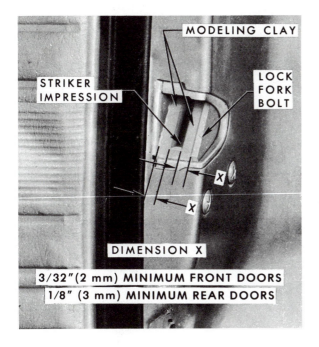

STRIKER
IMPRESSION

MODELING CLAY

LOCK
FORK
BOLT

X

X

DIMENSION X

3/32″(2 mm) MINIMUM FRONT DOORS

1/8″ (3 mm) MINIMUM REAR DOORS

FIGURE 11-12 Lock-to-striker engagement. (Courtesy of General Motors of Canada, Ltd.)

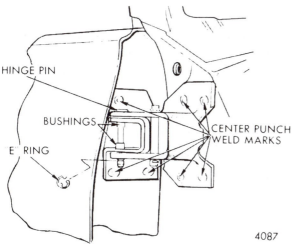

HINGE PIN

BUSHINGS

E RING

CENTER PUNCH
WELD MARKS

4087

FIGURE 11-13 Front door hinge E ring removal. (Courtesy of General Motors of Canada, Ltd.)

in the tool before compressing it to prevent it from slipping and causing damage or personal injury.

To install the hinge on the door after the position has been scribed on the door (Fig. 11-15), it is center-punched at the weld areas as in Fig. 11-16. A 1/8 in. (3 mm) pilot hole is drilled completely through the welds at the proper

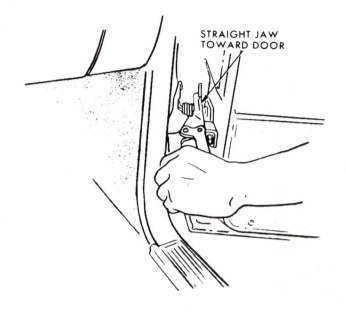

STRAIGHT JAW
TOWARD DOOR

FIGURE 11-14 Front door hinge hold-open spring installation using tool J-23497 or equivalent. (Courtesy of General Motors of Canada, Ltd.)

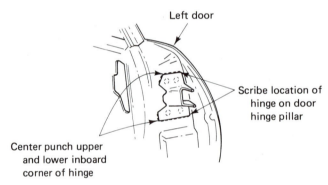

Left door

Scribe location of hinge on door hinge pillar

Center punch upper and lower inboard corner of hinge

FIGURE 11-15 Locating hinge on door hinge pillar (typical). (Courtesy of General Motors of Canada, Ltd.)

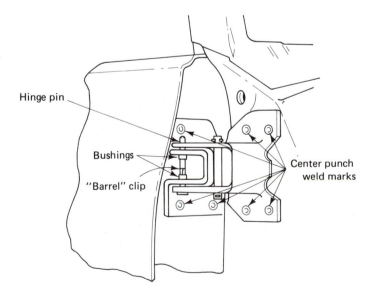

Hinge pin

Bushings

"Barrel" clip

Center punch weld marks

FIGURE 11-16 Weld-mark center punch locations (typical). (Courtesy of General Motors of Canada, Ltd.)

marks, this is then drilled out to 1/2 in. (13 mm), but only deep enough to penetrate the hinge base to release the hinge from the panel. A chisel is then driven between the hinge and the base to break it free from the panel. The new part is installed on the door but 1/2 in. (13 mm) holes are drilled into the attaching holes; this will provide a slight amount of adjustment on the door assembly, as the bolts used to attach it are 5/16 in. (8 mm) by 1½ in. (38 mm) [Fig. 11-17(A)].

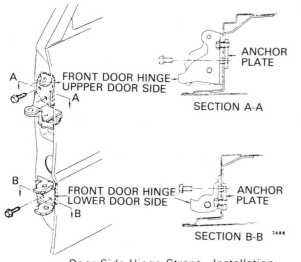

Door Side Hinge Straps - Installation

FIGURE 11-17 (A) Installation of door side hinge straps: (B) body side hinge straps—A style. (Courtesy of General Motors of Canada, Ltd.)

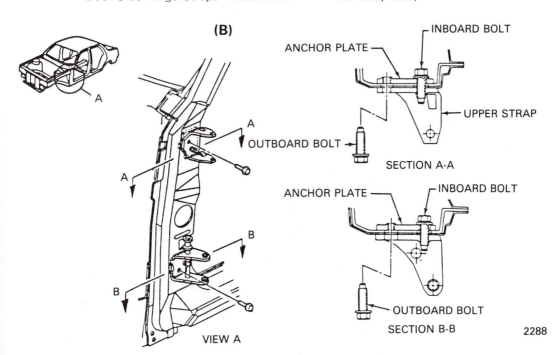

Figure 11-17(B) shows the service installation for the body side hinge straps on a typical front body pillar. Tapped anchors are not required to service A-style body hinge straps. A reinforcement is welded to the hinge pillar at the time of assembly.

Prepare the body hinge pillar as required for a replacement hinge strap. The service body hinge straps have only one bolt hole. To locate the other bolt hole, use the original hinge strap to make a paper template. Draw the original hinge strap on a piece of paper. Locate the centerline of the hole that is required. Push a sharp punch through the paper template at this location. Place the template on the service hinge and once the hinge is aligned with the template, center-punch a new hinge using the hole in the template as a locator. Using an 11/32-in. (or 8.5-mm) drill bit, drill a hole in the hinge strap. The holes in the body hinge pillar will provide for some movement when reinstalling the hinge strap. The surface of the hinge strap that mates with the body pillar is coated with a medium-bodied sealer. The bolt from inside the body through the hinge strap is started by hand; then the outside bolt through the hinge is installed. They should be torqued to 15 to 20 ft-lb (20 to 28 N · m); the inside bolt to 20 to 40 ft-lb (40 to 55 N · m). The door is then installed but should not be closed completely until a visual check is made to determine if the door or lock fork bolt engages properly with the striker. The area is then refinished to the proper color. If more information is required, check the manufacturer's manual.

UNIT 11-3: TRUNK LIDS OR HATCHBACKS

The trunk lid is used to close and seal the trunk opening from dust and water leaks. Figure 11-18 shows a typical trunk lid weatherstrip installation. In order to provide proper sealing, the trunk lid must come in contact with it when closed.

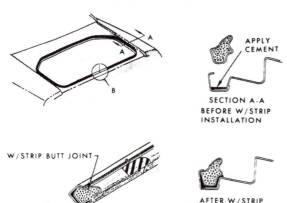

APPLY CEMENT

SECTION A-A
BEFORE W/STRIP
INSTALLATION

W/STRIP BUTT JOINT

VIEW B

AFTER W/STRIP
INSTALLATION

9679

FIGURE 11-18 Rear compartment weather strip assembly. (Courtesy of General Motors of Canada, Ltd.)

The trunk lid can be moved back and forth and sideways because of the slotted holes in the hinge and the tapped caged plates in the trunk lid. At times it is necessary to put shims between the bolts and the trunk lid to raise or lower the front edge. To raise the front edge, the shim is put between the hinge and the lid at the front bolt area. To lower it, the shim is put at the back area of the hinge.

Figure 11-19 shows a typical trunk lid hinge assembly, which uses torque rods to counterbalance the weight of the lid—to make the lid easier to raise and hold in the up position. The torque rods may be tightened by using a 1/2 in. (13 mm) pipe inserted over the end of the rod, or a tool like the one shown in Fig.11-20 may be used on some other types.

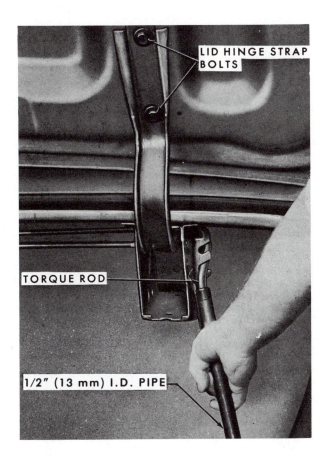

FIGURE 11-19 (Courtesy of General Motors Products of Canada, Ltd.)

The trunk lid latch and striker can usually be moved up and down and sideways to engage, direct, and hold the trunk lid in a closed position. Figure 11-21 shows a typical striker and trunk lid lock assembly.

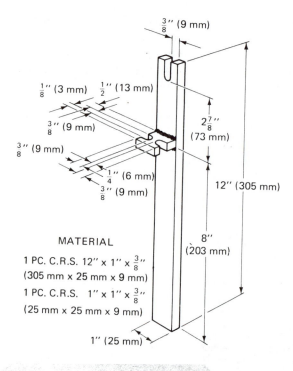

$\frac{3}{8}''$ (9 mm)

$\frac{1}{8}''$ (3 mm) $\frac{1}{2}''$ (13 mm)

$\frac{3}{8}''$ (9 mm)

$\frac{3}{8}''$ (9 mm)

$\frac{1}{4}''$ (6 mm)

$\frac{3}{8}''$ (9 mm)

$2\frac{7}{8}''$ (73 mm)

12'' (305 mm)

8'' (203 mm)

MATERIAL

1 PC. C.R.S. 12'' x 1'' x $\frac{3}{8}''$
(305 mm x 25 mm x 9 mm)

1 PC. C.R.S. 1'' x 1'' x $\frac{3}{8}''$
(25 mm x 25 mm x 9 mm)

1'' (25 mm)

FIGURE 11-20 (Courtesy of General Motors of Canada, Ltd.)

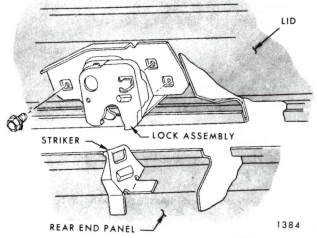

LID

STRIKER

LOCK ASSEMBLY

REAR END PANEL

1384

FIGURE 11-21 Rear compartment lid lock and striker. (Courtesy of General Motors of Canada, Ltd.)

UNIT 11-4: BUMPERS

The bumpers at the front end and back end are used to protect the vehicle in minor accidents. These bumpers are designed to withstand impacts as specified by federal government standards. Different manufacturers have used different methods to achieve these standards. Some use energy-absorbing devices such as shown in Figs. 11-22 and 11-23.

These bumpers are of a more complex nature than the bumper of previously manufactured automobiles. Some of these energy-absorbing devices are not designed to be repaired in case of failure, and the manufacturer's instructions should

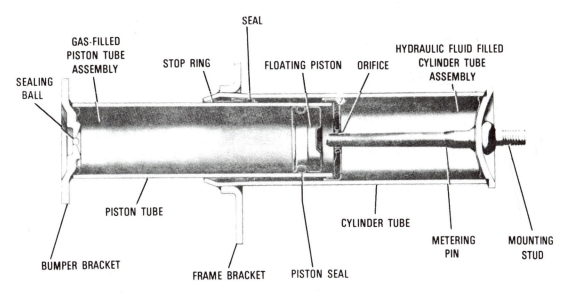

FIGURE 11-22 Energy absorber in extended position. (Courtesy of General Motors of Canada, Ltd.)

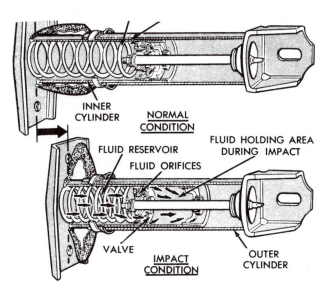

FIGURE 11-23 Impact energy absorber function. (Courtesy Chrysler of Canada.)

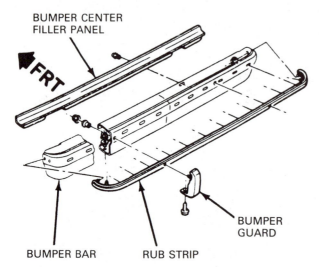

FIGURE 11-24   Rear bumper bar rub strip. (Courtesy of General Motors of Canada, Ltd.)

always be followed before repairs are attempted. The bumpers have also been heavily reinforced to meet the specifications. Figure 11-24 shows a typical rear bumper assembly.

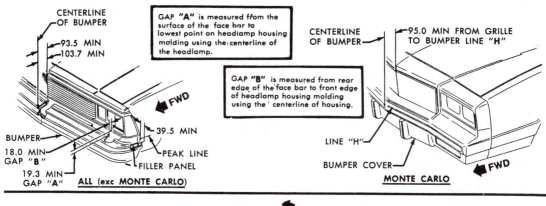

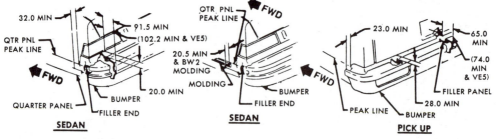

FIGURE 11-25   Chevrolet bumper alignment. (Courtesy of General Motors of Canada, Ltd.)

After a front or rear collision that is severe enough to distort and damage the automobile, the bumpers will need to be realigned to the automobile body to make them fit to the front-end sheet metal and frame horns. The specifications for one make of automobile are shown in Fig. 11-25, which shows the proper dimensions for adjusting these particular bumpers. For other makes of cars, manuals or another car of the same model and make should be compared to the particular car.

UNIT 11-5:   HEADLIGHTS

All cars manufactured are equipped with either a two-sealed-beam system or a four-sealed-beam system. When an automobile is involved in a front-end accident, the headlights should always be readjusted so that they provide the light necessary for driving at night.

In the two-sealed-beam system, the low and high beams are built into the same sealed beam. In the four-sealed-beam system, two sealed beams have both low and high beams; the other two sealed beams are used only on the high beam. The lights are changed from low beam, which is used mostly to drive in the city, to high beam, which is used for highway driving, by a beam control switch located on the floorboard near the left cowl trim panel.

Quick-disconnect terminals are used for the left and right sealed beams. The wiring harness is color coded so that like-colored wires are connected together; on some makes of cars, the connectors are also color-coded. Figure 11-26 shows a typical headlight system using the two sealed beams for each side of the front end of the car. The figure shows the adjusting screws that are used for both horizontal and vertical movement necessary to adjust the headlight. The screws that retain the bulb to the assembly are also shown.

Headlight adjustments should preferably be done when the gas tank is half full, with a person in the passenger seat at the front and the driver sitting on the left front seat at the steering wheel. The trunk should be unloaded except for the spare tire and the jack. The tires should also be checked to see if they have the recommended pressure. Before starting the adjustments, the car should be bounced by pushing at the center of the front and rear bumper to level the car.

If no headlight adjusting equipment is available, the following method can be used by laying out the floor layout and the wall layout (Fig. 11-27).

The headlight horizontal centerline is established by subtracting 20 in. (508 mm) from the actual measured height of the headlight lens center from the floor and by adding this dimension (dimension B, Fig. 11-28) to the 20 in. (508 mm) reference line obtained by sighting over the uprights. A horizontal line is drawn 2 in. (51 mm) below and parallel to the headlight horizontal centerline. The

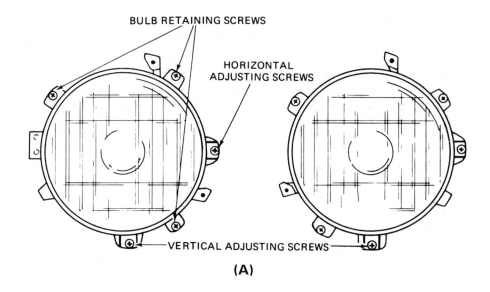

(A)

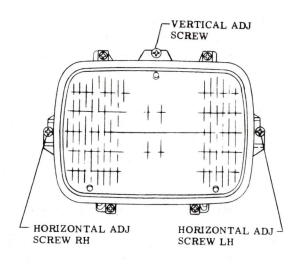

5 x 7 Headlamp System Aiming Screws

(B)

FIGURE 11-26 Headlight adjustment. [(A) Courtesy of Ford Motor Company of Canada, Ltd.; (B) courtesy of General Motors of Canada, Ltd.]

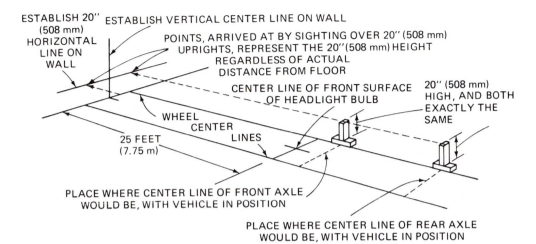

FIGURE 11-27 Floor and wall layout. (Courtesy of Ford Motor Company of Canada, Ltd.)

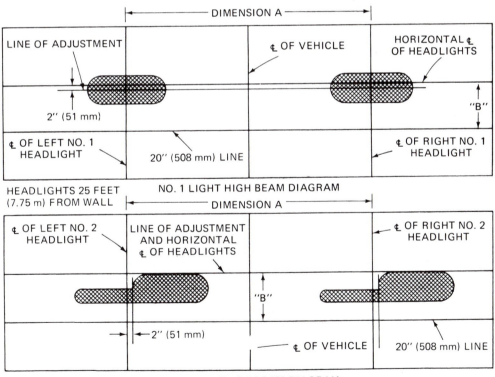

FIGURE 11-28 (Courtesy of Ford Motor Company of Canada, Ltd.)

headlight vertical centerlines are drawn on the screen as measured on the car (dimension A, Fig. 11-28).

The No. 1 headlight beam is adjusted as shown in Fig. 11-27 with the No. 2 headlight covered. Some states or provinces may not approve of the 2 in. (51 mm) dimension for the No. 1 headlights. The applicable law should be checked, for a 3 in. (76 mm) dimension may be required. In Canada, a 2 in. (51 mm) dimension in 25 ft. (7.74 m) distance is used.

The No. 2 headlights are adjusted by using the lower diagram in Fig. 11-28. Dimension B is the same for No. 2 lights as for No. 1 lights. Dimension adjustment of the No. 2 lights is the horizontal centerline of the No. 2. The headlights are turned to the low beam and each No. 2 light is adjusted as shown in Fig. 11-28, using the wall screen. Each beam adjustment is brought to final adjustment by turning the screw clockwise so that the headlights will be held against the tension springs when the operation is completed.

QUESTIONS

11-1 To what parts of the body should the fenders and hood be aligned?

11-2 What built-in adjustments are provided in the hinges of a hood to adjust the hood properly?

11-3 What part stops the hood from springing to the open position while the car is moving?

11-4 What movements are provided to align a door to fit the body opening?

11-5 Describe how a strap hinge is removed and replaced on a new-style body.

11-6 Describe how the different adjustments can be be used to align a misaligned front door.

11-7 Describe how a front door that has sagged down at the rear edge can be readjusted to fit the body opening.

11-8 Describe how a floor and wall layout can be laid out and used to aim headlights.

11-9 Describe how headlights should be adjusted.

12

Removing and Replacing Upholstery Trim and Headlinings

When repairs on automobile body panels are necessary, sometimes the repairman has to remove some of the trim, upholstery, or headlining to reach the inside of the body panels with the tools required to complete the operation.

Removal and Replacement of Door Armrest

Different types of armrests are available, and a typical one is shown in Fig. 12-1. Some armrests are attached or assembled to the door trim prior to installing the trim. Other armrests are an integral part of the door trim panel assembly and are therefore removed as an assembly. A third type is installed after the trim installation and is usually held by two or three long screws.

Door Trim Assemblies (General Motors)

Some models have a remote control mirror, and it is necessary to disconnect the controls in order to remove the trim panel. On some models, the escutcheon is retained to the trim pad or armrest with exposed screws. When the screws are removed, the cable can be pulled out far enough to disengage the nylon clip that secures the mirror controls to the escutcheon (Fig. 12-2). The inside door handles are retained by either screws or clips. In styles having screw-retained handles, the screws are either exposed or covered only by an applied-type armrest that can be removed by taking out several screws. Figure 12-3 illustrates various

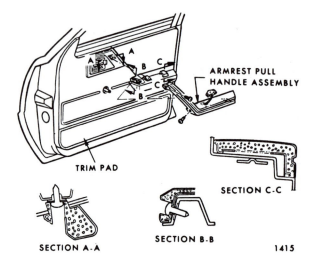

TRIM PAD

SECTION C-C

SECTION A-A

SECTION B-B

1415

FIGURE 12-1 Front door armrest and pull handle attachment—X shown, A similar. (Courtesy of General Motors of Canada, Ltd.)

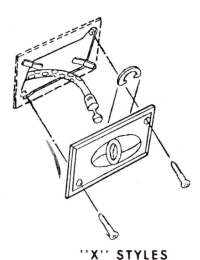

"X" STYLES

FIGURE 12-2 Typical remote control mirror cable and escutcheon attachment. (Courtesy of General Motors of Canada, Ltd.)

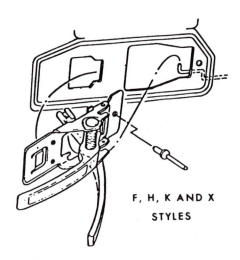

F, H, K AND X STYLES

FIGURE 12-3 (A) Typical door lock remote control handle installations; (B) typical window regulator handle assembly installations. (Courtesy of General Motors of Canada, Ltd.)

types of remote control handles. On styles with clip-retained handles, the clip is either exposed when the armrest is removed or it is hidden by the handle. Exposed clips can be disengaged from the remote control with a screwdriver. The clips that are hidden by the handle can be disengaged as follows: The door

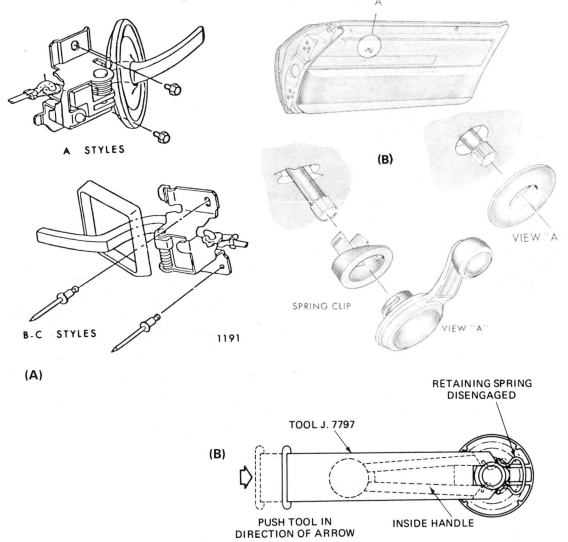

FIGURE 12-4 Door inside handle removal. Spring clip retained. (Courtesy of General Motors of Canada, Ltd.)

trim assembly is depressed sufficiently to permit the insertion of the tool between the handle and the plastic bearing plate (Fig. 12-4).

The door trim is held by various means, such as screws, spring clips, or plastic retainers. When these retainers are removed, it is necessary to take great care not to tear the trim when prying the panel from the door. Figure 12-5

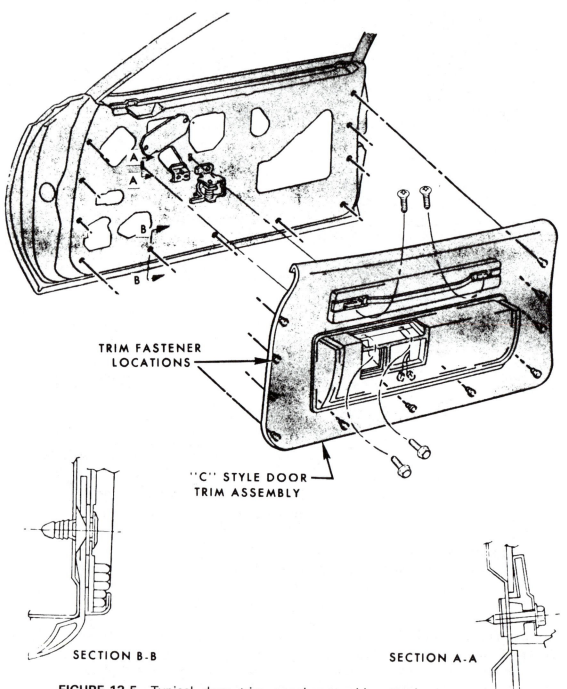

TRIM FASTENER
LOCATIONS

"C" STYLE DOOR
TRIM ASSEMBLY

SECTION B-B

SECTION A-A

FIGURE 12-5 Typical door trim panel assembly attachment.
(Courtesy of General Motors of Canada, Ltd.)

illustrates the different methods of holding the panels. A specially built tool or a narrow putty knife can be used to pry the panel away from the door frame gently. The inside door lock knob must be removed to enable the complete removal of the trim panel. To reinstall, the procedure is reversed; the regulator handles must be reinstalled in the proper position so that all handles have the same position when the windows are closed.

Trim Assemblies (Ford)

The armrest and trim assemblies are typical; the door lock knob is removed. The regulator handle retaining screw access covers must be removed in order to remove the retaining screws (Fig. 12-6). In most cars today, no garnish molding is used on the upper part of the trim panel. On the front doors, it may be necessary to remove the mirror remote control bezel if there is one. If the automobile has power windows, the switch lead wires must be disconnected from the switch and then the panel can be removed. If necessary, the water shield can then be removed.

To reinstall, care must be taken to daub sealer over each retaining clip hole to seal it when the panel is replaced. Sealer should also be applied around the

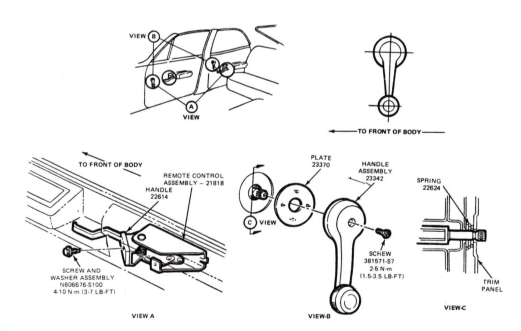

FIGURE 12-6 Typical door and window regulator handle installation. (Courtesy of Ford Motor Company of Canada, Ltd.)

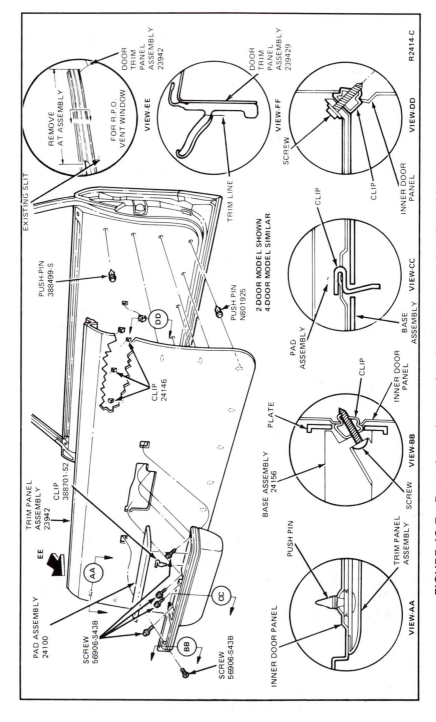

FIGURE 12-7 Front door trim panel and armrest—standard Ford/Mercury, two-door. (Courtesy of Ford Motor Company of Canada, Ltd.)

392

regulator shafts, door handles, and any other holes. The water shield must always be reinstalled carefully to prevent any leaks. The rest of the installation is the reverse of the removal. With the windows closed, the handles should be positioned as in Fig. 12-7.

Trim Assemblies (Chrysler)

The trim assemblies are typical, and their removal and installation do not vary too much. The regulator handle is removed by using a hex-head wrench to remove the screw in the handle (Fig. 12-8).

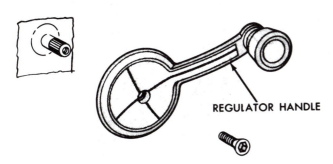

REGULATOR HANDLE

FIGURE 12-8 Window regulator handle. (Courtesy of Chrysler Canada, Ltd.)

Headlining Assembly

The headlinings in today's cars are of a formed style which is used by most manufacturers in one method or another. It consists of a molded substrate covered by replaceable foam and cloth or vinyl facings (Fig. 12-9). Some are in a one-piece assembly and some are in a two-piece assembly which uses a molding to close out the point of the front and rear sections.

The molding fits into a retainer which attaches to slots in a roof panel. The headlining is held in place partially with roof attaching clips. The final retention is accomplished when the interior molding and attaching screws that retain sun-shade brackets, dome lamp base, coat hooks, roof-mounted assist straps, and shoulder belt covers are installed.

To remove them, just undo the retainers, moldings, dome lamps, and so on, and then remove them from the car. To install, they are loaded into the car diagonally through the side window openings while taking great care not to overflex them, as damage results. The headlining is then aligned into its proper location and the removal steps or operations are reversed.

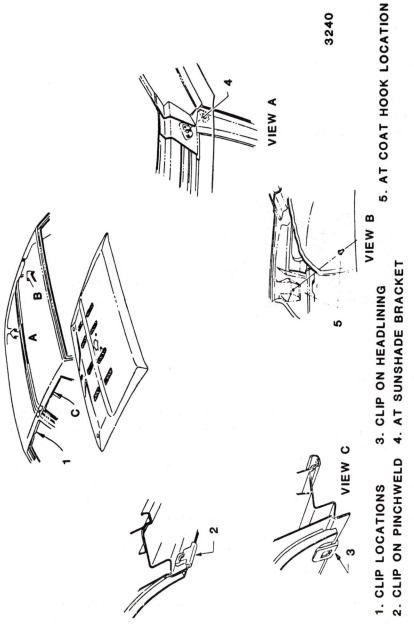

3240

VIEW A

VIEW B

VIEW C

1. CLIP LOCATIONS   3. CLIP ON HEADLINING   5. AT COAT HOOK LOCATION
2. CLIP ON PINCHWELD   4. AT SUNSHADE BRACKET

FIGURE 12-9 Formal headlining assembly. (Courtesy of General Motors of Canada, Ltd.)

QUESTIONS

12-1 What is used to hold the window inside handle on the regulator shaft on Fisher bodies?

12-2 How are the door trim panels held to the inner door panels?

12-3 What is used to hold the window regulator inside handle on the regulator shaft on recent Ford bodies?

13

Recovering and Repairing Vinyl Tops

UNIT 13-1: VINYL ROOF COVERS

The material used on tops of automobiles is a vinyl-coated fabric made in sections that are either dielectrically bonded or stitched at the seams. Depending on the body type, the fabric is applied to the roof panel via one of the following methods. A nonstaining vinyl-trim adhesive is used.

One material uses a padding that is cemented to the roof outer surface; next, the cover is applied over the padding and only cemented along the outer perimeter. In another method, the fabric is cemented entirely to the roof outer surface. Also, different types of cars use different moldings, a factor that will determine whether the fabric will extend into the back window, windshield opening, and drip molding. On the types where the cover extends into the openings, it is retained by cement, or by clips that are installed over weld or on studs. When the cover extends to the drip molding, it is retained by a flexible retainer or a drip scalp molding.

To remove the fabric roof cover, it may be necessary to detach the reveal moldings, drip scalp molding, flexible retainers and clips, rear quarter belt reveal moldings, and certain other moldings and nameplates. The reveal molding clips across the top of the windshield and the back window openings must then be removed. It may also be necessary to remove the molding clips along the bottom of the back window opening when the fabric extends below the windows. If one of the clips is not accessible, the fabric must be trimmed around the clip. The

396

drive nail and self-sealing screws that are present in the windshield and back window openings have to be removed with care; therefore the glass edge should be taped with two or three thicknesses of cloth tape. The nails are removed by inserting a screwdriver under the heads of the nails to loosen them. Diagonal cutters can then be used to pull them out, but care should be taken not to enlarge the holes in the roof panel.

In fabric removal, the application of heat to the cemented areas will help to loosen the fabric. Care must be taken not to heat the fabric over 200°F (93.2°C), because it may lose its grain or blister or become shiny.

If the roof panel has a pad, it must not be damaged when removing the fabric. The fabric is loosened from all cemented edges and detached from the roof panel. If any of the padding is damaged, it must be repaired; if any sections have to be removed, a special solvent can be used to loosen and clean the adhesive. Softening of the paint finish must be avoided when using the solvent.

To install a new fabric cover, the car must be masked to protect the finish from the glue, especially if the glue is to be sprayed on. On a top with no pad, the cement has to be checked to ensure that a smooth surface is present. Any excess glue must be removed; otherwise it will highlight through the fabric cover after installation.

A new fabric top should be installed at a temperature of about 72°F (22.2°C). Doing so will help the fitting and remove wrinkles from the new cover. If the top must be installed at a lower temperature, pliers like those used for installing headlinings can be used to help remove wrinkles. The centerline of the roof panel is measured and marked at the windshield and back window openings. The fabric cover is laid on the roof panel and then folded over lengthwise at the center location. It should then be marked at this location at the front and rear. The cover is then laid, lining side upward, on a clean, flat area.

A nitrile-type, vinyl-trim adhesive is applied to the part of the lining side of the cover that touches the metal portion of the roof. If there is a pad, the glue should overlap it by approximately 1 in. (25 mm). If there is no pad, the lining is completely and evenly covered. It is recommended that the glue be sprayed. If spraying equipment is not available, however, a brush or a mohair-type roller may be used. The cement is allowed to dry thoroughly on the fabric.

The cover is laid and aligned to the centerline of the roof and the marks in the cover. The proper amount of material overhang at the windshield and back window opening [usually about 2 in. (51 mm)] is determined. One-half of the cover is folded over the centerline, and adhesive is applied to the exposed half of the roof panel. Then, starting at the middle of the centerline, the fabric is cemented toward the drip molding while the cement is still wet. As the cover is being cemented, sufficient pressure and tension must be applied to avoid wrinkles and air bubbles. After one side is finished, the same operation is performed on the other side.

It will be necessary to cut relief notches in the cover at all weld-on studs; angle cuts are made as required in the back window opening. If the reveal molding clip could not be removed, the cover is trimmed around the clip and cemented down behind the clip (Fig. 13-1, views C and D).

FIGURE 13-1 Typical roof cover (unpadded). (Courtesy of General Motors of Canada, Ltd.)

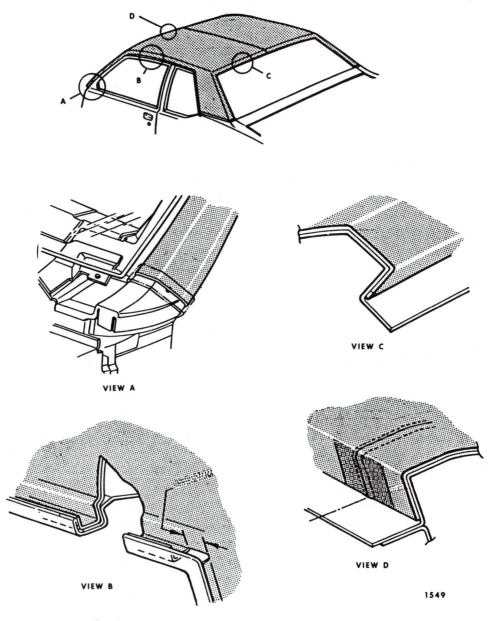

VIEW A

VIEW B

VIEW C

VIEW D

1549

Different operations will be needed to complete the job, depending on the type of body being worked on. When the job is finished, however, all areas that need cement should have a good bond with the roof panel, be free from wrinkles, and be trimmed.

All protective material is now removed, and any moldings and nameplates that were removed are now reinstalled. If any creases or fold marks are present in the cover after installation, they will usually disappear after a while. If air bubbles or wrinkles are present, they are pierced with a small needle; then a dampened shop towel is spread over the area. A flat-type electric home iron is used at low heat; it is applied to the surface with back and forth strokes until the bubble or wrinkle disappears. Care must be taken that the towel does not dry out, for too much heat will permanently damage the cover.

This information applies to bodies built by Fisher, but it also applies fairly closely to other makes. A manufacturer's repair manual should be checked for extra information that may be required for that particular make of car.

UNIT 13-2: REPAIRING FABRIC ROOFS

Some automobiles that have vinyl fabric tops may require repairs for gouged, cut, scuffed, or torn tops. With the proper methods, repairs can be performed that should be satisfactory to the customer if it is done properly. The first method uses a Teflon-coated graining tool with a heat control (Fig. 13-2) and the proper vinyl repair patching compound. The second method uses a heat gun, a graining die, and a fabricated plastic body filler (Fig. 13-3).

To repair the fabric, use a Teflon-coated graining tool and a kit such as shown in Fig. 13-4. The pallet knife is used as a trowel for applying vinyl repair patching compound. A razor or sharp knife is used to remove frayed edges from

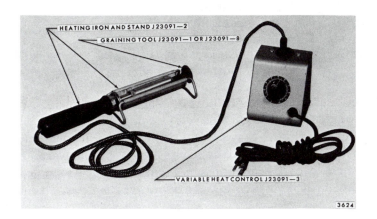

FIGURE 13-2 Fabric roof cover repair tool. (Courtesy of General Motors of Canada, Ltd.)

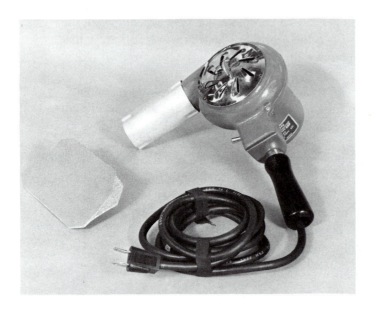

FIGURE 13-3 Fabric roof cover repair die and hot-air gun. (Courtesy of General Motors of Canada, Ltd.)

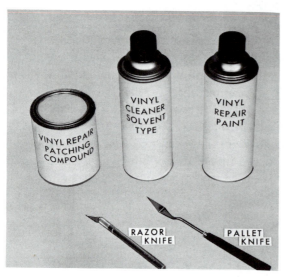

FIGURE 13-4 Fabric roof cover repair materials and tools. (Courtesy of General Motors of Canada, Ltd.)

the damaged areas before the application of the vinyl patching compound. An all-purpose detergent vinyl cleaner is used to clean surface dirt, grease, and dust from roof covers. A solvent vinyl cleaner is used to remove wax, silicone, oil, and so on, from the repair area before applying paint. A vinyl repair patching compound, which is composed of a heat-curing, milky-colored, heavy-bodied plastisol, is used to repair damaged vinyl covers. An approved vinyl repair paint that is durable, weather-resistant, and pliable is used to refinish vinyl-coated fabrics.

Repair Procedure

With a setting of 60 ±2 on the variable heat control, the graining tool is preheated for 15 minutes or until a temperature of 300°F (148°C) is reached. The surface is prepared as follows: If the cover is dirty, the detergent vinyl cleaner is used to clean it. The areas adjacent to the repair area, such as body panels, moldings, and glass, are masked off. Use a razor knife to trim the damaged portion (Fig. 13-5). A minimum of trimming of the vinyl should be done at the damaged areas; no trimming is required on cuts, scuffs, or gouges.

TRIMMING FRAYED EDGES

FIGURE 13-5 Fabric roof cover repair trimming. (Courtesy of General Motors of Canada, Ltd.)

On the damaged areas where no trimming is required, some vinyl patching compound is applied to the edges [Fig. 13-6(A)]. Where trimming has been done, the compound is applied to the area being repaired and troweled flush with the surrounding area [Fig. 13-6(B)]. Any excess material should be removed with a clean cloth.

The graining operation is performed by applying the preheated graining iron over the damaged compound-filled area with just enough pressure to obtain the necessary depth of the graining on the fabric (Fig. 13-7). The graining tool is held there for approximately 1½ minutes. The amount of time to cure and grain the area will vary with a larger area taking slightly more time.

The iron should be held in a stable, perpendicular position during the graining operation. For larger areas of repair, the curing and graining is overlapped

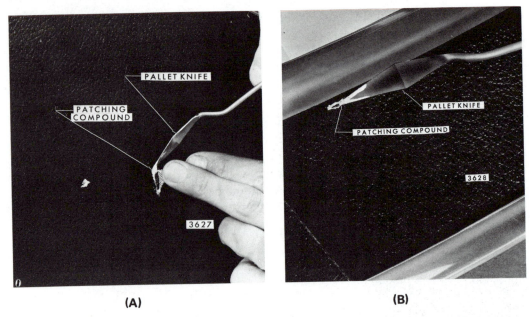

(A)   **(B)**

FIGURE 13-6 Vinyl repair patching compound application. (Courtesy of General Motors of Canada, Ltd.)

FIGURE 13-7 Vinyl patching compound curing and graining. (Courtesy of General Motors of Canada, Ltd.)

until all the area has been done. The graining tool must be cleaned with a solvent vinyl cleaner immediately after the graining operation is finished. A small amount of silicone is applied to prevent vinyl paint from adhering to the tool when it is used again.

Before applying vinyl paint, the area must be cleaned with a solvent vinyl cleaner using a soft lint-free cloth; this is done to remove any wax, oil, or silicone that could be present. The vinyl color is thoroughly mixed according to instructions; but if an aerosol is used, the spray pattern is tested on a piece of paper and then the color is applied to the repaired area using two or three light passes with a fanning motion to create a feather edge around the outside of the repaired area. Heavy wet coats should never be used.

Procedure Used with Fabricated Plastic Graining Die

In this procedure a die from plastic body filler and hardener is made by applying body filler that is mixed according to directions. The filler is spread on a previously prepared grain surface over an area 1/8 in. (3 mm) wide and 6 in. (152 mm) long. The material is spread from the center toward the outer edges. Immediately after, a scrap piece of vinyl, which is clean and of the same grain as the one which has to be repaired, is placed cloth side down over the mold using light finger pressure. In 10 to 15 minutes the filler will be cured. After the filler has cured, the entire mold is removed from the vinyl cover. The excess vinyl backing or unsatisfactory grain is trimmed off.

The area to be repaired is cleaned with a solvent vinyl cleaner and is allowed to dry thoroughly; remember to mask painted areas. Then using the razor knife, the frayed or damaged areas are trimmed to a minimum of 1/8 in. (3 mm) in width. The trimming is done with a taper if possible to facilitate the filling process and better adhesion.

The patching compound is applied in successive thin layers using the pallet knife. The heat gun is used to cure the compound, preferably at a 500°F (259°C) to 700°F (388°C) heat range as each coat is applied and cooled. It is filled and cured until the area is level to the surrounding area. The filler, although it is a milky substance, becomes almost transparent when fully cured. The heat should only be directed to the area until fully cured.

Too much heat could result in losing grain texture. To prevent any overheating, attention should be paid to the adjacent area exposed to the heat; when it becomes glossy, the vinyl has reached a working temperature. Then the graining die is pressed into the soft vinyl and the graining should be accomplished on the first attempt if possible to prevent loss of pattern uniformity. The mold is pressed with a steady even pressure to the back of the graining die; this provides an even impression.

When this operation is finished, the area is cleaned with a solvent cleaner and painted as previously explained.

Bubbles, Blisters, and Bulges

Sometimes a fabric top will have some bubbles, blisters, and bulges; this is usually caused by a separation of the cover from the roof in one spot where air is trapped under the vinyl. A hypodermic needle is inserted through the vinyl material in the bulged area so that it contacts the metal; the plunger should be completely depressed. The heat gun is then used to heat the adhesive under the bubble and to soften the vinyl. The heat should be held approximately 12 in. (305 mm) away from the surface and moved constantly to prevent overheating the vinyl. Check it by intermittently smoothing the surface by hand; if it is too hot, it should be cooled slightly. The plunger on the hypodermic needle is then pulled out to remove trapped air; if some air is still present, the plunger is removed and the bubble is pressed flat on the roof surface. If the vinyl does not stick, some vinyl adhesive is injected with the hypodermic syringe. The needle is then removed and the material is pressed smoothly in place. If any more information is required, a manufacturer's repair manual should be consulted.

QUESTIONS

13-1 Describe, step by step, the method used to install a fabric top.

13-2 What is the maximum temperature to which a fabric top can be heated?

13-3 Describe how a vinyl fabric top is removed and reinstalled.

13-4 Describe the method for repairing a cut in vinyl material by using a graining tool.

13-5 What type of material is used to remove the dirt from the vinyl?

13-6 What type of solvent is used to remove silicone, grease, and oil from the vinyl?

13-7 What is used to cut frayed edges?

13-8 What setting is used on the variable heat control?

13-9 What temperature is used with the heat gun?

13-10 What type of paint is used to refinish a repaired area, and how is the refinishing done?

14

Replacement of Glass and Weather Stripping

UNIT 14-1: REMOVING AND REPLACING WINDSHIELDS AND BACK WINDOWS

Frequently, windshields and back windows are broken in collisions and roll-overs or because of the twisting of the car body. Windshields are also broken by flying gravel, or vandals; they are also pitted by a sandstorm or industrial causes.

The windshields and back windows are usually held by a rubber weather stripping or a special adhesive butyl tape or urethane adhesive. Generally, moldings are placed around the opening on the outside. The outer moldings are called reveal moldings. Other companies have different names for these moldings. Thus, depending on the type of car being worked on, the proper term must be used when ordering parts.

The removal and replacement of the windshields and back windows follow the same methods rather closely. Methods may vary slightly for different makes of cars; however, many of the operations that are applied to one make of car can be applied to others as well. One of the first steps is to cover the seats, the dash, and the hood with a protective covering so as not to damage the upholstery and paint. Then the garnish moldings and the rear-view mirror are removed.

The center of the windshield and glass opening should be marked before removal. Next, the air-intake panel, if there is one, is detached; this is usually held by screws (Fig. 14-1). The wiper arms and outside or reveal moldings are

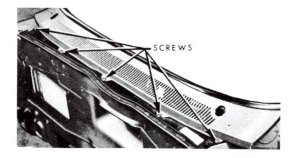

SCREWS

FIGURE 14-1 (Courtesy of General Motors of Canada, Ltd.)

detached; usually, special tools are needed to release the clips that hold the moldings. To remove the glass, break the seal between the rubber channel and the body-opening flange. A putty knife can be used to help force the lip of the weather stripping over the flange while applying hand pressure against the glass to push it out (Fig. 14-2). Only enough force to push the glass out should be applied. The cement and sealer must be removed from the body opening and the rubber channel. The windshield-opening flange should be checked for burrs or distortion, especially when the glass breaks without any valid reason or if the opening has been distorted from an accident. Special blocks are available to check the gap between the glass, the flange, and outer edge of the sheet metal. They are installed as shown in Fig. 14-3. The glass is then laid in the opening and the gap is checked. The gap between the pinch-weld flange and glass should be between 1/4 to 5/16 in. (6 to 8 mm) and from the outer edge the gap should be 5/16 to 3/8 in. (8 to 10 mm). If the opening has to be reshaped, the areas should be marked. Also, the centerline of the windshield and body should be marked so that the glass will be centered properly when permanently installed.

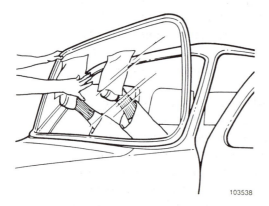

103538

FIGURE 14-2 Removing windshield from opening. (Courtesy of General Motors of Canada, Ltd.)

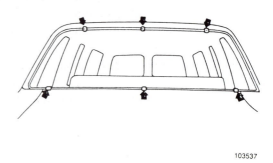

103537

FIGURE 14-3 Checking windshield opening. (Courtesy of General Motors of Canada, Ltd.)

When all necessary repairs have been made, repair areas should be primed, sanded, and painted to match the vehicle.

The installation of this type of windshield requires a number of cure-time steps. All cure times are minimum, unless otherwise indicated. When performing a step that requires a cure time to elapse, do not wait but make a note of the time and move on to a following operation that does not interfere with the timed sequence.

With a dry cloth, wipe the pinch-weld clean, making sure to remove previous urethane; then apply pinch-weld primer with a new applicator to the pinch weld [Fig. 14-4(B)]. The primer must be agitated and stirred prior to application

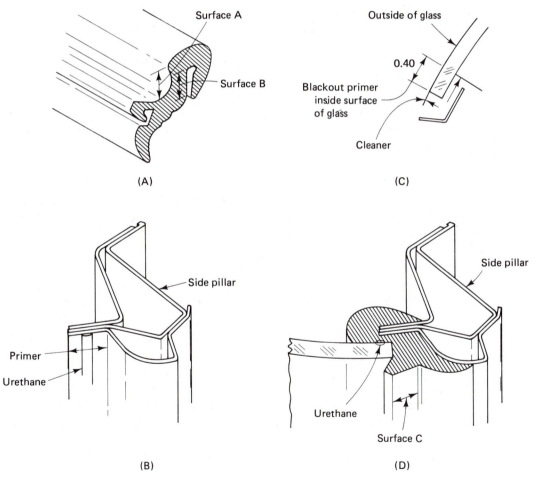

FIGURE 14-4 Windshield installation for a CK truck. (Courtesy of General Motors of Canada, Ltd.)

and allowed to cure for at least 30 minutes. The temperature of the pinch-weld flange should not exceed 160°F (38°C) at the time of primer application. A rubber cleaner must be applied to both channels of the rubber weather stripping [Fig. 14-4(A)]. This should be allowed to dry for 5 minutes; then both channels are wiped with a clean dry cloth.

The rubber primer is applied to both channels in the rubber weather stripping that were cleaned previously [Fig. 14-4(A)]. The primer is allowed to dry for at least 30 minutes. The surface of the glass on which black-out primer will be applied is cleaned around the edge of the inside surface with a clean alcohol dampened cloth and then allowed to dry. Never touch the edge of a plastic laminate material with a volatile cleaner. This could cause deterioration or discoloration of plastic laminate by wicking action.

The blackout primer is applied to the same area of the windshield glass that was cleaned before [Fig. 14-4(C)], and allowed to dry to touch. A 3/16 in. (6 mm) minimum diameter bead of urethane adhesive is applied around the pinch weld flange [Fig. 14-4(B)]. The windshield has to be installed within 20 minutes after applying the urethane. A mist of plain water is applied to the urethane bead on the pinch-weld flange, wetting it fully. The rubber weatherstrip is installed to the pinch-weld flange, then a 3/16 in (6 mm) minimum diameter bead of urethane adhesive is applied to the weather strip glass channel as shown in Fig. 14-4(D).

A mist of lubricant is applied to surface C or weatherstrip [Fig. 14-4(D)], wetting it fully. The windshield must be installed within 5 minutes after performing this operation. On windshields with an embedded antenna, the pigtail of the antenna should be taped to the inside surface of the windshield glass in a convenient position.

With the aid of a helper, the glass is lifted into the window opening of the weather stripping and then installed in it. Seat the windshield properly in the weather strip, then lubricate the lock strip channel and install the lock strip into the weather strip channel (Fig. 14-5). The lockstrip cap is then installed; it should be in the bottom center section of the windshield weather strip. The wipers, inside trim panel, rear view mirror, and radio antenna pigtail are all installed. The glass and all working areas should be cleaned thoroughly.

On late-model cars, a different method of installing windshields and some back windows has been used. The glass is glued to the opening pinch-weld flange by a urethane adhesive or butyl tape. As a result, companies employing this method use a different type of clip to hold the outside molding. This clip requires a special tool to engage the clip to permit the removal of the moldings (Fig. 14-6).

Special kits must be purchased to install this type of windshield or back window. These kits contain all necessary parts required for the installation. Gen-

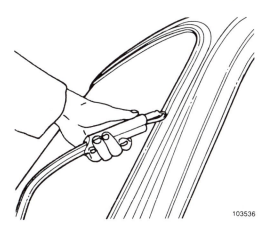

FIGURE 14-5 Installing reveal molding. (Courtesy of General Motors of Canada, Ltd.)

103536

eral Motors used two methods and a special adhesive caulking material. One method is called the extended method. The second, the short method, is used when the glass has to be changed and the adhesive remaining on the pinch-weld flange is good enough to be used as a base for the new adhesive. When the

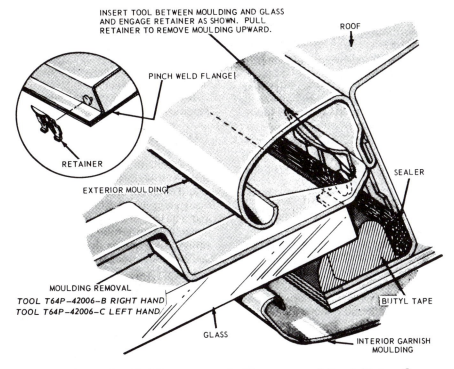

INSERT TOOL BETWEEN MOULDING AND GLASS AND ENGAGE RETAINER AS SHOWN. PULL RETAINER TO REMOVE MOULDING UPWARD.

ROOF

PINCH WELD FLANGE

RETAINER

SEALER

EXTERIOR MOULDING

MOULDING REMOVAL
TOOL T64P–42006–B RIGHT HAND
TOOL T64P–42006–C LEFT HAND

BUTYL TAPE

GLASS

INTERIOR GARNISH MOULDING

FIGURE 14-6 Molding removal. (Courtesy of Ford Motor Company of Canada, Ltd.)

adhesive remaining after the glass has been cut out is in poor condition or if metal work has to be done on the flange, the extended method must be used. That is, the urethane remaining on the flange is removed and new urethane and spacers are installed. Some companies use a butyl tape to glue to the glass. This tape has to be removed when the glass is changed and a new tape installed. The tape is peeled away from the body pinch-weld flange; it is then grasped and pulled directly away (Fig. 14-7). General Motors uses a rubber-sealing strip dam on the windshield when windshields are installed at the factory. The reason is to stop any excessive squeeze out of the urethane material, but this practice is not used in the repair field. It comes in a tube and is forced out by a caulking gun. A special primer is used on the remaining caulking material so that new urethane material sticks to the old material. In the extended method or when using butyl tape, another special type of primer is used on the flange to provide better adhesion for the tape or caulking adhesive.

The method used to detach this type of installation once the moldings and all necessary parts are removed is the same for all companies. On cars having an electric grille defogger or radio antenna in the glass, the wires must be disconnected and taped to the inside of the glass for the defogger and to the outside of the glass for the antenna.

Either steel music wire or an electric hot knife or cold razor knife is used to cut the adhesive. The electric hot knife is inserted through the glue, close to the glass. It is then pulled, which will cut the glue (Fig. 14-8). The knife should be held as close to the glass as possible, but excessive pressure should not be used because the glass might crack.

FIGURE 14-7 Butyl tape removal. (Courtesy of Ford Motor Company of Canada, Ltd.)

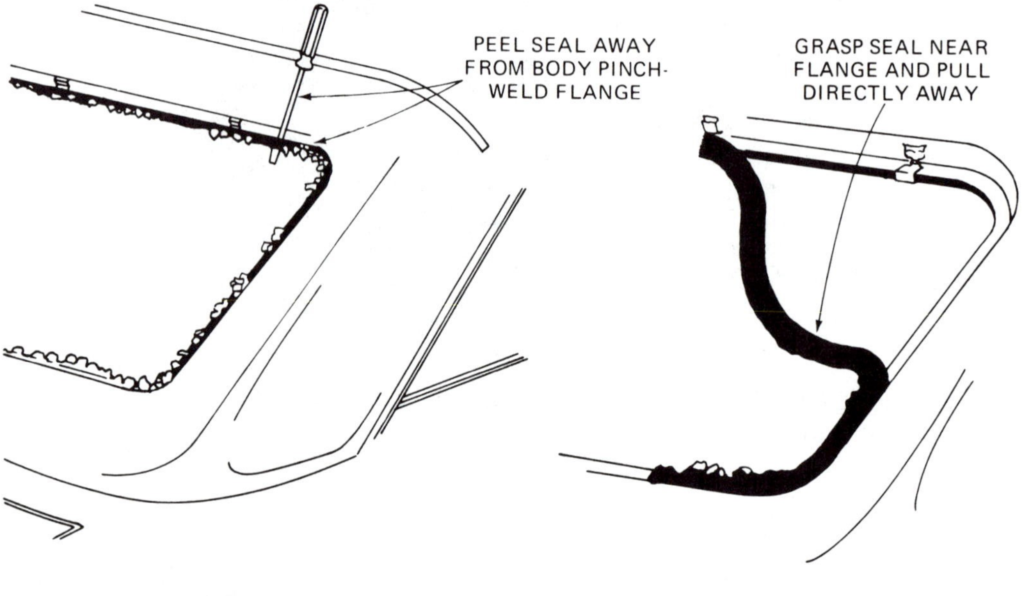

PEEL SEAL AWAY FROM BODY PINCH-WELD FLANGE

GRASP SEAL NEAR FLANGE AND PULL DIRECTLY AWAY

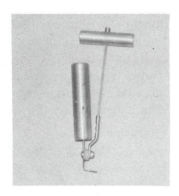

(A)

(B)

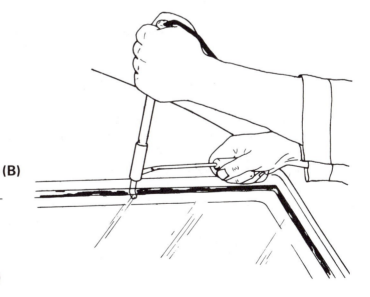

FIGURE 14-8 (A) Cold-knife removal method; (B) electric hot-knife removal method. (Courtesy of General Motors of Canada, Ltd.)

When two people are removing the glass, piano wire is inserted through the glue, close to the glass, and each end is tied to a short piece of wood, which will serve as handles. If the short method is used, the wire is held close to the glass to prevent cutting an excessive amount of adhesive from the window opening. The wire is pulled carefully through the adhesive material around the entire perimeter of the window. The wire must be kept under tension throughout the cutting operation in order to prevent kinking or breaking (Fig. 14-9).

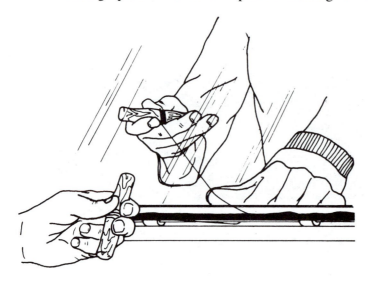

FIGURE 14-9 Cutting adhesive caulk material. (Courtesy of General Motors of Canada, Ltd.)

If only one man removes the glass, the wire is inserted through the adhesive material at the inner upper edge of the glass and then through the adhesive material at the inner lower edge. Handles are attached to each end of the wire and the adhesive can then be cut (Fig. 14-10).

On Chrysler cars, or other cars using butyl tape or adhesive, all the remaining tape or adhesive on the flange has to be cleaned thoroughly. Steel wool is used to remove the remaining flakes and the old primer of the fence. A nonoily solvent can be used to clean the surface thoroughly before priming (Fig. 14-11).

Manufacturers that use urethane adhesive use it because its tensile strength psi is greater than that of butyl tape. In fact, glass that is installed with urethane at the factory should never be repaired with any other material than urethane. Butyl tape will allow the glass to move in the opening, and sooner or later a water leak will develop. Or, because of the moving of the glass, the butyl tape will gradually move away from the fence and could at worst cause the glass to break. The materials used in installing windshields or back windows are shown in Fig. 14-12. They are urethane E primer, urethane glass cleaner, and urethane E adhesive.

FIGURE 14-10 One-man wire removal method. (Courtesy of General Motors of Canada, Ltd.)

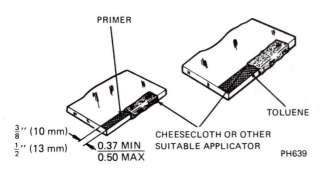

PRIMER

TOLUENE

$\frac{3}{8}''$ (10 mm)
$\frac{1}{2}''$ (13 mm)

CHEESECLOTH OR OTHER SUITABLE APPLICATOR

0.37 MIN
0.50 MAX

PH639

FIGURE 14-11 Cleaning glass surface. (Courtesy of Chrysler Canada, Ltd.)

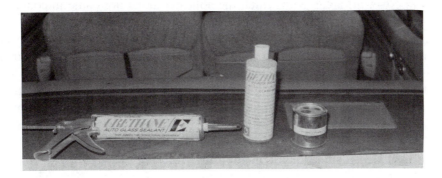

FIGURE 14-12 Material required for urethane installation.

If the removed glass is to be used again, it should be laid on a protected bench or holding fixture. All remaining caulk is removed with a putty knife or razor blade; any remaining traces can be removed with thinner. The edge of laminated glass should not come into contact with a volatile cleaner, for this may cause discoloration of the plastic laminate.

Before the glass is installed, the molding clips should be checked; any damaged clips must be repaired or changed. Any clip that is bent more than 5/16 in. (2 mm) from the body metal must be repaired or changed. If the clips are retained by screws, they must be sealed to prevent any water leaks.

If the short method is used on General Motors cars, the glass is installed in the opening, to check the relationship of the glass to the adhesive. If more than 1/8 in. (3 mm) of gap exists, it must be shimmed; otherwise more caulking material will have to be applied. The glass should be positioned in the opening and a piece of tape is then applied over each side edge of the glass and the body pillar (Fig. 14-13). The tape is slit vertically at the edge of the glass. These marks can be used to align the glass during the installation.

GLASS ALIGNMENT TO OPENING

FIGURE 14-13

The urethane E primer is applied on the fence with a brush. Care must be taken to cover all areas with which the adhesive must not come in contact (Fig. 14-14). A different primer is used for butyl tape, but the method is the same.

All glass spacers should be checked for damage; if damage exists, the spacers should be replaced. Loose or new spacers are glued with caulking material adhesive in the proper location. Figure 14-15 shows the proper location for the spacers on General Motors and Chrysler cars. The gap between the glass and pinch-weld flange should not be less than 3/16 in. (5 mm) or more than a 1/4 in. (6 mm).

The primer is applied on the original adhesive or on the pinch-weld flange in the extended method or the method used on other cars (Fig. 14-16). Primer should not be spilled on the paint or upholstery, for it may mar the surface. If any is spilled, it should be removed immediately.

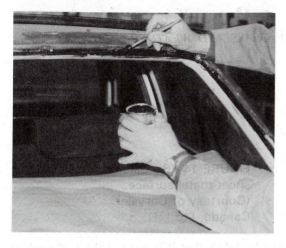

FIGURE 14-14 Applying urethane E primer with brush.

It once cures [?], care must be taken so that it is not too thick. If applied [...]
[faded text overlapping figure]

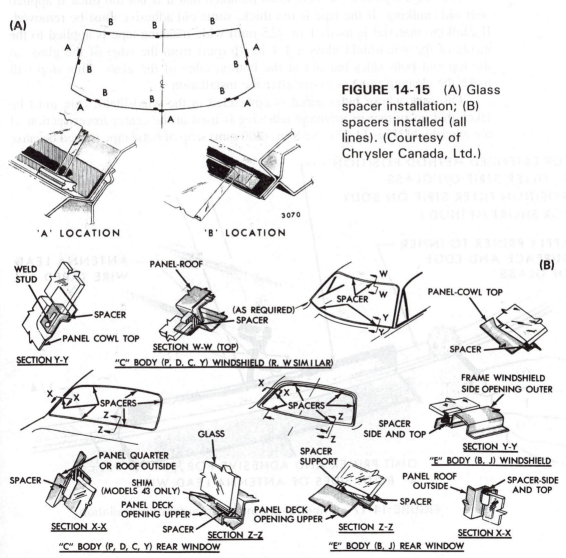

FIGURE 14-15 (A) Glass spacer installation; (B) spacers installed (all lines). (Courtesy of Chrysler Canada, Ltd.)

(A)

'A' LOCATION   'B' LOCATION

3070

(B)

WELD STUD — SPACER — PANEL COWL TOP

SECTION Y-Y

PANEL-ROOF — SPACER (AS REQUIRED) SPACER

SECTION W-W (TOP)

"C" BODY (P, D, C, Y) WINDSHIELD (R, W SIMILAR)

W W SPACER Y Y

PANEL-COWL TOP — SPACER

X X SPACERS Z Z

SPACER — PANEL QUARTER OR ROOF OUTSIDE — SHIM (MODELS 43 ONLY) — PANEL DECK OPENING UPPER — SPACER

SECTION X-X

SECTION Z-Z

"C" BODY (P, D, C, Y) REAR WINDOW

GLASS

X X SPACERS Z Z

SPACER SUPPORT — SPACER — PANEL DECK OPENING UPPER

SPACER SIDE AND TOP

FRAME WINDSHIELD SIDE OPENING OUTER

SECTION Y-Y

"E" BODY (B, J) WINDSHIELD

PANEL ROOF OUTSIDE — SPACER — SPACER-SIDE AND TOP

SECTION Z-Z

SECTION X-X

"E" BODY (B, J) REAR WINDOW

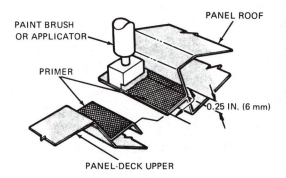

PAINT BRUSH
OR APPLICATOR

PANEL ROOF

PRIMER

0.25 IN. (6 mm)

PANEL-DECK UPPER

FIGURE 14-16 Cleaning sheet-metal surface. (Courtesy of Chrysler Canada, Ltd.)

If a butyl tape is used, care must be taken that it is not too thick if applied over old caulking. If the tape is too thick, some old adhesive must be removed. If caulking material is used, 1 in. (25 mm) wide masking tape is applied to the inside of the windshield glass a 1/4 in. (6 mm) from the edge of the glass, at the top and both sides but not at the bottom edge of the glass. This step will make the cleanup process easier after the installation.

On a car whose radio aerial is embedded in the windshield, care must be taken that no primer or urethane adhesive is used at the center lower section of the windshield (Fig. 14-17). An 8-in. (200 mm) strip of butyl tape is used because

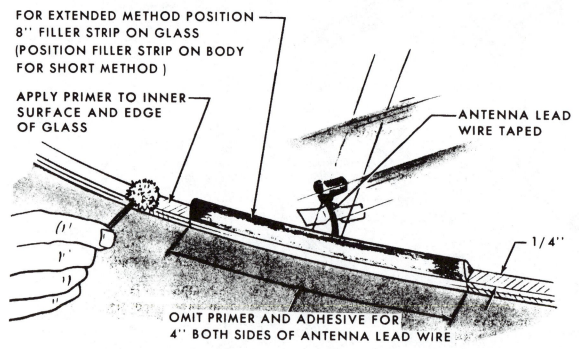

FOR EXTENDED METHOD POSITION
8'' FILLER STRIP ON GLASS
(POSITION FILLER STRIP ON BODY
FOR SHORT METHOD)

APPLY PRIMER TO INNER
SURFACE AND EDGE
OF GLASS

ANTENNA LEAD
WIRE TAPED

1/4''

OMIT PRIMER AND ADHESIVE FOR
4'' BOTH SIDES OF ANTENNA LEAD WIRE

FIGURE 14-17 Embedded windshield antenna installation.

it will not interfere with radio reception. It is also important that the primer should be allowed to dry for at least 5 minutes.

The surface of the glass on which adhesive material is applied is thoroughly cleaned with urethane glass cleaner (Fig. 14-18), or with a clean alcohol dampened cloth around the edge of the inside surface. This should be allowed to air dry before the primer is applied around the periphery of the glass, as in Fig. 14-17. Care should be taken not to apply the primer in the center lower section if the windshield has an aerial in it.

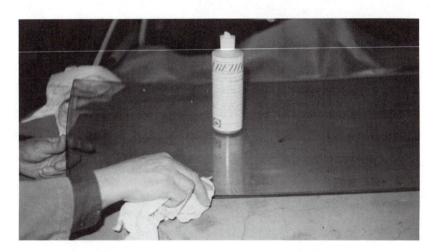

FIGURE 14-18 Cleaning the windshield.

The short method is used when the adhesive remaining on the fence has not been damaged too much. On some windshields it is almost impossible to locate the exact area at the lower part where the bead of adhesive should be applied. Here, the bead is put on the fence of the opening and the rest of the glass is done in the regular method. A smooth, continuous bead of adhesive material is laid around the entire inside edge of the glass. The material should be between 1/8 to 3/16 in. (3 to 5 mm) in diameter.

When the extended method is used, a bead 3/8 in. (10 mm) high and 3/16 in. (5 mm) wide is applied to the fence (Fig. 14-19); if spacer blocks are unavailable, the adhesive is given an overnight cure. A bead 3/8 in. (10 mm) high and 3/16 in. (5 mm) wide is used on the inside edge of the glass (Fig. 14-20).

If a butyl tape is used, it must be applied not more than 1/16 in. (2 mm) from the opening edge of the flange. The tape must not be stretched when fitted to the corners; it should be spliced at the side of the glass opening (Fig. 14-21).

During installation, the glass should be held by suction cups or lifted by hand. If no suction cups are used, the glass is carried with one hand on the inside

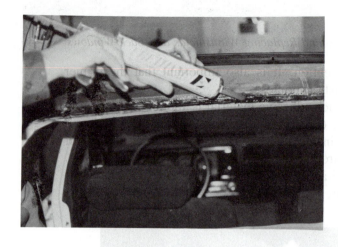

FIGURE 14-19 Applying adhesive to fence.

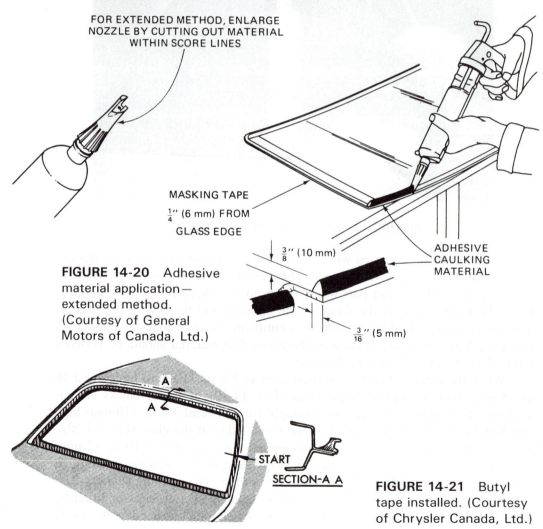

FOR EXTENDED METHOD, ENLARGE NOZZLE BY CUTTING OUT MATERIAL WITHIN SCORE LINES

MASKING TAPE $\frac{1}{4}$'' (6 mm) FROM GLASS EDGE

$\frac{3}{8}$'' (10 mm)

ADHESIVE CAULKING MATERIAL

$\frac{3}{16}$'' (5 mm)

FIGURE 14-20 Adhesive material application— extended method. (Courtesy of General Motors of Canada, Ltd.)

A

A

START

SECTION-A A

FIGURE 14-21 Butyl tape installed. (Courtesy of Chrysler Canada, Ltd.)

of the glass and one hand on the outside. The glass is placed in a horizontal position when the opening is reached. While the glass is held by one man, the second man reaches with one arm around the body pillar and supports the glass while the first man assumes the same position (Fig. 14-22). The tape is used as a guide to position the glass in the opening on the lower supports.

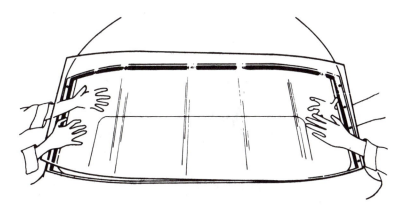

FIGURE 14-22   Glass installation. (Courtesy of General Motors of Canada, Ltd.)

The glass is firmly pressed to wet-out and set the adhesive material, but care should be taken to avoid an excessive squeeze-out of adhesive because it could cause an appearance problem. By using a small, flat-bladed tool or a disposable brush, extra material, if it is needed, is paddled around the edge of the glass to ensure a watertight seal and to fill any voids. On windshields equipped with embedded antenna additional material should be paddled at the edges of the butyl strip. Care should be taken to avoid the area near the antenna lead pigtail. On installations using butyl tape it is well advised that the edge of the glass be sealed with an appropriate sealer to fill any voids.

The car should be water tested by using a soft spray of warm water around the perimeter of the glass. If there are any leaks, extra adhesive is paddled at the leaking point with a flat-bladed tool (Fig. 14-23). At no time should a hard stream of water be used against the fresh adhesive. On urethane installations care should be taken that the glass lower supports be installed properly to stop the glass from sliding down. A rubber spacer should be cemented between both right and left sides of the glass and metal to ensure that the glass will remain centered in the opening while the adhesive material is curing. All moldings are then reinstalled, the tape on the inside is removed, and the area is cleaned up.

On all windshield installations using urethane, the vehicle must remain at normal room temperature for 6 hours in order to complete the proper curing of the adhesive material.

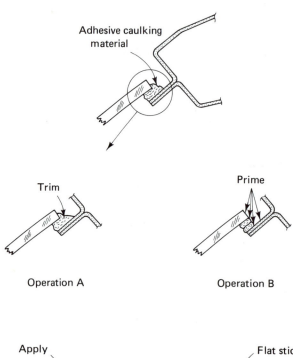

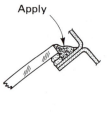

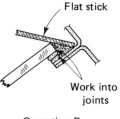

FIGURE 14-23 Adhesive-caulked glass water leak correction. (Courtesy of General Motors of Canada, Ltd.)

On a lot of late-model cars a vinyl reveal molding is used (Fig. 14-24) and it is retained to the body by urethane adhesive. To remove this molding, slide the escutcheon located at the top centerline of the molding to one side; this will expose the butt joint of molding out of the urethane. When the molding is removed about 3 in. (75 mm), grasp the molding by hand and slowly pull the molding away from the body until it is removed.

The original molding may be reused by doing the following (Fig. 14-25): Trim the lower barb off the molding using a razor blade or knife. A clear primer from a urethane kit is applied to the lower portion of the molding before reinstallation.

If the original molding cannot be reused due to damage, it should be discarded and replaced with a new one. The new molding has a shorter shank and will not bottom out when installed. Fit new molding to body before doing the

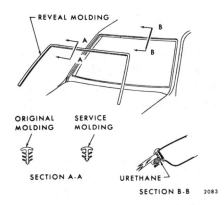

FIGURE 14-24 Windshield vinyl reveal molding for A styles. (Courtesy of General Motors of Canada, Ltd.)

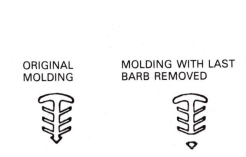

FIGURE 14-25 Reveal molding barb removal. (Courtesy of General Motors of Canada, Ltd.)

actual installation. Enough urethane is applied to the cavity between the body metal and glass to retain the molding. Use a container filled with lukewarm water and flood the cavity filled with urethane. Moisture is the catalyst for the adhesive and will speed up the cure of the material.

The centerline at the top of the glass is located; the installation of the molding is started there by pressing the molding into place using hand pressure. The escutcheon is then reinstalled, and a second application of water on top of the molding is done. If required, masking tape may be applied over the molding to keep it flush with the glass while curing.

UNIT 14-2: WEATHER STRIP MAINTENANCE

The weather strips used on doors and door frames, as well as on other parts, perform an important job on an automobile body. The weather strip seals or bridges the gap between a movable panel, such as a door, and the door frame. It seals the gap to keep out dust, rain, and air. Therefore, since it has to perform a very important task, it must be serviced properly.

The various automobile companies use a variety of methods to attach the weatherstrip to the panels—weather strip adhesive, wire clips, screws, plastic clips, and special grooved retainers. All these methods may be used, or only one or two, depending on the manufacturer. In order to remove the weather stripping, one uses whatever process is appropriate for the method used to attach the weather stripping to the panel. For example, when the weather strip has been attached with adhesive, a putty knife can be used to break or cut the bond of the adhesive to the panel.

Before installing the weather strip, the contact area on the weather strip and panel should be cleaned with a nonoily solvent. The adhesive should be applied thinly to the panel and the weather strip, on the areas where both surfaces will meet. The adhesive should be allowed to dry until it becomes tacky before the weather strip is pressed to the panel.

The weather strip should only be glued at the same location as it was at the factory. The weather strip is sometimes held to the panels by a combination of adhesive, clips, and plastic retainers [Fig. 14-26(A)]. On some cars, a body-caulking compound is used to help seal certain areas. After the weather strip has been installed, all excess adhesive should be removed.

Some of the weather strips are bulbous and are installed on the body pinch-weld flange [Fig. 14-26(B)]. They are usually retained by adhesive or friction. To remove them it is necessary to break the adhesive bond and then pull them off.

On certain models, especially hardtop sedans, a weather strip retainer is used to hold the weather strip (Fig. 14-27). This type of retainer is usually held on the body with screws, and a sealing compound or polyurethane strip is applied between it and the body to prevent water leaks. The weather strip is normally held at the ends with screws that must be removed to service it. The cement bond has to be broken with a flat-bladed tool as the weather strip is pulled carefully out of the retainer.

Before a new weather strip is installed, the retainer should be cleaned thoroughly to remove the old adhesive. A bead of adhesive is then applied to the outboard flange of the weather strip retainer where necessary. The weather strip is positioned to the front part of the retainer and the screws or plastic fasteners are installed. The weather strip is then inserted into the rest of the retainer by using a flat-bladed tool, the inboard lip first and then the outboard lip. All hardware that was removed can now be reinstalled.

The weather strip on some newer cars is retained with nylon fasteners to the door panels. The fasteners are a component part of the weather strip; they secure it to the panel by being engaged into piercings in the panel. The fasteners have serrations around the stem that retain the fastener in the piercing and also seal the openings to prevent water leaks. A tool like the one shown in Fig. 14-28 is used to remove them from the piercings. In addition to these fasteners, a certain amount of adhesive is used in certain areas to retain the weather strip to the door panel (Fig. 14-29). When the weather strip is reinstalled, all the nylon fasteners should be examined for damage. If damage exists, they should be changed. If the weather strip is damaged in the areas where the fasteners are

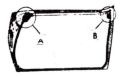

(A)

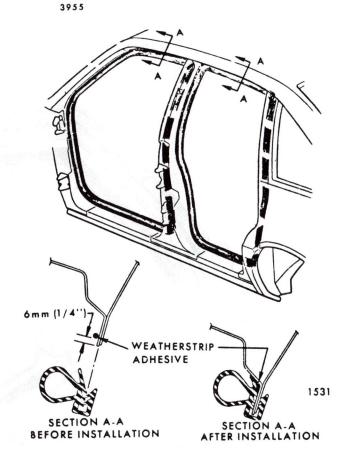

FIGURE 14-26 (A) Door weather strip, coupe styles; (B) front and rear door opening weather strip installation. [(A) Courtesy of General Motors of Canada, Ltd.)]

(B)

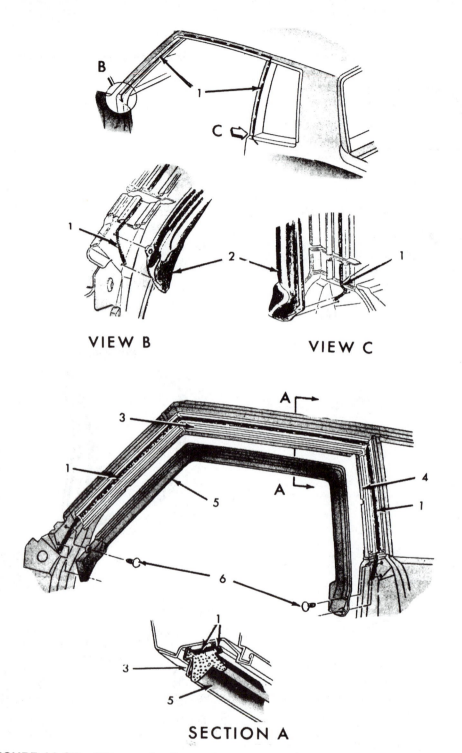

VIEW B

VIEW C

SECTION A

FIGURE 14-27 Slide roof rail weather strip and retainer, A-37 style shown. 1, Weather strip adhesive; 2, end details of weather strip; 3, slide roof rail weather strip retainer; 4, body lock pillar weather strip retainer; 5, weather strip; 6, plastic nail fasteners.

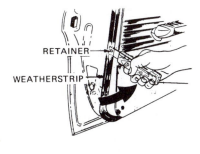

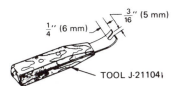

FIGURE 14-28 Door weather strip removal. (Courtesy of General Motors of Canada, Ltd.)

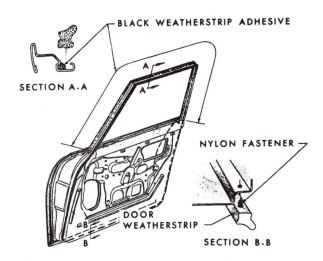

FIGURE 14-29 Door weather strip. (Courtesy of General Motors of Canada, Ltd.)

inserted, it may be necessary to replace it. Generally, it is replaced if two or three areas are damaged. If the weather strip is not changed, it will be difficult to keep the weather strip in the proper contact area. To install the fasteners into the piercings, tap them with a hammer or a blunt caulking tool.

When it is difficult to get the weather strip to touch the door frame or other flange, it is sometimes necessary to use shim stock to raise the weather strip so that it will make better contact with the area of the frame and thus provide a good seal.

The door drain hole slots are sometimes sealed with a flat weather strip that will let water out but will not let dust enter the door (Fig. 14-30). To remove the strip, a flat-bladed tool is used to pry the retaining plugs from the inner panel piercings. To reinstall, a blunt-pointed tool, such as an ice pick, is inserted into the strip-retaining plugs and they are pushed into the panel piercings.

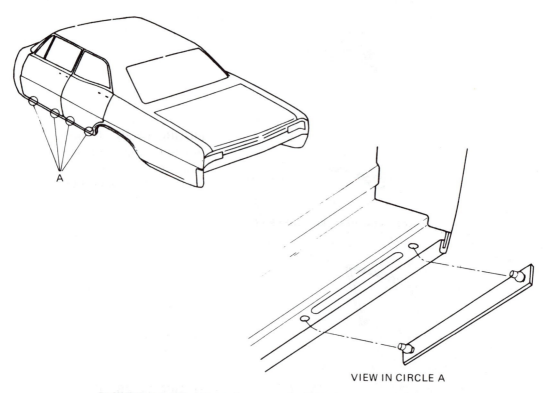

VIEW IN CIRCLE A

FIGURE 14-30   Door bottom drain hole sealing strips. (Courtesy of General Motors of Canada, Ltd.)

Glass-run channel-sealing strips are used to seal between the door inner and outer panels and the window at the beltline. Strips are attached to the door trim panel on the inside and to the door panel on the outside. They are usually attached with staples to the trim panel, and clips or screws are used to attach them to the door panel. To remove the strip, it is usually necessary to lower the window as low as possible. If it is not low enough, the stops on the window will have to be removed to permit the window to be lowered more. If screws are used to hold

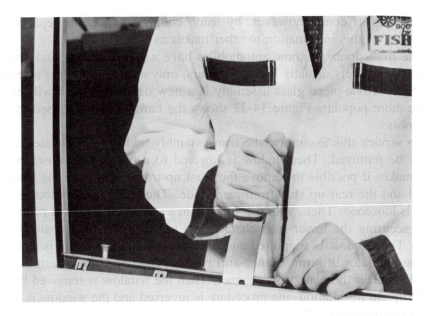

FIGURE 14-31 Clip-retained glass-run channel strip assembly removal. (Courtesy of General Motors of Canada, Ltd.)

the strip, a screwdriver is used, but if clips are used, a tool such as the one shown in Fig. 14-31 can be used to remove it. The area adjacent to the strip should be protected with tape to prevent marring the surface. The tool is fitted over the tang of the clip; the clip can then be disengaged from the slots in the flange of the door. To install the strip, it is positioned so that each clip tang starts from the slots; then the clips are engaged by pressing down.

To fabricate such a tool, a slot 1/4 in. (6 mm) wide and 3/8 in. (10 mm) deep is cut in a flat-bladed tool similar to a headlining inserting tool.

UNIT 14-3: DOOR AND GLASS SERVICE

Door and glass servicing represents an important part of the work a body man will be required to do. He not only has to service doors and glass after an accident but also has to repair, change parts, and align the windows and doors. Many different types of regulators, locks, lock cylinders, and vent assemblies are used, each with a specific function.

When certain parts on doors are out of alignment or are worn, they require servicing. The information in the following pages deals with some of the more popular types of doors; however, by using common sense, the repairman can apply much of this information to other makes as well.

The front doors on some automobiles have a vent assembly and a window assembly; on others, usually late-model cars, only a one-piece glass assembly is used. Since a one-piece glass assembly is a new development, it will probably become more popular. Figure 14-32 shows the hardware that is used in one of these doors.

To service this assembly, the trim assembly and the inner water deflector have to be removed. The window is lowered to a one-quarter down position, which makes it possible to remove the front up-travel stop from the lower sash channel and the rear up stop from rear guide. The rear guide to door-attaching screws is loosened. Then, with the window in a three-quarter down position, the screws securing the lower sash channel run to the lower sash channel are removed. The window is supported and the lower sash channel run is disengaged from the regulator lift-arm balance-arm rollers. The regulator lift arm is pushed inboard, to clear the glass sash channel. Then the window is removed by lifting straight up. In installation, the procedure is reversed and the window is adjusted for proper alignment.

When the window is removed, the regulator can be serviced if necessary. If the lock needs servicing when the door trim is removed, it is usually necessary to disconnect the remote control and lock cylinder. The rear window channel is also disconnected and moved away. This step will give the clearance required to take out the lock assembly. The lock assembly can only be removed after all the screws holding it to the door panel are removed. To reinstall, the procedure is reversed.

On some of the newer models a new type of regulator is used. The following discussion describes removal and servicing of these units.

The window is raised to full-up position and the glass is taped to the door frame using a cloth-backed body tape. The bolts holding the lower sash channel on the glass to the regulator sash are removed. The rubber down stop is removed from the bottom of the door by pulling carefully. The regulator handle is attached and the regulator is run to the full-down position. The regulator sash is removed by rotating 90° and pulling the outboard.

While supporting the glass, the tape is removed and the glass is lowered to full-down position. The front edge of the glass is disengaged from the front glass run channel retainer (item 14, Fig. 14-33). The glass is slid forward and tilted slightly to remove the guide from the retainer in the run channel. With care the glass is raised while tilting it forward and removing the glass inboard of the upper frame.

If the tape in this regulator needs replacing, insert a thin flat-bladed screwdriver into the slot at the top of the guide. Press down on the screwdriver and

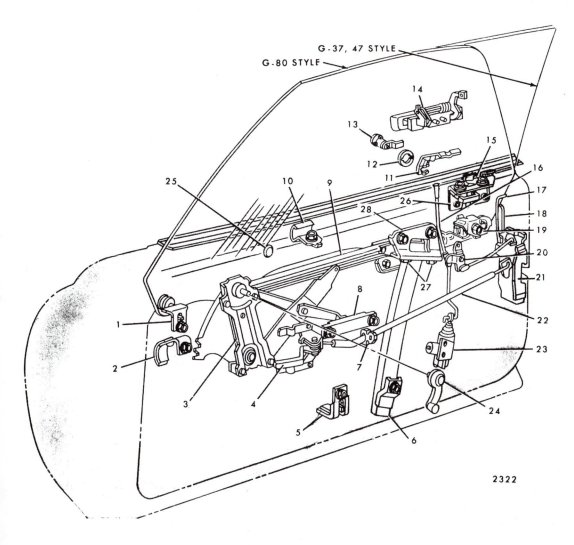

G-37, 47 STYLE
G-80 STYLE

2322

1. Front Up-Travel Stop (on Inner Panel)
2. Glass Stabilizer (on Inner Panel)
3. Manual Window Regulator
4. Inside Remote Handle
5. Down-Travel Stop
6. Vertical Guide Cam Assembly
7. Silencer
8. Inner Panel Cam
9. Lower Sash Channel Cam

10. Front Belt Stabilizer and Trim Retainer
11. Lock Cylinder Retainer
12. Lock Cylinder Gasket
13. Lock Cylinder Assembly
14. Outside Handle Assembly
15. Rear Belt Stabilizer Pin Assembly (on Inner Panel)
16. Inside Locking Rod

17. Outside Handle to Lock Connecting Rod
18. Lock Cylinder to Lock Connecting Rod
19. Rear Up-Travel Stop (on Inner Panel)
20. Bell Crank
21. Door Lock
22. Inside Handle to Lock Connecting Rod
23. Power Door Lock Actuator
24. Manual Window Regulator Handle

25. Plastic Stabilizer Button (on Glass)
26. Plastic Stabilizer Guide (Riveted to Glass)
27. Vertical Guide Upper Support (Lower) Screws
28. Vertical Guide Upper Support

FIGURE 14-32 Door hardware—G coupe styles. (Courtesy of General Motors of Canada, Ltd.)

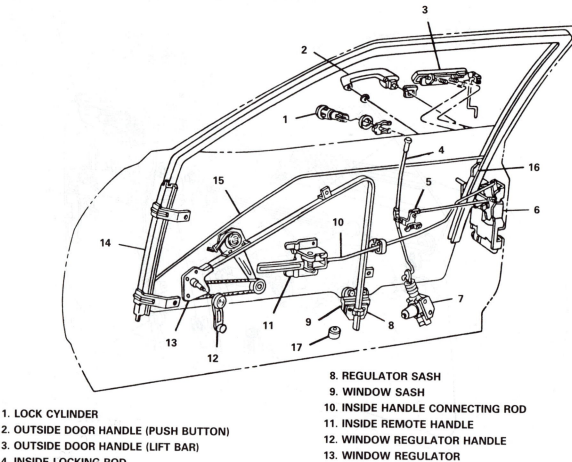

1. LOCK CYLINDER
2. OUTSIDE DOOR HANDLE (PUSH BUTTON)
3. OUTSIDE DOOR HANDLE (LIFT BAR)
4. INSIDE LOCKING ROD
5. LOCKING ROD BELL CRANK
6. DOOR LOCK
7. DOOR LOCK ACTUATOR
8. REGULATOR SASH
9. WINDOW SASH
10. INSIDE HANDLE CONNECTING ROD
11. INSIDE REMOTE HANDLE
12. WINDOW REGULATOR HANDLE
13. WINDOW REGULATOR
14. FRONT RUN CHANNEL
15. DOOR GLASS
16. PLASTIC GUIDE
17. RUBBER DOWN STOP

FIGURE 14-33 Front door hardware—B, D-37, 47, 69 styles typical.

pull forward to disengage the block from the guide. Using your thumb, push up on the guide from the block. The block is removed from the tape and the guide and sash are allowed to drop to the bottom of the door. The tape is removed from the tabs using a flat-bladed screwdriver. The regulator crank is used to turn the regulator to remove the tape from the regulator (Fig. 14-34).

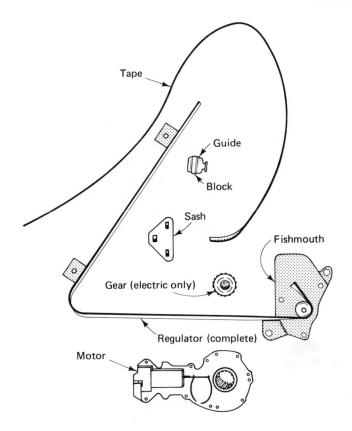

FIGURE 14-34 Tape drive regulator service parts—electric shown, manual similar. (Courtesy of General Motors of Canada, Ltd.)

The new tape is cut to the length needed and then inserted into the fishmouth of the regulator to attach it to the gear and then run through the regulator. Position the end of the tape at the center of the access hole. The last hole on the tape must fit over the last tab on the regulator housing; this is required for proper glass travel. The procedure for reinstallation is to replace the parts in the opposite order of disassembly.

The lubrication of door hardware is one of the most neglected services. The hinges, locks, and all hardware should be lubricated with a suitable white lithium soap grease where required (Fig. 14-35).

The window glass requires servicing when it is broken or when part of the channel assembly is broken. To remove the channel from the glass, a special tool (Fig. 14-36) can be used. If none is available, the bottom of the channel is heated slightly with an acetylene torch, which makes removal fairly easy. When the channel is warm, a flat screwdriver can be inserted between the glass and the channel. Care must be taken that only a slight amount of pressure is exerted; otherwise, the glass may crack or break. To reinstall the channel once the repairs

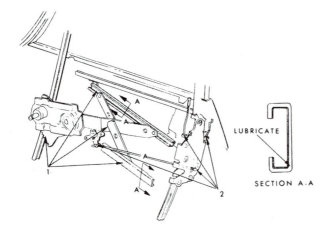

LUBRICATE

SECTION A-A

FIGURE 14-35 Door window regulator and cam lubrication, closed styles. (Courtesy of General Motors of Canada, Ltd.)

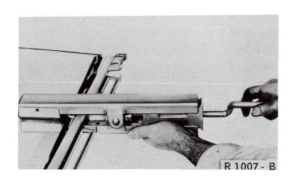

R 1007 - B

FIGURE 14-36 Glass channel replacement. (Courtesy of Ford Motor Company Canada, Ltd.)

have been made, a strip of the proper thickness of packing is applied to the bottom of the glass. The top part of the glass should be rested on a piece of soft wood or carpet, with the glass in a vertical position. The channel is then positioned on the glass and light blows are used to force the channel on the glass. A rubber hammer should be used if possible. If the channel is loose on the glass, a thicker packing can be used or the gap in the channel can be closed a little to provide the proper width.

When adjusting the windows on a hardtop, the vent assembly (if there is one) is adjusted to fit the roof pillar at the front. The adjustments are provided with slotted holes, thereby allowing forward-and-backward and up-and-down movement. The tilting of the top of the assembly is accomplished by an adjustable stud; this tilts the assembly in and out as required.

The window must be fitted to the vent assembly at the forward edge; the rear guide provides adjustment at the rear. These adjustments are either slotted holes or adjustable studs. The up-and-down travel of the window movement is controlled by stops that are adjusted so that the window will only go up and down as required. The equalizing arm and bracket are used to control the raising and lowering of the window; it will not tip ahead or backward at the wrong angle.

The rear door window is adjusted in much the same manner as the front door, for the hardware used is very similar. The window must be adjusted so that it fits the rear edge of the front window and the weatherstrip on the rear pillar and roof rail.

After the window is adjusted, the door should be opened and closed to check if the front edge of the rear window slips into the proper position at the rear edge of the other front window. The windows should be adjusted so that they fit the weatherstripping.

To remove the window glass in some Ford models, it is necessary to remove the door trim panel, water shield, lower window stop, and the screws retaining the glass channel bracket to the glass channel (Fig. 14-37). The forward edge of the glass assembly is tilted up, and then the glass assembly can be removed from the door. The channel assembly can be removed from the glass, by undoing the retaining bolts. To reinstall, the procedure is reversed. The glass and channel assembly is positioned into the door. The channel bracket is positioned to the glass channel and the retaining screws installed. The lower glass stop is installed and adjusted; then all hardware and the trim panel can be reinstalled.

The procedure to remove the glass from the hardtops is similar except that once the glass is out, the weather strip retaining screw is removed from the front of the glass assembly. The two remaining screws from the rear lower edge of the upper glass frame, as well as the two retaining screws from the top front edge of the lower glass frame and the channel, are removed. The channel is then removed from the glass.

To reinstall the glass, a new glass tape is positioned on the glass to the channel frame and the retaining screws are then installed. The removal procedure is reversed to reinstall the glass. Figure 14-38 shows typical hardtop model door hardware.

The regulators, or any other part, can be serviced by following the general practice of the servicing of the front doors.

To remove the quarter glass, it is necessary to remove the rear seat, window regulator handle, trim panel, and water shield. The glass lower frame to glass-attaching screws are aligned with the access holes (Fig. 14-39). While supporting the glass, the lower frame to glass-attaching screws are removed; then the glass is lifted out of the panel. The spacers are removed from the openings in the glass. To install, the procedure is reversed. It may be necessary to align the down-stop bracket and bumper, as well as the pivot bracket assembly and the up stops that are attached to the regulator idler arm. All other parts, such as the glass lower frame, regulator, and tracks, can then be serviced.

Rear Door Window Mechanisms—Single Tubular Run

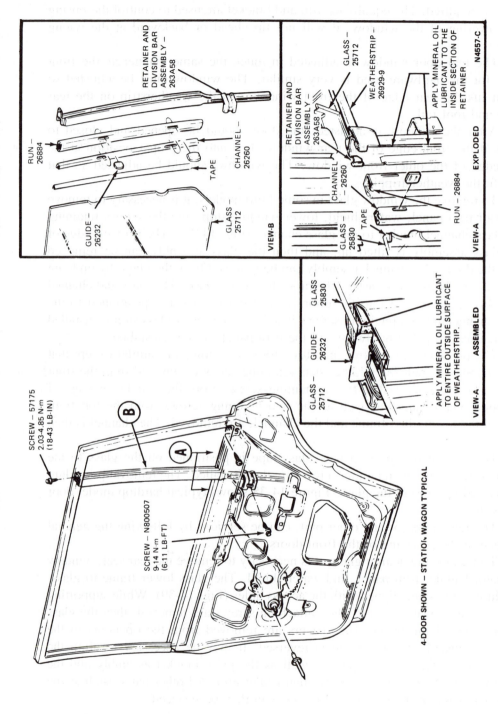

FIGURE 14-37 Rear door division bar, stationary window, Ford/Mercury. (Courtesy of Ford Motor Company of Canada, Ltd.)

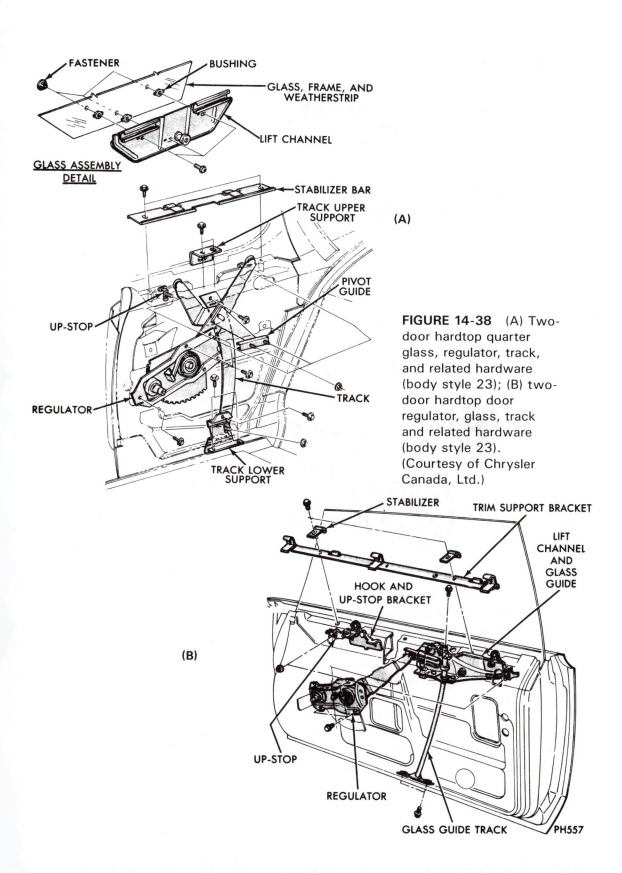

FASTENER

BUSHING

GLASS, FRAME, AND
WEATHERSTRIP

LIFT CHANNEL

GLASS ASSEMBLY
DETAIL

STABILIZER BAR

TRACK UPPER
SUPPORT

(A)

PIVOT
GUIDE

UP-STOP

REGULATOR

TRACK

TRACK LOWER
SUPPORT

FIGURE 14-38 (A) Two-door hardtop quarter glass, regulator, track, and related hardware (body style 23); (B) two-door hardtop door regulator, glass, track and related hardware (body style 23). (Courtesy of Chrysler Canada, Ltd.)

STABILIZER

TRIM SUPPORT BRACKET

LIFT
CHANNEL
AND
GLASS
GUIDE

HOOK AND
UP-STOP BRACKET

(B)

UP-STOP

REGULATOR

GLASS GUIDE TRACK

PH557

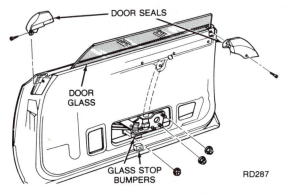

Glass Attachment Nuts

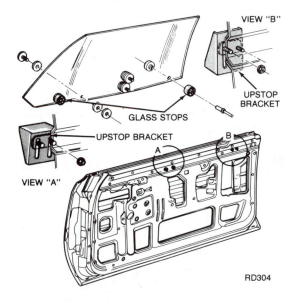

FIGURE 14-38 (cont.) (C) Glass attachment nuts; (D) glass and upstop positioning. (Courtesy of Chrysler Canada Ltd.)

Some of the side glass is held on the lower sash by bolts, nuts, and rivets. Some manufacturers also use channel bonding adhesive. The window is removed by using regular methods. Then the sash channel and glass are cleaned thoroughly with an adhesive cleaner. The position of the sash on the glass must be marked very carefully, for once the sash and the glass are joined together by the adhesive and the adhesive has cured, it will be impossible to move the glass from the sash.

A two-part adhesive, such as 3M channel bonding adhesive or equivalent, is used to bond the channel to the glass. Approximately 1½ tablespoons of the adhesive are thoroughly mixed (following the instructions on the package) and placed into the entire length of the channel as indicated in Fig. 14-40. The glass stabilizer clips are installed as shown, and then the glass is installed into the sash

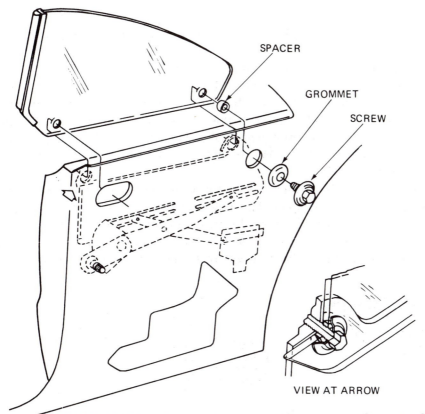

SPACER

GROMMET

SCREW

VIEW AT ARROW

FIGURE 14-39 Glass replacement. (Courtesy of Chrysler Canada Ltd.)

FIGURE 14-40 Glass-to-channel bonding.

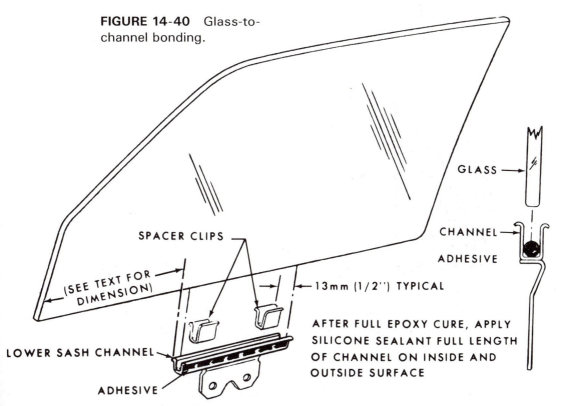

GLASS

CHANNEL

ADHESIVE

SPACER CLIPS

(SEE TEXT FOR DIMENSION)

13mm (1/2") TYPICAL

LOWER SASH CHANNEL

ADHESIVE

AFTER FULL EPOXY CURE, APPLY SILICONE SEALANT FULL LENGTH OF CHANNEL ON INSIDE AND OUTSIDE SURFACE

at the determined position or location. The sash channel and glass are immediately taped together with a cloth-backed tape in order to prevent any movement.

After the adhesive has been allowed to cure for one hour, a thin bead of silicone adhesive is applied to each side of the glass full length of the channel surface to prevent water entrapment in the channel. The glass is then reinstalled by using the proper method, and the door is closed by installing the parts that were removed.

The lock cylinder, which is found in front doors and trunk lids, is usually held in the panels by a retainer. This retainer has to be disengaged with a pointed tool like a screwdriver. On some doors, the cylinder can be removed once the linkage is disconnected. On other cars, it can be removed without removing the trim panel. Figure 14-41 shows a type that cannot be removed from outside the

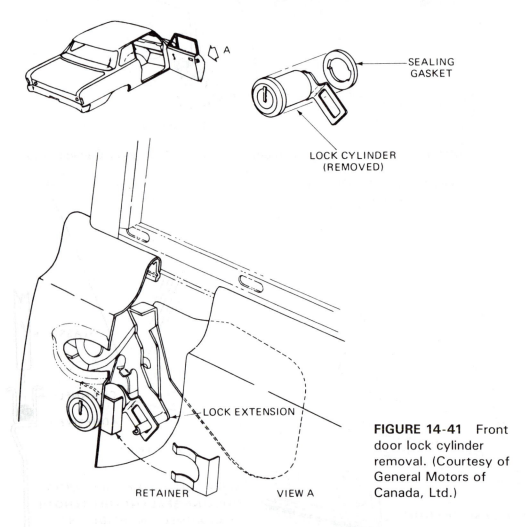

FIGURE 14-41 Front door lock cylinder removal. (Courtesy of General Motors of Canada, Ltd.)

door panel. To remove it, one has to remove the trim panel. If the gasket is damaged, it should be changed before the cylinder is reinstalled. To install, the procedure is reversed. The lock is usually lubricated with a dry graphite lubricant.

UNIT 14-4: ADHESIVE-BACKED MOLDINGS

Most body side moldings are bonded with a urethane and hot-melt adhesive system to the body panels. But some body side moldings are attached with foam or butyl adhesive tape to the body panels. Frequently, because of accidents, the adhesive-backed moldings on some panels have to be removed, repaired, or replaced with new moldings, if they are damaged. If it is not damaged, the two-sided adhesive tape must be removed from the molding and the adhesive must be cleaned thoroughly with naphtha or other nonoily solvent. Once the molding is dry, the two-sided tape is then applied to the back of the molding. Care must be taken not to touch the adhesive side or get any dirt on it. The protective film on the tape should not be removed until it is time to install the molding on the vehicle.

To ensure a quality repair or installation with new or old moldings, the panel surface should be between 70 and 90°F (21 to 32°C). The panels on which the moldings are to be applied must be free and clean of any wax or oil film. Therefore, the affected areas should be washed with detergent and water, wiped completely dry, and then wiped with oil-free naphtha or alcohol.

When moldings are to be installed on a vehicle on which there are no moldings, the repairman must decide where the moldings should be installed. Figures 14-42 to 14-44 give different examples of where the trim moldings can be installed. The trim moldings are usually applied to the widest points on the contour of the car. If the car has a ridge, the trim molding is applied either directly below or above but never on this ridge. When an automobile has a ridge or character line on the side panels which does not form a straight line, but

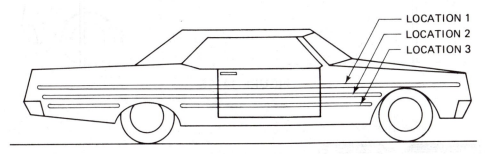

LOCATION 1
LOCATION 2
LOCATION 3

FIGURE 14-42

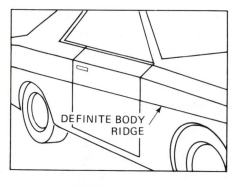

FIGURE 14-43

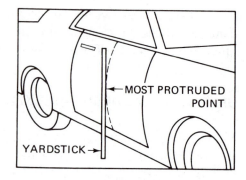

FIGURE 14-44

sweeps up toward the rear and front over the wheel openings, the installation can be carried out as in Fig. 14-43. In other cases, the trim moldings can be installed on the most protruded points as in Fig. 14-44.

A yardstick and a felt pen or a piece of masking tape are used to mark the location where the trim molding is to be installed. Care must be taken to ensure that the molding is applied level to the ground surface. A length of masking tape can be applied in a straight line from the front to the back of the vehicle on the side panels either directly below or above where the molding is to be applied, as in Fig. 14-45.

Starting with either the front or back fender, the proper length required for the panel is cut. Care is taken to keep the tips at least 3 in. (80 mm) from the front or rear edge of the car. The required length is cut with a single-edge razor blade. The section at the doors should be cut at a 45° angle where required so that the door will open freely (Fig. 14-46).

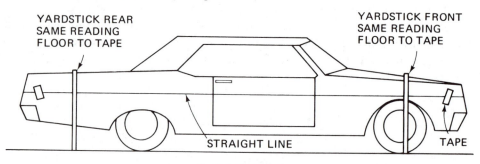

FIGURE 14-45

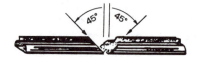

FIGURE 14-46

The release liner or protective film is peeled off for approximately 6 in. (150 mm). Starting at the door edge opening, the repairman lightly tacks on the trim molding along the guideline (Fig. 14-47). The other panels are all done the same way.

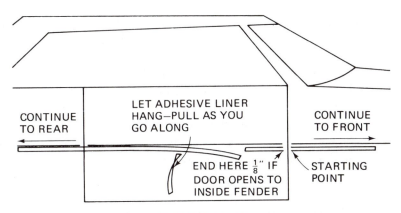

FIGURE 14-47

The trim is then checked to see if it has been applied in a straight line. Then, using a soft cloth, the repairman applies heavy pressure along the entire length of the molding (Fig. 14-48). The car should not be washed for one week so that the tape will set properly.

FIGURE 14-48

UNIT 14-5: WOOD-GRAIN TRANSFERS

Wood-grain transfers have become popular on many types of vehicles. They have a semigloss finish, are made of vinyl, and are designed to adhere to an acrylic painted surface because they have a pressure-sensitive adhesive on the back.

Replacement transfers are available through the appropriate automobile dealers. In ordering transfers, it is important to state not only the make but also the style and the applicable panel. The transfers are usually sold in rolls that are long enough to cover a certain portion of the vehicle.

When a transfer has to be replaced because it has been damaged, all the parts affected and the adjacent panels and openings must be washed. In addition, all the moldings, clips, handles, side marker lamps, and so on, and/or overlapping parts must be washed. A pointed or sharp instrument should never be used during transfer removal because it could gouge the underlying paint finish.

A heat gun facilitates the removal of the transfer because it softens the adhesive and the vinyl. The removal operation should be started at an edge by peeling back the transfer as a sheet from the surface of the panel. Too much force should not be used. Gradually heating the areas to be removed makes it easier to peel the transfer in most cases, as in Fig. 14-49.

FIGURE 14-49 Removing transfer with heat.

In reinstalling a transfer, care must be taken so that the panel is clean and free from imperfections. If the panel has been repainted, it should be allowed to dry thoroughly. Solvents remaining in a fresh paint film can lead to subsequent blistering. Acrylic painted surfaces should be scuff-sanded with No. 320 (9/0) or No. 400 (10/0).

Acrylic painted surfaces should be cleaned by using a good grade of de-waxing solvent. The surface is wiped with a cloth dampened with solvent and then with a dry, clean, absorbent cloth. The surface is allowed to dry and then compressed air can be used to blow any dirt away from the affected area of repair.

The transfer is prepared for installation by first making a template as follows: Tack-tape a suitable sheet of paper to the outer panel. Align it with the centers of the horizontal molding attaching clip holes. Following this line the template can be marked and cut to the right size. With the template flush to the panel, mark the front, rear, and bottom edges of the panel on the template. On styles on which "planking" grain is used or on which lines run the whole length of the vehicle the chaining or planking must be marked on the template.

Put the template on a table and draw another line of the front, rear, and bottom panel edges approximately 5/8 to 3/4 in. (16 to 19 mm) from the panel edges. Trim the excess paper from the marked edges by cutting it with scissors. Mark the front of the template also on the underside of the template.

Unroll the service transfer and position it on a table with the backing paper on top and with the outer wood-grain pattern running from left to right. Position the prepared template on the service transfer and mark the perimeter cut lines on the backing of the service transfer. On styles that use planking grain or lines, mark the upper one too. Make sure that the inner side of the template is up and that the wood grain pattern runs from left to right before marking the trim line on the service transfer. Then, following the marked lines, cut out the transfer.

Position the transfer on the repair panel and mark the center of the transfer and panel for proper vertical and lateral alignment (Fig. 14-50). Peel the paper backing from the transfer and lay the transfer face down on a clean table. Using a clean sponge, apply an ample wetting solution made of water and liquid detergent to the transfer adhesive and to the repair panel surface.

Center the transfer and align it with the center mark and the center of the horizontal molding clip holes. Press down lightly across the top. On styles using planking grain or lines, make certain that the upper plank lines or grain lines align with the lines on the adjacent panels. Use a squeegee on the center of the transfer. Press firmly at the center for a distance 3 to 4 in. (76 to 102 mm). Then squeegee upward over the same spot.

Raise one side of the transfer from the panel up to the secured spot at the center. Position the transfer close to the panel along the clip attaching holes. Working from the center, squeegee the transfer into place. Use firm, short, overlapping strokes. First squeegee laterally with overlapping strokes and then work horizontally across the top. Finish securing the opposite upper edge of the transfer the same way.

With one hand, lift the unsecured lower area of the transfer from the panel. If the transfer sticks prematurely, break the bond with a fast, firm pull. Position the transfer close to the panel at the center and squeegee at the center and downward approximately 2 in. (51 mm) and then laterally over the same area.

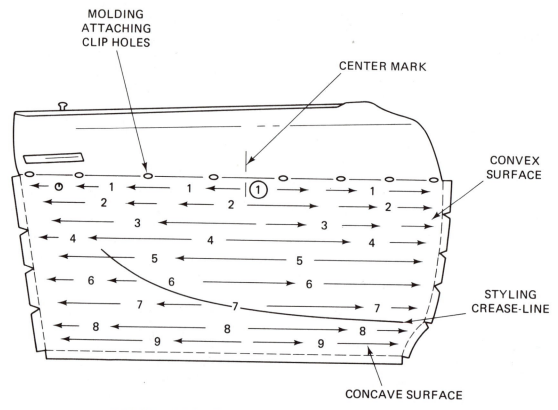

FIGURE 14-50 Transfer installation sequence (right door shown).

Repeat this operation by working toward each end of the panel. Bonding of the transfer is made by means of firm overlapping strokes (Fig. 14-50).

It may be necessary to apply the wetting solution periodically to the panel to facilitate raising and positioning the transfer during squeegee operations. Continue progressively downward in small increments completely across the transfer until the bottom is reached. Cut 90° notches in the transfer edges as needed in the lower corners and cut V notches in the transfer sides where necessary.

Apply a light coating of vinyl trim adhesive to the door hem flanges or any surface that is covered at the back with transfer material. Do not use excessive amounts of adhesive. Heat the inboard side of the door hem flanges and transfer and then fold them over as required on the hem flanges. Apply pressure as required to the transfer and hem flanges. Do not pull or stretch more than necessary because tearing could result.

FIGURE 14-51 Applying heat to transfer.

Apply heat to the transfer at the door handle holes or any other depression. Press firmly into these areas in order to obtain a good bond (Fig. 14-51). Using a sharp knife or razor blade, cut out the excess at the door handles or marker light holes or any other opening (Fig. 14-52).

Inspect the transfer from a critical angle. Use adequate light reflections to detect irregularities that may have developed during installation. Remove any air or moisture bubbles by piercing each bubble at an acute angle with a fine needle and then press the bubble down. Install all previously removed parts and clean the car.

FIGURE 14-52 Cutting excess transfer.

QUESTIONS

14-1 Describe the method used to remove and replace the weather strip type of windshields on bodies.

14-2 Why should a windshield opening be checked with checking blocks after a vehicle has been rolled over?

14-3 What method is used to hold and seal windshields and back windows on recent Ford, General Motors, and Chrysler automobiles?

14-4 What is a spacer dam, and how is it installed?

14-5 Describe the method used to remove the glued windshield using steel music wire.

14-6 Why should the edge of the windshield glass not come in contact with a volatile cleaner?

14-7 Describe how glass can be aligned to the opening before final installation.

14-8 Describe how a water leak is repaired when a windshield is glued with caulking material.

14-9 Describe the methods used to hold weather stripping on automobiles.

14-10 What method should be used when applying adhesive to hold weather stripping to a panel?

14-11 Describe the method used to remove a ventless front door glass assembly.

14-12 Describe how a side window glass is removed and reinstalled to the channel.

14-13 What type of lubricant is used in lock cylinders?

14-14 Describe how trim moldings are installed on vehicles that do not have any moldings.

14-15 With what material is an area cleaned before the molding can be reinstalled?

14-16 From what are wood-grain transfers made?

14-17 Describe how wood-grain transfers are installed on a panel.

15

Repairing Collision Damage

When a vehicle with collision damage is brought into the shop, the first thing that should be done is to disconnect the battery in case of shorts in the wiring. When the vehicle is jacked up, it should always be supported with safety stands so that the car will not fall on any employee that might be working on it. The floor should always be as clean and clear of obstructions as possible, because numerous accidents occur in shops that have a poor cleaning attitude.

With the frequent use of torches in the body shop, the dangers of a fire are always present unless precautions are taken to avert such occurrences. The owner should make sure that the proper fire extinguishers are on hand and that all staff know where they are and how they should be used. All rags that are soaked with oil, grease, or paint should be stored in proper containers and not in any corner where they could cause spontaneous combustion. Grease, oil, or any slippery substance should be cleaned off the floor regularly, because in addition to being a fire hazard the substance can also be a safety hazard. A worker or customer could slip and hurt himself seriously.

One of the most important features in any body shop is good lighting to reduce eye strain and also help the employees perform a satisfactory repair job, whether it is bodywork or painting. The shop should also be heated and ventilated to remove as much dust as possible from the air, especially with the fiberglass and plastic fillers used today.

UNIT 15-1:   REPAIRING FRONT-END COLLISION DAMAGE ON CONVENTIONAL AND UNITIZED AUTOMOBILES

In repairing any type of collision damage, the repairman should first familiarize himself with the particular job on hand before proceeding with repairs. He should study and diagnose the damage that has occurred from all angles and determine the direction of the damaging force or impact as well as which section or parts were damaged by the direct impact and which were damaged as a result of the direct damage. He should also consult the shop foreman or check the repair estimate to see how the repairs are to be made. He must know beforehand what parts are to be repaired and what parts are to be replaced if he is to carry out the necessary repair operations in their proper order or sequence and do this efficiently.

In front-end collisions, where the frame or chassis has been damaged, this part must first be aligned before any of the sheet-metal parts can be reinstalled once they have been repaired. In cases of severe damage, where the damaged frame must either be replaced completely or repaired and aligned, it is often necessary to remove all the front-end sheet-metal parts. Each part is removed separately, or the parts can be removed in one unit (conventional body construction) by loosening the radiator support from the front of the frame and the fenders from the cowl, as indicated by the arrows in Fig. 15-1. Before any of the front-end parts are removed, however, and this applies to standard as well as unitized

FIGURE 15-1

(A)

(B)

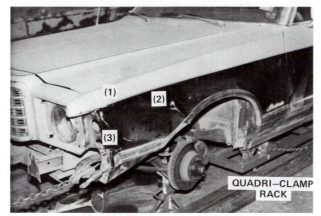

QUADRI—CLAMP RACK

FIGURE 15-2 (A) Pulling out a damaged bumper with a pulldozer; (B) pulling out a damaged fender with a pulldozer and quadri-clamp anchoring rack.

high-strength-steel (HSS) automobiles, they should be pulled out and roughly aligned, using the damage dozer (Fig. 15-2). This step not only corrects much of the direct damage as the bumper and front section of the fender are pulled forward, but it also repositions and aligns much of the indirect damage that has occurred to the bumper brackets, inner construction of the front fender, grille panel, underpans, and supporting brackets, thus making their removal, repair, and replacement much easier.

The front fender is roughed-out and aligned by bumping out the simple and collapsed rolled buckles with a large, heavy (sledge) hammer or dolly, starting (with the nonelastic or permanently deformed metal) in the crown area marked 1 (Fig. 15-3) and gradually proceeding downward until all of the crown has been brought out. The damage to the bordering fender flange (collapsed hinge buckle formed) in area marked 2 is aligned next. The simple hinge buckles in the damaged area marked 3 and the remaining lower front portions and side of the

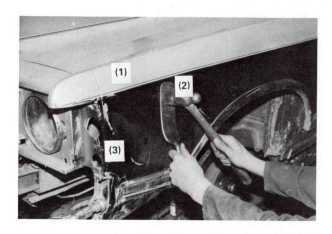

FIGURE 15-3 Spring-hammering high ridges.

fender are aligned the same way. All high ridges are spring-hammered simultaneously, as each buckle is brought out (Fig. 15.3), and the fender is straightened by alternately dinging and hand-feeling the metal and shrinking any excessively high or stretched areas.

In detecting surface irregularities by means of hand feeling (used in both metal-straightening and metal-finishing operations), both the surface of the metal and hand of the repairman must be clean, dry, and free of dust, dirt, asphalt, oil deposits, disk-sanding paint particles, and body metal fillings. The auto body repairman places his hand flat on the metal, with his forearm quite low to its surface, as shown in Fig. 15-4. By sliding his hand lengthwise and crosswise and in all directions over the work, using long strokes, he is able to detect or

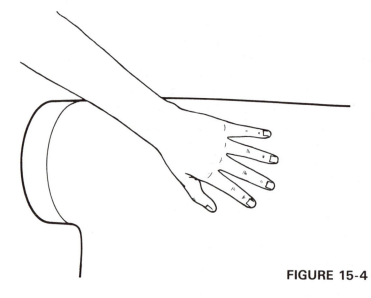

FIGURE 15-4

feel any hollows or high spots that may be present. It must be remembered, however, that it is with the center (palm) of the hand and not the tips of the fingers that these irregularities are detected or felt. When it is no longer possible to see or feel any high or low areas, the disk sander is used to remove the paint from the straightened surface and to outline any irregularities still present. These are then removed by alternately picking and filing the metal until perfectly smooth. The repaired metal is then disk-sanded as described in Chapter 6.

Many of the newer unitized (HSS) automobiles have front fenders of double-panel construction (Fig. 15-5), with little access to the outer panel, making replacement necessary when damaged extensively. Depending on its location, minor damage is usually repaired.

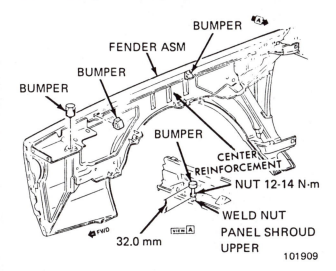

FIGURE 15-5 Double panel or reinforced fender. (Courtesy of General Motors of Canada, Ltd.)

All underpans, wheelhousing panels, and brackets that are either bolted or spot-welded to the front fenders (Fig. 15-6) must be aligned and straightened to fit properly. Generally, these parts do not require metal-finishing, but any cracks or breaks in the metal should be welded and protected from corrosion by means of painting or undercoating. On the newer automobiles of unitized (HSS) construction, many of these parts are made of plastic, so they cannot be repaired if badly damaged, making replacement necessary. However, parts with only minor tears or breaks can often be welded as described in Unit 9-2.

The grille is removed from its surrounding outer sheet-metal shell, composed at times of upper and lower panels (illustrated by 9 and 10 in Fig. 15-7), which are also straightened and metal-finished if not too badly damaged. All repaired, bare metal surfaces must be covered with a coating of primer or primer surfacer or completely refinished before the grille and its surrounding moldings are installed.

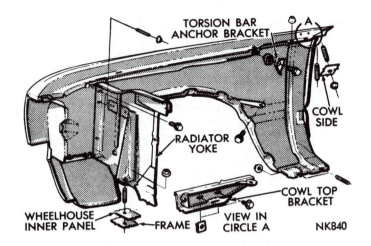

Fender Attaching Points

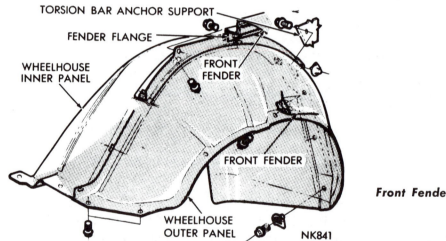

Front Fender Wheelhouse

FIGURE 15-6   (Courtesy of Chrysler Canada Ltd.)

In repairing the radiator support (11 and 12 in Fig. 15-7), the radiator must first be removed from its support and repaired, recored, or replaced by a completely new radiator. It should not be installed, however, until all other repair operations to the front-end have been completed, in order not to subject it to unnecessary vibration and abuse. Installing the radiator last often makes the assembling of parts much easier for the repairman.

The radiator support can often be straightened, depending on the extent of the damage and on its construction. It is straightened by first checking its center

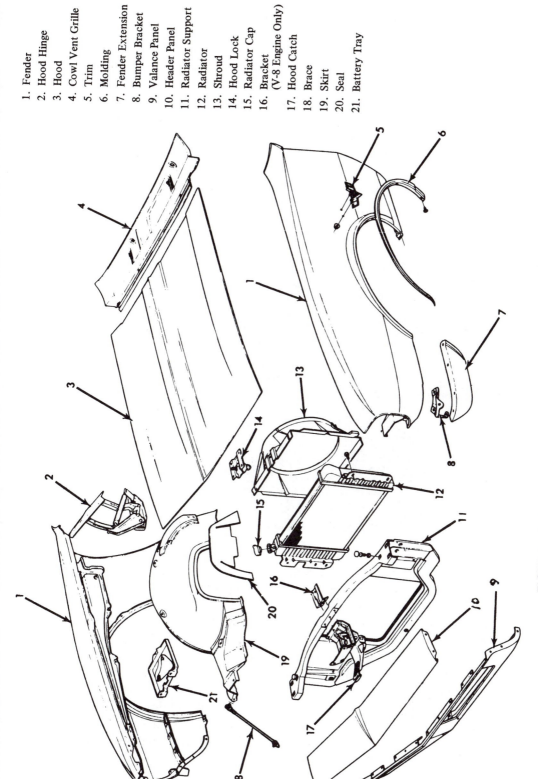

1. Fender
2. Hood Hinge
3. Hood
4. Cowl Vent Grille
5. Trim
6. Molding
7. Fender Extension
8. Bumper Bracket
9. Valance Panel
10. Header Panel
11. Radiator Support
12. Radiator
13. Shroud
14. Hood Lock
15. Radiator Cap
16. Bracket
    (V-8 Engine Only)
17. Hood Catch
18. Brace
19. Skirt
20. Seal
21. Battery Tray

FIGURE 15-7 (Courtesy of General Motors of Canada, Ltd.)

opening for squareness, by taking diagonal measurements from one top corner to the opposite lower corner of the radiator support, using jig holes, mounting nuts, mounting brackets, or accurately measured-off chalk marks as reference points. Hydraulic jacking equipment or the pulldozer (Fig. 15-8) is used in swaying and squaring the radiator support, in the direction of the shorter diagonal measurement reading obtained. The support is normalized by hammering down any folds or wrinkles in the metal, either cold or in conjunction with heat (carburizing flame), making sure that all breaks in the support have been welded beforehand. The radiator support is allowed to cool off completely before the hydraulic pressure is released. This step will eliminate all possibilities of the support returning to its former bent or distorted out-of-square position.

FIGURE 15-8

Great care must also be taken to reshape and straighten all outer portions of the radiator support correctly, especially the areas onto which the fenders, side panels, underpans, and headlights are fastened. Doing so will eliminate many of the alignment problems so often encountered and will ensure a better fit between the hood and fenders.

The radiator support on both older and newer unitized (HSS) automobiles is solidly spot-welded into position on the front side rails at the factory, its lower section serving as a front cross-member (Fig. 15-9). If only slightly damaged, it is aligned and straightened as on standard automobiles, but if badly damaged it is removed completely by breaking all spot welds. It is replaced with a new panel that is accurately fitted into position using centering gauges and then spot-welded in with a MIG welder (Fig. 15-10).

FIGURE 15-9 Spot-welded radiator support.

FIGURE 15-10 Fitting radiator support using centering gauges.

The front bumper face bar, which has already been removed, is aligned in an arbor press (Fig. 15-11) and straightened with a suitable hammer and dolly. In another method the face bar can be placed on an anvil and hammered smooth with a heavy, smooth-faced ball or cross-peen hammer, depending on its thickness, rigidity, and contour. It is metal-finished in the usual manner before being

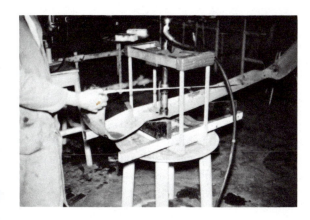

FIGURE 15-11

rechromed. Be sure to straighten the face bar accurately so that little or no further twisting of its surface is required after it is rechromed and installed on the car. Twisting of the surface once the bar has been installed might cause the chrome to crack. Cracking can be prevented by bolting the face bar in place on the automobile, checking its fit, and making the necessary adjustments before it is rechromed.

If the damage to the bumper brackets is only minor, they are usually straightened. If extensively damaged, however, the brackets are replaced with new ones.

Many high-strength-steel (HSS) constructed automobiles have bumper fascia (face bars) made of thermosetting plastic and bumper reinforcements made of martensitic steel (Fig. 15-12). Fascia with minor damage such as small punctures, gouges, and tears can be repaired using the structural adhesive repair method (Unit 9-2), but manufacturers recommend that bumper reinforcements be replaced rather than repaired.

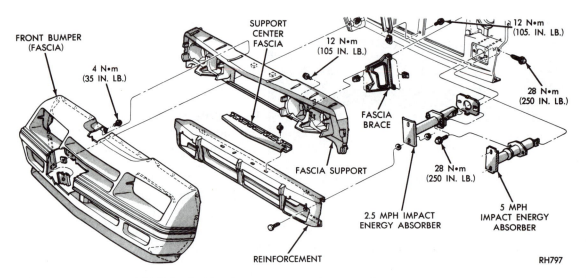

FIGURE 15-12 Front bumper fascia. (Courtesy of Chrysler Canada Ltd.)

Strongly reinforced hoods and adjoining cowl air-intake panels are generally not repaired when badly damaged. But if only minor damage has occurred, with very little if any damage to the large flat central section of the hood, it can be repaired by aligning and roughing-out both the inner construction and the outer panel simultaneously by using hydraulic jacking equipment [Fig. 15-13(A)] or the damage dozer [Fig. 15-13(B)]. This operation can be performed either on or off the automobile, with or without a straightening fixture.

(A)

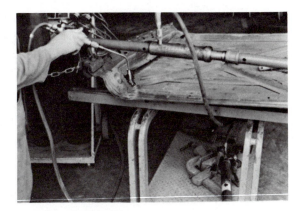

FIGURE 15-13   (A) Using hydraulic jacking equipment; (B) roughing out hood with the damage dozer.

(B)

After the hood hookups have been made, the paint is removed from all sharp buckles, bends, and ridges in both the inner construction and the outer panel, using the torch and a steel wire brush. The torch, which is then adjusted to a carburizing flame, is used to heat up the buckles, bends, and ridges to a blue color. The buckles, in turn, are stretched out and hammered down as the hood is pushed back to its original shape and contour.

CAUTION: When working on HSS bodies, do not overheat or overpull hood inner construction.

NOTE: The crown of the outer panel on the hood must be accurately roughed out and aligned to as near its original height and shape as possible before any spring-hammering and straightening of the flat, more central portions of the outer panel is attempted. (See the discussion on shrinking false stretch in Chapter 5.)

All accessible dents, V channels, valleys, and ridges in the outer panel are eliminated and straightened by bumping, dinging, and spring-hammering, respectively, while those in enclosed and inaccessible areas are removed and straightened with spoons, pick bars, or picks, or they are pulled out and roughly straightened by using body solder, pull plates, or pull rods (Fig. 15-14) or by means of the nail welder and slide hammer method (Fig. 15-15).

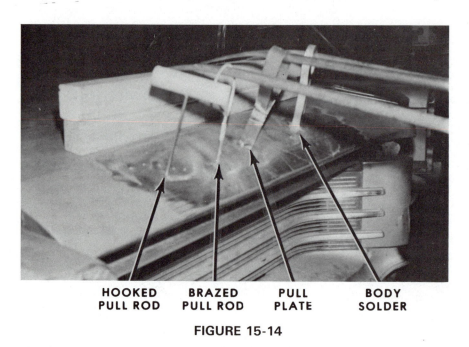

| HOOKED PULL ROD | BRAZED PULL ROD | PULL PLATE | BODY SOLDER |

FIGURE 15-14

Accessible areas are metal-finished in the usual way, while inaccessible, roughly straightened areas are either solder- or plastic-filled as described in Chapters 7 and 8.

Before the repaired front-end parts are assembled, any damage to the cowl, front doors, and windshield must be corrected. If the front doors are out of adjustment and do not close properly, either the front door opening will have to be aligned [Fig. 15-16(A)] or the door hinges will have to be adjusted or straightened, depending largely on the make and model of the automobile and the type of hinges used. All damage to the cowl assembly must be repaired so that the

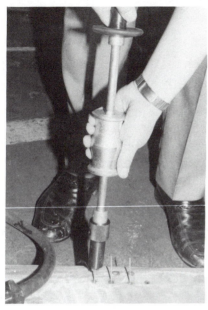

FIGURE 15-15 Spot-welded nails and slide hammer being used to roughly align a panel.

front fenders, hood, and windshield will fit and function properly [Fig. 15-16(B)]. If the windshield has been broken and there is no visible evidence or reason for its breaking, the pinch-weld flange around the window opening should be closely examined for sharp metal high spots that might cause the windshield to break before it is replaced with a new windshield, as described in Chapter 14. All body seams and panel joints on the front end are sealed with a brushable seam sealer or medium-bodied sealer, and all studs and brackets are sealed with caulk. All panels are then painted or undercoated as at the factory (Fig. 15-17).

After all damaged front-end parts have been repaired, assembled, and adjusted properly, the radiator is installed and filled with a coolant before the automobile is moved into the paint shop for refinishing.

Front-end damage on newer unitized, high-strength-steel automobiles is also pulled out as much as possible, before the front bumper, grille, radiator, battery, hood, and front fenders are individually removed. Often the motor, transmission, and front suspension also have to be removed so that indirect damage extending as far back as under the rear seat area of the floor pan, cowl assembly, rack and pinion steering mounting panel, strut towers, and side rails can be repaired.

In correcting minor front-end damage, the side rails, front fender inner panels, strut towers, and radiator support are usually simultaneously pulled back to their original position and straightened, while under tension, using centering and strut tower gauges with a body and frame straightening machine (Fig.

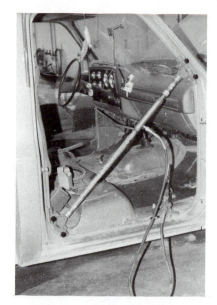

(A)

(B)

FIGURE 15-16 (A) Using hydraulic pushing setup to correct a door opening; (B) pulling cowl assembly forward and out with power pull.

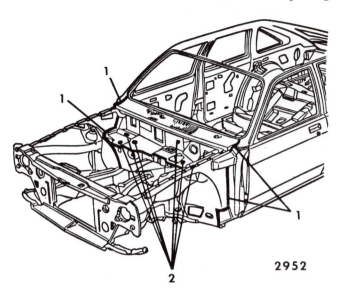

2952

1. **APPLY A BRUSHABLE SEAM SEALER OR MEDIUM-BODIED SEALER**

2. **STUDS AND BRACKETS MUST BE SEALED WITH CAULK**

FIGURE 15-17 Sealing the front end. (Courtesy of General Motors of Canada, Ltd.)

15-18) or a pulldozer anchored by means of the cross-tube and underbody clamps or the quadri-clamp rack (Fig. 4-40).

In correcting major front-end damage, where the previously mentioned parts are badly damaged (crushed and torn) (Fig. 15-19), the parts are simultaneously pulled out to their approximate position, and all adjacent sheet-metal panels to

FIGURE 15-18 Body and frame straightening machine pulling out a damaged side rail and adjacent parts.

FIGURE 15-19 Front fender inner panel, side rail, strut tower, and radiator support badly damaged.

which they are spot-welded are accurately aligned and straightened, while under tension, before they are removed and replaced with new parts (Fig. 15-20). All damage to the floor, cowl assembly, and strut towers is corrected first and in the order mentioned, so that all doors fit, open, and close properly. This is accomplished by simultaneously applying multiple corrective pulls with a body and frame straightening machine to the top of the cowl assembly, strut tower, side rail, and fender inner panel (Fig. 15-21), aligning and straightening all folds, buckles, and creases, one by one, while panels are kept under tension, until all parts are brought back to their correct shape and position. Their correct position

FIGURE 15-20 Major damage being pulled out with a body and frame straightening machine.

FIGURE 15-21 Applying multiple pulls with a body and frame straightening machine.

is determined by means of centering gauges and the strut tower gauge, mounted on the automobile body according to the manufacturer's specification.

The Korek frame and body straightener is also used in applying multiple corrective pulls in repairing front-end collision damage (Fig. 15-22) and will handle all types of damage fast and easily.

FIGURE 15-22 Korek body and frame straightener applying multiple pulls. (Courtesy of Blackhawk Division of Applied Power, Canada Ltd.)

The pulldozer can be used in correcting major front-end damage, just as it is in minor damage correction, but because it is incapable of applying as many multiple corrective pulls at one time and in several different directions, many different pulling hookups have to be made, making the repairing of the front end more cumbersome and much slower.

When the strut tower, fender inner panel, all reinforcements, and side-rail assembly have to be replaced, all parts from the cowl forward are removed by breaking spot welds by either cutting them out using an electric or pneumatic drill with a spot-weld cutter, or by partially drilling the spot welds, weakening them, and then breaking them with a pneumatic chisel (Fig. 15-23).

FIGURE 15-23 Strut tower, inner fender panel, and side rail being removed.

All the outer, overlapping, joining edges on the new replacement panels are then cleaned of all primer and paint using either a disk grinder or power-driven wire brush. Holes for plug welding are punched with a hole-punching tool, duplicating factory spot welds as much as possible, before the new panels are fitted together and firmly clamped into position on the body (cowl assembly) of the automobile (Fig. 15-24).

FIGURE 15-24 Joining edges on replacement panel cleaned and plug weld holes being punched.

The centering gauges and the strut tower gauge are again mounted, rechecking that all replacement panels are correctly positioned before they are firmly plug-welded in place.

Damaged side rails, if repairable, after having been roughed-out, are straightened cold whenever possible, using spoons, picks and punches, caulking irons, or either the Shortie ram or the Wedgie ram, as shown in Figs. 4-7 and 4-20.

CAUTION: If a side rail or any structural member cannot be straightened cold, remember that it is made of high-strength steel (HSS) and must not be overheated. Use a temperature-indicating crayon and apply heat sparingly with an oxy-acetylene torch using a neutral flame. Keep the heat concentrated on the repair area so as not to destroy the structural strength of the side rail.

Sometimes it is advantageous for the repairman to open up the side rail to gain access to the damaged area, especially when the damage is located in a double-constructed or reinforced area of the side rail (Fig. 15-25). Access is gained by breaking the spot welds along the top and bottom of the side rail and vertically cutting the side at one end of the portion to be removed, and pulling or bending it away from the rest of the side rail; or by cutting it vertically at both ends and removing the side completely. The damaged section of the side rail is then repaired quite easily and its removed side is also straightened before it is MIG-welded back in place.

FIGURE 15-25 Opened up side rail and reinforced area.

The fender inner panel is welded and straightened wherever necessary or is replaced with a new panel. It and the new radiator support are cleaned in preparation for welding, before being fitted and clamped into position on the side rails, by means of centering gauges according to the manufacturer's specification and solidly MIG-welded together (Figs. 15-26 and 15-27).

NOTE: Manufacturers recommend that all structural load-bearing panels, such as rails, rocker panels, strut towers, and pillars on unitized (HSS) automobiles should never be sectioned. They should be cut off and replaced at factory joints or seams, unless instructed otherwise. However, outer body panels that do not provide structural support or strength can be sectioned.

FIGURE 15-26 Radiator support being prepared for installation on side rails and inner fender panels of automobile.

FIGURE 15-27 All parts fitted and clamped in position ready for MIG welding.

Some unitized (HSS) automobiles are built with a side and cross-member assembly (Fig. 15-28) or engine cradle as it is often called. It supports the motor and transmission, and from it the lower control arms pivot. It is fastened to the side rails by means of isolation mounts. In front-end collisions, where damage to the side rails occurs, this assembly will generally be damaged also. It should therefore always be checked for misalignment. If only slightly out of alignment, it is generally repaired, but if damaged extensively, it is always replaced with a new assembly.

All welds and panel joints are thoroughly cleaned with a hand or power-driven wire brush and treated with a metal conditioner before a brushable seam or medium-bodied sealer and an asphaltic undercoating are applied (Fig. 15-29). The cowl assembly, strut towers, inner fender panels, and radiator support are also refinished, before the motor, transmission, and front suspension parts are installed.

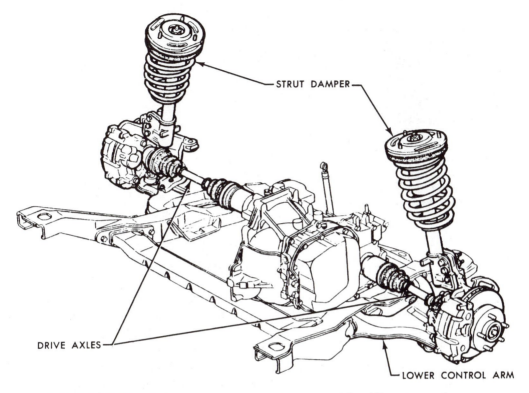

FIGURE 15-28 Side and cross-member assembly. (Courtesy of General Motors of Canada, Ltd.)

FIGURE 15-29 All welds and panel joints sealed with brushable seam sealer.

All front-end sheet-metal parts, such as front fenders, grille, headlights, battery, bumper isolators, front bumper, and radiator are installed and adjusted before the automobile (Fig. 15-30) is moved into the paint shop.

FIGURE 15-30 Automobile ready for refinishing in the paint shop.

UNIT 15-2: REPAIRING SIDE COLLISION DAMAGE

In repairing an automobile that has been severely damaged directly in the center of the side [Fig. 15-31(A)], the first thing the repairman must do—after carefully studying and diagnosing the damage—is to remove the front and rear doors, seats, and trim from the center post; if the turret top is damaged, remove the headlining either partially (only on the damaged side) or completely, whichever is more practical. The floor mats, floor pan insulators or heat shields, must also be removed so that hydraulic jacking equipment and the damage dozer or frame-straightening machine can be used in correcting the damage that has not only occurred to the sill or rocker panel assembly and floor but also to the center body pillar, doors, turret top, and roof rail.

Generally, the sill or rocker panel assembly and floor have been driven in to such an extent that the repairman has no alternative but to replace the rocker panel completely [Fig. 15-31(B)].

Heavy plates are spot-welded to the damaged rocker panel if it is repairable, or holes are cut into its side. By properly anchoring the end of the horizontal telescoping beam of the damage dozer either to the base of the center body pillar on the opposite side of the body or to the frame side rail, and then applying a steady and uniform pull at various points along the damaged rocker panel assembly or base of the center body pillar (Unit 4-6, Figs. 4-41 and 4-43), the damage to the floor and rocker panel is gradually pulled out. A variety of rams and spreaders shown in Fig. 4-6 are also simultaneously employed.

When a frame-straightening machine is employed, the damage is pulled out by applying a number of corrective outward pulls on the driven-in floor, rocker panel, and post, and simultaneously exerting another stretching pull (lengthwise)

(A)

FIGURE 15-31 [(B)
Courtesy of Ford
Company of Canada,
Ltd.)

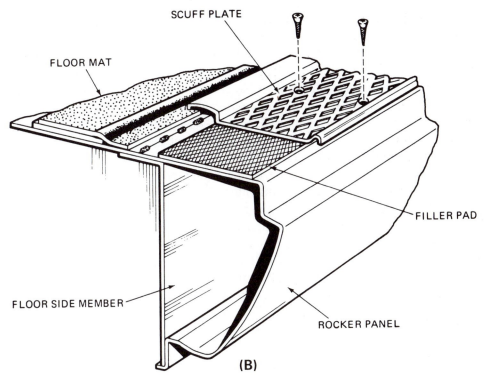

SCUFF PLATE

FLOOR MAT

FILLER PAD

FLOOR SIDE MEMBER

ROCKER PANEL

(B)

on the damaged side, using chains hooked to the top and bottom hinge areas of
the cowl so as to bring the side back to its original length (Fig. 15-32).

The procedure above is generally followed in the correction of all major
side collision damage, especially in the repairing of late-model, high-strength-
steel automobiles.

FIGURE 15-32

Remember that, whenever possible, the stretching pull applied on the damaged floor and rocker panel should always be greater than the outward pull exerted. Any breaking of spot welds or tearing of metal encountered while pulling should immediately be MIG-welded, before corrective pulling is resumed.

All folds and creases in the floor panel and surrounding metal are gradually eliminated, one by one, by spring-hammering and straightening them while under constant pulling pressure, using body pull hooks, pull plates, and pull clamps together with chains, at the cowl, center pillar, and rear door areas.

The turret top and roof rail can also be aligned and roughed-out by applying an outward pull on the top section of the center pillar, just where it joins the roof rail, using body- and frame-straightening equipment [Fig. 15-33(A)]. This can also be done without repositioning or changing the damage dozer hookup (Unit 4-6, Fig. 4-41) by merely using another hydraulic jack, positioned farther up on the damage dozer tower [Fig. 15-33(B)]. As the turret top and roof rail are slowly pulled out, the crown of the roof panel and surrounding damaged areas are roughed-out and straightened by lifting the sheet metal (V channels and valleys) with the hydraulic jack and attachments (Fig. 15-34) and spring-hammering the ridges and metal dinging, as previously described.

After the floor has been straightened, the rocker panel assembly is removed completely with a pneumatic chisel, the cutting torch (wherever its services are required), a spot-weld cutter, or by drilling out the spot welds (Fig. 15-35).

NOTE: Most manufacturers of 1980- or later-model automobiles with structural members made of high-strength steel recommend that if a torch or cutoff grinder must be used in the removal of a damaged body section or on salvage parts, at least 2 inches (50.8 mm) of additional metal be left on the part to be used. Once the part has been removed, the heat-affected area is cut off at the factory seams

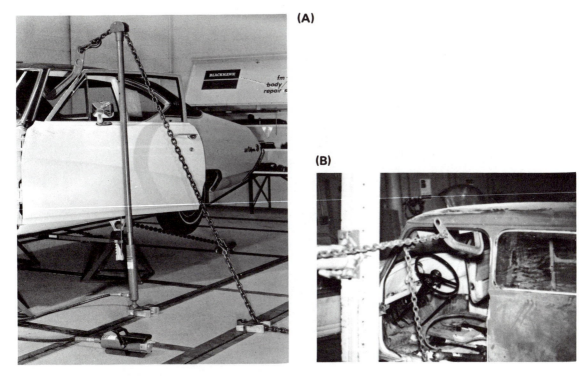

FIGURE 15-33 Pulling out the turret top and roof rail.

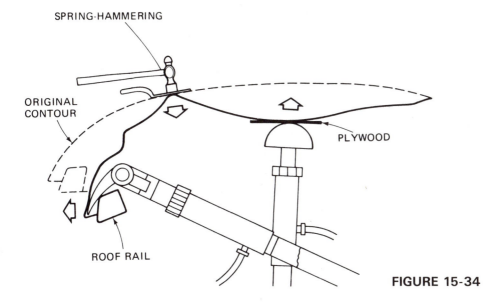

FIGURE 15-34

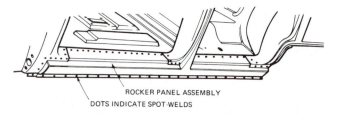

ROCKER PANEL ASSEMBLY
DOTS INDICATE SPOT-WELDS

FIGURE 15-35 Rocker panel assembly being removed.

using a pneumatic chisel so as not to destroy the properties of the high-strength steel.

The replacement rocker panel assembly and bottom of center door pillar are tack-welded into position and their locations accurately rechecked by hanging the new replacement or repaired doors on the body before they are solidly spot-welded into place with the MIG welder (Fig. 15-36).

When spot-welding high-strength-steel replacement panels, always try to duplicate factory methods, as much as possible. Use the same number and size of spot welds and place them in precisely the same location as at the factory. Following this procedure not only gives a factory-like appearance to the installation, but ensures the original structural strength of the repair.

Rocker panels on models older than 1980, if not too badly rusted out or damaged, can often be repaired by merely replacing the outer section with a slip-over repair panel (Fig. 15-37). The old or covered-up portion need not necessarily be removed, just roughly aligned, enabling the new panel to fit properly. Its top edge is then either spot-welded or pop-riveted into place, and its bottom edge

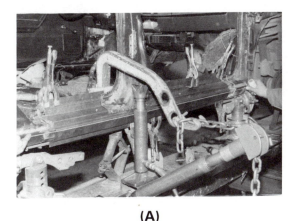

(A)

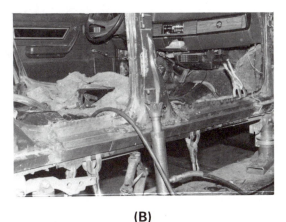

(B)

(C)

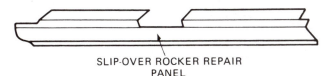

FIGURE 15-36 (A) Fitting and clamping replacement rocker panel into position on body before tack welding; (B) bottom of center pillar raised into position on rocker panel for spot welding; (c) doors hung in openings on body.

SLIP-OVER ROCKER REPAIR PANEL

FIGURE 15-37

is spot-welded to the vertical portion of the old rocker panel assembly (Fig. 15-38). The overlapping panel joint at the rear quarter panel is first spot-welded, sunk down, solder-filled, and metal-finished in the usual way.

Another method of repairing localized damage in rocker panels is by cutting a door into the upper section of the rocker panel directly underneath the scuff plate. This step provides access to the damaged area and enables the repairman to straighten and metal-finish the panel quite easily (Fig. 15-39).

The body must now be checked for alignment. If the opposite side of the automobile has not been damaged and its doors, trunk lid, and hood fit and

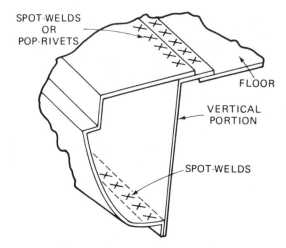

FIGURE 15-38

FIGURE 15-39

function properly, the diagonal measurement readings obtained from its door openings can be used in aligning the door openings on the damaged side (described and illustrated in Unit 15-3).

The front and rear doors are frequently repaired by replacing their badly damaged outer panels with new repair panels. The outer panels are removed by using a disk sander, with a No. 24 (3) grit closed-coat sanding disk to grind down the edges (hem) of the door panels and separate them from the door frame flange (Fig. 15-40). The door panels are cut at the top, either at the belt line

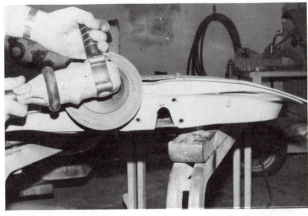

FIGURE 15-40 Grinding through outer edges (hem) of door panels.

(which often is covered with a chrome molding) or at the bottom portion of the window opening (Fig. 15-41). The door is then turned over in its straightening fixture and the remaining portions of the spot-welded flange are removed from the door frame flange by back and forth bending, hammering on the vise grips, or the pneumatic chisel (Figs. 15-42 and 15-43). Any damage to the framework (inner construction) of the doors must now be corrected before the new repair panel, which has been accurately cut down to the required size (partial replacement) and has had anticorrosion material and seam sealer applied to its inner surface (Fig. 15-44), is positioned and tack-welded into place at points A and B, as shown in Fig. 15-41. The repair panel is fitted and clamped firmly to the door frame flange at points C, D, E, and F with vise-grip welding clamps. The toe dolly is held tightly against the outer edge of the repair panel, just next to each of the welding clamps, and the repair panel flange is turned over the door

FIGURE 15-41 Door replacement panel.

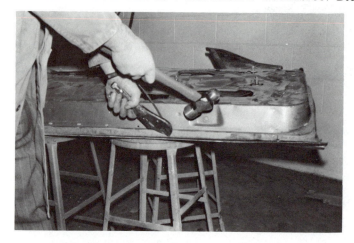

FIGURE 15-42 Removing spot-welded flange with a hammer and vise-grips.

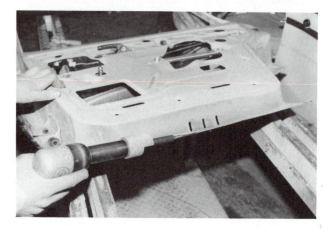

FIGURE 15-43 Spot-welded flange (hem) being removed from door frame with pneumatic chisel.

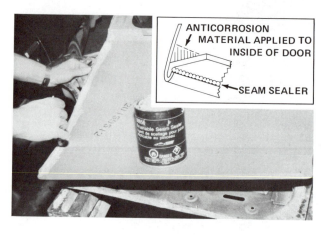

ANTICORROSION MATERIAL APPLIED TO INSIDE OF DOOR

SEAM SEALER

FIGURE 15-44 Applying seam sealer to outer edge of door panel.

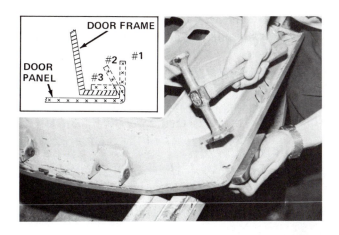

FIGURE 15-45 Turning over the door frame flange.

frame flange with the body hammer (Fig. 15-45) and tack-welded before the vise-grip welding clamps are removed. The door is then hung on its hinges and its alignment and fit are checked on the automobile.

The door must fit perfectly into its opening, and any twist or bends in its framework or inner construction must be eliminated before the remaining portions of the repair panel flange are turned over and spot-welded every 1½ to 2 in. (38 to 51 mm). The tack-welded butt joints at points A and B are welded completely and the door is metal-finished before it is installed on the automobile.

When the panel is replaced at the belt line, either a plain or a recessed lap joint may be used in joining the new panel to the upper section of the door panel. Pop rivets or metal screws spaced approximately 2 in. (51 mm) apart are used to keep the panel in alignment while it is being spot-welded.

Frequently, in major side collisions, door hinges damaged beyond repair must be replaced. Some are fastened by means of bolts, making removal and installation of new hinges rather simple and easy. Others are solidly welded to both the door frame and the door pillar, making replacement more difficult. The removal and installation of welded door hinges is described and illustrated in Chapter 11 (Figs. 11-13 to 11-17).

On many of the older automobiles, a badly damaged door can often be repaired when it is supported on either a straightening fixture or a stand and a hydraulic corrective force or pull is applied by means of a pulldozer [Fig. 3-20(B)]. As the stretching pull is applied, both the outer panel and the inner construction are aligned and straightened simultaneously, eliminating the need for cutting, complete removal, and welding back of the door's inner panel that would otherwise have been necessary.

Manufacturers of automobiles of later than 1980 models recommend that doors with no damage to framework or guard rails or beams be repaired or repaneled, depending on the extent of damage, but that doors with damage to framework and guard rails made of high strength and martensitic steel be replaced rather than repaired.

When the upper framework or window opening has become damaged and pushed out of shape, it can be corrected by positioning the hydraulic jack in the opening (Fig. 15-46). Pressure is then applied and the framework is pushed or forced back as well as up. The window frame is then spring-hammered, normalizing the metal and greatly reducing the springback of the framework when the pressure is released.

FIGURE 15-46

The turret top, which was roughed-out and straightened earlier to make alignment of the body possible, is now metal-finished, starting with the crown of the roof panel and gradually working toward its center, until all irregularities in its surface have been eliminated and the turret top is restored to its original shape and contour.

All joints and panel seams in the floor panel, rocker panel, and door pillars are sealed with a brushable sealer and undercoated or primed and painted, as at the factory, before the headlining, upholstery, floor pan insulators or heat shields, floor mats, seats, center pillar, and door trim are generally installed and the automobile refinished.

UNIT 15-3: REPAIRING TURRET-TOP DAMAGE

When the turret top on an automobile has not been damaged too badly and only minor repairs to its supporting inner construction or roof rails are necessary, the turret top is generally repaired. When the roof rails onto which the turret top (roof panel) is spot-welded (Fig. 15-47) have been extensively damaged also,

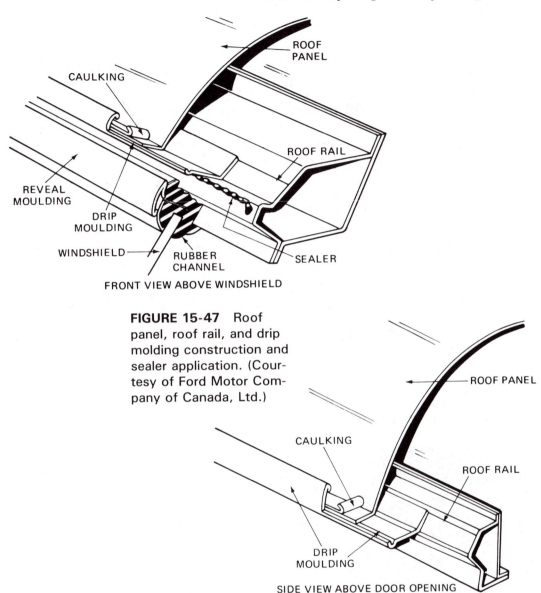

FIGURE 15-47 Roof panel, roof rail, and drip molding construction and sealer application. (Courtesy of Ford Motor Company of Canada, Ltd.)

however, it is advisable to replace rather than repair both the turret top and the roof rails.

Turret tops on many of the newer automobiles are of double-panel construction: an outer and an inner panel, with no access to the outer panel. When extensively damaged, replacement is necessary. Minor damage, such as that caused by hailstones, if not too extensive, is usually repaired by filling the pits with plastic-filler or body solder (Chapters 7 and 8).

Repairing of the damaged turret top is started by first preparing it for the straightening operation. This process involves removing the seats, headlining, trim panels, and wind cord from all body pillars and door openings. The floor mats, windshield, and rear window glasses are then removed, as well as any broken door glasses. The dashboard, instrument panel, and parcel rack behind the lazyback of the rear seat are covered with heavy wrapping paper, blankets, or canvas to protect them from being soiled and scratched while the necessary repairs are being made.

In order to repair the turret top, the insulation and sound-deadening material, which generally consists of sheets of spun fiber glass or asphalt-saturated felt paper, must be removed. Before this step can be taken, however, the turret top's reinforcing cross braces or bows must be removed, after their exact locations on the inside of the roof rails have been clearly marked off. The insulation is removed by heating up the turret top from the outside with the welding torch, adjusted to a carburizing flame using a large tip. When sufficiently hot, the adhesive on the inside becomes soft, allowing the insulation to come off clean and easy without tearing, so that it can again be put back after the turret top has been repaired.

Next, the turret top's inner construction is aligned and straightened. Roof rails that have not been badly bent or crushed, but merely pushed down, can quite easily be raised and restored to their original shape and position by using the hydraulic jack and suitable attachments (Fig. 15-48). If the roof rails have

FIGURE 15-48

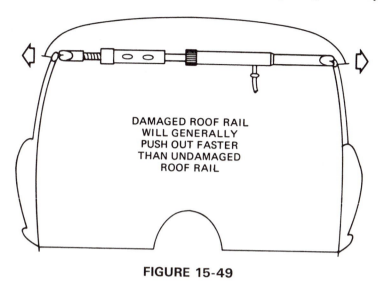

DAMAGED ROOF RAIL
WILL GENERALLY
PUSH OUT FASTER
THAN UNDAMAGED
ROOF RAIL

FIGURE 15-49

not only been pushed down but also driven inward, decreasing the distance between the roof rails and damaging the curvature of the side and crown of the turret top at the drip molding, the damage is corrected by positioning the hydraulic jack between the roof rails and spreading them apart (Fig. 15-49) until the right curvature of the side rail is obtained.

When the windshield header-bar reinforcement has been driven down and back, causing the windshield opening to decrease in both length and width, it is corrected by means of hydraulic jacking equipment (Fig. 15-50). A similar push-

FIGURE 15-50

ing setup is employed in aligning and straightening the rear window reinforcement.

Great care must be exercised when using hydraulic jacking equipment so as not to squash and buckle the inner construction when it is repositioned and aligned. This condition can be avoided by using sufficient padding material, generally pieces of hardwood, angle iron, or steel plates, to spread the force or pressure over a large area.

After the inner construction has been aligned and straightened, the damaged turret top (roof panel) is gradually raised with a hydraulic pushing setup and a small piece of plywood or Masonite (Fig. 15-63), starting at its outer edges and gradually working round and round toward its center, as indicated by the numbers in Fig. 15-51. In pushing up damaged metals, especially on turret tops, heavy-duty extension tubes are used, together with a slip-lock extension, in obtaining the desired length. The floor panel is well padded with suitable pieces of wood and the flex head at the top end of the pushing setup allows the angle of the plywood or Masonite to change as the roof panel is pushed up.

The turret-top metal is aligned, shaped, and straightened as it is pushed up by spring-hammering all high ridges (Fig. 15-52), metal dinging and shrinking wherever necessary. Before the turret top can be metal-finished, however, the whole body of the automobile must be aligned.

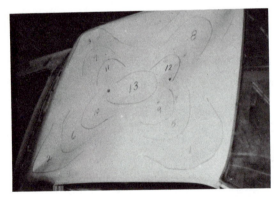

FIGURE 15-51

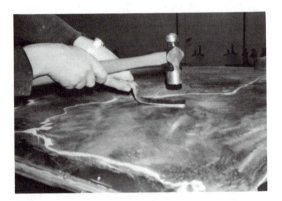

FIGURE 15-52

Body Alignment

Before checking the alignment of a badly damaged automobile body, the repairman must be sure that all frame misalignments have been corrected. Upholstery and glass must be removed and all badly damaged areas roughed-out. All sills, door pillars, roof rails, header bars, and other reinforcing brackets must be straightened. If it is necessary to remove any of the damaged parts in order to straighten them, they must be reinstalled and welded solidly back into place before any attempt is made at aligning the body.

NOTE: All welding of structural members on newer automobiles of high-strength-steel construction should be done *only* by the MIG welding process.

Parts that have been severely damaged (with sharp bends and folds) may have to be heated in order to keep them from cracking or breaking as they are straightened. The damaged areas should not, however, be heated to more than a dull or cherry red under any circumstances.

There are two ways of aligning or squaring up an automobile body—by using a tram rod (Fig. 15-53) or with a steel measuring tape. The alignment is

TRAM ROD

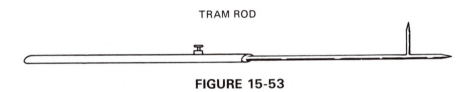

FIGURE 15-53

determined by taking two opposite diagonal measurements, using either body bolts or accurately measured-off chalk marks as reference points. It is very important that all measurements be taken from bare metal areas. If the two opposite diagonal measurements are the same, that particular section or area of the body is in alignment (Fig. 15-54). When an automobile has been damaged on both sides, it is rather difficult to align the body because both sides are out of alignment. In such a case, the correct diagonal measurements are obtained from an

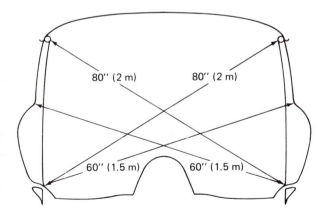

80″ (2 m)   80″ (2 m)

60″ (1.5 m)   60″ (1.5 m)

FIGURE 15-54

undamaged automobile of similar make, year, model, and body style, and the damaged body is aligned accordingly.

If the two opposite diagonal measurements are not the same, it not only indicates that the body is out of alignment in that particular section or area but also shows that the body must be forced over (using hydraulic jacking equipment) in the direction of the shorter diagonal reading. The distance that the body will have to be forced over will, in most cases, be a little more than half the difference between the two diagonal measurement readings. This will compensate for a certain amount of springback that generally occurs when the corrective pressure of the hydraulic jack is released. (Figures 15-55 and 15-56 clearly illustrate some of the reference points from which diagonal measurement readings of various sections of an automobile body are taken.)

The turret top is metal-finished by removing the paint and outlining the low spots with the disk sander, using either a No. 16 (4) or No. 24 (3) grit open-coat sanding disk. The low spots are raised with a suitable pick hammer and dolly, starting with the outer crown area and gradually working round and round toward the center of the roof panel (Fig. 15-57). When most of the low spots, outlined by the disk sander, have been raised, the turret top is filed, picked, and filed again (Fig. 15-58) until all damaged metal has been filed completely smooth and finished perfectly. The turret top is then given a final disk sanding, using a No. 24 (3) grit closed-coat disk first, followed by a sanding with a No. 36 (2)

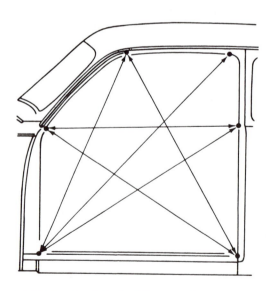

FRONT DOOR OPENING MEASURING POINTS

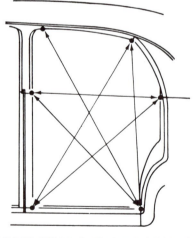

REAR DOOR OPENING MEASURING POINTS

FIGURE 15-55 (Courtesy of Ford Motor Company of Canada, Ltd.)

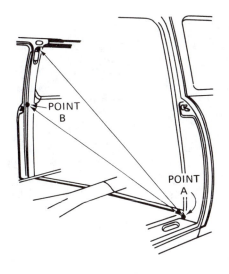

LOCK PILLAR DIAGONAL MEASURING
POINTS (TUDOR AND COUPES)

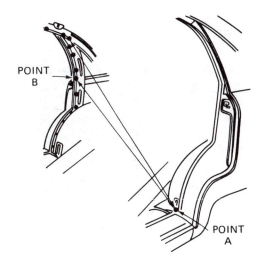

REAR LOCK PILLAR DIAGONAL MEASURING
POINTS (FORDOR)

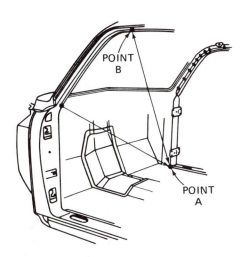

FRONT PILLAR DIAGONAL MEASURING
POINTS (FORDOR, TUDOR AND COUPES)

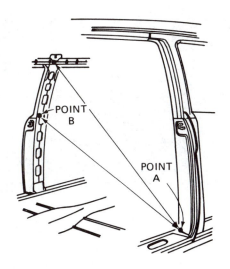

CENTER PILLAR DIAGONAL MEASURING
POINTS (FORDOR)

FIGURE 15-56

FIGURE 15-57

FIGURE 15-58

grit disk, and finished with a No. 50 (1) grit closed-coat disk (Fig. 15-59). The roof rails above the doors and the windshield and rear window openings, after they have been carefully checked to ensure proper fit of their glasses, are also metal-finished whenever necessary.

FIGURE 15-59

All bare metal areas that are covered up or concealed by the turret top's insulation upholstery, moldings, and glass, and particularly all welded and shrunk areas, must be thoroughly cleaned and primed before the parts and materials are again installed. If, however, the damage to a turret top is so extensive that it cannot be repaired and must be replaced with either a similar used turret top from another automobile or with a new roof panel, the damaged roof panel must not be removed before all damage to the turret top, its inner construction (roof rails, windshield, and rear window upper reinforcements), and body pillars have been roughed-out and aligned as previously described. The turret top is then removed from the rest of the body by locating and breaking the spot welds and beads along the eave troughs and panel joints (Fig. 15-60).

The paint is removed by heating it with the welding torch, using a carburizing flame in the areas of the spot welds and while still hot, brushing the paint away with a steel wire brush. This process will bring many of the hidden, hard-to-locate spot welds into full view. Solder-filled panel joints are generally quite easily located by either looking at or feeling the inner surface of the roof panel. The spot welds are weakened by partially drilling through them with a 1/4 in. (6 mm) drill and then breaking them by hand, with a hammer and cold chisel,

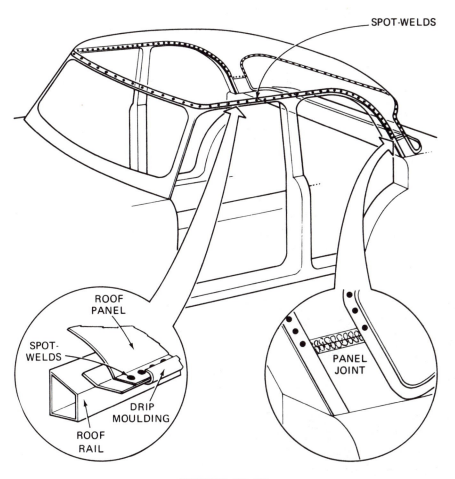

FIGURE 15-60

or with the pneumatic chisel. Besides the paint, the solder fills used in metal-finishing the panel joints must also be removed by melting the solder and either brushing or wiping the joints until all traces of body solder have been removed. The spot welds, which can now be clearly seen, are broken in the same way. After all turret-top spot welds have been broken, the roof panel is removed from the automobile and all necessary repairs to the roughed-out roof rails, windshield, and rear window reinforcements are carried out. The replacement panel is fitted and held down tightly in its proper position by means of self-locking welding clamps or C clamps, while it is first tack-welded and then checked once more for fit before it is solidly spot-welded into place. Great care must be exercised on older automobiles of mild steel construction when spot-welding the roof panel with an oxyacetylene torch so as not to apply excessive heat and warp its outer edges. This condition can be prevented by drilling 1/4 in. (6 mm) holes through the outer flange of the replacement panel, approximately 1 in. (25 mm) apart, before it is placed on the automobile, or by MIG spot welding as recommended for high-strength-steel. The flange is then simply spot-brazed to the adjoining inner construction and the holes neatly filled as the turret top is welded into place, giving it a factory-like appearance.

All panel joints are solder-filled and all minor irregularities in the turret top, eave trough or drip molding, windshield, and rear window openings are metal-finished. The spot-welded turret-top flange is properly sealed all around in the area of the eave trough or drip molding.

All welds and covered-up bare metal areas are primed before the insulation, headlining, windshield, rear window, upholstery, floor mats, and seats are installed and the automobile is moved to the paint shop.

Another method, probably one of the fastest and most economical methods, of repairing turret top or rollover damage (Fig. 15-61) is by replacing the turret

FIGURE 15-61

top completely as one whole unit or assembly with a used salvaged assembly, rather than by repairing and replacing individual parts.

After the body has been prepared for the straightening operation by removing all glass, seats, headlining, trim panels, and floor mats, the body is brought into alignment by correcting the windshield, door, deck-lid, and rear window openings, making certain that all doors open and close properly (Fig. 15-62).

FIGURE 15-62

The damaged roof panel is roughed-out first (after the body has been brought into alignment) and then the windshield pillars, center door pillars, and rear-quarter window (sailing) panels on both sides of the automobile and the salvaged roof replacement assembly are very accurately marked off (Fig. 15-63) with a measuring tape, scratch awl or marking pencil, a right-angled flexible piece of heavy paper or cardboard used as a square, and masking tape.

The roughed-out roof panel is then removed by running the panel cutter

FIGURE 15-63 **(B)**

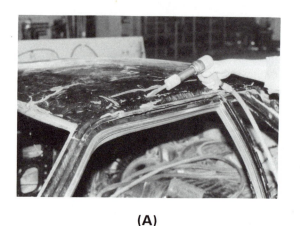

(A)

(B)

FIGURE 15-64

around its outer edges (Fig. 15-64), exposing the turret top's inner construction and body pillars, making the portions of the turret top remaining on the car much lighter in weight and cutting at the marked-off lines much easier. Cutting is done with either a hacksaw or panel cutter, whichever is more practical (Fig. 15-65). The salvaged turret-top assembly is also prepared for installation in the same manner.

FIGURE 15-65

After the remaining portions of the turret top have been removed from the automobile, the salvaged replacement assembly is lifted onto the car, positioned, and firmly clamped down by using vise-grips, welding clamps, or C clamps, and MIG tack-welded firmly in place (Fig. 15-66).

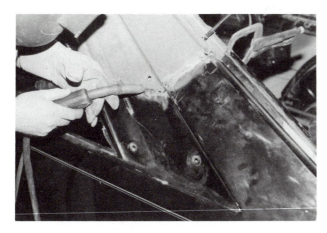

FIGURE 15-66

After the overall size and shape of all body openings have been rechecked, including the opening and closing of all doors, the turret top is solidly welded in position (Fig. 15-67) with a continuous-wire-feed MIG welder.

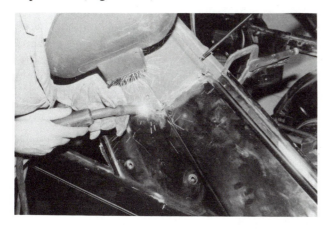

FIGURE 15-67

All welded pillar and panel joints are metal-finished by either countersinking or forging of the weld beads wherever possible and more practical, by leveling or cleaning the weld beads with the disk grinder and filling them and all surrounding surface irregularities with body solder or plastic filler (Fig. 15-68).

The top of the doors' "glass-opening" framework, which was roughed-out and straightened earlier to make possible accurate alignment and fitting of doors in their respective openings, is metal-finished at this time.

The undersides of all weld-joints, body-opening flanges, and all other bare metal-finished areas that will be covered up by chrome trim, glass, or upholstery are well primed before the glass, headlining, trim panels, upholstery, seats, and floor mats are reinstalled and the automobile is moved into the paint shop.

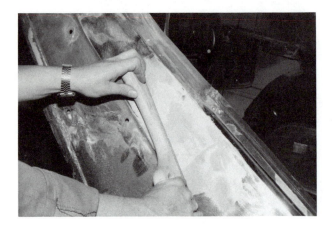

FIGURE 15-68

UNIT 15-4: REPAIRING REAR-END COLLISION DAMAGE

An automobile that has been badly damaged in the rear so that its bumper, quarter panels, deck lid, floor, and wheelhousings have been driven in and forward, bending its frame and causing an overlapping of the rear doors and the quarter panels (Fig. 15-69) can generally be restored to its original condition if the repair operations are carried out in their proper order or sequence and with the right equipment.

FIGURE 15-69 Typical rear-end collision damage.

The first step in repairing this type of damage is to prepare the automobile for the roughing-out and straightening operations by placing it on supporting safety stands, high enough so that the damage can be accurately diagnosed with measuring equipment (centering and tracking gauges) (Fig. 15-70), and then

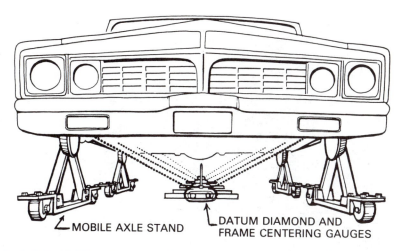

MOBILE AXLE STAND   DATUM DIAMOND AND
                                 FRAME CENTERING GAUGES

FIGURE 15-70 Automobile placed on safety stands. (Courtesy of Chart Industries, Ltd.)

repaired using alignment equipment, such as the damage dozer (Fig. 15-71) or the body and frame straightener (Fig. 15-72). The damaged frame or side rails in unitized construction, being the strongest members in the rear section of an

FIGURE 15-71

FIGURE 15-72   (Courtesy of Blackhawk, Division of Applied Power Industries, Canada Ltd.)

automobile, are first pulled out. Pulling can be done by using a damage dozer, which is hooked to the bumper, bumper bracket (after the bumper face bar and guards have been removed), or a pull plate bolted to the side rail, with the other end of the horizontal beam anchored to the center section of the body or frame as shown in Fig. 15-73 and described in Chapter 10. One of the latest and strongest methods of anchoring portable body and frame straighteners, especially when repairing automobiles of unitized, high-strength-steel construction, is the quadri-clamp anchoring rack (Fig. 15-74). The rack enables the repairman to apply single and also multiple corrective pulls and prevents additional unwanted damage to the underbody (rocker panels) of the automobile while pulling. They can also be pulled out using frame- and body-straightening equipment and similar hookups (Fig. 15-75). The damage to the frame and quarter panels in a rear end collision can also be corrected by firmly fastening the automobile in a stationary frame-straightening machine and then attaching hydraulic pulling rams to the vertical towers and the frame and quarter panels (Fig. 15-76). All pulling must be done slowly and very carefully (at the proper angle), stopping frequently not only to inspect the damaged frame (or side rails) and adjoining sheet-metal sections but also to align and roughly straighten them (spring-hammering and metal-

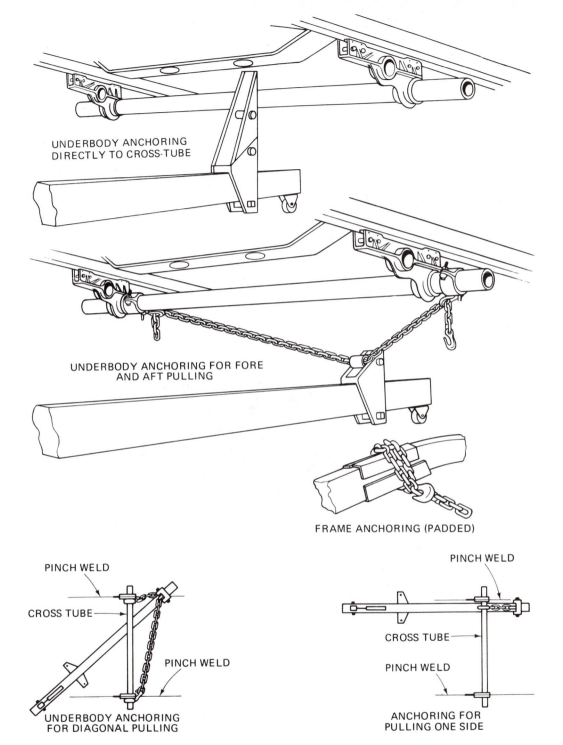

UNDERBODY ANCHORING
DIRECTLY TO CROSS-TUBE

UNDERBODY ANCHORING FOR FORE
AND AFT PULLING

FRAME ANCHORING (PADDED)

PINCH WELD

CROSS TUBE

PINCH WELD

UNDERBODY ANCHORING
FOR DIAGONAL PULLING

PINCH WELD

CROSS TUBE

PINCH WELD

ANCHORING FOR
PULLING ONE SIDE

FIGURE 15-73 Methods of anchoring the damage dozer. (Courtesy of Blackhawk, Division of Applied Power Industries, Canada Ltd.)

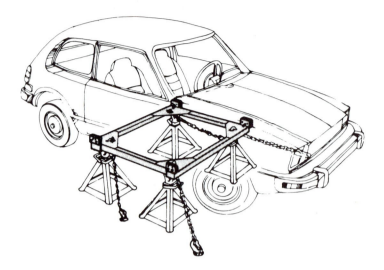

FIGURE 15-74 Quadri-clamp anchoring rack. (Courtesy of Blackhawk, Division of Applied Power Industries, Canada Ltd.)

FIGURE 15-75 (Courtesy of Blackhawk, Division of Applied Power Industries, Canada Ltd.)

dinging) as each panel is pulled back to its original position and shape. This operation tends to normalize the sheet metal into its drawn-back position and greatly minimizes the elastic or springback property that sheet metal possesses.

FIGURE 15-76
(Courtesy of Bear
Manufacturing Co.)

It must be mentioned, however, that in most instances a number of changes in positioning of the damage dozer and several different hookups (Fig. 15-77) will be required before all the damage is roughed-out, aligned, and corrected.

FIGURE 15-77   View of
several different
corrective hookups.

The frame alignment or centering gauges, which were previously installed and used in determining the extent and type of damage that has occurred, should be visually checked regularly as the damage is being pulled out and alignment progresses (Fig. 15-78).

FIGURE 15-78   Centering gauges mounted and ready for checking.

NOTE: It is very important that all structural panels, especially on automobiles of unitized (HSS) construction, to which the rear suspension components are directly mounted, be accurately brought back to their original position and shape so that the proper relationship of the rear suspension parts, not only to each other but also to the front suspension parts, is restored (Fig. 15-79).

FIGURE 15-79   View of trunk floor and rear suspension mounting structural panels.

In rear-end collisions, with no frame, side rail, or floor damage but where the quarter panel has been badly damaged (Fig. 15-80), the damage is repaired by applying corrective stretching pulls directly on the quarter panel. It is roughed-out, aligned, and straightened, while under tension, or replaced if necessary.

FIGURE 15-80

Sometimes, as already described for front-end collision repairing (Fig. 15-25), a side rail that has been badly buckled and bent will not only have to be opened up for straightening, but to make access to the repair area easier, a section of the roughed-out quarter panel (which will later be replaced) is also cut away (Fig. 15-81).

After the side rails, center floor pan, and deck lower panel have been pulled out and roughly aligned and straightened as much as possible, the damaged

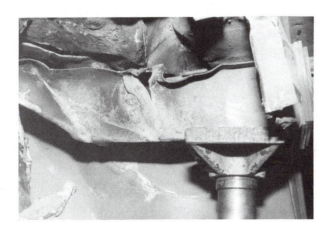

FIGURE 15-81   Cutaway quarter panel to gain access to damaged side rail.

FIGURE 15-82
Stretching out quarter
panel, wheelhousing, and
adjacent panels to
correct rear door
opening.

quarter panels are pulled out, using the frame-straightening machine (Fig. 15-82). By stretching out or pulling back the quarter panels, the vertical floor pan extensions, the lower turret-top panel, the rear door locking pillars, and to some extent the wheelhousings are repositioned (Fig. 15-83).

The wheelhousings generally require additional assistance and are pushed back into their proper positions and shape by placing the hydraulic jack with

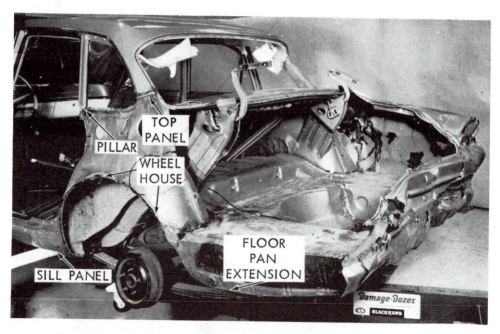

FIGURE 15-83 (Courtesy of Blackhawk, Division of Applied Power Industries, Canada Ltd.)

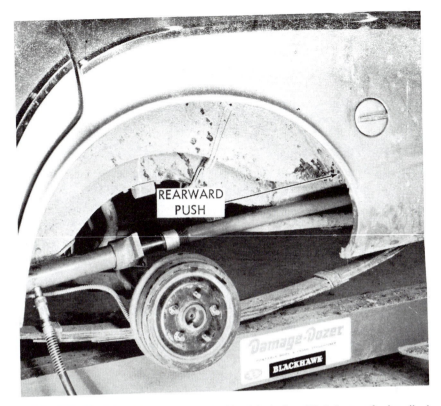

FIGURE 15-84 (Courtesy of Blackhawk, Division of Applied Power Industries, Canada Ltd.)

suitable attachments in the wheelhousings and stretching them (Fig. 15-84), or restricting them from becoming elongated by means of a practiclamp and ratchet hoist puller ("come-along"), or a pulling ram setup (Fig. 15-85). After the wheelhousings have been pushed back into their proper positions, and while the

FIGURE 15-85
Restricting wheel-housing from tearing or elongating.

tension of the hydraulic jack is still on the quarter panel, all high ridges caused by the bulging out of the quarter panels at their sides are spring-hammered and both wheelhousings and quarter panels are simultaneously aligned and roughly straightened. This step eliminates the overlap of the rear door and the quarter panel, making the door opening large enough for the door to open and close properly.

After all the damaged sheet metal has been roughly aligned, the number of body panels that can be repaired or that will have to be replaced will depend greatly on the extent and severity of the rear end collision.

If the damage is so great that all sheet metal except the side rails and wheelhousings have to be replaced, however, the damaged panels are then removed with the pneumatic chisel (Fig. 15-86). The side rails, rear cross-member,

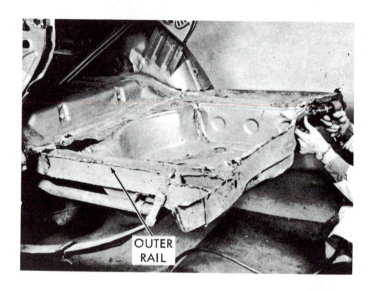

FIGURE 15-86 (Courtesy of Blackhawk, Division of Applied Power Industries, Canada Ltd.)

wheelhousings, and floor pan (over the differential housing) are straightened perfectly now that all areas are accessible and aligned according to factory specifications (Fig. 15-87 and 15-88). Replacement quarter panels can be installed as received from the manufacturer [Fig. 15-89(A)], which necessitates the removal of a portion of the vinyl top covering, eave-trough chrome molding, and also the rear window glass, or they can be cut down in size and installed without removing any parts [(Fig. 15-89(B)]. The new quarter panels, some manufactured with the vertical floor pan extensions already spot-welded to them, are then placed into position on the body (Fig. 15-90) and aligned so that the new deck lid fits properly before they are tack-welded into place (Fig. 15-91). Before the new

FIGURE 15-87 (Courtesy of Blackhawk, Division of Applied Power Industries, Canada Ltd.)

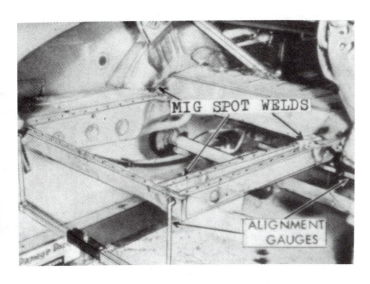

FIGURE 15-88
(Courtesy of Blackhawk, Division of Applied Power Industries, Canada Ltd.)

FIGURE 15-89

(A)

(B)

deck lid can be installed for fitting on the automobile, however, the deck lid hinges, which are also badly bent, are straightened quite easily. In most cases, the hinges will bend as shown at points A and B in Fig. 15-92. The bend at point A controls the upward and downward position of the deck lid, while the bend at point B controls the forward and backward position of the deck lid.

If the sharpness of the bend at A is increased by bending the hinge in the C direction, the deck lid is raised up higher in its opening, when in its closed position. If the bend in the hinge at point A is decreased, by bending it in the D direction, the deck lid is lowered in its opening.

On the other hand, if the hinge at point B is bent in the E direction, the deck lid moves forward in its opening, but when bent in the F direction, the deck lid moves farther back in its opening.

Generally the hinges, if repairable, can be straightened without removing them from the car (Fig. 15-93). The hinges are merely stabilized and kept from moving at either points A or B and bent by lifting up or pulling down on the deck lid.

(A)

(B)

FIGURE 15-90 (A) Quarter panels and trunk lower panel being fitted onto the body; (B) deck lid positioned and fitted in trunk opening.

FIGURE 15-91 Panels are tack-welded into position as indicated by arrows.

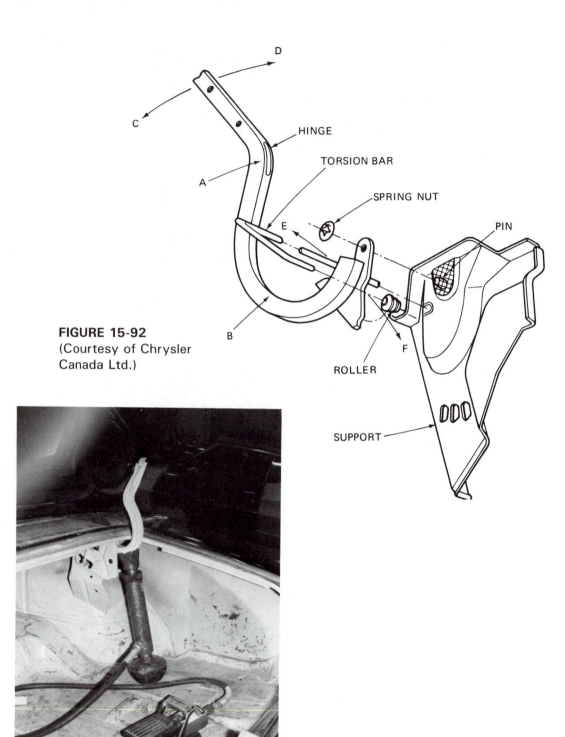

D

C

HINGE

TORSION BAR

SPRING NUT

PIN

A

E

FIGURE 15-92
(Courtesy of Chrysler
Canada Ltd.)

B

F

ROLLER

SUPPORT

FIGURE 15-93

If the quarter panel is rusted-out or badly damaged in only one particular area, it is often repaired by installing a partial replacement instead of replacing the whole quarter panel, as illustrated in Fig. 15-94. The size of the replacement section is clearly marked off on the quarter panel, allowing enough metal to flange the edges of the opening, after the damaged section has been cut out with the pneumatic chisel.

After the opening edges have been flanged, the replacement section is fitted into position and kept in alignment by means of metal screws or pop-rivets while the new section is spot-welded into place.

The quarter panel is then metal-finished by solder-filling the recessed lap joints and finishing in the usual manner. The deck lower panel is similarly positioned and tack-welded in place on the car. Body straps are frequently used with either a hydraulic pulling ram, ratchet hoist puller ("come-along"), or a

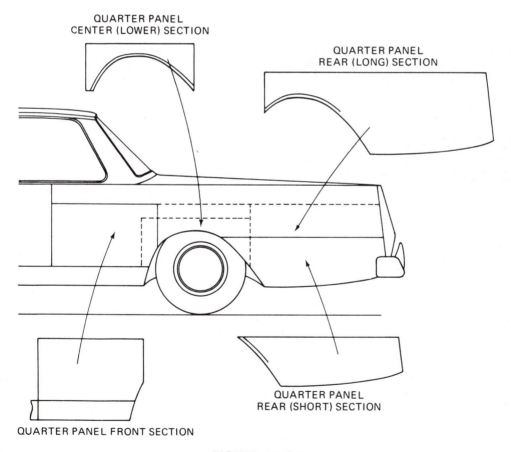

FIGURE 15-94

friction jack in pulling the quarter panels or front fenders together [Fig. 15-90(A)]. The damaged floor pan, which sometimes has to be removed in order to complete the straightening of the side rails, is also spot-welded (Fig. 15-95). The body is given another final check for alignment before all replacement panels are solidly welded in place. The deck lid opening, which may sometimes undergo slight changes due to expansion and contraction of metal when the new replacement panels are solidly welded into place, often has to be corrected by spreading the quarter panels apart with the hydraulic jack (Fig. 15-96).

The rear window opening also has to be checked for alignment, first by taking diagonal measurements from a point in the lower corner of one side to a point in the upper corner of the opposite side, using inner-construction holes or joints as reference points. The outer edge of the rear window glass is then covered with several layers of masking tape to prevent chipping the glass as it is placed into the opening; its curvature is checked with that of the window frame.

A twist in the framework of the rear window opening, which may cause the

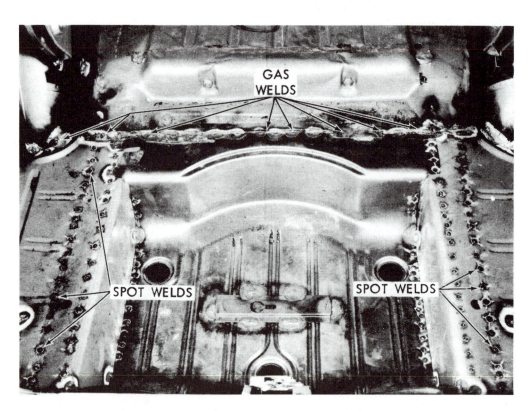

FIGURE 15-95   (Courtesy of Blackhawk, Division of Applied Power Industries, Canada Ltd.)

FIGURE 15-96

installed glass to crack, can be located by either gluing or taping a number of small rubber spacers, all of equal thickness, into position at various points on the pinch-weld flange. The rubber dam, used on later-model automobiles (Fig. 15-97), can also be used instead of the rubber spacers. The glass, when placed

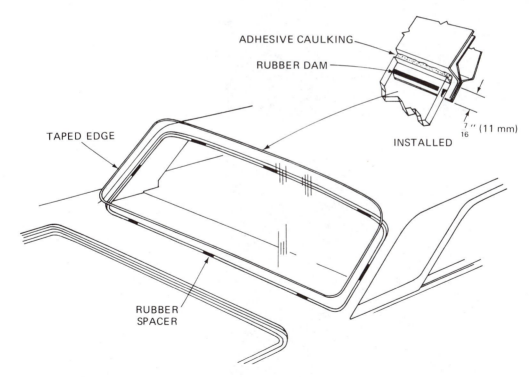

FIGURE 15-97 (Courtesy of Chrysler Canada Ltd.)

into the opening and properly centered, should lie flat and square, making solid contact with all the rubber spacers or the dam if the window opening is properly aligned.

All straightened sheet-metal and replacement panels are then metal-finished by first grinding down all spot-welds to a smooth finish, hammering out all small dents, and solder-filling or plastic-filling the panel joints (Fig. 15-98). The rear window glass is now installed, and all body joints, seams, and openings are carefully sealed with a high-grade sealer to prevent moisture, water, and dust from entering the interior of the automobile (Fig. 15-99). If the sealing operation is performed before the automobile is refinished, the body sealer is also covered with a coat of paint, which gives a factory-finished appearance to the repaired automobile (Fig. 15-100) after all the remaining parts have been installed.

FIGURE 15-98

FIGURE 15-99 Sealing body joints, seams, and openings.

FIGURE 15-100 Repaired automobile ready for delivery.

QUESTIONS

15-1 What are the important facts a repairman must have before he starts repairing a damaged automobile?

15-2 What operation must be carried out before front-end parts are removed?

15-3 How is the front fender bumped out?

15-4 What is meant by *hand-feeling* a metal surface, and in what operations is it used?

15-5 Are underpans and wheelhousing panels also metal-finished? If not, how are they repaired?

15-6 Out of what material are many of the underpans and wheelhousing panels on the newer, unitized, high-strength-steel automobiles made, and how are they repaired?

15-7 What methods are used in straightening damaged radiator supports?

15-8 If the radiator support is not repaired properly, what problems will the repairman encounter?

15-9 How is a badly damaged radiator support on older and newer unitized (HSS) automobiles replaced?

15-10 Describe the proper way used in aligning, straightening, and metal finishing a bumper face bar before it is rechromed.

15-11 How are fascia bumpers on late-model automobiles repaired?

15-12 How are the sharp buckles, bends, and ridges eliminated from the inner construction and outer panel of a hood?

15-13 What methods are used in roughing-out inaccessible outer panels on hoods?

15-14 Describe and illustrate with a sketch how a front door opening is aligned.

15-15 What precautionary measure should be taken when the windshield has been broken in a front-end collision and there is no visible evidence or reason for its breaking?

15-16 In minor front-end damage on unitized (HSS) automobiles, how are the front fender inner panels, strut towers, side rails, and radiator support pulled out and straightened?

15-17 In repairing major front-end damage, what damage is repaired first, and how is this accomplished?

15-18 Why is repairing of front-end damage with a pulldozer more cumbersome and slower than with a body and frame straightener or frame machine?

15-19 What equipment is used to determine the correct position of the strut towers, front fender inner panels, side rails, and the radiator support as they are pulled out and straightened or replaced?

15-20 How are the outer, overlapping, joining edges of replacement panels cleaned in preparation for welding?

15-21 How is a side rail or any structural member repaired if it cannot be straightened cold?

15-22 How can the overheating of high-strength steel be avoided?

15-23 Describe how an inaccessible, reinforced area on a badly damaged side rail is straightened.

15-24 Is the sectioning of load-bearing structural members and panels recommended, and how should they be installed?

15-25 What protective treatment is given all welds and panel joints before the motor, transmission, steering, and suspension parts are installed?

15-26 In repairing side collision damage, how are the floor and rocker panels repaired?

15-27 In what way are the roof rail and turret top aligned?

15-28 If a cutting torch is used in the removal of a body section or salvage parts, how should the cutting be done?

15-29 How are the top and bottom edges of the new rocker panel fastened to the old rocker panel assembly?

15-30 Can localized damage to rocker panels be repaired? If so, how?

15-31 Describe how a replacement panel is installed on a door.

15-32 What tools and equipment are involved in aligning and straightening the inner construction and outer panel of a badly damaged door?

15-33 Is the repairing of doors with badly damaged framework and guard rails on automobiles later than 1980 models recommended, and why?

15-34 Describe and illustrate with a sketch how the window opening on a door is corrected.

15-35 What preparations must be made before a damaged turret top can be repaired?

15-36 How are badly bent roof rails repaired?

15-37 What hydraulic setup and attachments are used in pushing up a turret top, and how is this operation carried out?

15-38 Describe how a badly damaged body is aligned.

15-39 What type and grit of sanding disks are used in metal-finishing a turret top?

15-40 Why must the roof rails, windshield, and rear window openings be metal-finished?

15-41 In what way are covered-up or concealed bare metal areas protected before parts are installed?

15-42 What method is employed in breaking the spot welds when a turret top has to be replaced?

15-43 Describe how a replacement roof panel is prepared for spot welding and how it is positioned and held in place.

15-44 How are the newly installed roof panel and adjoining parts metal-finished?

15-45 What is one of the fastest and most economical methods of repairing turret-top damage?

15-46 Briefly describe the method discussed in Question 15-45.

15-47 Why should an automobile with extensive damage to its rear end be placed on safety stands?

15-48 Describe how the damage to the rear end is roughed-out and aligned.

15-49 What equipment provides the strongest method of anchoring portable body and frame straighteners?

15-50 When repairing rear-end collision damage, especially on automobiles of unitized (HSS) construction, why is it so important that all structural panels be accurately straightened?

15-51 How are damaged panels removed that have to be replaced?

15-52 What kind of equipment is used in repairing side rails and the rear cross-member?

15-53 Describe and illustrate with a sketch how a deck lid hinge is straightened.

15-54 How are partial and whole quarter-panel replacements made?

15-55 What type of jack and attachments are used in aligning the quarter panels and the deck lid?

15-56 Explain how a rear window glass is used in checking the alignment of its opening.

15-57 Why should all the body panel seams be sealed, and why must this be done before the automobile is refinished?

16

Spray Painting Equipment

Spray guns are used to such an extent in our world that it could be said that we live in a spray-painted world. From the giant diesel locomotive to automobiles and perfume dispensers, the greatest portion of paint and varnish is applied with the spray gun. The reason this method is so widely accepted is that it increases production rates and produces high-quality finishes at lower production costs.

The application of paint by the spray method is a mechanical operation, but it requires that the methods used be handled properly. The process is not complicated if logically approached; in fact, it is rather simple. Unfortunately, there is a shortage of competent, trained painters with a complete knowledge of the industry. Many fail to realize that the equipment is manufactured with a great deal of care and designed to do specific jobs and that procedures, techniques, care, and cleaning are essential in achieving trouble-free operations. Also, they fail to realize that paint is formulated for specific uses and consequently must be used, treated, and handled in such a manner to achieve desired results.

The equipment involved in spray-paint operations must be considered from both the technical and practical aspects. It is not a conglomeration of items but rather a carefully selected coordinated group whose purpose is to do the best possible job.

UNIT 16-1: AIR COMPRESSORS

A compressor is the lifeline of the spray-finishing industry. It serves one main purpose; it compresses air, which operates sanding machines, and cleaning and dusting equipment as well as the spray gun. An air compressor is designed to supply air continuously at a determined pressure and a minimum volume in cubic feet (liters) per minute. There are two general types: the single-stage compressor and the two-stage compressor.

Single-Stage Compressor

A single-stage air compressor can be of a single- or twin-cylinder design (Fig. 16-1). Air is drawn from the atmosphere and is compressed in one stage to final tank pressure. The transition of the air is from the atmosphere through the compressor aftercooler and then through the check valve to the supply tank. The single-stage compressor is generally used where a 100 psi (690 kPa) maximum or less is desired. Single-stage compressors can be used at over 100 psi (690 kPa) pressure, but their efficiency is considerably less and they are a great deal more costly to operate. As a rule, this type of compressor is approximately 60 percent efficient.

FIGURE 16-1 [Courtesy of DeVilbiss (Canada) Limited.]

Two-Stage Compressor

A two-stage compressor has a large cylinder where the air is compressed to an intermediate pressure and then delivered through an intercooler to a small cylinder (Fig. 16-2). Here it is compressed to its final pressure and then delivered through an aftercooler to the air receiver. Two stages are used when pressure exceeds 100 psi (690 kPa). The advantage of a two-stage compressor after 100 psi (690 kPa) is reached is higher efficiency; example: working pressure 200 psi (1380 kPa)-80 percent efficiency. The higher pressure will also permit faster operation of tools, more air stored in the air receiver, and greater air delivery. The volumetric efficiency of average single- and two-stage compressors is as follows:

Single Stage

Maximum working pressure 75 lb (518 kPa)	75%
Maximum working pressure 100 lb (690 kPa)	70%
Maximum working pressure 125 lb (862 kPa)	65%
Maximum working pressure 150 lb (1035 kPa)	60%

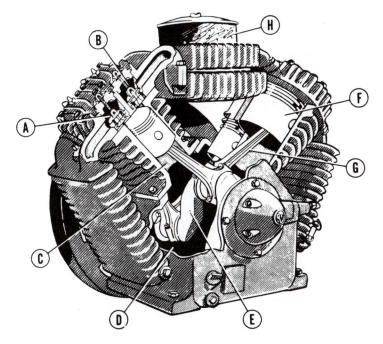

FIGURE 16-2   The principal parts of a piston-type compressor. Intake (A) and exhaust (B) valve assemblies, cylinder (C) and crankcase (D), crankshaft (E), piston (F), and connecting rod assembly (G), and air-intake filter (H). [Courtesy of DeVilbiss (Canada) Limited.]

Two Stage

Maximum working pressure 100 lb (690 kPa)	80%
Maximum working pressure 125 lb (862 kPa)	80%
Maximum working pressure 150 lb (1035 kPa)	80%
Maximum working pressure 175 lb (1210 kPa)	80%

These, then, are the two main types of air compressors. They can be driven electrically or by gas; they can be stationary or portable, horizontal or vertical, or air-cooled or water-cooled.

In selecting an air compressor, the air requirements are determined by listing all the equipment that is operated by air. How much air will each one require, and how many hours will each piece operate in an 8-hour day? Now select a compressor that will cope with the air requirements with approximately 10 percent surplus.

The emphasis must be placed on cooling because keeping a compressor operating as cool as possible is the major factor in determining efficiency. It is very important to select the right size so that the compressor will run intermittently throughout the day and therefore run cooler.

To find the proper size of compressor needed, consult Tables 16-1 and 16-2. Every air tool in the shop must be taken into consideration when calculating the amount of air used, and how much time it is used in a normal 8-hour day. When the total amount of air for the shop has been tabulated and the highest pressure used found, consult Tables 16-3 and 16-4 to find the right size of compressor.

Installation of a Compressor

A compressor crankcase should be filled with a good grade of oil to the proper level, SAE No. 10 for ordinary conditions and SAE No. 20 for temperatures above 100°F (37.8°C). The oil should be changed every 2 or 3 months and the level should be checked every week. The bearings on the electric motor should be oiled weekly unless they are life-lubricated bearings.

The belt should be checked for proper tension and alignment so that the proper power transmission is achieved. All dust should be blown away from the cooling fins, including the intercooler and aftercooler. The air-intake strainer should be cleaned once a week. The safety valve handle on the tank should be lifted at least once a week to check if it is functioning properly. The flywheel should be checked for tightness on the crankshaft. The tank should be drained of moisture every day, especially in high-humidity areas (Fig. 16-3).

A compressor, if properly cared for, will last a long time; but if trouble develops, consult the manufacturer's manual supplied to the purchaser.

TABLE 16-1 Operating consumption and air requirements chart (English units).

Type Device	Air Pressure Range (psi)	Average Free Air Consumption (cfm)
Air filter cleaner	70–100	3.0
Air hammer	70–100	16.5
Body polisher	70–100	2.0
Body sander	70–100	5.0
Brake tester	70–100	3.5
Carbon remover	70–100	3.0
Car rocker	120–150	5.75
Car washer	70–100	8.5
Dusting gun (blowgun)	70–100	2.5
Engine cleaner	70–100	5.0
Fender hammer	70–100	8.75
Grease gun (high pressure)	120–150	3.0
Hoist (1 ton)	70–100	1.0
Hydraulic lift*	145–175	5.25
Paint spray gun (production)	70–100	8.5
Paint spray gun (touch-up)	70–100	2.25
Pneumatic garage door	120–150	2.0
Radiator tester	70–100	1.0
Rim stripper	120–150	6.0
Spark plug cleaner	70–100	5.0
Spark plug tester	70–100	0.5
Spray gun (undercoating)	70–100	19.0
Spring oiler	70–100	3.75
Tire changer	120–150	1.0
Tire inflation line	120–150	1.5
Tire spreader	120–150	1.0
Transmission and differential flusher	70–100	3.0
Vacuum cleaner	120–150	6.5

*For 8000 lb capacity. Add 0.65 cfm for each additional 1000 lb capacity.

Source: Courtesy of DeVilbiss (Canada) Limited.

TABLE 16-2 Operating consumption and air requirements chart (metric units).

Type Device	Air Pressure Range (kPa)	Average Free Air Consumption (liters/min)
Air filter cleaner	480–690	85
Air hammer	480–690	467
Body polisher	480–690	57
Body sander	480–690	141
Brake tester	480–690	99
Carbon remover	480–690	85
Car rocker	830–1035	163
Car washer	480–690	241
Dusting gun (blowgun)	480–690	71
Engine cleaner	480–690	141
Fender hammer	480–690	248
Grease gun (high pressure)	820–1035	85
Hoist (900 kg)	480–690	28
Hydraulic lift*	1000–1210	149
Paint spray gun (production)	480–690	241
Paint spray gun (touch-up)	480–690	64
Pneumatic garage door	830–1035	57
Radiator tester	480–690	28
Rim stripper	830–1035	170
Spark plug cleaner	480–690	141
Spark plug tester	480–690	14
Spray gun (undercoating)	480–690	539
Spring oiler	480–690	106
Tire changer	830–1035	28
Tire inflation line	830–1035	42.5
Tire spreader	830–1035	28
Transmission and differential flusher	480–690	85
Vacuum cleaner	820–1035	184

*For 3630 kg capacity. Add 18.4 liters/min for each additional 454 kg capacity.

TABLE 16-3 Compressor capacity chart (English units).

Compressor (psi)		Free Air Consumption of Total Equipment (cfm)		Compressor[‡]
Cut-in	Cut-out	Average Service Station or Garage Use*	Continuous Operation[†]	(hp)
80	100	Up to 6.6	Up to 1.9	1/2
		6.7–10.5	2.0–3.0	3/4
		10.6–13.6	3.1–3.9	1
		13.7–20.3	4.0–5.8	1½
		20.4–26.6	5.9–7.6	2
		30.5–46.2	8.8–13.2	3
100	125	46.3–60.0	13.3–20.0	5
		60.1–73.0	20.1–29.2	7½
		73.1–100.0	29.3–40.0	10
		100.0–125.0	40.1–50.0	15
120	150	Up to 3.8	Up to 1.1	1/2
		3.9–7.3	1.2–2.1	3/4
		7.4–10.1	2.2–2.9	1
		10.2–15.0	3.0–4.3	1½
		15.1–20.0	4.4–5.7	2
140	175	Up to 11.9	Up to 3.4	1
		12.0–18.5	3.5–5.3	1½
		18.6–24.2	5.4–6.9	2
		24.3–36.4	7.0–10.4	3
		36.5–51.0	10.5–17.0	5
		51.1–66.0	17.1–26.4	7½
		66.1–88.2	26.5–35.3	10
		88.3–120.0	35.4–48.0	15

*These figures are not to be regarded as the capacity of the compressor in free air output but instead they are the combined free air consumption of all the tools in the shop, as well as tools anticipated for future added equipment. A factor has been introduced to take into account intermittent operation of tools likely to be in use simultaneously in the average shop or service station.

[†]These figures are to be employed when the nature of the device is such that normal operation requires a continuous supply of compressed air. Therefore, no factor for intermittent operation has been used, and the figures given represent the compressor capacity in free air output.

[‡]Do not use a compressor of less than 1½ hp if the pneumatic equipment includes a lift of 8000 lb capacity.

Source: Courtesy of DeVilbiss (Canada) Limited.

TABLE 16.4 Compressor capacity chart (metric units).

Compressor Pressures per kPa	Free Air Consumption of Total Equipment (liters/min)		Compressor (watts)
Cut-in Cut-out	Average Service Station or Garage Use*	Continuous Operation†	
550–690	Up to 187	Up to 53.8	374
	190–297	56.6–85	558
	300–385	87.8–110	746
	388–575	113–164	1,120
	578–753	167–215	1,492
	865–1300	249–374	2,238
690–862	1305–1700	376–566	3,730
	1725–2065	569–826	5,600
	2066–2832	829–1130	7,460
	2832–3540	1135–1420	11,190
830–1035	Up to 107	Up to 31.1	374
	110–206	34–59.5	558
	210–286	62.4–82	746
	290–424	85–122	1,120
	427–567	125–161	1,492
966–1210	Up to 337	Up to 96.2	746
	340–524	99–150	1,120
	526–685	153–195	1,492
	688–1030	198–294	2,238
	1035–1445	298–482	3,730
	1446–1870	484–748	5,600
	1871–2490	750–1000	7,460
	2500–3400	1002–1360	11,190

*These figures are not to be regarded as the capacity of the compressor in free air output but instead they are the combined free air consumption of all the tools in the shop, as well as tools anticipated for future added equipment. A factor has been introduced to take into account intermittent operation of tools likely to be in use simultaneously in the average shop or service station.

†These figures are to be employed when the nature of the device is such that normal operation requires a continuous supply of compressed air. Therefore, no factor for intermittent operation has been used, and the figures given represent the compressor capacity in free air output.

Source: Courtesy of DeVilbiss (Canada) Limited.

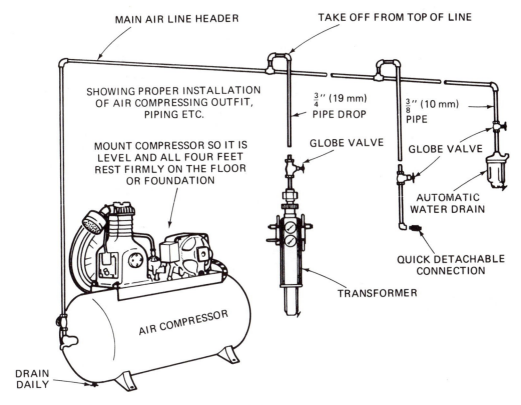

MAIN AIR LINE HEADER

TAKE OFF FROM TOP OF LINE

SHOWING PROPER INSTALLATION
OF AIR COMPRESSING OUTFIT,
PIPING ETC.

$\frac{3}{4}''$ (19 mm)
PIPE DROP

$\frac{3}{8}''$ (10 mm)
PIPE

MOUNT COMPRESSOR SO IT IS
LEVEL AND ALL FOUR FEET
REST FIRMLY ON THE FLOOR
OR FOUNDATION

GLOBE VALVE

GLOBE VALVE

AUTOMATIC
WATER DRAIN

QUICK DETACHABLE
CONNECTION

TRANSFORMER

AIR COMPRESSOR

DRAIN
DAILY

FIGURE 16-3   [Courtesy of DeVilbiss (Canada) Limited.]

UNIT 16-2: AIR TRANSFORMER

A transformer is a device (Fig. 16-4) that condenses air, oil, and moisture; regulates and strains the air; and provides outlets to which spray guns, dusters, etc. can be connected. The transformer separates the oil and moisture by mechanical means and air expansion, allowing only clean, dry air to reach the spray gun. If any moisture or oil passes through the spray gun onto the freshly painted surface, it will ruin the paint finish. Therefore a transformer is a must in the refinishing field. A transformer is the only way to control pressure at the gun to give the desired atomization.

Transformers are usually hooked up off the main line at least 25 ft (7.75 m) from the compressor. The workings of a transformer are relatively simple. The air enters at the back of the transformer main pressure line. By adjusting the pressure regulator knob until the desired pressure is reached, a diaphragm

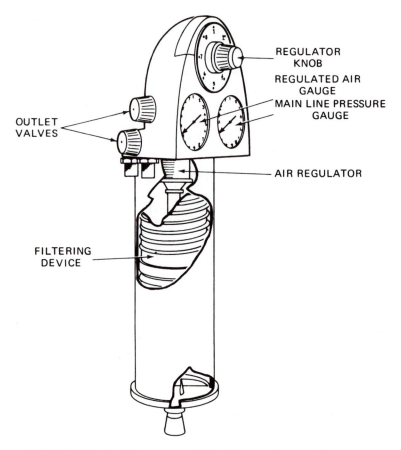

FIGURE 16-4   [Courtesy of DeVilbiss (Canada) Limited.]

opens that allows air to pass through a metal filter. Water separators and baffle condensers clean the air of its impurities and then it passes out through the regulated side to the spray gun. Drain the transformer daily if necessary.

Installation of Air Transformer

The air transformer should be bolted securely to the spray booth or to some similar sturdy object near the operator for convenience in reading the gauges and operating the valves. It should be installed at least 25 ft (7.75 m) from the compressor and the takeoff should always be from the top of the air line. Piping should slope toward the compressor air receiver or a drain leg, installed at the

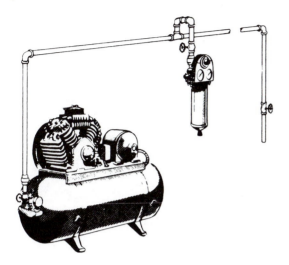

FIGURE 16-5 Piping should be as direct as possible if a large number of fittings are used; large-size pipe should be installed to help overcome excessive pressure drop. [Courtesy of DeVilbiss (Canada) Limited.]

end of the air line or at the end of each branch, to provide for drainage of moisture from the air line (Fig. 16-5). Use piping of sufficient size for the volume of air passed and the length of pipe used (Tables 16-5 and 16-6). The pipe must always be of the recommended size or larger. Otherwise, excessive pressure drop will occur.

TABLE 16-5 Minimum pipe size recommendations (English units).

Compressing Outfit		Main Air Line	
Size (hp)	Capacity (cfm)	Length (ft)	Size (in.)
1½ and 2	6–9	Over 50	3/4
3 and 5	12–20	Up to 200	3/4
		Over 200	1
5–10	20–40	Up to 100	3/4
		Over 100 to 200	1
		Over 200	1¾
10–15	40–60	Up to 100	1
		Over 100 to 200	1¾
		Over 200	1½

Source: Courtesy of DeVilbiss (Canada) Limited.

TABLE 16-6 Minimum pipe size recommendations (metric units).

Compressing Unit		Main Air Line	
Size (watts)	Capacity (liters/min)	Length (m)	Size (mm)
1120 and 1492	170–255	Over 15	190.6
2238 and 3730	340–566	Up to 61	190.6
		Over 61	254
3730–7460	566–1130	Up to 30.5	190.6
		Over 30.5 to 61	254
		Over 61	318
7460–11,190	1130–1700	Up to 30.5	254
		Over 30.5 to 61	318
		Over 61	382

Source: Courtesy of DeVilbiss (Canada) Limited.

UNIT 16-3: HOSES

Fluid Hose

Two types of hoses are available in the finishing industry: an air hose and a fluid hose.

A fluid hose is always black in color with a special solvent-resisting liner that is almost impervious to all common solvents in paints, lacquers, and other finishing materials that readily attack ordinary composition hose (Fig. 16-6). For production finishing, 3/8 in. (10 mm) ID hose is used for large guns. For maintenance finishing, 1/2 in. (13 mm) ID hose is used for large guns and 5/16 in. (8 mm) ID hose is used for smaller outfits.

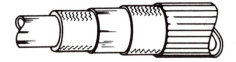

FIGURE 16-6 [Courtesy of DeVilbiss (Canada) Limited.]

Air Hose

An air hose usually has a red rubber cover or orange braid; the orange-braided hose is generally used on small outfits (Fig. 16-7). Using the improper size of hose will result in an excessive drop in air pressure, which will starve the spray gun.

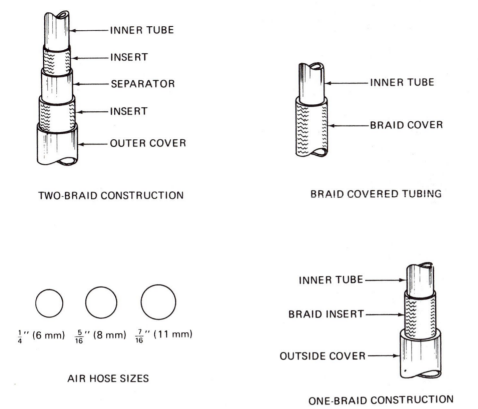

FIGURE 16-7 [Courtesy of DeVilbiss (Canada) Limited.]

Tables 16-7 and 16-8 should be consulted to find the proper size of hose. Too often a spray gun is blamed for functioning improperly when the real cause of trouble is an inadequate supply of compressed air at the gun.

UNIT 16-4: SPRAY BOOTHS

In many areas it is not only recommended, but is a code requirement that all spray painting must be done in a spray booth. In the past, cross-draft spray booths were used in the refinishing industry. These booths leave a lot to be desired, especially since the air velocity must be adequate to remove paint fumes and provide a safe working environment, but yet low enough to allow for a good paint job. OSHA and NFPA require a design velocity of a 100 fpm (30.48 m/min).

TABLE 16-7 Table of air pressure drop (English units).

| Size of Air Hose (ID) | Air Pressure Drop at Spray Gun (lb) | | | | | |
	5 ft Length	10 ft Length	15 ft Length	20 ft Length	25 ft Length	50 ft Length
1/4 in.						
At 40 lb pressure	6	8	9½	11	12¾	24
At 50 lb pressure	7½	10	12	14	16	28
At 60 lb pressure	9	12½	14½	16¾	19	31
At 70 lb pressure	10¾	14½	17	19½	22½	34
At 80 lb pressure	12¼	16½	19½	22½	25½	37
At 90 lb pressure	14	18¾	22	25¼	29	39½
5/16 in.						
At 40 lb pressure	2¼	2¾	3¼	3½	4	8½
At 50 lb pressure	3	3½	4	4½	5	10
At 60 lb pressure	3¾	4½	5	5½	6	11½
At 70 lb pressure	4½	5¼	6	6¾	7¼	13
At 80 lb pressure	5½	6¼	7	8	8¾	14½
At 90 lb pressure	6½	7½	8½	9½	10½	16

Source: Courtesy of DeVilbiss (Canada), Limited.

TABLE 16-8 Air pressure drop (metric units).

| Size of Air Hose (ID) | Air Pressure Drop at Spray Gun (kPa) | | | | | |
	1.53 m Length	3.05 m Length	4.58 m Length	6.10 m Length	7.63 m Length	15.3 m Length
64 mm						
At 276 kPa pressure	41	55	65	76	88	165
At 345 kPa pressure	52	69	83	97	110	123
At 414 kPa pressure	62	86	100	115	131	214
At 482 kPa pressure	74	100	117	134	155	234
At 551 kPa pressure	84	114	134	155	175	255
At 620 kPa pressure	97	129	152	174	200	272
79 mm						
At 276 kPa pressure	15.5	19	22.4	24.1	27.6	58.6
At 345 kPa pressure	20.7	24.1	27.6	31	34.5	69
At 414 kPa pressure	25.9	31	34.5	38	41.4	79.4
At 482 kPa pressure	31	36.2	41.4	46.6	50	90
At 551 kPa pressure	38	43	48.3	55	60	100
At 620 kPa pressure	44.8	52	58.5	65.5	72.5	110

Source: Courtesy of DeVilbiss (Canada) Limited.

The speed at which this air is moving makes it difficult for the intake air filters to remove all the dust which is pulled into the booth by the exhaust fan in a negative-pressure booth. The intake air filters of self-sealing types are designed to be efficient at an air velocity of 125 fpm (3810 cm/min) at 70°F (21.1°C).

The life expectancy of the intake filters varies according to the amount of air going through them plus the temperature of the air. The higher the velocity and the temperature, the quicker the filter material will break down and start shedding some fibers. Therefore, it is necessary that a program suited to the shop conditions be followed as to when these filters have to be replaced.

The filters are provided to give a smooth, even flow of clean air, which in turn envelopes the vehicle being painted and carries away spray fumes and evaporating solvents. The exhaust fan must be of sufficient size to meet the air velocity required by OSHA and NFPA and also local codes.

The paint-arresting filters in the exhaust remove the paint overspray in the air being exhausted outside. These filters must be of good quality and must be changed as required; otherwise, they choke off the air to the exhaust fan.

In a booth with the interlocks, the diminished flow will cut off the air to the spray gun. This will necessitate changing the filters. Clogged filters increase the load on the exhaust fan and could catch on fire if the conditions were right for spontaneous combustion; they should be disposed of in a safe manner.

Figure 16-8 show a typical cross-draft spray booth which is used in industry. In recent years a new type of booth has appeared on the North American continent. This type of booth was developed in Europe. It is called a down-draft spray booth (Fig. 16-9). The down-draft spray booth is designed on the same principle as an automotive production-line down-draft booth. The replacement air passes through filters in the ceiling and flows around the vehicle and through gratings in the floor (Fig. 16-10). This varies from conventional spray booths,

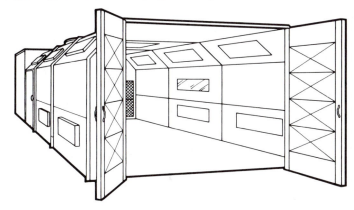

FIGURE 16-8 Cross-draft spray booth. [Courtesy of DeVilbiss (Canada) Limited.]

FIGURE 16-9 Down-draft spray booth. [Courtesy of DeVilbiss (Canada) Limited.]

FIGURE 16-10 Airflow in a down-draft booth. [Courtesy of DeVilbiss (Canada) Limited.]

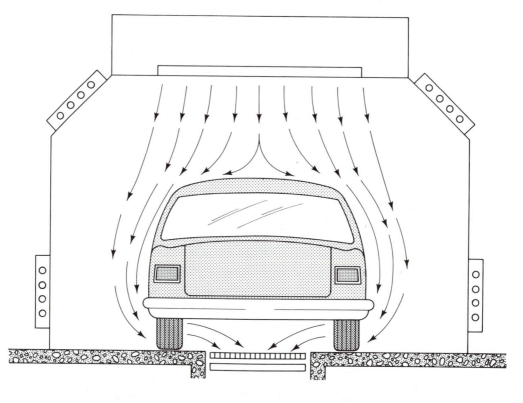

where the airflow is from one end to the other across the vehicle. The airflow pulls the overspray down and away from the painter into the pit instead of along the length of the vehicle being sprayed. This minimizes the chance of overspray and contaminants on a freshly painted vehicle and spoiling the finish. This type of spray booth will give a superior quality to the painted vehicle and draw the overspray away from the painter, giving a finish comparable to an original factory finish. Due to a better filtration system and different airflow, it helps to eliminate two major causes of unsatisfactory refinish jobs: airborne dirt and a bad painting environment.

A spray booth should have walls that are smooth; this will eliminate dust clinging to them. The booth should be fireproof and should have an unobstructed working area as well as an access door so that the painter can go to and from the spray booth without opening large doors. Explosion-proof lighting switches and interlocks must also be provided, because sparks could cause a fire to start.

The proper type of fire extinguishers must also be provided according to most codes. Many different types of booths exist, ranging from bench-type dry booths to large water wash installations; the latter are ordinarily used in large production shops.

In any new installation it is recommended and in some areas it is the law that all new booths be provided with an air-makeup unit which is capable of heating all replacement air used in the booth. Figure 16-11 shows a typical new installation as well as the air movement inside of the booth. The type of system is a positive type of installation; that is, slightly more air enters the booth than is exhausted according to code. This provides for a controlled environment, less dirt to contend with, and a controlled air temperature.

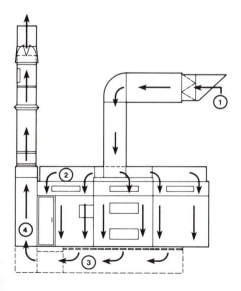

FIGURE 16-11 Typical new installation.

FIGURE 16-12 Typical exhaust fan. [Courtesy of DeVilbiss (Canada) Limited.]

All booths must have an exhaust fan of sufficient capacity to exhaust the required amount of air, again according to code. The fan should have the blades cleaned and bearings greased as often as required. Figure 16-12 shows a typical exhaust fan.

UNIT 16-5: INFRARED BAKING EQUIPMENT

To speed up the drying of enamels, many shops have installed infrared baking equipment. Many cars are refinished in enamel because it is a cheaper process than using lacquer. Enamel dries to a hard glossy finish and needs no polishing after painting. The baking units can be from a single bulb to portable units that do only a section to traveling ovens that are used in either a spray booth or a specially ventilated drying room (Fig. 16-13). The traveling ovens usually go

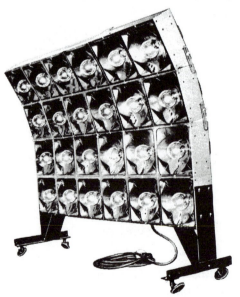

FIGURE 16-13

FIGURE 16-14 Traveling baking equipment. [Courtesy of DeVilbiss (Canada) Limited.]

back and forth on tracks; the movement is reversed by stop plates that are placed at the proper distance on the floor for the size of the object being force-dried (Fig. 16-14). The air movement must always be maintained in the booth when the oven is used. If the oven is in a special drying room, the car is put in it for the required drying time.

There are different types of drying. Although varying somewhat with different materials, the distinction generally recognized in the trade is as follows:

1. Air-drying temperature—less than 100°F (37.8°C). Air-drying temperature is the vaporization of the solvents, which normally takes from 8 to 10 hours.

2. Force-drying temperature—from 100 to 180°F (37.8 to 82.2°C). Force-drying refers to the method whereby the automobile is placed in a convection-type oven. By movement of the heated air, heat is transferred to the painted surface. The surrounding air must always be hotter than the vehicle. Air temperature is generally 165°F (73.2°C).

3. Baking temperature—above 200°F (93.3°C). Baking temperature, in contrast to radiant heat sources, gives off energy in the form of infrared rays. The air between the source and the object does not absorb an appreciable amount of this radiated energy. In an infrared oven, as soon as the lamps are turned on, the radiated energy is immediately transformed into heat upon reaching the painted surface, which instantly

becomes hotter than the surrounding area. Metal temperature is 220°F (104°C).

Enamel jobs will be ready for delivery in approximately 30 minutes when they are baked out. Lacquer-based undercoats and color coats are ready to sand or polish after 10 minutes in any weather. Enamel topcoats have better gloss, hardness, and color life when they have been baked in temperatures of 200°F (93.3°C) or more. Lacquers usually have a better gloss if they are baked also.

Improved Quality

Although the *drying from the inside out* aspect of infrared baking has been somewhat oversold, it is definitely true that infrared does have penetrating power and that this penetration of the paint film itself results in more uniform drying. There is also less possibility of surface pigment discoloration and much better flow-out, since paint film temperatures of from 200 to 230°F (93.3 to 110°C) are practicable with infrared equipment in the refinishing field. The quality of enamels is greatly improved due to the considerable amount of polymerization (a curing of the resins) that takes place during short baking cycles. Baked enamels are harder and more durable and have considerably longer color life.

After an infrared treatment, lacquer-based primer surfaces are dried much faster and allow easier sanding. Similarly, a force-dried lacquer color coat has better gloss with less rubbing. Infrared drying ensures fewer come-backs and rework because of improperly dried undercoats or finish coats.

One of the characteristics of lamp-type infrared units is the fact that different colors and materials have varying abilities to absorb near-infrared energy. Light colors will require a somewhat longer drying time than dark ones because a part of the energy is reflected rather than absorbed. Similarly, certain parts of automobiles, such as glass, plastics, and adhesives, have very poor infrared absorptive characteristics compared to paint or metal. This peculiar characteristic of near infrared permits the actual baking of the paint film on a car with temperatures in excess of 200°F (93.3°C) without any damage whatsoever to the more critical parts, such as glass, plastics, or the gasoline in the tank.

A smaller type of oven will require a longer time to dry a paint job. This information should be obtained from the distributor who sells the equipment.

UNIT 16-6:   RESPIRATORS

Respirators should be worn at all times when painting is being done (Fig. 16-15). The fumes from thinners, reducers, and paint are toxic and must be

FIGURE 16-15 [Courtesy of De-Vilbiss (Canada) Limited.]

removed as much as possible. One type of respirator is made to be worn over the nose and mouth. This type is further subdivided into several different types. Another type fits over the head like a hood; clean air is fed into it to push out all toxic fumes or dust. This type of hood respirator is usually only worn in shops or in types of work where extreme dust or fume conditions are present. Some respirators that fit over the mouth and nose are only made to remove dust and not toxic fumes. A good respirator is usually equipped with replaceable filter elements, which are not expensive and which increase the life of the respirator.

The paint being sprayed is more toxic if paint hardeners and gloss improvers are used. Some paints contain lead as well as other toxic materials, but when hardeners are used, isocyanates are introduced into the air that the painter must breathe. This product could irritate the lungs, as well as the eyes and skin, so washing your hands after using catalyzed paint is highly recommended. The wearing of a positive-pressure-air-supplied respirator type TC 19C NIOSH/MESA is strongly recommended (Fig. 16-16). If this type is unavailable, use a vapor/ particle type that meets the specifications as being effective for isocyanate vapor or mist.

To supply a positive-type respirator, it is imperative that the air supplied meet the code. Air from a compressor cannot be used unless a purifying and filtration device is installed in the air line before the respirator. Air coming from a compressor may contain carbon monoxide as well as oil and water. Therefore, caution is the word and the practice if the painter does not want to damage his health.

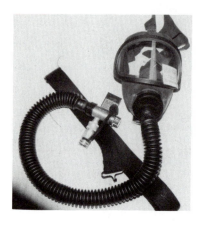

FIGURE 16-16 Positive air-supplied respirator.

QUESTIONS

16-1   What is a compressor, and what purpose does it serve in a body shop?

16-2   What is the difference between a single-stage and a two-stage compressor?

16-3   Should the compressor tank be bled of humidity? Why?

16-4   What is the purpose of an air transformer?

16-5   What size pipe will be required for a 4 hp (3 kw) compressing outfit with pipes that are over 200 ft (60.96 m) long?

16-6   What color is a fluid hose?

16-7   Why should painting always be done in a spray booth?

16-8   What is the difference in air movement between a cross-draft spray booth and a down-draft booth?

16-9   At what velocity must air move through a booth to meet OSHA and NFPA requirements?

16-10   What parts of your body can isocyanates affect?

16-11   What type of respirator must be worn when spraying paint that contains isocyanates?

16-12   What purpose does the exhaust fan serve in a spray booth?

16-13   For what purpose is the infrared equipment used in a refinishing shop?

16-14   How does the infrared accomplish the drying of paints?

16-15   What is the purpose of a respirator: to remove fumes and dust from the air, to help the painter to breathe dirty air, or to help the painter see the job better?

17

Paint Materials

SAFETY TIP

It is common knowledge that accidents are usually caused by negligence. Only by paying careful attention to accident causes can they be reduced. Many of the products used in a body shop are highly combustible—lacquers, reducers, thinners, and many other dangerous chemicals. Moreover, because the vehicles are sometimes dismantled in assemblies, they clutter up the floor or the alleys between the cars.

Combustibles are always a fire hazard and the containers holding such products as thinners, reducers, and paints should be kept closed and stored in fireproof cupboards. There should also be no welding or smoking close to the paint area, and proper signs signifying such restrictions should be prominently displayed. All painting should be done in a spray booth with exhaust fans that meet the requirements of local laws.

UNIT 17-1: REFINISHING MATERIALS

The materials used in the refinishing of an automobile body or panel are numerous. It must be understood, however, that the various car manufacturers do not all use the same products. Just a few years ago the standard finish coats were either nitrocellulose lacquer or synthetic enamel. These products left something to be desired, and thus new top-coat products were formulated: acrylic lacquer, acrylic enamel, and polyurethane enamel. Considering the number of products available, a refinisher must be well versed in their uses and application.

The compositions of automotive coatings are similar in some respects, whether they are acrylic lacquer, acrylic enamel, or conventional enamel. They are all composed of a pigment or pigments dispersed in a vehicle that is composed of a resin or resins and solvents.

The acrylic lacquer vehicle or binder contains more ingredients than an

537

enamel. Synthetic enamel consists of an alkyd resin and pigment or pigments and solvents. Acrylic enamels consist of an alkyd resin which is fortified with an acrylic resin and solvents. An acrylic lacquer consists of an acrylic resin, cellulose resin, a plasticizer, and solvents.

How do these ingredients differ, and what are the differences? The resins in both synthetic enamel and in acrylic enamel are chemically related. Alkyd resin in a synthetic is a combination of a drying oil such as linseed oil, a polyhydric alcohol such as glycerine, and a dibasic acid such as phtholic anhydride. This resin is soft and sticky even when there are no solvents present. It will react with the oxygen in the air to become a hard, tough material.

As stated above, acrylic enamel resin is an alkyd resin similar to that used in synthetic enamel, but is further modified with an acrylic resin. In contrast to an unmodified alkyd resin, this resin is not soft and sticky when no solvents are present. However, it reacts further with oxygen to become harder and tougher. Both synthetic resin and acrylic enamel resin are no longer soluble in solvents after a few days' exposure to the air.

The resins used in acrylic lacquer are hard nonsticky materials that tend to be slightly brittle. This deficiency is overcome by the use of a plasticizer, a liquid that is a solvent for these resins, softening them slightly and making them tough and flexible. An acrylic resin is chemically any polymer whose basic monomers are chemical derivatives of acrylic acid. An acrylic acid resin can range from soft resins soluble in mineral spirits to very hard resins such as Plexiglas, insoluble (or essentially so) in any type of solvent. Those useful in lacquers are readily soluble and about midway in hardness. A cellulosic resin is any resin derived from cellulose (pure cotton). These vary from hard and brittle to hard and tough.

You may wonder why industry does not use one or the other of these resins and have a simple formula. Industry could but it would sacrifice some desired properties. The proportions of components are selected to give best exterior durability with desired adhesion, flexibility, and polishing characteristics.

The other component of the vehicle is the solvent. The types used are classified chemically as:

- *Aliphatic hydrocarbons:* mineral spirits, VM&P naphtha
- *Aromatic hydrocarbons:* toluene, xylene
- *Esters:* ethyl acetate, butyl acetate
- *Ketones:* acetone, methyl ethyl ketone

Selection of the proper solvent is a matter of knowing what resins are soluble in what type of solvent and then blending fast-evaporating, medium-evaporating, and slow-evaporating types to give the desired drying rate. This is not a simple operation and requires a great deal of skill and knowledge.

The pigmentation of automotive paints requires a great deal of knowledge and experience. About 90 different pigments are used at manufacturing plants to obtain factory package colors. These pigments can range from inexpensive earth colors such as oxide yellow, to chemically complicated vat dyestuffs, which are very expensive.

Knowledge gained from experience enables the manufacturer to blend these ingredients to come up with very high quality enamels and lacquers that enable the body shop to produce high-quality repairs.

The paint used in shops generally consists of thinners or reducers, the binder, and the pigment. The thinners and reducers evaporate quickly, depending on the way they are formulated. The binder is the part that carries the pigment and that forms the protective film. The pigment is the part that gives the paint the color, as well as its hiding qualities.

Nitrocellulose or acrylic lacquer dries by the evaporation of the thinner. Each is fairly soluble even when dry and when recoated with the same product. They usually form a good bond between recoats without having to be sanded too much. Lacquer dries from the top down to the bottom surface, sets up fast, and becomes hard in a short time. These factors are important for the shop that is usually cool and that has a problem with dust.

Lacquers have a hard finish and good gloss; but if they are applied too thickly, they are liable to crack, especially when subjected to a considerable change of temperature. Acrylic lacquers have a better gloss retention and are a harder and tougher finish than nitrocellulose lacquer. Consequently, they are better suited for the glamour colors used today.

Synthetic or acrylic enamels dry from the evaporation of the reducer; then the binder is oxidized and polymerized by the oxygen in the air and the heat from the sun. Enamels dry from the inside out and to a full gloss; they do not need to be polished. They are usually soft because they require a long time to dry; once dry, however, the film becomes very hard and practically insoluble to ordinary solvents. In recent years the manufacturers have introduced chemicals which when added to the paint speeds up the hardening to eliminate lifting when recoating. This catalyst also improves the gloss, appearance, adhesion, flexibility, and the flow of the paint film. The sanding of the old surface must be well done to provide a suitable base for the adherence of the new paint film. The paint area must also be clean, for enamel does not dry very fast.

Acrylic and alkyd enamels contain certain solvents which evaporate rapidly after spraying. This evaporation gives the initial "set" to enamels. Then, as oxygen is "breathed" into the paint film, it creates a reaction with the dryers

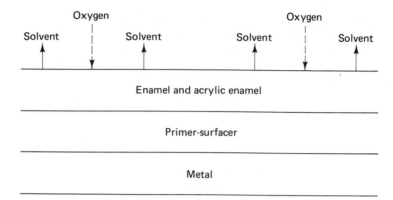

FIGURE 17-1   (Courtesy of Sherwin Williams Company Inc. Canada.)

which starts the cure cycle for the film. Although the film is apparently dry within a few hours, the total cure process requires several weeks (Fig. 17-1).

Surface Preparation

Spray painting, like brush painting or any other type of finishing, requires that the surface be properly prepared before paint is applied. Therefore rust, oil, grease, and water must be removed from all surfaces that are to be spray-painted. Any carelessness in surface preparation will result in a defective paint job. Also,

FIGURE 17-2   (Courtesy of C.I.L. of Canada, Ltd.)

where a high-quality finish is required, paint will not hide or eliminate bad defects in the original surface, including any holes or bumps. The life of a finish and the appearance of that finish will depend considerably on the conditions of the surface over which the paint is applied. Students should learn the steps to a perfect finish thoroughly, step by step. The first step is to wash the car with a good cleaning solution (Fig. 17-2).

Preparing Bare Metal

It is important to realize the necessity of having the metal absolutely clean before applying any undercoats. Some painters rub their hands over the area to determine the effects of sanding without realizing that they are transferring oil from their hands to the surface. Oil comes from the skin and shop tools; even if one's hands are freshly washed, a fine oily film will be left on the surface.

If there is any rust on the metal or a suspicion of rust because the bright steel has been allowed to stand for a day or so before being primed, no priming should be done until the metal has been treated with a metal conditioner that will neutralize the rusting action. This step is essential if peeling and doing a job over again are to be avoided.

If any soldering has been done on the job, the soldering acids should be neutralized; otherwise, blistering and peeling will occur. Wash off metal and soldered areas with a good metal conditioner before applying primer or primer surfacer (Fig. 17-3). This step is good insurance against peeling. When using a product such as Metal Prep, be sure to dilute with water as specified. Leave the solution on the metal for a minute or two and then wash the surface with water and dry it immediately.

FIGURE 17-3 Applying metal conditioner.

Preparing an Old Paint Surface

If a repaint job is to be done over old paint, obviously the first thing to determine is whether or not the old paint has good adhesion. You can check that by sanding through the finish and feather edging a small spot. If the thin edge does not break or crumble, it is safe to assume that the old paint is going to adhere.

The next step is to make sure that no wax is embedded in the finish. Gasoline is often used to clean up a job, but it is a poor wax solvent and will not remove deeply embedded wax. Before the job is sanded, it should be cleaned with a good wax and grease remover which should be applied to small sections of the body at a time and should be wiped up with a clean cloth while it is still wet. When no more scum comes off on the rag, it can be assumed that the wax and grease remover have dissolved all the old wax and floated it up to where it can be removed.

The third step is to feather-edge stone bruises, scratches in the paint, and the edge of the paint where body repairs were performed. A No. 80D to No. 120D (1/0 to 3/0) grit production paper used on a vibrator sander or a circular foam disk sander on which the sandpaper is glued will do a good job. Feather edging means to wear the paint surface to a taper (Fig. 17-4). A good rule for feather edging a paint surface is to taper the surface 2 in. (51 mm) for every coat of paint. The taper should be very gradual so that no edge is felt. This sanding

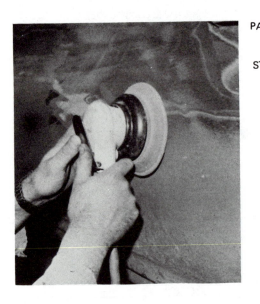

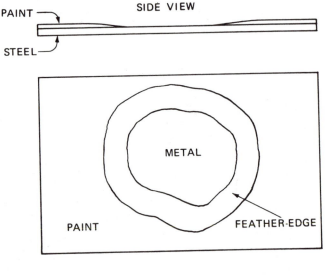

FIGURE 17-4

will help to remove any rust present, but it should also be treated with metal conditioner. These areas might require some filling with primer surfacer and putty.

The next step is to determine whether the old finish is lacquer or enamel. Lacquer color coats can be determined by wetting a cloth with a good grade of thinner and wiping it over the surface. If the paint dissolves after a few rubs, you can be almost certain it is lacquer.

To find out if it is nitrocellulose or acrylic lacquer, some perchlorethylene should be put on a rag. If some color comes off the old finish, it is acrylic; if it does not come off, it is nitrocellulose. On the other hand, if there is no color transfer, it is enamel.

If the finish is lacquer, certain precautions must be taken in preparing the car to prevent swelling of the old coat if it is to be recoated with lacquer. Swelling usually occurs where sanding has been done, and unless the new solvents are prevented from reaching the old surface, no amount of care will prevent the sanding scratches from showing.

The best thing to do under the circumstances is to seal down the old finish after the necessary sanding has been done and the bare metal spots properly treated with a sealer or primer sealer. This material has good adhesion to the old finish and will prevent penetration of the solvents used in the finishing coats. If it is necessary to use primer surfacer for filling the rough spots, this should be applied before the sealer coat. Under these circumstances an approved sealer is applied (Fig. 17-5) on the old finish after the necessary metal conditioning, priming, and sanding are done. This sealer can be used over alkyd, acrylic enamel, polyurethane enamel, and acrylic lacquer.

Some manufacturers recommend that a sealer be applied before painting an acrylic lacquer film with more acrylic lacquer. This is also applied if the repainting is done with synthetic or acrylic enamel (Fig. 17-6).

FIGURE 17-5 Acrylic sealer.

FIGURE 17-6 Synthetic primer-sealer.

The acrylic enamels and super enamels used on original finishes by some manufacturers are a very hard finish. Thus a thorough sanding job must be done before repainting; otherwise, the paint will not adhere properly.

When repairing over an old enamel finish, be sure that you do not use too coarse a sandpaper and that the old surface has been scuffed to provide a good tooth for the new finish. Unless the old enamel is in good condition, it is better to use a primer surfacer as the first coat. This will take care of the problem of adhesion and provide for sanding over any rough areas. Some old enamels are quite brittle, and it is a good idea to check adhesion very carefully before proceeding with any new coats.

A word here about sanding may be timely. Modern primer surfacer and glazing putties will fill almost any rough surface, but much time and material can be saved if the metal is quite smooth before these materials are applied. A good practice is to finish the metal or feather-edge with a very fine sandpaper or disk. There are no shortcuts—the finish will always reflect the care used in preparation.

When the paint surface is in poor condition because of cracking, blistering, or some other cause requiring that it be stripped completely off the metal surface, a paint and varnish remover is used. Paint removers are designed to remove varnish, enamel, and lacquer finishes from old surfaces. This product is toxic and should only be used in well-ventilated areas. Rubber gloves should be worn and all contact with the skin should be avoided. Some of these products are flammable and they should be used away from open flames, sparks, or excess heat.

One prevalent condition is from metal rusting, usually at the wheel openings, lower section on the fender, and quarter panel, or bruises. One of the most effective ways to clean these areas is to use a sandblaster (Fig. 17-7). Sandblasting brings the rusted areas back to a shiny surface which can then be refinished.

Sanding the Metal

Another method is to use a circular rotation sander polisher using a foam pad with a sandpaper disk that has adhesive on the back of it that will stick to the pad. The sandpaper disk is replaced when it is worn out. Usually a No. 36 (1½) grit disk is used to sand the paint off. This is then followed with a No. 80 (1/0) grit that will leave the surface smooth. Care must be taken not to gouge the metal with the disk (Fig. 17-8).

Sand scratches are probably the most annoying problem around a paint shop. Many otherwise beautiful paint jobs are spoiled because of some sand scratches in a prominent place. Unfortunately, they do not show up until after the color coat is applied, and then it is usually too late to correct them. If we understand

FIGURE 17-7

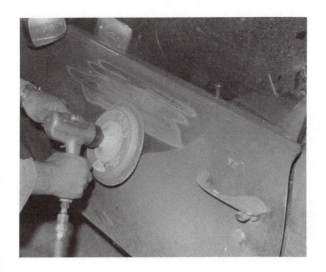

FIGURE 17-8

what causes them and do not try to hurry the job too much, most of them can be avoided.

The first and prime requisite for a good paint job is smooth metal. The metal finisher or bump man can make it doubly hard for the painter if the metal is not properly finished. Careless filing or bearing down too hard on the coarse disk will leave furrows that are hard to fill. The best practice is to sand the rough spots and welds down with a coarse disk and finish off with a fine disk. Do not worry about getting the metal too smooth; metal that appears smooth will have plenty of tooth for the primer to adhere to. Furrows and deep scratches create uneven shrinkage of the filler coats and therefore require a great deal more sanding. Also, more surfacer will have to be applied, and the more coats that are applied, the slower the drying time, thereby prolonging the operation.

Primers

Primer is made to provide adhesion to special surfaces. It has poor filling qualities and should not be used for this purpose. Lacquer-, enamel-, and epoxy-based primers are available and they are designed for special purposes.

There are different types of primers which can be used. The most popular is the nitrocellulose primer-surfacer in the average shop, primarily because it fills well, comes in different colors, dries fast, and is easy to sand (see Fig. 17-9). But it lacks the rust and corrosion resistance of an alkyd primer-surfacer and does not provide the tough flexible film of an alkyd surfacer; consequently, it is recommended for the smaller repair areas.

Alkyd enamel primer-surfacer is excellent in all respects but one. It requires a dry time of 2 to 3 hours before sanding, and overnight if it is to be wet-sanded. Its main use is for priming vehicles in cases where the paint could lift if lacquer primer-surfacer were used or on commercial vehicles.

When painting with polyurethane enamel, which is often used on flat trucks and trailers, an epoxy zinc chromate primer should be used. The adhesion is

FIGURE 17-9

superb, it is corrosion resistant, and it has great chemical resistance. Most primer-sealers, as the name implies, may be used on bare substrates, but can also be used over old finishes as a sealer. This material is a two-part system which after being mixed must be used within 3 days.

The crisis in the energy field as well as new pollution standards have forced both car and paint manufacturers to develop new products to meet the needs of the buying public. Most manufacturers now use a seven-stage zinc phosphate metal treatment; then the bodies are primed using an electric deposition system with either polyesters or epoxy esters. These types of primers are usually baked at 350 to 400°F (176 to 205°C) for 30 to 40 minutes. Some companies will apply a surfacer which is also baked for the required time. These are then wet-sanded using a No. 400 (10/0) grit sandpaper. For example, zinc chromate primer is used for aluminum and galvanized metal as a first coat. Primer is usually applied to the metal and only in a special case would it be used over another primer.

Another type of primer is used to increase adherence to steel, aluminum, aluminum alloys, galvanized metals, and zinc- and cadmium-plated metals. This is a vinyl wash primer which must be used on metal which is clean of paint, corrosion, grease, and oil, and treated with the proper metal conditioners.

This primer must be sprayed at the proper air pressure in a thin coat after it has been reduced to the proper viscosity according to manufacturer's directions. The metal should be visible through the prime coat as too heavy a coat will tend to ruin its adhering qualities. It must be allowed to dry for 30 minutes before it is recoated with primer surfacer and it must not be sanded.

This primer is mildly corrosive and if it comes in contact with the skin, eyes, or clothing, it should be rinsed off immediately with cold water. It has a pot life of 8 hours; therefore, no more should be mixed than can be used during that period of time.

Primer-Surfacers

The answer to a refinisher's dream would be a paint that would stick to anything (grease and dirt included), that would fill out all file marks, dings, and scratches, and finally that would flow out absolutely smooth without any sags and would require no rubbing or polishing. Unfortunately, no one has yet discovered a paint with all these qualities.

To design a paint that will stick to everything is a large order. In fact, to produce a paint that will stick to clean metal and remain bonded to it is by no means a simple problem. Adhesion is not a temporary proposition. Many materials will adhere to metal for a short period; but as soon as they begin to harden, the bond is destroyed.

A primer surfacer is recommended to improve the surface condition by filling the surface imperfections. Filling is a matter of placing sufficient materials on a surface so that after it dries and shrinks the surplus material may be sanded off to the level of the low spots. To accomplish this, fillers or surfacers carry a very high solid content that includes pigments, as well as other materials, and they are so formulated that when sprayed on a surface they build up the film thickness very rapidly.

Priming materials or finish coats cannot be formulated with such high solid contents without sacrificing other qualities. The one exception to this statement is modern primer-surfacer, where a surfacer has been formulated to possess the adhesive properties of a primer. Regardless of what is used as a finishing coat—lacquers or synthetic enamels—the paint will not materially improve the roughness of the original surface (Fig. 17-10). To obtain a smooth job means to start with a smooth surface, so we use a primer for good adhesion and a surfacer or putty for filling the rough surface (Fig. 17-11). Then we sand the surface until all the high spots are brought down to the level of the low points. If some of the metal shows before we reach the low spots, we have to spray more primer-surfacer and resand until the surface is smooth (Fig. 17-12). Primer-surfacers should be reduced according to the manufacturer's recommendation, using a good-quality thinner. It should be sprayed at around 45 psi (310 kPa) or less at the spray gun. The spray gun should be held approximately 6 in. (152 mm) away from the surface.

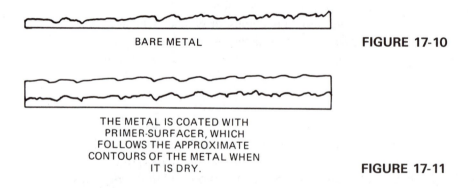

BARE METAL

FIGURE 17-10

THE METAL IS COATED WITH
PRIMER-SURFACER, WHICH
FOLLOWS THE APPROXIMATE
CONTOURS OF THE METAL WHEN
IT IS DRY.

FIGURE 17-11

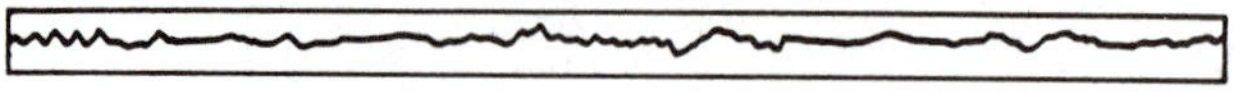

SANDING WILL PRODUCE A FLAT
SMOOTH SURFACE LEVELING OFF
HIGH SPOTS. IF IT IS NOT
THOROUGHLY DRY BEFORE SANDING
SHRINKING WILL OCCUR OVER
DEEP FILLS PRODUCING UNEVEN
SURFACES AND SHOWS FILE MARKS.

FIGURE 17-12

Putties

The purpose of glazing putty is for filling, especially for filling very rough surfaces that cannot be filled satisfactorily by the surfacer or primer surfacer. A glazing putty is similar to a surfacer except that it is much higher in solids and thus has greater filling properties. Putties are not a cure-all and sometimes too much is expected of them. Rough metal and deep scratches and holes should be sanded down or filled with solder or plastic filler. Two or three applications of putty, allowing 15 to 20 minutes between coats, will produce better filling than one heavy coat. Glazing putty is usually applied by using a wide glazing knife or a squeeze (Fig. 17-13). Always remember to apply enough pressure to obtain proper adherence.

FIGURE 17-13

Sanding

After the primer-surfacer has dried thoroughly, the next thing to consider is the sanding operation. The use of coarse sandpaper, such as No. 220 or No. 240 (6/0 or 7/0), will produce scratches in the primer surfacer that will be hard to fill by the final finish coat. The only reason this coarse paper is used by the painter is to speed up the sanding. With present-day surfacers, sanding is so easy that it is not necessary to use paper coarser than No. 320 (9/0). In order to get even fewer scratches, the use of No. 400 (10/0) paper is recommended for the final sanding when the top coat is acrylic lacquer (but not for enamel).

Keep the sandpaper clean and do not grind the sanding grit into the paint film. Sand in long, even strokes and always in the same direction. If you sand in a circular motion, these sand marks will show through the color coats.

Cleaning

In cleaning automobile bodies, care should be taken to clean carefully around the moldings, hinges, and handles where wax or grease may collect. These seams, moldings, cracks, and so on, should be blown out with high air pressure. This step will remove sediment and moisture, which would later cause the paint film to bridge and break.

A small, clean paintbrush is handy for this operation. If paint remover is necessary, make sure that all the paint remover is cleaned out of cracks and crevices where it is likely to collect.

Special Metals

Galvanized aluminum must be treated with a metal conditioner which will etch the metal and remove rust, oils, and acid-soluble contaminants. Always follow the manufacturer's directions when using a metal conditioner.

Automotive Thinners and Reducers

Thinners and reducers are specially developed thinning and reducing agents that are used with lacquer and enamel finishing materials. Generally thinners are used to thin lacquer-based products to spraying viscosity. Reducers are used to reduce enamel products to a spraying viscosity. These products should never be inter-mixed because they are formulated to do specific jobs.

Enamel reducers and lacquer thinners are necessary for the application of lacquer and enamel automotive finishes. Since they become dissipated by evaporation, they do not become part of the paint film. The solvent value and the rate of evaporation of the thinners and reducers play an important part in the durability, appearance, and application of the paint film.

When using a poor thinner formula a painter is at the mercy of the variation in temperature and humidity. If the conditions are not perfect, the weak slow solvent will be the last in the undercoat. This will kick the undercoat out of the solution and the adhesion will be very bad. In Table 17-1 it is shown that large

TABLE 17-1   Composition of good and poor thinners.

	Percent by Volume	
Type of Solvent	Good Thinner	Poor Thinner
Strong fast solvent	35	20
Weak fast solvent	35	50
Strong medium solvent	10	0
Weak medium solvent	0	10
Strong slow solvent	20	10
Weak slow solvent	0	10
	100	100

Courtesy of Sherwin Williams Inc. Canada.

amounts of strong fast and strong medium solvent are used in a good thinner. This will dissolve the top coat well. In the poorer thinner the 20 percent strong fast solvent will make it borderline for solvency.

The biggest problem in a top-coat thinner is in the slow and medium solvent area. The strong slow solvent in the good thinner will give good flow-out and gloss. The poor or cheaper thinner has only 20 percent slow solvent, but half of it is weak in solvency, which will cause poor gloss, flow, and adhesion. In the poor thinner, if the weak medium and weak slow solvent are the last to evaporate, the lacquer job will fail.

It must be kept in mind that all strong solvents are more expensive to produce than weak solvents. Therefore, economic considerations tend to force manufacturers to produce solvents of various qualities to be sold at different prices.

A poor thinner or reducer can cause a multitude of problems for the painter because it must dissolve or reduce the coating through the entire solvent evaporation phase. A poor thinner or reducer can cause curdling or kickout, seediness, dulling gloss, chalking, cracking or splitting, sand scratch swelling, blushing, poor adhesion, blistering and pinholing, poor settling properties, and poor color matches.

Only with a balanced mixture of active and latent solvents and dilutants will reducers and thinners have the ability to dissolve various ingredients in enamels and lacquers. It is also necessary that they evaporate at the proper rate for ease of application and good flow-out without sags or runs. Each agent has a very specific function to perform.

Active solvents are the base for all thinners and reducers. They have the ability to dissolve or reduce completely the viscosity of lacquer or enamel finishes as received from the manufacturer.

In a refinish shop, a good grade of thinners and reducers should always be used. Low-priced thinners and reducers often contain an excess of cheap dilutants, which will cause lack of adhesion, brittleness of the paint film, or chalking and checking.

If too much cheap, fast-evaporating solvent is used in a thinner or reducer, it will seriously affect the gloss and flow-out of the product being applied, as well as cause orange peel and blushing problems in lacquer.

The use of too much cheap, slow-evaporating solvent or dilutant may cause slow drying and other application problems. The thinners and reducers used in a shop should always match the conditions, such as cold or heat, of the different shops.

The latent solvents are the slower-acting solvents, which are relatively weak when used alone. They are blended with the active solvents to provide the extra measure of control necessary for the application of lacquers and enamel products.

The dilutants are a nonsolvent type of material and are primarily used as extenders. They also help the reducer and thinner to be more effective when the proper types are used in the right proportions.

To produce well-balanced lacquer thinners and enamel reducers, the blending of the proper types and in the proper proportions of the solvents and dilutants must be done very carefully, because each of these products has its own characteristics and many different types are available.

Vinyl Guard

Several manufacturers produce different types of vinyl guard. This material is used to repair and protect behind the wheel opening on the front lower fenders, lower portion of door panels, and lower sections on quarter panels. Each manufacturer has its own method of application; some require that their product be top-coated with paint and some do not require any painting after application because their material is transparent. Therefore, the repairman must follow the directions on the label of the can. Figure 17-14 shows a quart of vinyl guard and a lower section of an automobile finished with vinyl guard.

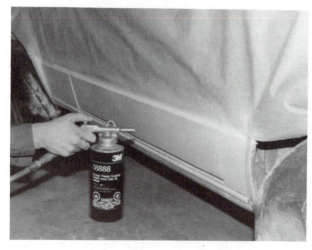

FIGURE 17-14

The area to refinish is usually governed by a character line or sometimes a molding which is used as a natural cutoff line to mask off the area which does not require refinishing. If there is rust on the outer panels or if the paint is badly chipped, it will probably be necessary to strip the paint off, sand-blast the rust, and then use metal conditioner on the affected areas. A vinyl wash primer should be used to prime the metal. When the area is dry, a primer-surfacer is used. After this has thoroughly dried, a pressure feed gun is used to apply the vinyl guard to the panels. This usually takes about 2 hours to dry. Then the area can be painted, if required, the color of the automobile using the proper materials.

Care must be taken to mask the required areas properly so that only the areas requiring refinishing will be painted with vinyl guard.

Trunk Splatter

When sections such as quarter panels or trunk lower panels are changed, they must be refinished as they were finished in the factories. Many manufacturers use a multicolored interior finish that resists abrasion and moisture. This product is designed to duplicate original finishes in passenger car trunks.

The area to be painted is masked and, for best results, the paint is poured into the cup of a pressure feed gun. The paint is sprayed at package consistency on the required parts (Fig. 17-15). The area is unmasked when the paint is fairly dry. A factory-type finish is left over the repaired areas. When spraying operations are finished, the gun is cleaned thoroughly by following the instructions on the paint can label.

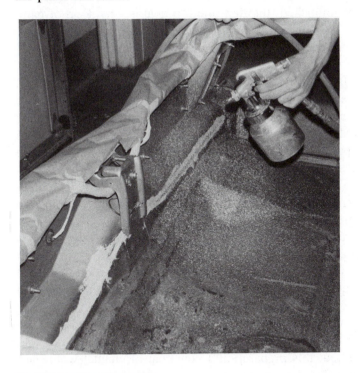

FIGURE 17-15

Rubbing Compounds

Rubbing compounds are used to remove dirt nibs, spray dust, and orange peel, and to improve gloss in lacquer finishes. They can also be used on fully cured enamel surfaces. The rubbing compound is a fine abrasive in a neutral medium of creamy consistency. It can be used either by hand or by machine to polish a surface. It can also be used to clean the surface of the paint when it is to be blended in or spot repaired.

Tack Rag

A tack rag is made from a piece of cheesecloth that is dipped into a nondrying varnish. It is put into a special paper envelope to stop the varnish from drying out. The automobile body should be rubbed properly from end to end with the tack rag, for it will pick up dust remaining after the body has been blown off.

Top Coats

When the vehicle is to be refinished, the first thing to note is what kind of paint is on it. It could be acrylic lacquer, nitrocellulose lacquer, acrylic enamel, enamel, or polyurethane enamel. A general rule is to use the same product as that already on the vehicle unless the vehicle is stripped to the bare metal.

The different manufacturers use different types of paints, such as alkyd enamel, acrylic enamel, urethane enamel, waterborne acrylic enamel, or acrylic lacquer. All these paints are types that can be baked at high temperatures. They are also using what is called a base coat/clear coat, which is formulated from many different types of paints and is used mainly for metallic colors. The base coat/clear coat system makes the paint richer looking, helps it retain its gloss longer, and has that deep look which is very attractive to customers. The clear coat also protects the paint film from contaminants in the air, such as acid rain or other chemicals that are being emitted from different sources.

Acrylic lacquer or nitrocellulose lacquer need not necessarily be sanded, when it is recoated with acrylic lacquer. As a rule, the surface is not free from imperfections; therefore, it should be sanded to give the surface good bond and appearance. If acrylic lacquer is to be used over baked enamel, the surface should be sealed with a sealer.

Acrylic enamel or synthetic enamel has to be sanded and prepared properly before repainting in order to provide the necessary adhesion to resist peeling and chipping of the film. Without this preparation a new coat of enamel would not give very good satisfaction. Enamel can be spot painted if the proper techniques and products are used in certain cases.

A customer's desires will probably dictate what type of top coat will be used. He should be informed as to the results that can be expected with the different materials. In this way, his satisfaction is usually assured.

UNIT 17-2:   MIXING AND MATCHING COLORS

One of the most important jobs in the painting process is the mixing and matching of colors. To find the color required to repaint a vehicle, the tag on the body must be checked for the original finish (Figs. 17-16 and 17-17). If the customer wants a different color, it is mixed according to his wishes. Once the painter has this information, he either orders the paint from a supplier or he mixes it. The code book that is supplied with a paint-mixing system is consulted to find the amount and the type of colors that have to be mixed together to produce the desired color.

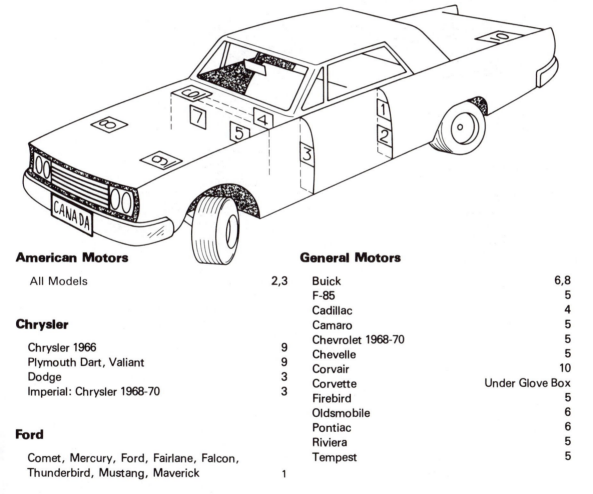

American Motors

All Models	2,3

Chrysler

Chrysler 1966	9
Plymouth Dart, Valiant	9
Dodge	3
Imperial: Chrysler 1968-70	3

Ford

Comet, Mercury, Ford, Fairlane, Falcon, Thunderbird, Mustang, Maverick	1

General Motors

Buick	6,8
F-85	5
Cadillac	4
Camaro	5
Chevrolet 1968-70	5
Chevelle	5
Corvair	10
Corvette	Under Glove Box
Firebird	5
Oldsmobile	6
Pontiac	6
Riviera	5
Tempest	5

FIGURE 17-16   Where to find the paint job identification on Canadian and U.S. cars.

Great Britain

BMC	9
Ford of England	4
Land Rover	4
Rootes: Imp	15, 16
All Others	15
Rover	4
Triumph: 1200, 2000	5
All others	12
Vauxhall	11

Sweden

Volvo: 122, 123	8
All others	11

Japan

Datsun	17
Honda	11
Toyota	5

France

Renault: R8, R10, Caravelle	6
R4, R16	3
Peugeot: All models	4, 6
Citroen: All models	7
Simca: 1000 (1967)	9
1000, 1100, 1301/1501	4
1200	13

Germany

Mercedes: To 1964 Except SL	12
After 1964 Except SL	2, 10
SL Models	5, 10
Volkswagen	1

Italy

Fiat	14

FIGURE 17-17 Where to find the paint job identification plate on imports.

Mixing the Colors

When using a power mixer (Fig. 17-18), the paint should be mixed for at least a minute. Some pigments are heavier than others, and they have to be mixed enough so that they are mixed thoroughly in the binder. Pigments give the color and opacity and they vary in weight. Some pigments are many times heavier than the vehicle, a factor that makes them settle faster than some of the others. The heavier the viscosity of a paint, the slower the pigment will settle. When a color has been reduced to the spraying consistency, the heavier pigments will settle to the bottom. This fact will change the shade of the color unless it is used immediately after mixing.

FIGURE 17-18 Mixing paint.

Factory-mixed paint is used by some refinish shops because the colors are usually a good match to the paint that is on the car. These colors are very carefully formulated at the factory. If the paint has been in stock for a long time, the pigments have probably settled to the bottom and become hard. The binder should be poured out and then the pigment should be broken up and remixed into the binder.

The viscosity of the paint shipped by manufacturers is usually heavy and it has to be reduced to spraying viscosity. When reducer or thinner is added, it should always be poured in slowly, stirring the paint at the same time.

Manufacturers' recommendations should always be followed as to the amount of reducer or thinner to be used in their products. Using the wrong amount could ruin the paint job.

Matching Colors

The hardest job a painter has to do is to match the color. If a complete refinish is to be done, the problem is not so great; but if only a part is to be done, the problems of matching the color can sometimes be very difficult. A car that stands outside with no protection will fade a lot faster than one that is stored in a garage part of the time. Some colors will fade lighter but some will darken.

To offset this change in a color, a painter has to be able to tint the color and try to match the weathered color. This step is not always possible, for some colors are almost impossible to match. Some colors from a tinting system [Fig. 17-19(A)] will behave according to the tint that is put in. Other colors have to be added very carefully because a slight amount will affect the color greatly.

Metallics are harder to match because, depending on the way the car was painted at the factory or the amount of weathering it has had to withstand, the amount and type of light can affect the color greatly as well as the angle that the color is looked at. It must also be remembered when trying to match the color that a lot of metallics have a certain amount of clear binder added to the color.

(A)   **(B)**   **(C)**

FIGURE 17-19   (A) Typical tinting system; (B) acrylic lacquer tinting system; (C) urethane tinting system. (Courtesy of Du Pont Canada Inc.)

To discover how much the color has changed, always look at the door jambs and compare the color to the paint that is in the can. Another method is to clean the oxidized paint on part of the surface. A piece of paper with a hole in it can be used to restrict the area that is sprayed as a test. Looking and comparing the color should give a clue as to what changes must be made in the formulation.

Always start with a small amount of paint, no more than is required for the job. Then, after it has been checked for match, if it is not the exact shade, start adding the tinting toners in very small amounts from the suitable colors of the tinting system (Fig. 17-19) required (see Table 17-2). Always remember, once the color matches, to add some drier to the paint to offset the extra paint added. In matching colors, the paint should be approximately at spraying viscosity.

To further explain the matching of colors, it must be realized that color consists of different pigments and dyes that are mixed together to produce a shade of a color. The car manufacturers choose a multitude of different colors and develop a standard for every color which will be used in the factory to paint the vehicles that are manufactured for customers.

The paint manufacturers develop what is known as factory package paint. The rest is mixed on a tinting system in either the jobber's establishment or at the body shop according to a formula. At the factory a computer is used as well as the eye (which is the most sophisticated device) to tint a color to match the color standard.

The best light for a body shop to use when matching color is natural sunlight (see Figures 17-20 and 17-21). These figures demonstrate a condition in color matching called metamerism, in which two colors appear identical under one lighting condition but not under another. For example, a painter sprays a panel inside a body shop. It looks pretty good for match, but the car is pulled out of the shop and the customer sees a glaring mismatch. The painter should be helped to determine the best location in the shop to view color match. Help him find the location where A and B are most likely to match. The painter should be shown why he should take the car outside to make a final *judgment*. Remind the painter of the quality match of the manufacturers and that they take this condition into account when they do their color matching.

Colors usually darken after drying, so a certain amount of consideration must be given when tinting the color, especially with enamel. Enamels dry much slower than lacquers, which creates a certain problem; it takes longer to find the true color. Another point to consider is the thickness of the film; light pastel shades will usually be lighter when a heavy film is sprayed.

Lacquers are usually sprayed to a film thickness of about 3.0 to 3.5 mils (7.6 to 8.8 μm); enamels are generally a little thicker, up to 3 to 4 mils (7.6 to 10.1 μm). This thickness includes the undercoat; more film thickness than this will at times make the film crack during great temperature changes. When the

TABLE 17-2 Common reasons and remedies for color mismatches.

I. Reasons for color mismatches:
   A. Car manufacturer: car's color has drifted from standard.
      1. New finish being used.
      2. Different supplier of original-equipment color or material change by the supplier.
      3. Equipment problem at the plant: color not properly agitated or spray equipment faulty.
      4. Vehicle baked too long or not long enough, or oven temperature too low or too high.
      5. Too little or too much paint applied.
   B. Aftermarket supplier—paint company.
      1. Color was not originally matched to standard.
      2. Change in raw material—pigment.
      3. Not properly mixed at the factory.
   C. Jobber.
      1. Color not properly mixed.
      2. Wrong color mixed.
   D. Painter.
      1. Color not properly stirred.
      2. Improper painter technique.
      3. Too much paint or not enough.
      4. Wrong color ordered.
   E. Color is faded or the film is degraded from weathering. No matter what the reason or who is to blame, the problem becomes the painter's.

II. How to solve color match problems:
   A. Learn to describe color correctly and in the proper sequence.
      1. Lighter–darker.
         a. Side angle.
         b. Direct.
      2. Cast: the effect a color gives when looking at it.
         a. Redder.
         b. Bluer.
         c. Greener.
         d. Yellower.
      3. Brighter–grayer.
   B. Learn to compare the original paint to the color that is being sprayed.
      1. Say that the car's finish is darker than the color being sprayed; always allow the color to dry before making an adjustment. Test for color description.
   C. Adjust painter control variables.
      1. Before any color is tinted, adjust lightness ar darkness.
      2. The cast will be slightly affected by changes in lightness or darkness. If the cast is right, then:
      3. Adjust for brightness or grayness.
   D. Adjust the color for lightness or darkness.
      1. Methods to lighten a color:
         a. After spraying a wet coat, follow with a coat at 1/2 trigger or adjust the fluid control valve for less material flow.
         b. Raise the air pressure at the gun in 5 psi (35 kPa) increments.

TABLE 17-2   (cont.)

    c. Add more thinner—at least 25 percent—and use a faster thinner than that currently in the mix.

    d. Let the thinned color set for 10 minutes in the spray cup; pour the top 1/2 off into a clean container, stir up the remaining material, and spray.

    e. Add additional poly to the color.

  2. Methods to darken a color:

    a. Double coat the panel, wetting the surface. Open up the fluid valve and reduce the fan size slightly.

    b. Lower the pressure at the gun in 5 psi or 35 kPa increments.

    c. Add 2 oz or 60 ml of retarder per thinned cup.

    d. Let the thinned color set for 10 minutes, pour the top portion off into a clean spray cup, stir, attach gun, and spray.

    e. Add the predominant dark color to the mix.

E. If after adjusting the color for lightness or darkness, the cast is off, tinting for correct cast is required.

  1. Steps involved in tinting for correct cast:

    a. Decide how the original finish is off compared to the material you sprayed; for example, the original finish is redder than the material sprayed. In being off in cast, a color can only be described as being redder, yellower, greener, or bluer.

    b. Use the chart to decide on what tint color for the appropriate system should be used.

    c. Each color can vary in cast in only two directions. See Chart 17-1.

F. Once the color necessary to correctly adjust the cast is determined, the amount must be calculated.

  1. The first tinter should be determined from the chart, indicating the least amount of the particular tint necessary to effectively change the color.

  2. The color should be thoroughly mixed, the gun triggered to clear the chamber, and the small panel sprayed, allowed to dry, and checked with the original-equipment (OE) panel. Add additional tint in the specified increments and repeat the process.

G. After the color is correct in lightness–darkness and cast, the final adjustment must be made.

  1. *Note:* It is impossible to make a color brighter without throwing the previous corrections off.

  2. The only way a color can go at this point is to the grayer or dirtier side.

  3. Too gray a color, follow this procedure:

    a. Spray a wet coat followed by a coat that is sprayed at 1/2 trigger at a slightly greater distance, lifting the metallic to the surface.

    b. Add a small amount of white mixed with a very small amount of black.

H. Once these three corrections are made in the proper sequence, the color will match the OE panel.

III. *Test* the color match as follows: On one corner of the OE panel, effectively blend the color into the panel.

A. Use blending clear or blending solvent.

B. Tape off one corner of the panel at least 6 in. into the panel and spray the color simulating a panel repair.

Chart 17-1.

(1) Colors either greener or redder in cast:
    (a) Blues
    (b) Yellows
    (c) Golds
    (d) Purples
    (e) Beiges
    (f) Browns

(2) Colors either yellower or bluer in cast:
    (a) Greens
    (b) Maroons
    (c) Whites
    (d) Blacks
    (e) Grays

(3) Colors yellower or redder in cast:
    (a) Bronzes
    (b) Oranges
    (c) Reds

(4) Colors bluer or greener in cast:
    (a) Aqua
    (b) Turquoise

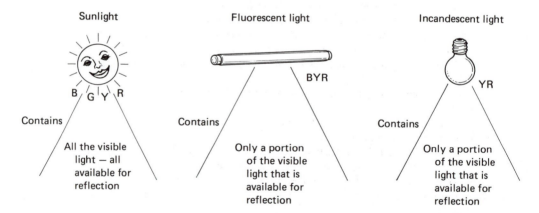

FIGURE 17-20 Those parts of the light spectrum available for reflection under different forms of light. B, Blue; G, green; Y, yellow; R, red. When working inside the body shop, the most effective lighting can probably be had with Durotest Company's Color Classer fluorescent bulb. (Courtesy of Sherwin Williams Company Inc. Canada.)

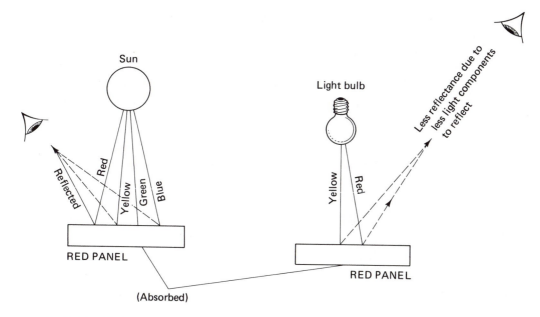

FIGURE 17-21   How we see color and why. (Courtesy of Sherwin Williams Company Inc. Canada.)

film is too thick, it loses some elasticity and will crack as the metal expands and contracts.

Spraying Viscosity (Viscosity Cup)

Altogether too many painters fail to concern themselves with the spraying viscosity of paint materials. The average painter pays little or no attention to the paint manufacturer's recommendations of the amount of thinning or the type of thinners specified. He uses a number of so-called systems of reduction, such as adding reducers until the paint runs off the stirring stick at a certain rate that has been preestablished in the painter's mind. Unfortunately, the viscosity varies considerably from job to job and is sometimes reflected in poor gloss, hiding, excessive fade, and metallic color shades.

What is viscosity, and how can it be checked? Viscosity is frequently stated in terms of length of time it takes for a known quantity of paint to flow through a certain size of orifice.

It is important to remember that temperatures strongly influence viscosity, and therefore paint should be stored at room temperature. If it is not possible, remember that paint must be brought to room temperature before reducing. A cold paint will be thick. When thinner is merely added to bring it down to spraying viscosity, we usually find paint that has poor hiding qualities or it may run off the job, especially on a vertical surface.

Several easy-to-use viscometers are manufactured, and one of them should be part of the refinisher's equipment. Perhaps one of the most popular is the No. 4 Ford Cup. This cup holds 100 cc and has a cone-shaped bottom with a 5/32 in. (4 mm) orifice (Fig. 17-22).

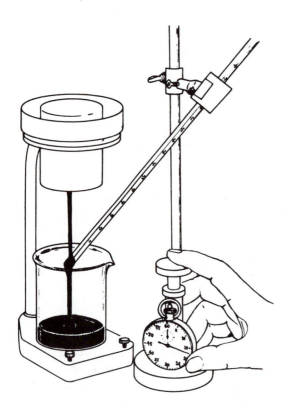

FIGURE 17-22 [Courtesy of DeVilbiss (Canada) Limited.]

Method of Using Viscosity Cup

1. Check temperature of material—approximately 70°F (21.1°C).

2. Read the paint manufacturer's directions for proper reduction. Add the reducer, stirring until the thinner and material are well mixed.

3. Place a finger over the orifice in the bottom of the cup and fill with material at hand. A stopwatch is used to time the number of seconds it takes the cup to empty or the flow of material to break.

Different materials have different spraying viscosity. For example, lacquer will spray best and give good hiding and flow-out at 19 to 20 seconds. Alkyd enamel will show its best qualities at 24 to 25 seconds.

Unfortunately, a number of paint shops will never use a viscosity cup, but the importance of measuring the amount of thinners according to the paint manufacturer's directions cannot be stressed too strongly.

Consistent control will give each job uniform hiding, gloss, better flowout, and good gloss retention, It is interesting to know that car manufacturers and paint companies control viscosity to within a variation of 1 second from the desired viscosity.

Overreduction and underreduction of paint can result in a good many cases of excessive orange peel, sags or runs, mismatches with metallic shades, and poor hiding.

When mixing colors to match, add only a small amount of color at a time. This is very important when mixing metallic colors. Sometimes, when adding extra color to metallics, it is necessary to add some extra-clear vehicle to the paint in order to keep the high gloss.

Stirring

For years paint manufacturers have stressed this one point: *stir thoroughly before using*. Yet many in the refinishing field fail to do so, and 95 percent of complaints of color fading and other problems are a result of this failure.

Do not use sharp sticks or screwdrivers for stirring. Use at least a 1 in. (25 mm) wide flat, clean stirring stick or steel spatula, and mix from the bottom up, making sure that all pigments are in suspension and completely mixed.

Another method sometimes employed is to box the material—that is, pouring from one container to another until all pigments are mixed.

UNIT 17-3:   MASKING

When an automobile is to be painted, certain areas must be covered in order to protect those areas that are not to be painted—for example, the chrome moldings, nameplates, windows, and even the weather-stripping in certain cases.

Many manufacturers of masking tape and paper have produced good-quality products that will serve the purpose at the lowest cost possible. Using good products and methods will cut the amount of time required to mask an automobile.

Masking tape must be capable of adhering to many surfaces, such as paint, chrome, glass, and upholstery. The tape must also be easy to remove from the surface. The adhesive on the tape must always come off with the tape. It must also be able to resist water from wet sanding, as well as paint and reducing agents. Masking paper must be of high quality in order to resist water, paint, and reducer. The paper must be able to resist rough handling, seepage, or the penetration of the paint to the panels that it protects.

Special apron dispensers are used in many shops to speed up the work of masking (Fig. 17-23). These apron dispensers apply the tape to the paper as it is pulled from the roll. Approximately half the width of the tape is applied to the paper's edge and the other half is free for application to moldings. A cutting bar is provided on the dispenser to cut the paper and tape at the length desired. These dispensers come in various widths so that different widths of paper can be used.

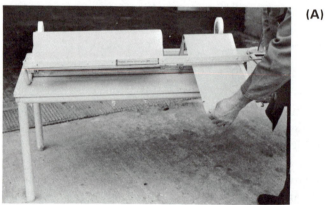

(A)

(B)

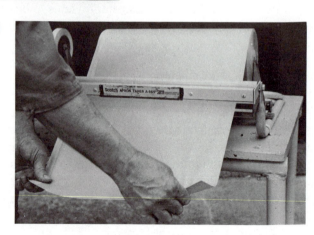

FIGURE 17-23

Tips on Masking Paper and Tape

Tape should always be applied to clean areas. If dust, silicone, rubber lubricants, and similar items are present, the surface must be cleaned thoroughly. Tape must never be stretched unless curves are being masked; it should be laid on the surface and pressed down. On all edges, it should be laid down as close to the edge as possible, so that no paint will seep under the tape and ruin the adhesive. The tape should not be so close to the surface being painted that it shows a line after painting operations.

Tape should not be removed or applied at temperatures below 50°F (10°C), for temperatures below that figure will not give good results. The tape should be removed as soon as the paint is no longer sticky—at a 90° angle to the surface if possible. Tape should not be allowed to come into contact with high heat or be exposed to the sun for long periods. Tape and paper should be stored in cool, dry areas. Taped aprons should not be pulled taut; a certain looseness should be allowed for shrinkage.

On freshly painted surfaces, when contact between paper and surface cannot be avoided, two thicknesses of masking paper should be used. A gap should be left between the first and second layers if possible. Masking paper should not be placed over newly painted areas for at least 24 hours and then it should be removed as soon as possible after the painting is finished.

Masking Upholstery

When the door jambs have to be painted, it is necessary to cover the upholstery, windlacing, weather stripping, lock, and striker plate (Fig. 17-24). A 6 in. (152 mm) pretaped apron is ideal for this operation. If the rubber is not perfectly clean, it might be necessary to coat it with clear lacquer before applying tape. With the edges covered, a spray gun can be used to paint the area.

Masking Headlights or Taillights

To mask headlights, use a 6 in. (152 mm) apron. The tape edge is applied to the edge of the seal beam or its retaining ring, forming a circle (Fig. 17-25). The paper is then folded toward the center, and a strip of tape is pressed down from edge to edge across the center to hold the paper flat. The same method can be used for taillights and parking lights, but for some a 3 in. (76 mm) apron or less is very often sufficient.

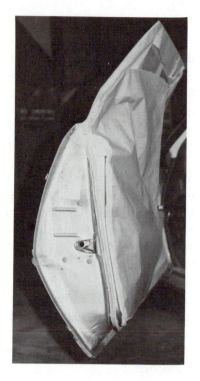

FIGURE 17-24

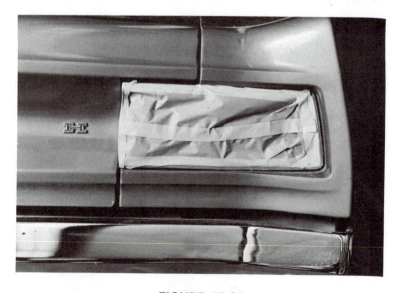

FIGURE 17-25

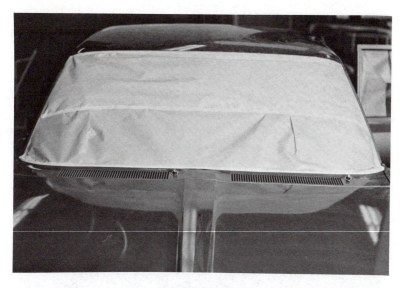

FIGURE 17-26

Windshields and Rear Windows

On windshields or rear windows, a 24 in. (610 mm) apron, or a combination of a 12 and a 16 in. (305 and a 406 mm) apron, will cover most rear windows or windshields (Fig. 17-26). A pretaped apron that is slightly larger than the window should be used. The taped edge is pressed to the chrome molding or rubber; the contour of the window should be followed. The extra paper at the edge is folded inward and toward the window; the loose edges are fastened with a 3/4 in. (19 mm) tape. If two aprons are used, the top one must always overlap the lower apron to prevent spray dust seepage.

Grilles and Bumpers

On most late-model cars, grilles and bumpers can usually be covered in one operation (Fig. 17-27). Whenever this is possible, an apron of suitable width is used to cover both at the same time. If this is not possible, the edge of the grille is covered with 3/4 in. (19 mm) tape and then the rest is covered with a taped apron of the right width. The bumper is covered with the right size apron and the lower loose edges are gathered up and taped together.

Door Handles, Moldings, and Ornaments

Masking tape of the required width is used on these items (Fig. 17-28). The narrowest width possible is used for economy as long as complete coverage is

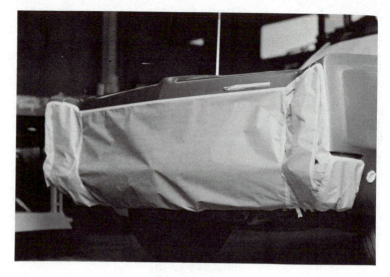

FIGURE 17-27

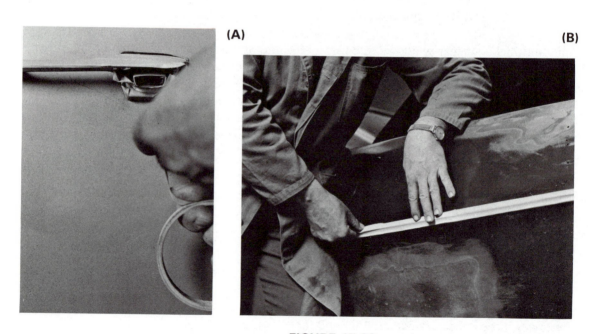

(A)

(B)

FIGURE 17-28

attained. A 2 in. (51 mm) apron with 3/4 in. (19 mm) tape is used if the molding is wider than 2 in. (51 mm). Door handles are covered lengthwise to facilitate ease and speed in the removal of the tape.

Side Windows

A 3/4 in. (19 mm) tape is laid on the molding edge of windows and then a taped apron of the proper width is used (Fig. 17-29). The bottom is taped first and then the top. If the proper-size apron is not available, a second apron is used from the top edge. Pick up all slack and tape it, and then seal the edges between the two aprons with tape.

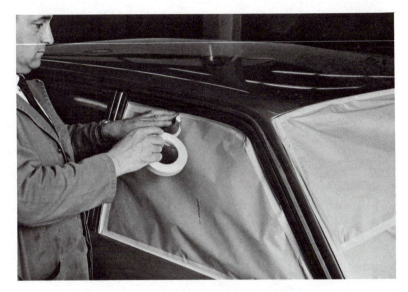

FIGURE 17-29

Masking Aerials

A tube can be formed with paper and this is slipped over the aerial and taped to the bottom (Fig. 17-30). Another method is to use a tape of the proper width, which is run up one side and then the other and pressed together.

Masking Wheels

A 6 in. (152 mm) pretaped apron with 1/2 in. (13 mm) pleats every 4 to 6 in. (101 to 152 mm) is used to mask a wheel quickly (Fig. 17-31). The taped edge of the apron is placed on the tire next to the rim. Short strips of tape are used to fasten the paper to the tire.

FIGURE 17-30

FIGURE 17-31

QUESTIONS

17-1 Do lacquers form a good bond between recoats without sanding?

17-2 Whick dries faster, enamel or lacquer?

17-3 By which method do enamels dry: polymerization only, evaporation only, or polymerization and oxidation?

17-4 What is the advantage of acrylic lacquer over the nitrocellulose lacquer?

17-5 What method should be used to find the type of paint that is already on an automobile?

17-6 What is used to remove silicones and grease from a paint surface?

17-7 What should be used to etch and clean the bare metal?

17-8 Describe the method that should be used to feather-edge paint.

17-9 When should a sealer be used?

17-10 What is used to strip paint from metal?

17-11 For what purpose is primer surfacer used on an automobile body?

18

Spray Guns

In the refinishing of automobiles, the spray gun is king; its uses are practically unlimited. In the application of paint, it gives a beautiful smooth finish, free from brush marks. It is a precision-built piece of equipment; if treated properly, it will last a long time.

UNIT 18-1:   ATOMIZATION AND VAPORIZATION

A spray gun in operation produces atomization and vaporization. Atomization is the process of breaking up the solids in the paint and depositing these solids on the surface in the form of tiny spheres or globules (Fig. 18-1). Vaporization is the gassing off of the thinners or reducers in the paint, a process that takes place between the gun and the surface being coated (Fig. 18-2). It is important for the spray gun to atomize the material properly; therefore maximum atomization is desirable. Vaporization, which results in a loss of paint thinner or solvent, is not desirable; therefore it should be held to a minimum. This brings us to the basic rule in spray painting. A production gun should be held 6 to 8 in. (152 to 203 mm) away from the surface being coated. There is one exception, however—metallic colors, where the gun is held 12 to 14 in. (305 to 356 mm) away when applying the final coat (Fig. 18-3).

A number of fundamental motions in the use of the spray gun are very important and must be followed if a good finish is to be obtained. The importance

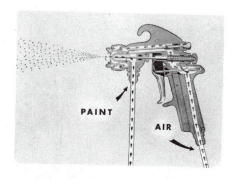

FIGURE 18-1 [Courtesy of DeVilbiss (Canada) Limited.]

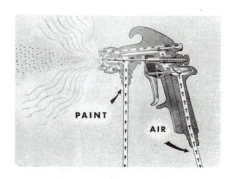

FIGURE 18-2 [Courtesy of DeVilbiss (Canada) Limited.]

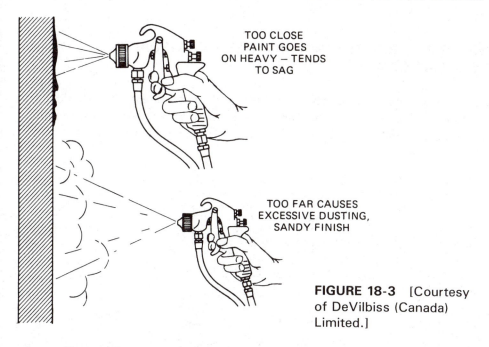

FIGURE 18-3 [Courtesy of DeVilbiss (Canada) Limited.]

of gun distance is the major cause of poorly painted articles. A good guide to correct gun distance is to use the span of a man's hand, which will be approximately 8 in. (203 mm). If the gun is held too close, flooding will result. If held too far, excessive overspray and dry spray occur (Fig. 18-4). The next thing to consider is the speed of the gun as it is moved across the surface to be painted. Most operations require the application of a full coat of material. This means that the gun should be moved fast enough to obtain production but slow enough to put on a good finish. A definition of a wet coat is *all the paint that can hang on a vertical surface without sagging* (Fig. 18-5).

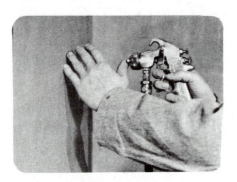

FIGURE 18-4 [Courtesy of De-Vilbiss (Canada) Limited.]

FIGURE 18-5 [Courtesy of De-Vilbiss (Canada) Limited.]

UNIT 18-2: PROPER STROKING AND TRIGGERING OF THE SPRAY GUN

To achieve proper stroking, the gun must at all times be held perpendicular to the surface being coated. If the gun is tilted, there will be a flooding condition nearest the gun and dry spray at the bottom of the pattern (Fig. 18-6).

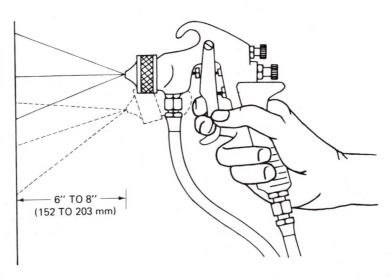

6" TO 8"
(152 TO 203 mm)

FIGURE 18-6 Spray gun should be held perpendicular to the surface, as shown here by solid lines. Tilting the gun up or down gives an uneven spray pattern. [Courtesy of DeVilbiss (Canada) Limited.]

Triggering is the method used when beginning or ending a spray stroke. A spray gun is designed with two pressures on the trigger—first and second. In first pressure, the air is allowed to pass through the gun by opening only the air valve. The second pressure pulls the fluid needle back, allowing the material to enter the airstream.

At the start of a stroke, the trigger is pulled back all the way and the gun is moved only the length of the panel, or within the comfortable reach of the operator. The trigger is then released back to first pressure and the gun is placed in position to begin another stroke. If the operator does not release the trigger at the end of each stroke, there will be a buildup of paint at each end, which may result in sags (Fig. 18-7).

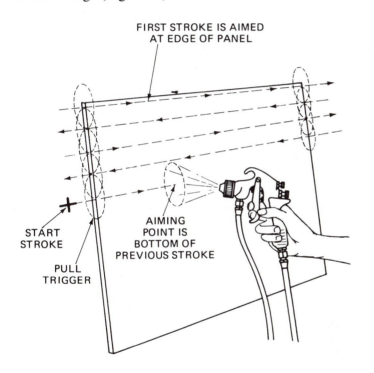

FIRST STROKE IS AIMED
AT EDGE OF PANEL

START
STROKE

AIMING
POINT IS
BOTTOM OF
PREVIOUS STROKE

PULL
TRIGGER

FIGURE 18-7 When spraying a panel, use alternate right and left strokes, triggering the gun at the beginning and end of each stroke. The spray pattern should overlap one-half the previous stroke for smooth coverage without streaks. [Courtesy of DeVilbiss (Canada) Limited.]

UNIT 18-3: OVERLAPPING, BANDING, AND ARCING

When spraying, always overlap the area 50 percent. Overlapping is accomplished by aiming the air horns directly at the bottom or top of the last spray stroke; otherwise streaks will appear on the sprayed surface. This is particularly true when metallic paint is sprayed (Fig. 18-8).

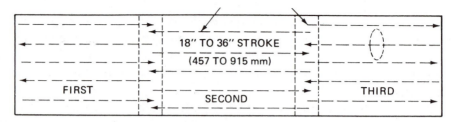

FIGURE 18-8 Long work is sprayed in section of convenient length, each section overlapping the previous section by 4 in. (102 mm). [Courtesy of DeVilbiss (Canada) Limited.]

If the painter has only one panel to paint on an automobile, it should be banded at the edges (Fig. 18-9). This method reduces the amount of overspray that does not reach the surface to be painted. Either this overspray is exhausted through the exhaust fan or it falls on the spray booth floor. The painter sprays a band at each end of the panel vertically; then the panel is sprayed with horizontal strokes. The painter triggers the gun at the appropriate time in his stroke. The bands will help him overcome any arcing that could be present in his stroke. This method will give a good flow-out of the painted surface and cut the waste of material. It is well-known that approximately 30 percent of the material is wasted, especially if proper triggering and gun stroking are not applied to the

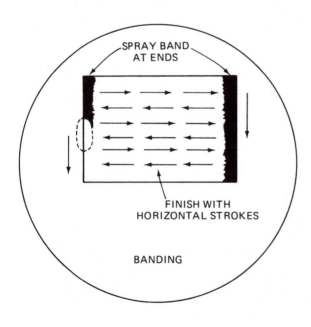

FIGURE 18-9 Banding— vertical bands sprayed at the ends of a panel prevent overspray from horizontal strokes. [Courtesy of DeVilbiss (Canada) Limited.]

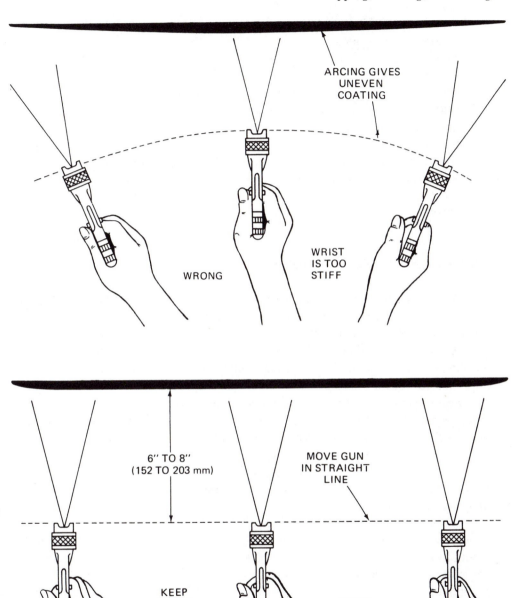

ARCING GIVES
UNEVEN
COATING

WRONG

WRIST
IS TOO
STIFF

6" TO 8"
(152 TO 203 mm)

MOVE GUN
IN STRAIGHT
LINE

KEEP
WRIST
FLEXIBLE

RIGHT

FIGURE 18-10 [Courtesy of DeVilbiss (Canada) Limited.]

job by the painter. The stroke must always be a smooth and steady movement by the painter at all times.

Arcing means that the gun is swung in a stroke in which the gun may be 6 to 8 in. (152 to 203 mm) from the surface in the center of the swing, but at the end of the stroke it could be perhaps 16 in. (406 mm) away from the surface. The results are an excessive overspray and poor flowing-out of the painted surface (Fig. 18-10). When spraying a radius or curved surface, the gun must follow in a path that has the same radius as the surface being coated, maintaining the correct gun distance. For slender work, adjust spray pattern to fit the job—avoid excessive overspray. Spray technique is the most important phase of spray painting, and the various rules and methods just outlined should be practiced until they become fixed working habits.

UNIT 18-4: TYPES OF SPRAY GUNS

A spray gun is a mechanical means of bringing air and paint together. It atomizes or breaks up the paint stream into a spray and by ejection applies a coating to a surface to preserve or beautify.

All spray guns suitable for first-class work have an assortment of fluid tips, needles, and air caps that make them adaptable for any type of material. It is important to have a gun that has been specifically designed for the job at hand.

Spray guns are precision instruments. They are constructed as accurately and listed as carefully as precision tools and gauges. When completely assembled, each spray gun is tested for general operation. It is adjusted for atomization, spray-pattern size, and uniformity with the paint and accessory equipment for which the gun was designed. If given a reasonable amount of care, it will produce good results for years. Neglect and carelessness are responsible for the majority of spray gun difficulties.

A wide choice of spray guns is available. A production-type gun should be chosen, whether it be used on a suction cup attachment or pressure-type equipment. Smaller guns are used for spot spraying and touch-up. When used for complete overall refinishing, these guns are not fast enough to make the job profitable.

The way in which the paint is supplied to the nozzle of the spray gun will decide if it is a suction-feed or pressure-feed type. These two types can be further subdivided into bleeder and nonbleeder and external and internal mix guns.

Suction Feed

Suction feed is designed to create a vacuum and thus draw the material from the container, better known as the suction cup. This system is generally limited to

1 qt (1 liter) and used only with paint (Fig. 18-11). A vacuum is created when the trigger is pulled, allowing air to flow out of the orifice surrounding the fluid tip. The paint is then pulled from the container out through the fluid passage. This vacuum is augmented by the opening in the lid of the fluid container, allowing atmospheric pressure to exert itself on the material. On suction-type guns the fluid tip will always protrude approximately 1/32 in. (1 mm) beyond the air cap (Fig. 18-12).

FIGURE 18-11
[Courtesy of De-
Vilbiss (Canada)
Limited.]

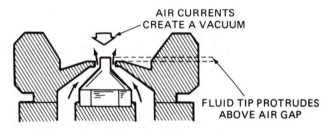

AIR CURRENTS
CREATE A VACUUM

FLUID TIP PROTRUDES
ABOVE AIR GAP

FIGURE 18-12 Suction or gravity feed cap.
[Courtesy of DeVilbiss (Canada) Limited.]

Pressure Feed

In this type of system, the material is placed in a closed container to which direct air pressure is admitted. A hose leads from the container to the spray gun and the paint is thus forced through the spray nozzle. This method is employed where large quantities of the same color are used; it is slightly faster than the suction feed. A paint container can be from 2 qt to 60 gal (2 to 227 liters). It has a gauge on the container to show the pressure at which the diaphragm is set to let air exert pressure on the material. On pressure-type guns, the fluid tip does not extend beyond the air cap (Fig. 18-13).

FLUID TIP IS FLUSH WITH AIR CAP

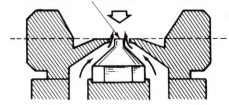

FIGURE 18-13 Pressure-
feed cap. [Courtesy of
DeVilbiss (Canada) Lim-
ited.]

Bleeder Type

Bleeder means an intentional discharge of air from the spout of the gun that prevents air pressure from building up in the hose. This type of gun is used where there is no pressure control device, such as an automatic unloader or pressure switch on the compressor. The air valve on this gun is designed to remain open even after the trigger has been released, shutting off the fluid (Fig. 18-14).

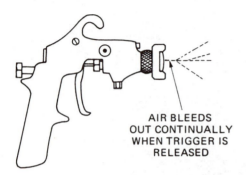

AIR BLEEDS
OUT CONTINUALLY
WHEN TRIGGER IS
RELEASED

FIGURE 18-14 Bleeder-type system. [Courtesy of DeVilbiss (Canada) Limited.]

Nonbleeder Type

This type of gun is used when air is supplied from the tank or compressor having pressure control. The gun is equipped with an air valve that shuts off the air as well as the fluid when the trigger is released. This gun is used in automotive maintenance work in applying industrial finishes and is more popular than the bleeder type (Fig. 18-15).

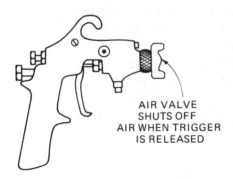

AIR VALVE
SHUTS OFF
AIR WHEN TRIGGER
IS RELEASED

FIGURE 18-15 Non-bleeder-type system. [Courtesy of DeVilbiss (Canada) Limited.]

External Mix

As the name implies, the air and the fluid are mixed outside the air cap (Fig. 18-16).

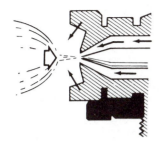

FIGURE 18-16 External mix. [Courtesy of De-Vilbiss (Canada) Limited.]

Internal Mix

With this method, the air and fluid are mixed inside the air cap. It should be remembered, however, that this gun is limited to slow-drying materials that will not build up and dry inside the cap (Fig. 18-17). The only advantage of internal mix over external mix is less overspray. Internal mix always involves pressure feed equipment.

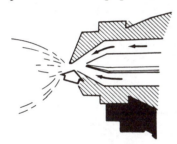

FIGURE 18-17 Internal mix. [Courtesy of De-Vilbiss (Canada) Limited.]

Air Caps

Air caps are at the front of the gun (Fig. 18-18). They direct the air into the material stream to atomize or break up the material and form it into a suitable spray pattern. All caps can be divided into external or internal mix. In the internal mix, air and material mix inside and are ejected through a slot (Fig. 18-17). In external mix, air is ejected through spreader horns through a center orifice and sometimes auxiliary orifices (Fig. 18-19).

Multiple Jets

Multiple jets have five, seven, nine, or more orifices: a center orifice, one in each horn, plus twin auxiliary jets. The size of the air cap is determined by the type of material being sprayed and the air requirements. Multiple jets offer better atomization for viscous materials, such as synthetics and heavy-bodied lacquers (Fig. 18-20).

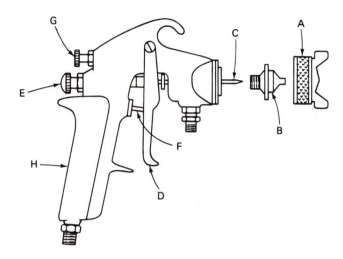

FIGURE 18-18 The principal parts of a spray gun. The principal components are the air cap (A), fluid tip (B), fluid needle (C), trigger (D), fluid adjustment screw (E), air valve (F), spreader adjustment valve (G), and gun body (H). Guns equipped with a removable spray head will also have a socking bolt. [Courtesy of DeVilbiss (Canada) Limited.]

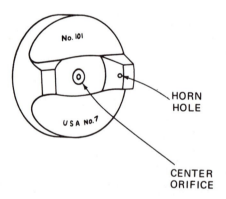

FIGURE 18-19 Conventional air cap—three-hole type. [Courtesy of DeVilbiss (Canada) Limited.]

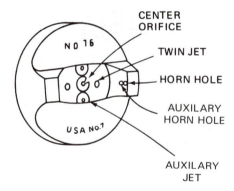

FIGURE 18-20 Multiple-jet air cap. [Courtesy of DeVilbiss (Canada) Limited.]

Fluid Tips

Fluid tips meter and direct the material into the airstream. They provide a self-aligning concentric ball and cone seat for the air cap and equalize the air leaving

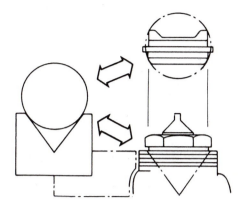

FIGURE 18-21 [Courtesy of DeVilbiss (Canada) Limited.]

the center orifices of the cap (Fig. 18-21). In selecting a fluid tip, consideration should be given to several factors. Heavy, coarse material requires large nozzle size tips to eliminate clogging. Very thin material that sags readily is applied at low atomizing pressure with a small nozzle to prevent excessive material application.

Fluid Needles

Fluid needles control the amount of material flow and are always the same number as the fluid tip, that is, FF tip, FF needle; EX tip, EX needle (Fig. 18-22).

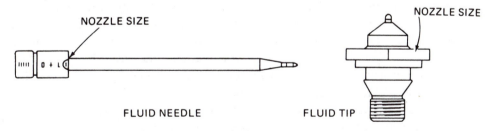

FIGURE 18-22 [Courtesy of DeVilbiss (Canada) Limited.]

Spreader Adjustment Valve

The spreader adjustment valve controls the amount of air allowed to the air horns. This, of course, will be used when changing from a round spray pattern to a flat elliptical pattern or any desired pattern in between (Fig. 18-18).

Fluid Needle Adjustment

This adjustment controls the movement of the fluid needle and will meter the amount of material through the nozzle. This valve is generally used with at least the first thread in sight (Fig. 18-18).

Air Valve

This valve in the gun body controls the air and is opened or closed by the pull and release of the trigger (Fig. 18-18).

Baffle

The baffle ensures an even distribution of air inside the air cap.

UNIT 18-5: CLEANING SPRAY GUNS

Cleaning the spray equipment can be done easily if a few simple rules and procedures are established. On the suction-feed gun, loosen the cup from the gun; and while the fluid tube is still in the cup, unscrew the air cap two complete turns, hold a rag over the cup, and pull the trigger. This process diverts the air pressure to the fluid or passageways forcing the material back in the cup. Then empty the cup of the material and replace with thinner. Usually about a pint (1/2 liter) of thinner will be adequate; spray the thinner through the gun the same as paint (Fig. 18-23). The suction action will lift the material out of the cup and through the fluid tube and flush the thinner down through the fluid passageway inside the gun. The air cap is then taken off the gun and carefully cleaned with a soft-bristle brush, such as a toothbrush, using thinner if necessary (Fig. 18-24). Avoid placing the entire gun in thinner, for this will wash out the lubrication in the various packings in the gun and contaminate the inside air passageways. Consequently, the gun will operate either inefficiently or not at all.

Pressure Feed

On the pressure-feed gun, additional steps are involved. The first operation is to blow back the system. This is done by releasing the pressure in the paint container and undoing the container from the top. Now go up to the spray head and hold a cloth over the front end of the gun and pull the trigger. Since the cloth is restricting the airflow to the atmosphere, the air will turn around and push the

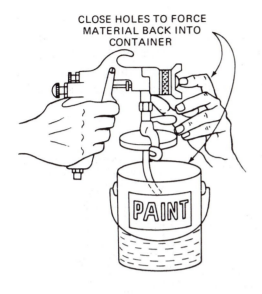

CLOSE HOLES TO FORCE
MATERIAL BACK INTO
CONTAINER

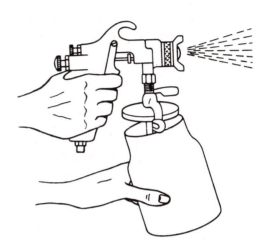

CLEAN CUP OUT THEN
SPRAY SOLVENT THROUGH GUN

FIGURE 18-23 Cleaning the spray gun. [Courtesy of DeVilbiss (Canada) Limited.]

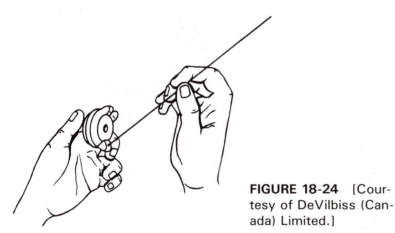

FIGURE 18-24 [Courtesy of DeVilbiss (Canada) Limited.]

paint from the gun through the fluid hose back into the paint container. This blow-back can also be accomplished by unscrewing the air cap retaining ring three full turns and pulling the trigger.

This blowing-back operation is done to empty the paint out of the gun and fluid hose. Remove the paint from the pressure paint container and pour in a quart (a liter) of thinner or reducer used for thinning the material. It will not be necessary to atomize, so the atomization air can be turned off. Pull the trigger, thus allowing the thinner to be forced by the pressure back through the hose and gun. Any paint that may have accumulated on the outside of the gun should be wiped off with a thinner rag or brush.

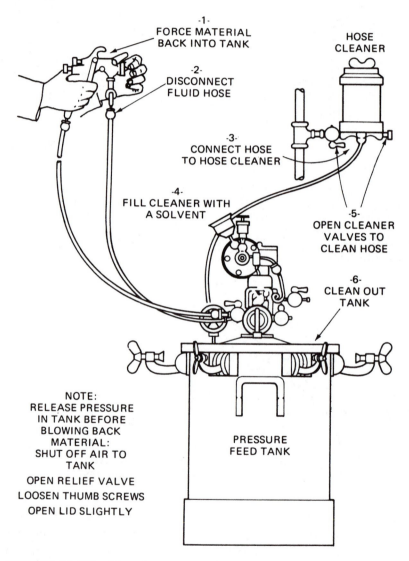

FIGURE 18-25 Cleaning spray gun—pressure feed. [Courtesy of DeVilbiss (Canada) Limited.]

A hose cleaner, which will save both time and thinner, is available to do this same fluid tube and gun cleaning operation. It is important to remember that all spray equipment should always be clean. Any paint used should be properly strained before going into the system, to avoid plugging up the inside of the fluid tip in the spray gun (Fig. 18-25).

Spray Gun Lubrication

The spray gun needs to have a number of its parts lubricated at regular intervals, depending on how often it is used. The fluid needle packing, the air valve stem, and the trigger bearing screws should be oiled. The fluid needle packing should occasionally be softened with oil. The fluid needle spring should be coated with light grease (Fig. 18-26).

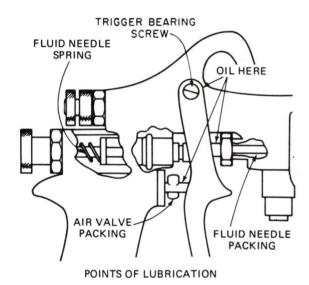

POINTS OF LUBRICATION

FIGURE 18-26 Points of lubrication. [Courtesy of DeVilbiss (Canada) Limited.]

UNIT 18-6: HOW TO PAINT WITH A GUN

A production type of spray gun can either be suction or pressure and is used in the refinishing of a panel or a whole body. If the gun is a suction feed, it will probably have a fluid tip with an orifice of 0.070 in. (1.78 mm) or larger; up to 0.085 in. (2.1 mm), if faster application is desired. Different sizes of air caps use different amounts of air. An air cap to fit a 0.070 in. (1.78 mm) fluid tip will use approximately 12 cu ft (340 liters) of air at 60 psi (414 kPa).

On certain makes of pressure-feed guns the same size of air cap and fluid tip can be used. A pressure-feed gun usually needs a slightly lower air-atomizing pressure than the suction feed because all the air that goes through the air cap is solely used to atomize the paint.

Spray guns used in shops have two controls that have to be adjusted before painting (Fig. 18-18). These controls are used by the painter to control the amount of fluid and pattern of the spray. When the spreader-adjusting valve is closed, no air reaches the horns in the air cap, and the result is a round spray pattern. The spreader-adjusting valve should be opened enough so that a proper spray pattern is formed to suit the job to be done.

The fluid valve, when closed, will stop the paint from entering the air-stream coming out of the air cap. This valve should only be opened for the amount of paint that is required for the job. For spot work, use only a minimum flow; whereas for painting a panel, a maximum flow is used.

Pressure

The air pressure used at the gun is adjusted to the required pressure at the regulator on the transformer, taking into consideration the pressure drop caused by the hose. The pressure that should be used on different products will vary according to the manufacturer's recommendation. Table 18-1 can be used if the recommended pressures are not known.

TABLE 18-1   Suggested spray-gun pressures.

Product	Air Pressure at Gun	
	psi	*kPa*
Primer surfacer enamel or lacquer base	40–45	276–310
Acrylic, enamels	55–65	380–455
Enamel alkyd	55	380
Lacquer, nitrocellulose	45	310
Lacquer, acrylic	45	310
Urethane enamel	60–70	420–490

The pressure used must sometimes be increased or decreased, depending on the viscosity of the material that is to be sprayed. If the pressure used is too low, the surface will be rough or have an orange peel effect. Too high an air pressure will cause overatomization, resulting in dry spray and orange peel, because the air forces too much of the solvent to evaporate. The result will be a poor flow-out of the painted surface.

UNIT 18-7: TROUBLESHOOTING

Sags or runs are caused (Fig. 18-27) by holding the gun too close to the surface, the viscosity of paint being too low, or the speed of stroke being too slow. Other causes are strokes overlapping too much or by not using enough air pressure.

Dry spray is caused (Fig. 18-28) by the air pressure being too high, the viscosity of the paint being too high, the speed of stroke being too fast or not overlapping enough, or the gun being held too far away from the panel.

FIGURE 18-27 [Courtesy of DeVilbiss (Canada) Limited.]

FIGURE 18-28 [Courtesy of DeVilbiss (Canada) Limited.]

Proper flow-out (Fig. 18-29) will result when correct air pressure is used, the viscosity of the paint is right, the spray gun is used with the proper stroke and proper overlapping, and the gun is held at the proper distance from the panel.

Excessive orange peel is caused (Fig. 18-30) by viscosity of the paint being too high, using too high or too low air pressure, or using a poor reducer or thinner.

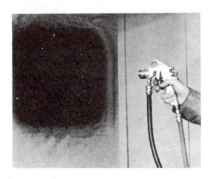

FIGURE 18-29 [Courtesy of DeVilbiss (Canada) Limited.]

FIGURE 18-30 [Courtesy of DeVilbiss (Canada) Limited.]

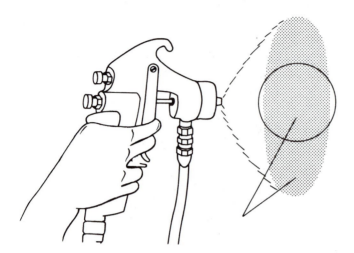

FIGURE 18-31 Normal spray patterns. [Courtesy of DeVilbiss (Canada) Limited.]

The first thing a painter must do once the mixed paint is in the gun cup is to check his spray pattern (Fig. 18-31). The fluid valve is opened to give sufficient flow and then the spreader adjustment is opened to get the proper spray pattern. If the gun does not give the proper spray pattern, then the painter must know what to look for.

1. When the spray pattern is top heavy, it is the result of horn holes being partially plugged, an obstruction on the bottom of fluid tip, or dirt on air cap seat or fluid tip seat (Fig. 18-32).

2. When the spray pattern is bottom heavy, it is caused by horn holes being partially plugged, an obstruction on the top side of fluid tip, or dirt on air cap seat or fluid tip seat (Fig. 18-32).

3. Heavy right-side pattern is caused by right-side horn holes partially clogged, dirt on right side of fluid tip, or on twin jet air cap, the right jet clogged (Fig. 18-33).

4. Heavy left-side pattern is caused by left-side horn holes partially clogged, dirt on left side of fluid tip, or on twin jet cap, the left jet clogged (Fig. 18-34).

5. Heavy center pattern is caused by too low a setting of the spreader adjustment valve, or with twin jet cap, too low an atomizing pressure or material is too thick; with pressure feed equipment, too high a fluid pressure for the atomization air being used or the material flow is in excess of the normal cap's capacity. The nozzle could be too large or too small for the material used (Fig. 18-35).

TOP HEAVY

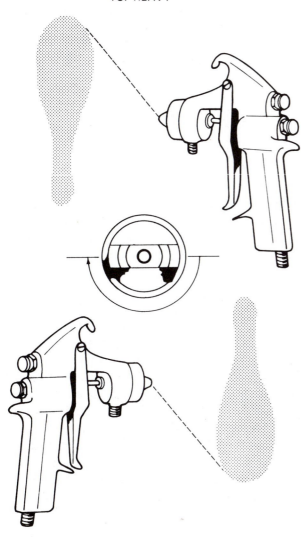

FIGURE 18-32 [Courtesy of DeVilbiss (Canada) Limited.]

BOTTOM HEAVY

FIGURE 18-33

FIGURE 18-34

FIGURE 18-35

6. Split spray pattern is due to air and fluid not being properly balanced. Reduce width of spray pattern by means of the spreader adjustment valve or increase fluid flow (Fig. 18-36).

FIGURE 18-36

Remedies for 1 to 4

To determine if the obstruction is on the air cap or fluid tip, make a test spray pattern—rotate the air cap half a turn and spray another pattern. If the defect is inverted, then the obstruction is on the air cap; but if it is not inverted, then the obstruction is on the fluid tip. Clean the air cap and check the fluid tip for a fine burr or dried paint inside the opening.

Remedies for 5 or 6

If the adjustments are out of balance, readjust atomizing pressure, fluid pressure, and spray width adjustment until the desired spray is obtained.

The causes of a jerky or fluttering spray (Fig. 18-37) are lack of sufficient material in container, the container is tipped at an excessive angle or an obstructed fluid passageway, the fluid tube could be loose or cracked, or the fluid tip or seat could be damaged. These conditions apply both to a suction or pressure-feed gun. The following conditions only apply to a suction feed. The material viscosity is too high or the air vent in the cup lid is clogged. The coupling nut or cup lid could be loose, dirty, or damaged. The fluid needle packing nut is either dry or loose or the fluid tip is resting on the bottom of the cup.

UNIT 18-8:   PRACTICE SPRAYING

The best way to get the feel of handling a spray gun is by using it. The wrist, arm, and body must be able to flex at the right time. Therefore practice spraying panels with the gun, using water as the fluid. When painting panels, a certain method should be used to save material and time.

It must be remembered that the spray gun should be held the proper distance, be as perpendicular as possible to the surface, and follow the contours of the

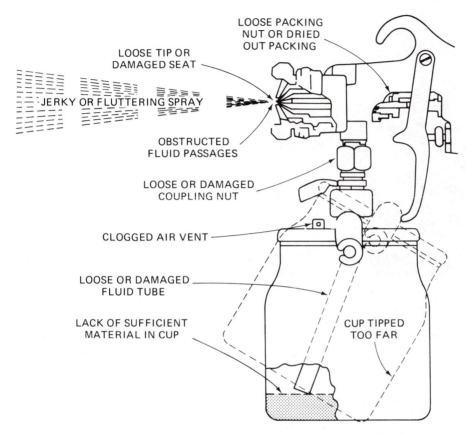

FIGURE 18-37   Causes of jerky or fluttering spray. [Courtesy of DeVilbiss (Canada) Limited.]

body or panel. A smooth and steady motion must be used; the speed of travel must be just right to cover the surface properly. Overlapping of the previous stroke must be 50 percent, and no arcing of the gun must be done at the start and finish of the stroke.

Spraying a Door

The top of the door frame is painted first and then the painting proceeds down toward the bottom of the door. If only one door is painted, the edges should be banded; also, care must be taken when spraying near the door handle, for a little too much paint will cause a sag to occur (Fig. 18-38).

FIGURE 18-38   Spraying
a door panel.

Spraying a Fender

The hood edge and the body flange of the fender are done first, then the front
part around the headlight, and then the crown, progressing downward to the
bottom (Fig. 18-39).

Spraying a Quarter Panel

The edges should be done first; then the painter should stand halfway along the
panel and spray the panel in long, continuous strokes. If this is impossible, divide

FIGURE 18-39   Spraying
a fender.

FIGURE 18-40 Spraying a quarter panel.

the area in half. Great care must be paid to the overlapping at the center when it is done with this method. If too much paint is loaded in the center, a sag will occur (Fig. 18-40).

Spraying a Hood

The cowl edge is done first and then the front of the hood. Next, standing along the side of the fender, start at the center and progress toward the edge; both sides are done the same way (Fig. 18-41).

FIGURE 18-41 Spraying an engine hood.

Spraying a Turret Top

To paint a top, a painter usually stands on a bench to enable him to reach the center of the top. The windshield edge is done first on one side; then painting progresses from the center to the outer edge. The back and side are done after one side is completed. The other side is done using the same method (Fig. 18-42).

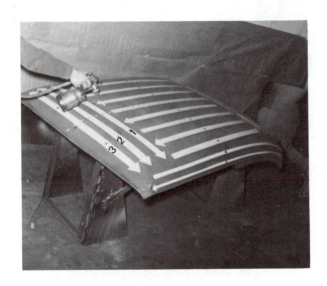

FIGURE 18-42 Spraying a turret top.

Complete Refinishing

When refinishing a car completely, the order in which the different sections of the car are painted may vary and this is left to the preference of the painter. Generally, however, in a cross-draft booth, the sections farthest from the exhaust fan are painted first. This procedure keeps a minimum amount of spray dust from settling on the already painted sections and results in a glossier finish. The turret top is painted first (Fig. 18-43). Then the doors on either the right or left side of the car are painted. Next the rear quarter panel on the same side is painted, followed by painting the deck lid and trunk lower panel. The opposite side of the car is painted starting at the quarter panel and then the doors and front fender. The hood, grille shell, valance, and opposite fender are painted last.

But in a down-draft booth, since the air is moving from the ceiling down toward the pit under the vehicle, a painter must change his methods. To be able to keep the edge of the paint film wet, he should paint the roof first, then the hood and the trunk lid. Then the right side followed by the lower trunk panel

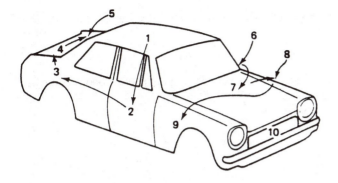

FIGURE 18-43 Spraying a complete automobile in a cross-draft spray booth.

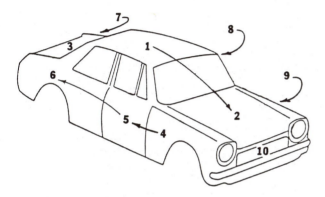

FIGURE 18-44 Spraying an automobile in a down-draft spray booth.

and the left side moving toward the front, which is finished last, as shown in Fig. 18-44.

QUESTIONS

18-1 What is *atomization*?

18-2 What is *vaporization*?

18-3 In general, how far should a production gun be held from the surface when spraying: 4 to 6 in. (102 to 152 mm), 6 to 8 in. (152 to 204 mm), or 12 to 14 in. (305 to 357 mm)?

18-4 What is *overlap*?

18-5 What is *arcing*?

18-6 How does a suction-feed gun pull the paint out of the container?

18-7   What is the difference between an air cap on a suction-feed and a pressure-feed gun?

18-8   What purpose does an air cap serve on a spray gun?

18-9   What is the main difference in painting a vehicle in a cross-draft booth compared to painting in a down-draft booth?

19

Refinishing Procedures

The majority of refinishing complaints arise from the fact that almost everyone tries to find the universal product, the shortcut, the cure-all—when no such method or item exists.

Each product is formulated for a specific purpose and must be used and handled in such a way as to fit properly into the complete refinishing system. This holds true in every stage of the refinishing procedure—from the beginning of the job, when the refinisher tests the condition of the surface to be painted, until the final coat of refinish material is dry and the job is ready for delivery to the customer.

The complete refinishing procedure is divided into five well-defined stages:

1. Examination and testing of the surface

2. Surface preparation and conditioning

3. Selection and preparation of materials

4. Application of the products

5. Final finishing touch

UNIT 19-1: DETERMINING THE CONDITION OF A SURFACE

There are numerous ways of determining the condition of a surface. For example, compounding and polishing a small area is helpful. In some cases, sanding will reveal a weak, crumbly film, or examination of suspected areas with a magnifying glass will often reveal checks or cracks in the film that are invisible to the eye. A test patch may be treated with lacquer thinner to aid in determining the type of finish on the vehicle. In the final analysis, however, it is frequently the refinisher's own judgment that determines whether the old finish is sound or whether it will be necessary to remove all or part of it in order to provide a solid foundation for the refinishing procedure (Fig. 19-1).

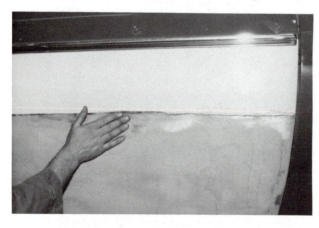

FIGURE 19-1 Checking the condition of the paint.

The first step in getting a car ready for painting is the thorough cleaning of the surface to free it from dust and dirt accumulations. The car should be washed with a cleaning solution and plain water (Fig. 19-2). After it has dried out, a solvent to remove grease, oil, and wax is used over the whole body (Fig. 19-3). A great amount of care is required when doing it. A good supply of rags is needed, for only a small area can be done at a time with the same rag. Pour some solvent on a rag and be careful not to touch the container with the rag; if the rag is contaminated with silicone, the solvent in the can could become contaminated. Wet an area of approximately 3 × 4 ft (914 × 1220 mm) and wipe immediately with a dry rag. Discard the rag and use a different rag for the next area. The whole body of the car should be done in this way. If the car has a surface that is heavily waxed, it may be necessary to apply the solvent with a fine pad of steel wool to remove the film.

All surface breaks in the paint film, such as areas where stone bruises are present or body work has been done, must be feather-edged using either a random

FIGURE 19-2 Washing the vehicle using a pressure washer.

FIGURE 19-3 Cleaning the surface with a wax and grease remover.

orbit or a regular vibrator. No. 80D (1/0) to No. 120 (3/0) production sandpaper can be used. The edge is tapered gradually (Fig. 19-4) until no edge is felt on the break in the paint film. Of course, there is always an exception to some procedures. When a paint film is very thick, the edge is feather-edged or ground out to a sharp angle, or if a deep enough imperfection is present, it should be filled with a plastic body filler which is sanded level to the paint surface.

If the paint surface is in good condition, sand with either No. 320 (9/0) wet and dry sandpaper or No. 280 free-cut sandpaper if alkyd enamel is to be used for the top coat. However, if acrylic enamel or urethane enamel is to be used, No. 360 wet and dry sandpaper should be used. For acrylic lacquer a No. 400 (10/0) wet or dry sandpaper should be used. Usually, one series lower of free-cut sandpaper can be used when dry sanding (Fig. 19-5).

FIGURE 19-4 Feather edging using a random orbit sander.

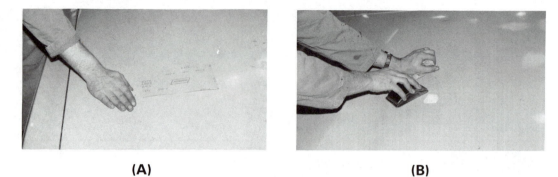

(A)   **(B)**

FIGURE 19-5   (A) Sanding with free-cutting sandpaper; (B) wet sanding with a block.

The broken-paint film areas should be back-sanded first to remove the marks the power sanders have left on the paint film near the edge of the break. Then the rest of the vehicle can be sanded using the wet-sanding method or by dry-sanding, usually with a random orbit sander. In the wet-sanding method the sanding should be started at the highest part of the vehicle that requires sanding. As each part is sanded, the panel should be washed. Always use enough water when wet sanding, as the water not only cleans the sandpaper, but provides a lubricant for the sandpaper to slide over.

When sanding a vehicle, all sanding should be done as much lengthwise as possible, as this will help to prevent sand-scratch marks in the old finish from showing up if some of the sanding is done crosswise. Great care must be taken when sanding near moldings, door handles, and so on. All gloss must be removed from the old finish so as to give a surface which has tooth, to give the paint mechanical adherence to the old finish.

When wet sanding of a panel is finished, a squeegee can be used to remove the excess water from the paint surface, leaving practically a dry film behind. Rinse and dry the body of the car thoroughly.

If the paint film is not in good shape due to cracking, crazing, or other paint failure and has to be removed, a paint and varnish remover is used (Fig. 19-6). Before using the paint remover, all joints, moldings, and panel edges should be protected with masking tape and paper where appropriate. This is to stop the paint remover from running into the joints, under the molding, or along the edges of the panels. This will stop the paint remover from removing paint where it is not required.

The paint remover is usually applied with a paintbrush in one direction only to eliminate breaking the film and trapping air in the remover. It must be applied thick enough to remain wet while it performs its task. Enamel will usually lift

FIGURE 19-6 Using paint remover.

up from the primer and sometimes to the bare metal. Lacquer will dissolve and become fairly fluid. In either case a putty knife is used to scrape off the old finish. Some primers, such as epoxy primers or baked enamels, will not be lifted or dissolved by paint removers. The vehicle or panel affected should then be rinsed off thoroughly using water; this neutralizes the paint remover.

When the panel is dry, the metal is then sanded with a random orbit sander or an orbital vibrator using No. 80D to No. 120D (1/0 to 3/0) grit production paper or free-sanding paper.

Paint remover should always be used in a well-ventilated area, as the fumes are quite toxic. If necessary, wear a proper respirator.

If the paint remover does not remove the affected material, a polishing machine using a foam pad and stick-on No. 40 (1½) or No. 80D (1/0) disk can be used to remove the paint. The coarse disk is used first, followed by the finer grit so as not to leave deep gouges in the metal after the paint removal is finished (Fig. 19-7).

FIGURE 19-7 Using a disk sander to remove paint.

UNIT 19-2: PREPARATION OF BARE METAL

The bare metal should be washed to clean it; then scrub the area with an appropriate metal conditioner, using a wire brush, steel wool, or cloths. Rinse with clean water and wipe dry with cloths, or blow dry using compressed air. The type of metal will determine the type of metal conditioner that should be used. It is important that the area be washed off thoroughly to remove all traces of phosphoric residue, if a good bond with the paint is to be formed (Fig. 19-8). The metal conditioner etches the metal to provide a good base for adhesion. When properly cleaned and etched, the metal will lose its brightness and change to a gray color.

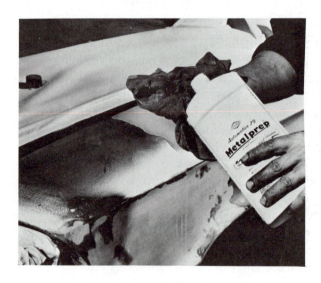

FIGURE 19-8 (Courtesy of C.I.L. of Canada, Ltd.)

Priming the Surface

The bare metal must be primed as soon as possible to prevent a recurrence of rusting and oxidation. A vinyl wash primer (Fig. 19-9) should be used as a first primer on all bare metal. It should be stirred properly, as the solids in the binder have a tendency to settle to the bottom of the can rather quickly. It must be reduced according to the manufacturer's recommendations. The material must be mixed as the catalyst is gently poured in or it will jell. It has about an 8-hour pot life.

The vinyl wash primer has excellent adhesion and will provide corrosion protection for most substrates. It is applied in a thin see-through coat; the metal should be fairly visible through it. It can be used over steel, aluminum, fiberglass,

FIGURE 19-9 Vinyl wash primer and reducer.

plastic, and galvanized and Zinco sheet metal. It is sprayed at a pressure of 40 to 45 psi (276 to 310 kPa) of air pressure at the gun, keeping a distance between the gun and the metal of approximately 6 to 8 in. (152 to 200 mm).

Primer or primer-surfacer should always be reduced according to manufacturer's recommendation (Fig. 19-10). Most lacquer-based primer-surfacers are reduced with 1 part of primer-surfacer to 1 to 1½ parts of thinner. The thinner used should be the right type for the shop conditions present, whether slow, medium, or fast evaporating. This mixture is then sprayed on the bare metal in sufficient light coats to obtain sufficient film thickness for satisfactory sanding (Fig. 19-11). Heavy coats should not be applied, and sufficient time should be

FIGURE 19-10 Mixing and reducing primer-surfacer.

FIGURE 19-11 Spraying primer-surfacer.

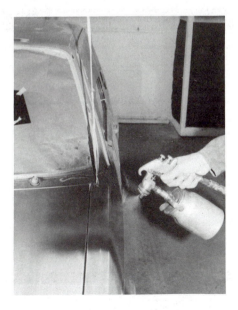

allowed to let the primer-surfacer flash off between coats. Between 40 and 45 psi (276 to 310 kPa) of air should be used at the gun. Undercoats form the important *middle layer* of the refinishing system. They must provide good adhesion to the surface and form a solid foundation for the color coats at the same time.

The key to the selection of the undercoats is *compatibility*. Consideration must be given to the surface on which they are to be applied and to the type of color coat that is to follow. Furthermore, if several undercoats are used to form the complete undercoat system, they must be compatible with one another.

Vinyl wash primer should be recoated with a primer-surfacer for most uses after allowing it to dry for 20 to 30 minutes. If it is not coated within 4 hours, it will have to be resprayed with vinyl wash primer all over again, and this would waste material. Vinyl wash primer should always be the first step in coating the surface, as it will save having to redo some jobs due to its tremendous adhesion and corrosion resistance.

Primer-surfacers are applied to basic types of substrates as an undercoat. These are rough surfaces, repairs of painted substrates, auto body steel, most plastic, and fiberglass. A primer surfacer must not only prime the surface to improve adhesion of the top coat, but must also fill feathered areas and other imperfections in the substrate (Fig. 19-12). Primer surfaces must be sanded to provide a smooth surface with the appropriate grit according to the top coat to be used. Figure 19-13 shows the qualities a good primer-surfacer must possess to achieve the job required of it.

LACQUER TOPCOAT

SEALER

ENAMEL UNDERCOAT

SUBSTRATE

FIGURE 19-12 A primer-surfacer is a primer that also fills small flaws in the substrate. (Courtesy of Du Pont Canada Inc.)

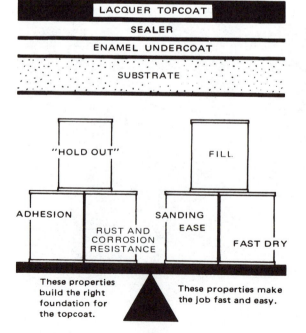

"HOLD OUT"   FILL

ADHESION   SANDING EASE

RUST AND CORROSION RESISTANCE   FAST DRY

These properties build the right foundation for the topcoat.

These properties make the job fast and easy.

FIGURE 19-13 A good primer-surfacer is a balance of many properties. (Courtesy of Du Pont Canada Inc.)

A good primer-surfacer is easy to sand smooth, has a fast film buildup, holds out for the top coat, and must be fast drying, usually around 30 minutes if applied properly.

If too thick a coat is applied on top of another, the top layer will dry, trapping solvents in the material. This will cause sand-scratch swelling and could also cause solvent popping at a later date (see Table 19-1).

TABLE 19-1   How to use label directions on containers.

Reduction Percentage	Proportions of Thinner to Paint
25	1 part thinner to 4 parts paint
33	1 part thinner to 3 parts paint
50	1 part thinner to 2 parts paint
75	3 parts thinner to 4 parts paint
100	1 part thinner to 1 part paint
125	5 parts thinner to 4 parts paint
150	3 parts thinner to 2 parts paint
200	2 parts thinner to 1 part paint
250	5 parts thinner to 2 parts paint
300	3 parts thinner to 1 part paint

Courtesy of Sherwin Williams Company Inc. Canada.

Refer to the paint label for the proper reduction percentage so that there will be no danger of over- or underreducing. Table 19-1 shows you how to convert these percentages to the proper proportions of paint and thinner.

Putties are used to fill slight imperfections in the metal-finished surface. They are usually applied in thin coats with a glazing knife or squeegee (Fig. 19-14). Putty is applied over primer-surfacer; if applied in thin coats, it will dry

FIGURE 19-14 Applying glazing putty.

in a few minutes. If it is applied in a thick coat, the surface will dry but solvents will be trapped underneath. This will cause shrinking as the solvents evaporate. If it is too thick, it could also split and open up to the surface.

Some putties require coating with primer before painting, but others need not be primed. Putties are sanded with anywhere from No. 80D (1/0) production paper to No. 320 (9/0) wet or dry sandpaper, depending on the product, the shop, and the methods used.

Sealers are used by some shops, depending on the products used. Different manufacturers recommend various methods that must be used with their undercoat preparation before the color coat. Sealers are used to prevent sand scratches and sand-scratch swelling and sinking in when refinishing over sanded baking enamels or acrylic lacquers. Sealer is sprayed in one or more wet coats, using an air pressure of 35 to 40 psi (241 to 276 kPa) at the gun. The sealer should then be given the proper amount of time to dry before it is top-coated with nitrocellulose or acrylic lacquers, alkyd or acrylic, or urethane enamels.

UNIT 19-3: AUTOMOTIVE ENAMELS

Automotive top coats must always be strained before using. Straining can be done when the paint is poured into the paint cup. It should then be reduced with the proper reducer, made to match the conditions of the shop (Fig. 19-15). If the temperature is under 70°F (21°C), a fast evaporating reducer should be used. If the temperature is between 70 and 85°F (21 and 29.4°C), use a medium-evaporating reducer. When the temperature is above 85°F (29.4°C), a slow-evaporating reducer is used.

When the slow-drying reducer is not available, an antiwrinkling additive can be used in alkyd enamel in hot and humid weather. This additive is also used when the car is to be baked after painting. Follow manufacturer's recommendations for the amount to add.

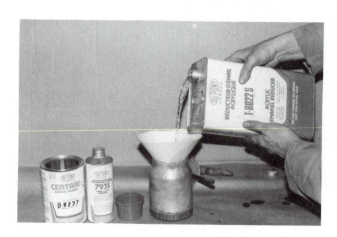

FIGURE 19-15 Mixing and stirring enamel.

FIGURE 19-16 Spraying enamel.

Reduce the alkyd enamel to the proper spraying viscosity and apply a light medium wet first coat; follow this in 10 to 20 minutes by a full wet coat. This coat is sprayed at a pressure at the gun of 50 to 60 psi (345 to 419 kPa) (Fig. 19-16). If the color is metallic, it has to be mist-coated with a mixture reduced by 1 part enamel to 1 part reducer. This mixture is sprayed on to obtain the desired uniform metallic finish.

Alkyd enamel dries dust-free in 20 to 40 minutes and tack-free to handle in 6 to 8 hours; overnight drying will give a fairly hard surface. If a super hardener or catalyst is used, the enamel dries much quicker and can be fairly hard in 2 to 3 hours. This helps to speed up production, as the paint is tack-free in about 1 hour after painting is finished. If the paint is force-dried, it is usually tack-free to handle in 30 minutes to 1 hour, depending on the size of the baking oven.

Table 19-2 can be followed to find the proper reducer for the temperature.

NOTE: When temperature is above 85°F (29.4°C) and the relative humidity is high, add 1½ to 2½ oz (33 to 71 g) of antiwrinkling additive to each quart (1 liter) of alkyd enamel. Then the enamel is reduced in the normal ratio with the proper reducer for air-dry or force-dry application. Remember that thinners should never be used in enamel. Thinners are liable to make the film brittle and give a poor gloss. Enamel may be polished with a paste wax after 90 days.

TABLE 19-2 Recommended temperature ranges for use of enamel reducers. (Courtesy C.I.L. of Canada, Ltd.)

	4.4	7.2	10.0	12.8	15.6	18.3	21.1	23.9	26.7	29.4	32.2	35.0	37.8		82.2	°C
SHOP TEMPERATURE	40	45	50	55	60	65	70	75	80	85	90	95	100	TO	180°	F.
FAST-FLO REDUCER				/////	/////	/////	---	---	---	---	---	---	---	---	---	
MEDIUM DRY							/////	/////	---	---	---	---	---	---	---	
SLOW DRY								/////								
LOW BAKE									/////	/////	/////	/////	/////	/////	/////	
SHOP TEMPERATURE:	40	45	50	55	60	65	70	75	80	85	90	95	100	TO	180°	F.
	4.4	7.2	10.0	12.8	15.6	18.3	21.1	23.9	26.7	29.4	32.2	35.0	37.8		82.2	°C

UNIT 19-4: METALLIC COLORS

One of the major problems confronting the automobile refinisher today is metallic colors. It is well known that the gun technique, mixing, reduction, and distance the gun is held from the surface all play a major role when spraying these so-called glamour shades. Metallic color has a great deal of acceptance and eye appeal with the buying public, and as long as the demand for these shades exists, car manufacturers will continue to use them.

It is not our intention to say that these colors are delicate and troublesome. If a refinisher is familiar with the difficulties and, in some cases, follows a few simple recommendations, he can overcome a good many of the problems.

Metallic color must be sprayed exactly opposite to straight color. That is, the first coat applied is medium wet, or what could be termed a *flow coat*, with the gun held 6 to 8 in. (152 to 203 mm) from the surface, followed by one or two light coats with the gun held 12 to 14 in. (305 to 356 mm) from the surface. The reason for the greater gun distance is to eliminate dappling streaks and shadows.

Certain metallic colors are very transparent and often give the painter problems. Transparent colors have poor hiding qualities. If a color change is being done using one of these transparent colors, the body of the car must be all the same color. This can be achieved by either priming the body completely and taking care not to cut through during sanding operations so that there will be the same color throughout. Another method is to use a nonsanding pigmented sealer and coat the body completely. Or the body of the car can be based with a solid color to hide the old paint film.

Care must be taken to tack off the car body to keep it clean. Primer sealers must be recoated within a certain amount of time to achieve maximum adherence of the paint film. When the same color is being used and primer spots are present, a first coat is applied but not so heavy as to cause runs or sags. Then the primer spots showing through are sprayed with a fairly dry spray. One spot is done per application. The spots are done one after another by applying successive coats and moving from one spot to another between coats in order to allow the reducer to flash off. This procedure is followed until the spots are well hidden. Then the second coat is applied at the regular distance or three panels are done one after the other. Usually the paint has set up enough so that these panels can be blended in to eliminate all traces of irregular metallic variations. The gun is usually held from 12 to 14 in. (305 to 356 mm) from the surface. The paint job is done in this fashion until it is completed. The repairman should then check for uniformity of the metallic flakes in the paint film throughout.

Sometimes the last panel painted looks different from the other panels. To overcome this, it is sometimes necessary to open the front door to a half-open position and repaint the door with one coat. This stops the overspray from going onto the adjacent panel which is too dry to absorb the last coat of spray. This procedure usually gives a very satisfactory job and a uniform metallic pattern.

Spraying Metallics to Match

Almost everyone will agree that by employing different gun techniques they can create infinite numbers of shades from the same can of paint. Dry spray will cause the color to lighten; whereas wet spraying will cause it to darken. Consequently, if the operator can predetermine the correct gun technique for a certain finish on an automobile, he can in all probability cut his rework down considerably. He can do so by testing the color on a panel, creating two or three variations and then allowing the panel a short drying period. He can then match this panel against any flat surface of the original finish. There is a possibility that not one of the variations will match, but one will be closer than the others. By using a similar technique, although changing enough to allow for the difference on the panel, he should come very close. This process is suggested where there is considerable trouble in matching due to excessive fade.

This method will prove itself on cars that (1) have been exposed to the elements for some time, (2) have been stored inside most of the time, and (3) have been parked outside all the time.

Although the color is the same, there will be a distinct difference in shades that will necessitate a different technique.

Metallics are very sensitive to reduction, film thickness, and changes in air pressure. A painter, if he is to achieve good matches, must be on guard against all these hazards and eliminate as much guesswork as possible, especially in film thickness, uniformity of metallic particles, viscosity, gun technique, and atomizing air pressure.

The material in the can is usually a good match to the manufacturer's standards, but it may still be a poor match if it is not properly prepared and applied. There are two very basic causes of mismatch. The first is the painter's failure to stir the paint thoroughly before and after reducing the viscosity. Any flakes or pigment left in the bottom of the can or the spray cup will affect the sprayed-out color.

The second cause is the painter's failure to apply the same degree of wetness as was applied to the original finish. If the original color was sprayed wet and the repair is sprayed drier, it will lighten the color. The reason for this is that when a wet coat is sprayed, the metallic flakes have time to position themselves deeper in the paint film before it flashes. This method produces a darker and stronger shade of color (Fig. 19-17).

FIGURE 19-17   Using a dry spray method will trap metallic particles at various angles near the surface of the paint film; this will cause a high metallic color effect.

When the paint is sprayed dry, the metallic flakes remain trapped closer to the surface of the drying film. This produces a lighter shade and a more metallic-looking finish (Fig. 19-18). Most new vehicles are sprayed with a wet spray, and some manufacturers use a clear coat on top of the regular paint to produce what is called the "wet look." The color shines more and is of a darker shade.

FIGURE 19-18   A wet spray will allow sufficient time for the metallic particles to settle in the paint film, which will produce a strong pigment color effect.

Different methods are used to achieve the desired result. Gun adjustments, spray techniques, and using proper reducer or thinner are all different ways of controlling the wetness of the spray material. If a couple of coats have been applied over the repaired area and the color is too light and metallic looking, then the color is darkened by spraying a few wet coats.

This can be done by using different spraying techniques or adjustments, for example, decreasing the spray gun pattern or distance, opening the fluid adjusting valve slightly more or reducing the spray pattern height, using less flash-off time between coats, or slowing down the speed of the stroke.

If the repair area is too dark, a few lighter, drier coats are applied so that the color will become lighter and will look more metallic. This can be achieved by reversing the techniques used to darken the color: increasing the spray gun pattern or distance, closing the fluid adjusting valve or increasing the width of the spray pattern, using more flash-off time between coats, or increasing the speed of the stroke.

If these techniques do not solve the dryness or wetness problem, then a different evaporation rate of thinner or reducer should be used. The amount of air pressure used will also cause different shades of color. The higher the pressure air used, the lighter the color will be; the lower the air pressure, the darker the color will be.

When making a metallic repair it is difficult to foresee how accurate the match will be. Before spraying the color on the vehicle it is wise to spray some color on a piece of sheet metal and let it dry a bit and then compare the color with the color on the car body.

UNIT 19-5: ACRYLIC ENAMEL

Acrylic enamel is more widely used today than ever before in the refinish field. Over the past few years it, and some of the products used with it, has been greatly improved. Figure 19-19 shows some of the products used to repaint a vehicle.

FIGURE 19-19

The preliminary steps for preparing the car are the same as those for enamel, but some manufacturers require that a finer paper be used. After the car body has been cleaned and is ready to receive the acrylic paint, care should be taken to follow the methods and recommendations on the can label. Some manufacturers insist that a sealer be used over all substrates, that is, over all paint films except enamel. On a good enamel surface it is not absolutely necessary, but to ensure a good bond between the paint films it is strongly recommended that a sealer be used at all times.

First, the paint is stirred thoroughly and then the proper catalyst is poured into the paint following the manufacturer's recommendations as to the amount required per quart (liter) of enamel. The paint is then reduced according to the manufacturer's recommendations using the proper reducer for the temperature. Products from other companies must not be intermixed because one product may react with another product.

The reduced material is then poured through a strainer in the gun cup to ensure that there will be no dirt in the paint. The right amount of air pressure must be used. This varies from one manufacturer to the other. Some acrylic enamels are applied by using a two-coat system and others are applied by using a three-coat system. The one shown in Fig. 19-19 requires a three-coat system. The first coat, which is a medium-wet coat over the primed or sealed surface, is allowed to dry for 20 minutes. This coat is followed by two medium wet coats. For metallics, a final mist coat can be applied if necessary to eliminate streaking and mottling or to lighten the color. This final mist coat is made of the same material as used previously. No additional reducer is required. It should be applied immediately after the last coat in order to prevent a hazy, pinched effect and also loss of gloss.

Once the catalyst has been added to the acrylic enamel, the mixture should be used as soon as possible (within 3 hours under normal shop conditions). The pot life can be increased by reducing the paint immediately after the catalyst has been poured in and stirred. Pot life decreases as the temperature and humidity increase and it also varies depending on the color. If the viscosity should begin to increase, additional reducer can be added as required.

Most acrylic enamels can be baked once the catalyst has been added without adding any further additives. They can usually be baked at a temperature of 180°F (or 83°C) maximum for not more than 20 minutes. The solvents should be allowed to evaporate for 15 minutes before baking is started. A 20-minute bake at 180°F (83°C) is approximately equivalent to 24 to 48 hours of air-dry time.

Most acrylic enamels will dry dust-free in 30 minutes under normal conditions and tack-free in 2 hours. Under most conditions, the painted vehicle may be moved within 2 hours and put outside in 4 hours if the weather permits. If the weather is not good, the unit should be left inside overnight.

When two-toning is required, the vehicle can usually be taped within 5 to 7 hours. Most acrylic enamels may be recoated after 5 to 7 hours under normal drying conditions. The masking tape should be removed immediately after the final color has been applied to prevent tape marking. All possible masking paper contact with fresh material should be avoided.

The spray gun and equipment should be cleaned immediately, preferably with a lacquer thinner. All catalyzed paint should be disposed of in the proper manner because it will harden and be of no use to anybody.

Acrylic enamel and alkyd enamel do not easily lend themselves to spot repairing except on a recent paint job. If the acrylic enamel has dried overnight, it can be spot repaired with acrylic lacquer or acrylic enamel. If there are any dry areas in the paint job, they can usually be compounded after 24 hours; a check should be made first on a small area by using a fine grit polishing compound. If there are any fisheyes, the proper fisheye eliminator should be used. When painting with a paint that has a catalyst, hardener, or accelerator added to it, proper respirating equipment should be used and the painting should be done in a well-ventilated booth.

UNIT 19-6: POLYURETHANE ENAMEL

Alkyd enamels have been used on fleet equipment for many years, but today polyurethane enamel is being used by many fleets.

Polyurethane enamel gives a faster drying time to speed ease of repair, gives better initial gloss, resists fading, resists chemicals, gasoline, and solvents, has a harder surface, washes better, and since it tends to shed dirt easier, fewer washings are needed.

The metal is prepared by following the proper methods. Usually, a vinyl wash primer is applied to a thickness that is still transparent. Complete hiding is not necessary. This primer is allowed to dry 20 to 30 minutes at room temperature before recoating with the special epoxy primer. If the vinyl wash primer is allowed to dry more than one hour, it will be necessary to recoat again with vinyl wash primer.

Epoxy primer requires an activator, which is mixed in the required proportions and left to stand for the required time before using. This mixture is thinned with the proper thinner and in the recommended proportions. The pot life of epoxy primer is usually up to 3 days at room temperature. It must not be stored at below 50°F (10°C).

The primer is applied in one or two full wet coats in order to achieve a desirable dry thickness. It should be allowed to dry 2 to 4 hours. For best top-coat appearance, it is sanded. If it is allowed to dry more than 24 hours, it must

FIGURE 19-20

be sanded prior to top-coating. Figure 19-20 shows the materials used for this type of paint job.

Imron takes an activator which is mixed as follows: 1 part activator to 3 parts pigmented Imron. If desired, a dry time activator may be added to the mixture at the rate of 5 oz/gal (140 ml to 4 liters approx.) to provide a faster hard dry and tape time.

This activator is recommended at all times but especially when using Imron metallics 580S clear or black. Usually, no more reduction is required, but, if necessary, the material may be reduced with the proper reducer at the rate of 4.7 oz (139.7 ml) per activated gallon (4 liters). This will increase flow-out, leveling, and gloss (especially on large areas). The average pot life is approximately 8 hours at normal room temperature.

The solid colors are applied by using 50 psi (323 kPa) at the gun. A medium wet coat is sprayed first and is allowed to tack up. This is followed by a full second coat. On metallic colors 65 psi (420 kPa) is used at the gun and a light-medium coat is applied as a tack coat. This is allowed to set 20 minutes and then a second light-medium coat is applied. The material is then reduced 15 percent with the proper reducer and a light-medium coat is applied. If desired, another light-medium coat of the reduced material may be applied.

Imron metallic colors should be clear coated with the proper Imron clear material after an overnight dry (12 to 18 hours), but the metallic top coat should not be sanded before the clear material is applied.

All of these materials are very toxic. Therefore, a painter should always wear the proper respirating equipment and painting should always be done in a well-ventilated spray booth.

The dry time for two-toning at 68°F (20°C) with accelerator is approximately 2 to 4 hours and without accelerator it is approximately 6 to 10 hours.

This paint can be force dried without additives to a temperature up to 250°F (121°C). If there are any fisheyes, only fisheye eliminator made for this product should be used.

As soon as the paint job is finished, the spray equipment should be cleaned immediately with lacquer thinner. All unused paint that has accelerator in it should be disposed of or thrown in the garbage as it will jell up and become hard.

UNIT 19-7: ACRYLIC LACQUER

Acrylic lacquers provide a superior finish because they combine the advantages of lacquer and the qualities inherent in acrylic resins. Acrylic lacquer dries by evaporation and requires compounding and buffing in order to bring out the gloss.

The most outstanding characteristics of acrylic lacquer are its superior gloss retention and its exceptional good resistance to color fade under exposure. The main reason acrylic lacquers are used is because they can tolerate larger amounts of aluminum in their formulation, thus offering a wide color selection.

The basic steps for preparing are the same as those for other paints, but a finer grit of paper is used and a sealer sometimes has to be used. A fresh can of acrylic lacquer must be stirred thoroughly and then it must be reduced with the recommended thinner and in specified amounts. Temperature and humidity not only affect the evaporation rate but also the choice of thinner. On hot, humid days or in baking, a retarder is added to the mixture to prevent blushing of the lacquer film and to increase gloss (Fig. 19-21).

The lacquer is strained in the gun cup and then it is sprayed with a spray gun that does not have too many holes in the air cap. A pressure of 45 psi (310 kPa) is used at the gun. Usually, one or two coats are sprayed first and the solvents are given time to evaporate before more lacquer is sprayed on. This method allows the first and second coats to seal the surface and it will go a long

FIGURE 19-21 Materials required for acrylic lacquer paint job.

way to prevent sand-scratch swelling. At no time should the spraying be done without allowing sufficient time for the solvents to evaporate. Succeeding coats can then be applied by allowing each coat to flash off before applying the next coat. Only as many coats as required to achieve proper hiding and the proper level of gloss should be applied, for too much thickness causes the paint film to crack or craze.

For metallic colors, a final mist coat consisting of 1 part lacquer to 9 parts thinner is applied and spray techniques are adjusted to achieve the desired metallic effect. The lacquer will be tack-free in approximately 15 minutes at 70 to 80°F (21.0 to 26.7°C) and it will hard-dry in 1½ hours. If force-dried at 180°F (82.2°C), the lacquer will hard-dry in 30 minutes to 1 hour.

When a clear coat is being applied, the clear material is thinned according to the manufacturer's recommendations and two coats are usually sprayed on. Care should be taken to overlap properly because overlapping will give the desired gloss and deep look to the paint job.

UNIT 19-8: REFINISHING INTERIOR PLASTIC TRIM PARTS

Interior paintable plastic trim components are divided into three general types: polypropylene plastic, ABS plastic, and vinyl plastic (polyvinyl chloride).

It is important that a painter be able to identify each plastic so that he can paint it satisfactorily. Manufacturers do not approve complete painting of soft seat cushion and seat back trim cover assemblies of vinyl construction. The plastic used most widely on the interior of bodies, with the exception of the soft seat cushion and back trim cover assemblies, is polypropylene.

Below are two tests that will help the painter determine the identity of a given plastic.

- *Test for ABS plastic or polypropylene:* With a sharp blade remove a sliver of plastic from a hidden back side portion of the part. Hold the sliver of plastic with tweezers or lay it on a clean noncombustible surface and then ignite the plastic.

    Observe the burning closely. Polypropylene burns with no readily visible smoke. ABS plastic burns with a readily visible black smoke residue that will hang temporarily in the air.

- *Test for vinyl plastic:* Using a suitable flame, such as provided by a propane torch or equivalent, heat a copper wire until the wire turns red. Touch the back side or hidden surface of the part being tested with the heated wire. Some of the plastic will be retained on the wire. Return the wire and retained plastic to the flame. Observe for a green-blue flame, which indicates that the plastic being tested is vinyl.

To paint polypropylene plastic parts involves using a special primer (329S, Fig. 19-22). Because polypropylene plastic is hard, it should be color coated with conventional interior acrylic lacquer after the primer has dried. If the proper primer is not used on these parts, the color coat will usually fail and there will be peeling problems.

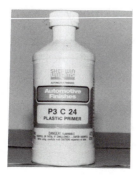 

FIGURE 19-22

The parts must be washed thoroughly with a paint finish cleaning solvent such as Acryli-Clean, Pre-Kleano, Prep-Sol, or equivalent. All label directions should be followed. A thin wet coat of polypropylene primer is applied according to the directions on the label. The wetness of the primer is determined by observing the gloss reflection of the spray application in adequate lighting. The primer application must cover all edges. The primer is allowed to dry 1 minute minimum and 10 minutes maximum.

During the flash-off time period (1 to 10 minutes) conventional interior acrylic lacquer color is applied as required and is allowed to dry before the part is installed. Applying the color during the flash-off time range will provide the best adhesion of color coats.

The rigid or hard ABS plastic parts require no primer because conventional interior acrylic lacquers adhere satisfactorily to this material. The part is washed thoroughly with the proper paint finish cleaning solvent. The interior acrylic lacquer color is applied according to trim combination. Only enough color is applied for proper hiding and to avoid washout of the grain effect. The part is allowed to dry before installation.

Painting Vinyl and Flexible (Soft) ABS

The outer cover material on flexible instrument panel cover assemblies is made mostly of ABS plastic that is modified with PVC or vinyl. The same material is used on many padded door trim assemblies, but the soft cushion padding under the ABS covers is usually urethane plastic foam.

Flexible vinyls are most widely used in seat trim, some door trim assemblies, headlinings, and so on. They are coated fabrics. Hard vinyls are used on seat back assist handles, coat hooks, exterior molding inserts, and some door trim panels.

The paint system for flexible ABS plastic and vinyl includes an interior vinyl color and a clear vinyl top coat. Neither primer sealer nor primer is required. The parts are washed thoroughly with a vinyl cleaning and preparation solvent, such as Vinyl Prep Conditioner, Vinyl Prep, or equivalent. The cleaner is wiped off with a clean, lint-free cloth while the cleaner is still wet.

As soon as the surface is wiped dry, the interior vinyl color is applied in wet coats. Enough flash time must be allowed, and between coats all label directions must be followed. The proper color is found by using the trim color code, and only enough color is used for proper hiding and to avoid washout of the grain effect.

Before the color flashes off completely, one wet double coat of vinyl top coat is applied. When this top coat is being applied, care must be taken so that appropriate level of gloss matches the adjacent parts. The instrument panel should be covered with a nonglare vinyl. A clear coat is applied to control gloss requirements and to prevent the color from rubbing off after drying. The panel is allowed to dry before it is installed.

To paint flexible parts such as filler panels between the bumper and fender, a flex agent must be used. The part is prepared as usual, then 155S (Fig. 19-22) is sprayed on it and left to dry following the manufacturer's recommendations. Then 1 part 155S is added to 1 part acrylic lacquer and 1 part thinner in the gun cup; this must be well mixed. This material is sprayed on the part in successive coats with flash-off time between coats. To spray this material, a pressure of 25 to 35 psi (175 to 245 kPa) is used at the gun.

If unsure of the method to be used, check the part for the International Organization Code. Then compare to Tables 19-3 and 19-4 and find the proper materials for refinishing the different types of plastics.

If no code is present, the commonsense approach should be used; that is, divide the types of materials. For example, for the exterior, is it flexible or hard? If it is for the interior, is it flexible or hard? Exterior hard (rigid) parts should be treated as fiberglass when in doubt as to their makeup.

TABLE 19-3 Plastic refinishing systems for interior use.

Symbol	Name	Primer*	Top Coat†
ABS	ABS (acrylonitrile/butadiene/styrene)	None	A/L
CPE	Chlorinated polyethylene	P3C24	A/L
EP	Epoxy	P2A43-P2N44	A/L
EP DM	Ethylene/propylene diene monomer	P3C24	A/L plus V2V297
E/P EPM	TPO, TPR (thermoplastic rubber)	P3C24	A/L plus V2V297
E/VAC	Ethylene/vinyl acetate	P3C24	A/L plus V2V297
MF	Melamine	P2A43-P2N44	A/L
PA	Nylon	P2A43-P2N44	A/L
PE	Polyethylene	P3C24	A/L
PF	Phenolic	P2A43-P2N44	A/L
PP	Polypropylene	P3C24	A/L
PPYO PPO	Noryl	P2A43-P2N44	A/L
PS	Polystyrene	P2A43-P2N44	A/L
PUR	Polyurethane, thermoset	None	A/L plus V2V297
PVC	Vinyl	None	Vinyl color
SAN	Styrene acrylonitrate	None	A/L
TPUR	Polyurethane, thermoplastic	None	A/L plus V2V297
UF	Urea-formaldehyde	P2A43-P2N44	A/L
UP	Polyester/thermoset	P2A43-P2N44	A/L

*P2A43-P2N44 is an acrylic-type primer-surfacer; P3C24 is a polyolefin primer.

†A/L is an acrylic lacquer; V2V297 is a flexible additive for acrylic lacquer. Use V2V297 when the plastic is flexible.

Source: Courtesy of Sherwin Williams Company, Inc., Canada.

If the exterior is flexible (semirigid), the addition of a flexible additive to the paint will be required. Interior hard (rigid) parts can all be painted except polycarbonate (Hexan), as solvents will weaken the integrity of the material. The majority of the plastic parts that need refinishing will be polypropylene, which requires the use of a plastic primer.

If the interior is flexible (semirigid), the use of vinyl color is recommended. The second choice will involve the use of acrylic lacquer interior color and flexible additive.

To paint vinyl surfaces, such as the vinyl on roofs of cars, it is necessary first to mask them off properly to protect the vehicle from overspray. The vinyl is then cleaned using a good grade of wax and grease remover and left to dry. Then two or more thin coats of the vinyl color at package consistency (Fig. 19-23) is sprayed on or until enough depth of shade has been acquired at 30 to 35 psi (210 to 245 kPa) at the gun. Allow a flash-off time of 8 to 10 minutes between coats. The finish should be left to dry for 1 hour prior to weather exposure or use.

TABLE 19-4 Plastic refinishing systems for exterior use.

Symbol	Name	Primer*	Top Coat†
ABS	ABS (acrylonitrile/butadiene/styrene)	P2A43-P2N44	A/L
		E2R34-E2A35	A/E
		E2R27-E2A28	CA/E
CPE	Chlorinated polyethylene epoxy	P3C24‡	A/L, A/E, CA/E
		P2A43-P2N44	A/L
		E2R34-E2A35	A/E
		E2R27-E2A28	CA/E
EP DM	Ethylene propylene diene monomer	P3C24‡	A/L plus V2V297
			CA/E
E/P EPM	TPO, TPR (thermoplastic rubber)	P3C24‡	A/L plus V2V297
			CA/E
E/VAC	Ethylene/vinyl acetate	None	A/L plus V2V297
			CA/E
MF	Melamine	P2A43-P2N44	A/L
		E2R34-E2A35	A/E
		E2R27/E2A28	CA/E
PA	Nylon	P2A43-P2N44	A/L
		E2R34-E2A35	A/E
		E2R27-E2A28	CA/E
PE	Polyethylene	P3C24‡	A/L, CA/E or
			V2V297 plus A/L
PF	Phenolic	P2A43-P2N44	A/L
		E2R34-E2A35	A/E
		E2R27-E2A28	CA/E
PP	Polypropylene	P3C24‡	A/L, CA/E or
			V2V297 plus A/L

PPYO PPO	Noryl	P2A43-P2N44	A/L
		E2R34-E2A35	A/E
		E2R27-E2A28	CA/E
PUR	Polyurethane, thermoset	None	A/L plus V2V297
	(If factory primed)	None	CA/E
	(If unprimed)	E2G973-R7K242	CA/E
PVC	Vinyl	None	Vinyl color
SAN	Styrene acrylonitrile	P2A43-P2N44	A/L
		E2R34-E2A35	A/E
		E2R27-E2A28	CA/E
TPUR	Polyurethane, thermoplastic	None	A/L plus V2V297
(TPU)	(If factory primed)	None	CA/E
	(If unprimed)	E2G973-R7K242	CA/E
UF	Urea-formaldehyde	P2A43-P2N44	A/L
		E2R34-E2A35	A/E
		E2R27-E2A28	CA/E
UP	Polyester/thermoset	P2A43-P2N44	A/L
		E2R34-E2A35	A/E
		E2R27-E2A28	CA/E

*P2A43-P2N44 are acrylic-type primer-surfacers; P2A43-P2N44 are acrylic enamel primer sealers; E2R34-E2A35 are vinyl wash primers for unprimed plastic.

†A/L, Acrylic lacquer; A/E, acrylic enamel; CA/E, catalyzed acrylic enamel. V2V297 is a flexible additive for acrylic lacquer for use in lacquer for flexible plastics. Use V6V241 or V6V247 POLASOL in acrylic enamel for flexible plastics.

‡P3C24 polyolefin plastic primer is recommended for limited automotive exterior plastic types where no other primer will gain adequate adhesion. The use of P3C24 for wider exterior applications must have laboratory approval.

Source: Courtesy of Sherwin Williams Company, Inc., Canada.

FIGURE 19-23 Vinyl color.

UNIT 19-9: RUBBING AND POLISHING

Reduce the compound to a creamy consistency. Using a medium-grit rubbing and polishing compound, rub the surface of the vehicle. Some people prefer to use No. 400 grit (10/0) paper and bar soap to remove the dry spray and the slight orange peel effect on the surface (Fig. 19-24). Once this is done, a fine compound is used to bring the gloss up. If the rubbing is done by hand, a soft cloth moistened with water should be used. The cloths will have to be changed frequently (see Table 19-5).

FIGURE 19-24

If machine polishing is used, spread the compound evenly over the surface, which has been wet with water (Fig. 19-25). Add water frequently. Using the edge of the buffing wheel, move back and forth rapidly with light, overlapping strokes. Use light pressure to avoid burning or cutting through the finish. Clean pad from time to time to prevent the compound from caking.

TABLE 19-5 Procedures for rubbing and polishing.

Acrylic Lacquer	Nitrocellulose Lacquer
	1. Wet sand with No. 400 grit (10/0) paper to remove heavy orange peel if necessary.
1. Apply medium rubbing and polishing compound.	2. Apply medium rubbing and polishing compound.
2. Apply fine polishing compound.	3. Apply fine polishing compound.
3. Polish with cleaner and polish.	4. Polish with cleaner and polish.

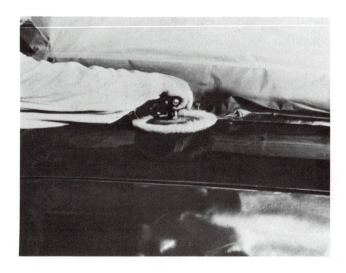

FIGURE 19-25 (Courtesy of C.I.L. of Canada, Ltd.)

After compounding, use a cleaner and polish or cornstarch with the buffing wheel to increase the gloss of the finish. A hard paste wax may be used after 60 days.

UNIT 19-10: SPOT REPAIR USING ENAMEL OR ACRYLIC LACQUER

Spot repairing with enamel can be done, provided that the right methods are used. It can be done in certain areas on the body but should not be attempted on large flat panels.

Using panel edges, contour changes, or molding where possible, mask off to protect the remainder of the vehicle from overspray. Where there is no natural break, mask well beyond the area to be repaired to allow enough room for color blending and feather-edging. The area should then be cleaned with a silicone polish remover by scrubbing a small area; wipe dry while the solvent is still wet. If the solvent should dry, rewet the surface and wipe immediately; change cloths frequently. The area should be wet-sanded to remove all gloss; start by using No. 320 (9/0) paper and give the final sanding with No. 400 (10/0) or finer. Do not sand beyond the area to be covered with top coat. If cut-throughs occur during sanding, feather-edge well back from bare metal areas.

If bare metal is exposed, treat with metal conditioner as usual; then prime by using lacquer-type primer (Fig. 19-26). A wet coat should be applied, using a medium spray fan and 15 to 20 psi (103 to 138 kPa) at the gun. The work should be done from the center of the repair area out toward the fringe, building up with succeeding coats to bring the low area up level to the paint surface, if necessary. Let the primer surfacer dry for the required time and then sand, using

FIGURE 19-26

No. 400 (10/0) paper. Next, apply a fine polishing compound reduced to creamy consistency with water (Fig. 19-27). A soft cloth moistened with water should be used to polish the area around the repair area to remove primer surfacer; overspray and prepare a blending edge. The polished area should then be cleaned with a silicone polish remover, using clean cloths. The area should be tacked off with a tack cloth.

If the spot repair is done with enamel, the procedure is as follows. Reduce enamel as usual; then apply it in medium wet coats, using a medium spray fan and pressure of 15 to 20 psi (103 to 138 kPa) at the gun. Work from the center

FIGURE 19-27

of the repair area out toward the edge (Fig. 19-28). If the job is done with acrylic lacquer or nitrocellulose lacquer, apply two single wet coats to the primed area only, allowing flash-off between coats. Use a medium fan and a pressure of 15 to 20 psi (103 to 138 kPa) at the gun. Follow with two to four additional single wet coats, advancing farther into the fringe area with each coat. Allow to flash between coats; stay well within the area that was polished previously. Immediately following application of the top coat, either enamel or acrylic lacquer, spray some blending reducer or regular reducer or acrylic thinner. Start spraying from just outside where the spray dust is visible in toward where spray dust ends. Do not apply reducer or thinner to the main repair area to avoid reflow, which could

FIGURE 19-28

alter the color. If used correctly at low pressure, this method will melt most of the overspray. A liquid cleaner and polish can be used to remove any overspray left on the enamel surface, after drying for 24 hours. On acrylic lacquer, the spot repair must be polished with a fine rubbing compound to remove overspray and obtain a good gloss (Fig. 19-29). This is done when the spot repair has dried for the required amount of time. A liquid cleaner should then be used for further polishing on the repaired area. The same procedure for acrylic lacquer can be used to repair acrylic enamels. The sanding job must be done as well for acrylic enamel as for enamel. Acrylic enamel needs a good surface to be able to provide good adhesion on the old surface. All these products can be either air-dried or force-dried.

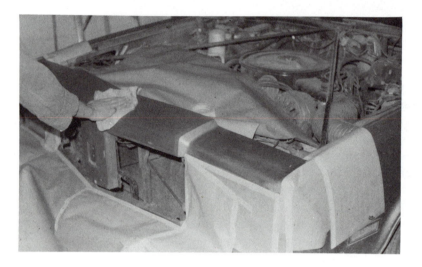

FIGURE 19-29

Recently, new methods for repairing acrylic lacquer have been developed. When done properly, they provide excellent color matches. These methods are called the modified conventional method and the metallic color control method. The modified conventional method is used for partial panel repair and the other method is used for spot repair.

The preparation steps are the same as for the other methods, but feather-edging solvent is used with a cloth to feather-edge the broken area. The work is carried out from the center to the outer edges by sanding with No. 400 (10/0) paper. The edges are compounded to remove sand scratches and then washed with a rag that is soaked with a little water and silicone polish remover. The next steps are the same as for acrylic lacquer until the time has come for the color coat.

The modified conventional method requires that two guns be used. One gun contains the acrylic lacquer color, which is composed of the acrylic lacquer, plus the thinner and 5 percent of retarder. The second gun contains the same mixture of thinner but only 5 percent of color. The purpose of adding 5 percent color is to allow uniformity of wetting the surface and to prevent beading of the thinner. An air cap with only a few holes should be used on both guns so that the material does not become overatomized.

To help prevent sand scratches, a dry, dusty color coat from the first gun is applied on the primer edges. This dusty coat is obtained by closing the fluid valve completely and then opening it a quarter turn. The spreader valve should be opened to give the widest fan possible in relation to the size of the repair area. A thorough wipe with a tack rag is required on this coat before proceeding. For large primed areas, it is advisable to apply a normal color coat first, followed immediately by a mist coat from the second gun. This mist coat is allowed to flash off before the next step is undertaken.

A medium-wet coat from the mist coat thinner gun is applied and then followed with a color coat from the other gun. It will be noted that the wetter the color coat, the darker the color obtained. This coat is then sprayed with a medium wet mist coat; the two steps are repeated until the color being applied matches the color on the car. The final mist coat used will probably require a cross coat to obtain uniform wetness, and it should be applied to a larger area than the color coat to allow complete blending in with the factory finish. The finish is then allowed to air-dry overnight or to air-flash 30 minutes; it is then force-dried for half an hour at 180°F (82.2°C) and allowed to cool before polishing.

The metallic color control is normally used for smaller body repairs and paint defects, such as mottling, streaks, and off-color. If the existing defect reaches bare metal, the same preparation steps as for the other method should be applied.

Two guns are again necessary; the first gun contains the color and the second gun contains the mist coat. The thinner used is generally a different mixture than that used previously. The thinner or thinner blend used is a very important aspect of the metallic color control method. A thinner that will flash-off in approximately 60 to 70 seconds when it is applied under the following conditions is necessary.

A specially prepared primed panel is used; one double pass of thinner is sprayed on the panel at an atomizing air pressure of 35 to 40 psi (241 to 276 kPa). A normal opening on the spreader valve is used. The fan in the booth should not be running when this check is made. The flash-off is timed, and if necessary the blend is adjusted as detailed below. The acrylic lacquer thinner normally recommended should be used for this application. If the temperature and humidity conditions are such that an adjustment of flash-off time is required, up to 10 percent of retarder may be used to slow down flash time and up to 50 percent of a faster evaporating thinner may be used to speed up flash time. This blend of thinner is used both in the color coat gun and in the mist coat gun.

Using the mist coat thinner gun, a medium wet mist coat is applied to the repair area as well as to the surrounding area. This coat is immediately followed with a dry, dusty color coat from the other gun. This dusty coat is obtained by closing the fluid valve completely and then opening it a quarter of a turn. The spreader valve should be opened to give the widest fan possible in relation to the size of the repair area. Two or three dry passes with the gun may be made, followed immediately by careful tack wiping of the surface to remove loose overspray. This step is followed again with a medium wet coat from the mist gun and then back to dry dusty color coat and a further tack-off. This step is repeated until a suitable color match is obtained. The final coat is always a mist coat.

The metallic color control method offers about a 50 percent reduction in air-dry time compared with conventional repair methods. With lamps, the force-dry time is about 10 minutes. After the surface has cooled from force drying, compounding may be required. Use a fine polishing compound and then a polish to obtain a finish that is comparable to the original finish. Care should be taken in buffing because it is possible to rub through.

UNIT 19-11:   ACRYLIC ENAMEL AND LACQUER BASE COAT/CLEAR COAT

Acrylic Enamel

Recently, manufacturers have introduced what is called base coat/clear coat paint on their vehicles. The base coat/clear coat system contains mica pearl and/or aluminum flakes and is commonly known as the base coat. Some paint manufacturers have acrylic enamel base coat/clear coat materials in both acrylic enamel and lacquer. We will discuss the application of the acrylic enamel base coat/clear coat system (Fig. 19-30).

The preparation is the same as for acrylic enamel top-coat application. The enamel from one manufacturer is reduced 75 to 100 percent with an acrylic enamel reducer selected for shop temperature and conditions. The catalyst is added [4 oz (125 ml)] to 1 qt (1 liter) of unreduced paint. The sprayable pot life is about 6 hours at 75°F (24°C).

The paint is applied in two or three light color coats, enough to achieve hiding and uniformity of the color. A 20-minute flash-off time should be allowed between coats; the base coat will not be glossy. After a 2-hour drying time it is

FIGURE 19-30 Materials for base coat/clear coat acrylic enamel.

coated with an acrylic urethane clear with catalyst added to it according to the manufacturer's recommendations. To increase flow-out a retarder may be added to it. The pot life is about 6 hours.

Two medium-wet coats should be applied, allowing a 15-minute flash time between coats. The clear coat should be allowed to dry for 16 hours before delivery.

Sanding of the base coat should be avoided, but if required because of dirt or imperfections, rebase-coating the sanded area may be necessary. Light controlled coats using a blending technique will work best. Should imperfections show up in the base coat after the first coat of clear is applied, the clear can be sanded if it is dry, usually about 3 hours. Using heat, the affected area can be sanded 1 hour after coating. If there are dirt problems in the second coat of clear, the times are double.

Color sanding and buffing can be performed the next day. Use color-sanding ultrafine 1200 grit sandpaper to sand if required. To buff, a clean pad is necessary, at approximately 1800 rpm using a medium- to heavy-duty liquid compound followed by a polish.

Some of the urethane clear can be used over an acrylic enamel paint job to enhance the glamour of the color. Figure 19-31 shows the materials required. At least a 2-hour waiting period is required after top coating with the enamel, but not more then 24 hours; otherwise, the surface will have to be scuff-wet-sanded with No. 1200 grit sandpaper before applying the clear.

FIGURE 19-31 Materials to clear-coat acrylic enamel.

The vehicle top coat must be clean before applying the urethane clear, which must be activated with the catalyst following the manufacturer's recommendations. Do not mix more than 1 qt (1 liter) or more material than can be used in an hour. If additional flow-out is required when refinishing large surfaces or in temperatures of 75°F (24°C), 5 ounces of flow reducer can be added.

Two medium-wet coats should be applied at 55 to 60 psi (380 to 420 kPa) at the gun with a temperature of 65 to 70°F (18 to 21°C). A third, medium coat may be applied if required, allowing a 5 to 10 minute dry time between coats under normal conditions; the time may be extended under cooler conditions.

Heavy coats of acrylic enamel should be avoided, as this could affect through-dry and the appearance of the paint film. The finish should be allowed to set up before removing the vehicle from the spray booth. For the best film performance the finish should be allowed to air-dry overnight indoors or to bake 20 to 30 minutes at 140 to 160°F (60 to 71°C). The masking tape should be removed as soon as the clear coat is touch-dry or after baking, to avoid film pulling away from the edges. (See Fig. 19-34.)

If the finish has to be repaired, allow 24 hours of drying time. To minimize feather-edge lifting, apply the repair primer, color, and the clear coat carefully, using faster solvents and light dry coats. All necessary steps to clean and prepare the area must be followed, as well as using the proper materials (Fig. 19-32).

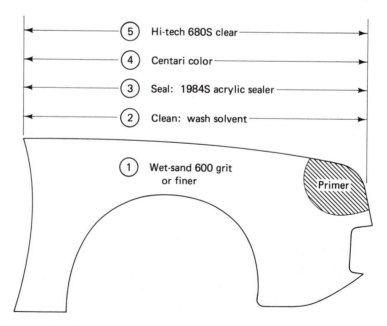

FIGURE 19-32 Schematic of fender with steps 1 to 5. (Courtesy of Du Pont Canada Inc.)

If the clear coat must be blended into the original panel, 2 parts base coat thinner to 1 part activated clear must be used. With an air pressure of 35 to 40 psi (245 to 275 kPa) at the gun, blend the area carefully into adjacent areas. This should be allowed to dry overnight and the blend should be carefully compounded with fine polishing compound so as not to cut through. If fisheye eliminator is required, it should be used very sparingly.

Acrylic Lacquer

With the change in technology, factory finishes (OEM) are glamorous and much more durable than ever, due to the introduction of the lacquer base/clear coat system. The paint manufacturers have introduced materials that can be used in body shops (Fig. 19-33).

FIGURE 19-33 Materials required to repair base coat/clear coat.

In the acrylic lacquer system a concentrated acrylic color with special thinners, and urethane clears with its activator and flow reducer, have been introduced. This material is not hard to work with as long as instructions are followed.

The preparation of the area is the same as usual for lacquer except that the final sanding should be done with No. 600 grit or finer sandpaper. For the newer finishes and waterborne acrylic enamel a midcoat adhesion promoter must be used—on (OEM) factory acrylic enamel on the complete panel, or in a blend area if the panel has to be blended in.

The sealer is used on older finishes but should never be used together with 222S. Then the base coat lacquer is stirred thoroughly and thinned with the appropriate medium. Coats are applied to a visual hiding and mottle-free appearance using 40 to 45 psi (275 to 310 kPa) at the gun and allowing sufficient dry time between coats.

The film buildup should be kept to a minimum and heavy wet coats of base color should be avoided, as such coats could affect the final color and film appearance. The color coats should be tack-wiped between coats, and if necessary a solid ground coat should be used for transparent base coat colors.

The final color should not be overthinned, as it could affect the color match and the metallic orientation or color effect. The final base coat color must not be sanded prior to clear-coating. Under normal shop drying conditions, allow the base coat color to dry for about 15 minutes before clear-coating with the clear. The urethane clear is activated according to the manufacturer's directions, in this case 1 part activator is slowly added to 4 parts clear while it is being mixed. No more material should be mixed than will be needed in a 1-hour period.

Under most circumstances no further reduction will be necessary, but if additional flow is required when refinishing large surfaces or in temperatures above 75°F (24°C), up to 5 ounces of flow reducer can be added per activated quart can or liter of clear.

The spraying viscosity of the clear should be between 17 and 19 seconds in the same cup. The pot life of the mixture may vary from 2 to 4 hours depending on the shop working temperature. It should be used within 1 hour after mixing and should always be strained before application.

The clear should be applied in two medium-wet coats at 55 to 60 psi (380 to 420 kPa) of pressure at the gun and can be followed with a third medium-wet coat if it is required. A 5 to 10 minute dry time between coats should be allowed under normal conditions; in a cool shop, extend the dry time.

To ensure a proper cure, the temperature of the surface to be refinished should be at least 65 to 70°F (18 to 21°C). The finish should be allowed to set up before removing the vehicle from the spray booth. The masking tape is removed as soon as the clear is touch dry or after baking, to avoid the film pulling away from the edges. It should be allowed to air-dry overnight indoors or baked 20 to 30 minutes at 140 to 160°F (60 to 71°C).

Figure 19-34 shows a step-by-step procedure to repair a base coat/clear coat if it needs to be repaired.

It must be remembered that after the area is compounded, it must be washed with a wash solvent and then tack-wiped. If the clear must be blended into the area beyond the repair area, it should be compounded and then washed with a wash solvent.

To blend the clear, add 2 parts base coat thinner to 1 part activated clear, with air pressure set at 35 to 40 psi (245 to 275 kPa) at the gun. Blend out over the prepared area using light, thin coats. Thinner alone should not be applied to the blend area. The blend area should be left to dry overnight before compounding very carefully to prevent cutting through the clear.

In the case of two-toning, apply all colors first, then double mask the required area to prevent penetration of the solvents through to the finish. The area is then unmasked and the colors are tack-wiped; then the clear is applied over the required areas.

A vehicle that has been refinished completely, or even if only a fender has

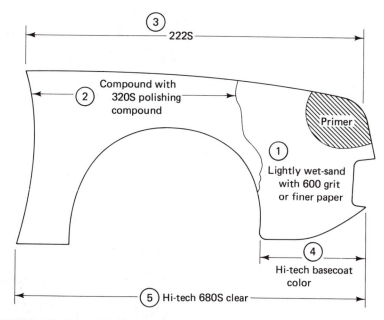

FIGURE 19-34 Basic steps for repair of base coat/clear coat. (Courtesy Du Pont Canada Inc.)

been refinished, should be cleaned thoroughly inside and out. A vacuum cleaner can be used to clean the inside of the body and the trunk. Windows and chrome should be cleaned of all overspray and dust. If necessary, the tires should also be refreshed with tire dressing.

These steps will create a favorable impression with any customer, which will mean repeat business if all aspects of the job are done properly.

UNIT 19-12: TROUBLESHOOTING AND PAINT FAILURES

The purpose of this section is to acquaint the new painter with paint failures so that he can recognize the causes and correct them.

Cracking. Fine, minute cracks in the finish usually appear only on the surface of the paint film. This condition is generally caused by too heavy a film of lacquer top coat or by sudden temperature changes. The surface has to be sanded and refinished (Fig. 19-35).

Shrinking and splitting. This new condition is caused by the contraction and cracking of the material. Shrinking and splitting is caused by applying material

FIGURE 19-35 (Courtesy of C.I.L. of Canada, Ltd.)

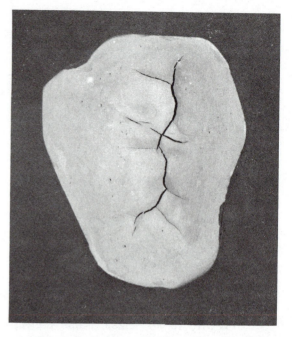

FIGURE 19-36 Shrinking and splitting of putty. (Courtesy of C.I.L. of Canada, Ltd.)

in heavy coats or insufficient dry time between coats. The putty must be removed in the affected area and applied as directed (Fig. 19-36).

Blistering. This condition is caused by oil or moisture in spray lines or temperature variations between shop materials and surface to be painted or by high humidity conditions. To repair the area, remove the blisters and sand down to the metal. Treat the metal, prime, and top coat (Fig. 19-37).

Cratering and crawling. Surface blemishes in a freshly painted surface where the paint has receded from small areas are usually found in the form of small round patches. This condition is caused by oil or moisture in spray lines or silicone contamination from products used in some surface operations. To repair on freshly painted surfaces, wash off with solvent, clean thoroughly, and repaint. If the surface dries before condition is noted, sand and refinish damaged areas (Fig. 19-38).

Fisheyes. Small craters on the finished surface, sometimes as large as a dime and circled by a noticeable ring are caused by silicone contamination on the surface. To repair, wash off while paint is still wet; clean thoroughly and repaint (Fig. 19-39).

Pinholing. Breaks in a dry paint film no larger than the head of a pin, exposing the surface underneath, are caused by oil or moisture in equipment or

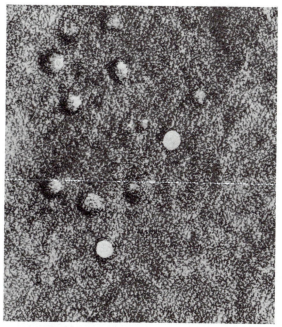

FIGURE 19-37 Blistering. (Courtesy of C.I.L. of Canada, Ltd.)

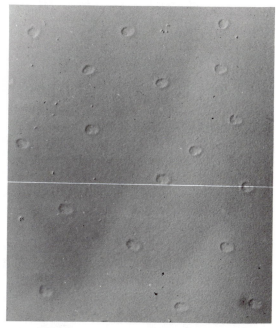

FIGURE 19-38 Cratering and crawling. (Courtesy of C.I.L. of Canada, Ltd.)

FIGURE 19-39 Fisheyes. (Courtesy of C.I.L. of Canada, Ltd.)

FIGURE 19-40 Pinholing. (Courtesy of C.I.L. of Canada, Ltd.)

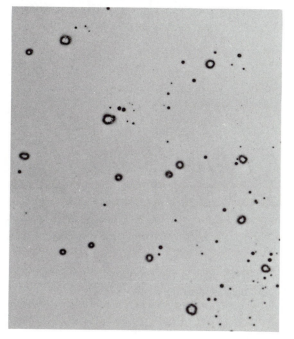

material applied to a cold surface or by using too fast an evaporating solvent, causing surface dry or incorrect reduction. To repair, sand the damaged area and refinish (Fig. 19-40).

Runs and sags. A paint film that has drooped under its own weight and displays a thick edge or wrinkle at the lower part is caused by too heavy an application of paint or paint reduced too much. To repair, wash off with solvent before the material dries and repaint. Should the surface dry, sand and refinish (Fig. 19-41).

Wrinkling. The buckling of a paint film at its surface causes a shriveled appearance and occurs when the film is dry on the surface but remains soft underneath. This is caused by applying material in heavy coats, particularly in hot, humid weather, or by not adding retarder before force-drying. To repair, allow to dry thoroughly, sand the affected areas to remove surface wrinkles, and refinish (Fig. 19-42).

Sand-scratch swelling. *Sand-scratch* swelling is an exaggerated reproduction of sanding marks in the underlying finish of the new top coat. The marks are distorted or swollen and usually occur over the original finish. They rarely appear on primed areas. They are also caused by solvent penetration into underlying

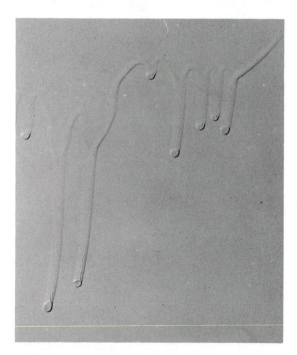

FIGURE 19-41 Runs and sags. (Courtesy of C.I.L. of Canada, Ltd.)

FIGURE 19-42 Wrinkling. (Courtesy of C.I.L. of Canada, Ltd.)

surface. Sand-scratch swellings are caused by improper cleaning, using too coarse a grade of sandpaper, or using gasoline for wet sanding. To repair, allow to cure thoroughly, wet-sand with No. 400 (10/0) paper. Apply one or two wet coats of sealer and respray with top coat (Fig. 19-43).

Rub-through. Burning of lacquer finishes through the primer during compounding operation is caused by not applying enough material to allow proper compounding or excessive rubbing and compounding. To repair, sand the affected areas and repaint (Fig. 19-44).

Bleeding. Bleeding is the migration of soluble dyes of pigments from an old finish into a newly applied finish as a result of solvent action. This condition is caused by failing to test the old surface to determine if it is a bleeding color. To repair, use of a bleeder sealer will sometimes be sufficient to overcome the problem. In most cases, however, it is necessary to remove the paint in the affected area and resume refinishing procedures (Fig. 19-45).

Hand or finger prints. Hand or finger marks appearing in the finish are caused by touching or wiping the surface with bare hands prior to finishing. Avoid contacting the surface once it has been prepared for painting. To repair, remove the finish and repaint (Fig. 19-46).

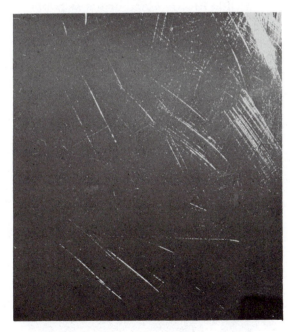

FIGURE 19-43 Sand-scratch swelling. (Courtesy of C.I.L. of Canada, Ltd.)

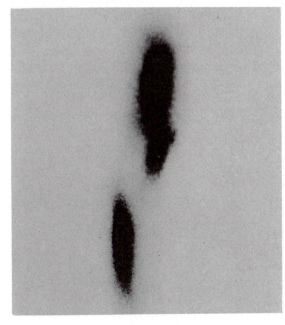

FIGURE 19-44 Rub-through. (Courtesy of C.I.L. of Canada, Ltd.)

FIGURE 19-45 Bleeding. (Courtesy of C.I.L. of Canada, Ltd.)

FIGURE 19-46 Hand or finger prints. (Courtesy of C.I.L. of Canada, Ltd.)

FIGURE 19-47 Rain or water spotting. (Courtesy of C.I.L. of Canada, Ltd.)

FIGURE 19-48 Corrosion (rust). (Courtesy of C.I.L. of Canada, Ltd.)

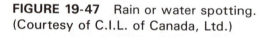

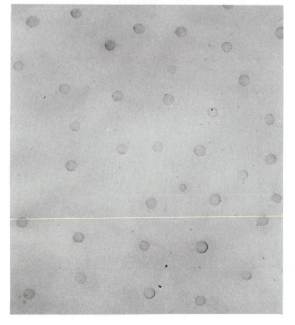

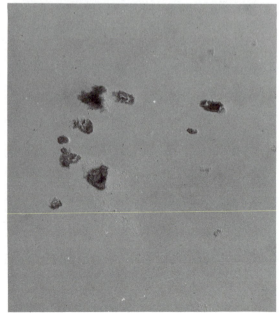

Rain or water spotting. Small circular imprints in finish that are low in gloss are caused by premature exposure of the freshly painted vehicle to rain or sunshine or washing the vehicle too soon after applying paint. To repair, allow to dry, wet-sand, and refinish (Fig. 19-47).

Corrosion. Corrosion on metal surfaces is caused by improper cleaning and treatment of metal, by touching metal with bare hands after cleaning, or by moisture and chemicals attacking the metal through breaks in the film. This results in subsequent blistering or peeling. To repair, remove the paint to the bare metal, clean thoroughly, and repaint. For more information, check a refinisher's manual (Fig. 19-48).

QUESTIONS

19-1 What is the main reason for paint failures?

19-2 What steps can be used to help determine the condition of the surface to be refinished?

19-3 What type of product is used to clean the surface to be painted? What method is used?

19-4 What is used on bare metal to etch it before paint is applied to it? How should it be used?

19-5 What is the reason that primer or primer surfacer should be applied on the bare metal as soon as possible? How should it be applied?

19-6 What is used to fill slight imperfections?

19-7 What is the reason that sealers are used?

19-8 What product is used to reduce automotive enamels: thinners, reducers, or solvent?

19-9 How long does it take for enamel to dry to be dust free: 5 minutes, 30 minutes, or 50 minutes?

19-10 What system is used to spray metallic colors, and how far is the gun held for the last coat?

19-11 How can the color in metallics be changed?

19-12 How much air pressure is used to spray acrylic lacquer?

19-13 What methods can be used to remove the orange peel effect on acrylic lacquer finishes after spraying to obtain a high gloss?

19-14   Is it necessary to wash an area that has been polished with a polishing compound with a wax and polish remover before painting? Why?

19-15   What causes blistering in a paint job?

19-16   What causes fisheyes in a paint job? How can it be overcome?

19-17   What causes sand-scratch swelling? What can be done to overcome it?

19-18   How many guns are used to spray when using the modified conventional method to repair acrylic lacquer?

19-19   The modified conventional method is used to repair what type of area?

19-20   How long should it take for the thinner to flash-off in using the metallic color control method?

19-21   Why is it necessary to use the tack rag so often when using the metallic color control method?

19-22   Describe the method used to determine if a trim part is made from ABS plastic or polypropylene.

19-23   What is the purpose of adding a catalyst to enamels?

19-24   If a catalyst is used, how long must acrylic enamel dry before it can be taped?

19-25   Describe how an acrylic enamel base coat/clear coat can be repaired using an acrylic enamel base coat/clear coat system.

19-26   Describe how an acrylic lacquer base coat/clear coat can be repaired using an acrylic lacquer base coat/clear coat system.

19-27   Describe how an acrylic lacquer base coat/clear coat system can be repaired using an acrylic lacquer base coat/clear coat system.

19-28   Describe how to spot repair a damaged acrylic lacquer base coat/clear coat area on the front part of the fender.

20

Body and Trim Care

UNIT 20-1: BODY SEALING AND MAINTENANCE

Car owners will complain at times about dust and water leaks. To the average person, correcting these problems seems routine, but they can often prove to be time-consuming projects.

It is usually easy to find out where the water or dust comes inside the body, but sometimes it is difficult to discover where the water and dust enters the body. When the area is located, it is normally not too hard to repair if the proper products are used.

When car owners and repairmen talk about body sealing, they usually refer to the rubber seals around the windshield or rear window; the weather stripping around doors, deck lids, and tail gates; or the grommets, boots, and molded plugs used in many areas of the body.

These areas come to mind first because they are the areas that are more prone to leaking. But it must be remembered that the body of a vehicle is built from many parts that are welded together. These parts, when welded together, form many seams that have to be sealed with sealing compounds. This sealing of these parts usually makes the shell of the body water and dust free. This sealing generally lasts the life of the vehicle; but if it should break down, then it has to be resealed.

The side windows cannot be sealed so tight as the windshield because they have to move up and down. The water enters at the outside bottom edge of the glass at the belt weatherstrip, and it drops to the bottom of the door or body panel. The bottom of these panels are provided with special holes to let the water out.

Since some of the water will deflect toward the inside panels, a plastic water shield is installed to prevent the water from damaging the inside trim panels. These water shields must always be replaced, so that the water will drain properly out of the panel.

Car body sealing can be handled by two different procedures: one for water and dust leaks and the other for wind noise leaks. Sometimes, however, wind noises will be corrected when a dust or water leak is corrected.

When checking for wind noises, the car is either test-driven to put it under the conditions causing the noise or the car body can be pressurized while standing still. When the leak is caused by a body or weather strip leak, either method can be used. If air turbulence is the source of the noise, then the only way to locate the noise is to test-drive the vehicle.

Water and Dust Leak Testing

Before any testing is done, the general area should be checked for things that are obviously wrong, like loose or torn weatherstrips, gaps or holes in body joints, or improperly fitted doors and windows. Water and dust leaks usually leave traces (Fig. 20-1). If the weatherstripping does not contact properly or if some floor plugs are loose, telltale traces of dust will be evident. If it is water

FIGURE 20-1 Check for traces of road splash. (Courtesy of Chrysler Canada Ltd.)

FIGURE 20-2 Weatherstrip makes even contact. (Courtesy of Chrysler Canada Ltd.)

that is leaking in, the upholstery will be wet or rust might show up at some body joints.

The first defect that must be corrected is the alignment of the doors. The weatherstrip has to be compressed slightly so that proper contact is made with the door frame (Fig. 20-2). The hinges and striker plate may have to be readjusted in order to achieve a proper fit. On hardtop models and convertibles, the windows must also make a good seal with the weatherstripping. In some cases, it is necessary to shim the weatherstripping with special stock shims to achieve a good seal between a door and the car body.

Water Leak Testing

Water testing is commonly done in an area like a wash rack, where the runoff will not cause a mess. An air hose should also be available to dry off with air the tested areas that must be repaired. Water testing can be used for finding dust and water leaks; some noise sources can also be traced by this method.

Only a small stream of water is required from the hose (Fig. 20-3). Never use a high pressure because the force of the stream will force water past good-sealing weatherstripping. Have another person in the car to check as the water test is started. He will be able to see where the water seeps through; the area should be dried and repaired before progressing further.

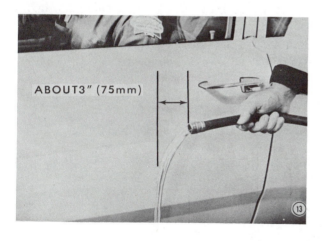

ABOUT 3" (75mm)

FIGURE 20-3 Adjust flow to get small stream. (Courtesy of Chrysler Canada Ltd.)

The test should always start at the bottom of the panel and gradually work up (Fig. 20-4). On some cars it is necessary to roll back the wind cord to watch where water might seep past the weatherstrip. The area of the leak should be marked with tape or chalk to facilitate the finding of the area after the door is opened.

FIGURE 20-4 Test low points first. (Courtesy of Chrysler Canada Ltd.)

If the weatherstripping is sealing the opening, water should then be run along the bottom of the window at the beltline weatherstripping. The trim panels should be checked for dampness, if it is damp. This is usually caused by the water shield not having been reinstalled properly or it could be torn or missing. The water shield should be installed so that the bottom edge is in the slot that is provided at the bottom and all sides and top edges glued to the panel (Fig. 20-5). The same test can be used for any area of the body. When doing deck lids, it is sometimes necessary to have somebody inside the trunk with a flashlight to notice where the water comes in (Figs. 20-6 and 20-7). The inside man should keep a careful check, especially at body joints or where moldings are installed.

The water test is used for any area of the body. It will be effective if done properly. It must be remembered that it is always started at the bottom of the

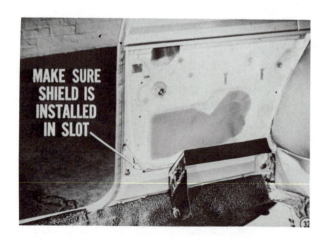

FIGURE 20-5 Flap directs water to drains. (Courtesy of Chrysler Canada Ltd.)

FIGURE 20-6   Use a light to spot leaks. (Courtesy of Chrysler Canada Ltd.)

FIGURE 20-7   Flow water around deck lid. (Courtesy of Chrysler Canada Ltd.)

panel and gradually moved toward the top. In some cases, it is necessary to remove the kick panels to find leaks in the front and side sections of the cowl, for much of the construction is double walled. The area in which the leak is occurring can be found and repaired. When the mats on the floor of the car become wet, the cause is generally water entering through a leak in the floor (Fig. 20-8). The seats and the floor mats will have to be removed. Because it is almost impossible to test the floor area with a water test, the best method is to look for traces of leaks from inside the body. The seams and plugs should be inspected carefully for traces of dust and water leaks. If the leak does not come from the floor, then it will be necessary to check all areas around the body with a water test.

LOOK FOR TRACES OF LEAKS

FIGURE 20-8 Check floor and wheelhousing seams. (Courtesy of Chrysler Canada Ltd.)

Chalk Testing

Another method to check weatherstrip leaks is by using a soft chalk. Open the door and rub some soft carpenter's chalk on the weatherstripping sealing surface; then close the door. The door is then opened; a line of chalk should be visible on the body surface that was contacted by the weatherstrip edge in an unbroken continuous line if the seal is okay.

When not enough chalk is transferred, use some body wax on the body surface that comes in contact with the weatherstrip. The wax will pick up the chalk and this will leave a distinct imprint. If rechalking is necessary, the wax that has been transferred to the weatherstrip will have to be removed. On light-colored cars, use a dark chalk; on dark-colored cars, use a white chalk. If the chalk test shows up some low areas on the body surface, it will be necessary to build up these areas to provide proper contact with the weatherstripping. The chalk test will also show high spots on the contact surface with the weatherstrip. These high spots have to be finished smooth and all areas that have been reworked must be refinished (Fig. 20-9). If some sizable areas show no contact, it will be necessary to move or shim the weatherstrip until it provides contact.

On hardtop models, the chalk test may not be too successful; the paper test is used instead. A flexible strip of paper of about 2 in. (51 mm) wide should be used. Clamp the paper in between the glass and weatherstrip in several places. There should be a slight resistance when the paper is pulled out; if there is none, a possible leaking area must be repaired (Fig. 20-10). This would mean that the front vent wing assembly and door glass have to be realigned to obtain a proper fit. The chalk test can be used for deck lids and tailgates, but it must be remembered that good alignment is the requisite to any body sealing job.

FIGURE 20-9   Level low spots with plastic solder. (Courtesy of Chrysler Canada Ltd.)

FIGURE 20-10   Pull-out should have slight resistance. (Courtesy of Chrysler Canada Ltd.)

Powder Testing

White powder may also be used to check for leaks. All that is needed is white powder and a syringe to blow the powder around the door, deck lid, and tailgate. The syringe should not be squeezed too hard because all that is required is a light amount of powder (Fig. 20-11). If the test reveals a slight amount of powder inside the weatherstrip, or on its contact surface, the weatherstrip is not sealing properly and it will be necessary to align the panel to provide a good seal (Fig. 20-12).

FIGURE 20-11   Blow in powder with syringe. (Courtesy of Chrysler Canada Ltd.)

FIGURE 20-12 Powder inside seal shows leak point. (Courtesy of Chrysler Canada Ltd.)

FIGURE 20-13 Do not leave a mess after testing. (Courtesy of Chrysler Canada Ltd.)

The powder test will sometimes show up conditions that cause leakage, conditions not shown by chalk or water test. After the job has been completed, always clean the vehicle (Fig. 20-13).

Wind Noise Leak Testing

Wind noises will not cause the mess and damage that a water or dust leak will cause. A wind noise can be nerve-wracking, and it can also cause a cold draft. Today's cars are a lot quieter than cars built 10 years ago. If there is a wind noise, it will disturb the customer and he will want it repaired.

Surprisingly, most wind noises are caused by air leaking out of the vehicle. If the windows are closed and the cowl vents are open, the forward motion of the vehicle will pressurize the interior of the body. The air actually enters the car faster than it can leave (Fig. 20-14). On some hardtop models, the top of the windows lose contact with the weatherstrip at high speed because of the pressure built up inside the body (Fig. 20-15). Pressurizing the inside of the body will not cause any trouble if the weatherstripping does a good job of sealing the body. If an area does not have good contact and lets the air out of it, however, it may cause an objectionable noise. Oncoming air can also create noises if the sealing of the chamber is poor; this condition will also cause water and dust leaks.

There is another kind of wind noise, one caused outside the car by air turbulence. This condition results from loose moldings, protruding moldings, and gaps between moldings and rubber seals. Masking tape can be used to close

FIGURE 20-14 Forward motion pressurizes interior. (Courtesy of Chrysler Canada Ltd.)

FIGURE 20-15 Pressure can force windows outward. (Courtesy of Chrysler Canada Ltd.)

off suspected areas or to change their shape when the test is made to find the source of the noise.

As with water and dust testing, check door and glass alignment or any suspected area first. The next step is a road test, preferably on a quiet smooth road where the car can be driven at cruising speed. Close the doors and windows, shut off blower fan and radio, and open ventilation ducts to pressurize the body while driving.

Drive the car up to a cruising speed and listen for noise from outgoing air; this noise will vary with the speed of the car. The ventilation ducts should be closed and the test continued; if the noise is still present, it is caused by air coming into the car. The noise will be louder on the windy side of the car and a draft of air might even be felt. If closing and opening the ventilation ducts have no effect on the noise, then the cause is outside the car and may be hard to find.

WIND NOISE AREAS

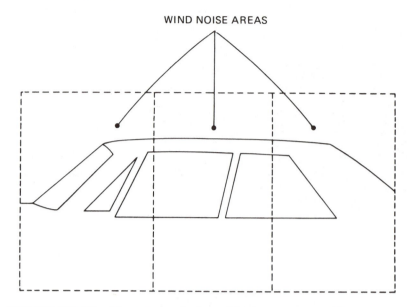

FIGURE 20-16 Most noise is found in upper areas. (Courtesy of Chrysler Canada Ltd.)

Most causes of wind noises are found in the upper area of the body down to approximately a foot below the beltline (Fig. 20-16). The area of the car that seems to cause most wind noises is the vent wing assembly or the front part of the top of the front door. Place some mastic sealer on the door frame at the front from the top to the bottom of the window (Fig. 20-17). This step will seal that part of the door completely from the outside when the door will be closed. Masking tape should be used to seal the vent assembly completely and also the

FIGURE 20-17 Block off test area with mastic. (Courtesy of Chrysler Canada Ltd.)

space between the door and door pillar (Fig. 20-18). The car should then be test-driven; if the noise is gone, keep the car at the same speed and remove the tape at the pillar slowly. If the noise comes back, the source should be close by. Mark the area with chalk so that the spot will be easy to find when the car is back in the shop. If no wind noise is noticed after the tape is removed from the pillar, remove the tape slowly from the vent wing. As soon as the noise is heard, the source of it is close (Fig. 20-19). Another method of listening for wind noise is to use a rubber hose of a small diameter, moving the free end along the suspected area while listening for the sound at the other end (Fig. 20-20).

FIGURE 20-18 Seal pillar and vent with tape. (Courtesy of Chrysler Canada Ltd.)

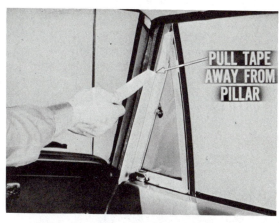

FIGURE 20-19 Remove pillar seal first. (Courtesy of Chrylster Canada Ltd.)

FIGURE 20-20 Use hose to listen for leaks. (Courtesy of Chrysler Canada Ltd.)

Body Sealing Tips

Common sense and the application of testing procedures will help to find most body leaks. With experience, however, the repairman can repair leaks that show up in certain conditions without bothering to test them. Visual inspection is the first step at all times, but the source of the trouble may not be so obvious as a loose weather strip or an open hole.

If the headlining is wet on the sides, look for pinholes in the drip rail. The pinhole is usually caused by an air bubble under the sealer. The bubble finally breaks and the holes let water enter inside the body (Fig. 20-21). Windshield and rear window leaks will usually necessitate removal of the moldings. The rubber seal around the glass should be pried away with a thin, blunt tool to break any existing bond remaining (Fig. 20-22). The rubber should then be blown clean and dry with air. A good-quality windshield sealer should then be used between the rubber and glass. The rubber should then be pressed to the glass so that a good bond is achieved; the moldings are then reinstalled. Auto body sealer is used to embed windshield and back window rubber in the grooves. It is also used for sealing retaining clips for moldings.

FIGURE 20-21 Seal voids or pinholes closed. (Courtesy of Chrysler Canada Ltd.)

On a body that has the windshield glass cemented to the body, it is necessary to remove the moldings to repair the leaking area. A coating of semiliquid cement should be applied on the area after it has been cleaned and dried thoroughly. The cement should be allowed to set before water-testing the area; if no other leaks are found, the moldings should be reinstalled.

Weatherstripping on doors or deck lids will sometimes come loose and must be repaired in order to provide a good seal. Clean the weatherstrip and body with lacquer thinner; then apply a thin even coat to both surfaces (Fig.

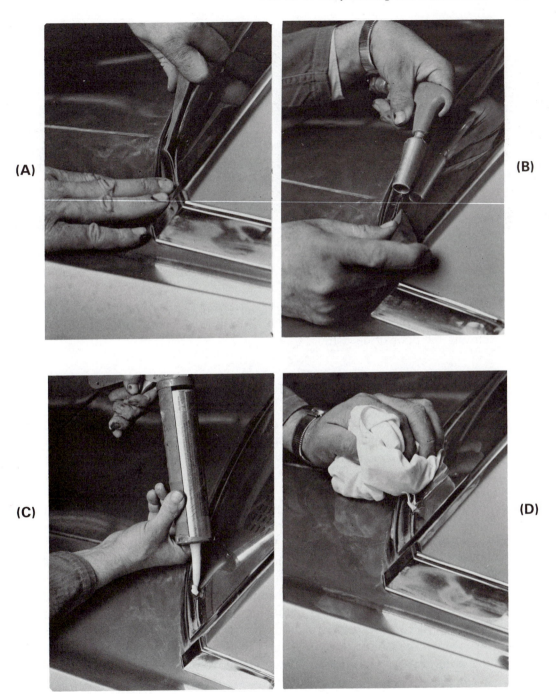

(A)

(B)

(C)

(D)

FIGURE 20-22

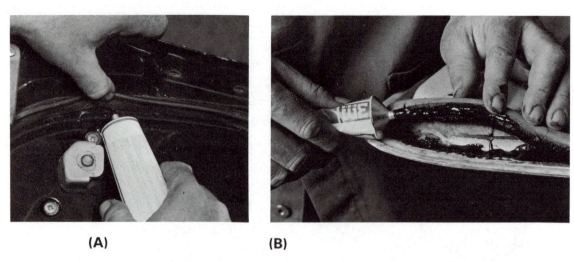

(A)   (B)

FIGURE 20-23

20-23). Bind them firmly at once, but allow at least 3 hours of drying time before closing the door or deck lid.

UNIT 20-2: ELIMINATION OF RATTLES

Rattles and squeaks are normally caused by loose or rubbing sheet metal, loose bolts and screws, and loose or improperly adjusted bumpers, hoods, and doors. The shock-absorber mounting bolts could be loose or the exhaust system could have a broken mount. The jack, tire, or any article in the trunk can be responsible if it is not properly held down.

The customer may think that the noise comes from the front end of the car, when actually it is caused by something in the back. This effect is caused by the sound traveling through the body. It is only through a careful examination and a test drive of the vehicle that the noise can be located. Once the area has been located, necessary repairs or adjustments are then carried out.

Most of the repairs consist of readjustment of parts, welding of broken parts, replacement of parts, and the tightening of bolts. A rubber mallet can also be used to strike the suspected parts or area from which the noise is emitted. No damage will be caused as long as the parts being struck are hit on an edge. The jolt from the blow will cause the metal to move or vibrate, giving out a rattle or a squeak.

The hood should be checked for proper alignment at the front and back; any paint knocked off an edge is suspected of hitting another edge. The hood latch pin should be checked for alignment and fit; any missing rubber bumpers should be replaced. Flutter of the back of the hood is usually caused by the hood not fitting tightly on the back seal; readjust hood to fit. The grille, moldings, wheelhousing, and bumper brackets should be checked for tightness.

The body has many areas that can cause rattles and squeaks, such as the dash, steering column, seat tracks, lazyback, doors, and the hardware inside them. The weatherstripping can sometimes cause squeaks when it becomes too dry; lubricate with a silicone lubricant. Door hinges need to have lubricant, otherwise they will rust in the linkage and jam. The body bolts might be loose, thus causing the body to shift, or they may not be shimmed properly.

A careful examination, plus good workmanship in the repairs required, is the best way to remove rattles.

Cleaning the Exterior

The outside of a vehicle should be washed frequently to remove the accumulation of dust, dirt, and road salt. The finish should never be wiped dry because the dust that accumulates on the rag will act like sandpaper to scratch the paint. The finish should be washed with clear water, not with the harsh detergents used by many of the car wash stations. These actually tend to diminish the gloss on the paint.

A good polish can be used to shine the finish after washing, a step that will help the finish to shed dirt. Remember that a vehicle should be washed and polished in the shade rather than in the sunlight.

Moldings and bumpers are usually chrome-plated to preserve them, but many moldings today are made of aluminum and even plastic. These bright surfaces should not be rubbed or cleaned with a material that is too abrasive, thereby causing them to deteriorate. A preservative should be put on the bumpers to help these particular parts to withstand road salts and corrosion.

UNIT 20-3: CLEANING OF UPHOLSTERY

Approximately four different types of trim materials are used in automotive bodies. The four most widely used materials are (1) polyurethane foam, (2) coated fabrics (vinyl or nylon), (3) genuine leather, and (4) plain fabrics such as broadcloth or patterned fabrics that are made from natural or synthetic fibers, such as nylon or rayon.

An accumulation of dust and dirt particles should never be allowed to remain on upholstery; it should be removed frequently. A whisk broom or vacuum cleaner is used, except on fabrics having raised tapestry patterns where a whisk broom would damage the fine threads. Flocked headliners are cleaned with a whisk broom and volatile cleaners. Detergents will leave rings.

Before any attempt is made to remove spots or stains from upholstery fabrics, the age and nature of the stain, as well as the effect the stain-removing agents may have on the color and general appearance of the fabric, must be determined as accurately as possible.

To obtain the best results, stains should be removed as soon as possible from the upholstery. If they are allowed to stand for some time, they will become set and removal will be more difficult. The three types of cleaners commonly used are volatile cleaners (colorless liquids), detergents, and neutral soaps (non-alkaline). Volatile cleaners have a great solvent power to dissolve oil, grease, and road grime. Detergents will generally loosen stains satisfactorily; however, the use of an improper type of detergent may damage the color or the finish of fabrics.

Cleaning Fabrics with Volatile Cleaners

Care should be taken not to use too much solvent and to apply it only with clean cloths. It is the solvent that does the work—so only a minimum of pressure is applied. All loose particles of dirt and soil should be brushed away; then dampen a clean cloth with a volatile cleaner. Open the cloth and allow a portion of the cleaner to evaporate so that the cloth is just slightly damp.

With very light pressure and a circular motion, rub the stained area, starting at the outer edge and working toward the center until the entire area has been covered. Change to a clean portion of the cloth every few strokes. Next, use a clean white blotter to blot stained area to remove any excess cleaner. Change to a new portion of the blotter each time stained area is blotted. The blotting action should be repeated until no stain is transferred to the blotter surface.

Before proceeding, wait several minutes to allow most of the volatile cleaner to evaporate, for the stained area should be saturated. This step will avoid the danger of the cleaner penetrating to the padding under the upholstery. Certain cleaners will deteriorate sponge rubber, which is often used in padding. If part of the spot remains, work the area again until it has been satisfactorily removed. If a ring should form on the fabric when removing a stain, the entire area of the trim assembly should be cleaned and allowed to dry completely before using.

Some volatile cleaners are toxic and harmful; hence, safety precautions should be used. Always use them in a well-ventilated area. Avoid prolonged or repeated breathing of vapors from cleaner or prolonged and repeated contact with the skin. Always keep cleaners away from the eyes and mouth. Some cleaners are flammable, and every precaution should be taken in handling them. Manufacturer's directions must always be followed explicitly.

Cleaning Fabrics with Detergents

Make a solution of detergent in lukewarm water, working up thick, frothy suds. With a clean cloth or sponge, dampened with lukewarm water, apply suds only to the surface of the upholstery, using light to medium pressure. Repeat several times, applying more suds with a clean portion of the cloth or sponge. With a second clean cloth, dampened with lukewarm water, rub over the area with medium pressure to remove excess detergent and loose material.

With a clean, dry cloth, wipe off all excess moisture; a vacuum may also be used. The upholstery is allowed to dry partially; then, if necessary, repeat the preceding treatment to remove the stain. When the upholstery is satisfactorily cleaned, allow it to dry completely before using.

Precaution for Cleaning Fabrics

Solutions containing water are not recommended for general cleaning of broadcloth. Water has great destructive powers on the high face or high gloss finish of broadcloth, causing the nap to curl and roughen to such an extent that the finish is destroyed or made very unsightly. In some cases where it is necessary to use a solution containing water to remove a stain, however, the resultant disturbance to the finish of the material may be preferable to the stain.

Do not use a cleaning solvent such as colored gasoline or one containing tetraethyllead or acetone, lacquer thinners, enamel reducers, or nail polish removers. Do not use laundry soaps, bleaches, or reducing agents like chloride of lime, Javelle water, hydrogen peroxide, sodium hydrosulfite, potassium permanganate, chlorine or chlorine water, sulfurous acid (sulfur dioxide), or sodium thiosulfate (photographer's hypo). The use of these agents tends to weaken fabric and to change its color. Too much cleaning fluid should not be used as some interior trim assemblies are padded with rubber and volatile cleaners are generally solvents for rubber. The application of too much cleaner may destroy these rubber pads or leave a solvent ring.

Cleaning Genuine Leather and Coated Fabrics

Care of genuine leather and coated fabrics is relatively easy but is an important matter. The surface should be wiped occasionally with a dry cloth, and whenever dirt accumulates the following cleaning instructions should be used. Lukewarm water and a neutral soap are used. The thick suds are applied to the surface with a piece of gauze or cheesecloth. The area is wiped with a damp cloth to remove the residue of the soap; it should then be wiped dry with a soft cloth.

Polishes and cleaners used for autobody finishes, volatile cleaners, furniture polishes, oils, varnishes, or household cleaning and bleaching agents should never be used on these fabrics.

Cleaning Headlining Material

Normal soilage such as dirt and fingerprints can be removed with a cleaning solution of approximately 2 oz (58 g) of white detergent powder mixed in a gallon (4 liters) of water. Immerse a clean cellulose sponge in cleaning solution. Wring the sponge out thoroughly, leaving suds only; then clean soiled area carefully. Rinse off the cleaned area with sponge and clean water—*do not soak* the cleaned area.

Soilage such as cements, sealers, and grease can be removed by first cleaning the soiled area with a detergent solution as described above—*do not rinse*. Leaving suds on the soiled area, clean area with a clean cloth that has been dipped in a good volatile upholstery cleaner and thoroughly wrung out (naphtha cleaner is recommended). Then clean soiled area again with detergent suds and rinse as described earlier.

Cleaning Folding Top and Fabric Roof Cover Material

The top should be washed frequently with neutral soap suds, lukewarm water, and a brush with soft bristles. Rinse top with sufficient quantities of clear water to remove all traces of soap.

Care must be taken to keep the soaps and cleaners from running onto the body finish, for they may cause streaks if allowed to run down and dry.

If the top requires additional cleaning after using soap and water, a mild foaming cleanser can be used. Rinse the whole top with water; then apply a mild foaming-type cleanser to the entire top. Scrub with a small, soft bristle brush, adding water as necessary until the cleanser foams to a soapy consistency. Remove the first accumulated soilage with a cloth or sponge before it can be ground into the top material. Apply additional cleanser to the area and scrub until the top is clean. After the entire top has been cleaned, rinse the top generously with clear water to remove all traces of cleanser. If desired, the top can be supported from the underside during the scrubbing operations.

After cleaning a convertible top, always be sure the top is thoroughly dry before it is lowered. Lowering the top while it is still wet or damp may cause mildew and unsightly wrinkles.

Do not use volatile cleansers or household bleaching agents on the top material.

Volatile cleaners may be used in certain instances when stubborn sealer or cement stains are encountered. *Extreme caution* must be exercised, however, for damage to the fabric finish may result.

Cleaning Floor Carpets

Thoroughly brush or vacuum the floor carpet. In many instances, the floor carpet may require no further cleaning. If the carpet is extremely soiled, remove it from the car and thoroughly vacuum to remove loose dirt. Then, with a foaming-type upholstery cleaner, clean approximately 1 sq ft (0.9 sq m) of carpet at a time. After each area is cleaned, remove as much of the cleaner as possible with a vacuum cleaner. After cleaning the carpet, use an air hose to "fluff" the carpet pile; then dry the carpet. After the carpet is completely dried, use an air hose to fluff the carpet pile again.

If not extremely soiled, the carpet may be cleaned in the car by applying a sparing amount of foaming-type upholstery cleaner with a brush.

If oil or grease spots are still present on the carpet, they may be removed by using the volatile cleaner. The cleaner must be used very sparingly, however, for it may have a tendency to remove some of the dye coloring.

Removal of Specific Stains from Automotive Upholstery
(Courtesy General Motors of Canada, Ltd.)

Some types of stains and soilage, including blood, ink, and chewing gum, require special treatment. For these and other stains, specific instructions are outlined in succeeding paragraphs. It must be expected, particularly where water treatment is specified, that discoloration and finish disturbance may occur. In some cases, the fabric disturbance may be preferable to the stain itself. By following the procedures outlined with normal care and caution, reasonably satisfactory results can be expected.

Blood

Do not use hot water or soap and water on bloodstains, for they will set the stain, thereby making its removal practically impossible. Rub the stain with a clean cloth saturated with cold water until no more of the stain will come out. Care must be taken so that clean portions of cloth are used for rubbing the stain.

This treatment should remove all the stain. If it does not, apply a small amount of household ammonia water to the stain with a cloth or brush. After a lapse of about 1 minute, continue to rub the stain with a clean cloth dipped in clear water.

If the stain remains after the use of water and ammonia, a thick paste of cornstarch and cold water may be applied to the stained area. Allow the paste to remain until it has dried and absorbed the stain. Then pick off the dry starch. Brush the surface to remove starch particles that remain. Several applications of starch paste may be necessary for bad stains.

Candy

Candy stains, other than candy containing chocolate, can be removed by rubbing the affected area with a cloth soaked with very hot water. If the stain is not completely removed, rub area lightly (after drying) with a cloth wet with volatile cleaner. This step will usually remove the stain.

Candy stains resulting from cream and fruit-filled chocolates can be removed more easily by rubbing with a cloth soaked in lukewarm soapsuds (mild neutral soap) and scraping while wet with a dull knife. This treatment is followed with a rinsing by rubbing the spot with a cloth dipped in cold water.

Stains resulting from chocolate or milk chocolate can be removed by rubbing the stain with a cloth wet with lukewarm water. After the spot is dry, rub it lightly with a cloth dipped in volatile cleaner. Using a clean white blotter, blot area to remove excess cleaner and chocolate stain. Repeat blotting action until stain is no longer transferred to surface blotter.

Chewing Gum

Harden the gum with an ice cube, and scrape off particles with a dull knife. If gum cannot be removed completely by this method, moisten it with a volatile cleaner and work it from the fabric with a dull knife while gum is still moist.

Fruit, Fruit Stains, Liquor, and Wine

Almost all fruit stains can be removed by treatment with very hot water. Wet the stain well by applying hot water to the spot with a clean cloth. Scrape all excess pulp, if present, off the fabric with a dull knife. Then rub vigorously with a cloth wet with very hot water. If the stain is very old or deep, it may be necessary to pour very hot water directly on the spot, following this treatment with the scraping and rubbing. Direct application of hot water to fabrics is not recommended for general use since discoloration may result.

If the foregoing treatments do not remove the stain, allow the fabric to dry thoroughly. Then rub lightly with a clean cloth dipped in a volatile cleaner. This is the only further treatment recommended.

Soap and water are not recommended, for they will probably set the stain and cause a permanent discoloration. Drying the fabric by means of heat (such as the use of an iron) is not recommended.

Grease and Oil

If grease has been spilled on the material, remove as much as possible by scraping with a dull knife or spatula before attempting further treatment.

Grease and oil stains may be removed by rubbing lightly with a clean cloth saturated with a volatile cleaner. Be sure that all motions are toward the center of the stained area, to decrease the possibility of spreading the stain. Use a clean white blotter and blot area to remove excess cleaner and loosened grease or oil. Repeat blotting action until the grease or oil stain is no longer transferred to blotter.

Ice Cream

The same procedure used in removing fruit stains is recommended for the removal of ice cream stains. If the stain is persistent, rubbing the spot with a cloth wet with warm soapsuds (mild neutral soap) may be used to some advantage after the initial treatment with hot water. This soap treatment should be followed with cold water. After this dries, rubbing lightly with a cloth wet with volatile cleaner will clear up the last of the stain by removing fatty or oily matter.

Nausea Stains

Sponge with a clean cloth, dipped in clear cold water. After most of the stain has been removed in this way, wash lightly with soap (mild neutral), using a clean cloth and lukewarm water. If odor persists, treat the area with a water–baking soda solution (1 teaspoon baking soda to 1 cup of tepid water). Then rub with another clean cloth dipped in cold water. If any of the stain remains after this treatment, gently rub clean with a cloth moistened with a volatile cleaner.

Shoe Polish

On types of shoe dressings containing starch, dextrin, or some water-soluble vehicle, allow the polish to dry; then brush the spot vigorously with a brush. This will probably be all the treatment necessary. If further treatment is required, however, moisten the spot with cold water; after it has dried, repeat the brushing operation.

Paste or wax-type shoe polishes may require the use of a volatile cleaner. Rub the stain gently with a cloth wet with a volatile cleaner until the polish is removed. Use a clean portion of the cloth for each rubbing operation and rub the stained area from outside to center. Blot the stained area to remove as much of the cleaner as possible.

Tar

Remove as much of the tar as possible with a dull knife. Moisten the spot lightly with a volatile cleaner, and again remove as much of the tar as possible with a dull knife. Follow this operation by rubbing the spot lightly with a cloth wet with the cleaner until the stain is removed.

It is possible that the cleaner will dissolve the tar, thereby causing it to bleed. Generally tar will stain trim materials, and this type of stain will be very difficult to remove.

Urine

Sponge the stain with a clean cloth saturated with lukewarm soapsuds (mild neutral soap) and then rinse well by rubbing the stain with a clean cloth dipped in cold water. Then saturate a clean cloth with a solution of 1 part household ammonia water and 5 parts water. Apply the cloth to the stain and allow solution to remain on affected area for 1 minute; then rinse by rubbing with a clean wet cloth.

Lipstick

The compositions of different brands of lipsticks vary, a fact that makes these stains very difficult to remove. In some instances, a volatile cleaner may remove the stain. If some stain remains after repeated applications of the volatile cleaner, it is best to leave it rather than try other measures.

Ball Point Ink

Sponge the stain with cool water; work a detergent into it and rinse. Generally, this type of stain will be very difficult to remove.

QUESTIONS

20-1 What is the reason a water shield is installed in the doors of an automobile?

20-2 What are the first things to check for before doing a water test?

20-3 How long should the stream of water coming out of the hose be?

20-4 When checking for water leaks, should the test be started at the top of the panel, the center of the panel, or the bottom of the panel?

20-5 What should be checked for leaks in the floor of a car?

20-6 What other method can be used to check for weatherstrip leak?

20-7 On hardtop models, where will the windows lose contact: at the side, the center, or the top?

20-8 Where is the wind noise most prevalent in an automobile?

20-9 What is used to seal a suspected area of wind noise?

20-10 What is used to cement weather strip that has become loose? What method should be used?

20-11 What is one of the most frequent causes of rattles and squeaks?

20-12 What methods should be used to remove a bloodstain?

20-13 What method should be used to remove chewing gum?

20-14 What should be used to remove tar?

21

Management, Estimating, and Shop Safety

UNIT 21-1: SHOP MANAGEMENT

A suitable stock of materials must be maintained for efficient shop operations. A proper stock room utilizing a minimum–maximum balance system as a basis for quantity purchasing is important and will save many headaches and losses in shop morale and efficiency, besides reducing material costs.

A requisition system should be set up so that each shop worker can obtain materials only when approved by the shop foreman. A carefully worked out material control system is essential for economical use of materials.

Caution is necessary in maintaining a stock of perishable organic finishing materials—the oldest materials must be used first. As new stock arrives, similar older material in stock should be rotated so that it will go out first. If it is not rotated, important changes will occur in the paint material, instead of pigment settling, viscosity increase, loss in drying speed, and so on. Therefore it is advisable to date shipments and to initiate a system of stock rotation.

Cleaning rags have been found to be a large cost item. A supply source should be investigated; a laundry service is well worthwhile to permit reuse. Next to paint, masking tape is the largest material cost item. Tape is perishable and should be purchased carefully to avoid inferior materials. Special tape suitable for baking temperatures should be used with the infrared oven. Tape widths from 1/2 to 2 in. (13 to 51 mm) should be maintained in stock; the 3/4 in. (19 mm) width is normally used in the greatest quantities.

Sanding disks and sandpaper are also a major cost item, but money can be saved by careful purchasing and commonsense use. For example, after using a 9 in. (225 mm) disk, cut it to 7 in. (175 mm), thereby getting twice as much out of the same disk.

Cost Accounting and Analysis

General accounting will provide the basis for profit and loss statements of assets and liabilities. Only by proving more detailed operational information can management properly analyze the source of profits or losses, correct any weak spots, plug loss leaks, and improve the overall operation of the business.

The primary elements in the cost of running a business are material, direct labor, and overhead. These three items are collected from subsidiary records and recorded on the job cost sheet. Comparison with the estimate or standard cost will reveal the profit or loss on each job. Finished job costs are not compiled for historical purposes but rather as a guide by which management can readily distinguish between profitable and unprofitable work. The efficiency of various workmen, the accuracy of estimating, the use of materials, and other data of value in rating will show the trend of costs and consequent profit or loss.

To realize the full benefits of cost accounting, the shop supervisors and personnel giving estimates, as well as the management, should take an active interest in closely following the cost figures. It cannot be over-emphasized that in order to maintain an effective control over costs it is necessary to know the facts regarding costs.

An effective cost accounting system need not be burdensome to a refinishing shop, and its usefulness will soon be appreciated. The basic elements are well-kept labor cost records, sufficiently detailed estimates, and a good record of materials and parts going into each job.

Personnel

Even though it does not show on the balance sheet, an efficient, productive labor force is one of the biggest assets of a refinishing shop. A new shop should pay considerable attention to building such an asset in the shortest possible time. Sound training and subsequent good supervision are essential in reaching this goal.

It is more prudent to employ top-notch body men and pay higher wages than to have incompetent, mediocre workers and pay lower wages. Some semiskilled labor, such as apprentices, can be useful in the shop for certain jobs. The skilled men can then be kept on productive work.

The same condition is true in the refinishing shop—skilled workers will be worth their higher pay by producing better quality work. Roughly three men for every two complete automobiles per day are required. Intelligent and conscientious spray men can save the shop considerable rework by inspecting the car for defects in preparation and repairing before color coat is applied. This skilled labor should form the nucleus of the labor force.

UNIT 21-2: ESTIMATING

A good estimator is the most effective sales promoter, and by pricing accurately he can play an important role in achieving good profits. Consequently, this job has become one of the most important in the organization. To be able to provide an accurate estimate, the estimator must have thorough knowledge and experience in all phases of auto body repairs.

An accurate estimate for each car is not always possible, for hidden damage cannot be seen. If such damage is present, such as damage to the transmission, power steering, and power brakes, these assemblies should be left open on the estimate sheet. Good, detailed estimate sheets are necessary not only to provide records but also to give a good impression to the customer.

Most collision work is done for insurance companies, and two estimates are usually required for each job. The lowest estimate generally gets the job. The insurance company will usually consider the price as a contract with a fairly firm price except for some items that may have been left open for inspection. The estimate must be made with all necessary information filled out. Each part to be repaired or replaced must be included, as well as the time necessary to do the work. All parts, materials, and the shop labor rate are included in the estimate at a retail rate.

To establish the retail rate of labor, the shop overhead, made up of such things as supervision, supplies, and depreciation on equipment, must be known. Then the cost of labor and the profit required to keep the business going must be added.

The average wage paid to the skilled tradesman in many areas is about 40 percent of the labor rate when flat rates are used in a shop. This will mean that the highly skilled tradesman will make more money than the apprentice because he usually can do the job in less time. Some parts of the country pay a higher percentage, but this depends on the individual shop. Other shops will use a weekly or monthly wage, plus a bonus after so many hours of work.

Since a tremendous amount of supplies are used in a body shop, this factor raises the overhead of the shop. Therefore, the retail rate for labor is usually calculated by multiplying the wages of the body man by two and one-half. It is estimated that the overhead can run from 40 to 50 percent of the retail rate, leaving between 10 to 20 percent as shop profit.

The estimating of the 1970s will not be sufficient for the cars of the 1980s. The new vehicles have been totally redesigned; the power trains are now placed completely in the front on front-wheel-drive automobiles. The manufacturers use slightly different methods of construction to achieve their aims for their vehicles. The steel has changed and the methods to repair them have also had to change. The steel is lighter gauge, HSS, HSLA, Galvaneal, galvanized, and zinc coated, to name a few. The amount of plastics has also increased tremendously; therefore, the cars are lighter.

The first damage is, of course, the direct damage, that is, the area that was hit (Fig. 21-1). A system should be followed to ensure that no area or damaged part be missed, if at all possible.

The parts required, plus price, remove and replace, or repair times are listed. Damage in the newer cars affects the body in a different way than in the older cars. The damage will spread to a wider or longer zone than on the older-style vehicles. A car hit on the rail hard enough will collapse, gradually absorbing the impact as it crumples (Fig. 21-2).

FIGURE 21-1 Direct damage.

FIGURE 21-2 Collapsed rail and cradle.

Depending on the force, the impact that is absorbed will probably distort the side engine shields or aprons (Fig. 21-3). The damage may also distort the floor, driving it up and back; this will bend the metal and pop some spot welds (Fig. 21-4).

FIGURE 21-3   Damaged engine shield.

FIGURE 21-4   Distorted floor.

Due to the amount of high-strength steel used in supporting members, the estimator will have to decide which part can be repaired, or replaced in whole or in part by splicing and welding in new parts. The McPherson struts towers should be checked and measured to determine if they have moved (Fig. 21-5). These measurements are available from manufacturers' specifications drawings.

When making an estimate on these vehicles, it is imperative that a vehicle that has been in even a slightly serious accident be raised off the floor and put

FIGURE 21-5   Measuring and checking McPherson strut towers.

on safety stands. This is to enable the estimator to be able to get underneath to check for areas that may be damaged, such as bent, distorted, or even broken parts that can be seen and checked (Fig. 21-6). Some reinforcements may have been driven back, causing them to distort, bend, and break spot welds. The door-to-fender gap should be checked because the fender may have been driven back as well as the engine shield (Fig. 21-7).

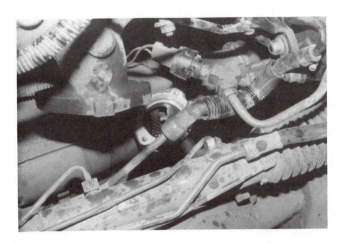

FIGURE 21-6   Damaged rack and pinion steering and speedometer gear housing.

FIGURE 21-7   Fender-to-door gap distorted.

The next area to examine is the door gaps, especially at the top of the windshield pillar (Fig. 21-8). This would indicate if the cowl has moved back, thereby causing an uneven gap at the top front part of the door. This would also help to indicate that the frame has sagged at the cowl area. With this wide gap at the top of the pillar, it is very possible that the pressure exerted on the roof panel could be warped, due to the changes of position on the pillar.

All primary damage is fairly easy to locate, but the secondary and hidden damage is harder to find. In this type of construction, accuracy is very important; the maximum tolerance is 1/8 in. (3 mm). Follow your check list carefully each time a vehicle is evaluated; this will minimize chances for errors. If possible, all electrical systems should be operated as well as starting the engine to check power equipment for damage.

FIGURE 21-8 Gap between door and windshield pillar.

A steering and suspension check should be conducted if possible. The rack and pinion steering and the McPherson strut are quite simple, but often misunderstood. These systems are based on a straight-line principle and a simple bounce-rebound check will determine if there is any damage to the components of either system. The rest of the vehicle must be checked panel by panel to see if the accident has distorted any panels. It is possible that the fuel tank may have been damaged or that the rear bumper gaps may have changed due to the impact or secondary damage traveling through the vehicle to the rear (Fig. 21-9).

FIGURE 21-9 Bumper showing uneven gap between the body lower line.

If in doubt on some of the mechanical components, such as the engine or transmission trans-axle, leave them open for inspection on the estimate.

The estimator must then check his collision manual and enter the part number as well as the parts required, the labor time, the paint time, and any sublets to other firms. It is important that this be done well, with the fewest mistakes possible, as it could make a difference to the insurance company as well as the customer.

Flat Rate

Flat-rate manuals are books that give the times required for different operations when a car is repaired. The flat-rate time is the time required to remove and replace or overhaul an assembly. These times are based on new cars where no bolts are rusted. Therefore the estimator must add extra time for rust, cutting parts, reaching attached bolts, removing and replacing of undercoat, and also removing of some special materials found on some replacement parts.

It is also necessary to estimate the time required to repair adjacent parts that cannot be aligned by shifting the assembly. The plugging of holes that are not required in the used parts, the removal of brackets from an old part to weld onto the new part, and the cleaning of broken glass or checking the windshield or back window opening are all operations that require extra time above the flat-rate schedule.

The time given in flat-rate manuals is given in tenths of an hour in most cases. The hour is divided into 10 parts of 6 minutes, so this will mean that the shops and employees will also be paid accordingly in tenths of an hour on many jobs.

On most jobs there are combination or overlap operations; that is, part of a job is done while doing another job. For example, a fender is removed from a vehicle, the time to R&R (remove and replace) is 2.3 hours, but to remove this fender one side of the bumper must be dropped; since the bumper is also damaged, it must also be R&R'ed completely and the time given to R&R the bumper is 0.9 hour. Therefore, the R&R of the fender becomes the major operation; the minor operation is the bumper. Since the body man is getting paid to remove or lower one side already, this creates an overlap of payment of the job. To obtain a proper payment on the minor operation, the flat-rate time is cut by one-third, giving the body man 0.6 hr to complete the R&R of the bumper. In making an estimate, the estimator must be careful to deduct for this overlap time because this could cause his estimate to be out of line from what it should be if it is not taken off.

In making an estimate, the estimator must also use good judgment in recommending repair or replacement for a part. It must be remembered that to replace a part will double the cost of repair for that panel. The estimator must not allow himself to be influenced too much by the customer. If the insurance company feels that the panel can be repaired, the company will certainly insist that it be done. Also, the customer must be assured that the repair of the panel will give as good a job as a replacement, for the panel must be repainted regardless of repair or replacement.

To be competitive in his estimate, the estimator must be able to figure out the amount of time required to align and metal-finish the panel to provide a satisfactory repair. Only through having a thorough knowledge of all phases of repair work can the estimator give an accurate and reasonable amount of time for labor required for the repair of the vehicle. By looking, checking, and feeling different bumps and bends with his hands, the estimator must be able to picture in his mind the operations necessary for the repair of the particular damage that was caused by the impact. He must remember that the damage is always removed in the reverse order to which it occurred. A fairly general rule for time for the repair of metal is that the estimator must figure the amount of time required to align the panel and its reinforcement, plus usually 1 hour per square foot (0.09 sq. m) to repair ordinary damage and 1½ hours per square foot (0.09 sq m) for badly creased metal.

The estimator must be able to picture in his mind how much metal will be left to metal-finish on the particular panel after the alignment and roughing-out have been completed. It would be very possible to have overlap in doing these operations between alignment, roughing-out, and metal-finishing and only through experience will an estimator be able to provide estimates that are fair to the customer, the shop, and the employee.

It is also necessary to charge for some of the cost of the materials used in the body shop; this could mean the difference between profit and loss for the shop on certain jobs, for many materials do get used in any shop. In many areas a charge of 10 to 15 percent of the body labor is put on the estimate because the customer pays for the materials used.

For the refinishing of the panels, the estimator has the flat-rate manual to follow. This part of the estimate is not too complicated to do. The only thing to watch out for is overlap in the painting of adjacent panels. The amount of overlap removed is usually either 0.2 or 0.4 from the minor operation. Some estimators will take 0.2 from the estimate when some adjacent panels need to be repainted. This would depend a great deal on the flat-rate manual used.

There is also a charge for supplies in the paint shop, because as in the body shop the amount of materials used accounts for quite a sum of money for each job. For enamel jobs, most shops charge around $11.00 or slightly more per man-hour of labor on the particular job. For acrylic lacquer, a surcharge of around 15 to 20 percent could be charged because the material is more expensive to buy than enamel.

To finish the estimate, the estimator must not forget the sublet, that is, any work that may have been done in another shop, such as radiator repairing, straightening wheels, towing, or chrome plating. The amount is then entered in the proper column and the estimate can be given to the customer or sent to the insurance company.

UNIT 21-3: SHOP SAFETY

It is common knowledge that accidents are usually caused by negligence. Only by paying careful attention to accident causes can they be reduced. Many of the products used in a body shop are highly combustible—lacquers, reducers, thinners, and many other dangerous chemicals. Moreover, because the vehicles are sometimes dismantled in assemblies, they clutter up the floor or the alleys between the cars.

Combustibles are always a fire hazard and the containers holding such products as thinners, reducers, and paints should be kept closed and stored in fireproof cupboards. There should also be no welding or smoking close to the paint area, and proper signs signifying such restrictions should be prominently displayed. All painting should be done in a spray booth with exhaust fans that meet the requirements of local laws. The painter should always wear a suitable respirator and have the exhaust fan on when painting or working with thinners and reducers. The inhalation of thinner, reducer, or paint fumes could possibly result in physical ailments.

With the frequent use of torches in the body shop, the dangers of a fire are always present unless precautions are taken to avert such occurrences. The owner should make sure that the proper fire extinguishers are on hand and that all staff know where they are and how they should be used. All rags that are soaked with oil, grease, or paint should be stored in proper containers and not in any corner where they could cause spontaneous combustion. Grease, oil, or any slippery substance should be cleaned off the floor regularly, because in addition to being a fire hazard the substance can also be a safety hazard. A workman or customer could slip and hurt himself seriously.

When a vehicle with collision damage is brought into the shop, the first thing that should be done is to disconnect the battery in case of shorts in the wiring. When the vehicle is jacked up, it should always be supported with safety stands so that the car will not fall on any employee that might be working on it. The floor should always be as clean and clear of obstructions as possible, because numerous accidents occur in shops that have a poor cleaning attitude.

When a welding torch is not being used, it should be shut off because it could set a fire or seriously burn a fellow workman if he should come in contact with it. One of the most dangerous things to weld is a gas tank that has not been steamed properly, for there is a good chance that it will explode on contact with the flame. One of the best methods to repair a gas tank is to use a soldering iron and do a solder repair instead; it is much safer.

One of the most important features in any body shop is good lighting to reduce eye strain and also help the employees perform a satisfactory repair job, whether it is body work or painting. The shop should also be heated and ventilated to remove as much dust as possible from the air, especially with the fiberglass and plastic fillers used today.

A basic staff rule of safety should be that no staff should be horsing around, running, or playing practical jokes, because the jokes and tricks get worse and worse until somebody gets hurt. A first aid kit should be available at all times; it should be stocked with all basic items required to render first aid for simple injuries.

The proper tools should always be used to do the job that needs to be done. Files should never be used to pry or hammer with, for they are made of a very hard steel and are very brittle. Hammer handles should always be checked for tightness; a loose hammer handle could cause the hammer to fly off and hurt somebody or even break a windshield. Chisels with mushroomed heads should be either discarded or repaired to provide a proper area for hitting it.

Wrenches should be tight fitting, for loose wrenches will slip when they are put under great tension, thus causing injury to the workman.

When any grinding is done, a face mask or goggles that cover the eyes should be worn at all times. A body grinder can be a very dangerous tool if not used properly; the disk can disintegrate and hurt the operator or any other person in the vicinity. Compressed air is a very useful tool. If used improperly, however, it could cause serious injury to a person if some particles of dust are blown in his eyes.

The good shop owner will find that it pays big dividends in morale and work output if he runs a safe, clean, and orderly shop. In addition to a more orderly flow of work, he will keep his employees for longer periods of time.

QUESTIONS

21-1 Why should a requisition system be used in a shop?

21-2 Why is it necessary to keep a stock record and rotation system?

21-3 What are the three principal elements that must be considered in running a business?

21-4 Is it better to employ top-notch tradesmen rather than mediocre employees?

21-5 Faulty paint jobs are caused to a great degree by what conditions?

21-6 What factors must be considered besides the flat-rate time when making an estimate?

21-7 How is the hour divided in flat-rate manuals?

21-8 What is the difference between a major and a minor operation?

21-9 What is the general rule for estimating sheet-metal work?

21-10 What is overlap?

21-11 Why should combustibles be stored in fireproof cupboards?

21-12 What can happen when grease- and paint-soaked rags are stored in a corner?

21-13 Why should vehicles always be supported by safety stands when they are jacked up?

21-14 Is it safe to weld a gas tank without cleaning it?

21-15 Is it a good practice to wear a safety mask when grinding? Why?

Appendix A

Hand Tools
for Metalworking

SAFETY TIPS

The proper tools should always be used to do the job that needs to be done. Files should never be used to pry or hammer with, for they are made of a very hard steel and are very brittle. Hammer handles should always be checked for tightness; a loose hammer handle could cause the hammer to fly off and hurt somebody or even break a windshield. Chisels with mushroomed heads should be either discarded or repaired to provide a proper area for hitting.

Wrenches should be tight fitting, for loose wrenches will slip when they are put under great tension, causing injury.

All tools used in autobody repairing are generally divided into two categories: hand tools and power tools. In this Appendix the more common and most frequently used hand tools are discussed. It is of the utmost importance for a metal repairman to understand and know the purpose and type of work for which each individual hand tool is designed and used if he is to become a fully experienced tradesman.

In sheet-metal repairing, the *bumping* hammer and the dolly block, or *dolly* as it is generally called, are the basic hand tools used in restoring damaged surfaces to their original contour.

Types of Hammers and Their Uses

Many different types of hammers are available to the metal repairman today: Each hammer is designed for a specific purpose. Hammers used in auto body repairing are divided into four classes or categories, based on the particular operation for which each is used. Metal work is generally carried out in three distinctive steps or operations: (1) the "alignment and roughing-out," (2) the "bumping and dinging," and (3) the "metal-finishing" operations. A fourth class of hammers, called *special* hammers, used in performing special repair operations, such as trimmer's hammers, composition head hammers, and wood and rubber mallets, is also available.

The alignment and roughing-out operation involves the repositioning and straightening of the inner construction or reinforcement of an automobile body section, assembly, or part and aligning and roughly reshaping the damaged outer sheet metal with the surrounding undamaged areas. This process will often require not only the use of auto body hammers but also hydraulic jacking equipment as well.

A bumping hammer is used in the bumping operation to level and smooth out the already roughed-out damaged area further, restoring it to as near its original shape and contour as is possible by *eye* and *feel*.

The pick hammer is employed in the metal-finishing operation in which small low spots still present after the bumping operation has been completed are raised by *picking* (using the pick end of the hammer) and thereby creating a perfectly smooth and level repaired surface.

Curved-face hammers are ideal in bumping concave surfaces; square-face hammers are used in bumping straight-line constructed panels.

Because each hammer is equipped with a limited number of working faces, several kinds of hammers must be used in sheet-metal repairing if it is to be done efficiently.

Hammers vary in weight from lightweight to heavy-duty and choosing the right weight hammer for the job on hand will not only make the job much easier but will enable the repairman to do a better job in considerably less time.

It is very important that hammers be well balanced. This factor offers greater ease of handling and accuracy of control, which is so very necessary if additional damage is to be prevented during the repair operations. Hammer faces should also be kept smooth at all times. Use body hammers only for metal bumping. This will not only prolong the life of the hammer but will enable you to do better body work.

The heavy-duty bumping hammer (Fig. A-1):   Sometimes called a heavy-duty shrinking hammer, equipped with a round face and also a square face. It is used for getting into tight places when roughing-out metals, for forging and shrinking of welds, for roughing-out badly creased metals, and for general alignment of the heavier gauged sheet metals. The corner of the square face can be used as a pick to force up low areas on damaged panels. If it is necessary to make a small

FIGURE A-1 (Courtesy of H. K. Porter, Inc.)

shrink and the area cannot be reached with a dolly, either face of the hammer can be used as a dolly inside the fender, door, or panel and another hammer can be used on the outside to complete the shrinking operation.

The light bumping hammer (Fig. A-2): Similar in shape and size except that it is lighter in weight. It is used for metal finishing, turning of flanges on replacement door panels, working out flat-surfaced metals, light shrinking on turret tops, and metal-finishing car hoods.

FIGURE A-2 (Courtesy of H. K. Porter, Inc.)

The balanced dinging hammer (Fig. A-3): Light bumping hammer, very useful in general metalworking. It is made with either two round faces or with one round and one square face. It is used for roughing-out such metals as fenders, doors, and turret tops; shrinking fender flanges and edges of doors; and in bracket

FIGURE A-3 (Courtesy of H. K. Porter, Inc.)

alignment. It is sometimes used as a dolly for shrinking metals. The square face lends itself to the alignment of straight-line constructed sheet metals.

The short pick hammer (Fig. A-4):   Equipped with a round face and a pick combination head and is used for light picking and metalworking in tight or restricted areas, such as fender skirts and flat-surface panels, and for shrinking on metals.

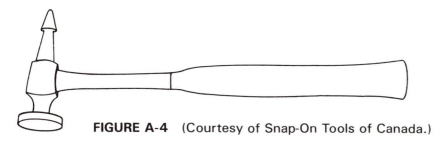

FIGURE A-4   (Courtesy of Snap-On Tools of Canada.)

The long pick hammer (Fig. A-5):   Used for general auto body work. It has a long round pick and a flat round face head, which is ideal for metal-finishing. It should, however not be used for roughing-out metals. It is primarily used in the alignment of sheet metals after they have been roughed-out and for picking in the metal-finishing process.

FIGURE A-5   (Courtesy of Snap-On Tools of Canada.)

The straight chisel pick hammer [Fig. A-6(A)]:   Used on modern auto bodies and has a round face and a chisel-pick head. It is used on fenders and for reshaping beads, moldings, headlight inset reveals, and louver work and is especially handy in fitting panel edges and flanges in the welding process of replacement panels and straight-line construction.

FIGURE A-6(A)   (Courtesy of Snap-On Tools of Canada.)

STRAIGHT CHISEL PICK HAMMER.

The curved chisel pick hammer [***Fig. A-6(B)***]*:*   Used in straightening and metal-finishing (picking) sharp corners around beads and moldings, rolled fender flanges, and outer edges of turret tops and in raising low areas partially obstructed by body braces or framework, which can only be reached by curved, offset swinging of the pick.

CURVED CHISEL PICK HAMMER.   **FIGURE A-6(B)**

The long roof pick hammer (Fig. A-7):   Equipped with an extra long pick and used for working deep-crowned surfaces on fenders, doors, turret tops, and quarter panels.

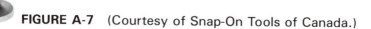

FIGURE A-7   (Courtesy of Snap-On Tools of Canada.)

The reverse-curve light bumping hammer (Fig. A-8):   Equipped with two single-crown faces, with one face running in exactly the opposite direction to the other. It is used for aligning and straightening sharp concave surfaces, such as the reverse curves on fenders, headlights, doors, and quarter panels on late-model automobiles.

FIGURE A-8

The heavy-duty fender bumping hammer (Fig. A-9): Designed for heavy work in roughing-out high-crowned metals such as fenders and restricted areas where a long reach is required. It can also be used in conjunction with extra-heavy cross-peen hammers and sledgehammers in offset roughing-out operations on rocker panels, wheelhousing, cowls, quarter panels, and badly dented bumper face bars.

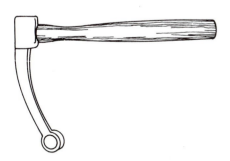

FIGURE A-9

The cross-peen hammer, or blacksmith hammer (Fig. A-10): Equipped with a round, flat face at one end and a cross peen at the other. The round face of the hammer is used in striking heavy blows in roughing-out and aligning operations, either by itself or in conjunction with a flat piece of hardwood or steel plate, spreading the force of the blow over a larger area. It is also used in driving cold chisels, punches, and various body spoons. Its cross-peen end is used in straightening right-angled frame members, bumpers and bumper brackets, and straight-line construction.

FIGURE A-10

The ball-peen hammer (Fig. A-11): Available in various weights and sizes. It also has a round, flat-faced end and a ball-peen end. The ball-peen end is used in bumping out and stretching of metals and in setting (mushrooming) the ends of rivets. The round-faced end is used for and will handle practically all jobs that the similar end on a cross-peen hammer will.

FIGURE A-11

The sledgehammer (Fig. A-12):   Very similar in design and construction but much larger and heavier than a cross-peen hammer. Another type that is available is equipped with two round flat faces. Both types are used for extra-heavy work, such as required in straightening and aligning strong inner construction on auto bodies and straightening frames, cross members, heavy body and bumper braces, and brackets.

FIGURE A-12

Dolly Blocks and Their Uses

Dolly blocks, or dollies, are made of high-grade steel and are used as anvils or backing-up tools in roughing-out and bumping operations. They are held on the inside of the damaged panel and pressure is applied by the repairman's arm. When a hammer blow is struck on the outside of the panel, the dolly will rebound slightly on the inside. It will, however, immediately return after the blow has been struck because of the tension in the repairman's arm. The repairman can then reposition the dolly for the second and each succeeding blow thereafter that may be required in the reshaping of the damaged area.

Dolly blocks are designed for a specific purpose. Each is equipped with only a few working faces and, because of the different types of panel constructions and body panel contours, quite a number of different dollies must be employed in order to do efficient work. Dollies are available with a high, medium, low, and flat crown or a combination of several crown-working faces. In choosing the right crowned dolly for a particular surface, a dolly with a slightly smaller radius than the original crown should be used.

Like hammers, dollies should be well balanced for ease of handling and accuracy of control. They should be of the right weight in order to avoid unnecessary fatigue. They should be easily held and gripped securely by the hand, and they should be suitable for working many different contoured surfaces and panel constructions. The working faces should be kept smooth and free from tar, undercoating, and nicks to avoid distorting and further damaging surfaces being repaired.

The general-purpose dolly (Fig. A-13):   Has many faces and may be used for roughing-out metal on crown parts of fenders, different curvatures on car bodies; straightening fender flanges, moldings and beads; shrinking flat and crowned surfaces; and for forging welds.

FIGURE A-13 (Courtesy of H. K. Porter, Inc.)

The low-crown dolly (Fig. A-14): Generally used on sheet metal that has been worked a lot and has become thin. It is also used for shrinking thin metals because the dolly has weight and is easy to handle on flat-surface metals. It may be used on the inside of doors, on hoods, on flat and crowned surfaces of fenders, and on turret tops.

FIGURE A-14

The heel dolly (Fig. A-15): Derives its name from its shape. It is very good for the forming and shaping of large beads in metals and aligning high- and low-crown metals as well as straight-line construction and flat-surface panels.

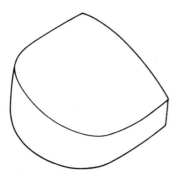

FIGURE A-15 (Courtesy of Snap-On Tools of Canada.)

The toe dolly (Fig. A-16): Specially designed combination flat dolly used for shrinking flat surfaces on door panels, fender skirts, turret tops, and car hoods and also for forming beads and flanges on the bottom of fenders. It is excellent in working out unfinished metal panels because the dolly is perfectly flat on one

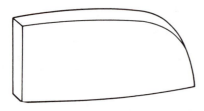

FIGURE A-16 (Courtesy of Snap-On Tools of Canada.)

side and low crowned on the other side. Excessive hammering on the dolly should be avoided, however, so as not to stretch the metal.

The beading dolly (Fig. A-17):   Used in forming different size beads on metals. The larger end of the dolly is used for larger and wider beads, while the smaller end is for the narrower beads. It is sometimes used to knock out smaller dents in sheet metals.

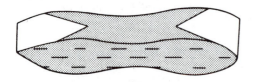

FIGURE A-17

The wedge dolly (Fig. A-18):   Designed for working out crowned surfaces on turret tops and wide fender flanges. It may be used in working out metals enclosed by bracket or inner construction; roughing-out small dents in turret tops, especially behind roof rails and header bars; and for shrinking in different places on car bodies.

FIGURE A-18

Picks, Punches, and Their Uses

Picks and punches are used in metal-finishing damaged auto body sheet metal that has been aligned and straightened and whose minor irregularities or low spots cannot be raised in the usual manner by means of pick hammers.

The short curved pick (Fig. A-19):   Medium length with a curved pointed end and used for working through holes in the inner construction of doors and rocker and quarter panels, by turning and applying pressure on the handle to force out and bring up small damaged or low areas.

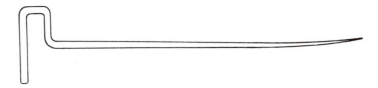

FIGURE A-19   (Courtesy of H. K. Porter, Inc.)

The long curved pick (Fig. A-20):   Similar to the short curved pick except that it is longer and is used to get at damaged areas requiring a longer reach.

FIGURE A-20   (Courtesy of H. K. Porter, Inc.)

The long tee handle chisel bit pick (Fig. A-21):   Long pick bar that can be inserted between inner and outer panels that have very little space between them. It may be used as a dolly when shrinking or in bringing out damaged areas, where the inner construction and outer panel are close together.

FIGURE A-21   (Courtesy of H. K. Porter, Inc.)

The deep-throat straight pick (Fig. A-22):   Used in applying an off-set corrective force, such as the raising of low spots in the center section of a trunk lid or on door panels behind door hinge mounting brackets and other reinforced inner construction.

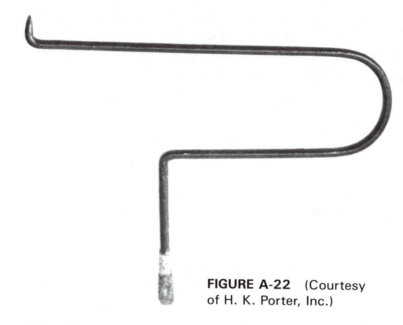

FIGURE A-22 (Courtesy of H. K. Porter, Inc.)

The curved finishing punch (Fig. A-23): Used in hard-to-get-at places where an offset blow is required, such as door pillars, header bars, outer areas of door panels, and rocker panels.

FIGURE A-23 (Courtesy of H. K. Porter, Inc.)

The hooked finishing punch (Fig. A-24): Used where the insertion hole can be made at nearly the same level as the panel that is being repaired. It may also be employed in raising low areas in window reveal panels of doors and in trunk lid work.

FIGURE A-24 (Courtesy of H. K. Porter, Inc.)

The piercing punch (Fig. A-25): Sharp, long, tapered punch used to punch holes in the inner construction of auto bodies (generally behind weatherstripping on doors), through which picks and pick bars may be used to raise damaged areas and low spots.

FIGURE A-25

Types of Body Spoons and Their Uses

Body spoons are available in many different sizes and contours and each is designed for a specific purpose.

Body spoons are generally divided into three classes: back-up spoons, driving spoons, and surfacing spoons.

Body spoons are designed so that they can be used in prying out dents in restricted and confined areas. They can also be employed as dollies in metalworking areas where there is insufficient space between the inner construction and the outer panel, thus preventing the use of the ordinary dollies.

Some spoons are designed especially for the straightening of ridges and other high surfaces. In this operation, commonly called *spring-hammering*, the spoon is used in conjunction with a hammer. The spoon is held directly on the ridge and is struck squarely with the hammer. The spoon spreads the blow over a large area, straightening out the ridge in a quick and efficient manner and preventing any additional damage to the panel.

The working faces of spoons should be kept smooth and clean. Use of masking tape or celluloid, such as that used on frost shield, between the spoon and the work will often prevent the marking up of painted surfaces.

Types of Back-Up Spoons

The double-end lower back and quarter-panel spoon (Fig. A-26): Large spoon used for removing dents on quarter panels around rear pillars, behind inner construction and back-panel strainers, and center and lower sills. It can also be used for prying out doorsill flanges and releasing buckled metals on turret tops, back decks, and quarter panels.

FIGURE A-26   (Courtesy of H. K. Porter, Inc.)

The double-end door and side-apron spoon (Fig. A-27): Has a longer, wider face. It is shaped to reach in behind the inner construction of doors, quarter panels, and cowl areas. It may also be used as a pry or a dolly in the alignment of metals.

FIGURE A-27   (Courtesy of H. K. Porter, Inc.)

Types of Driving Spoons

The double-end heavy-duty driving spoon (Fig. A-28):   Made of high-grade steel with a specially molded square face at each end of this spoon, on which hammer blows can be given. It has a variety of uses, such as setting inside seams on front fenders; bumping top rail panels, headlights and hood louvers; straightening and finishing drip moldings, quarter-panel moldings, deck panels, and other beading work. It may also be used for the shrinking and alignment of metals and as a dolly in roughing-out work.

FIGURE A-28   (Courtesy of H. K. Porter, Inc.)

The double-end heavy-duty driving and fender beading tool (Fig. A-29):   Designed primarily for straightening all reverse beads on fenders without wire-reinforced flanges and hood flanges and in aligning inner construction on auto bodies. This spoon may also be used as a dolly for working out as well as shrinking deep-crowned fenders and doors.

FIGURE A-29   (Courtesy of H. K. Porter, Inc.)

Types of Surfacing Spoons

The flat light dinging surfacing spoon (Fig. A-30):   Used for spring-hammering operations with a mallet or ball-peen hammer for surface finishing or hammering down high ridges left as a result of indirect damage. It prevents the nicking of these high ridges, bringing them into general alignment without causing any further damage to the metal surface.

FIGURE A-30   (Courtesy of H. K. Porter, Inc.)

The low-crown radius surfacing spoon (Fig. A-31):   Used to spring-hammer reverse-crown surfaces. Its face has a low-crowned radius required for concave surfaces.

FIGURE A-31   (Courtesy of H. K. Porter, Inc.)

The molding surfacing spoon (Fig. A-32):   Has a gently tapering, half-round face and is used in reshaping and eliminating high ridges on damaged sharp concave surfaces by means of spring-hammering, without any danger of nicking the metal.

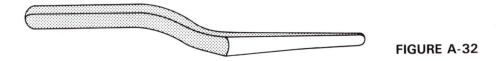

FIGURE A-32

Caulking irons (Fig. A-33):   Of various shapes and sizes, generally made of round, rectangular, or hexagonal stock steel, used as driving irons or sets in conjunction with either ball or cross-peen hammers of varying weights in the reshaping (smoothly roughing-out and straightening) of flanges, beads, straight-line constructed ridges, and bends on body panels and frames which cannot be straightened as efficiently with conventional driving spoons because of their re-stricted location or complicated shape and contour.

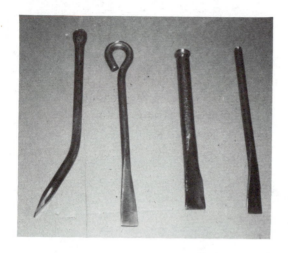

FIGURE A-33

The ezy-edger (Fig. A-34): Used for the straightening of edges of drip mold-ings, doors, trunk lids, hoods, grilles, and louvers. There are hooks on either end, one end for straight pulling and prying and the other for offset pulling, prying, or bending. This tool is designed to prevent marking of surface edges and is most frequently used in opening up panel flanges on fenders, doors, hoods, and trunk lids.

FIGURE A-34 (Courtesy of H. K. Porter, Inc.)

Types of Body Files and Their Uses

Body files of various types are used in the metal-finishing operation. They serve a purpose similar to that of a plane in woodworking. They are used in accurately locating surface irregularities (high and low spots) on damaged areas after they have been *bumped* out. They are also employed in creating a smooth surface after all high and low spots have been removed by means of picking. This surface is then given a final sanding with the power disk grinder, completing the metal-finishing operation. Following is a description of the five different types of body files used in auto body shops today.

The adjustable flexible file and holder (Fig. A-35): Used in metal-finishing to locate minor irregularities after the damaged area has been roughed out and properly aligned. It is used by the autobody mechanic to locate high and low

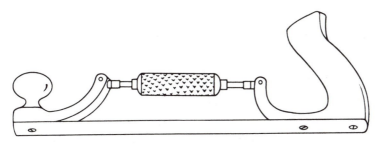

FIGURE A-35   (Courtesy of Snap-On Tools of Canada.)

spots. The file holder is adjustable to provide a means of bending the file to conform to the curvature or shape of the panel, whether it be flat, concave, or convex. Care should be taken not to flex the file too much, however, so as not to break it. The mounting screws should be loosened and then retightened after the file adjustment has been made.

The standard cut file and holder (Fig. A-36):   14-in. (356 mm) curve-tooth, flat file mounted on a straight, solid, wooden holder that is ideal for straight filing of flat and crowned surfaces. This file is easy to handle, has a superior cutting action, and is preferred by many auto body repairmen.

FIGURE A-36   (Courtesy of Snap-On Tools of Canada.)

The bead or reveal molding file (Fig. A-37):   Used in repairing the upper portions of doors, around window openings, small beads and moldings, and restricted areas, where the standard cut file cannot be used. It is equipped with different-shaped file blades approximately 4 in. (102 mm) long that can be easily mounted and interchanged in the holder.

FIGURE A-37   (Courtesy of Snap-On Tools of Canada.)

The hog file (Fig. A-38): Used to check the straightness of sharp concave surfaces, ridges, and moldings.

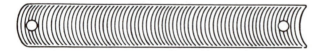

FIGURE A-38

The half-moon file and holder (Fig. A-39): Used in metal-finishing large concave surfaces.

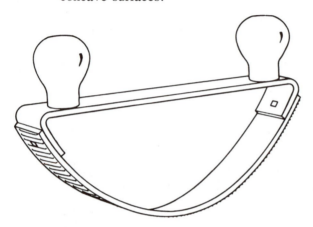

FIGURE A-39

Types of Door Handle Removing Tools and Their Uses

The old- and late-model door handle tool (Fig. A-40): Can be used on all old- and later-model automobiles, except Chrysler products. The outward appearance of old and new style handles is identical, but the construction of the inside flange is different. The hook end of the tool works on old style handles to push the pin out. It is a great timesaver.

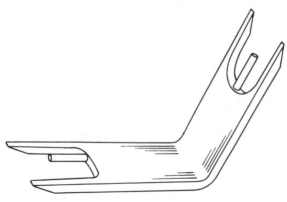

FIGURE A-40 (Courtesy of Snap-On Tools of Canada.)

The clip-type door handle tool (Fig. A-41):   Used for the removal of clip-type retainers on General Motors and Ford cars. It fits both old and new style retainers. The offset handle provides clearance. The retaining clip is held by jaws, which are forced over it when the tool is inserted to release the inside door handle.

FIGURE A-41   (Courtesy of Snap-On Tools of Canada.)

The plier-type door handle tool (Fig. A-42):   Used for the removal of clip-type retainers used on General Motors cars. The slim jaws slip between handle and escutcheon plate to hold the clip. Handles are also offset to provide clearance. This tool is approximately 8 in. (203 mm) long.

FIGURE A-42   (Courtesy of Snap-On Tools of Canada.)

The Chrysler door handle tool (Fig. A-43):   Used for older model Chrysler cars only. They use a spring clip that cannot readily be disengaged with any other tool. The two prongs are 5/64 in. (2 mm) thick and are tapered for easy entry between handle and plate. A raised wall makes contact with the spring clip, forcing it out of the handle shaft groove to release the handle. Offset shape provides hand clearance. This tool is also available in plier form.

FIGURE A-43   (Courtesy of Snap-On Tools of Canada.)

Vise-Grip Wrenches and Their Uses

The standard vise-grip wrench (Fig. A-44):   Indispensable for all types of work. The double-action jaws lock on work. It grips all shapes and will not slip. It works in close quarters and at any angle. It substitutes for vise clamps. It is used for holding new quarter panels, rocker panels, and door panels in position when replacing same. It will hold objects up to $1\frac{1}{8}$ in. (29 mm) square and round work up to $1\frac{5}{8}$ (41 mm) in diameter.

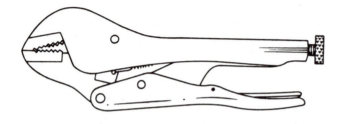

FIGURE A-44   (Courtesy of Peterson Mfg. Co., Inc.)

The vise-grip wrench with wire cutter (Fig. A-45):   Eight tools in one. It serves as an adjustable end wrench, thin-nosed pliers, pipe wrench, portable toggle press, locking wrench clamp, vise, and bolt cutter. It can also be used on the same type of work as the standard vise grip.

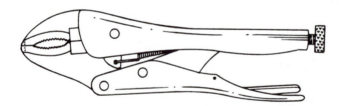

FIGURE A-45   (Courtesy of Peterson Mfg. Co., Inc.)

The vise-grip bending tool (Fig. A-46):   With its wide jaws is ideal for sheet-metal work. It provides a solid grip for twisting, bending, shaping, or pulling. It eliminates tiresome hand gripping. It is useful in stretching upholstery without danger of unraveling material. It has 8 in. (203 mm) long jaws, $3\frac{1}{8}$ in. (79 mm) throat, and is $1\frac{3}{4}$ in. (44 mm) in depth.

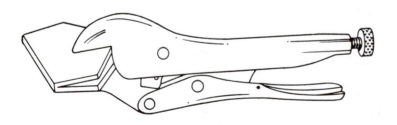

FIGURE A-46   (Courtesy of Peterson Mfg. Co., Inc.)

The vise-grip C clamp (Fig. A-47): Much faster than the ordinary C clamp. The end screw provides quick jaw-opening adjustment up to 3½ in. (89 mm). Just align pieces to be clamped. Place vise grips in position—a squeeze of the hand locks work in position. It will hold awkward pieces easily, such as replacement quarter panels and turret tops on cars.

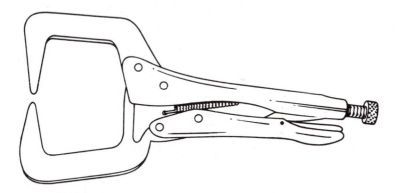

FIGURE A-47 (Courtesy of Peterson Mfg. Co., Inc.)

The vise-grip welding clamps (Fig. A-48): Used to align parts almost instantly. The parts are held in a position that leaves both hands free. Special V-shaped jaws provide perfect visibility and working room. They are ideal for fender work, soldering, riveting, drilling, and so on. They are very useful for students to hold metal while practicing welding on the bench.

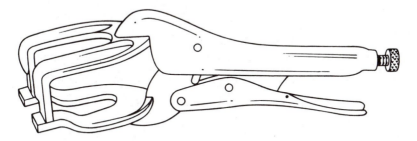

FIGURE A-48 (Courtesy of Peterson Mfg. Co., Inc.)

QUESTIONS

A-1 Into what categories are auto body hand tools generally divided?

A-2 What are the basic hand tools used in sheet-metal repairing?

A-3   Into what four classes or categories can auto body hammers be divided?

A-4   List and describe the steps in which metalwork is carried out.

A-5   What kind of hammers are used in *bumping* straight-line constructed panels and what kind are used in *bumping* concave surfaces?

A-6   What is the reason for using several kinds of hammers in sheet-metal repairing?

A-7   Why do auto body hammers vary in weight?

A-8   Why is it so important that an auto body hammer be well balanced?

A-9   Are body hammers also designed for driving nails and punches?

A-10 Why should hammer faces be kept smooth?

A-11 What other name is often given to the heavy-duty bumping hammer?

A-12 List the uses of the heavy-duty bumping hammer.

A-13 What is the main difference between the light- and heavy-duty bumping hammers?

A-14 With what type of faces is the balanced dinging hammer made?

A-15 What type of face is used in the alignment and repair of straight-line constructed sheet metals?

A-16 The short pick hammer is used for picking and metalworking what areas on an automobile?

A-17 Should the long pick hammer be used in roughing-out metals?

A-18 What are the uses of the curved chisel pick hammer?

A-19 What hammer is used for working deep-crowned surfaces on fenders, doors, turret tops, and quarter panels?

A-20 Dolly blocks are used for what purpose in roughing-out and bumping operations?

A-21 Explain how dolly blocks are used in roughing-out and bumping operations.

A-22 With what kind of working faces are dollies available?

A-23 In what way is the right dolly determined for a particular job?

A-24 Why should the working faces of the dolly be kept smooth?

A-25 What dolly is equipped with many faces and has a wide range of uses?

A-26 What kind of dolly is used in working sheet-metal that has become thin?

A-27 Name the dolly used in forming and shaping large beads and aligning high- and low-crown metals as well as flat surface panels?

A-28 What dolly is used in forming beads and flanges on fenders and working out unfinished metal panels?

A-29 What are the ends of the beading dolly used for?

A-30 For what operations is the wedge dolly most suited?

A-31 In what particular operation in auto body repairing are picks and punches primarily used?

A-32 How are picks used in bringing up or raising small low areas?

A-33 What pick is used when an extra long reach is required?

A-34 What pick is used as a dolly for shrinking and also bringing out damaged areas where the inner construction and the outer panel are close together?

A-35 What are the uses of the deep-throat straight pick?

A-36 What special tools are used in raising outer areas of door panels where an off-set blow with a pick hammer is required?

A-37 What is the purpose of the piercing punch? How is it used?

A-38 Into what three classes are body spoons generally divided?

A-39 What are body spoons generally used for?

A-40 How can a painted surface be protected when a spoon is used on it?

A-41 Name the spoon that is shaped to reach in behind inner construction of doors, quarter panels, and cowl areas.

A-42 What are the uses of the double-end heavy-duty driving spoon?

A-43 What tool is used in straightening reverse fender beads and hood flanges and working deep-crowned fenders and doors?

A-44 What tools are used in spring-hammering metals? Why are they employed?

A-45 What are caulking irons used for?

A-46 Name the tool used in opening up panel flanges on fenders, doors, hoods, and trunk lids?

A-47 What are body files used for in autobody repairing?

A-48 Make a list of the different types of body files and their uses.

A-49 List the different types of door handle removing tools, and describe how each is used.

Appendix B

Conversion Tables

METRIC TABLES

Linear	One METER (m) : 10 decimeter (dm) : 100 centimeter (cm) : 1000 millimeters (mm)
	1000 meters : One kilometer (km)
Square	One SQUARE METER (m^2) : 100 square decimeters (dm^2) : 10,000 square centimeters (cm^2) : 1,000,000 square millimeters (mm^2)
Cubic	One CUBIC METER (m^3) : 1000 cubic decimeters (dm^3) : 1,000,000 cubic centimeters (cm^3)
Capacity	One LITER (l) : 10 deciliters (dl) : 1000 centiliters (cl)
	100 Liters: One hectoliter (hl)
Weight	One KILOGRAM (kg) : 100 decagrams (dkg) : 1000 grams (g)
	100 Kilograms : One metric cent (q)
	1000 kilograms : One ton (t)
Pressure	KILOGRAM PER SQUARE CENTIMETER (kg/cm^2)
	One kilogram per square centimeter : One ATMOSPHERE (atm)
Temperature	CENTIGRADE degree (°C) : CELSIUS degree (°C)

CONVERSION TABLE
INCH FRACTIONS AND DECIMALS TO METRIC EQUIVALENTS

INCHES Fractions	INCHES Decimals	m m	INCHES Fractions	INCHES Decimals	m m	INCHES Fractions	INCHES Decimals	m m
-	.0004	.01	-	.4331	11	31/32	.96875	24.606
-	.004	.10	7/16	.4375	11.113	-	.9843	25
-	.01	.25	29/64	.4531	11.509	1	1.000	25.4
1/64	.0156	.397	15/32	.46875	11.906	-	1.0236	26
-	.0197	.50	-	.4724	12	1 1/32	1.0312	26.194
-	.0295	.75	31/64	.48437	12.303	1 1/16	1.062	26.988
1/32	.03125	.794	-	.492	12.5	-	1.063	27
-	.0394	1	1/2	.500	12.700	1 3/32	1.094	27.781
3/64	.0469	1.191	-	.5118	13	-	1.1024	28
-	.059	1.5	33/64	.5156	13.097	1 1/8	1.125	28.575
1/16	.0625	1.588	17/32	.53125	13.494	-	1.1417	29
5/64	.0781	1.984	35/64	.54687	13.891	1 5/32	1.156	29.369
-	.0787	2	-	.5512	14	-	1.1811	30
3/32	.094	2.381	9/16	.5625	14.288	1 3/16	1.1875	30.163
-	.0984	2.5	-	.571	14.5	1 7/32	1.219	30.956
7/64	.1093	2.776	37/64	.57812	14.684	-	1.2205	31
-	.1181	3	-	.5906	15	1 1/4	1.250	31.750
1/8	.1250	3.175	19/32	.59375	15.081	-	1.2598	32
-	.1378	3.5	39/64	.60937	15.478	1 9/32	1.281	32.544
9/64	.1406	3.572	5/8	.6250	15.875	-	1.2992	33
5/32	.15625	3.969	-	.6299	16	1 5/16	1.312	33.338
-	.1575	4	41/64	.6406	16.272	-	1.3386	34
11/64	.17187	4.366	-	.6496	16.5	1 11/32	1.344	34.131
-	.177	4.5	21/32	.65625	16.669	1 3/8	1.375	34.925
3/16	.1875	4.763	-	.6693	17	-	1.3779	35
-	.1969	5	43/64	.67187	17.066	1 13/32	1.406	35.719
13/64	.2031	5.159	11/16	.6875	17.463	-	1.4173	36
-	.2165	5.5	45/64	.7031	17.859	1 7/16	1.438	36.513
7/32	.21875	5.556	-	.7087	18	-	1.4567	37
15/64	.23437	5.953	23/32	.71875	18.256	1 15/32	1.469	37.306
-	.2362	6	-	.7283	18.5	-	1.4961	38
1/4	.2500	6.350	47/64	.73437	18.653	1 1/2	1.500	38.100
-	.2559	6.5	-	.7480	19	1 17/32	1.531	38.894
17/64	.2656	6.747	3/4	.7500	19.050	-	1.5354	39
-	.2756	7	49/64	.7656	19.447	1 9/16	1.562	39.688
9/32	.28125	7.144	25/32	.78125	19.844	-	1.5748	40
-	.2953	7.5	-	.7874	20	1 19/32	1.594	40.481
19/64	.29687	7.541	51/64	.79687	20.241	-	1.6142	41
5/16	.3125	7.938	13/16	.8125	20.638	1 5/8	1.625	41.275
-	.3150	8	-	.8268	21	-	1.6535	42
21/64	.3281	8.334	53/64	.8281	21.034	1 21/32	1.6562	42.069
-	.335	8.5	27/32	.84375	21.431	1 11/16	1.6875	42.863
11/32	.34375	8.731	55/64	.85937	21.828	-	1.6929	43
-	.3543	9	-	.8662	22	1 23/32	1.719	43.656
23/64	.35937	9.128	7/8	.8750	22.225	-	1.7323	44
-	.374	9.5	57/64	.8906	22.622	1 3/4	1.750	44.450
3/8	.3750	9.525	-	.9055	23	-	1.7717	45
25/64	.3906	9.922	29/32	.90625	23.019	1 25/32	1.781	45.244
-	.3937	10	59/64	.92187	23.416	-	1.8110	46
13/32	.4062	10.319	15/16	.9375	23.813	1 13/16	1.8125	46.038
-	.413	10.5	-	.9449	24	1 27/32	1.844	46.831
27/64	.42187	10.716	61/64	.9531	24.209	-	1.8504	47

Millimeters

10 20 30 40 50 60 70 80 90 100 110 120 130 140 150

CONVERSION TABLE
INCH FRACTIONS AND DECIMALS TO METRIC EQUIVALENTS

| INCHES | | | INCHES | | | INCHES | | |
Fractions	Decimals	m m	Fractions	Decimals	m m	Fractions	Decimals	m m
1 7/8	1.875	47.625	-	3.0709	78	-	4.7244	120
-	1.8898	48	-	3.1102	79	4 3/4	4.750	120.650
1 29/32	1.9062	48.419	3 1/8	3.125	79375	4 7/8	4.875	123.825
-	1.9291	49	-	3.1496	80	-	4.9212	125
1 15/16	1.9375	49.213	3 3/16	3.1875	80.963	5	5.000	127
-	1.9685	50	-	3.1890	81	-	5.1181	130
1 31/32	1.969	50.006	-	3.2283	82	5 1/4	5.250	133.350
2	2.000	50.800	3 1/4	3.250	82.550	5 1/2	5.500	139.700
-	2.0079	51	-	3.2677	83	-	5.5118	140
-	2.0472	52	-	3.3071	84	5 3/4	5.750	146.050
2 1/16	2.062	52.388	3 5/16	3.312	84.1377	-	5.9055	150
-	2.0866	53	-	3.3464	85	6	6.000	152.400
2 1/8	2.125	53.975	3 3/8	3.375	85.725	6 1/4	6.250	158.750
-	2.126	54	-	3.3858	86	-	6.2992	160
-	2.165	55	-	3.4252	87	6 1/2	6.500	165.100
2 3/16	2.1875	55.563	3 7/16	3.438	87.313	-	6.6929	170
-	2.2047	56	-	3.4646	88	6 3/4	6.750	171.450
-	2.244	57	3 1/2	3.500	88.900	7	7.000	177.800
2 1/4	2.250	57.150	-	3.5039	89	-	7.0866	180
-	2.2835	58	-	3.5433	90	-	7.4803	190
2 5/16	2.312	58.738	3 9/16	3.562	90.4877	7 1/2	7.500	190.500
-	2.3228	59	-	3.5827	91	-	7.8740	200
-	2.3622	60	-	3.622	92	8	8.000	203.200
2 3/8	2.375	60.325	3 5/8	3.625	92.075	-	8.2677	210
-	2.4016	61	-	3.6614	93	8 1/2	8.500	215.900
2 7/16	2.438	61.913	3 11/16	3.6875	93.663	-	8.6614	220
-	2.4409	62	-	3.7008	94	9	9.000	228.600
-	2.4803	63	-	3.7401	95	-	9.0551	230
2 1/2	2.500	63.500	3 3/4	3.750	95.250	-	9.4488	240
-	2.5197	64	-	3.7795	96	9 1/2	9.500	241.300
-	2.559	65	3 13/16	3.8125	96.838	-	9.8425	250
2 9/16	2.562	65.088	-	3.8189	97	10	10.000	254.000
-	2.5984	66	-	3.8583	98	-	10.2362	260
2 5/8	2.625	66.675	3 7/8	3.875	98.425	-	10.6299	270
-	2.638	67	-	3.8976	99	11	11.000	279.400
-	2.6772	68	-	3.9370	100	-	11.0236	280
2 11/16	2.6875	68.263	3 15/16	3.9375	100.013	-	11.4173	290
-	2.7165	69	-	3.9764	101	-	11.8110	300
2 3/4	2.750	69.850	4	4.000	101.600	12	12.000	304.800
-	2.7559	70	4 1/16	4.062	103.188	13	13.000	330.200
-	2.7953	71	4 1/8	4.125	104.775	-	13.7795	350
2 13/16	2.8125	71.438	-	4.1338	105	14	14.000	355.600
-	2.8346	72	4 3/16	4.1875	106.363	15	15.000	381
-	2.8740	73	4 1/4	4.250	107.950	-	15.7480	400
2 7/8	2.875	73.025	4 5/16	4.312	109.538	16	16.000	406.400
-	2.9134	74	-	4.3307	110	17	17.000	431.800
2 15/16	2.9375	74.613	4 3/8	4.375	111.125	-	17.7165	450
-	2.9527	75	4 7/16	4.438	112.713	18	18.000	457.200
-	2.9921	76	4 1/2	4.500	114.300	19	19.000	482.600
3	3.000	76.200	-	4.5275	115	-	19.6850	500
-	3.0315	77	4 9/16	4.562	115.888	20	20.000	508
3 1/16	3.062	77.788	4 5/8	4.625	117.475	21	21.000	533.400

Millimeters

METRIC CONVERSION EQUIVALENTS

Linear Measure

Inch to metric			Metric to Inch		
1 inch	25.400	millimeters	1 millimeter	0.0393700	inch
1 inch	2.540	centimeters	1 centimeter	0.393700	inch
1 foot	304.800	millimeters	1 meter	39.3700	inches
1 foot	30.480	centimeters	1 meter	3.2808	feet
1 foot	0.3048	meter	1 meter	1.0936	yards
1 yard	91.4400	centimeters	1 kilometer	0.62137	mile
1 yard	0.9144	meter			
1 mile	1,609.35	meters			
1 mile	1.609	kilometers			

Area

Square Inch to Metric			Metric to Square Inch		
1 square inch	645.16	square millimeters	1 square millimeter	0.00155	square inch
1 square inch	6.4516	square centimeters	1 square centimeter	0.1550	square inch
1 square foot	929.00	square centimeters	1 square meter	10.7640	square feet
1 square foot	0.0929	square meter	1 square meter	1.196	square yards
1 square yard	0.836	square meter	1 square kilometer	0.38614	square mile
1 square mile	2.5889	square kilometers			

Cubic Measure

Cubic Inch to Metric			Metric to Cubic Inch		
1 cubic inch	16.387	cubic centimeters	1 cubic centimeter	0.0610	cubic inch
1 cubic foot	0.02832	cubic meter	1 cubic meter	85.314	cubic feet
1 cubic yard	0.765	cubic meter	1 cubic meter	1.308	cubic yards

Capacity

Imperial to Metric			Metric to Imperial		
1 fluid ounce	28.413	milliliters	1 milliliter	0.035195	fluid ounce
1 fluid ounce	0.2841	liter	1 centiliter	0.35195	fluid ounce
1 pint	0.56826	liter	1 deciliter	3.5195	fluid ounces
1 quart	1.13652	liters	1 liter	0.88	quart
1 gallon	4.546	liters	1 hectoliter	21.9969	gallons

Weight

Avoirdupois to Metric			Metric to Avoirdupois		
1 grain	64.7989	milligrams	1 gram	15.432	grains
1 ounce	28.35	grams	1 dekagram	0.353	ounce
1 pound	0.4536	kilogram	1 kilogram	2.2046	pounds
1 short ton (2000 lbs.)	907.200	kilograms	1 metric cent	220.46	pounds
1 short ton (2000 lbs.)	9.072	metric cents	1 ton	2204.6	pounds
1 short ton (2000 lbs.)	0.9072	ton	1 ton	1.102	short tons

METRIC CONVERSION EQUIVALENTS

Pressure

Pounds/Inches to Metric		Metric to Pounds/Inches	
1 pound per square inch	0.0703 kilogram per square centimeter	1 kilogram/square centimeter	14.223 pounds/square inch
1 pound per square inch	0.0703 atmosphere (metric)	1 kilogram/square centimeter	1 atmosphere

Temperature

Canadian to Metric		Metric to Canadian	
1 Fahrenheit degree (°F)	1.8 × (°C) plus 32	1 centigrade (Celsius) degree (°C)	0.556 × (°F minus 32)

SANDPAPER AND SANDING DISK CONVERSION CHART

	Silicone Carbide	Aluminum Oxide	Garnet	Emery	Flint
Very fine	600				
	400	400–10/0			
	320	320–9/0			
	280	280–8/0	8/0		
	240	240–7/0	7/0		
	220	220–6/0	6/0		4/0
Fine	180	180–5/0	5/0	3/0	3/0
	150	150–4/0	4/0	2/0	2/0
	120	120–3/0	3/0		
	100	100–2/0	2/0	1/0	1/0
				1/2	1/2
Medium	80	80–1/0	1/0	1	1
	60	60–1/2	1/2	1½	
	50	50–1	1	2	1½
Coarse	40	40–1½	1½	2½	2
	36	36–2	2	3	2½
	30	30–2½	2½		3
Very coarse	24	24–3	3		
	20	20–3½	3½		
	16	16–4			
	12	12–4½			

Appendix C

Glossary of Terms

Abrasive: Substance used to wear away a surface by friction.

Abrasive coating: In closed coat paper, the adhesive is completely coated with abrasive, and in open coat paper, the adhesive is partially exposed, for the abrasive is not put on the paper close together.

Acid core: Solder in a tubular wire form in which the interior contains a flux.

Acrylic resins: A synthetic resin that has excellent color retention and clarity and that is used in both lacquer and enamel.

Active solvent: An ingredient of lacquer thinners that is a solvent for nitrocellulose.

Adhesion: Sticking together of two surfaces, such as top coat to primer and primer to metal.

Air drying: A lacquer or enamel is said to be air drying when it is capable of drying hard at ordinary room temperatures and without the aid of artificial heat.

Alligatoring: Term describing lacquer or enamel films in which the finish has cracked into large segments resembling alligator hide. Similar to checking, crazing and cracking.

Aluminum oxide: Sharp and hard abrasive that is made by fusing mineral bauxite at high temperatures.

Anticorrosive and inhibitor: Protective coatings applied on metal surfaces to retard or prevent corrosion and said to be anticorrosive or corrosion inhibitive.

Assembly: A number of auto body parts that are either bolted or welded together forming a single unit.

Atomize: The extent to which air at the gun nozzle breaks up the paint and solvents into fine particles.

Backfire: A malfunctioning of the torch causing the flame to go out with a loud snap or pop.

Backhand welding: When the torch, in the case of a right-hand operator, is moved in the opposite way from left to right instead of right to left as in the usual practice.

Baking: Application of heat to cure and dry a coating. In the refinishing trade, baking is used to speed up the drying of air-drying lacquers and enamel and is sometimes called force drying. The metal temperature in refinish baking usually does not exceed 180°F (82.2°C).

Binder: The portion of the paint that helps to bind the pigment together.

Bleeding: The action whereby the color of a stain or other material works up into succeeding coats and imparts a certain amount of color. This is characteristic of certain red pigments used in lacquers and enamels. A nonbleeding color is one that is not soluble in materials used over it and, consequently, does not work up into succeeding coats.

Blending: Mixing together of two or more materials or the gradual shading off from one color to another. *See* Tint.

Blistering: A bubbling up of the paint film in the form of small blisters.

Blushing: White or grayish cast that sometimes forms on a lacquer film as it dries, particularly under conditions of hot, humid weather.

Body files: A variety of files used in accurately locating surface irregularities (high and low spots) on damaged areas after they have been "bumped" out. Also used in trimming down solder and plastic-filled areas.

Bodying: Thickening in the package, usually due to evaporation of solvents or volatile material because of excessive heat during storage.

Body solder: It is an alloy of tin and lead. Its properties may vary but the most common mixture consists of 30 percent tin and 70 percent lead, or 30/70 solder as it is usually called.

Body straps: Are specially designed straps made out of strong vulcanized belting material equipped with wide hooks that snugly fit around the flanges of various body panels. They are used in repositioning and pulling different assemblies and parts closer together.

Boiling point: The temperature at which the vapor pressure of a liquid exceeds the atmospheric pressure and the liquid begins to boil.

Bonding strips: Narrow strips of laminated fiberglass bonded to the inner surface of the replacement panel and the adjoining body panels. When properly installed, the strips greatly strengthen the joint and make alignment of the replacement panel with the rest of the body panels much easier.

Braze welding: When bronze welding, rod in a molten stage is deposited on metals that are heated to a cherry red, similar and dissimilar metals are bonded together.

Bridging: The ability of an enamel or lacquer to cover a crack, void, or other small gap.

Buffing compound: A soft paste containing fine abrasive in a neutral medium, used to eliminate fine scratches and polish lacquer.

Burning: Condition resulting from rubbing a lacquer film too hard. The heat generated by the friction of the rubbing pad may soften the lacquer and cause it to stick to the pad, thus permanently marring the finish.

Butt weld: Two pieces of similar metal are aligned closely edge to edge. The edges are tack welded first and then by running a good bead are solidly fused together.

Caking: Gathering of sanding dust into solid cakes sticking to sandpaper. *Compare* Gumming.

Camber: Is the inward or outward tilt of the wheel at the top. It is the tire wearing angle measured in degrees and is the amount the center line of the wheel is tilted from true vertical.

Carbonizing flame: Used mostly for heating parts and for soldering. It burns more acetylene than oxygen through the torch. Its inner core is whitish in color and has a feather. Sometimes also called a reducing flame.

Case hardening: A surface coating that will dry hard on top and remain more or less soft underneath. *Compare* Heaving.

Cast: The tendency of one color to look like another.

Caster: The backward or forward tilt of the king pin or spindle support arm at the top. It is the directional control angle measured in degrees and is the amount the center line of the spindle support arm is tilted from the true vertical.

Catalyst: A substance that causes or speeds up a chemical reaction when it is mixed with another substance and that does not change by itself.

Caulking compound: A semi- or slow-drying plastic material used to fill crevices or seal joints.

Chalking: The formation of soft white powder on the surface of a finish, which may be removed by friction of the finger or similar methods.

Checking: Small, irregular cracks going partly or completely through a paint film. Like ''alligatoring,'' only very fine cracks. *Compare* Cracking and Crazing.

Chipping: A term used to express the condition of the finish flaking off or chipping away from the underneath surface.

Chipping hammer: A special hammer used in removing slag deposits from a weld so that it can be inspected for quality.

Closed-coat disk: One on which the abrasive grains are very densely spaced. Used in disk sanding and polishing repaired sheet metal.

Cold cracking: Cracking of a paint job resulting from a sudden drop of temperature.

Collapsed hinge buckle: Formed whenever a simple hinge buckle extends and crosses over a stamped-in reinforcing flange, bead, or ridge on a flat or reverse-curved (concave) surface of an auto body panel. Will also form when box-constructed members and assemblies, such as the side rails on automobile frames, rocker panels, roof rails, and a variety of body pillars, are forced to bend and buckle.

Collapsed rolled buckle: Formed whenever a hinge buckle extends or crosses over into the crowned surface of a panel, causing the metal to collapse and shrink severely and a general shortening up in the overall length of the panel to occur.

Color retention: A paint of a certain color, when it is exposed to the elements and does not change, is said to have good color retention.

Compartment: A separate enclosure or section, such as the engine, passenger and luggage compartment, on an auto body.

Compatibility: The ability of two or more materials to blend into a homogeneous mixture and, upon drying, a homogeneous film.

Compressor: A machine used to compress air from atmospheric pressure to a high pressure.

Cone mandrel: Special attachment used with an abrasive cone in sanding hard-to-get-at concave surfaces around headlights, fender flanges and trim moldings.

Connectors (male and female):   Attachments used in coupling two or more extension tubes together and to the various rams.

Conventional body construction: A type of construction where the body and frame are two entirely separate units held together at various points by means of body bolts.

Corrosion: The chemical reaction of air, moisture, or corrosive materials on a metal surface. Usually referred to as rusting or oxidation.

Coupler (quick detachable):   Permits the removal of the coupler tube without the loss of hydraulic fluid from the ram making it possible to use the same pump with a variety of rams and spreaders.

Coverage: The quality some colors have to cover other colors and the area a certain quantity of paint will cover.

Cracking: Crevices or ruptures going completely through a film. This is in contrast to alligatoring or checking, where crevices slowly work their way down from the surface.

Cratering: Surface blemishes in a freshly painted surface, usually in the form of small round patches.

Crawling: The action of a finishing material when it appears to creep or crawl away from certain spots and leaves them uncoated.

Crazing: Very fine minute cracks on the surface that are usually interlaced.

Cross-coat: *See* Double head-coat.

Cut: "Cut" as applied to surface coating denotes both the dissolving of solid material in a solvent and the reducing of the viscosity of liquid by the addition of a thinner. Can also refer to sanding down a film as in "cut and polish."

Datum line: Is an imaginary line that appears on frame blueprints or charts to help determine correct frame height.

Diamond: A frame misalignment resulting from a heavy impact on the corner of either side rail of the frame, that is sufficient to push the side rail back. As a result the cross members are pushed out of a right angle with the side rail.

Dilutants: Dilutants are volatile liquids that are not solvents for nitrocellulose. They are used in nitrocellulose lacquer to lower viscosity and give certain other desirable properties. In most cases, dilutants act as a solvent for the resins contained in the lacquer.

Dinging: Reshaping and levelling out of damaged metal by means of on- and off-the-dolly hammering after the metal has been unlocked and roughed-out.

Dinging hammer: A specially built hammer used for the removal of the smaller dents on body panels.

Direct damage: Is the damage that occurs to the area that is in direct contact with the damaging force or impact.

Dirt nibs: Small specks of foreign material in a dried film of finishing material are called dirt nibs. They should be removed by scuff sanding.

Disintegrate: The dried film of a finishing material completely breaks down.

Disk sander: A power sanding tool used for grinding, sanding, and polishing repaired metal areas. It is manufactured in either the 7 in. (178 mm) standard or the 7 and 9 in. (178 and 229 mm) heavy-duty model and is available with a round, flexible, molded rubber backing pad 5, 7, and 9 in. (127, 178, and 229 mm) in diameter.

Disk trimmer: A special tool used to cut down a worn-out sanding disk to a somewhat smaller size, giving it a fresh cutting edge.

Dolly: A tool that is made in different shapes, usually held in one hand on inner side of a dented panel while the outer side is struck with another dolly or dinging hammer.

Door panel flange: The 90° projecting edge all around the edge of a door replacement panel, by means of which the replacement panel is attached to the door frame or inner construction.

Double head-coat: Usually called one coat but meaning an application of material sprayed horizontally and immediately followed by an application sprayed vertically. Also called a cross-coat.

Driers: The salts of certain metals or metallo-organic compounds, which when added to an enamel, paint, varnish, or oil hasten the drying or hardening of the film through proper ventilation.

Dry spray: This term is used if in applying a finish by spray the atomized paint is not absorbed in the film, leaving a rough, dry finish.

Ductility: Refers to the property whereby a material can be worked or bent without breaking.

Dust free: When a film has dried so it will no longer allow dust to penetrate and stick to the finish, it is said to be dust free.

Elastic metal: All V channels, valleys and buckles extending outward from the area of direct damage but not including the extreme outer high ridges that bound them are called elastic metal.

Electrode: A special type of flux-coated welding rod used in arc welding.

Electrode holder: The electrode holder is located at one end of the electrode cable. It consists of a well-insulated handle that protects the operator from shocks, and to which a spring-loaded clamp is attached that firmly grips and holds the electrode.

Enamel: A pigmented alkyd varnish usually characterized by a glossy surface. Dulux is such a pigmented synthetic resin solution.

Epoxy resins: Resins obtained by the condensing reaction that occurs between phenols and epichlorohydrin.

Evaporation: The escape of solvents from the paint into the air.

Excess acetylene flame: *See* Carbonizing flame.

Face bar: The large chrome-plated extrusions that provide protection for both front and rear of an automobile and which are generally held in position by means of brackets bolted to the side rails of the frame (frame-horns).

Fade: Denotes the change in the color of a surface coating where and when such a coating has been subjected to sunlight. It is a dying away or bleaching action.

False stretch: The bulge formed in the flatter areas of an outer panel whenever the collapsed rolled buckle in the crowned surface of that panel extends into the flatter, more central portions of the panel (in the area of indirect damage). Even after the damage has been roughed-out and straightened as accurately as possible, false stretch cannot be completely eliminated.

Feathering (feather edging):   The term is used in motor car finishing when sanding down a surface to a very fine edge; that is, when one coat of material is made gradually thinner around the edge until it finally disappears.

Feeling (the metal):   Used in detecting surface irregularities. The repairman slides the palm of his hand back and forth over the work and is able to detect or feel any hollows or high spots that may be present.

Fender flange: The outer rim or bend along the lower edge of a fender that gives shape and strength to the side of the fender.

Ferrous metal: Any metal composed of or containing iron.

Fiberglass: Very fine filaments of glass that are spun together; it is used as insulation and for repairs on automobile and truck bodies.

Filing: Pushing or drawing a file back and forth over the surface of the work in order to detect high and low spots (surface irregularities) or to wear down a surface to an exact size and shape.

Fillet weld: *See* Lap weld.

Filling: A method of repairing inaccessible areas of an auto body by either using body solder or plastic filler.

Film: A layer of applied coating material.

Film thickness: *See* Mil.

Finish coat: The last coat of paint to be applied will usually determine the amount of gloss.

Fisheyes: A kind of cratering appearing on the surface. Sometimes as large as a 10-cent piece circled by a noticeable ring.

Fish plate: The repairing of a cracked frame rail by first of all welding the cracks and then reinforcing the rail by welding another plate that covers and extends well beyond the repaired area.

Flaking: A term used when the finish does not knit properly to the undercoating, causing the finish to chip off the work by breaking into small pieces.

Flange: A projecting edge, rim, or bend on the outer edge of a panel that strengthens it.

Flash-back: A malfunctioning of the torch when the flame goes inside the torch and it starts to hiss and squeal.

Flash off: The rate of evaporation of the thinner or reducer.

Flat: A term used to designate a finish that has no luster or gloss.

Flex-heads: Sometimes called rubber bases; conform to any contour, and are most often used as a terminal point for pushing against concave surfaces.

Flint paper: An inexpensive but short-working-life abrasive paper, not used extensively in body shops.

Flood: The floating of a pigment to the surface of a coating, giving a changed color to the surface and lack of uniformity in color appearance through the film.

Fog coat: A thin, highly atomized coat applied in such a way as to obtain a fast flash-off of the thinner and thereby achieve a minimum penetration of the thinner into the old finish.

Force dry: *See* Baking.

Forging: A repair operation used in restoring welded butt joints to as near as possible the same thickness and molecular structure as that possessed by the surrounding sheet metal.

Frame alignment: Is the procedure by which the frame of a car, truck or bus that has been damaged in an accident, or from wear, is restored to the manufacturer's specifications.

Frame centering gauges: Used in determining the type of misalignment that has occurred and also the extent of the damage.

Frame horns: The extending ends of the side rails of a frame to which the bumper brackets are fastened.

Front-end sheet metal: All parts from the cowl assembly forward are considered front end sheet metal. This includes the grille, the hood, and right and left fender and the front bumper assembly.

Fusion weld: The operation in which two pieces of the same kind of metal are made into one is called fusion welding.

Garnet paper: A hard, sharp, red abrasive; more expensive than flint paper but will last much longer.

Garnish moldings: The moldings that fit around the inside of door, windshield and rear window openings, generally held in position by counter-sunk metal screws.

Gel: The general consistency of a jelly; the material being soft but not free flowing. The term ''gel'' is generally applied to a vehicle as contrasted to false body caused by pigmentation.

Glazing: The application of a filler by means of a putty knife, the material being filled into the depression but scraped off the higher areas.

Gloss: A term used to express the shine, sheen, or luster of a dry film.

Grille: An open-work structure made out of plastic, die cast, aluminum or stamped out of sheet which is then chrome-plated. Although it covers the air intake opening in front of the radiator, the grille allows the air to pass freely through it.

Gritty: A product is said to be gritty when it contains large particles, either from insufficient grinding, which would mean seed, or by the presence of large, hard particles of foreign materials.

Ground cable: The ground cable clamped to the work allows the electric current produced by the welding machine to flow through the electrode cable and the electrode to the work when the arc is formed. The current completes its circuit by flowing through the ground cable back to the welding machine.

Guide coat: A coat of a different color from the other coats is used to serve as a guide coat in rubbing or sanding to determine when a smooth surface has been reached.

Gumming: A condition where the sandpaper becomes clogged by the abraded surface coating. *Compare* Caking.

Hairlining: A term used to describe very fine lines or checks on the dried surface coating of a finished material.

Header bar: The framework or inner construction that joins the upper sections of the windshield, pillars, forms the upper portion of the windshield opening and reinforces the turret top panel.

Headlining: Different types of materials used to cover the inner surface of the roof in a car.

Heaving: *See* Lifting.

Hide glue: Made from animal hides and used in making abrasives that can only be used in ''dry'' sanding and grinding work.

Hiding: The hiding power of a finishing material is a measure of its opacity or its ability to cover solidly over another color as to obscure or prevent the original color from showing through.

High-crown metal: The outward curving portion of a body panel.

Hinge pillar: The framework or inner construction to which the door hinges fasten.

Hood panel: The large metal panel that generally fills in the space between the two fenders and closes off the engine compartment so that rain cannot fall on the engine.

Humidity: The water vapor present in the air in varying amounts.

Hydraulic oil: A special type of oil used in hydraulic jacks that does not deteriorate and destroy the rubber seals in the jack or its hose.

Indirect damage: Any damage that occurs as a result of direct damage.

Induction baking: Heat used for baking finishes; it is induced by electrostatic and electromagnetic means.

Industrial fallout: Chemical compounds present in the air, which are deposited on the horizontal surfaces of vehicles and which under certain circumstances will affect the finish, particularly metallics.

Inner construction: The framework and inner panels that hold and reinforce the outer body panels.

Jig: A mechanical device for holding work in its exact position while it is being welded.

Jigsaw: A narrow-bladed saw usually driven by an electric motor; it is used to cut body panels.

Knit: Adhere or bond together.

Lacquer: A refinishing material that dries by the evaporation of the thinner.

Lap: The point where one coat extends over another.

Lap weld: A type of weld made by overlapping two pieces of metal and joining them by running a bead along only one of the edges.

Leveling out: Flowing or settling to a smooth, uniform surface.

Lifting: Disruption of a paint film by the application of a succeeding coat, caused by the solvents of the succeeding coat penetrating and partially dissolving or swelling the preceding dried film.

Listing bows: Slightly tempered, bowed steel rods that are inserted into headlinings to keep them in proper position inside the passenger compartment.

Livering: The coagulation of paint into a viscous liver-like mass.

Low-crown metal: The portion of a body panel with just a very small amount of outward curve.

Luster: Gloss or sheen or brightness of a finish.

Mash: A type of frame damage in which a portion of the side rail is bent down causing buckles to be formed on its underside.

Masking paper: A paper designed to prevent paint bleed-through and resist water-soaking to a certain degree.

Masking tape: A special paper that is coated with adhesive; used to protect body parts or to attach masking paper to the car.

Metal conditioner: An acetic acid preparation that is used to prepare metal, remove rust, and etch the metal slightly to provide a good adherence between the metal and the paint.

Metal finishing: Is an operation in which hidden surface irregularities are detected and removed by means of filing and picking the straightened metal until all low spots have been eliminated and a perfectly smooth and level surface is obtained.

Metallic: General term applied to finishes containing aluminum particles.

Metal stamping: A process of manufacturing auto body parts in which straight sheets of metal are placed in between dies operated by huge presses and "die-formed" or "stamped" into the finished part.

Mil: Measure of film thickness equal to 0.001 in. (0.025 mm).

Milkiness: Cloudy, whitish—not clear.

Mist coat: A light spray coat of lacquer thinner or other volatile solvent by itself or with very little color in it.

Modified unitized body construction: A form of body construction consisting of half frame and half unitized body construction.

Muriatic acid: Sometimes called hydrochloric acid. A strong acid used for cleaning metal and when "cut" (treated with zinc bar), is used for soldering.

Natural mineral abrasive: Abrasives made from materials found in nature.

Nitrocellulose: "Gun cotton," "pyroxylin," a compound of nitrogen and cellulose prepared from nitric acid and cotton or wood fiber.

Nonelastic metal areas: Areas in auto body panels that have been permanently deformed and that will not spring back to their original shape after stresses and strains have been released.

Non-ferrous metals: Metals that contain no iron.

Normalizing: The removing of stresses and strains in metal. This is done by hammering, heating up the metal, or by a combination of both.

Opaque: A material is opaque when it is impervious to light. Not transparent.

Orange peel: The term used to describe an uneven, pebbly surface somewhat resembling the skin of an orange; appears in a paint film that has been applied by spray.

Original finish: The paint the car manufacturer applies at the factory.

Overlap: The amount of the spray pattern that covers the previous spray swath.

Overspray: *See* Dry spray.

Oxidation: The drying of an oil, varnish, or synthetic resins by the absorption of oxygen from the air. The act or process of combining with oxygen.

Paint film: The coating of paint that is applied to a material.

Paint remover: A fast-acting blend of solvents used to remove enamels, lacquers, and varnish.

Pebbling: Excessively large orange peel.

Peeling: Loss of bond or adhesion of a paint film from the surface to which it is applied.

Perchloroethylene: A solvent used in determining whether the finish is acrylic lacquer, nitrocellulose lacquer, or enamel.

Phenolic resin: A resin that is based on the reaction between formaldehyde and phenol.

Picking: Raising up low spots with the sharp-pointed end of a pick hammer.

Picks: Special tools used in the metal-finishing operation for raising (prying up) low spots located in the more central areas of inaccessible body panels.

Pigment: Any fine, insoluble, dry, solid particles used to impart color.

Piling: Heaping, or applying too heavily.

Pinch weld flange: The flange that is formed when the framework and outer panels are clamped and spot-welded together as found on windshield and rear window openings.

Pinholing and pitting: Minute hollows or holes no larger than the head of a pin in a film produced by the bursting of trapped air, moisture, or thinner during drying.

Plastic filler: A compound of resin and fiberglass used to fill dents on car bodies.

Plunger: The male threaded part, that acts like a piston moving in and out of the ram body and onto which different lengths of extension tubing and attachments can be connected.

Polychromatic: A term used by some paint manufacturers for color coats that contain aluminum powder in flake form.

Polyester filler: A special kind of putty-like filler used in filling slight imperfections and low spots on fiberglass panels.

Polyester resin: A bonding liquid that forms a good bond with fiberglass surfaces only.

Poor adhesion: A paint system that has poor bond to the underlying surface.

Powdered fiberglass: Actually is processed fiberglass that has been crushed into a powder. It not only gives bulk but also strength to the filler.

Pressure-feed gun: A spray gun equipped with a separate paint container that is pressurized and connected to the spray gun by means of two hoses.

Prime coat: The first coat in a paint system—its main purpose being to impart adhesion.

Pull plates: Several types of special plates that can be bolted, soldered or braze-welded onto the damaged panel. The damaged area can then be pulled out by attaching the hydraulic jack to the pull plates in a variety of pulling combinations.

Pull rods: Are rods that are equipped with hooks on one end and handles on the other. The hooked ends are inserted into small holes drilled in areas of direct damage (creases) and used in roughly aligning the areas of direct damage before they are soldered or plastic filled.

Punches: Special tools used in driving shafts and pins and in aligning holes in panels so that they can be bolted together. Different punches are used in the metal-finishing operation; for raising (prying up) low spots located around the outer edges of inaccessible body panels.

Putty knife: Special knife used in applying glazing putty.

Pyroxylin: *See* Nitrocellulose.

Quarter panel: The side panel, which (in 4 door sedans) is generally a quarter of the total length of the automobile and which extends from the rear door to the end of the car.

Quenching: The cooling of a shrink spot or solder fill with a wet rag or sponge.

Radiator support: The large vertical panel which not only ties the two front fenders together and holds them in position on the frame but to which also the radiator is bolted.

Rain or water spotting: Marks on a surface due to rain or water absorption.

Reduce: Lower or make less in consistency. To cut.

Reducer: Commonly referred to as the volatile substance used to thin the viscosity of enamel prior to application.

Relative humidity: The condition of the atmosphere with reference to its content of water vapor.

Retarder: A slow evaporating thinner used to retard drying.

Rocker panels: Are assemblies of box-type construction, located directly below the doors, that are not only spot-welded to the cowl assembly in front and to the rear quarter panel assembly at the rear, but also to the side of the under-body section.

Roof rails: The framework or inner construction that reinforces and supports the sides of the roof panel or turret top.

Rosin: A natural gum or resin; residue of the distillation of crude turpentine.

Run-sags: When too many or too heavy coats are applied at one time, causing the film to droop under its own weight.

Sag: A type of frame damage in which one or both side rails bend and sag at the cowl, causing buckles to be formed on the top of the side rails.

Sander: A power-driven tool, some with a rotary action, others with an orbital motion, used with abrasives to sand car bodies.

Sand scratches: The reproduction in the top coat of the sanding marks in the underlying surface.

Sand-scratch swelling: An exaggerated reproduction and distortion of the sanding marks in the underlying surface.

Sealer: A paint product used to prevent bleed-through of previous coat or the sinking in of the new paint, resulting in loss of gloss.

Seediness: Being gritty or sandy, or full of small grains.

Separation: Nonuniform mixture.

Serrated saddle: An attachment used to protect the threads on the extension tubing and the ram plunger. Its serrated face serves as a base that does not slip or slide easily when pressure is applied.

Setting-up: The period during which the solvents are evaporating from the film flowing ceases, and the film surface becomes tack free.

Shrinkage: Contracting of the surface.

Shrinking: Is an operation by means of which stretched areas on damaged auto body parts and panels are disposed of and brought back, as nearly as possible, to their original shape and size.

Shroud: A sheet-metal or plastic part used on cars to direct the suction of the cooling fan.

Sidesway: A type of frame damage in which one or both of the siderails are bent sideways.

Silicon carbide: An abrasive made by fusing silica and coke in an electric furnace. The abrasive is very hard, shiny black, and iridescent.

Simple hinge buckle: Formed when flat sheet-metal is forced to bend either inward or outward by a damaging force or impact. It is similar to the bending of a hinge on a door and the change in the grain or molecular structure of the metal that occurs will vary greatly, depending on the sharpness of the bend.

Simple rolled buckle: The outer ridges formed at either end of a hinge buckle that extends or crosses over into the crowned surface of an auto body panel.

Single coat: Usually referred to as a coat of paint. Once over the surface with each stroke overlapping the previous stroke 50 percent.

Sinking in: The term applied when one coat is partially absorbed by the previous one.

Skinning: The oxidation, hardening, or drying of a paint at the surface of the liquid while in its container.

Slide hammer: A weight that slides along a bar until it hits a stop. The bar usually has attachments to pull dents out, and the impact that results when the weight hits the stop helps to pull the dent out.

Solder: A mixture of lead and tin used to fill dents and joints on body panels.

Soldering salts: A type of non-acid flux employed in the tinning of metal.

Solids: The part of the paint that does not evaporate and stays on the surface.

Solution: A homogeneous liquid or mixture of two or more chemical substances.

Solvency: Ability or power of causing solution. Ability to dissolve.

Solvent: Any liquid in or by which a substance can be dissolved.

Specific gravity: The weight of a certain amount of liquid compared to the same amount of water at the same constant temperature.

Speed file: A special file that has a straight solid base about 2¾ in. (70 mm) wide and 17 in. (432 mm) long onto which strips of sandpaper are fastened. This file is used in sanding down solder- and plastic-filled areas to their final shape and contour.

Spoon: A tool that is designed to perform the same work as a Jolly, but is thin, wide, and fairly long and can be used in areas that have very little clearance.

Spotting or spot repair: In repair work, the ability of a lacquer to blend in with the damaged film surface thereby making the repair unnoticeable.

Spray gun: A device that mixes paint and compressed air to atomize and control the spray pattern as the paint leaves the fluid needle and cap.

Spreader toes: Attachments designed to anchor combinations against frame members, braces, and the heads of body bolts.

Spring-hammering: The elimination of high ridges generally formed at the outer edges of indirect damage by means of hammering them down with a surfacing spoon and bumping hammer.

Squeegee: A rectangular piece of rubber approximately 2 in. (51 mm) wide, 3 in. (76 mm) long, and 3/16 in. (5 mm) thick. It is used in applying glazing putty and plastic filler on concave surfaces.

Standard body construction: *See* Conventional body construction.

Steering axle inclination: The inward tilt of the king pin or spindle support arm (ball joint) at the top. It is a directional control angle measured in degrees and is the amount the spindle support center line is tilted from the true vertical.

Strength: Tinting power of a pigment or paint.

Striker plate: The part that is installed on the door frame in which the lock engages to lock the door.

Suction-feed gun: A spray gun that has the paint container connected directly to it. It is designed to create a vacuum and thus draw the paint from the container.

Surface drying: The drying of the top coat while the bottom coats have remained soft.

Sweating: Separation and appearance at the film surface of the oil in lacquer.

Symmetrical: A regular, well-balanced arrangement of parts on opposite sides of a line or plane, or around a center or axis.

Synthetic resin: Any resin not produced by nature; man-made.

Tack coat: The first enamel coat. A full coat that is to dry only until it is quite sticky.

Tack-free: That period of time in drying at which the surface of the film will not fingerprint; yet the film is not dry and hard throughout.

Tack rag: A cloth impregnated with varnish; used as a final cleanup to remove dust before applying the finishing paint.

Tack welds: Short welds placed at intervals along a break or the joining edges of two pieces of metal, keeping the metal in alignment while the bead is run.

Template: A pattern made from a part so that another part can be made to the exact same shape.

Thermoplastic: Type of plastic that can be softened with the application of heat, can be reshaped, and can also be welded.

Thermosetting: Type of plastic that is permanently set; cannot be softened with the application of heat; cannot be reshaped, and cannot be welded. Minor damage can often be repaired with a structural adhesive.

Thickness of film: The measurement of a film usually expressed in mils of the distance from top to bottom, or at right angles to its surface. A mil is 0.001 in. (0.025 mm).

Thinner: Commonly known as a lacquer solvent, which reduces the viscosity of a lacquer to spraying consistency.

Tint: A mixture of two or more pigments. *See* Blending.

Tinting color: A finishing lacquer or enamel in which only one pigment or color is normally used.

Toe-in: The distance the front of the front wheels is closer together than the rear of the front wheels.

Toe-out: The distance the front of the front wheels is farther apart than the rear of the front wheels.

Tooth: A roughened surface that affects adhesion of the coating.

Top coat: The last or final color coat.

Toxicity: Pertaining to poisonous effect.

Tram gauges: Gauges used to accurately measure and diagnose body and frame collision damages for all conventional and unitized vehicles.

Turning radius: A tire wearing angle measured in degrees. Is the amount one front wheel turns sharper than the other on turns.

Twist: A type of frame damage in which both side rails are bent out of alignment, so that they do not run horizontally parallel to one another.

Undercoat: A material used to protect the underbody sections of a vehicle.

Unitized body construction: A type of construction in which the frame and body are made out of a large number of sheet-metal panels of varying sizes and shapes assembled and welded into a single unit.

Unlocking the metal: The unfolding and reshaping of the V channels, valleys and buckles as gently as possible, without further stretching, creasing or upsetting the metal.

Upsetting: The application of heat on metal that is restricted from expanding in all directions and yet allowed to contract in all directions when it cools.

Vehicle: The liquid portion of a paint.

Viscosity: Consistency or body of a liquid.

Volatile: Capable of evaporating easily. That portion which readily vaporizes.

Weathering: The change or failure in paint caused by exposure to the weather.

Wheel balancing: The proper distribution of weight around a tire and wheel assembly to counteract centrifugal forces acting upon the heavy areas in order to maintain a true-running wheel perpendicular to its rotating axis.

Wheelhouses: The deep curved panels that form the compartments in which the wheels rotate. They are generally bolted to the front fenders and spot-welded to the rear quarter panels.

Wind cord: *See* Windlace.

Windlace: Special trim used around the edge of the door opening as a decoration and to help to reduce drafts.

Windshield header bar: The reinforcement above the windshield to which the roof is attached.

Wrinkling: The term used when a paint film buckles at its surface, causing a shriveled appearance.

Yield strength: The resistance a particular type of material possesses to permanent stretching.

Index